VIOLENCE AND TERRORISM 91/92

Second Edition

Annual Editions

A Library of Information from the Public Press

Editor

Bernard Schechterman
University of Miami

Bernard Schechterman is a professor and former chairperson in the Department of Politics and Public Affairs at the University of Miami. He received a B.Soc.Sci. from the University of Wisconsin (Madison) in 1948, an M.A. from Indiana University (Bloomington) in 1950, and a Ph.D. from Indiana University (Bloomington) in 1973. He is Chief Editor of *The Political Chronicle*, an editor with *The Journal of Political Science*, and an editorial consultant with *The Middle East Review*. He co-authored the book *Multidimensional Terrorism* (1987) with Martin Slann.

Editor

Martin Slann
Clemson University

Martin Slann is a professor of political science at Clemson University. He received an A.B. from the University of Miami in 1964, an M.A. from the University of Connecticut in 1966, and a Ph.D. from the University of Georgia in 1970. He is co-editor of *Morality and Conviction in American Politics: A Reader* and co-author of *The American Republic: Politics, Institutions, and Policies*. He is also the author of *Eight Nations: An Introduction to Comparative Politics*, and the editor of the *Journal of Political Science*.

Cover illustration by Mike Eagle

The Dushkin Publishing Group, Inc.
Sluice Dock, Guilford, Connecticut 06437

The Annual Editions Series

Annual Editions is a series of over fifty volumes designed to provide the reader with convenient, low-cost access to a wide range of current, carefully selected articles from some of the most important magazines, newspapers, and journals published today. Annual Editions are updated on an annual basis through a continuous monitoring of over 200 periodical sources. All Annual Editions have a number of features designed to make them particularly useful, including topic guides, annotated tables of contents, unit overviews, and indexes. For the teacher using Annual Editions in the classroom, an Instructor's Resource Guide with test questions is available for each volume.

VOLUMES AVAILABLE

Africa
Aging
American Government
American History, Pre-Civil War
American History, Post-Civil War
Anthropology
Biology
Business and Management
Business Ethics
Canadian Politics
China
Comparative Politics
Computers in Education
Computers in Business
Computers in Society
Criminal Justice
Drugs, Society, and Behavior
Early Childhood Education
Economics
Educating Exceptional Children
Education
Educational Psychology
Environment
Geography
Global Issues
Health
Human Development
Human Resources
Human Sexuality
Latin America
Macroeconomics
Management
Marketing
Marriage and Family
Microeconomics
Middle East and the Islamic World
Money and Banking
Nutrition
Personal Growth and Behavior
Psychology
Public Administration
Race and Ethnic Relations
Social Problems
Sociology
Soviet Union and Eastern Europe
State and Local Government
Third World
Urban Society
Violence and Terrorism
Western Civilization, Pre-Reformation
Western Civilization, Post-Reformation
Western Europe
World History, Pre-Modern
World History, Modern
World Politics

Library of Congress Cataloging in Publication Data
Main entry under title: Annual editions: Violence and terrorism. 1991/92.
1. Terrorism—Periodicals. 2. Violence—Periodicals. I. Schechterman, Bernard, *comp*. II. Slann, Martin, *comp*. III. Title: Violence and terrorism.
303.6′25′05 ISBN 1-56134-032-4

Second Edition

Manufactured by The Banta Company, Harrisonburg, Virginia 22801

Editors/ Advisory Board

Members of the Advisory Board are instrumental in the final selection of articles for each edition of Annual Editions. Their review of articles for content, level, currentness, and appropriateness provides critical direction to the editor and staff. We think you'll find their careful consideration well reflected in this volume.

To the Reader

In publishing ANNUAL EDITIONS we recognize the enormous role played by the magazines, newspapers, and journals of the *public press* in providing current, first-rate educational information in a broad spectrum of interest areas. Within the articles, the best scientists, practitioners, researchers, and commentators draw issues into new perspective as accepted theories and viewpoints are called into account by new events, recent discoveries change old facts, and fresh debate breaks out over important controversies.

Many of the articles resulting from this enormous editorial effort are appropriate for students, researchers, and professionals seeking accurate, current material to help bridge the gap between principles and theories and the real world. These articles, however, become more useful for study when those of lasting value are carefully *collected, organized, indexed,* and *reproduced* in a *low-cost format*, which provides easy and permanent access when the material is needed. That is the role played by *Annual Editions*. Under the direction of each volume's *Editor*, who is an expert in the subject area, and with the guidance of an *Advisory Board*, we seek each year to provide in each *ANNUAL EDITION* a current, well-balanced, carefully selected collection of the best of the public press for your study and enjoyment. We think you'll find this volume useful, and we hope you'll take a moment to let us know what you think.

Terrorism is an international curse of the late twentieth century. Its causes are as varied and as complicated as its manifestations. Governments and citizenries have come to accept the phenomenon of terrorism as one of those hazards of life that is not completely resolvable.

The articles in this reader were chosen in an effort to represent the several categories of terrorism and the multiplicity of terrorist organizations. One primary criterion for their selection was succinctness. There are simply too many ways to track and analyze terrorist groups and activities to concentrate at length on particular facets in one introductory reader.

The readings are authored by reputable journalists and academicians, most of whom have written extensively on terrorism. Their views are not always in agreement with one another and some of their suggestions or analyses may not be agreeable to the student. They are, however, both informed and informative. These articles should stimulate thoughtful inquiry into the subject of terrorism.

However disconcerting political terrorism may be, it remains a constant in international and often domestic politics. Terrorism may not be an indefinite reality, but it is one that certainly has demonstrated staying power. For this reason it is of singular importance that we learn what terrorism really is, what motivates terrorists ideologically, and how the goals of terrorism as well as its outrages can be understood and countered.

This volume is organized in nine units. Unit 1 is devoted to the difficult task of defining and conceptualizing both "terrorism" and "terrorists." Unit 2 introduces and explains the more pronounced reasons for terrorism. Indirectly, this unit's articles also make the point that terrorism may have no realistic termination; hatred is a long-term as well as a destructive emotion. Unit 3 explores the different categories of terrorism, with a particular emphasis on the most effective and lethal type: state-sponsored and state-supported international terrorism. Unit 4 is a new section developed for this edition and one that naturally complements Unit 3. State terrorism is a mass killer and during this century it has destroyed more lives than any other human endeavor. Unit 5 is also new and its essays deal with both the actuality of and the potential for terrorism in the United States. America is neither immune from nor totally open to terrorism. Unit 6 is a brief but pertinent consideration of the relationship between terrorism and the news media. The emphasis here is on the dilemma every free society faces: although the coverage of terrorism is newsworthy, it also encourages future terrorism. Unit 7 emphasizes one of the more frightening characteristics of terrorism: as the articles in this section reveal, terrorism is frequently well financed and organized to maximize resources through networking, intimidation, and even illicit drug trafficking. Unit 8 is the largest collection of articles and attempts to assure the reader that something is being done about terrorism's threat and to explain what the limits and successes are in countering terrorism. These articles identify and analyze what individuals as well as governments do and can do to thwart those who would harm them. Terrorism will remain a permanent and dangerous threat to international peace and political stability. In light of this fact, the articles in Unit 9 are devoted to potential and projected trends in terrorism.

We hope that this volume acquaints the student with terrorism. Ideally, it will be an acquaintance that will foster further inquiry into this omnipresent global phenomenon.

Your comments have produced an improved second edition of *Annual Editions: Violence and Terrorism 91/92*. Your further opinions and suggestions are still welcome and will help shape future editions. Please fill out and return the article rating form on the last page of this book. Any anthology can be improved; this one will continue to be.

Bernard Schechterman

Bernard Schechterman

Martin Slann

Martin Slann
Editors

Contents

Unit 1

The Concept of Terrorism

Five articles examine the phenomenon of terrorism in the context of today's world security.

Unit 2

The Causes and Scope of Terrorism

Six articles discuss the more prevalent lethal causes and scope of contemporary terrorism.

The concepts in bold italics are developed in the article. For further expansion please refer to the Topic Guide and the Index.

Unit 3

The Terrorists: International, State-Sponsored, and State-Supported

Eleven selections examine the vicious forms of violence generated by state-sponsored terrorism, and the extent to which a government can go to put pressure on its citizenry.

Unit 4

State Terrorism

Eleven articles consider the extent to which a nation's government can exercise terrorism.

The concepts in bold italics are developed in the article. For further expansion please refer to the Topic Guide and the Index.

Unit 5

Terrorism in America

Seven articles examine how terrorists impact on American domestic society.

Unit 6

Terrorism and the Media

Five selections examine the critical connection between terrorism, the media, and the audience.

Unit 7

Tactics, Strategies, and Targeting

Eight articles discuss how terrorists share tactics and strategies. Terrorists organizations, if they are to be successful, need logistical and financial support.

Unit 8

Countering Terrorism

Eleven articles examine methods used to counter terrorism, from legalistic to retaliation through force.

Unit 9

Trends and Projections of Terrorism

Three articles discuss the possible future of terrorism.

The concepts in bold italics are developed in the article. For further expansion please refer to the Topic Guide and the Index.

Topic Guide

This topic guide suggests how the selections in this book relate to topics of traditional concern to students and professionals involved with the study of violence and terrorism. It can be very useful in locating articles that relate to each other for reading and research. The guide is arranged alphabetically according to topic. Articles may, of course, treat topics that do not appear in the topic guide. In turn, entries in the topic guide do not necessarily constitute a comprehensive listing of all the contents of each selection.

TOPIC AREA	TREATED IN:
Abu Nidal Organization (ANO)	4. Terrorism: Myths and Reality 16. Interview With Abu Nidal
African Terrorism	9. Terrible Toll of Human Hatred 46. Linkages Between Sunni and Shi'i
Airline Hijackings/ Bombings	5. Unmasking Terrorism 16. Interview With Abu Nidal 17. A Terrorist Talks About Life 41. Terrorism and the Media 55. International Crime 59. On the Trail of Terror 60. Fighting International Terrorism 65. Terrorist Threat to Commercial Aviation
Biological/ Chemical Weapons	13. Arming the IRA 52. Will Terrorists Use Chemical Weapons? 59. On the Trail of Terror 66. Growing Threat of Terrorism
Diplomats	41. Terrorism and the Media
Eastern Asian Terrorism	6. "Holy Wars" 9. Terrible Toll of Human Hatred 20. Selling of Terrorism 21. C.I.A. Tie Asserted in Indonesia Purge 30. Chinese Repression Threatens Tibet's Buddhist Tradition 31. Government Declares War on Tamils 32. What Became of Burma's Dissident Students? 49. Narco-Terrorism
Ethnic Rivalry	9. Terrible Toll of Human Hatred 13. Arming the IRA 16. Interview With Abu Nidal 17. A Terrorist Talks About Life 18. Neo-Nazis Stage Attacks 19. Interview With Martin McGuiness 22. As Peru Votes 28. Political Violence in Guatemala 30. Chinese Repression Threatens Tibet's Buddhist Tradition 31. Government Declares War on Tamils 48. The IRA 53. Terrorism and Public Opinion 67. Contrasting Ethical Foundations
Extradition	60. Fighting International Terrorism
Freedom Fighters	1. Defining Terrorism 3. How to Tell a Terrorist
Hezbollah	14. Rafsanjani May Hold Key that Releases the Hostages 15. Out From the Cellar 47. Why Hostage-Taking Is So Popular
Hostage-Taking	14. Rafsanjani May Hold Key that Releases the Hostages 15. Out From the Cellar 46. Linkages Between Sunni and Shi'i 47. Why Hostage-Taking Is So Popular 57. Hezbollah Frustrates a Gulliver-Like U.S. 63. Terror and Negotiation
Human Rights Violations	24. Iraq's Human-Rights Toll 25. Iran's Dismal Record
International Terrorist Groups (Mercenaries)	13. Arming the IRA 16. Interview With Abu Nidal 17. A Terrorist Talks About Life 19. Interview With Martin McGuinness 38. Borders Open to Terrorist Threat 46. Linkages Between Sunni and Shi'i 48. The IRA
Irish Republican Army (IRA)	13. Arming the IRA 19. Interview With Martin McGuinness 48. The IRA 53. Terrorism and Public Opinion
Latin American Terrorism	22. As Peru Votes 27. El Salvador's Rights Record Challenged 28. Political Violence on the Rise in Guatemala 29. Death Squads Seek Negotiations 49. Narco-Terrorism 50. Peru's Shining Path Terrorism 51. Colombian Journalists vs. Drug Terrorists 53. Terrorism and Public Opinion 54. Counterterrorism in the 1990s 55. International Crime 64. Mission Improbable
Lebanese Groups	14. Rafsanjani May Hold Key that Releases the Hostages 15. Out From the Cellar 46. Linkages Between Sunni and Shi'i

TOPIC AREA	TREATED IN:
Media	41. Terrorism and the Media 42. Manipulation of the Media 43. Terrorism on TV 44. Silent Treatment for Terrorists 45. Lessons From the British Experience
Narco-Terrorism	22. As Peru Votes 29. Death Squads Seek Negotiations 38. Borders Open to Terrorist Threat 49. Narco-Terrorism 50. Peru's Shining Path Terrorists 51. Colombian Journalists vs. Drug Terrorists 54. Counterterrorism in the 1990s 55. International Crime 66. Growing Threat of Terrorism
Palestine Liberation Organization (PLO)	8. As Palestinian Revolt Continues 16. Interview With Abu Nidal 17. A Terrorist Talks About Life 46. Linkages Between Sunni and Shi'i 59. On the Trail of Terror 62. Diminishing the Threat
Religious Extremism	6. "Holy Wars" 7. Terrorist Mentality 9. Terrible Toll of Human Hatred 14. Rafsanjani May Hold Key that Releases the Hostages 46. Linkages Between Sunni and Shi'i 57. Hezbollah Frustrates a Gulliver-Like U.S. 67. Contrasting Ethical Foundations of Terrorism
Revolutionary (Domestic Terrorism)	2. 'Terrorism' 3. How to Tell a Terrorist 4. Terrorism: Myths and Reality 5. Unmasking Terrorism 7. Terrorist Mentality 8. As Palestinian Revolt Continues 13. Arming the IRA 18. Neo-Nazis Stage Attacks 19. Interview With Martin McGuinness 22. As Peru Votes 34. Stopping Terrorism 35. Skinheads Target the Schools 36. New Extremists 38. Borders Open to Terrorist Threats 39. Officials Say They Have Leads in Killings 40. Environmentalist Hurt 50. Peru's Shining Path Terrorists 51. Colombian Journalists vs. Drug Terrorists 53. Terrorism and Public Opinion 54. Counterterrorism in the 1990s 56. When Reality Came Unglued 67. Contrasting Ethical Foundations of Terrorism
Soviet Union and Eastern Europe	16. Interview With Abu Nidal 59. On the Trail of Terror
State-Sponsored and State-Supported Terrorism	2. 'Terrorism' 5. Unmasking Terrorism 12. What Constitutes State Support to Terrorists? 13. Arming the IRA 16. Interview With Abu Nidal 17. A Terrorist Talks About Life 20. Selling of Terrorism 21. C.I.A. Tie Asserted in Indonesia Purge 33. Who Killed Jonathan Moyle? 46. Linkages Between Sunni and Shi'i 47. Why Hostage-Taking Is So Popular 49. Narco-Terrorism 57. Hezbollah Frustrates a Gulliver-Like U.S.
Tactics	44. Silent Treatment for Terrorists 46. Linkages Between Sunni and Shi'i 47. Why Hostage-Taking Is So Popular 48. The IRA 49. Narco-Terrorism 50. Peru's Shining Path Terrorists 51. Colombian Journalists vs. Drug Terrorists 52. Will Terrorists Use Chemical Weapons? 53. Terrorism and Public Opinion 57. Hezbollah Frustrates a Gulliver-Like U.S. 65. Terrorist Threat to Commercial Aviation 66. Growing Threat of Terrorism
Terrorist Funding	16. Interview With Abu Nidal 17. A Terrorist Talks About Life 46. Linkages Between Sunni and Shi'i 50. Peru's Shining Path Terrorists
Training	29. Death Squads Seek Negotiations 46. Linkages Between Sunni and Shi'i
Urban Terrorism	35. Skinheads Target Schools 39. Officials Say They Have Leads in Killings 53. Terrorism and Public Opinion
West European Groups	4. Terrorism: Myths and Reality 18. Neo-Nazis Stage Attacks 26. Destasifying Germany 53. Terrorism and Public Opinion 56. When Reality Came Unglued 59. On the Trail of Terror

The Concept of Terrorism

This section of the book has two primary goals: (1) to place the phenomenon of terrorism in some context of political modes of violence, and (2) to shed light on the actual meaning and boundaries of this form of activity.

"Defining Terrorism" reviews the ongoing debate and variations in the attempt to define terrorism (and the terrorist act). Drawing upon the comprehensive literature on the subject, the author delineates the contentious issues and helps to facilitate the defining process.

Articles 2 through 5 take up, among other things, the continuing controversy among those who study terrorism as to how to define it. There is widespread concurrence on the general characteristics of terrorism, and divisions on certain factors beyond these basics. The minimalist approach focuses on three ingredients: perpetrator, victim, and an audience deliberately affected by the violent act. Of the three, the victim remains the subject of the most contentious debate. The official American concept of terrorism stresses that an assault against a noncombatant civilian victim is clear-cut evidence of a terrorist act. The maximalist approach, favored by the Israelis and others, includes the presence of passive military targets alongside civilians as a basis for labeling an attack a terrorist act. The definition becomes crucial to statistical compilations, especially trend and geographic pervasiveness analysis, as well as to the question of countering terrorism (see Unit 8).

The American concept of terrorism (articles 2 and 4) places a heavy emphasis on the criminal nature of the act as well as the threat to the rule of law and democratic systems. The British view, discussed in article 3, also stresses the threat to democracy, but concentrates equally on the obligations and rights of people. This view makes moral condemnation of terrorism even more significant.

"Terrorism: Myths and Reality" helps negate some popular notions that, particularly in the United States, contribute to and reinforce the government's definition and perception of terrorism. These involve classification as well as patterns of behavior.

"Unmasking Terrorism: The Fear of Fear Itself" places great stress on a critical ingredient of terrorism and terrorist objectives—the creation of a climate of fear, in which the ultimate goal is the intimidation and coercion of the public, especially in open and democratic societies. Aside from the personal fears of physical harm, the most dangerous ramification is the disruption of the ordinary life-styles of citizens in free societies.

Looking Ahead: Challenge Questions

Why are there basic difficulties in reaching agreement on the characterization and definition of terrorism?

What ideas are central to the American definition of terrorism? Which of these may be misleading?

Where does terrorism fit on a continuum of organized modes of political violence in today's world?

Unit 1

DEFINING TERRORISM

Peter C. Sederberg

Peter C. Sederberg, Ph.D. is professor of political science at the University of South Carolina.

A weary cliche, yet a most persistent myth in the study of terrorism stresses the subjectivity that supposedly afflicts efforts to define the phenomenon. The aphorism "one man's terrorist is another man's freedom fighter" suggests that all attempts to formulate the concept will be hopelessly compromised by essentially arbitrary personal or political bias. Consequently, any analysis based on such dubious conceptual foundations will be distorted and most likely vacuous.

The emotional baggage attendant on the term leads it to be used more for condemnation rather than clarification. To successfully attach the label "terrorist" to one's opponent constitutes a moral and political victory (Jenkins, 1985). Such victories, though, are purchased at high cost for critical discourse on the problem. Christopher Hitchens (1986, p. 68) argues that the terrorist label "disguises reality and impoverishes language and makes a banality out of the discussion of war and revolution and politics." Little wonder, then, that some conclude that the "very word terror is a hindrance in the investigation of violence" (Bell, 1978a, p. 39).

This lamentable condition induces some commentators to abandon the quest for a working definition. Laqueur (1977, p. 5) argues that a comprehensive definition is unlikely to be found in the foreseeable future but asserts that "to argue that terrorism cannot be studied without such a definition is manifestly absurd." On somewhat similar lines, Geoffrey Levitt (1988) suggests that the deductive approach to terrorism may produce a certain political satisfaction but is too vague to serve as a basis for practical responses to terrorism. As a pragmatic alternative, he suggests a inductive approach that simply identifies a series of criminal acts to be addressed. From a different ideological position, other critics assail terrorist definitions as simply rhetorical weapons used to castigate opponents of the established order (Chomsky and Herman, 1979; Herman and O'Sullivan, 1989).

While the critics of the concept make valuable points, we need either some kind of working definition in order to delimit the boundaries of terrorism from other forms of conflict behavior (Gibbs, 1989; Provizer, 1987; Wardlaw, 1982, 1989; Weinberg and Davis, 1989) or else be prepared to abandon the term to the mindless pleasures of the politicians. Unfortunately, the lack of consensus produced by the combination of inherent ambiguity and polemical pressure results in a plethora of definitions. Alex Schmid (1983), in a comprehensive review of the literature at the time, identifies over a hundred competing definitions. When he published a second edition (1988), the situation had worsened, ironically, in part, in response to a survey on the definitional problem he conducted.

To sort through this morass, we first review several problems afflicting various definitions, thereby suggesting some means for assessing comparative worth. We then suggest a kind of "middle range" strategy that allows us to distinguish terrorism from other forms of coercive conflict, though not without a certain degree of irreducible ambiguity. Somewhat paradoxically, if we can be clear about the areas that lack clarity, we will possess a better understanding of the terrorist phenomenon than we would if we embraced a definition that obscures its own obscurities.

Perhaps the most easily recognized definitional flaw consists of the failure to distinguish between presumed terrorist activities and other forms of coercive action not normally (or usefully) considered terrorist. Brian Crozier (1974, p. 4) suggests that terrorism is " 'motivated violence for political ends' (a definition that distinguishes terrorism from both vandalism and non-political crime)." Unfortunately, it doesn't distinguish it from any other tactic of internal or external warfare. Similarly, a CIA study (1978, p. 1) defines international terrorism as "the threat or use of violence for political purposes when (1) such action is intended to influence the attitude and behavior of a target group

From *Terrorism: Contending Themes in Contemporary Research,* by Peter C. Sederberg, 1991. From the forthcoming *Annual Review of Conflict of Knowledge,* published by Garland Publishing, New York, NY.

wider than its immediate victims, and (2) its ramifications transcend national boundaries." The blunt edge of this instrument eliminates the distinction between a PLO hijacking and the Battle of Midway in World War II. Other examples of the tendency to conflate terrorism with a variety of other forms of coercion include Russell, Banker, and Bowman (1979), Lodge, (1981a), U.S. Department of Defense (1986; quoted in Schmid, 1988), and Falk (1988).

A second definitional shortcoming arises when terrorism, however characterized, is primarily associated with one side or the other in a political struggle. Not surprisingly, given the nature of the dominant political agenda, terrorism is often identified with revolutionary dissent. Take, for example, the effort of the U.S. Department of Defense (1983, p. 1220) to confine terrorism to "the unlawful use or threatened use of force or violence by a revolutionary organization against individuals or property with the intention of coercing or intimidating governments or societies, often for political or ideological purposes." This definition manages to be both vague and tendentious. Other definitions that seem to be compromised by too close an identification with the established order are those of Lodge (1981a) and Buckelew (1986).

Given the polemical purposes frequently served by the terrorist label, those identifying with various dissident struggles castigated as terrorist have attempted to appropriate the term for their own purposes. Falk (1986, pp. 135–137) argues that the manipulation of political language serves to disguise the indiscriminate violence of what he calls "First World Terrorism." Noam Chomsky (1988, p. 1) makes a somewhat similar point when characterizing the Fifth Freedom; "the freedom to rob, to exploit and to dominate, to undertake any course of action to ensure that existing privilege is protected and advanced." Finally, Goren (1984, p. 13) quotes a definition of terrorism offered by an ad hoc group of nonaligned nations which condemns, among other things, "acts of violence and other repressive acts by colonial, racist, and alien regimes against peoples struggling for their liberation. . . ." Proponents of this definition clearly intend that the actions of the South African and Israeli regimes be considered as terrorist.

Somewhat less contentious than explicitly defining one side or the other in a political struggle as terroristic are those definitions that single out the nature of the victims as being central to the understanding of the terrorist act. Unfortunately, the definitions stress different characteristics such as being "innocent" (Friedlander, 1980; Netanyahu, 1986), noncombatant or civilian (Francis, 1981; Sederberg, 1989), symbolic (Crenshaw, 1981; Singh, 1977; Thomton, 1964), or arbitrarily chosen (Kupperman and Trent, 1979; Wilkinson, 1974). Whatever the superficial similarities, these traits are not equivalent to one another. A civilian victim may not be "innocent" (whatever that means). Noncombatants may not be civilians; they might be prisoners of war. Symbolic victims might be combatants, and if they are symbolic, they cannot be chosen arbitrarily, but for their symbolic value.

If the pitfall of political identification is avoided, definitions sometimes slip into circularity. For example, Crelinstein (1987) defines terrorism as "the deliberate use of violence and the threat of violence to evoke a state of fear (or terror) in a particular victim or audience." Other definitions that stress the fear-inducing character of the act include Duvall and Stohl (1988), Mickolus (1980), and Wardlaw (1982). Now the question of why acts considered terrorist are often capable of inspiring a state of terror in disproportion to their actual threat is an important area for research (see below), but to define terrorism as action causing (or intended to cause) terror fails to provide much of a basis for distinguishing terrorism from other forms of coercive conflict. Such definitions obscure the many purposes beyond brute terror for which terrorism is used or make the character of the action dependent on the success it achieves in causing terror in the target.

In all, Schmid (1988) identifies twenty-two elements that appear in the 109 definitions he analyzes. In an effort of cumulation, if not synthesis, he (p. 28) offers a definition that incorporates sixteen of the twenty-two elements:

> Terrorism is an anxiety-inspiring method of repeated violent action, employed by (semi-) clandestine individual, group, or state actors, for idiosyncratic, criminal, or political reasons, whereby—in contrast to assassination—the direct targets of violence are not the main targets. The immediate human victims of violence are generally chosen randomly (targets of opportunity) or selectively (representative or symbolic targets) from a target population, and serve as message generators. Threat- and violence-based communication processes between terrorist (organization), (imperiled) victims, and main targets are used to manipulate the main target (audience(s)), turning it into a target of terror, a target of demands, or a target of attention, depending on whether intimidation, coercion, or propaganda is primarily sought.

Although an impressive effort at summarization, the definition's convoluted and somewhat contradictory nature diminishes its utility.

A variety of problems, then, impede our efforts to develop an analytically useful definition of terrorism. First, an understandable, but confusing, tendency to intermingle explanation, justification, and condemnation mars many definitions. Second, the confusion between the action (terrorism), the actor (the terrorist), and the effect (terror) detracts from the ability to distinguish between terrorism and the larger class of coercive behavior of which it is a part. In this regard, definitions should focus on the act, and recognize that issues of actors and effects are areas for inquiry, not definitional attributes. Finally, the option of focussing on various subspecies of terrorism fails to specify what it is about these subspecies that make them terrorist. Though we may be able to formulate some policy response to particular activities, we would be forced to abandon the search for a more general understanding.

If we are to rescue the concept of terrorism from the polemicists, as well as address the concerns of those who believe it to be an empty category, we must specify those characteristics that distinguish terrorism from other coercive tactics used within or between political communities. Two traits, each drawing upon fairly well-established rules of war, seem to hold some promise (Walzer, 1977). The most well-established limits on the conduct of warfare involve the targets selected and the means chosen to attack those targets. Specifically, the targets of attack should be combatants, and the weapons used against these targets should be highly discriminating.

The principle of noncombatant immunity and the ban on indiscriminate means are certainly interrelated; nevertheless, they raise distinct issues. Terrorism may be seen as a tactic of severe coercion that deliberately violates these two rules of war: Noncombatants are the targets, and the means used to attack these targets are relatively indiscriminate. These two criteria, then, suggest two propositions and two qualifying exceptions (Sederberg, 1989, p. 37):

Proposition One: Discriminating acts of coercion aimed at combatants are not terrorist.
Exception One: At some point, attacks on combatants may become so indiscriminate (counterforce nuclear war) that they become terrorist in effect, if not intent.
Proposition Two: Undiscriminating and severe coercive attacks deliberately aimed at noncombatants are terrorist.
Exception Two: At some point, attacks against noncombatants may become so discriminating in choice of target (e.g., a tyrant) and means, that they are not usefully labeled terrorist (George, 1988).

The value of this definition lies both in its clear specification of what tactics are or are not terrorist and in its explicit identification of the areas where disputes are likely to arise (i.e., indiscriminate attacks on presumed combatants; highly discriminate attacks on noncombatants). Moreover, by treating terrorism as a tactic, it incorporates recognition that all contenders in a political struggle may yield to the terrorist temptation. Two key questions remain open, however: Who is a noncombatant? and, how indiscriminate is too indiscriminate? These probably cannot be convincingly resolved by definitional fiat, but although they remain open to debate, provisional determinations need not be arbitrary, but should be supported by reasoned elaboration.

The characteristics we have suggested for distinguishing terrorism from other coercive tactics, however, suggest why terrorism has the common consequence of spreading fear far in excess of the concrete damage done or the probabilities of being a victim. The distinction between combatants and noncombatants is, perhaps, the last firebreak of a civil order. Once breached, no one can feel secure. Terrorism, moreover, often involves innocuous targets, such as airplanes, railway depots, and department stores, places that people normally consider safe. Terrorist acts cause not only substantive damage, but also they undermine the confidence people have in the familiar. Now every place must be viewed with suspicion, if not alarm.

If we abandon the concept of terrorism to the ideologues or ignore the differences between terrorism and other forms of coercion, we hamper the possibilities for successful political action to contain this particular tactic. Only if we have a sensible and reasonably clear idea of the distinctive traits of terrorism can we pursue questions of who uses it and why.

'TERRORISM'—A TERM NOTORIOUSLY DIFFICULT TO PIN DOWN

Rushworth M. Kidder

Staff writer of The Christian Science Monitor

Just exactly what *is* "terrorism"?

Following the American bombing of Libya, the word is being bandied about on all sides. The United States and its allies refer to the regime of Col. Muammar Qaddafi as "terrorist," while Libya and its friends describe the US action as "terrorism."

In fact, the term is notoriously difficult to pin down.

"The great difficulty when you get into [discussions of terrorism is that] right away you run into problems with definitions," notes Noel Koch, a specialist in terrorism at the US Defense Department.

Last summer, when Vice-President George Bush convened his Task Force on Combatting Terrorism, the group spent a number of days simply trying to agree on a definition. The final report notes that "terrorism is a phenomenon easier to describe than to define." The problem, terrorism experts say, is that the term shifts according to one's viewpoint. The United Nations has struggled long and hard over the problem, since it is often said that "one man's terrorist is another man's freedom fighter." Terrorism, a pejorative term, is often described by those who favor it as "paramilitary action," as "resistance to occupation," or as part of a "war of national liberation." Nevertheless, experts on terrorism interviewed recently in the US, Europe, and the Middle East agree on some common elements.

"The crucial element," says Prof. Paul Wilkinson of the University of Aberdeen, Scotland, "is the deliberate attempt to create fear, intensive fear, in order to coerce the wider target into giving in to what the terrorist wants." Prof. Eytan Gilboa of Hebrew University in Jerusalem notes that "we have to make a distinction between the accidental killing of innocent civilians and an official deliberate policy of hurting civilians."

He notes that civilians are often killed both in guerrilla warfare and in terrorism.

"The question is if you do it by accident or if you do it on purpose," he says. "In my understanding of it, terrorism means that you do it on purpose." British scholar Brian Crozier calls attention to different forms of terrorism.

"There's disruptive terrorism," he says, and "there's theatrical terrorism to draw attention to the cause. And there is a very important form of terrorism which is nearly always overlooked, and that's what I call coercive terrorism: terrorism against the terrorists' own side."

In that category, for example, come the numerous bombings and assassinations carried out by various Palestinian groups against one another.

Other scholars emphasize that terrorism needs both a political motive and an audience. The motives underlying common crime are more often individual rather than political. And common crime usually involves only two parties (the criminal and the victim), whereas terrorism, which seeks to amplify and spread fear, has three: the victim, the criminal, and the audience, usually reached through the news media.

Other terms commonly used in discussions of terrorism include:

• **State-sponsored terrorism.** This term is applied when an established government supports the activities of terrorist organizations. It is usually reserved for cases in which the sponsoring nation uses the terrorists to further its own policy goals beyond the territory in which the terrorism occurs. Libya, Syria, and Iran are generally recognized as major state sponsors of terrorism, although some experts believe much of the funding and support for international terrorism can be traced to the Soviet Union and its East bloc allies.

- **State terror.** This term covers acts of violence and intimidation perpetrated not by small groups of clandestine terrorists but by the military and political apparatus of the state itself. Nazi Germany practiced state terror, as do many communist countries. The term is open to broad interpretation: Palestinians on the Israeli-occupied West Bank accuse Israel of practicing state terror, and Libya accuses the US of the same thing.

Selected US definitions

Department of Defense, 1983
"The unlawful use or threatened use of force or violence by a revolutionary organization against individuals or property with the intention of coercing or intimidating governments or societies, often for political or ideological purposes."

FBI, 1983
"The unlawful use of force or violence against persons or property to intimidate or coerce a government, the civilian population, or any segment thereof, in furtherance of political or social objectives."

State Department, 1984
"Premeditated, politically motivated violence perpetrated against noncombatant targets by subnational groups or clandestine state agents."

Department of Justice, 1984
"Violent criminal conduct apparently intended:
- To intimidate or coerce a civilian population.
- To influence the conduct of a government by intimidation or coercion.
- To affect the conduct of a government by assassination or kidnapping."

The Vice-President's Task Force on Combatting Terrorism, 1986
"The unlawful use or threat of violence against persons or property to further political or social objectives. It is usually intended to intimidate or coerce a government, individuals, or groups or to modify their behavior or policies."

How to tell a terrorist

Three questions to ask before you start mumbling about "freedom fighters"

Terrorism is nothing new—its modern era was kicked off a century ago by Russia's *narodnaya volya* bombers and assassins—and it is not about to go away. Despite the prophecies of all of President Reagan's critics, America's bombing of Libya in April has apparently had the welcome result of reducing Libyan terrorism. But in the past fortnight Spain has suffered two Basque terrorist bombings, one of which killed ten people, and West Germany an attack by the Red Army Faction that killed a senior executive of the electronics company Siemens. Peru's centre-left democracy no longer goes many days without a bomb blowing up in its people's faces.

There will be more attacks. The magic of terrorism has always been its power of magnification: an act of violence which would be too puny to be noticed if it were directed against the armed forces of a state can be turned into a psychological blow strong enough to shake a society if it is directed against a few ordinary and unarmed people. Thanks to the modern technologies of weapons, television and travel, the enlarging power of terrorism has never been greater. The spiritual heirs of those nineteenth-century anarchists who invented "propaganda by the deed" would not dream of walking away from deeds that now yield so much propaganda.

The democrats' task

Democracies, not tsars and the like, are almost always the target of terrorism these days. The main danger for democracies in their next-to-unending fight against it is that their peoples will not have a clear enough picture of their enemy: so that democratic governments may not be as tough as they need to be to contain the threat. Few people now succumb to the romantic picture of the terrorist. But many still think that "one man's terrorist is another man's freedom fighter." He isn't. The democracies victimised by terrorism must keep the difference clear if they are to mount effective attacks on terrorists and the states that back them.

The main reason terrorists and freedom fighters blur in many people's minds is that attacks on non-combatants are a frequent by-product, and occasionally a centrepiece, of military strategy in modern wars. It has been a long time since non-combatants did not predictably die in a military attack. Sometimes their deaths are intended: it is hard to call the Dresden and Hiroshima bombings in 1945 anything but terrorism. Yet the second, at least, helped to end a terrible war.

Several things nevertheless distinguish terrorist violence from the legitimate use of force to attain political ends. The first distinction is between perpetrators. States have repeatedly shown themselves capable of committing terrorist acts, including ones directed against their own citizens. But the force used by a state, especially in its conflicts with other states, has to be weighed in a different balance from the force used by freelancers who take it upon themselves to conduct politics with the bomb and the gun. Among other things, whole societies speak for larger interests than a few individuals do.

Violent resistance to the authority of the state is often justified: not a few of today's presidents and prime ministers were yesterday's guerrillas. Yet not every use of force is warranted, even against a ghastly government. The second ground for distinguishing terrorism from other insurrectionary action is the intentions of those carrying out the violence. Military operations mounted by armies or guerrillas will frequently lead to the deaths of non-combatants, because they are in or around the military target being aimed at; but harming them is not normally the purpose of the operation. The whole point of an act of terrorism, by contrast, is to attack targets that have no military value. A terrorist intends to harm non-combatants: they are the means by which he exerts his effect on others.

This suggests the third, and strongest, reason for distinguishing terrorism from other uses of force. The essential feature of modern terrorism is the severing of the link between the target of violence and the reason for violence. All varieties of terrorism strain that link, but not all cause it to snap. This is why some terrorists are more sympathetic than others. The nineteenth-century Russians who assassinated cabinet ministers stand at one end of the terrorist scale; so do the bombers of Dresden and Hiroshima. At the other end

From *The Economist*, July 26, 1986, pp. 9-10.

stand the Palestinian hijackers who last year put a bullet through the head of a wheelchair-bound American on board an Italian cruise ship because they wanted to get back at Israel.

It may seem ghoulish to make judgments about the relative virtues of different kinds of terrorism; but it makes a difference in how firmly the West should respond to international terrorism. (Apart from help such as extradition treaties, each country has to handle the national sort on its own.) A terrorist attack is less awful the closer the connection between the target and the grievance, and the fewer the democratic opportunities there are for remedying the grievance. Airline hijackings are always unacceptable; so are attacks in countries, such as Britain and Spain, where the complaint can soon be put to the vote. South African blacks who mount attacks against the white government of their own country have a better case to argue.

The international terrorism that democracies must be utterly merciless about is the kind in which the victim of the terror and the reason for it are complete strangers. The West should prepare for more of it, because unfortunately it is also the kind that technology has made especially attractive to terrorists.

Terrorism: Myths and Reality

L. Paul Bremer III

Following is an address by L. Paul Bremer III, Ambassador at Large for Counterterrorism, before the Norwegian Atlantic Committee, Oslo, Norway, February 4, 1988.

The impact of terrorism has spawned a huge volume of literature and commentary. There are scores of self-styled experts and consultants. Analyzing and explaining terrorism has become a growth industry.

Of course, we should try to understand terrorism. But much of what has been written and said about terrorism has created a mythology which instead has served to confound the public and, in some cases, to romanticize terrorists. If we are to have a sound counterterrorism policy we must know the facts.

Three myths, in particular, confuse thinking about terrorism.

- Solve the "underlying problems" and terrorism will cease.
- Terrorists are crazy.
- Vigorous action against terrorism only increases it.

Today I will address these myths and tell you about the American Government's strategy for countering terrorism.

Myth One: Solve the Underlying Problems and Terrorism will Cease

Too often terrorist acts are followed by guilt-ridden responses which begin by pointing out the wrongs done to the terrorists and end by declaring that there is no solution until the "underlying problem" is solved. This argument, often made by well-intentioned people, closely parallels the line of reasoning put forward by terrorists. Stripped of glossy phrases, the terrorists' argument goes something like this:

- Had we been treated justly, there would be no violence.
- We seek justice.
- Whatever we do in pursuit of justice is, therefore, justified.

This line of reasoning is not only arrogant—leaving the judgment of right and wrong to the terrorists—but unsupported by the facts. Let us examine some cases.

Again and again, terrorist attacks in the Middle East have been specifically designed to derail progress in dealing with the region's deep problems.

- In 1948, UN mediator Count Bernadotte was assassinated as he worked on a cease-fire during Israel's war for independence.
- In the early 1950s, King Abdallah of Jordan was assassinated in part because of his talks with Israel.
- In 1974, while then-Secretary of State Kissinger was negotiating a disengagement agreement on the Golan Heights, Palestinian terrorists seized and killed 32 Israeli school children in the town of Ma'alot.
- President Anwar Sadat was assassinated in large part because he made peace with Israel.
- In 1983, the Abu Nidal Organization (ANO)—at the urging of Syria—conducted a series of attacks against Jordanian interests when Jordan seemed to be taking a more moderate approach to a Middle East settlement.

It is not just in the Middle East that terrorism has increased as underlying problems are dealt with.

- Basque terrorism in Spain has dramatically increased as its demands for Basque autonomy have been realized. In 1975, the year Franco died, Basque terrorists killed 16 Spaniards. Five years later, after the implementation of democratic rule in Spain and the granting of significant autonomy in the Basque region, Basque terrorists killed 96 Spaniards—a sixfold increase.
- In Turkey, Kurdish terrorists, in addition to kidnaping and murdering Kurdish village guards and headmen, have attacked bridges, roadbuilding equipment, and other elements of an economic infrastructure which was improving conditions for impoverished Kurds in southeast Turkey.

Terrorism occurs in the most free and just societies ever known to mankind.

- In the Federal Republic of Germany, the Badder-Meinhof gang and the Red Army Faction have practiced terror. France has been beset by the terrorism of the Direct Action group. Terrorists have also been active in other democratic, free countries—Belgium, Italy, Canada, and Japan.
- In the United States, there have been terrorist actions by the Weathermen, the Order, the Aryan Brotherhood, and the Symbionese People's Liberation Army.

Individuals frequently join groups because of a need to "belong." Moreover, it is not at all clear that terrorists themselves are motivated by a desire to solve underlying problems. In fact, recent psychiatric research makes it clear that many individual terrorists are not motivated by their so-called cause. For example, Dr. Jerrold M. Post of George Washington University concludes that the "cause" is not the fundamental reason most terrorists join up. The "cause" provides the rationale, but the motivation is the terrorist's desire to belong to a group.

Social isolation and personal failure are frequently seen in preterrorist histories. Studies in Italy and Germany have shown that members of the Red Army Faction and the Red Brigades often came from incomplete family structures and had shown a high frequency of educational and job failure. Fully a third had been convicted in juvenile court before they joined a terrorist group. While the leadership remains focused on the political goal, many of the rank and file join not out of deep ideological commitment to a "cause" but because the terrorist group, in effect, offers a "home," a "family."

Another example of this phenomenon is found in the Basque ETA [Basque Fatherland and Freedom] organization. In the Basque region, only 8% of the population is from mixed Spanish-Basque heritage, and children

Reprinted from U. S. Department of State, *Current Policy #1047*, February 4, 1988, pp. 1-3.

from mixed marriages are not well accepted in Basque society. Yet fully 40% of ETA members are from mixed heritage.

Causes can be addressed without giving in to terrorism. Of course, we cannot and should not ignore underlying problems while we devote ourselves to countering terrorism. No country has done more to promote a peace settlement in the Middle East than the United States. We recognize the legitimate grievances of many groups, but nothing justifies terrorism. Recognizing a grievance does not require accepting terrorism as the solution.

We do not have the luxury of choosing between policies which counter terrorism and those which seek to resolve underlying issues. We must do both.

Myth Two: Terrorists are Suicidal Lunatics

A second myth is that terrorists are crazy. A corollary is that they are willing to die for their cause, so arresting and imprisoning terrorists will have no deterrent effect. Both elements of this myth are incorrect.

Most terrorists are not crazy. In fact, it is their sanity which makes them dangerous. They are calculating fanatics. They may use unstable people in their operations, but it is their ability to calculate and plan which makes them dangerous. Terrorism is rarely "mindless."

Nor does their distortion of good and evil make terrorists insane. Russian terrorist Mikhail Bukanin put it this way:

> To the revolutionist, whatever aids the triumph of the revolution is ethical; all that hinders it is unethical and criminal.

Let us look at a few examples.

- The 1985 Rome and Vienna airport massacres, carried out by the Abu Nidal Organization with Syrian and Libyan assistance, were not the work of lunatics. The attacks were not random but directed against the El Al counters. The purpose was to terrify El Al passengers and travelers to Israel, thus weakening Israel's economy and "furthering the revolution."
- Last October, the notorious Peruvian terrorist group, *Sendero Luminoso*, occupied a small village in the Department of Ayacucho and captured eight members of the local civil defense force. After a mock trial, the villagers were tortured and beheaded. Such grotesque treatment of the very people whose support *Sendero* seeks might seem counterproductive. Actually, it is an example of "enforcement terrorism." The intention is to terrify the *campesinos* into supporting *Sendero* or, at a minimum, to prevent them from collaborating with the government in any way.
- "Enforcement terrorism" is widespread in the Middle East. Most Palestinian terrorism over the years has been directed against rival Palestinians and other Arabs. For example, while the Abu Nidal Organization's goal is the destruction of the state of Israel, only 14% of its attacks have been against Israeli or Jewish targets. Sixty-three percent of all attacks have been against Palestinian and Arab targets. Clearly, "enforcement" is a major goal for the ANO. And most of what they are enforcing is a hard line against negotiation or accommodation with Israel.

Few terrorist attacks are intended to end in the death of the terrorist. Spectacular bombings, such as those against the Marine barracks and the U.S. Embassy in Beirut have drawn attention to suicide attacks. Yet, in fact, very few terrorist attacks are deliberately suicidal.

According to a study of terrorist missions between 1968 and 1974, less than 2% of all terrorist attacks are genuinely suicidal. In about a third of the cases, the terrorists were willing to die but preferred to live. In more than 60% of the cases, elaborate escape plans were made. In spite of prominent suicide attacks since that study, recent events do not suggest dramatic variations in these figures.

So terrorists make careful calculations about their attacks. They intend to escape unharmed. Their rationality means that forceful action to deter terrorists can have a beneficial effect. But this brings us to the last of the myths.

Myth Three: Forceful Action Against Terrorists Only Fuels Terrorism

It has been argued that jailing terrorists only leads to attacks to free them, that military action only leads to counteraction. This is a myth, and a dangerous one, because it can paralyze us into inaction. The reality is that forceful action is a necessary element of any successful response to terrorism.

By forceful action, I mean not just military responses but aggressive law enforcement practices and stiff sentences when terrorists are convicted. Since the acts that terrorists commit—murder, arson, kidnaping, air piracy—are invariably crimes, the law is a tool for us to use. Yes, in the short run we may face reprisals when we imprison terrorists. But over time, the rule of law will prevail.

One of the reasons that we have so little domestic terrorism in the United States is that the FBI [Federal Bureau of Investigation] and the Justice Department have, for years, brought the full weight of the law to bear on organizations like the Aryan Brotherhood and the Symbionese Liberation Army. Tough law enforcement measures in Europe, including stiff sentences for convicted terrorists in France, Spain, Italy, the Federal Republic of Germany, and the United Kingdom in the past year, coincide with a 40% decline in international terrorism there.

But sometimes international realities limit the use of the law. Simply put, our writ did not run to Qadhafi's headquarters, so we turned to other means to defend ourselves.

Here too, many people fell victim to the myth that forceful action increases terrorism. For example, a day after the U.S. strike on Libya on April 15, 1986, 97 Western terrorism experts meeting at a seminar in Aberdeen, Scotland, unanimously agreed that the United States had committed an error. Neither the morality of nor the justification for the strike was at issue; efficacy was. The experts' view was that the air strike would just stimulate Qadhafi to more terrorism.

These experts were dead wrong. We believe that as many as 35 attacks planned by Libya were averted within weeks after the attack. Yes, Qadhafi still practices terrorism. And he continues to assassinate his dissidents abroad. Recently, he was caught in October trying to ship 150 tons of arms to the IRA [Irish Republican Army]. But Qadhafi clearly reduced his planning for attacks on us after the bombing.

Moreover, military actions have nonmilitary consequences far removed from the scene. While some friendly governments questioned the wisdom of our limited attack, the message of U.S. resolve was unequivocal and as surely understood in Western capitals as in terrorist training camps. Overall, there was a dramatic drop in Middle East-sponsored terrorism in Europe following our Libya attack and the accompanying diplomatic and political measures we and our allies took. . . .

UNMASKING TERRORISM

THE FEAR OF FEAR ITSELF

Rushworth M. Kidder

Boston

WHEN "The Color Purple" went to the Cannes Film Festival in France this month, director Steven Spielberg and star Whoopi Goldberg stayed home.

The Italian Open tennis tournament began yesterday in Rome, but there were no junior players from the United States: The US Tennis Association had decided not to send any.

A trade delegation from the state of Washington canceled a European trip just days before it was to have begun.

TWA is closing down its Cairo-Athens and Cairo-Rome connections; Pan Am has laid off 212 employees and canceled new services planned for the Chicago-Frankfurt and Los Angeles-Paris routes; and US travel agents are reporting 20 to 30 percent declines in trips to Europe.

The reason in each case: fear of terrorism.

In the past year, terrorism has made its mark on America as never before. A relatively small number of committed terrorists, operating thousands of miles from America's borders, have succeeded in changing the way the most influential nation on earth lives, works, and relaxes.

The present upsurge in concern began, perhaps, with the 17-day ordeal of TWA's Flight 847 in the Middle East last summer. Watching the hijacking unfold in lurid detail on network television, ordinary Americans were reminded once again how much they, too, were susceptible to terrorism.

Americans had seen plenty of terrorism before, of course. But much of it had been directed at government officials and other obvious targets. The takeover of the US Embassy in Tehran, Iran, in 1979, although of much longer duration than the TWA incident, involved diplomats, not ordinary folks. The truck-bombing of the Marine barracks in Beirut in 1983, though far more lethal, involved uniformed servicemen.

> Terrorism, so often sponsored by nations and magnified by the media, plants seeds of fear throughout the world. And fear can imprison free men and women more surely than the stoutest walls.

But TWA 847 seemed different. Ordinary Americans from places such as Indianapolis, Little Rock, Ark., and Albuquerque, N.M., became hostages. The terrorists, given plenty of television air time, explained their deadly purpose with new force.

So the nation was already primed with concern when, in October, New York passenger Leon Klinghoffer was brutally murdered by the Palestinian hijackers of the Italian cruise ship Achille Lauro. The spiral of fright rose another notch when, in December, five Americans perished in the wanton massacres by Palestinian gunmen at the Rome and Vienna airports.

Could not *something* be done? Must the Western world stand by helplessly while trained terrorists strike out at will against innocent people?

The occasion for response came after a discothèque frequented by US soldiers in West Berlin was bombed April 5. US intelligence traced the cause to Libyan agents in East Berlin. On April 14, US planes bombed Libya.

Never before in the Western world's two-decade-long battle against modern terrorism had military force been directed against a government. Terrorism had moved into the big leagues.

Historians will long debate the wisdom of the Reagan administration's decision to send in the bombers.

Will the strike help limit terrorism, by sending messages that states supporting ter-

From *The Christian Science Monitor,* May 13, 1986, pp. 17-19. Reprinted by permission from *The Christian Science Monitor* ©

ter'ror-ism:
n. [Fr. *terrorisme*] **1.** the act of terrorizing; use of force or threats to demoralize, intimidate, and subjugate, esp. such use as a political weapon or policy **2.** the demoralization and intimidation produced in this way

—Webster's New World Dictionary

"...the unlawful use or threatened use of force or violence by a revolutionary organization against individuals or property with the intention of coercing or intimidating governments or societies, often for political or ideological purposes."

— Department of Defense, 1983

"...the unlawful use of force or violence against persons or property to intimidate or coerce a government, the civilian population, or any segment thereof, in furtherance of political or social objectives."

— FBI, 1983

"...premeditated, politically motivated violence perpetrated against noncombatant targets by subnational groups or clandestine state agents."

— State Department, 1984

"...violent criminal conduct apparently intended: (a) to intimidate or coerce a civilian population; (b) to influence the conduct of a government by intimidation or coercion, or (c) to affect the conduct of a government by assassination or kidnapping."

— Department of Justice, 1984

"...the unlawful use or threat of violence against persons or property to further political or social objectives. It is usually intended to intimidate or coerce a government, individuals or groups or to modify their behavior or policies."

— The Vice President's Task Force on Combatting Terrorism, 1986

Terrorism's central weapon is fear itself. It consists of an attempt by the weak to gain dominion over the strong.

And since its ultimate target is not the victim but the public at large, terrorists seek access to channels of communication.

rorist groups cannot escape without penalty? Or will it provoke new fury and new attacks on Americans?

Will the attack drive wedges between America and friendly nations, or will the unified stand against terrorism articulated at the recent Tokyo summit prove to be a bellwether for tougher stands in general?

Is terrorism best fought with military force? Or does it take better police work, tougher security, and more preventive intelligence?

Should Americans seek to emulate the successes of the British and the Italians, who have managed to diminish the incidents of Irish Republican Army (IRA) and Red Brigades terrorism by strict adherence to the law? Or is the world now fighting a new kind of terrorism — masterminded by puppeteers controlling suicidal operatives and sweeping across international borders — that demands a new kind of response?

Finally, can terrorism be fought without altering the fabric of free democracies? Or must protection of liberty involve curtailment of individual freedoms? These questions have been the subject of scores of Monitor interviews conducted over the past five months in London, Belfast, and Aberdeen; Bonn, Cologne, Bremen, and Hamburg; Paris, Milan, and Rome; Tel Aviv and Jerusalem; and Washington and Boston.

From discussions with politicians, government officials, past and present intelligence analysts, police and military officers, counterterrorism specialists, academics, security consultants, clergymen, journalists, terrorist sympathizers, and ordinary citizens, the following points come to the surface:

- Terrorism's central weapon is fear itself. It consists of an attempt by the weak to gain dominion over the strong. And since its ultimate target is not the victim but the public at large, terrorists seek access to formal or informal channels of communication.
- Terrorism stems from some of the basest elements of human nature — hatred, revenge, and territoriality. Yet it often comes in the guise of religious or political movements, a just attempt to gain a homeland or a remedy for past injustices.
- It is essentially a problem affecting the free world, not the communist bloc. The US State Department conservatively counts 695 terrorist incidents worldwide in 1985. Only one took place in Eastern Europe. And although only four occurred in North America, American targets overseas were involved in about 25 percent of all terrorism. Of the 695 total,

the vast majority took place in the Middle East (310), Europe (184), and Latin America (125).

• Terrorists are becoming more sophisticated in weaponry, selection of targets, use of intelligence, and manipulation of the news media. The gunmen themselves are beginning to use home video equipment to make tapes for release to commercial networks. The terrorist of the future, writes expert Neil C. Livingstone, "may more likely be armed with an Apple II home computer than a Polish-made WZ63 machine pistol."

• Terroists are building new alliances. Isolated groups are beginning to come together in what John Newhouse, a New Yorker writer, has dubbed "a freemasonry of terrorism." A meeting in Tripoli in early February at which Libya's Col. Muammar Qadaffi was host brought together 22 Arab terrorist groups. An unrelated meeting, in Frankfurt, West Germany, from Jan. 31 to Feb. 2, brought together several hundred participants from 11 European countries to discuss "anti-imperialist and anti-capitalist resistance in Western Europe" and to review strategy with "comrades" from the Middle East and Central America.

• Terrorists are shifting to a new target: the tourist. Robert Kupperman of the Center for Strategic and International Studies at Georgetown University in Washington, D.C., notes that "the real story in terrorism [these days] is the tourism business." In the 1970s, embassies and military installations were frequently attacked. These targets, subsequently "hardened," may soon become even more secure: The US State Department is proposing to spend $4.4 billion to build 79 new embassies and renovate 175 others. A second source of targets, the international business community, has also hardened itself: A Rand Corporation terrorism expert, Brian M. Jenkins, notes that businesses in America spend $21 billion a year on security. So terrorists, seeking softer targets, increasingly look to tourists. Estimates are that countries around the Mediterranean lost $1 billion in canceled bookings in 1985, with Greece alone losing $300 million.

• Much of modern terrorism is tied to the Arab-Israeli conflict — involving two cultures whose dominant religious teachings both make room for revenge. But many observers agree that the solution to terrorism does not lie simply in resolving the Palestinian problem. Even if that problem were solved tomorrow, they say, Middle Eastern terrorism would continue at the hands of militant Shiite fundamentalists. Terrorism would also continue from other groups: Sikhs, Tamils, Basques, Irish Republicans, the Boricua Popular Army in Puerto Rico, the Red Army Faction in West Germany, and the M-19 in Colombia, to name a few.

• Terrorism appears to be more than a passing phenomenon. "It's a problem to be managed, not to be solved," says Ambassador Edward Marks, a counterterrorism specialist on leave from the State Department

The Rand Corporation's Mr. Jenkins cites new sources of frustration and new levels of state sponsorship as reasons for the rise in terrorism. He also notes a widening arena: By the mid-1980s, terrorist incidents were occurring, on average, in 65 countries each year — up from 29 countries in the late 1960s.

• Most experts agree there is plenty of room for strong counterterrorist measures. Noting that terrorism is most effective when the public lets fear take over, many observers urge that it be kept in perspective — noting, for example, that the 23 American lives lost overseas last year in terrorist incidents are greatly overshadowed by the 18,000 murders in the US each year.

They note, too, that the presence of conditions in which political violence seems to flourish does not mean that terrorism will necessarily occur. "People who have lost their homelands don't automatically turn to terrorism," notes Rand Corporation scholar Paul B. Henze. "We have enormous groups of these people around the world who haven't gone to [terrorism] at all."

ACTS OF TERROR?

'THE Boston Tea Party was a historical event or a terrorist act, depending on which side you sat." When he speaks to American audiences, former Italian intelligence official Franco Ferracuti uses that line to point up the difficulty of defining terrorism.

From the gunman's point of view, "terrorist" is a dirty word. Journalists in Northern Ireland, seeking interviews with

Defining the types of terrorism

State terrorism
Acts of terror perpetrated by governments using their own military or police forces. The best-known example is probably Nazi Germany. More recent examples include the slaughter of 20,000 Islámic fundamentalists by Syrian troops in Hama in 1982 and the widespread use of violence by several Latin American governments.

State-sponsored terrorism
Support of quasi-independent terrorist groups by sympathetic governments. Most terrorist groups receive some state support such as funds, training, arms, intelligence, or safe houses. Examples include the Palestinian Saiqa organization (largely controlled by Syria) and the Salvadorean FMLN (which gets support from Cuba).

Acts of war
Open military hostilities between governments, whether declared or not. Unlike terrorism, war usually avoids attacks on civilians and primarily involves conflicts between uniformed soldiers. Since few such wars are fought today, other terms have arisen, such as low-intensity conflict, involving a political-military struggle short of war.

Idiosyncratic terrorism
Disturbed individuals, acting without accomplices and without criminal or ideological motivation, can also terrorize. Examples include the San Ysidro, Calif., massacre at a MacDonald's restaurant in 1984 or even John Hinckley's attempted assassination of President Reagan. Such acts are not, however, usually considered "terrorism."

Criminal acts
A term reserved for acts of lawlessness where the motive is personal rather than ideological gain. Crime usually involves only the victim and the perpetrator, who usually wants to remain of sight. Terrorism involves a third party, the public. This distinction blurs in organized crime, where victims are sometimes shot in public to make a point.

FILE PHOTO/AP

Terrorist act? Grand Hotel, Brighton, England, after '84 bombing of British Cabinet members by Irish Republican Army: when targets are political, most experts call it terrorism.

FILE PHOTO/REUTERS

Act of war? US Marine barracks at Beirut International Airport after '83 explosion of a Shiite suicide truck-bomb: If the target is soldiers, is it terrorism or guerrilla warfare?

Provisional Irish Republican Army officials, are careful to use such terms as "paramilitary activist." Palestinians on the West Bank see themselves as resisting unlawful occupation, while rebels in El Salvador think of themselves as freedom fighters.

Among students of terrorism, the term lies somewhere on a scale stretching from crime to war. Most definitions (see box), include four elements: the method (force and violence), the perpetrator (a revolutionary or conspiratorial group), the target (governments and civilian populations), and the purpose (to coerce and intimidate for political ends).

Scottish scholar Paul Wilkinson, seeking to distinguish terrorism from crime, cites "the deliberate attempt to create fear, intensive fear, in order to coerce the wider target into giving in to what the terrorist wants." By "wider target" he includes the public at large.

Israeli scholar Eytan Gilboa, seeking to distinguish terrrorism from war, emphasizes "a deliberate policy of hurting civilians" as opposed to unintented injury.

And the Bush Commission report, noting that "terrorism is political theater," emphasizes the terrorists' need for publicity.

Despite such definitional efforts, there is still plenty of slippage. The mining of the Gulf of Suez in 1984, presumably by the Libyans, is usually called terrorism. But the United States administration does not use the term for the 1984 mining of the harbor in Nicaragua by Central Intelligence Agency-backed "contras."

FILE PHOTO/AP

Criminal act? Abortion clinic, Washington, D.C., after '85 bombing: because no "conspiratorial enterprise" can be found, the FBI does not define antiabortion attacks as terrorism.

Such definitional difficulties sometimes stem from ideological differences: Both the United Nations and the Bush Commission reportedly spent inordinate amounts of time trying to define terrorism.

Different definitions can lead to practical problems. Italian officials say they know of 290 left-wing and 65 right-wing Italian terrorists who are still at large, and complain that the majority live openly in France. But France, citing a tradition of asylum dating back to the French Revolution, is loath to extradite any "terrorist" who might, in fact, be a political exile.

The Causes and Scope of Terrorism

This section assesses the overall scope of contemporary terrorism and examines its most prevalent, as well as most lethal, causes. Terrorism, in its modern sense, is the result of both excessive resentment and extreme self-righteousness. Many terrorists are genuinely convinced that their cause (which is usually associated with their ethnic or religious community or ideological convictions) has been systematically betrayed and exploited by powerful and nefarious forces. They consequently feel justified in victimizing others with similar atrocities. According to their beliefs, they have been left no choice in the matter by a cruel and insensitive world.

It is this perspective that eliminates the possibility of compromise or flexibility. Terrorists view the world in terms of good and evil. One does not negotiate or "work through the system" with evil; one can only destroy evil, root and branch. Thus, for example, extreme Palestinian nationalists regard Israel as an abomination that cannot be reduced or dealt with, but only eliminated once and for all.

Terrorism, then, represents an absolutist approach to resolving political problems. It is also indicative of a decidedly anti-Western bias. A great deal of contemporary terrorism is motivated, justified, and inspired by fundamentalist religious doctrine. " 'Holy Wars': The Ominous Side of Religion in Politics" provides an explanation of the theological rationale for indiscriminate and gratuitous violence. It is difficult to overestimate the influence of fanaticism inspired by religious zealotry.

The perception of being morally wronged, sometimes passed on for generations, is compounded by the fact that terrorists are simply unpleasant individuals. "Unmasking Terrorism: The Terrorist Mentality" characterizes them as aggressive, lonely, frustrated, and dogmatic people who tend to oversimplify issues. Terrorism for such individuals is the ultimate expression of a chip on the shoulder. Whether religiously or ideologically motivated, a sense of self-righteousness can be a powerful catalyst for violence.

The next article provides an incisive commentary on the relentless conflict between the Israelis and the Palestinians and tries to explain the delicate distinctions between levels of violence and varieties of terror.

"The Terrible Toll of Human Hatred" reveals how terrorists can easily take advantage of ethnic and religious distrust and suspicion to completely wreck a country. The ability of terrorists to take advantage of human misery should not be underestimated by any society desirous of avoiding Lebanon's fate.

Prospects for terrorism in the 1990s are examined in "International Terrorism." The inescapable conclusion is that terrorism will not be easily or soon eradicated. While this is regrettable there is also the hope that terrorism can be effectively fought against.

Finally, "Explaining Terrorism" helps to explain what we are up against in terms of the social psychology of terrorism. Destructive behavior is a complicated and frightening phenomenon.

Looking Ahead: Challenge Questions

Why does the religious fundamentalist surge that has inspired much of the political unrest in the Middle East and elsewhere over the last several years involve an antagonism toward the West? How is it that this antagonism also has secular roots?

How can a terrorist be profiled? What are the more pronounced personal, ideological, and psychological characteristics?

Why does terrorist violence seem relentless and endemic in several societies across the globe? What are the historical, ethnic, and religious dimensions of this violence?

What is the more or less current status of international terrorism? Which countries assist terrorism, and which attempt to frustrate it?

Are terrorist acts so abhorrent to the entire world community that assassination of terrorists is actually justified, even for democratic societies?

What do terrorist organizations realistically expect to achieve? Do they understand their limitations? Can they be expected to resort to future violent acts if they receive at least some of what they want? What if they do not?

Unit 2

"Holy Wars": The Ominous Side of Religion in Politics

Suicide bombings. Hostage-taking. Killing civilians. To many extremists, religion justifies such acts. The growth of Sikh militancy shows how conflict intensifies as economic and political grievances take on religious overtones. When the issues no longer seem just of this world, violence becomes harder to defuse by conventional means. The last in a five-part series traces the emergence of religious militancy and discusses how best governments can learn to handle the trend.

Robin Wright
Special to The Christian Science Monitor

Robin Wright is a senior associate at the Carnegie Endowment for International Peace.

New Delhi

AIR-INDIA Flight 182, carrying 329 from Toronto to Bombay, simply disappeared from Irish radar screens monitoring the Atlantic on June 23, 1985. It had exploded in midair.

Last June, New Delhi witnessed its worst violence in two years when gunmen separately opened fire at a children's birthday party and at late-night strollers; 12 were killed and 20 injured. Three weeks later, 72 Hindus were hauled off two rural buses and gunned to death.

The incidents, for which Sikh extremists were held responsible, reflect the most ominous side of religion in politics. As David Rapoport, a political scientist at the University of California, Los Angeles, said: "The most striking development in terrorist movements in recent years is the reemergence of theological concepts."

The relationship between religion and violence is not new. History is littered with holy wars and inquisitions. The words "assassin," "zealot," and "thug" derive from fanatic groups that thrived centuries ago within Islam, Judaism, and Hinduism.

But violence inspired by or linked to religious movements, a constant in 1980s headlines, has historically been limited to regional issues and impact. Today, it has global impact.

A series of suicide bombings by Shiite Muslim extremists in Lebanon and Kuwait led to the erection of concrete barriers 8,000 miles away – around the White House. The United States, Canada, Britain, and West Germany have all witnessed protests by Sikh militants, who were also linked to an assassination plot against Indian Prime Minister Rajiv Gandhi during his 1985 visit to the US.

The emergence of Sikh militancy reflects three characteristics about the relationship between religion and violence:

- Minorities, either within a nation or a religion, are more susceptible to mobilization because of perceived threats to their identity or survival. Sikhism, a monotheistic faith that grew out of Hinduism in the 16th century, constitutes only 2 percent of India's 800 million people. Sikhs have long feared absorption by the dominant Hindus.

Elsewhere, Lebanon's Maronite Christian minority has balked at giving up its edge in government – a key Muslim demand to end the 12-year civil war. Iran's Shia are a majority domestically, but represent only 10 percent of Islam, and the minority sense of persecution has been a dominant Shia theme for 13 centuries.

• Increased religious militancy within one sect can heighten consciousness and militancy in others, creating a cycle difficult to break. Sikh and Muslim militancy in India has led to new Hindu activism, evident during cross-country marches in 1983 to "save Hinduism."

Sikh violence led to a 1984 Army raid on the Golden Temple, the Sikhs' holiest shrine, in which more than 1,000 people were killed. Prime Minister Indira Gandhi was assassinated four months later by her Sikh bodyguards. That in turn triggered a Hindu massacre of 2,500 Sikhs.

Last May, Prime Minister Rajiv Gandhi dissolved the moderate Sikh state government and imposed President's rule (federal rule), which was extended Monday for six months by Parliament. But over the past several months the killings, now a fact of daily life in Punjab, have already exceeded all those in 1986.

Elsewhere, Christian minorities in Egypt and Nigeria have become restive under pressure from Islamic majorities. The worst sectarian strife in Nigeria's post-independent history erupted last March. Sudan's 12-year peace was shattered when minority Christians and animists renewed the civil war after the 1983 imposition of Islamic law.

• Goals centering on economic, ethnic, or political issues can evolve into nonnegotiable religious demands.

The Sikh issue became a major political factor in the 1960s with demands for a separate Punjabi-speaking province. Mrs. Gandhi, then new to the premiership, agreed, though mainly to win new allies for a clash with her Congress Party bosses. (Ironically, religious movements in the 1960s and early '70s were often cultivated by governments for their own purposes. Egypt's President Anwar Sadat, who was killed by Muslim fanatics in 1981, had encouraged Islamic movements in the 1970s to counter leftist groups.)

But Mrs. Gandhi – and her son, who succeeded her – did not follow through on several subsequent pledges to moderates. After two decades of political disappointments, a five-man Sikh council last year proclaimed Punjab the independent state of Khalistan ("land of the pure"), and declared holy war on the government.

Militants belonging to such groups as the Khalistan Liberation Force are a tiny minority within a minority. Most Sikhs reportedly do not support secession, though they back less militant political demands.

But as the newsweekly India Today concluded: "What started as a violent political agitation has now assumed the trappings of an insurgency that could rip to shreds the delicate weave that sustains the country's democracy and integrity."

Despite its martial traditions, Sikhism, like all other major religions, promotes nonviolence and proscribes killing. The extremists' actions are now justified for a greater truth, rather than merely for social or political gain.

'BY identifying a temporal social struggle with the cosmic struggle of order and disorder, truth and evil, political actors are able to avail themselves of a way of thinking that justifies the use of violent means," explained Mark Juergensmeyer of the Department of Religion at the University of California, Berkeley. "The pattern of religious violence of the Sikhs could be that of Irish Roman Catholics or Shiite Muslims or fundamentalist Christian bombers of abortion clinics in the US. There are a great many communities in which the language of cosmic struggle justifies acts of violence."

Lasting reconciliation seems beyond immediate reach. Among Sikh militants, the individual's inner struggle with belief and the community's struggle to defend the faith have become inseparable from the greater conflict in the universe between order and chaos. The issues are no longer just of this world or this moment.

The Sikh case illustrates how the intensity of religious violence is more difficult to defuse than secular conflicts and that it is potentially a greater long-term threat than are secular ideological disputes.

Religious belief is so deep-rooted and so basic to life, especially in the troubled third world, that the sophisticated arsenal of an earthly power cannot "defeat" it by conventional means, if at all.

NEEDED: A NEW APPROACH TO TACKLING RELIGIOUS VIOLENCE

THE religionization of politics has emerged at a time that the world's dominant powers have arguably never been so ill equipped to cope with the trend.

The United States is constitutionally secular. The Soviet Union is ideologically atheist. Both have so far largely ignored the policy implications of religion in politics. US intelligence sources concede that no government body regularly monitors global religious trends. Nor is any US policymaking body – eight years after Iran's Islamic revolution – now consistently examining the religious dimension in foreign policy.

Yet US and foreign analysts warn that the trend needs urgent attention. "For many years, people didn't take religion seriously, certainly not as a political force," said Ehud Sprinzak of Jerusalem's Hebrew University. "This kind of attitude no longer has a place in modern thinking. Religion today is as powerful or as potentially powerful as it was in the Middle Ages, particularly in the third world."

"It's incredibly naive to think that you can conduct successful policy or intelligence-gathering without anyone to make sense of the religious dimension," said sociologist Anson Shupe, co-editor of "Prophetic Religions and Politics."

In developing policy, analysts have identified common threads among disparate movements that should be considered:

• One of three factors – political repression, economic inequality, or social upheaval – has usually reached crisis proportions in all areas where religion has become a political force. Ethnic or military disputes are a fourth common factor.

"We know now that when social systems fail, people often turn to fundamentalism. They return to a way they have always known, but not practiced or seen as a political option," said Mr. Sprinzak.

• Societies that are politically secular or where modernization is heavily emphasized, particularly in the third world, are most prone to religion in politics.

"Take any one of the world faiths in which this process is occurring. There was once a social order that made sense. What they perceive to have happened is that those traditional world views were overthrown or eroded by the secularization process," commented University of Virginia sociologist Jeffrey Hadden.

• The strongest early movements grew up around religions – such as Roman Catholicism in Christianity and the Shia of Islam – in which clergymen directly intercede between man and God, and thus have tangible temporal power over their flocks. These faiths appear more susceptible to mobilization.

Specialists in several nations suggest that a whole new policy approach – by the superpowers and countries with politicized religious movements – is needed. Different regional flash points require varying solutions, but analysts suggest a number of steps to cope with religiously inspired opposition or violence:

First, differentiate between fundamentalists or activists who demand change and extremists who use violence, a distinction rarely understood. "Talk to fundamentalists and address their problems; at the same time try to cut popular support for the extremists," Sprinzak advised. "Even the craziest religious fundamentalists may have reasonable grievances. Remove the grievance and they automatically lose support."

Tahsin Bashir, an Egyptian analyst and former diplomat, added that governments "must attend to the problems of newly urbanized, disinherited youth in the third world. Don't allow the religious groups to answer their needs. Develop a creative and concrete program to show that this is not the only alternative."

Several specialists suggested that external military force or internal repression are not long-term "cures." "The Egyptian government started fundamentalism by arresting and torturing people, giving them a reason for anger. Some were guilty, but most were not. Jihad and other movements were born in [former Presidents] Nasser's and Sadat's prisons," said Cairo columnist Fahmi Huwaidi.

Second, learn to recognize the signs and try to prevent movements from festering, thus preempting evolution from dissent to violence. "Extremist movements take a long time to develop. they are not born extremist and they do not resort immediately to violence," Sprinzak said. "The question is to be able to identify movements before they mature."

'A danger foreseen is half avoided.'
Writer and physician
Thomas Fuller

Third, deemphasize modernization's imitative aspects, and respect religious forces and cultural authenticity. "The modern world has never done the three things most religious groups in the third world are crying out for," said Dr. Ashis Nandy of India's Center for the Study of Developing Societies. "They've never received proper recognition. They've never been allowed full dignity. And they've never been granted equality. Those things would go a long way toward coexistence."

Fourth, improve education on religion. "We need more public awareness of different religious traditions," said Harvard Divinity School theologian Harvey Cox. "Very few people are aware that the same Supreme Court decision that ruled out prayer in the schools also explicitly invited teaching about religion."

Fifth, do not approach policymaking from the angle of fear. Many analysts believe that, despite their current potency and future potential, politicized religions will eventually settle down, as have other cyclical movements. Others contend they will run their course and possibly even eventually burn out for several reasons.

The utopian idealism that fundamentalist movements evoke is likely to wear off with time and exposure to hard realities. Nationalism and ethnicity are still strong alternative sources of identity. And doctrinal differences and clashes over tactics and local issues, which are growing among rival factions, are also likely to further fragment movements.

Khushwant Singh, a leading Sikh historian, commented: "Wherever there are three Sikhs, there are four political groups." In a similar vein, Dr. Muhammad Shalaan, a psychiatrist at Al Azhar University, Cairo, said: "Fundamentalists [in Egypt] differ so much among each other. They boycott each other in prayer and become so picky over doctrinal detail, group politics, and personalities."

Over time, the xenophobia evident in so many groups, which has led to tension and confrontations with both superpowers, is also likely to fade, if for no other reason than that today's "global village" makes isolation economically unfeasible.

Analysts offered a variety of opinions about the end product of religion in politics. Much, they cautioned, will depend on the way the trend is handled, both in individual nations and as a common phenomenon. But most agreed that, as a result of religion's growing influence in politics, the political themes and ways of life that have dominated the 20th century are rapidly – perhaps irrevocably – changing.

– Robin Wright

UNMASKING TERRORISM

THE TERRORIST MENTALITY

THE Shiite suicide bomber who drove her explosive-packed Peugeot into an Israeli Army convoy in South Lebanon last year was 16 years old. The Jordanian who tried to assassinate the vice-consul of the United Arab Emirates in Rome in 1984 was 22. Of the four hijackers of the Achille Lauro, all of whom were sentenced in Genoa, Italy, last November, the oldest was 23; the youngest, 19.

Rushworth M. Kidder

Tel Aviv

Terrorists, whatever their background or cause, have one thing in common: their age.

"Most of them are youngsters," says Prof. Ariel Merari, speaking of the Middle Eastern terrorists he has studied through the Project on Terrorism which he directs at Tel Aviv University.

Scholars looking at other parts of the world second his view. "The age of terrorism is the age of youth," says Jerrold M. Post, a psychiatrist who studies terrorism as director of behavioral sciences at Defense Systems Inc., a consulting firm based in Washington, D.C. "Apart from some of the leaders, you basically don't find middle-aged terrorists," he notes, citing research that puts the median age of terrorists at 22.5 years.

Dr. Lorenz Bollinger, a West German psychologist who conducted detailed interviews with imprisoned members of the Red Army Faction (RAF), sees elements of what he calls "adolescent crisis" among terrorists.

Experts remain divided about whether a particular terrorist mentality can be defined. On this one point, however, there is general agreement: The hand that actually carries the bomb or pulls a trigger is a young hand.

Why? In some cases, the answer is relatively simple. "In certain countries," says Prof. Paul Wilkinson of the University of Aberdeen, "whole families pass on to their children the message that this is the way you struggle for your rights, this is the way we work for the cause." The result, he says, is a "terrorist tradition" of inducting children into paramilitary activity at an early age.

Beyond that, students of terrorism can trace numerous threads.

Two broad types of terrorism

On one hand, Dr. Post points to the "nationalist-separatists," exemplified by the Spanish Basque group ETA and the Armenian Secret Army for the Liberation of Armenia. They live openly in their own communities — they are often lionized as heroes — and their goal is to establish a separate nation, usually as an act of loyalty to parents who have suffered under earlier political regimes.

On the other hand, says Post, are what he calls the "anarchic-ideologues," members of such groups as the RAF or Italy's Red Brigades. Living underground, often in rebellion not only against the state but against their own parents, they seek the wholesale destruction of the existing social order.

Increasingly, European specialists are finding it useful to add a third category: the spillover of terrorism from the Middle East. Often referred to as "international terrorism" (to distinguish it from the two domestic categories), it is characterized by state support and extensive training of commandos. International terrorism involves professional terrorists like Abu Nidal, who reportedly hires out his services to various states with little concern for ideology.

Reprinted by permission from *The Christian Science Monitor*, May 15, 1986, pp. 18-19.

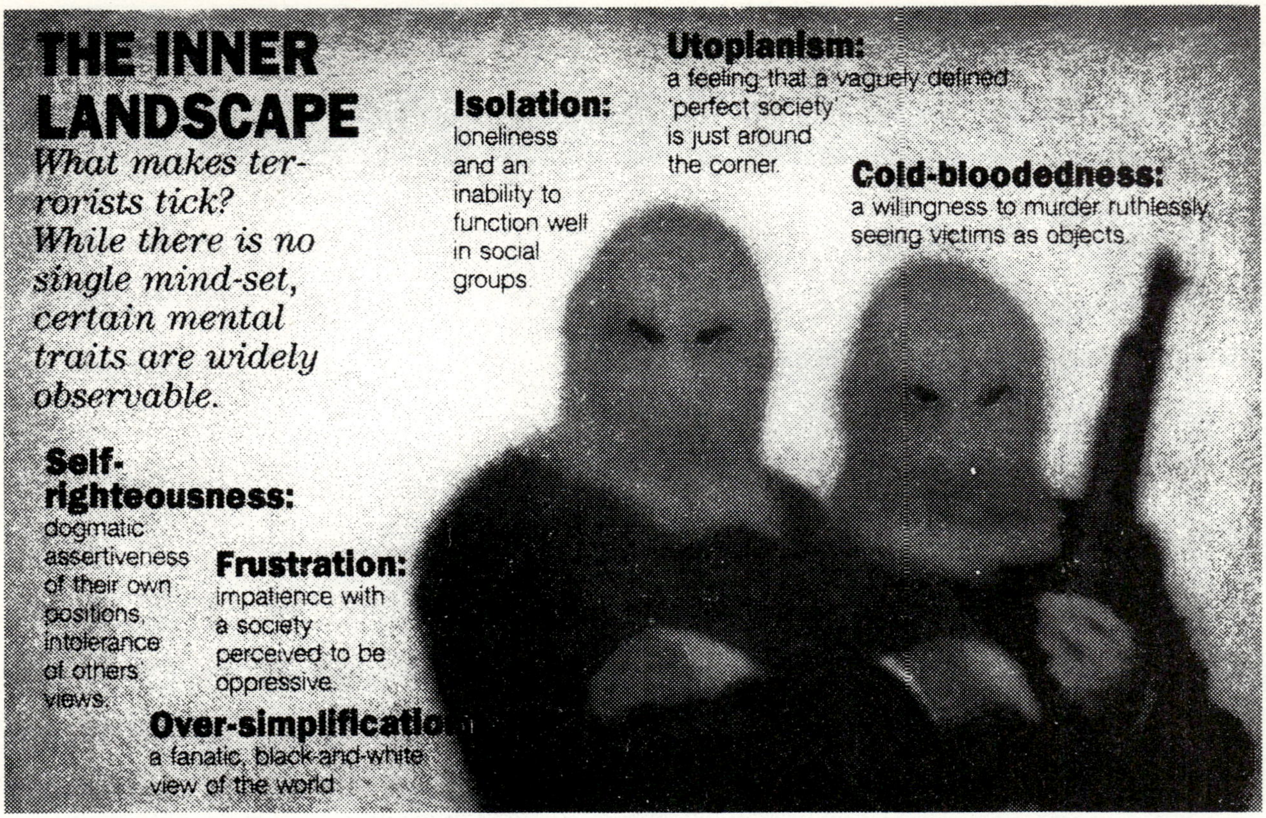

Because terrorists of these three types may resort to the same means, a bombing in Madrid may look much like one in Berlin or Beirut, and the perpetrators are often lumped together under the single label of "terrorist." The ensuing confusion illustrates the difficulty in finding a single definition for the term and leads to the adage that "one man's terrorist is another man's freedom fighter." The result is such a welter of differing behaviors and purposes that terrorist experts are often skeptical about identifying a universal mind-set.

"I don't see any reason to assume that there is more commonality among those that resort to *political* violence," says Dr. Merari, "than among those that resort to *criminal* violence." He adds that "even among terrorists of the same nationality, even among terrorists of the same terrorist group, there is not much reason to assume a common personality."

Nevertheless, he says, some common characteristics do emerge from studies of certain well-defined groups. His own research on Palestinian hostage-takers, for example, points to high levels of aggression, a disturbed family background, and early involvement in illegal activity.

Religious motivation

The difficulty, and the importance, of trying to define the terrorist mentality are illustrated by one key example: the influence of religion in terrorism.

Much of the recent violence generated in the Middle East is traceable to the brand of Shiite fundamentalism of the Iranian leader, Ayatollah Ruhollah Khomeini, especially to his approval of those who die for the cause.

Is the West, then, facing a particularly menacing threat in the form of suicidal terrorists? Dr. Merari plays down the threat. "Contrary to the image created by the media, and by the perpetrators themselves, religious fanaticism does not play a major role [in terrorism]."

Merari argues, and Israeli intelligence officials confirm, that much of the so-called suicide bombing is not carried out by fanatics who believe that by dying for a cause they will go straight to the presence of Allah. Interviews with would-be suicide terrorists who were captured alive indicate they were often tricked into believing they could escape before the bomb exploded or they were blackmailed into accepting the task, on threat of harm to their families.

Was the motive in attacking the US Marine barracks in Lebanon a religious one? In her recent book, "Sacred Rage: The Crusade of Modern Islam," veteran foreign correspondent Robin Wright offers one response. In Beirut a month after the bombing, Sheikh Fadlallah, perhaps the most influential Shiite leader outside Iran (and a man often accused of blessing young fanatics about to go forth on suicide missions), told her that "Suicide in such a way is forbidden in our religion."

Yet the extent to which religion plays a role remains a puzzle, even among the experts. One problem: inadequate understanding of the Muslim faith among Westerners.

"Don't underestimate the religious content of Islam," warns Franco Ferracuti, an Italian scholar and former government antiterrorism official. "That's the one variable that we seem to be losing sight of all the time."

Whatever the answer, one thing appears certain: Suicide attacks represent a new and challenging threat. Lord Chalfont, a former British Cabinet minister with antiterrorist experience in Cyprus, Malaya, and Palestine, observes: "The whole time that I have been involved in terrorist operations, which now goes back to 30 years, my enemy has always been a man who is very worried about his own skin. You can no longer count on that, because the terrorist [today] is not just *prepared* to get killed, he *wants* to get killed. Therefore, the whole planning, tactical doctrine, [and] thinking [behind antiterrorism measures] is fundamentally undermined." For example: The shootings last December at the Rome and Vienna airports were carried out by terrorists who had little if any thought of escaping.

A terrorist mind-set

Is there, then, a terrorist mind-set? From dozens of interviews over four months with longtime students of terrorist ideology and psychology, certain common characteristics begin to emerge. Not surprisingly, given the typical age of the terrorist, these characteristics are also often attributed to adolescence:

- Oversimplification of issues. Terrorists often reduce complex issues to black-and-white. Dr. Ferracuti points to the intensely intellectualized, inward-looking, and politically naive theorizing of many groups. The terrorist, he says, "no longer tests his ideas against reality by [engaging in] dialogue with people with different views." Instead, he lives out "a fantasy war," convinced that he has broad support from numerous like-minded followers.
- Frustration. Pent-up concerns about an individual's inability to change society figure strongly in this mind-set. Italian historian and journalist Giorgio Bocca notes: "They have no patience, these terrorists. They are totally absorbed in their cause. One of the slogans of one of these movements [I studied] was 'We want it all and we want it now.' "
- Self-righteousness. "They believe in [their] total rectitude," notes Professor Wilkinson, who adds that "intolerance, dogmaticism, authoritarianism, and a ruthless treatment of their own people who deviate from their own view are common to their mentality."
- Utopianism. Many terrorists seem to feel that a near-perfect future lies just around the corner, once the present order is destroyed. This utopianism, coupled with frustration at the slow pace of social change, often leads to political extremism on both the left and the right. "Unless you catch this utopian aspect," notes Professor Ferracuti, "it's difficult to understand the mind-set."
- Social isolation. Terrorists, says Dr. Post, are often "people who really are lonely." Terrorist groups use religious or political ideals to interest potential recruits. But those taking up political violence often share traits that are less religious or political than mental and emotional.

  For many of them, Post says, the terrorist group is "the first family they have ever had."
- Assertion of their own existence. Terrorist actions are often laden with symbolic overtones, involving the choice of captives, locations, weapons, and timing. They are frequently meant to send messages — and the message, quite often, is simply "I exist! Pay attention to me!" French criminologist Jacques Léauté calls terrorism "a communication system" in which frustrated people are "trying to express through violence their own message."
- Willingness to kill. Perhaps the most startling characteristic, however, is the coldbloodedness of some terrorist murders. Students of terrorism relate this characteristic to a harsh oversimplification that allows killers to see victims simply as objects — a habit of mind observed among Nazi killers during the massacre of Jews in World War II. Researchers have noticed, however, that captors who hold hostages for protracted periods tend to develop a kind of bond with them that makes coldblooded murder less likely.

As Palestinian Revolt Continues, Violence Declines

Joel Brinkley
Special to The New York Times

BETHLEHEM, Israeli-Occupied West Bank, May 3—It is 1 P.M. and Manger Square is swarming with tourists in search of souvenirs. But with the calm nonchalence born of routine, one by one all the Palestinian merchants show the customers out, then close and padlock their doors.

"This is life for us now," Mahmoud Abu Atah said of the strike as he brushed past the potential buyers he lost by closing early. "We don't even think about it any more."

For Mr. Abu Atah and other Palestinians who have been in open revolt for almost two and a half years, the daily commercial strikes that force merchants to go home at 1 P.M., the heavy presence of Israeli troops and the other conventions of the Palestinian uprising have become a numbing routine.

But even with the continued near-universal adherence to the cause, the Palestinian uprising has undergone one dramatic, through little noticed, change. If the first four months of this year are any indication, it has become significantly less violent.

More Intercommunal Killings

The number of Palestinians shot and killed by Israelis has fallen by more than half. At the same time, though, the number of Palestinians killed by other Palestinians on suspicion of cooperating with Israel has risen. In fact more Palestinians are being killed by their brethren than by the army—43 in January through April.

So far this year, Israeli troops have shot and killed 40 Palestinians, according to figures compiled by B'Tselem, or In the Image, an independent Israeli human rights organization. In that period last year, more than 100 Palestinians were killed by Israeli troops. It is not known how many Palestinians were killed by Palestinians then, since such statistics were not routinely collected until this year.

That number is far higher than either side would like, and almost a third of the dead were children, 16 years old or younger. But before this year, almost as many Arabs were killed in any single given month, on average.

Here in Bethlehem, Mahmoud, another souvenir salesman who would not give his last name for fear of problems with the Israeli authorities, scratched his head when asked when the last city resident died in intifada violence.

"I don't know," he said. "Three months ago, maybe four. You know, I hadn't thought about it. But it's been a long time."

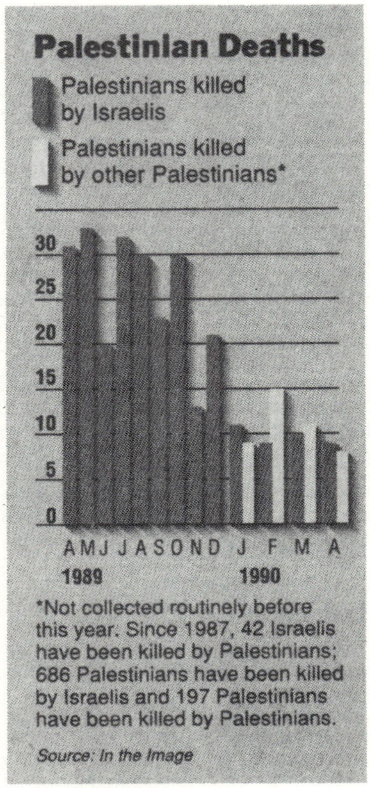

The New York Times

Bethlehem Deaths Fall

In fact, not one resident of the Bethlehem area has been killed since January, when four were killed by troops. In 1989, an average of three were killed every month.

Overall, across the West Bank and Gaza the number of intifada deaths has fallen to about one-third its previous level. Nine Palestinians died from Israeli gunfire in April, tying a record low number since the uprising began. In April 1989, 31 were killed.

The four consecutive months of comparative calm have brought many to believe that after 29 months the uprising may be entering a new, less violent phase—a product of military enforcement and popular fatigue.

But now Palestinians' killing one another has become the leading cause of violent death in the territories. With 43 of these killings this year, according to B'Tselem, many Palestinians fear that such violence will be the revolt's undoing, as happened with the Arab revolt of the 1930's.

Since the uprising began on Dec. 9, 1987, at least 686 Palestinians have been killed by Israeli soldiers or civilians. In addition, 197 have died at the hands of fellow Palestinians. And 42 Israelis and 3 foreigners have been killed by Palestinians.

Even with the decline in shooting deaths, no one, Israeli or Palestinian, is willing to suggest that the uprising is nearing an end. But "it's clear that it's not the same kind of intifada as it used to be," as an official of B'Tselem said.

And in fact, a sampling of intifada-related incidents today clearly shows that the revolt continues.

Israeli troops put the 190,000 residents of Nablus, the West Bank's largest city, under curfew today, meaning no one was allowed out of his home, so 10 Israeli legislators could carry out a religious ceremony at Joseph's Tomb.

In Ramallah, also in the West Bank, about 1,000 Palestinians demonstrated in the city center and then began pelting troops with stones. The army put Ramallah under curfew, too.

In Arab East Jerusalem, there were attacks on two Israeli vehicles, a police jeep and a civilian bus.

But today no one was reported seriously hurt or killed.

Reasons Are Offered

Israelis, Palestinians and independent observers can do no more than speculate as to the cause for the decline in deaths.

A senior Israeli security officer, who asked not to be identified, said: "I don't think the intifada is over, but several months ago it entered a stage where they just couldn't sustain the high level of violence any more."

Radwan Abu Ayyash, head of the Palestinian journalists association, agreed with that only in part.

"There are so many Palestinians in jail," he said, "so many Israeli soldiers scattered around the West Bank, that the Israelis have a tight grip on the Palestinians."

Peace Hopes Fading

In addition, Mr. Abu Ayyash cited the one explanation that was common to everyone interviewed: "So many Palestinians have been waiting, hoping for the peace process to start. Many hopes have been hung on that."

The fall of the Israeli Government last month encouraged many Palestinians who believed Shimon Peres and the Labor Party might take power.

The Terrible Toll of Human Hatred

War may come and go, but ethnic rivalries are forever

Don Podesta

Lord Justice Maurice Gibson and his wife, Cecily, were returning to their home in Belfast from vacation in Britain in April when a bomb blew apart their car, killing them both.

The same week, half a world away in Colombo, Sri Lanka, a bomb at a bus station killed more than 100 persons and injured 300.

The attacks against Gibson, 74, the second-ranking judge in Northern Ireland, and against innocent patrons at the Sri Lankan bus terminal were but two instances of the most enduring form of human hatred: ethnic and religious rivalry, which has spawned more than two dozen violent conflicts across the world.

From Belfast to Beirut to New Caledonia, well over half a million people have been killed in the last quarter of a century because they belonged to one ethnic group or religious sect rather than another.

These simmering conflicts rooted in the most basic forms of human identity, often do not command the headlines that rivet world attention on international wars and guerrilla insurgencies, but they frequently prove more vicious and intractable.

Unlike conventional war between nations, these wars have no definitive time frame. And while the rival combatants often lack the weapons of destruction available to the major powers, they often disregard any recognized rules of warfare, killing and maiming civilians through indiscriminate car bombings, grenade attacks and mass shootings.

Invariably, furtive attacks evoke the timeless question of whether the perpetrators are terrorists or freedom fighters. The violence assumes different forms in different places:

- More than a decade of unabated civil war in Lebanon among Maronite Christians, Druze and Shiite and Sunni Moslems has taken 125,000 lives, police and relief organizations say. The cost of reconstructing the Lebanese economy is estimated at $100 billion.
- More than 1,000 members of the Dinka tribe in southern Sudan were reported killed in March after 6,000 of them had fled fighting in the south. A civil war between southern Sudanese, who follow traditional tribal religions, and Sudan's government, based in the Moslem north, has taken thousands of lives in the past 30 years.
- In the Philippines, the military now considers a Moslem revolt a more formidable threat than the communist insurgency because the Moslems—unlike the communists—control territory and are better organized and better armed, with a ready flow of weapons from patrons in Libya and other Arab countries.
- Basque separatists in Spain have been responsible for about 500 deaths since 1968, when a policeman reputed to engage in torture became the first victim of the ETA (Basque Homeland and Liberty in its Basque language initials).

Why so much bloodshed in so many, diverse places for apparently similar reasons?

There are several possible answers, but many originate in one emotion: fear.

"Fear, not aggression, is a prime motivator of conflict," says Gary Weaver, who specializes in intercultural communications at American University's School of International Service. This fear, Weaver and others say, arises out of a sense of vulnerability, the feeling that the ethnic group might not survive.

"Both sides in many of these conflicts see themselves as the persecuted minority," Weaver says. "This drives them to the feeling that 'if we don't stand up and fight, we're just going to disappear,' and leaders capitalize on that."

The idea that each side in a conflict feels vulnerable has striking parallels in Ireland and Sri Lanka. In each case, the island has a religious minority overall that predominates in the north of the island and that traditionally represents a more prosperous part of the society than the majority in the south. In both cases, the majority in the country is a minority in the north.

The Roman Catholic minority in Northern Ireland comprises a majority on the island of Ireland as a whole,

From *The Washington Post National Weekly Edition,* June 8, 1987, pp. 9-10. © The Washington Post.

ETHNIC AND RELIGIOUS VIOLENCE AROUND THE WORLD

Europe

1. CORSICA: Separatists seeking autonomy from France have attacked the homes, offices and businesses of French mainlanders since the 1960s. On March 21, at least 54 bombs exploded in 14 different towns and cities on the island, ruled by the French since 1796.

2. CYPRUS: Turkish troops occupied the northern part of the island in 1974 following a Greek-backed coup, later creating an independent republic recognized only by Turkey. Thousands of Greeks and Turks have been expelled from each other's side of the island.

3. NORTHERN IRELAND: British troops and Protestant paramilitary forces continue to battle Catholic nationalists seeking end to British rule and unification with Irish Republic. Provisional wing of Irish Republican Army continues terrorist activities. More than 2,500 killed since 1969.

4. SPAIN: Basques seeking independence in three northern provinces have been responsible for about 500 deaths since 1968. Government in Madrid also faces a less violent movement for regional autonomy by Catalans in the northeast.

5. YUGOSLAVIA: Ethnic Serbs, a minority in the southern province of Kosovo, have clashed repeatedly with majority Albanians. Thousands have fled the area—about 2,000 in 1986 alone—amid charges that the Albanians want to create an ethnically pure province.

Africa

6. ANGOLA: Union for the Total Independence of Angola (UNITA), supported mainly by South Africa (also covertly by the United States), opposes the Cuban-backed Angolan government. Although this is largely an East-West political struggle, UNITA leader Jonas Savimbi's power base is in the Ovambo tribe, of which he is a chief. Thousands have been killed, 2,000 in 1985 alone.

7. CHAD: Decades of violence between Moslem, Arabic northerners and Christian, black southerners. More than 21,000 killed since 1965.

8. ETHIOPIA: Four different rebel groups fighting for independence. The largest are the Eritrean People's Liberation Front and the Tigray People's Liberation Front. More than 45,000 killed since the conflict began in early 1960s.

9. NIGERIA: Repeated outbreaks of religious and tribal violence between northern Moslems, from regions traditionally less developed and poorer than the south, and the Christians who dominate southern life.

10. SOUTH AFRICA: Phase of increased violence between 90 percent nonwhite population and the white minority government began in 1984. Violence among blacks and among tribal groups has overtaken security force action as the main cause of fatalities. About 3,000 killed from 1984–1986.

11. SUDAN: Resumption of bloody civil war has pitted northern Arabized Moslems against black southerners who follow traditional beliefs and Christianity. Main rebel group is the Sudan People's Liberation Army, backed by Ethiopia. About 3,000 killed since 1983.

12. UGANDA: Decades of fighting between ethnic, tribal groups and private armies. National Resistance Army, which seized power in January 1986, continues to fight scattered forces of previous Ugandan leaders. Attacks on civilians resulted in 250,000 deaths from 1983 to 1985.

13. ZIMBABWE: Government of Prime Minister Robert Mugabe, whose power base is in the Shona tribe, continues to fight Ndebele guerrillas who support Joshua Nkomo. More than 1,500 killed since 1980.

Asia

14. BURMA: At least 14 separatist and revolutionary armed groups have opposed the government since Burma became independent from Britain in 1948. Heaviest fighting now with the Karen National Liberation Army which seeks an autonomous state for 2 million to 3 million ethnic Karen.

15. INDIA: Ethnic and religious violence has plagued India since independence in 1947. Sharpest conflict today is with Punjab Sikhs who seek autonomy or independence. Approximately 5,000 died in Sikh-Hindu violence from 1984 to 1986. Government also faces militant Hindu groups and separatist struggles in the northeast. More than 10,000 killed across the country from 1983 to 1986.

16. IRAN: Kurds (3 percent of the country's population) seek autonomy or independence in Iran's northwestern region. Largest rebel group is the Kurdistan Democratic Party. Thousands killed since 1979.

17. IRAQ: Kurds (15 to 20 percent of Iraq's population), seeking autonomy, have expanded antigovernment attacks on oil installations and military facilities since 1980. Iraqi Army controls only major towns and roads in northern region of Kurdistan.

18. ISRAEL: Israeli troops fight Palestinian guerrillas in southern Lebanon, and violence continues between Israelis and Arabs in the Israeli occupied West Bank.

19. LEBANON: Bloody civil war between shifting alliances of Shiite and Sunni Moslem, Druze and Christian militias and Palestinian guerrillas has continued since 1975. Shiites oppose the minority Christians who traditionally dominated political and economic life. More than 125,000 killed since 1975.

20. NEW CALEDONIA: Kanak separatists oppose pro-French settlers in their quest to end French rule of the South Pacific island. Approximately 30 people killed during two years of violence beginning in late 1984.

21. PAKISTAN: Periodic separatist guerrilla campaigns since early 1970s by Baluchis and frequent rioting by Pathans and Sindhis against the Punjabi-dominated central government. Approximately 9,000 killed since 1972.

22. PHILIPPINES: Moslem insurgency began about 15 years ago for separate homeland on the southern islands of Mindanao and Sulu. Conflict today is far less violent than during the mid-1970s. Rebel leaders say 100,000 have been killed; government estimates exceed 50,000.

23. SRI LANKA: Torn by violence between militant Tamils and the Sinhalese-dominated government. Conflict rooted in Tamil claims that Sinhalese discriminate against Tamils, their culture and language. More than 4,500 killed since 1983.

24. SYRIA: Government faces opposition from Islamic fundamentalist groups—notably the (Sunni) Moslem Brotherhood. Minority Alawite Moslems dominate politics and economics, but 72 percent of the population is Sunni.

25. TURKEY: Kurds (20 percent of Turkey's population) seek autonomy in southeastern Turkey. The Syrian-headquartered Kurdish Workers' party has escalated attacks on civilians recently, killing more than 40 in 1987 alone.

By Michael Drew and Clarice Borio—The Washington Post

which helps explain the Protestant fear of being absorbed into an all-Irish republic.

In Sri Lanka, Tamils represent only 18 percent of the population, but the majority Sinhalese consider themselves a minority, because Tamil separatist guerrillas receive support and sanctuary from the Tamil population across the Palk Strait in India's state of Tamil Nadu.

Academics and diplomats cite other factors contributing to violence among ethnic groups or by minorities against central governments, including the need to assert group identity, particularly among those who do not have a state of their own; economic disparity among groups, and disproportionate or lack of representation in government. These are often products of a colonial legacy. Colonial rulers frequently selected members of particular tribes to fill administrative posts, leaving behind ill will toward the privileged group when they departed.

Sri Lanka offers a laboratory for the study of ethnic conflict. The Tamil minority, which practices the Hindu religion, developed during colonial times into the preeminent business and bureaucratic class.

"The Sinhalese have incredible anxiety about cultural extinction," says Bryan Pfaffenberger, associate director of the University of Virginia's Center for South Asian Studies. "They have a unique culture at the tip of South Asia, and 20 miles across the strait they face 50 million Tamils."

This cultural anxiety drove the Sinhalese-dominated government to declare Sinhalese the official language in 1956 and sparked rioting in 1983 that destroyed 2,000 Tamil factories and businesses. "It was an act of consummate economic self-destructiveness, because most of these factories employed Sinhalese," Pfaffenberger says.

"They systematically dismantled the whole system of Tamil advantage," says Joseph Montville, research director of the Foreign Service Institute's Center for the Study of Foreign Affairs. Montville attributes violent behavior in such circumstances to "psychological regression . . . causing people to get more desperate" and seek the shelter of the ethnic group.

Among the Protestants of Northern Ireland, he says, "there has always been a very precarious world view, kind of like the Afrikaners in South Africa or the slave holders in the United States before the Civil War. The Protestants are conscious of having committed wrongs and are scared to death of being made to pay for it."

Another aspect of the colonial legacy is that boundaries frequently cut across tribal areas. After independence, most African and Asian nations kept those boundaries, lumping together tribes with little in common or leaving ethnic groups in more than one country with no homeland of their own.

The classic case of a people left without a homeland by its colonial masters is Kurdistan, a land that lies in parts of five countries—Syria, Iraq, Iran, Turkey and the Soviet Union—but nowhere on any political map of the world.

The Kurds, 20 million strong today, have been battling for years for some sort of autonomy. The first recorded use of aircraft to bomb civilian targets was carried out by Britain's Royal Air Force against Iraqi Kurds in the wake of World War I, when the British and French reneged on promises to create a Kurdish republic after the dismemberment of the Ottoman Empire. In May, the Iraqi army was accused of using poison gas against Kurdish villages to stop an Iranian offensive involving anti-Iraqi Kurds.

In other cases, such stateless groups are driven to form separatist movements by beliefs that they are bearing more than their fair share of the tax burden or carrying the rest of the country economically. The Basque and Catalan regions in Spain, for instance, are much more industrialized than the rest of the country. In India's Punjab state, called the breadbasket of India, militant Sikhs are agitating for independence.

Experts are divided on the degree to which economic factors influence ethnic and religious conflicts, but it is clear that they play a significant role. On the theory that "a rising tide lifts all boats," some experts argue that if more jobs, housing and other economic benefits are made available in countries wracked by ethnic violence, the various groups would have less reason to fight. Others take issue with this approach, pointing out that perceptions of inequality in the distribution of new economic benefits only exacerbate tensions.

The conflict in Northern Ireland, which goes back to the time of King James I in the early 17th century, is certainly between Catholics and Protestants, for whom a massacre 300 years ago and a shootout last year are equally infamous. But the real battle is over economic and political power and has little to do with churches. Religion, like language, takes on a symbolic importance, serving to identify people as members of a group, and thus can become a matter of life and death.

Communist countries, despite their traditional restraints on freedom of expression, are not immune to this sort of violence. The Balkan countries, and in particular Yugoslavia, have long served as the crucible of some of the world's most intractable ethnic conflicts, which have ignited local wars in this century and helped trigger World War I. National and ethnic tensions recently have gained significance as a force to weaken Soviet dominance among communist-ruled countries.

In Yugoslavia, ethnic tensions have threatened survival of the communist government. The most serious conflicts have involved the rivalry between Serbs and Albanians in the Yugoslav province of Kosovo; the persecution of ethnic Turks by Bulgarians in parts of southern and eastern Bulgaria; and pressure on ethnic Hungarians and Germans in Romanian-ruled Transylvania.

Another aspect of East bloc ethnic conflicts is that they have been stimulated by governments as part of subtle efforts to gain greater independence from Soviet control. In the years after World War II, national conflicts and national identities alike were suppressed by strict Stalinist rule. In recent years, however, Eastern European communist regimes have stressed national traditions and differences.

One effect of this trend has been a loosening of Soviet influence over domestic policies of East European countries. Recognition of "different roads" to socialism has become a key part of Soviet leader Mikhail Gorbachev's policy toward Moscow's allies. In a press conference in April in Budapest, Kremlin ideology chief Yegor Ligachev declared that the Soviets will no longer act as arbitrators in national-based disputes between allies.

At the same time, rising nationalistic sentiment in Eastern Europe must worry Gorbachev as leader of a country that has many ethnic and national groups, ranging from large Moslem populations in Central Asia to three once-sovereign Eastern European nations conquered by the Soviets only 40 years ago. Some observers believe that the recent riots in the Soviet republic of Kazakhstan may mark the beginning of an era in which Soviet national and ethnic groups begin to assert themselves in a way similar to what has occurred in Eastern Europe during the 1980s.

Washington Post correspondents Karen De Young in London, Jackson Diehl in Warsaw, William Claiborne in Johannesburg, Jonathan C. Randal in Paris, Richard M. Weintraub in New Delhi, Keith B. Richburg in Southeast Asia and special correspondents Nora Boustany in Beirut and Tom Burns in Madrid contributed to this report.

International Terrorism

Background

The United States is a prime target of international terrorism because its policies, values, and culture are directly opposed by many terrorist groups and because the United States has an extensive official and commercial presence overseas. Other nations also are seriously threatened, and Israel, the Western democracies, and moderate Arab governments are major targets. State sponsorship of terrorist activity has greatly increased both the number of attacks and the resulting casualties. During 1980–89, 6,500 international terrorist incidents occurred worldwide, leaving 5,000 people dead and 11,500 wounded. There were 1,751 incidents against the United States, and US casualties for the decade were 570 dead and 576 wounded.

Terrorist Activity in 1989

The level of international terrorism in 1989 declined by about 38%—down from 1988's total of 855 attacks, the highest figure ever recorded. Last year, the citizens and property of more than 74 countries were attacked by international terrorists in more than 60 countries.

Attacks in the Middle East and by Middle Eastern-inspired terrorist groups outside that region accounted for more than half of the total. Terrorism decreased significantly in Western Europe, Latin America, and Asia. Attacks against US citizens or property, which accounted for 27% of the worldwide total during the past decade, also decreased.

Key Factors in Terrorism's Decline

Several factors contributed to the overall decrease in terrorist incidents reported in 1989.

► The Afghan government curtailed its terrorist campaign in Pakistan after Soviet troops were withdrawn.

► Yasir Arafat's renunciation of terrorism apparently resulted in a decline in operations by groups affiliated with the Palestine Liberation Organization.

► Dissension within the Abu Nidal organization and its focus on Lebanon decreased the group's terrorist operations.

► A number of countries involved in terrorism reduced their support for terrorists. (Iran was a notable exception to this trend.)

► Other positive trends included improvements in physical security at both official and non-official facilities, which frustrated terrorist targeting, and continuing cooperation on counterterrorist measures by both Western and other countries that has led to the imprisonment of additional terrorists.

US Policy

US counterterrorism policy was initially developed in the 1970s, and the three basic principles remain as valid today as they were then.

First, the United States makes no concessions to terrorists holding official or private US citizens hostage. Specifically, the United States will not pay ransom, release prisoners, or change its policies in response to terrorist demands. At the same time, the US Government will make every effort, including contact with the captors or their representatives, to obtain the release of hostages without making concessions. Making deals with terrorists only encourages more terrorism.

Second, the United States works with other countries to put pressure on terrorist-supporting countries (such as Iran, Libya, Syria, Cuba, South Yemen, and North Korea) to persuade them that such support is not cost free. These countries help

Reprinted from *GIST*, U.S. Department of State, June 1990.

terrorists by providing training, money, weapons, travel and identification documents, diplomatic pouch privileges, safe houses, and refuge. The United States, working with friendly countries, seeks to isolate terrorist-supporting countries by imposing economic, political, diplomatic, and—if all else fails—military pressures.

Third, the United States cooperates with friendly countries in developing practical measures to counter terrorism. These measures include:

- Identifying the terrorists by name and learning their goals, ideologies, sponsors, and areas of operation;
- Tracking them, particularly when they cross borders, and searching them for forged documents, weapons, and dangerous materials; and
- Apprehending, prosecuting, and punishing terrorists.

Although more needs to be done in these areas, we are beginning to see results. More terrorists are being caught before they can carry out their attacks, and more are being convicted and sentenced to stiff prison terms. Laws covering prosecution, exchange of evidence, and extradition are being applied more frequently.

The United States offers anti-terrorism training assistance to representatives of friendly governments trying to fight terrorism. More than 7,000 police and security personnel from nearly 60 countries have received such training since the program started in 1984. The United States also is working to provide more protection for American officials abroad and make US embassies and facilities overseas more secure.

Because most terrorism originates and is carried out abroad, international cooperation is the key to success in countering the terrorist threat, and high priority is given to improving this cooperation.

EXPLAINING TERRORISM

Peter C. Sederberg

Peter C. Sederberg, Ph.D. is a professor of political science at the University of South Carolina.

The lack of any consensus on a definition of terrorism or a typology of its significant forms hardly bodes well for the explanation of its occurrence. Indeed, the common characterization of terrorism as "senseless violence" suggests that no explanation is possible. No one, of course, really thinks terrorism is radically senseless; explanations emerge, if only of a conspiratorial or psychological sort, on the heels of every terrorist event. Nevertheless, respected commentators doubt whether true scientific explanations can be constructed for the myriad forms of terrorism (Laqueur, 1987; Wilkinson, 1976; 1979). Certainly, the absence of an accepted theory of civil violence in general does little to ameliorate the situation with respect to one of its particular forms (Rule, 1988).

Nevertheless, when explaining particular terrorist acts, analysts seldom content themselves with discrete, etiological interpretations; rather, comparisons and generalizations abound. These generalizations, unfortunately, cannot be facilely synthesized for at least three reasons: First, they focus on different levels of analysis; second, they reflect alternative, and somewhat incommensurate, methodological approaches; and third, they range from the essentially deterministic to the completely voluntaristic.

We cannot hope to resolve these incompatibilities; yet they can at least be organized and illustrated. Essentially, four broad types of explanation are drawn upon (in various combinations) to explain terrorist acts, whether dissident or regime: psychopathological, social psychological; sociopolitical; and strategic/tactical. These four also approximate a continuum from deterministic to voluntaristic positions.

Psychopathological Interpretations of Terrorism

Terrorist behavior, whether done in the name of change or preservation, certainly deviates from what we consider normal social interaction; therefore, we might conclude that some deviant personality could stand out from the background of "normal" people. From this perspective, certain people will be driven by their inner demons to engage in terrorism. In particular, the tendency to wreak havoc on the helpless seems to cry out for psychological explanation.

In his study of human destructiveness, Fromm (1973) distinguishes between defensive and malignant aggression; the former occurs in response to a threat to a vital interest, but the latter is simply bent on destruction. The two traits associated with malignant aggression are sadism and necrophilia. To illustrate the role played by such tendencies, Fromm explores in depth this century's three premier practitioners of terrorism: Hitler (a necrophilic), Himmler, and Stalin (both sadists). Similarly, Anthony Storr (1972; 1978) has developed an inventory of experiences that he argues contribute to the development of sadistic and paranoid personalities (again, assuming that these types possess the capacity to engage in terrorism for either regime or dissident). Billig's (1985) study of a leader of the Red Army Faction in West Germany hypothesizes that the inability to identify with an adequate father-figure contributed to both antiauthoritarianism and a tendency to overcompensate in his own ruthless exercise of power. In interesting contrast with the Freudian position of Fromm and Storr, Hennelly (1988) develops a Jungian interpretation of how a destructive personality develops. Other psychological theories on the development of the "terrorist personality" are summarized in Schmid (1988).

People who commit acts of terrorism, however, need not appear as demented monsters outside of the context where they commit these acts. Both the "terrorist" and "torturer," to paraphrase Rubenstein (1987), may be like the person next door, indeed, it may be the person next door. Lifton (1986) develops the concept of doubling to explain how people can in one part of their lives commit unspeakable horrors, yet otherwise appear unexceptionable, even admirable. Doubling allows for the organization of "an entire self-structure (or self-process) encompassing virtually all elements of [a person's] behavior" (p. 418). One self commits terrorism while the other, semi-autonomous self participates in the conventional world.

While psychopathology may offer some intriguing insights, it tends to discount the significance of the social and political environment. Indeed, under certain conditions, such as those of the death camps, terrorist acts may become the norm, and the deviant personality may be the one who resists committing acts of terrorism. In response to such difficulties, Freedman (198, p. 6) observes that "a psychological profile of a model terrorist cannot be drawn. The personalities are disparate. The context and circum-

From *Terrorism: Contending Themes in Contemporary Research*, by Peter C. Sederberg, 1991. From the forthcoming *Annual Review of Conflict of Knowledge*, published by Garland Publishing, New York, NY.

stances within which terrorism . . . has been carried out are diverse in chronology, geography, and motive." On one hand, certain contexts may encourage the manifestation of destructive personality tendencies. On the other, the stresses and strains of particular social conditions may also encourage different forms of destructive behavior. A fuller understanding of terrorism involves both questions of social psychology and political context.

The Social Psychology of Terrorism

With the possible exception of the lone psychotic, terrorism must be placed in the wider political and social context of which it forms a part. Terrorism represents one form of severe coercion selected from among the alternative coercive instruments available to the establishment for repression or the dissidents for resistance. Coercive repression or resistance are themselves aspects of social control or protest, each of which, in turn, reflects some kind of discontent or fear. From this perspective, terrorism does not arise in a vacuum, but is one of many different responses to discontent. Social psychological explanations focus on the origins of this discontent.

Fundamentally, if rulers and subjects live in happy harmony, then there would be no terrorism. This observation doesn't carry us very far, since under these conditions, no forms of protest or social control, coercive or otherwise, would be needed. Nevertheless, though discontent may not be sufficient to explain the occurrence of terrorism, the argument that it is necessary seems plausible, and so do the social psychological theories that purport to explain the origins of discontent.

Discontent is generally seen as a state of mind, one related to experience, but not automatically determined by experience alone. Discontent, rather, arises from the interpretation we give to our experience; basically, whether we find our expectations met. Some of the classic work in this area includes that by Davies (1979), Feierabend and Feierabend (1972), Gurr (1970), and Schwartz (1973). Concepts such as "relative deprivation" or "alienation" suggest why members of the relatively privileged middle classes in Europe and America, as well as more obviously deprived sectors, might be frustrated enough to resort to radical resistance, perhaps including terrorism. Recognition that members of the establishment might also find their expectations concerning the sanctity of privilege challenged by the dissidents and feel frustrated by a sense of relative powerlessness identifies a possible motivation for repressive terrorism (Duvall and Stohl, 1988; Rosenbaum and Sederberg, 1974). More recently, a number of studies focus specifically on the background experiences of those recruited into radical resistance (Crenshaw, 1981; Moxon-Brown, 1987; Thompson, 1989; Wasmund, 1986; Weinberg, 1986).

Socio-Political Influences on Terrorism

Deprivation, frustration, or alienation alone, however, cannot explain by themselves why people choose to respond with acts of severe coercion. Those alienated from the established order can, after all, withdraw, acquiesce, or engage in non-violent forms of protest. Those fearing the challenge of the dissidents have all the instruments of state control short of extreme coercion at their disposal. To address this issue, analysts identify a variety of socio-political factors which presumably encourage the choice of coercive responses, including terrorism.

A popular, but somewhat confused, explanation for internal terrorism of either dissidents or establishment blames external sponsors. The next section examines the complex issue of external manipulation and control. Here, we note only that this hypothesis continues a kind of determinism, in that although the external puppeteer presumably exercises deliberate choice, the perpetrators of terrorism are merely instruments.

Efforts to test various social psychological theories indicate that frustration by itself does not explain the choice of violence. Muller (1979) suggests a belief in the efficacy of violence, exposure to norms that validate violence, and alienation from the political system are more strongly related to the disposition toward dissident violence. Commitment to an ideology, either secular or sacred, provides a source for the validation of extreme coercion (Capitanchik, 1986; Drake, 1986; O'Sullivan, 1986; Rapoport, 1988; Wilkinson, 1986). Indeed, some evidence suggest that identification with an ideology may be a factor of considerable importance in overcoming the "free rider" problem (Rose, 1987).

While the justifications for dissident violence receive most of the attention, similar values presumably exist to validate destructive behavior on the part of members of the establishment (Smelser, 1971; Duster, 1971; Walter, 1969). The validation of establishment coercion, however, might tend to be less explicit, because support values may well be taken for granted and need not be formally justified. Sometimes, however, rationales for destruction will be articulated, as in the case of the Nazi "bioideology" that consigned the Jews to their doom (Lifton, 1986).

A somewhat related proposition suggests that alienated elements may learn from the success other groups appear to have with violent tactics (Hacker, 1981). Such "contagion" presumably could influence members of the establishment as well as the dissidents. The media, unsurprisingly, is often identified as the medium of this terrorist contagion (Livingstone, 1986; Redlick, 1979; Schmid and de Graff, 1982; Wardlaw, 1982, 1990).

Political ideology may justify violence and the media may publicize such rationales and images of apparent success, but people must still have the opportunity to act on their intentions. Theories of collective action (McAdam, 1982; Tilly, 1978) argue that radical protest requires that the dissidents possess adequate resources and that something weakens the regime's instruments of social control. Although the notion that democracies are inherently vulnerable to terrorism, because their adherence to legal and political niceties opens up a space for terrorist abuses, has gained some currency, more credible research suggests that both dissident and establishment terrorism are more prevalent in relatively divided and unsettled states, whether democratic or authoritarian (Targ, 1988; Duvall and Stohl, 1988). On the other hand, terrorism may not develop out of the particular weakness of one side or the other in a political struggle; rather, there may be a "general tendency toward equilibrium in the severity of coercion used by all groups contending for power" (Gurr, 1986). Finally, changes in the political context appear to play a role in the decline of terrorism (Ross and Gurr, 1989).

The Terrorists: International, State-Sponsored and State-Supported

Variations in the form terrorism takes include those that transcend borders and take place in other individual states. Transcending versions can include international state-sponsored or state-supported terrorism. In the last two instances, governments of particular states exert influence and seek to fulfill political objectives beyond their own territories by either directly sponsoring terrorist operations abroad or supporting those groups that parallel their goals. Sponsorship invariably means more than influence—it can translate into decision-making and control of the group's activities. Support usually refers to aiding and abetting existing terrorist groups that have degrees of independence or their own operational goals. Influence in the latter case moves both ways in the relationship. Admittedly, much of the literature fails to adequately differentiate the nuances between the two.

International terrorists may be territorially based but usually operate regionally or worldwide. Some have achieved nearly total independence, verging on a self-sustaining basis in their own right.

"What Constitutes State Support to Terrorists?" covers both versions of state sponsorship and state support, and places special stress on motivational aspects of government involvement before turning to the instrumental nature of these activities.

"Among the IRA: The Libyan Connection" explores the well-documented connection between the Libyan government and the Irish Republican Army (IRA) in the mid-1980s. A French investigation exposes the delivery of nearly 120 tons of arms and explosives to the IRA from Libya.

If a government is a sponsor state for terrorism, it can also stop its activities. In the aftermath of the Ayatollah Khomeini era in Iran, many Westerners are optimistic about the release of at least some Western hostages. The articles "Rafsanjani May Hold the Key That Releases the Hostages" and "Out From the Cellar" address the possibilities of the Iranian and Syrian governments influencing the release of the kidnap victims in Lebanon.

The preoccupation with the Middle East continues because of the number of terrorist incidents connected to the region, as well as the large number of governments sponsoring or supporting terrorists. In the next two articles, two of the most infamous recipients of such support, Abu Nidal and Abul Abbas, are interviewed and reviewed at length. Their commentaries are insightful, provocative, and disturbing.

"An Interview With Martin McGuinness of the Irish Republican Movement" provides a fascinating overview of the IRA movement, and again reveals the politics versus (or plus) terrorism choices open to dissenters.

The future appears somewhat ominous for the new Germany in "Neo-Nazis Stage Attacks" because of a revival of the extreme right and the transnational tendencies of the "skinhead" movement.

Beyond the Middle East and Europe are various other regional examples of state involvements in terrorist activities—including cooperation with each other in such endeavors. "The Selling of Terrorism: Profit From a Lucrative Export" explains how North Korea has become an arsenal for terrorist groups and for selected terrorist states. A disputed U.S. role in Indonesia's past is examined in "CIA Tie Asserted in Indonesia Purge" that raises some critical questions about democracies in state-supported terrorist activities. The elusive and mysterious Shining Path in Peru, and especially its leader, are the center of attention in "As Peru Votes, Insurgent's Mystique Casts Shadow." Can we draw analogies between this movement and other leftist terrorist groups in Latin America?

Looking Ahead: Challenge Questions

What are some prevalent reasons for governments indulging in state-sponsored terrorism? How is terrorism justified by the governments involved? How does religious extremism provide a motivation for state-sponsored terrorism?

How can state-supported terrorism be considered the most lethal and the most effective form of terrorism? How can the participation of states in terrorist activities be considered a rude reversal of the traditional purpose of the state?

How do governments contribute to and take advantage of other political systems? Through what means does state-supported terrorism accomplish this?

What are examples of some of the more notorious regimes that practice state-sponsored terrorism? How can terrorist groups benefit from the goals of such regimes? Besides contributing to political instability and violence, how does a regime practicing state-sponsored terrorism benefit financially?

What are the characteristics of extreme right-wing and left-wing terrorist organizations? Do they have anything in common? How do their goals differ?

Unit 3

امام خمینی
مجهز شوید به سلاح و صلاح که خدای بزرگ باشماست
قیام کنید و ابرقدرتها را از صحنه تاریخ و روزگار براندازیم

What Constitutes State Support to Terrorists?

Edward F. Mickolus

Despite the best efforts of governments worldwide to eradicate it, state-sponsored terrorism continues to dominate headlines. Whether we look at the scores of Afghan WAD/KHAD-supported attacks on Pakistani marketplaces,[1] or at almost two decades of Libyan-orchestrated depredations around the world, aid given to terrorists by governments continues to stymie our best efforts to protect ourselves. Indeed, many theorists have suggested that external support by governments is necessary to ensure the survival of terrorist bands, whose limited self-generated resources would otherwise cause these organizations to wither over time.[2]

Taking action to stop this official assistance to terrorists[3] has thus become a crucial component in legislative as well as non-traditional proposals to combat the overall phenomenon of terrorism. Many proposals as well as laws on the books call for actions against regimes which 'aid and abet terrorism'.[4] But where does one draw the line? If we are to go beyond mere name-calling, we need to determine what specific, observable actions draw our ire, and whether some actions are more reprehensible – and thus more critical to expose and combat – than others.

In addition to the policy question, the issue of state support raises methodological concerns which affect the conduct of our empirical research. As part of Vinyard Software's work in creating the ITERATE III dataset on international terrorist incidents,[5] we have wrestled with the issues of state support to terrorists: what constitutes evidence of support, and what constitutes a pattern of support? We have found in coding incidents that we may be faulted by some of our readers on criteria for inclusion. 'Some' evidence and 'overwhelming' evidence, as the US found when trying to get West European governments to move against Libya following the bombing of La Belle Disco in April 1986, is in the eyes of the beholder. If the US cannot get like-minded Europeans to agree on what a cancelled check and radio intercepts mean, it is doubtful that the far more disparate membership of the United Nations will take action against member states with goals parallel if not identical to their own.

The patron state issue also raises the broader question of what constitutes support for terrorists. Are we looking for specific-event assistance, or broader facilitation of terrorism without actually being involved in discrete incidents? Perhaps we (or the discipline as a whole) need a scale of types of behaviour/attitudes that governments can take which, volitionally or unintentionally, tend to make a terrorist's life easier. This article offers a scale of such actions, ranging from passive support to actual incorporation of the terrorist group into a quasi-official arm of a renegade government.

Motivations of Governments

As a first cut in constructing our scale, we can suggest several general degrees of government support/attitudes toward terrorists. In rough order of culpability/evil, there are:

- intimidated governments;
- ideologically supportive regimes;
- generally facilitative supporters;
- direct support in incidents by governments;
- official participation.[6]

To place regimes in any of these categories, we can examine specific observable behaviours made by governments which would lead us to infer the motivations of those governments. While we must always be mindful that these inferences can be faulty and we must consult multiple sources before feeling confident in these judgements, behaviours are, after all, what assist terrorists and what concern us here.

Refining our scale further to assign behaviours within each category, we can rank the behaviours in roughly ascending order of usefulness to the terrorists. One can quibble with the specific location of any given behaviour within these rankings; the scale is designed to be heuristic rather than theological.

Intimidated Governments[7]

In the first category we find governments which do not necessarily sympathize with the terrorists but whose actions, whether by inadvertence, inattention, ignorance, or intimidation, somehow assist terrorists. Examples of these acts appear below:

ACTS BY INTIMIDATED GOVERNMENTS WHICH DO NOT NECESSARILY SYMPATHIZE WITH THE TERRORISTS

1. Granting terrorist demands;
2. Refusal to sign/ratify bilateral/regional/universal anti-terrorist treaties;
3. Refusal to legislatively/juridically enforce #2;
4. Refusal to extradite on legal technicalities;
5. 'Quiet deals' by governments who permit terrorists to transit country in return for guarantee of no attacks on local soil.

Whatever one's rationale for granting terrorist demands, there can be little doubt that it directly assists terrorists. Indeed, such governments are giving the terrorists exactly what they request, a phenomenon almost unique among the behaviours along this scale. Wherever one stands regarding the debate on the merits of long-term deterrence versus short-term altruistic concern for hostages,[8] giving in starts governments on the slippery slope of terrorist assistance.

Other behaviours in this category are ones which the terrorists generally do not directly request, but which nonetheless assist them. Fence-sitting regarding anti-terrorist treaties, no matter how many other governments agree to them, tends to weaken the appearance of universal resolve to combat terrorists, and gives them the impression that if you attack the system at such vulnerable points, they can still win. We have put refusal to enforce such treaties, whatever the domestic political or constitutional excuses, higher on our list because this tergiversation gives terrorists the impression that perhaps all signatories were not really serious when they drafted the treaties.

Refusing to extradite on legal technicalities – vice political reasons, a greater offense on this scale – is similar to the previous entry on the scale, but gives more specific aid and comfort to the terrorists. Knowledge that they need not fear a probably tougher court in an aggrieved nation lessens overall terrorist fear of retribution.[9]

Quiet deals, while difficult to prove, are often cited by the Western press as explaining why terrorist attacks by foreign groups decline precipitously in certain countries. While the ploy does seem to buy a fragile peace for these countries, it bolsters terrorist resolve that their methods can work.

Ideologically Supportive Governments

Further along the scale are those governments whose motives are clearer. Far from being intimidated by the terrorists, they more openly embrace the

From *Terrorism and Political Violence*, Vol. 1, No. 3, July 1989, pp. 287-293. *Terrorism and Political Violence*, published by Frank Cass and Company, Ltd., England.

motives – if not yet the methods employed – of these bands. Their actions include:

ACTS BY IDEOLOGICALLY SUPPORTIVE GOVERNMENTS

6. Propaganda/rhetorical support to terrorist groups in media, international organizations;[10]
7. Permitting group to open office on local soil;
8. Refusal to extradite on political grounds;
9. Receiving visiting terrorist leaders on level normally given to heads of state;
10. Early release of incarcerated terrorists;
11. Failure to arrest hijackers who leave airplane on country's turf;
12. Granting of landing rights to hijackers;
13. Refusal to permit foreign hostage rescue squads into country;
14. Failure to arrest known terrorist transiting country.

Without belabouring the point with commentary on each entry, we shall simply note that these actions are more incident–specific than those earlier on the scale. Moreover, the given action requires a more formal decision by central governments which would more clearly understand the consequences of their actions in terms of assistance to terrorists.

Generally Facilitative Governments

Governments at this point on the scale have now decided that the actions of terrorist groups are in keeping with their own foreign policies. There can be no question of the sympathies of governments engaging in these actions. While not yet assisting in specific incidents, these governments are directly adding to the general capabilities of terrorists to conduct attacks. These actions include:

GENERALLY FACILITATIVE SUPPORT

15. Permitting group to set up safehouses/safehaven on local soil;
16. Permitting terrorists to conduct training on local soil;
17. General training by government of umbrella guerrilla bands which have terrorist appendages;[11]
18. Large monetary contributions to umbrella group's coffers;
19. Provision of arms to group or lax supervision of third party arms transfers.[12]

Incident-Specific Support

Governments engaging in these types of incidents are engaging in what Brian Jenkins has referred to as a type of surrogate warfare. While governments understand that they probably cannot win a conventional or nuclear battle with an adversary, they can conduct protracted conflicts with enemies through terrorist groups, which gives them the added benefit of deniability, however implausible. These actions include:

DIRECT SUPPORT TO TERRORISTS IN INCIDENTS

20. Providing false/true documents/passports/backstopping aliases/ cover stories;
21. Providing diplomatic pouch to move terrorist items;
22. Provision of non-lethal operational assistance – maps, safehouses, communications;
23. Direct financing for specific operation;
24. Direct training for specific operation;
25. Provision of weapons for specific operation;
26. Adding to terrorist demands during incident;
27. Payment of insurance/bonuses to terrorists after the fact.

Joint Operations

Finally, we find governments which incorporate the terrorist methodology – and sometimes the terrorist group – into the government repertoire of official (if covert) action. These actions have included:

OFFICIALLY-SANCTIONED PARTICIPATION OF GOVERNMENT PERSONNEL IN INCIDENTS[13]

28. Participation of intelligence/security service personnel in planning of operation;
29. Government personnel joining terrorist attack squad
30. Joining terrorist attack squad once incident has begun
31. Incarcerating hostages
32. Shooting at hostage rescue squads

Concluding Remarks

Using the above scale, the ITERATE III project treats behaviours 20–32 as triggering our listing the incident as having state support. Acts lower on the scale, while we may be displeased with them, do not constitute the type of patronage which we would find sufficiently notorious for our purposes.

This scale, of course, is not meant to be exhaustive, nor need one agree with the absolute ranking given one action in comparison with another action. The intention of the scale is to determine the relative demerit of a pattern of actions – the broad category is key, not the numerical position.

The author hopes that this scale helps contribute to a more focussed policy debate on what constitutes state aid to terrorists and what we should do to stop it.[14] If we can agree on these definitional and typological preliminaries, we may be on our way toward a more effective policy response, and make the world just a little bit safer from further terrorist attacks.

NOTES

1. Consult, for example, *Patterns of Global Terrorism: 1987* (Washington, DC: US Department of State, 1988), as reported in John M. Goshko, 'World Terrorism up 7 per cent, U.S. Says', *Washington Post* (23 Aug. 1988), p.10, which notes in passing the increase in incidents is due to 'a wave of high-casualty bombings in Pakistan carried out by . . . the Afghan intelligence service known as WAD'. The report notes the WAD conducted 127 attacks inside Pakistan, killing 234 persons and wounding 1,200.
2. Consult, for example, the directory of terrorist groups, and their extensive networks of external supporters, in Alex P. Schmid, Albert J. Jongman, *et al.*, *Political Terrorism: A New Guide to Actors, Authors, Concepts, Data Bases, Theories, and Literature* (Amsterdam: North-Holland, 1988).
3. Our discussion is confined to regime assistance to terrorist bands, not the separate issue of terrorism (or other forms of gross violations of human rights, usually of the local citizenry) by repressive regimes, of whatever ideological persuasion.
4. For a fuller discussion of these proposals, consult the works cited in Edward F. Mickolus, *The Literature of Terrorism: A Selectively Annotated Bibliography* (Westport, CT: Greenwood, 1980), pp.297–301, as well as Edward F. Mickolus with Peter A. Flemming, *Terrorism, 1980–1987: A Selectively Annotated Bibliography* (Westport, CT: Greenwood, 1988), pp.67–81.
5. ITERATE III (International Terrorism: Attributes of Terrorist Events) is a follow-on to earlier numeric datasets on international terrorism. Available from Vinyard Software, 2243 Beacon Lane, Falls Church, Virginia, USA, it covers the 1980–87 time-frame. A numeric dataset, compatible with the ITERATE I and II coding schemes, is available, as is a computer-searchable textual version, which describes each incident. For a more detailed description of the datasets, consult Edward Mickolus, Todd Sandler and Jean Murdock, *International Terrorism in the 1980s: A Chronology, Volume 1: 1980–1983* (Ames, Iowa: Iowa State University Press, 1988), and the companion work, Edward Mickolus, Todd Sandler and Jean Murdock, *International Terrorism in the 1980s: A Chronology, Volume 2: 1984–1987* (Ames, Iowa: Iowa State University Press, 1989).
6. A similar scale of counter-terrorist actions could be constructed, with many of the entries the reciprocals of the items which will be described below.
7. As is evident by the opening sentence of this section, not all of the governments engaging in these behaviours are intimidated by the terrorists. Some may even be sympathetic to the terrorists, and engage in some instances in behaviours further along the scale. However, the vast majority of governments which engage in these behaviours are probably trying to avoid trouble for their nationals and believe that concession, rather than confrontation, is the easiest way out.
8. For a more thorough discussion of this debate, see Edward F. Mickolus, 'Negotiating for Hostages: A Policy Dilemma', Vol.19, No.4, *Orbis* (Winter 1976), pp.1309–25.
9. International narcotics traffickers, particularly members of the Medellin cocaine cartel in Colombia, show similar concern about being extradited to the United States, and go to extreme lengths – including million-dollar bribes to judges, hiring a terrorist group to kill the majority of the Colombian Supreme Court, and conducting a no-holds-barred media and lobbying blitz against extradition treaties – to throw a monkey-wrench into extradition efforts.

   Our ire with governments which refuse to extradite can be tempered somewhat by offers such as that given by Ireland when it refused to extradite to the United Kingdom an accused Irish Republican Army gunrunner. Although he held that Patrick Ryan could not get a fair trial in the United Kingdom due to media sensationalism, Irish Attorney General John Murray offered the British the option of using a 1976 Irish law to press charges in an Irish court. See Karen DeYoung, 'Ireland Turns Down Request by Britain to Extradite Priest', *Washington Post* (14 Dec. 1988), pp.A-27, A-32.
10. Paul Wilkinson would put this behaviour even further along the scale, under Generally Facilitative or even Direct Support. Personal communication, 6 Oct. 1988.
11. The Soviet Union, for example, was frequently cited in the late 1970s and early 1980s by Western observers for having trained and armed members of the Palestine Liberation Organization, some of whose members later turned up on terrorist missions. While many could argue that the Soviets did not intend for their arms and skills to be used by terrorists and that they were only assisting a revolutionary group which happened to have terrorist appendages, such aid did, even if arguably inadvertently and indirectly, build terrorist capabilities.

12. While charges that Libyan leader Muammar Qadhafi has armed terrorists date back to his coming to power in September 1969, he none the less has continued these pursuits. The most recent evidence of Libyan arms collusion on a grand scale is the consignment of 150 tons of Russian-made SAM-7 ground-to-air missiles and other weapons destined for the Irish Republican Army which was intercepted in late 1987. However, senior Northern Ireland security chiefs believe that other shipments have been smuggled in. A senior Army official opined, 'We think it is almost certain they have the SAM-7's. I believe they are not using them at the moment because they do not have the sort of people of the calibre to use them and they are trying to do something about it.' The London Press Association article went on to say that 'A team of top provos is believed to be training in secret in one of Colonel Qadhafi's desert camps and others in isolated parts of the (Irish) Republic. The IRA may have already made an unsuccessful test firing in County Fermanagh. A helicopter pilot reported hearing a "woosh" and seeing what appeared to be a vapour trail.' 'IRA Believed to Have SAM-7 Missiles', *London Press Association* (21 Nov. 1988), reported in *Western Europe; FBIS-WEU-88-226* (Foreign Broadcast Information Service, 23 Nov. 1988), p.4.
13. The actions of the Iranian government during the takeover of the US Embassy in November 1979 to the end of the administration of President Carter come immediately to mind. The Iranians have kept busy since that incident, opening up camps for local and international terrorists at the Imam Hossein Post, the Manzarieh Camp, the Chamran Post, the Aqdassieh Post, the Qods Post, a Shiraz location, and the Najafabadi Camp. Consult Jack Anderson and Dale Van Atta, 'Khomeini Turns Attention to Terror', *Washington Post* (25 Nov. 1988), p E5.
14. Two strategies immediately come to mind, based upon this scale. One is to attempt to prevent certain types of actions, for example, for openers, the 32 listed in this article. Another complementary approach would key on the categorization of governments, and hinge on attempting to work out appropriate sanctions for these patterns of behaviours.

ARMING THE IRA

The Libyan connection

In 1985 and 1986 the IRA took delivery of nearly 120 tonnes of arms and explosives from Libya, including a tonne of Semtex explosive and 12 SAM-7 ground-to-air missiles. The weaponry has been used in Ireland, Britain and other European countries. These are the findings of a French judge, backed by further investigation by The Economist

IT WAS to be the gun-runners' last meeting with the judge. On a wet Paris morning in mid-March this year, the four-vehicle convoy, blue lights flashing, flanked by six police motorcyclists, swept south across the Pont au Change on to the Ile de la Cité, turned on to the Quai de l'Horloge, into Quai des Orfèvres and disappeared through a side-gate of the Palais de Justice.

In the courtyard, armed *gendarmes* and police circled the prison van. Out stepped the Irishmen, still handcuffed to police officers. They were escorted up flights of narrow stairs to the fourth floor, down long dingy corridors and through a bullet-proof glass door to the office of the *juge d'instruction*, the investigating judge. For the umpteenth time, the judge fired questions at them; for the umpteenth time, the Irishmen remained stony-faced and silent throughout the two-hour interview. No matter, the judge already had enough evidence to bring a case against them.

This week the judge passed his report to the prosecution service in Paris. His investigations had begun with the *Eksund*, a ship carrying arms to the IRA that was seized in October 1987, when it strayed into French waters off Brittany. Its five-man Irish crew was arrested. But the judge's investigation cast its net far wider than the *Eksund*, covering four previous—successful—shipments of arms from Libya to Ireland. His findings, a closely guarded secret, may embarrass the French government, which, despite an embargo on arms sales to Libya, has recently allowed the sale of aircraft spares there.

The painstaking investigation into the *Eksund* was carried out by the 14th section of the *parquet* (prosecution service) in Paris, the Service Central de la Lutte Antiterroriste, the central anti-terrorist service. The SCLAT was set up by the Chirac government in October 1986 after a series of bombings in Paris by the Iran-linked Hezbollah terrorists, which culminated in an explosion on the Rue de Rennes that killed seven people. Its brief is to pursue and prosecute terrorists nationwide.

A *juge d'instruction* has broad powers to call and question witnesses; his job is essentially to piece together the case (which, in the *Eksund* affair, comprises 4,000 pages of documents and statements, as well as the captured weaponry itself). His report is then sent to the *parquet*, and the official prosecutor decides if there is a case to answer. In the *Eksund* affair there is little doubt of that.

The *juge d'instruction* at SCLAT, Mr Jean-Louis Bruguière, has spent 2½ years investigating the *Eksund* and the four successful shipments of Libyan weaponry—120 tonnes of it—to Ireland. Further investigation by *The Economist* has uncovered not only details of the cargoes but the names of the Libyans who supervised their loading on board, the names of crew members on the boats that carried them, their final destination and how and where some of the arms and explosives have been used.

No buffoon

At the time when the *Eksund* was seized, its captain, Adrian Hopkins, a 49-year-old Dubliner, was portrayed as a sea-going buffoon who had incompetently allowed his ship to drift into French waters. He was a bit more than that. Although a travel company that he once ran went bust in 1980, stranding 400 tourists in the Canary Islands, Hopkins was an accomplished mariner. He was the skipper who carried through the four previous gun-running voyages.

The island of Malta figured prominently in all five voyages. The first run to Ireland was in August 1985. The boat was a converted yacht called the *Casamara*, sailing under the British flag. It had been souped-up with two speed-boat engines and carried, beside two lifeboats, three high-speed rubber dinghies, for transferring the arms to shore when it reached Ireland.

The *Casamara* had been in and out of Malta a number of times over the previous months, ostensibly making trips to Greece. It arrived back in Malta on August 7 1985 with a crew of two—Hopkins and another Irish national—and put to sea two days later. On the same day a Libyan ship, the *Samra Africa*, which had left Tripoli on August 6th and arrived in Malta on August 7th, also weighed anchor.

Among the *Samra Africa*'s crew were two men born in Donegal, Ireland. One called himself Denis Boyle. Also on board were two high-ranking Libyan officials, Hussein Abuzeed and Naser Ashur. The latter, also known as Ali Ashoud Naser, was the diplomat sent to negotiate the release of the staff of the Libyan People's Bureau in London after one of their number had shot and killed policewoman Yvonne Fletcher outside the bureau in 1984.

The two ships had a rendezvous off the nearby Maltese island of Gozo. The *Samra Africa*'s ten-tonne cargo was transferred to the *Casamara*. It comprised around 500 boxes, containing Russian Kalashnikov AK47 rifles, Taurus automatic pistols made in Brazil, other guns and ammunition, hand-grenades and seven Belgian-made rocket-propelled-grenade launchers (RPGs).

The *Casamara* headed straight for Ireland and Clogga Strand, a sparsely populated piece of coast some 40 miles south of Dublin on Ireland's eastern shores. The arms were offloaded at night in the high-speed dinghies. The IRA took delivery of them (and kept them: contrary to press speculation at the time that the *Eksund* was seized, none of the Libyan weaponry from this or later voyages was shared with other terrorist groups in continental Europe).

Less than two months later, Adrian Hopkins was back in Malta. The boat that sailed into Valetta harbour on October 2 1985 looked familiar. So it should have. Called the *Kula*, it was in fact the *Casamara* renamed and now under Panamanian colours, but with little else to camouflage its past. Things went much as before, except that this time when the *Kula* left Malta only Hopkins was on board. Off Gozo, he again met the *Samra Africa*, which was once again carrying an Irish national and Ali Ashoud Naser, as well as another Libyan offical, Mohamed Zeltini.

Another ten tonnes of arms were quickly transferred to the *Kula*. Among them were more Kalashnikov rifles, Webley pistols (originally the property of NATO forces), two more RPGS, hand-grenades and ammunition. Also on board were Russian-made "Dushkas"—12.70mm heavy anti-aircraft machineguns. This cargo too went to Clogga Strand.

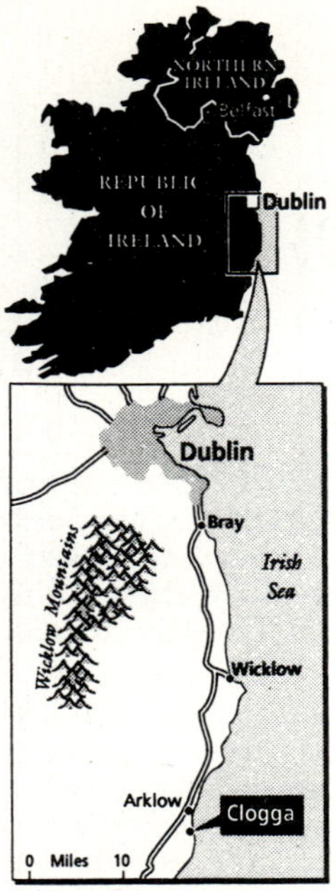

You bomb us, we'll blast you

Libya's leader, Colonel Moammar Qaddafi, had already been angered when his diplomats were thrown out of Britain after the murder of policewoman Fletcher. He was further enraged at the bombing of Tripoli by American F-111 aircraft based in Britain, which almost cost him his life, in April 1986. He was happy to step up arms shipments to the IRA.

On July 17 1986 the *Samra Africa* and the *Kula*, after a brief stay in Malta for both, met again off Gozo. The high-ranking Libyan sent along on the *Samra Africa* this time was the Tunisian-born Mohamed el-Amar Ramadan. On board the *Kula* were Hopkins, Boyle and another Irishman, who called himself Edward Friel. This time the cargo was larger—14 tonnes—and, as well as the usual Kalashnikovs, pistols, grenades and ammunition, there were also two Russian-made SAM-7 surface-to-air missiles. All were duly deliverd to Clogga Strand.

With success, the IRA became more ambitious, and perhaps less careful. The terrorists bought a new and bigger ship, the *Sjarmor*, which they renamed the *Villa* and fitted out with sophisticated navigational equipment and a long-range radio transmitter. Hopkins sailed it into Malta on September 29 1986 with a temporary crew. There he met Boyle, Friel, and another Irishman, Henry Edward Cairns. Three days later Boyle left on a flight for Tripoli.

Soon afterwards the *Villa* too left for Tripoli. Offshore there, more than 80 tonnes of arms were loaded aboard—more Kalashnikovs, ammunition, detonators, fuses, seven more RPGS, ten more SAM-7 missiles and one tonne of Czechoslovak-made Semtex-H plastic explosive. Colonel Qaddafir could afford to be generous with his Semtex. Last week in London Czechoslovakia's President Vaclav Havel said that his communist predecessors had supplied Libya over the years with 1,000 tonnes of Semtex, an ideal explosive for terrorist bomb-makers, because it is detectable neither by sniffer dogs nor X-ray machines.

Because the *Villa* was a much larger vessel, it could not be unloaded at Clogga Strand; its cargo was instead landed at Roadstone Pier, a nearby jetty. The landing went without a hitch. But the voyage into Tripoli may have been the IRA's undoing. It is possible that the transfer of arms, or at least the *Villa*'s presence in Libyan waters, was monitored by American spy satellites. More probably, agents of the French external counter-espionage service (DGSE) in Libya discovered what was going on. Whatever the source of information, the fun was nearly over.

Running out of sea

For the next trip the IRA, through Hopkins, bought an even bigger ship, a 50-year-old, 237-ton rust-bucket, from a Swedish shipowner. The terrorists paid £50,000, considerably more than she was worth.

The *Eksund* was delivered to Malta by a temporary crew, who, like those hired to sail other boats for the IRA, were unaware of their true purpose. Hopkins took delivery of the boat and teamed up with his own four-man crew. On October 12 1987 the *Eksund* left Malta, ostensibly for Gibraltar; in fact, it headed south, straight for Libya. When the *Eksund* sailed into and tied up in the port of Tripoli for loading on the nights of October 14 and 15 1987, one thing is certain: the French security services, including the internal DST (Direction de la Sûreté du Territoire), were aware of it.

Around 50 Libyan soldiers loaded the *Eksund*'s cargo—Kalashnikovs (from Romania), more than 1m rounds of ammunition, 430 grenades, 1,000 mortar bombs, 120 rocket-propelled grenades, 12 more Russian Dushkas, anti-tank missile launchers, 2,000 electric detonators, 4,700 fuses, two tonnes of Semtex and 20 SAM-7 missiles. While in Tripoli and for part of its journey through the Mediterranean, the *Eksund*, like the *Villa* before it, was under the protection of the Libyan navy and air force. Later it came under the eye of French spotter aircraft, which tracked it until it was intercepted in French territorial waters.

The French customs officers who boarded the *Eksund* on October 30th found on board Hopkins, Cairns, Boyle, Friel and one "William Finn". The last three turned out to be travelling on passports stolen from the Irish Department of Foreign Affairs in Dublin in 1984. "Boyle" was really James Doherty, an electrician from Donegal and a member of the IRA; "Friel" was James Coll, also from Donegal and an IRA member. The new face, "Finn", was in reality Gabriel Cleary, from Priorstown, County Dublin, one of the IRA's top bombmakers. All five men were initially questioned at the French naval base at Brest. Since then they have been held in Paris, being periodically shunted around the city's three jails, La Santé, Fresnes and Fleury-Mérogis. Their trial is expected to begin later this year.

Efforts to trace (through Interpol) and question the Libyans involved in the arms shipments came to nothing, but not because they were back in Tripoli. Some, in fact, were still in Malta at the start of the investigation. But Maltese red tape—if that is what it was—meant it was months before permission was given to question them. By that time they had fled. Some of them are now believed to be in Scandinavia.

Murder continent-wide

What happened to the arms carried on the four previous voyages? Some were immediately "re-exported" and hidden in caches in Britain and elsewhere. The French are sure that they figured in at least six incidents in continental Europe in 1988:

- In February 1988 Belgian police found 100 kilos of Semtex in the boot of a car in Brussels, along with detonators of the kind found on the *Eksund*.
- In March, after men from the British Special Air Service had killed three IRA terrorists in Gibraltar, the Spanish police found 70 kilos of Semtex and two electronic timers in a hire-car in Marbella. The timers were identical to those carried on the *Eksund*.
- In May 1988 three British soldiers who had crossed the border from West Germany for a night out at Roermond in Holland were shot dead with Kalashnikovs. The markings on the cartridge cases were identical to those found on ammunition from the *Eksund*.
- At Duisburg in West Germany in July 1988, two bombs exploded inside the perimeter fence of a British army barracks. Forensic tests showed that they were made of Semtex, with detonators identical to those found on the *Eksund*.
- Semtex, undoubtedly from the *Villa*, was used in an attack on barracks at Ratingen in West Germany, the home of 96 servicemen of the Royal Engineers' map-making unit. Forensic tests showed that the detonators were the same as ones found on the *Eksund*.
- Two suspected IRA terrorists arrested by West German police in September 1988, were carrying Kalashnikov rifles. Tests showed that one of these had been used in the Roermond murders.

The IRA was putting its Semtex to use in Northern Ireland and mainland Britain soon after it had taken delivery of the *Villa*'s Libyan cargo. For instance:

- In November 1986 seven mortar bombs containing Semtex were fired at an army observation post near Crossmaglen, in South Armagh, a stronghold of the IRA in Northern Ireland.

- In Lisburn, County Antrim, in June 1988, a 7½lb bomb placed under a van killed six off-duty soldiers on their way to a charity race.
- A 200lb bomb detonated in August 1988 at the roadside on the A5 from Belfast's Aldergrove airport to Omagh killed eight infantrymen travelling in an unmarked coach.
- A bomb placed inside an army barracks in 1988 in North London killed one soldier.
- A bomb was exploded at Deal barracks, in Kent, last September, killing 12 bandsmen of the Royal Marines.

So far, the security forces of Britain and the Irish republic have captured only a fraction of the arms and explosives supplied by Colonel Qaddafi—and even for some of that they have to thank good luck and bad weather.

- Semtex was first found in Britain by police in February 1987. Almost 200 pounds of the stuff had been buried in Macclesfield Forest in Cheshire.
- In 1988 the Gardai (the Irish police) were led to Five Fingers Beach in Donegal and a cache of 100 Kalashnikovs, Semtex and some of the heavy machineguns brought by the *Villa*.
- In December 1989 high winds and rough seas uncovered mortars and mortar bombs on a shore in County Wicklow, Ireland.
- In the same month another coastal cache of Semtex was found in Wales, not far from the spot where two years earlier police had arrested two Irishmen bringing arms ashore from a small fishing boat. The hoard included Semtex, detonators, timers and fuses, as well as an assortment of small arms and Kalashnikovs.
- An informer, in jail in Limerick on a charge of armed robbery, led Irish police to three small dumps in and near Manorcunningham, a village in Donegal. The find included rifles, shotguns, handguns, 2,600 rounds of ammunition, 20 pounds of Semtex and bombmaking paraphernalia.

Cross-Channel coolness

One difficulty for the British and Irish security forces is that they have been kept virtually in the dark about the French judge's findings. Although the French have two policemen on secondment to Scotland Yard, and there is one British policeman in Paris, relations between Britain's anti-terrorist squads and the French DST are cool. Mrs Margaret Thatcher recognised this when, in December 1989, she called for closer co-operation between the two.

French governmental attitudes towards terrorists, especially those with a Libyan connection, have softened since Mr Chirac's administration was replaced by a Socialist one in 1988. Publicly, the government condemns terrorism. But privately it is cosying up to Colonel Qaddafi, who at the end of 1989 intimated that he would like better relations with the British and Americans. Many fear that, after the sales of aircraft spares for the colonel's aging Mirage fighters, the French will soon ease their embargo on arms sales to Libya. France not only values the potential export earnings, but also needs Libyan co-operation if, as it wants to, it is to reduce its forces in Chad or pull out altogether.

The report of the *juge d'instruction* of section 14 of the Paris *parquet*, and the publicity of the Irishmen's trial, will not help to improve France's relations with Libya. It would be a pity if section 14, after its painstaking investigation into the Libyan/IRA connection, were to be in any way weakened.

Rafsanjani May Hold the Key That Releases the Hostages

SUMMARY: Anticipation swelled last month with the prospect that at least some of the American hostages in Beirut would be released. Such hopes have been high since Hojatoleslam Hashemi Rafsanjani became president of Iran. Although U.S. hopes were dashed, Washington is counting on his moderate reputation as the means of winning the freedom of the eight captives. Still, he must contend with a faction that resists any deals with the U.S.

"The situation within Iran is desperate. They must break the logjam of international isolation and get access to the Western market."

After a couple of months of reading the tea leaves, the Bush administration started getting excited in early March, thinking that the eight long-suffering American hostages in Beirut, or at least some of them, might soon be released.

White House Press Secretary Marlin Fitzwater said the administration was "encouraged" by events, including signals from Iran, which is widely believed to pull the strings of the shadowy Lebanon-based terrorist groups that hold the hostages. Others were close to ecstatic: "I am as optimistic as I have ever been," said Columbia University's Gary Sick, who was President Carter's Iran specialist on the National Security Council. "I think this is it. I really do."

Present and former government officials were not the only ones to get caught up in what one cynical expert calls "the hostage bubble." Teams of network television crews rushed off to Damascus, Syria, convinced that the time for release was nigh. The truth soon dawned, however: It was just another frustrating letdown in the chronicle of rising and falling hopes for the Americans and several dozen other foreigners being held prisoner in assorted basements and back rooms in war-torn Lebanon.

What all the optimists shared to some degree is the hope that one man can make a difference — Hojatoleslam Hashemi Rafsanjani, president of the Islamic Republic of Iran since the death of the Ayatollah Ruhollah Khomeini. Often described as a moderate, Rafsanjani is believed to have pragmatic reasons of his own for wanting the hostages freed. Along with President Hafez al-Assad of Syria, he is one of the few individuals who might have the means to effect the hostages' release. Whether Rafsanjani can deliver on these expectations in the near future, or ever, is now the crucial question in the hostage debate.

Rafsanjani's reputation as a moderate comes partly from his family background. Born in Rafsanjan, the central Iranian city from which his name is derived, he was one of nine children in a reasonably wealthy family that made its money through ownership of large groves of pistachio trees and in exporting.

Even today, the 55-year-old Rafsanjani has amicable relations with the *bazaaris*, the influential businessmen who run Tehran's traditional bazaar. Before the fall of Shah Mohammad Reza Pahlavi in 1979, Rafsanjani wrote a respected biography of Iran's first modern, Western-educated nationalist, Amir Kabir. "The Struggle Against Colonialism" quotes not a verse of the Koran.

In describing Rafsanjani, R. K. Ramazani, an Iranian-born professor of government at the University of Virginia and author of 11 books on Iran, points to the text of a speech Rafsanjani gave at an international conference in Tehran in November. "It is remarkable," Ramazani says. "It is most conciliatory. He says the only way to maintain security in the Persian Gulf region is on the basis of equality and reciprocity and noninterference with all neighbors."

Soon after taking office as president under Iran's revolutionary constitution, Rafsanjani began to enhance his power. Controlling about 50 percent of the 270-member Majlis, the parliament, he was able to replace 12 members of the 22-man Cabinet last August. In so doing, he promised to bring new blood into government to activate a huge reconstruction effort. "Rafsanjani is a tough, smart, clever politician," says a Bush administration official who watches Iran. "He is probably the most effective politician Iran has."

Experts also cite his cooperation during the 1985 hijacking of TWA Flight 847 in Athens as a reason for optimism. In Damascus at the time of the hijacking, he worked with the Syrians and leaders of several Palestinian groups to help free those hostages, an act for which Khomeini later had to protect him back home.

Since the beginning of Rafsanjani's presidency, there have been high hopes that Iran's position on the hostages will change, according to Shaul Bakhash, an expert on Iran and author of several books on the Persian Gulf region. If those hopes have not yet borne fruit, the administration official argues this is because Rafsanjani, due to internal politics and an omnipresent hard-line opposition, has had to move "carefully and slowly, a couple of steps forward and one back. He has had to change tactics and rhetoric to accommodate prevailing political currents, which is how he has managed to stay afloat for so long."

The official adds: "I think he does see the hostages . . . as interfering with his plans for improving relations primarily with the Europeans and perhaps ultimately with the United States."

Why he might want better relations is clear enough: Iran's economy is still shattered, and isolation from the Western world is no recipe for growth. Consumer goods are in short supply, inflation runs at 50 percent, the black market is pervasive; dissident Iranian expatriates report that the economic hardship has been so severe as to spark demonstrations.

"The internal situation within Iran is desperate," says Ramazani. "They must break the logjam of international isolation and get access to the Western market. The Iranians have many relationships, but they don't have the kind that counts."

Into that category falls the recent rapprochement between Tehran and Moscow. Although the trip was scheduled before Khomeini's death, Rafsanjani paid an official visit to Moscow shortly after the leader's funeral last spring. The visit was meant to antagonize Washington into taking a rash action to prevent Iran from entering the Soviet camp. It was met with a resounding silence by the Bush administration.

While in Moscow, Rafsanjani signed trade agreements reportedly totaling as much as $15 billion over the next decade. How useful the agreements will prove given Moscow's well-publicized economic problems is in question. Says Ramazani: "They're peanuts for what Iran needs in terms of reconstruction."

Besides the huge costs of repairing the damage from the eight-year war with Iraq, Iran must worry that the peace is not permanent. Negotiations are stalled while Iran has been cut off from buying arms in Western Europe. Iraq, at the same time, is stocking up in a serious way and may be close to joining the nuclear weapons club. Iraq has also successfully deployed long-range missiles and continues to stockpile poison gas.

Facing all these problems, Rafsanjani pushed through a budget in mid-March that allows Iran to borrow $5.4 billion abroad in the next year. The only problem is finding a place to borrow it, isolated as the country is because of the hostages and its state use of terrorism, which continues apparently with Rafsanjani's approval against Iran's own dissidents abroad and probably against Saudi Arabian diplomats.

In late February, Iran entertained a World Bank team in Tehran that came to determine whether the country could qualify for a lending program. "He needs the World Bank," says Bakhash. "To get into the World Bank, he needs American acquiescence, if not outright approval. Without the United States weighing in, it's impossible."

"I don't know if Iran is prepared at this stage to ask for major assistance, but they may be getting ready for that," says the administration official. "Certainly some of their actions have been designed to position them for that."

So what's stopping Rafsanjani? "He has to deal with a lot of people within his own government who are terribly opposed to any kind of relations with the United States," says another U.S. official. "They see the existence of hostages as a means to prevent any rapprochement."

Chief among the supposed hard-liners is former Interior Minister Ali Akbar Mohtashemi, one of several opposition leaders who have good contacts with the shadowy groups in Lebanon that hold hostages. He was one of several people Rafsanjani fired when the president rebuilt the Cabinet.

Another of the anti-Rafsanjani faction was one of the principal organizers of the takeover of the U.S. Embassy in 1979: Prosecutor General Mohammad Hossein Mousavi Khoeiniha. A young hard-line cleric, he is a leading figure in the Mohtashemi camp and is a close friend of Khomeini's son, Sayed Ahmed, another hardliner.

The suggestion of any relations with the United States is a contentious internal issue. Rafsanjani's opponents believe they have to keep stoking the Islamic revolution. They hold to Khomeini's line of keeping the outside world, particularly the United States, at arm's length. They feel that doing business with such countries will open Iran to foreign domination.

Still, there is broad agreement among all Iranian leaders on the tenets of Iran's foreign policy: nonalignment and radical Islam with Iran as leader of the world's Muslims. "Rafsanjani is no different from Mohtashemi on that," says Martin Kramer, a fellow at the Woodrow Wilson Center in Washington. "He believes that, with the world changing, Islam can emerge as a great power and that Iran can be at the center of that power. But that's a long road, and how you get there from here is the question."

Rafsanjani differs in figuring that Iran "can do business with the outside and maybe even the United States, but on Iran's terms, to ensure they won't be devoured," says the Bush administration official. "The Mohtashemis of Iran think that is basically a slippery slope. Once you do that, it's all over. You can't do that or you will have abandoned the revolution. International lending agencies, for example, are viewed as Trojan horses for the West to come in and take over the country again."

In pragmatic terms, Rafsanjani has to get something out of any dealings he has so he can take the profit back to his opposition and say, "Look at this. It was in our interest."

The problem with much analysis is that it may not be in Rafsanjani's power to get all the hostages released on his own say-so. Each of the three main groups holding Americans has its own agenda, apart from Iranian money and influence.

There are three logics at work, says Kramer. They are the fate of a group of prisoners in Kuwait, three of whom face the death penalty; the idea that keeping hostages in perpetuity is itself a guarantee of safety that also will keep Israel out of South Beirut; and the fate of 400 Shiite and Palestinian prisoners held in Israel and South Lebanon. "So some have an interest in making an exchange, and others say frankly that an exchange is out of the question," says Kramer.

No American hostages have been kidnapped since 1988 because, under Syrian influence, the groups have been told that they can keep the hostages they now have but cannot take anymore, says Kramer. Late last month, an American missionary, William Robinson, 59, was shot and killed at an orphanage he was running in Israel's self-declared security zone in southern Lebanon. In Beirut, the Lebanese Communist Party and the pro-Syrian Lebanese National Resistance Front claimed responsibility. Neither group has been linked to American hostages.

While continuing statements issued by a group that does hold hostages, the Islamic Jihad, have been consistent and are easy to read, many efforts at understanding what is happening tend more toward the tea leaf method, partly because there is no direct diplomatic contact between Iran and the United States.

Rafsanjani sends messages through statements in the Tehran Times, which he controls, and in his Friday sermons. On the anniversary of Khomeini's death sentence on Indian-born "Satanic Verses" author Salman Rushdie, Rafsanjani gave a sermon in which he hinted that Khomeini's opinion was the opinion of one jurist. Nonetheless, the contract on Rushdie remains.

At the same time, in a hastily called news conference earlier this year, Rafsanjani was the most conciliatory any Iranian has ever been on the hostage issue, saying there should be no conditions for their release.

Just what the United States can do other than wait is not easy to assess, say the experts. Iran has its own demands of Washington, particularly the release of billions of dollars that were seized by the Carter administration after the American Embassy in Tehran was taken by Iranian militants (**Insight**, Sept. 11).

The United States has said repeatedly that it is prepared to talk directly with the Iranians, but only to an authorized representative of that government, says the Bush administration official.

"It is going to be a long process," says Bakhash. "It will probably happen in bits and pieces. It will be slow and incremental."

Which hostages would be released and when is nothing but a guess, says the University of Virginia's Ramazani.

President Bush recently alluded to behind-the-scene operations that he said would intrigue anyone if the details were known. It is known that one of Rafsanjani's brothers, Mahmoud Hashemi, who heads the Middle East department at the Iranian Foreign Ministry, has been running interference among Iran, some Lebanese factions and Syria. Jimmy Carter's recent visit to Syria may show a willingness by Syria to try to do something about the impasse, says Ramazani.

But the idea of all hostages coming out together may go nowhere. It would be easier to get one or two released at a time, says Kramer. But successive U.S. administrations have said they will not be satisfied until all are freed. There were rumors for a while that some had been released and were being held in the Iranian Embassy in Beirut as a sort of halfway house to satisfy Washington until Rafsanjani could get them all.

They were not the only rumors, nor will they be the last.

— Richard Mackenzie

Out from the cellar

IN TIME, the release of the American university professor, Mr Robert Polhill, from his Lebanese cellar on April 22nd may be seen as the beginning of the end of a decade of political kidnapping in the Middle East. This is not because Mr Polhill was the first American hostage to be released from Lebanon in more than three years, nor because his freedom seemed to come without the payment of ransom to his jailers or his jailers' sponsors. It is because Syria and Iran, the two countries with most influence over Lebanon's kidnap gangs, seem to have agreed that hostage-taking no longer serves their wider interests in the world.

Syria's influence in Lebanon comes out of the gun-barrels of the 30,000 or so soldiers it keeps there. Iran has a far smaller armed presence, in the shape of several hundred Revolutionary Guards encamped in the Bekaa valley. The two countries are imperfect allies: Syria supports the Amal, or "Hope", movement among Lebanon's Shia Muslims, whereas Iran arms and inspires Hezbollah, the "Party of God", which is Amal's competitor. During the Gulf war, however, a shared fear of Iraq kept the two countries on friendly terms.

Now they share something else: a growing sense of isolation. Syria's President Hafez Assad no longer enjoys full-hearted Soviet support in his quest for "strategic parity" with Israel. He has antagonised many fellow-Arabs by his occupation of Lebanon and his coldness towards Mr Yasser Arafat of the Palestine Liberation Organisation. By portraying himself as the hostages' liberator, Mr Assad hopes to improve his standing in the West.

Iran's encouragement of the Lebanese kidnappers kept it isolated from the West and helped its Islamic revolution stay fiery—which is precisely what Ayatollah Khomeini intended. Since his death, however, President Rafsanjani, a pragmatist opposed to Iran's isolation, has sought western economic help for his war-shattered country. For him, if not for all the hardliners in his government, the western hostages in Lebanon have become a liability. Since the end of February Iranian newspapers have called repeatedly for their release. Iranian envoys to Lebanon, one of them Mr Rafsanjani's brother, are believed to have been instrumental in winning Mr Polhill's freedom.

If so, the wheel has turned full circle. It was in Iran, in 1979, that the hostage epidemic began. The students who stormed the United States embassy in Tehran, and held its staff captive for 444 days, discovered through hostage-taking a weapon powerful enough to destroy an American presidency. Their example was soon followed by admirers in Lebanon, where kidnap gangs have abducted nearly 90 foreigners since 1984. About 60 have escaped or were set free, another 11 died or were murdered in captivity. On most counts around 16 westerners—seven Americans, three Britons, two West Germans, two Swiss, an Irishman and an Italian—are still being held. (In addition, four Belgians are probably held in Libya.)

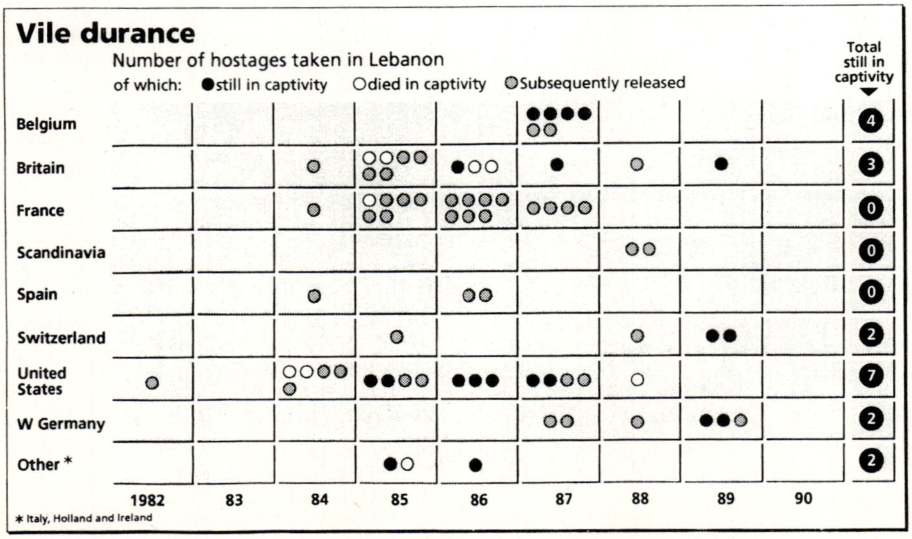

The links between Syria, Iran and the congeries of kidnapping gangs are murky. It serves the interests of all concerned to keep them that way. Syria and Iran routinely deny any involvement with hostage-taking, yet routinely advertise their "influence" with the kidnappers. There typically follows a complex game of duplicity, designed to extort cash or make western governments "adjust" their foreign policies. For Iran, this policy reached its apotheosis in the arms-for-hostages affair of 1985-86. That was when President Ronald Reagan lectured his allies against negotiating with terrorists or supplying arms to Iran while the men in his basement were doing those very things to bring a handful of hostages out of Lebanon.

What also seems clear through the murkiness is that the kidnappers, or some of them, have minds and local aims of their own, separate from the geopolitical interests of their sponsors. When Syria was poised once to storm a Hezbollah barracks in Beirut, Hezbollah held it off by threatening to murder its hostages. Some kidnappers are said to be common thugs, who sell their hostages on for profit. Others have taken hostages to trade against the freedom of relations facing trial in Europe.

Most western governments say that it is wrong to make any deals with hostage-takers, and then break their own rules. France, most recently, appears to have bought the freedom of a Frenchwoman, her daughter and her Belgian lover by sending Libya's Colonel Moammar Qaddafi lavish messages of praise plus three Mirage fighters it had been withholding. Only Britain adheres to a no-talks policy, in spite of domestic agitation for more flexibility on behalf of the British captives. One is Mr Terry Waite, the special representative of the archbishop of Canterbury, who became a hostage in Lebanon in 1987, while pleading for the release of those already there.

President George Bush, America's vice-president during the Iran-contra affair, nowadays handles hostage matters as gingerly as

Dark days at Dog River

FROM OUR CORRESPONDENT IN EAST BEIRUT

THIS year, Friday April 13th was not just Good Friday. It also marked the 15th year of civil war in Lebanon. In the Christian enclave shelling broke out in the morning, as usual. A cartoon in the local paper showed a civilian pleading to the Maronite patriarch: "Forgive them, for they know what they do." The patriarch has threatened many times to excommunicate the Christians who are fighting one another.

New battles erupted on April 24th. The battle lines are unchanged (see map). The "Lebanese Forces" militia of Mr Samir Geagea controls the Jounieh and Jubail regions in the north of the Christian enclave, plus the East Beirut quarters of Ashrafieh and Karantina (which includes the port and the militia's headquarters). General Michel Aoun's rival troops of the "official" Lebanese army control the area around Ras el Metn and the southern entrances into East Beirut.

At the checkpoints in and out of each zone cars form long lines. At the Dog River crossing between Jounieh (under Mr Geagea's control) and Dbayeh (General Aoun's northernmost point) eight lanes of traffic converge into a single-track railway bridge, which in turn leads on to a narrow and previously disused road that bypasses the Dbayeh tunnel, which is blocked with stones and sand. Traffic jams make easy targets for snipers. A school bus was hit last week by a rifle-grenade that killed 15 people, 11 of them children. The British ambassador's bulletproof Range Rover was hit three times in East Beirut. Each side uses its television station to blame the other for the indiscriminate sniping.

Women with guns and uniforms are becoming an increasingly common sight as militarisation spreads. Most shops are open, though shopkeepers keep one ear constantly on the indispensable radio, ready to lock up and rush home at the first newsflash. Owning premises has become a liability: many merchants have taken to selling fruit and vegetables from boxes and carts, and cartons of cigarettes from piles on the bonnets of their cars.

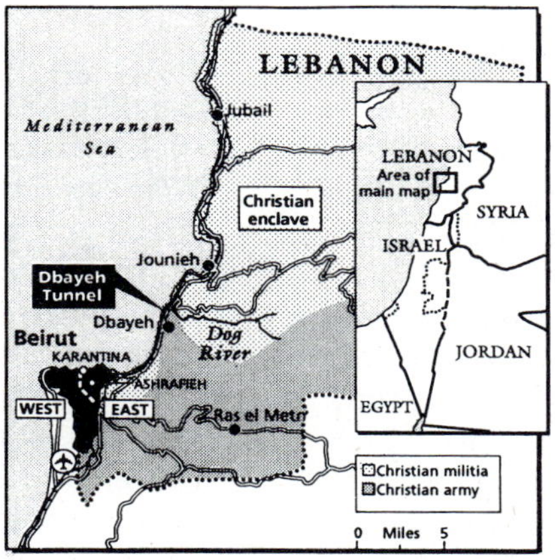

In the coastal town of Jounieh graffiti have appeared on the walls of the town hall singing the praises of "*il-hakeem*" (referring to "Doctor" Geagea, who was once a medical student) and denouncing General Aoun. Militiamen have commandeered the blue-grey jeeps of the Internal Security Forces, the impotent national police force, and painted out the Lebanese flags on their number-plates. One downcast policeman in Ashrafieh says he had been "made redundant" by teenage militiamen who have occupied the government building where he worked.

General Aoun still enjoys plenty of support in those areas of the enclave under his army's control and, more discreetly, in Mr Geagea's areas. His appeal rests on his defiance of Syria, his own powerful personality and the belief of many Christians that he still embodies what is left of Lebanon's legitimate government. A businessman says of the destruction of two recently bought beach chalets in Jounieh: "If the army destroys or takes my house, then OK, it's the legal army, but I wouldn't accept that the militia could do that."

a cat with a burnt paw. While stressing at every opportunity his refusal to bargain, he has let it be known that "goodwill begets goodwill". Once Mr Assad had deployed Syria's famous "influence" to help free Mr Polhill, he was indeed rewarded, on April 23rd, with a telephone call from Mr Bush.

The United States was hoping that Mr Polhill's release would be swiftly followed by the release of more hostages. But Iranian officials say that it is now America's turn to come up with a "goodwill gesture". They want Mr Bush to make Israel release the Lebanese prisoners it has taken in southern Lebanon (particularly Sheikh Abdelkarim Obeid, whom Israeli soldiers abducted last February) together with Palestinian gunmen and *intifadists* imprisoned in Israel.

As for Mr Bush's assertion that goodwill begets goodwill, some people in Hezbollah are unimpressed. This week the American House of Representatives followed the example of the Senate by calling Jerusalem the capital of Israel. "Now the Americans have proved their bad will on a very high level," said Sheikh Hussein Musawi in Beirut. Whatever the new thinking in Syria and Iran, a few men with guns will continue to see hostage-taking as a good way to make their mark on history.

Interview With Abu Nidal

Are you Abu Nidal or someone who is posing as Abu Nidal? How can I be sure you are Abu Nidal?

The information I will give you will prove that I am Abu Nidal.

There was an interview in the English press last year that you had died.

The secret service of the British would like to see me gone. This dastardly ghost which walks through the night, creates nightmares. The news of my death, from the Jordanian secret service together with the secret service of other Gulf states and the British secret service, was fabricated. Together with other imperialist governments and people in these circles consider me as dangerous as the atom bomb. However, as you see, I am not a ghost or a phantom, I am Abu Nidal in the flesh and blood.

Can you please give us some proof of your identity?

Let me show you here (he opens his shirt) the scar on my chest from an operation.

A heart operation?

Yes.

Where was this operation performed?

In the USA.

Under the name Abu Nidal?

Absolutely not. I used the name of a prominent Saudi Arabian; I had a false passport.

When was that?

At the end of 1977.

Is it not true, as the press reported, that you had this operation performed at a London hospital with 25 bodyguards?

That's absolutely false.

Why do you fight against the British?

Margaret Thatcher is on the side of Zionism. She helps the Arabian lands only because of the British industrial connection with Arab capital. British business is dependent on Arab capital. The British secret service is a simple information organization for the Israeli secret service, the Mossad; and hundreds of their agents, Israeli agents with British passports, wander through Arab lands for information. It is therefore no wonder we are against the government of Margaret Thatcher and she is one of our enemies.

What has that produced?

It has produced a connection between us and the IRA. The last assassination in Britain was an example of our connection. And the next case will prove it even further, however, I won't say any more about what we're planning for the future.

Who do you define as your enemy?

My enemy is the Zionists in my homeland, Palestine. My enemy is also the imperialist governments in any form. My enemy is also people responsible for the destruction and revision of Arab nations. My enemy is also the chaos and pressure put on Arab society and our younger generation. I just want to tell you of a dream we have . . . my dream, for a united Arab nation, freedom, righteousness, and equality.

Do you think that explosive use of terrorism for political ends is a legitimate means for this dream?

I think it's very legitimate; because the Zionists have broken up my land. In my eyes, what we do is against this destruction. For me I will fight this invasion and fight to rid my land of the Zionists. That is my philosophy. I, Abu Nidal, as an Arab, give you that as an answer.

Why do you hate the Americans so much?

If there is any absolute in this world, then it's the imperialism of Americans, of America. Without the help of the American imperialism, the Zionists never would have attained what they have. The Americans encourage a Gulf war and try to divide the Arabs. If we were to win our goals in the Arab lands, you would see an end to terrorism. You can be sure of one thing . . . given the chance we will destroy as much as we can that is American. Between us and the Americans is a war of life and death, and in the next few months and next few years we are going to give the Americans something to think about.

Reprinted from *Der Spiegel*, No. 42, 1985 by permission.

What do you want people to think of this last message or prophecy?

We want the world to know that all we want is our land that was stolen. We also want you to know that you can elect any president you want, a ballet dancer, a cowboy, or an actor, but when the American bombers fly over our land and bomb our people, you are committing terrorism and destruction, and you must answer for it.

Is President Reagan on your death list?

Of course he is. We would like to see an end to him. Reagan has spent hundreds of millions of dollars to protect himself in his White House. He has a feeling, rightly so, of fear. He'll always remain so.

But many Arabs in the Arab world welcome the American presence.

Unfortunately. They mostly are kings or sheiks in our region who have to ask the Americans if they can sleep with their own wife. How can you believe these people when their entire armies, flags and national hymn are something that the Americans have dreamed up and dictate like puppets?

Not only the Americans but the Soviet Union has an interest in Arab land, but you only criticize the Americans in your eyes. Why not also the Soviet Union?

The Soviets are more of a friend to the Arabs. Naturally they have an interest in our land but they do not condone the existence of the Zionists in Palestine. That is why we are more understanding of them.

If you are only an enemy of imperialism and Zionism, why is it that you seem to attack Jewish school children, synagogues and restaurants?

The question isn't if we attack civilians or civilian Jews that we meet in our actions. The question is, when we attack, unfortunately these people are there in situations where the Zionist secret service, Mossad, is situated.

You claim that the English, French and German ambassadors and embassies are centers of spying. Will you attack these embassies?

My methods will not be so cut and dried. For instance, French secret service has sort of two wings; one side must remain neutral between the Arabs and the Zionists. On the other hand, the American pressure forces them on the side of Zionism. I would like to tell the Germans not to forget about the French. I will give a warning to the French. In the next few months you will see action against the French.

What about the Germans?

We believe basically that the Germans work for the interests of the German people and not necessarily 100% for the CIA.

But will the German mentality stay the same? What will happen if the Germans go against the Arabs?

Much will happen. The answer will be for the Germans what is obvious.

What do you think the German agencies have against Arabs?

Much. When you have your government agencies read this article, they will know what I mean. For instance, the German government gives asylum to a reactionary Moslem brotherhood, and they support these people with asylum in your territory. These people are against our cause. They are a group of pure Islamic teachers who are forming a brotherhood to cleanse Arab lands of unpure Moslem thinking. The German government is giving these people asylum and we feel that by doing this, the German government is in danger of provoking a reaction for us.

However, our only wish is to give these Moslem brotherhood asylum.

That is not the case, I can sit here in this room I can telephone directly to Stuttgart to the central location of this Moslem brotherhood. I have seen the central brotherhood headquarters myself.

Can you please tell me have you been often in Germany?

Yes, I have visited Germany often. I know Germany from border to border and many cities.

You are known in this world as a very dangerous man. Many attacks have been credited to your organization, and under your leadership the attempted assassination of Shlomo Argov, an Israeli diplomat in London in 1982, was that your work?

Yes, absolutely.

It seems that after this attack the Israelis marched into Lebanon. Why, then, did you do this when you knew the consequences for the Palestinians?

The Israeli embassy in London was a central meeting point for the members of the secret service, Mossad. We have had the embassy under surveillance for a long time and I told my fellow fighters to strike, but not to injure any diplomats. They were only meant to strike against secret service agents.

But you must have known that the Israeli soldiers were massing on the northern border quite a long time; and that any attack or assassination would have had dire consequences.

You are absolutely right. The Israelis welcomed the assassination which gave them an excuse to invade. It also gave them the opportunity to involve the multinational troops of America, France, Great Britain and Italy into Lebanon.

Do you think that the Israelis had plans for the invasion of Lebanon?

Any blind man would know that they had plans for an invasion. The Israelis looked for an excuse to invade and the assassination of the ambassador was the spark they needed.

Yasir Arafat said that you were an agent for the Israelis and you caused them to invade Lebanon, that you were in a way, working for them.

You know what Arafat says sometimes makes me laugh. In different areas of Arab and international politics I am known as many things. Some people say I am in the service of the Zionists, of Israel, and even the CIA. Others say I work for the French secret service. The newest saying is that I work as an agent for Khomeini in Iran. Some other people say that I am an agent for Syria and that I am in the employ of King Fahd.

Well, who do you work for it you don't work for any of these people?

I must be very honest with you. Many sociologists and psychologists in the Eastern bloc have attempted to study the person, Abu Nidal. They wanted to find a weak point in my personality and they couldn't find anything. Now people are saying I work for every secret service in the world. I would just like to say one thing: I only work for one organization, el Fatah, a revolutionary organization.

How many people do you have in your organization, a dozen or hundreds?

You must believe me in all seriousness, but I cannot give you an answer.

How are you organized? How do you operate your commandos?

I can't open up my plans to you. They must be an absolute secret. I can't even tell my eight-year-old daughter how things really are.

Where do you get the money for your organization?

Parts of it comes from colleagues and sympathizers. We're not really soldiers. At the present time we have arranged some money from a Gulf state. And another part of the money comes from oil lands, based on oil bills.

The money you receive into your organization comes from different groups. Are you the sole individual who decides how it will be used or do you answer to other people?

You have to ask yourself that same question that you're asking me. Is it possible for me, one man, who is answerable to others, to be able to be the leader of an organization and to be able to walk the land and go from country to country without any bodyguards if I was answerable to other people?

Aren't you like Arafat?

No, I can walk in any Arab land or European land and travel as I wish. No Arab regime is informed where I go or who my friends are or how I plan to direct my colleagues.

You're a wanted man in many lands. Many secret agencies are looking for you. Can you tell us where you travel, to which lands?

I have traveled through the entire Arab world and to two African states.

Have you ever been in Israel?

Palestine is my land. In 1967 I was living in Nablus. After 1967 I lived in Jordan.

How are you able to keep your movements such a secret and escape so quickly when you're discovered in a land?

I never meet with people who send me to my grave. I really have no great personal ambition, especially a great political ambition. I am a man of principle and a goal and organizer to do my business.

You say you're not like Arafat, a man who seeks political exposure?

I've got to tell you that this is only my third interview in my entire life, and I am not any longer a young man.

You have been given a death sentence by Yasir Arafat. How do you explain that?

Since September 1970 we have been fighting. We don't understand each other correctly. In the beginning we tried to join together for goals of Fatah, my group, with his group, a democratic phase that ended in March 1974. Arafat and his group started a campaign against us where quite a bit of blood was spilling. We then at that time broke off Fatah from his group. Because of that break, and at that time 150 of my men lost their lives at the hands of Arafat's cold-blooded soldiers. You might say it was a power struggle. At that time I was told that I was given a death sentence by Arafat. He tried many times to kill me. And from that time on I have not been under the protection of any Arab regime. We stand alone against the threat of Arafat.

How do you judge Arafat today?

Arafat is like a puppet. On the one hand he tries to impress his Arab following, but on the other hand he's sort of a marionette for the Americans and the Zionists. He swings from side to side whenever he has to.

There was a time when you used to work for the Iraqis. Why haven't you continued this connection, why have you broken with them?

The problem was, that our alliance was broken for this reason: the Vatican at the time was sending out signals that perhaps the Palestinian people did have a righteous grievance in this region which the Iraqis of course opposed. I believe that tactically we should have used the Vatican since they were sympathetic to us. And believe me I really believe that the Vatican is a Christian organization that is compassionate to our cause.

It appears that all you see around you are liars and agents against you. Do you have any sympathy for the Syrians?

I am a great admirer of Syria. I hope someday we can have Iraq listen to us again and also Iraq has made us very sad. The military operation that has spilled much blood is unfortunately occurring. Our previous work together with Iraq was very important strategically for our group. That was important for us, and we would like to still see Iraq on our side in our fight.

Do you feel that you are Syrian or are you a Palestinian?

We are Syrian citizens and Syria for us is a mother nation. Syria is for us a story of comradeship and we are part of the geography. At one time half of Lebanon was part of Syria. You see in Lebanon, are really Syrian citizens. I myself am half Syrian. One of my parents came from Syria and one came from Palestine. The great kingdom of Syria is Jordan, and the kingdom of Syria was once Palestine, Iraq, Jordan and Syria. Jordan for instance didn't exist before the 1920s. Geographically, the kingdom of Syria was a territory with a Turkish border north, and Palestine in the south. Until then, Syria at one time also included what is known today as Israel.

Do you think that the kingdom of Syria should once again go back to its old borders which would mean the expulsion of Israel?

The closer we come to a united Arab state the greater our chance would be to expel the Zionists.

Don't you think there is a peaceful way to find a solution for Palestine?

There doesn't seem to be a peaceful way to solve a problem in this world. When you look at the Arab story throughout centuries, and see that peaceful solutions never work and it won't solve our problem.

Do you think then that an armed conflict is the only way to reach your goal?

I give you this. That the existence of Zionists in Palestine is incompatible with our dream. At this time the entire Zionists nation is mobilized against our children. They are ready with stones and knives to fight against us, as we are against them. For instance, the Camp David accords have been signed a long time ago. Through peaceful means since that time, nothing has happened to solve our problem. The successor to Sadat, Husni Mubarak is himself paying now for his lack of interest in the Arab history, or Arab story of what is happening today.

A short time ago, an Israeli ambassador was murdered in Cairo. Is this part of your revenge for the Egyptian lack of interest in Palestinian problems?

We cannot claim responsibility for this action. This was the action of the revolutionary Egyptians.

Can you give us a short synopsis of your background?

The story of my life is not very important but I'll give you a few details. I was born to a Syrian family in 1937. My father was a prominent businessman in Palestine. He was quite rich. He had 13 wives, I am the son of the eighth wife. My father had with these women 16 boys and eight daughters. Through his marriages, I am the uncle of over 300 boys and girls in that family. I studied for 3 years in a French high school in Jaffa. In that school, together with two Christian Arabs I was expelled and then went to Islamic school in Jerusalem. . . . The Egyptian army began shooting at us and we had to flee Palestine. My family got scattered.

What happened with you?

We had to spend nine months in a camp in the Gaza Strip. Later I was forced to become a worker for the Saudi Arabian company, Aramco. In Saudi Arabia I was arrested, tortured, and then evicted from the country.

Are you married? Do you have children?

Yes, I have three children.

Do you have many wives like your father, or just one?

For heaven's sake, just one. One is enough!

Which politician is your model?

Of the modern politicians I admire strongly the discipline and organizational talent of Chou En-lai.

Which revolution has influenced the most: the French, the Russian or the Islamic of Khomeini?

The technical and organizational preparation in the beginning phase of the Soviet revolution has influenced me the most. A good organization is decisive for a successful revolution. The political contents of the French revolution are overwhelmingly nice: freedom, equality, brotherhood. These maxims impress a repressed people.

And the Iranian revolution?

(He laughs)

What is your real name?

Sabri Chalil el-Banna.

In the press there are always lists of your terrorist acts. Therefore you have allowed under others, the Palestinians Said Hamami, Iss el-Din el-Kalak, and Naim Chudr to be killed.

You bring a very modest list, very modest. I say to you very clearly: Every Arab or Palestinian who has had contact with the Mossad will end as those three—liquidated. We have carried out nearly one hundred actions, without which we would have been much larger. The reason was always the same: contact with the Mossad.

They have never erred and killed an innocent?

Certainly not. We took every accusation to task beforehand. When he did not listen to us, we had him killed. Incidentally, Said Hamami was my nephew.

What have you attained with the murders? Have you gotten any closer to your goal?

That is not the question for me. When somebody has given away your land, your people, and your country, he receives the corresponding answer: All resistance fighters have acted so. What have the French resistance done with their traitors? We have never shot innocents or journalists.

That does not matter. You have allowed the shooting in 1978 of the famous Egyptian journalist, Sibai, in Cyprus.

You brought this up to me before the first time we spoke of this occurrence. We aimed not only for Sibai, but primarily for his intimate friend, President Sadat.

How so?

We designed a plan, in order to lure the Egyptian secret service and its head, Major Nabil, to Cyprus. Major Nabil was the boss of the so-called Republic Security, a secret service organization which is under the sole control of Sadat. Its main job was to protect the life of the president at any cost. Therefore we killed Sibai in Cyprus, and Sadat reacted exactly as we expected. He sent special troops with military weapons to Cyprus, led by Major Nabil. They were supposed to do a punishment raid on Cyprus against us. For that reason Sadat was defenseless. The further plan of action called for taking advantage of the opportunity to kill Sadat and his close friends. For particular reasons, the second part of our plan could not be carried out. There were shoot-outs at the airport at Cyprus, in which Major Nabil and half his elite troops came to the end of their lives. With the state funeral of Nabil and his people, Sadat dared, contrary to the announcements, to show himself.

Would you do something like that today?

Yes, for example with Ahmed Dscharallah, the chief editor of the Kuwaiti newspaper, El-Sijassa. . . . We have nothing against his commentaries and analyses, but his publishing house in Kuwait is not a press house but a whore house. We have often invited him, both written and orally to withdraw his outstretched hand. The corrupter had decided to accept an invitation to occupied Palestine. Every Arab should know: betrayal will be punished with death. The regime in Kuwait should not forget that Kuwait is an Arabic land and its oil is Arabic oil, not Zionist-American oil. We have shot Dscharallah. Hopefully he has understood the message.

How does it help you to hound people like Dscharallah? There are Arabic rulers who have permanent contact with the Israelis; for example, King Hussein and President Mubarak.

Who claims then, that Mubarak and Hussein can live safe and carefree? Almost daily the Egyptian secret service discover assassination plans against Mubarak. Our organization has made the decision to liquidate King Hussein, some attempts have failed. There was at one time arrogance among Sadat and Arafat's friend Issam el-Sartawi, who regarded themselves as immortal. Where are they today? Who would like to claim that Husni Mubarak and King Hussein will have a long life?

You had nothing to do with Sadat, but you liquidated Sartawi. What was his crime supposed to have been?

His fall lies crystal-clear. He built a peace committee with the Zionists. A member of this committee was the earlier Zionist police head, Peled. We possess perfect documents, which prove that Sartawi was an agent of the CIA. He was the right hand of Arafat, consequently we cut off Arafat's right hand.

Is every Jew and Israeli really your enemy?

Every Zionist is my enemy. But I make a distinction between Zionists and Jews. It is not so that every Jew is my enemy.

Do you not see that there are also factions in Israel which want peace with the Arabs?

The so-called Peace Now movement is not as eyewash. We do not believe them. Uri Avnery is a Zionist immigrant; he should go back where he came from—to Germany, in the area of Hannover. When he thinks honestly, then he should clearly distance himself from the Zionist ideology. Then we can believe what he says.

Do you also work together with European underground organizations?

Certainly. With the French Action Direct, the Belgian fighting communist cells, the IRA, the Basques, the German Red Army Group, and so on. Why not? What is wrong with it? The imperialists have united themselves and combat us everywhere. So have we also united under the motto: "Repressed, unite yourselves!"

What is the difference between struggle and terrorism in your eyes?

Fair struggle means the right of a people to fight against the usurpation of their land by all available means. Terrorism is the liquidation of innocent people without reason, by a group or organization or state power; for instance, the Palestinian camp Sabra and Schatila.

The PLO is split up now. Does the PLO have a chance, in your opinion, to defeat Israel's military?

Neither the Palestinians nor the PLO will ever be in position to achieve a military victory over the Zionists. The victory over the Zionists can only be reached through a general Arab strategy; all Arabs must participate so long as the Zionist organization exists. The Arabs will be forced to unite themselves to meet this danger. We Palestinians and Lebanese will be the igniter for the fight of all Arabs against the Zionists. We will kindle the great fire in the Near East.

Do you really believe in all seriousness that Syria would allow you to fight on their territory against Israel?

That is not the question, but there are many more: How will the conflict between the Arabs and the Zionists develop in the next years? How will the Syrian regime develop its relationship to the other power of this region? Also important is: will Syria develop to a base of our revolution or not?

What do you think of Qadhafi and Libya?

Muammar is a very good friend, a very righteous man. Our connection with him is very deep, our friendship is based on mutual respect. We dream of the same dream, a united Arab nation. He is a one of a kind individual, sort of a bird who sings and others sing along with him. Sometimes the other birds will join him in his song. His land is a strong basis against imperialism and Zionism. He despises American imperialism deep in his heart. For us he is a great help.

What side of his politics do you reject?

His political convictions are in line with ours basically. His formulations and definitions are the same as ours. Essentially, we are in full agreement with him.

Abu Nidal, we thank you for this interview.

A Terrorist Talks About Life, Warns Of More Deaths

PLF's Abbas, in an Interview, Applauds Saddam Hussein And Hints at New Actions

Tony Horwitz

Staff Reporter of The Wall Street Journal

BAGHDAD—A visit to the hideout of Abul Abbas, one of the world's most wanted men, begins with a rubber-burning drive down the back streets of the Iraqi capital.

The driver loops twice past an anonymous house in an anonymous neighborhood, honking each time so guards can check that the Mercedes isn't being tailed. On the third pass, the car veers into the driveway. Stern young men with submachine guns lurk in the bushes. At the door of the one-story villa, a guard frisks a visiting reporter and tests his tape-recorder—with the machine's microphone pointed at the journalist's neck.

Mr. Abbas, leader of the Palestine Liberation Front, waits in an office decorated with photos of his commandos setting off in speedboats to strike Israel. "I am sorry for the welcome," he says, gesturing at guards posted by his window. "This is my life."

'Battle for Palestine'

Mr. Abbas's life, as it unfolds in a three-hour interview over tea, Turkish coffee and two packs of Marlboro cigarettes, is the chilling tale of the making of a terrorist. It begins in a Palestinian refugee camp in Syria and leads to this Baghdad lair, where Mr. Abbas plotted the 1985 Achille Lauro hijacking and this year's attack on a Tel Aviv beach, which ended America's dialogue with the Palestine Liberation Organization.

Now, with his Iraqi patron, Saddam Hussein, under siege by U.S. forces, Mr. Abbas thinks the time may soon be ripe for renewed commando warfare.

"We see this as the battle for Palestine," he says of the Persian Gulf conflict. "Winning it will get us closer to home. Losing it will put us further away." Asked if terrorism is a necessary part of Saddam Hussein's struggle, he responds: "We use many ways to reach our aim."

In apparent anticipation of guerrilla strikes, the U.S. State Department took the unusual step of issuing a statement at 8:30 p.m. Friday saying, "The United States would view with utmost seriousness any Iraqi-sponsored terrorist attack." Iraq was restored to the department's list of governments sponsoring terrorism on Sept. 1.

A Symbol

Among radical Palestinian leaders, Mr. Abbas's position is exceptional. His rap sheet of what he calls "military operations"—and what the West calls terrorism—is exceeded only by the shadowy Abu Nidal and Ahmed Jebril, who is believed to have masterminded the bombing of Pan Am flight 103.

But Mr. Abbas also sits on the PLO's 15-man executive committee, and therefore has a voice within the Palestinian mainstream. "Abul Abbas is a symbol, to show that the PLO hasn't abandoned armed struggle," says Asad Abdul Rahman, a member of the PLO's parliament in exile.

To many in the West, Mr. Abbas is a much darker symbol: violent, uncompromising and determined to torpedo efforts at peacefully resolving the Arab-Israeli conflict. Helena Cobban, a Washington-based PLO expert and author of a leading book on the organization, describes Mr. Abbas as "a low-level thug" and a "mercenary gun-for-hire" who has no real political program. Long on the Iraqi payroll, he could become useful to Saddam Hussein if he decides to "activate the terror option," she says.

Although Mr. Abbas says he only strikes at Israeli "military targets," civilians often have been cut down in the crossfire. In a 1979 raid by PLF gunmen on the Israeli town of Nahariya, the four Israeli deaths included a four-year-old girl; a PLF commando crushed her skull with a machine gun.

Meeting an American in Baghdad for what he says is the first time, Mr. Abbas cuts an imposing, rather incongruous figure. Broad-shouldered and six feet four inches tall, he has the strong but softening build of a retired lumberjack. Ruggedly handsome, his thick black hair and mustache show no signs of gray at 41. His eyes don't give much away; in the dimly-lit office, they are so dark as to seem all pupil.

Mr. Abbas's manner is disarming. Soft-voiced, his face wrinkles easily into laughter. He speaks passable English and florid Arabic, filled with metaphor and rhythmic locutions. A graduate in Arabic literature from the University of Damascus, he also appears to be well-read. His favorite Western writer, he says, is William Shakespeare—"particularly the tragedies." He says he was a schoolteacher in Syria before becoming a full-time "freedom fighter."

The second career has left its mark. Brushing back his hair, Mr. Abbas reveals a jagged scar across his forehead, the result, he says, of an Israeli cluster bomb during the siege of Beirut in 1982. He also has a bullet wound in each thigh from guerrilla fighting in Jordan and the West Bank. "That's the life," he says, chuckling grimly.

Asked if he has personally killed anyone, he responds with a half-smile, "During the fight, you don't know what happens." He adds that what happens in the heat of battle "isn't just killing" because "this is war. Israel is our enemy."

As for innocents who have died in this war, he shrugs. "Accidents happen," he says.

'Ruthless Stunts'

Mr. Abbas welcomes the current Gulf conflict, which is gathering Palestinian extremists beneath the Iraqi tent in company with PLO Chairman Yasser Arafat. Last week, a leading radical, Syrian-based George Habash, made his first visit in 11 years to Baghdad, where he met with both Mr. Abbas and Saddam Hussein. Palestinian sources say Abu Nidal already is in Iraq. And Mr. Abbas predicts that others, such as Mr. Jebril, also may soon defect from Syria to Saddam Hussein's camp.

"I think Saddam will win, and we will win as Arabs," Mr. Abbas says. "When we support Iraq, we support our case as Palestinians."

While Mr. Abbas won't disclose what this support might include, past exploits give some clue to future attacks. "Ruthless stunts that often go wrong" is how one Palestinian official describes PLF operations.

The group has staged strikes on Israel by hang glider, by hot-air balloon, by rubber dinghy and, most notoriously, by seajacking the cruise liner Achille Lauro (which he says was to be taken to Israel, in part to free PLF fighters captured in the 1979 Nahariya attack).

It was during the bungled Achille Lauro mission, when a wheelchair-bound American passenger, Leon Klinghoffer, was killed, that Mr. Abbas became known internationally. The world's most wanted terrorist, with U.S. warrants out for his arrest for hostage-taking and piracy, he eluded a global manhunt, reportedly disguised in an Egyptair uniform. An Italian court later convicted him in absentia and sentenced him to life imprisonment.

No Regrets

Mr. Abbas is unapologetic for the death of the crippled Mr. Klinghoffer, who was shot in the head and back and pushed overboard. "Maybe he was trying to swim for it," Mr. Abbas coldly suggested in 1988. Asked about the incident again last week, he bristled. "Klinghoffer, always I hear about this Klinghoffer," he says. "Nobody knows all the people who die in Palestine. But this Klinghoffer is like Jesus Christ."

Mr. Abbas also has no regrets over the failed attack on a crowded Tel Aviv beach last May. It was Mr. Arafat's refusal to denounced Mr. Abbas following the attack that led the U.S. to suspend its dialogue with the PLO. Four commandos were killed and 12 captured in what Mr. Abbas says was an assault aimed at military targets. "For two years we say yes, yes, yes to America, without results," he says of the dialogue. "Political ways have stopped now. Only we will fight."

Mr. Abbas says he still would welcome a negotiated settlement to the Arab-Israeli conflict. But asked if he is prepared to recognize Israel, as Mr. Arafat has done, he responds: "For me, for our organization, we will not. We want our land now and to build our state. After that we will say."

Mr. Abbas's hard-line views reflect the militancy of a new generation of Palestinians. In contrast to other splinter groups, some Marxist and others fundamentalist, the PLF appeals to young militants devoted to action rather than to ideology. Members are carefully ranked, in military style, and tend to wear blue jeans, white shirts and combat boots.

One fiery-eyed lieutenant in Baghdad, who goes by the name of Abu Nahar, says he follows Mr. Abbas because the PLF "is focused, rational, not emotional." He adds that all members of the PLF, which may have a hard core of only 100, "must prove themselves in battle."

Videotaped Images

Mr. Abbas, ranked as secretary-general, is the youngest member of the PLO's executive committee and the only one born outside of what is now Israel and its occupied territories. His parents fled their village near Haifa in 1948, just after the founding of Israel. Mohammed Zaidan Abbas was born a few months later, in a Syrian refugee camp. The only image he has of his family's village is from videotapes taken by friends who have visited since.

Mr. Abbas says it is this separation from his homeland that has made him so radical. Members of the PLO's old guard, he says, "can balance between the truth and the dream. But for me, no. Everything is a dream. And dreams are always more powerful than reality."

As a university student, Mr. Abbas says, he wanted to be a professor of literature. But the 1967 Arab-Israeli war, and the occupation of the West Bank that followed, convinced him that "if I as a Palestinian do not fight now, then I am nothing."

While finishing his degree, and working briefly as a teacher, he plotted with other Palestinians and made several raids across the Jordan River. In 1968, he joined Mr. Jebril's Popular Front for the Liberation of Palestine-General Command, and combed the camps of Jordan for recruits.

From there, his rise through the PLO ranks was slow but steady, aided since 1983 by the Iraqis and also by his second marriage to a close relative of Farouk Kaddoumi, a leading Arafat adviser.

Once known as a playboy, he has settled down and talks proudly of the oldest of his three sons, a teen-age computer whiz. Palestinians in Baghdad say he is rarely seen anymore outside his closely-guarded compound.

"This is my life," he says, casting his glance around the cluttered office. Lieutenants slip in and out with whispered missives. Papers are piled on his desk, with spectacles perched on top. "I live only for my dream," he says.

Like so many Palestinians, Mr. Abbas takes a very long view of his dream of regaining his homeland. "There is an Arabic saying that revenge takes 40 years," he says. "If not my son, then the son of my son will kill you. Some day, we will have missiles that can reach New York."

Neo-Nazis Stage Attacks

Alienated East German youth form core of right-wing extremists

Reese Erlich and Maria Wetzel

Special to The Christian Science Monitor

LEIPZIG, EAST GERMANY

On March 17, 200 youths led by neo-fascist skinheads stoned a building occupied by East Berlin anarchists. The attack, one of many against leftists in recent weeks, was particularly bold because the anarchist building is next to a police station.

On Feb. 19 in Leipzig, about 50 people disrupted a church forum on anti-Semitism by chanting slogans claiming that the Nazi Holocaust against the Jews never happened.

On Feb. 5, hundreds of supporters of the far-right Republican Party demonstrated in Leipzig. The government had banned that party's participation in parliamentary elections.

Although the vast majority of East Germans reject such activities, right-wing extremism is growing in the country, say political party leaders and academic experts. Its support is found mainly among alienated youth.

The move away from Stalinist socialism will lead to political and economic turmoil, says Siegfried Hollitzer, a Leipzig activist who heads the Lutheran Church and Judaism Committee. Under such conditions, he says, "the soil is fertile" for the growth of fascist groups.

Until last year, government officials denied that any neo-fascist movements existed in East Germany. Minister of Culture Margot Honecker has said frequently that all East German youth had a strong socialist orientation.

But Ekkehart Sauermann, a political scientist at Martin Luther University in Halle-Wittenberg who has studied right-wing youth, says the phenomenon has existed for at least 10 years.

The government of Erich Honecker made scientific investigation of rightist extremism difficult, he says. But his study shows there are two main groups: skinheads and *faschos* (fascists).

The skinheads have adopted the bizarre dress and shaved heads of their West European counterparts. Some tend toward anarchism and others toward neo-fascism.

The skinheads are loosely organized and prone to spontaneous violence, such as the Berlin attacks on anarchists or "long-haired leftists."

The *faschos,* according to Mr. Sauermann, have no distinct appearance, but organize themselves into secret political groups. They hate foreigners (which they consider Jews to be) and homosexuals, and admire strong totalitarian leaders, such as Adolf Hitler.

There are several thousand skinheads in East Germany, according to the Central Institute for Youth Research in Leipzig. But Sauermann says there are probably closer to 20,000 skinheads and supporters. No academics have accurate estimates on the number of *faschos,* he says, because of their underground organizations.

How did such neo-Nazi movements develop in the stridently antifascist East Germany? Two young men just released from jail for neo-fascist activity offer some insights.

Rene Kalkbrenner and Oliver Schreiber, both 18, were parolled March 12 after serving two years for desecrating a Jewish cemetery. Their 1988 trial attracted international attention when the

Honecker government used it to demonstrate opposition to anti-Semitism.

For two months, the two youths and other friends had desecrated Lutheran and Jewish cemeteries and beat up homosexual men. While knocking over Jewish tombstones, they screamed out, "Heil Hitler" and "Jewish pigs."

Their nighttime forays began as drunken attempts to hold parties in graveyards, a common practice among some alienated youth. But they were also influenced by neo-fascist skinheads.

"We wanted to free Germany from foreigners," says Mr. Kalkbrenner. "We thought the Nazis had done things for young people, not like Honecker. In some ways I admired Hitler, because he had united the German people. People attended the Nazi rallies not because they had to, but because they wanted to."

Both men now say they have rejected those views as a result of study in jail and talks with East German Jewish journalist Salomea Genin. "We had never met a Jew before," says Mr. Schreiber. "It really made a difference."

Although the vast majority of East Germans reject such activities, right-wing extremism is growing in the country, say political party leaders and academic experts. It is found mainly among alienated youth.

Neo-fascist thinking is common among the skinheads and *faschos* he met in prison, says Schreiber. He says *faschos* have organized in many cities. Their secret groups sometimes extend citywide and even to regional networks.

"They have names, like the Saxon Front and SS Division Walter Kruger," he says. The latter group has Nazi uniforms and membership cards.

The *faschos* commanded the respect of other prisoners, says Schreiber, "because they know history, are intelligent, and cooperated with each other in jail."

Both Schreiber and Kalkbrenner are glad to see East Germany move away from the authoritarian government of the past, and want to see a stable, democratic Germany.

They predict that "right-wing extremism will grow" in the years ahead. What had been mainly a homegrown movement of alienated youth could now grow into a political force.

"Now with the borders open," says Schreiber, "it's easier for West German fascists to influence people."

An Interview With Martin McGuinness of the Irish Republican Movement

Richard Oliver Collin

Coastal Carolina College, University of South Carolina

I. MARTIN MCGUINNESS: FAMILY AND PERSONAL BACKGROUND

Observers of the Irish situation were stunned when Peter Brooke, Britain's Secretary of State for Northern Ireland, commented recently that a military victory over the Provisional Irish Republican Army no longer seemed possible, suggesting that the Government of the United Kingdom open talks with the IRA and its legal political organization, Sinn Fèin.

What kind of people lead the Provisional Irish Republican Movement, now the oldest and strongest of Western Europe's overtly revolutionary groups? To find the answer, I visited Mr. Martin McGuinness, currently Vice President of Sinn Fèin, and reportedly a former military commander of the Provisional IRA itself.

Together with Gerry Adams and Danny Morrison, McGuinness is one of the senior leaders in the Irish Republican Movement, but he seldom gives interviews and seems uninterested in achieving fame outside his own home town of Londonderry. Unlike most of his colleagues, McGuinness has no family background in the Sinn Fèin/IRA movement. He is happily married, and a committed, practicing Catholic. Press accounts have stressed his charisma and great speaking ability.

Since actual membership in the IRA is illegal, McGuinness quite naturally refused to discuss his participation in criminal activities, although specialists believe him to have served as the IRA's military leader during the most active years of Irish sectarian violence. He has, however, managed to achieve a reputation as a "humane" fighter, avoiding civilian casualties whenever possible, and ordering an end to the bestial IRA practice of knee-capping. In his beloved Londonderry, McGuinness arouses strongly contrasting emotions. Irish Catholics spoke of him with reverence, even people who otherwise disapproved of IRA violence. Protestant (or "Loyalist") members of the same community, however, saw him as a satanic presence and told me frankly and emphatically that he should be killed.

Sinn Fèin's Londonderry office is on Cable Street in the heart of an exclusively Catholic neighborhood called "Bogside," scene of many violent conflicts with the British Army and the Royal Ulster Constabulary (RUC). As I arrived, there was a group of British Army troops in full combat gear some fifty feet from the front door; a soldier openly "scoped" me with his rifle while another "squaddy" photographed me entering the building.

The Cable Street office functions as a kind of informal city hall for the Bogside. One of McGuinness' principal assistants is an American-born woman named Martha McClellan who runs what amounts to the Bogside social service bureau, dealing with housing and welfare issues. While I was waiting to see McGuinness, a Catholic waitress called to complain that she had been molested by her Protestant employer. She was promised that a Sinn Fèin committee would investigate and take appropriate action. Since the RUC were understandably reluctant to come into the Bogside to investigate non-political crime, Sinn Fèin also dealt with robberies, assaults, non-payment of child support, and similar problems. I was told that there were no drug problems in the Bogside because "bad things" happened to people who sold narcotics to Bogside youth. The office was busy, dusty, disorderly, and cheerful.

Martin McGuinness' private office was tiny and drab with a desk, two chairs, a file cabinet, and a telephone. McGuinness himself is a slender, athletic man of medium height, with curly, sandy hair and pale blue eyes. Dressed in jeans and a checkered sports

Reprinted with the permission of Richard Oliver Collin, Professor of Government at Coastal Carolina College, University of South Carolina, 1990. His most recent publication is *Winter of Fire: The Abduction of General Dozier and the Downfall of the Red Brigades.*

shirt, he looked considerably younger than his forty years. He was polite without being particularly friendly, and seemed impatient with my preliminary attempts at small talk. His voice is soft, and tinged with a strong local accent.

Throughout our conversation, McGuinness referred to Republic of Ireland as the "Twenty-six Counties." Like every other Ulster Catholic, he referred to his hometown by its old Irish name of "Derry," rather than the British-imposed title of Londonderry. He used the phrase "Republican Movement" to describe the combined forces of Sinn Fèin and the Provisional IRA. The following transcription is unedited except for the removal of a little preliminary chatter, some "ah's" and "um's," and a few redundant phrases.

II. JOINING THE REPUBLICAN MOVEMENT: (1968–1972)

Martin McGuinness joined the Sinn Fèin/Irish Republican Army at a particularly bleak moment in the movement's history. The Irish War of Independence (1918–1921) had left a strong IRA presence in Londonderry, but Derry Catholics were quickly subdued by threats of Protestant violence, and Republicanism became primarily a problem for the Republic of Ireland. A second generation of IRA men became active in the early post-war period, mounting the so-called "Border Campaign" (1956–1962), but failing to attract much support for the Movement. By the time of the late sixties "Civil Rights Movement," the IRA was regarded by most Ulster Catholics as part of the past.

In the 1960s, an attempt was made to translate Martin Luther King's strategies into an Irish context and the resulting Ulster Civil Rights Movement was led by Catholic moderates who disliked the IRA and wanted to avoid violence. Protest marches began in the summer and autumn of 1968, but a Royal Ulster Constabulary over-reaction during a 5 October 1968 march produced counter-violence from an angry Catholic Irish community, and the first serious fighting in Derry.

While inter-communal warfare in Belfast drove thousands of Irish Catholics from their homes, an increasingly radical Derry Republican Movement mounted a violent challenge to the RUC under the leadership of Sean Keenan, a man admired by the young Martin McGuinness. After the tumultuous "Battle of Bogside" in August of 1969, the British Army took responsibility for security in Northern Ireland while many young Derry Catholics like McGuinness joined the IRA.

There had always been a tension within the Republican Movement between socialists who sometimes seemed to prefer Marxist politics to guerrilla warfare, and romantic nationalists or "traditionalists" who saw their task as primarily military. In the sixties, Cathal Goulding's Dublin-based Sinn Fèin/IRA was clearly becoming a Marxist political organization rather than a revolutionary army. Deciding that Goulding's endless theoretical debates on Marxism were irrelevant to the problems of Ulster, a group of traditionalists created the "Provisional" Irish Republican Army in November of 1969. When many older militants were swept up by Britain's 9 August 1971 "Internment without Trial" program, youthful "Provisionals" like McGuinness and Belfast's Gerry Adams emerged into positions of leadership.

III. WITH THE IRA IN LONDONDERRY: (1972–1976)

As violence swept across Ireland in 1971, Martin McGuinness found himself operating with considerable autonomy in Derry, since IRA leaders in Belfast and Dublin were too occupied with local affairs to give much thought to Londonderry. Fire-fights with the Army and RUC were common, and McGuinness established a reputation for colorful martial valor, dashing from one end of the city to another with one hundred volunteers and an aging arsenal of Lee-Enfield rifles to fight pitched battles with regular British Army troops. For an eighteen month period, the IRA created a "Free Derry" out of the two principal Catholic sections of the city, the Creggan Estates and the Bogside, with Provisionals openly policing the streets with rifles.

Even McGuinness' enemies conceded that he was soldierly in his use of violence. In 1971–72, his forces methodically reduced the center of Londonderry to rubble with an exhaustible supply of home-made bombs, but took exceptional care to avoid "civilian" casualties, although they were ruthless when it came to British soldiers and members of the RUC.

For the generation represented by Martin McGuinness, any lingering doubts about legitimacy of violence vanished on "Bloody Sunday" (30 January 1972), when British Army paratroopers opened fire in the Bogside, killing fourteen Derry Catholics. Counter-violence continued into the summer of 1972, until the IRA declared a truce which would allow its leaders to visit Mr. William Whitelaw, then Home Secretary, a meeting the British Government has always denied holding. The truce quickly faltered, however, beginning a discouraging period during which McGuinness and his colleagues were either on the run or in prison. The number of IRA operations slowly decreased during the middle seventies, and the Dublin-based leadership of the IRA seemed unable to decide upon a focused agenda.

IV. LEADERSHIP IN THE IRA: (1976–1981)

The IRA is administered by a seven-person "Army Council," whose operations are coordinated by an Army Chief of Staff, regarded as the *primus inter pares* of the Republican Movement. In 1976, Martin McGuinness and others of the same generation of Ulster

Catholics rebelled against the leadership of the Dublin-oriented Republican Movement, demanding and achieving the creation of a virtually autonomous "Northern Command" which came into existence in November of 1976, allegedly with McGuinness as its first commanding officer. In 1977, McGuinness was given a seat on the Army Council, and after the arrest of Seamus Twomey in December of that year, McGuinness is reported to have become IRA Chief of Staff.

Under his direction, the IRA became smaller, shunting off its less active or less reliable people toward an enlarged and revitalized Sinn Fèin organization. In imitation of Britain's anti-terrorist SAS squads, new guerrilla cells, or "Active Service Units," were created, able to live and fight in the border areas. During this period, the IRA resumed a high level of operations, planning attacks on celebrated targets like Queen Elizabeth II, and striking successfully against Lord Mountbatten and his family on 27 August 1979, the same day they murdered eighteen members of the Second Battalion Parachute Regiment in County Down.

It is not clear how long McGuinness remained Chief of Staff, although some accounts maintain that he stepped down in 1979 in favor of his friend, Gerry Adams, who was released from prison that year. Other accounts suggest that he became Chief of Staff a second time, retiring only when he "surfaced" to run for office in 1981.

V. DOING POLITICS: (1981–1989)

In April of 1981, the dying hunger-striker Bobby Sands won election to the British Parliament. Before the end of the same year, the spectacle of ten imprisoned Republicans deliberately starving themselves to death brought the Movement enough legitimacy to wage war with both "a ballot sheet and an Armalite." While the move necessarily meant that his military leadership within the IRA would be curtailed or eliminated, Martin McGuinness successfully stood in 1982 for election to a Northern Ireland Assembly that had been created as part of Home Secretary James Prior's "Rolling Devolution" policy. Sinn Fèin won five of eighty seats with about ten percent of all votes cast.

While all the Sinn Fèin delegates ritually refused to take their seats, election to the Assembly began McGuinness's career as a politician. Although he is believed to have retained his position on the Army Council, he now concerns himself with building permits and trash removal and zoning regulations, the daily bread of a working community leader. He has run twice as the Sinn Fèin candidate for the House of Commons constituency of Foyle, losing both elections but achieving respectable results.

Collin: This is a question you will probably laugh at, but do you have any personal regrets at what you perceive to be the necessity of carrying out this war?

McGuinness: I hate war. I hate the fact that people have been killed. I hate the fact that IRA people have been killed. I also hate the fact that British soldiers have to die in this struggle. I hate the fact that RUC men have to die and I hate the fact that Irish people have to act in a military fashion against them. But I don't see any alternative! The alternative is for Irish people to sit back and accept continued British rule, accept that people like Margaret Thatcher are going to dictate my future, the future of my children, and the future of my country, that they're going to control the politics of this country, the economic life of this country. And I can't accept it. As an Irish Republican, I cannot accept that any English government has a right to rule me or my children. It's as simple as that! You're an American. If the Russians moved into America tomorrow, you would fight like hell! And you would be correct! Absolutely right, one hundred percent! I could not deny you the right to take up arms or explosives against an invading Russian army. Just as an American could not be expected to accept the degradation and humiliation of having another government, especially a government that has controlled this part of Ireland with such abominable ignorance and stupidity and allowed the Unionists to degrade us the way they have for the past seven or eight hundred years.

Look, there comes a time, when you say to yourself, and that's what happened to me, when you can't take no more, because you can't talk to these people! Of course, you go along, and they say, yes, we'll investigate this and we'll investigate that, but at the end of the day, you end up with bad situations happening. We had a fifteen year old killed last night in Belfast. Fifteen years of age! A passing RUC Landrover fired a plastic bullet, hit him in the chest, and killed him. It was on the radio this morning, saying that they were walking down the street and a plastic bullet was fired and Seamus Duffy was killed! Now that's the reality of life here. They would never go down a street in East Belfast, or another Loyalist area, or an English city, and fire a plastic bullet and kill someone because they would not be allowed to do it.

But it can happen here. You're only here for the next couple of days, but by next week after next, it will all be forgotten that Seamus Duffy was killed. And they can ride the storm if they can say, these people were terrorists and were carrying guns. Well, there comes a time when you can't take it any more. We just can't take it!

The Selling of Terrorism: Profit from a Lucrative Export

SUMMARY: North Korea, although very poor, manages to support the world's fifth-largest army. The country has few resources for export, but one — military expertise. North Korea provides training for terrorists abroad in addition to funneling materiel for battles around the globe.

Under the idiosyncratic leadership of strongman Kim Il-sung, North Korea looms as a military power of sobering proportions. Despite its relatively small population of 20 million, the country boasts the fifth-largest army in the world. Though impoverished, it spends about 25 percent of its gross national product on building its military. With possibly the largest commando group in the world, numbering some 100,000, North Korea has developed a considerable strategic reach. Says one U.S. official, "They are active in state-sponsored terrorism, and they teach guerrilla warfare around the world."

Kim's overriding ambition is the forced reunification of Korea. Checked by the presence of 40,000 U.S. troops stationed in the South, he has sought — with strong Soviet and Chinese backing — to enhance his military influence abroad.

A number of rumors are making their way through intelligence and diplomatic circles about the possibility of an expanded military presence by North Korea in southern Africa. The North Koreans have had a small number of advisers there since the early 1980s. For the past 18 months, though, the number has been as high as 1,000. Then, in mid-April, unconfirmed reports had it that Angolan leader Jose Eduardo dos Santos, who has been embroiled in a guerrilla war with Jonas Savimbi's anticommunist UNITA forces, had officially asked North Korea to take over military support operations there from Cuba, which has an estimated 35,000 troops in the country. African diplomats in Luanda, the Angolan capital, claimed that dos Santos had requested North Korea to "play an essential role" in the country and be ready to replace the Cubans "imminently." The request was allegedly delivered when dos Santos visited Pyongyang to reactivate a defense agreement.

With unusual speed, Angolan authorities moved to discredit the reports. In an interview on French radio, Luanda's ambassador to France, Luis Jose de Almeida, described as "idiotic" the idea of replacing Cubans with North Koreans. He claimed the reports were part of a disinformation campaign mounted by Savimbi.

But a senior Cuban military officer who defected to the United States in May told Vice President George Bush that 56,000 desertions occurred within the ranks of the Cuban military in the past three years alone. Many of those desertions are believed to have occurred in Angola. In a series of Radio Marti broadcasts to Cuba, Gen. Rafael de Pino Diaz said there is a feeling "that the war is lost" among the Cuban armed forces high command.

There have been no overt signs of Luanda's displeasure with Havana's military support. Even so, the North Korean presence may be set to expand. North Korean troops could be sent in to aid rather than replace the Cubans and abet "revolutionary struggle," as they have done throughout the Third World. Much of North Korea's military might has been stationed in black Africa, where the country has military forces in at least 10 countries.

In March, Zambia signed a new agreement with North Korea for the training of its defense and security personnel. The deal, signed in Lusaka, means that part of the Zambian military will train in North Korea until 1990. Zambian government and military leaders are reportedly pleased with the terms of the agreement, convinced that they have found a bargain. "North Korean training is the cheapest available," says Alfred Sayila, an Africa correspondent for Jane's Defence Weekly.

In other African countries, notably Zimbabwe, soldiers trained by the Northeast Asian nation have distinguished themselves chiefly by their violent excesses. In 1982 thousands of villagers were massacred in Matabeleland by Zimbabwe's notorious Fifth Brigade, trained and supported by North Korean forces.

Lucrative exports of military manpower and materiel have become a keystone of North Korea's strategic and economic policy. Straitened by a foreign debt totaling

$3 billion and beset by widespread shortages of basic consumer goods, the nation needs the hard currency it earns from overseas sales of military hardware and expertise. "It's a poor country with little to sell or trade other than the contents of its war chest," notes a State Department official.

Take the case of Iran as a prime example. Acting as a conduit for arms from the Soviet Union and China, Pyongyang has profited handsomely. Though estimates vary, North Korean deliveries of military hardware to Iran have been conservatively valued at more than $1 billion.

Following the 1984 visit of Iranian diplomat Mohammed Sadr to Moscow, it was reportedly agreed that, in return for a lessening of anti-Soviet propaganda in Tehran and renewed supplies of natural gas, the Soviets would provide military equipment, including several hundred heavy trucks. The shipments were to be sent through North Korea, enabling Moscow to preserve its special relationship with Iran's enemy, Iraq, and to play both sides in the Persian Gulf conflict.

Iranian pilots also may have received combat training in North Korea, and Pyongyang reportedly delivered two squadrons of MiG-21 fighter planes, which could be critical in any escalation of the aerial war over the gulf.

Under a $1.3 billion agreement concluded with Peking in April 1983, Pyongyang also has served as a proxy for the Chinese, transporting tanks, aircraft and spare parts to Iran.

Latin America has been another focus for the expansion of Kim Il-sung's military clout. Last year Pyongyang and Havana signed a 20-year Treaty of Friendship and Cooperation that pledges both countries to promote terrorism, revolution and Korean unification in the name of the "international communist movement." During a visit to Pyongyang after the agreement was signed, Cuban leader Fidel Castro heaped praise on the North Korean president and extended thanks to him "for having supplied our people with 100,000 automatic rifles and tens of millions of rounds of ammunition."

Since Cuba already possesses adequate stockpiles of Soviet-supplied small arms, this shipment (assuming there was one) might ultimately be for use in Nicaragua or elsewhere in Latin America, Western analysts speculate. North Korean weapons (and, in some cases, clandestine military advisers) have already turned up in Grenada, Puerto Rico, Mexico and Costa Rica.

North Korea's military prowess also has been applied to terrorism. By far the best-known, boldest and most devastating attack sponsored by Pyongyang was directed against the South Korean leadership of President Chun Doo-hwan. On Oct. 9, 1983, North Korean military personnel detonated a powerful bomb at the Martyr's Mausoleum in Rangoon, Burma. The explosion killed 17 South Korean officials, including the deputy prime minister and three other senior Cabinet members. Chun escaped death by only a few seconds.

In addition, Kim is operating dozens of training centers for international terrorists at home and abroad. In his country alone, he has established some 30 training camps. According to South Korean intelligence, the programs there, lasting from three to 18 months, offer instruction in special techniques such as rural guerrilla warfare.

Since 1969, these officials estimate, North Korea has trained about 5,000 foreign guerrillas on its soil. Graduates reportedly include members of the Sandinista National Liberation Front, the Angolan People's Movement for the Liberation of Angola, the Palestine Liberation Organization, the Mozambique Liberation Front, Italy's Red Brigades and West Germany's Baader-Meinhof underground.

North Korea offers on-the-spot training for terrorists abroad. South Korean intelligence estimates there are North Korean trainers in 34 countries in Latin America, Asia and Africa. Western estimates speak of "at least a dozen" in such countries as Libya, Algeria and South Yemen.

North Korean guerrilla warfare instructors in South Yemen, for example, are part of a 140-man military mission. They teach the use of explosives, bomb and booby trap construction, clandestine organization and communication, kidnap and assassination methods, and the use of infantry weapons including rocket-propelled grenade launchers. Many of the instructors are members of Kim's special forces, or commandos.

"The North Koreans are very selective about terrorist training, and they are very smart," says Neil Livingstone, who has written extensively about international terrorism. "They've been scrupulous in staying out of internal politics in communist countries." Their special forces have also been spotted recently in Nicaragua, he reports, where they train elite security units in counterinsurgency.

Kim's policies look set to stand the test of time. The 75-year-old leader, who revels in a personality cult that Stalin himself would have envied, has been grooming his son, Kim Jong-il, to succeed him. The younger Kim, by all accounts, is an enthusiastic supporter of his father. "We're in for more of the same," says a State Department official. "North Korea has set its agenda for the foreseeable future."

— *Maxine Pollack*

C.I.A. Tie Asserted in Indonesia Purge

Michael Wines

Special to The New York Times

WASHINGTON, July 11—A dispute has developed over a report that 25 years ago, United States officials supplied up to 5,000 names of Indonesian Communists to the Indonesian Army, which was then engaged in a campaign to wipe out the Communist Party in that country.

The House Intelligence Committee plans to investigate the report, which said that State Department and Central Intelligence Agency officials who served in Jakarta "described in lengthy interviews how they aided Indonesian Army leader Suharto" in his attack on the Indonesian Communist Party.

Gen. Suharto, now Indonesia's President, took control of the Government in October 1965, days after Communist insurgents launched an unsuccessful coup and killed six senior military officials. His army later encouraged and joined in a nationwide massacre of known and suspected Communists, which the C.I.A. has said claimed 250,000 lives before it ended in early 1966.

The article, distributed by the Washington-based States News Service on May 17, first appeared in The Spartanburg (S.C.) Herald-Journal on May 19, and has been published by other papers, including The Washington Post, in somewhat abridged form.

The author of the article, Kathy Kadane, quoted Robert J. Martens, who from 1963 to 1966 was a political officer at the United States Embassy in Jakarta, as saying that he had headed an embassy group of State Department and Central Intelligence Agency officers who for two years compiled lists of as many as 5,000 Communist Party members and sympathizers.

He was quoted as saying that the lists were turned over to an aide to the Indonesian Foreign Minister, who was known as an anti-Communist, once the massacre of Communists and others had begun.

The article also said that approval for the release of the names came from the top officials of the Embassy, including Ambassador Marshall Green.

Release of a List: Who Approved It?

There is no question that a list of names was provided to the Indonesians. The dispute was focused on whether the decision to turn over the names was that of an individual American Embassy officer, or was coordinated with the Central Intelligence Agency and approved by senior embassy officers.

Did an agency or Ambassador approve a list's release?

Also, there is some disagreement over the significance of the action—whether the turning over of several thousand names was important information for the Indonesian Army.

Mr. Martens, who is retired from the Foreign Service and now lives in Maryland, acknowledged in an interview that he had passed the lists of names to the Indonesians. But he contended in a letter to the editor of The Washington Post that "I and I alone decided to pass those 'lists' to the non-Communist forces."

"I neither sought nor was given permission to do so by Ambassador Marshall Green or any other embassy official," he said in the letter.

"I also categorically deny that C.I.A. or any other classified material was turned over by me. Furthermore, I categorically deny that I 'headed an embassy group that spent two years compiling the lists.' No one, absolutely no one, helped me compile the lists in question."

He said in the letter that the lists were gathered entirely from the Indonesian Communist press and were available to everyone.

Mr. Green, who later became Assistant Secretary of State for East Asian and Pacific Affairs, called the Kadane account "garbage."

"There are instances in the history of our country, and specifically in the Far East, where our hands are not as clean, and where we have been involved," he said in Washington, where he lives in retirement. "But in this case we certainly were not."

Ms. Kadane said tape-recorded interviews support "every point of the story that was published," and the editor of States News Service, Leland Schwartz, said: "The news service stands behind the story and we feel that there is no question that what we said took place, took place. This comes from principals at the time."

Responding to a New York Times reporter's request, States News Service, which provides articles on Federal Government activities to local and regional newspapers, furnished transcripts of several key interviews used to prepare the article. They appear ambiguous on the central accusation: that Mr. Green and others approved releasing to the Indonesians a list of Communist Party members.

What Was U.S. Role In Frenzied Killing?

The Indonesian coup attempt and the massacre occurred against a backdrop of political intrigue and virulent anti-Americanism in Jakarta, where the Government was then controlled by a charismatic pro-Communist dictator, President Sukarno. Mr. Sukarno had actively supported the three million-member Indonesian Communist Party, also known as the P.K.I., as a counterweight to General Suharto's growing influence as head of the military.

In October 1965, one day after a coup attempt by Communist forces was beaten back by General Suharto, Communist forces killed six senior military officers. In response, army units marched into Communist strongholds and, joined by anti-Communist civilians, began a frenzied round of killing. Mr. Sukarno retained titular control for another six months before being ousted by General Suharto.

In an interview, Mr. Martens said he told Ms. Kadane that he acted without approval because he wanted to avoid embassy red tape at what he believed was a critical time.

"I felt it necessary and useful to provide people standing up to this Communist takeover the means to understand what was happening," Mr. Martens said. "If we had any purpose in the world except to be bureaucrats, that was the sort of thing I felt we ought to be doing."

Ms. Kadane agrees that Mr. Martens told her that he acted alone, but contends that Mr. Green and two other officials then at the United States Embassy—the deputy chief of mission, Jack Lydman, and the political section chief, Edward Masters—acknowledged in interviews that they approved Mr. Martens's action in advance.

In interviews with The New York Times, Mr. Lydman, Mr. Masters and the two senior C.I.A. officials in Jakarta at the time of the coup denied any involvement in Mr. Martens's action.

According to the transcripts of Ms. Kadane's tape-recorded interviews, Mr. Green said he had no recollection that Mr. Martens had compiled lists of Communist Party members. Asked whether he had approved the transfer of such a list to the Indonesians, he replied, "I have no recollection of such a thing."

When Ms. Kadane said that others had confirmed it, he replied, "Well, I wouldn't gainsay it," and added, "I told you I couldn't remember it."

Role of 'Top People': One Memory Fails

But the transcripts do not show conclusively that others confirmed Mr. Green's involvement. Indeed, they suggest that some embassy officials did not see the lists as sensitive or of great value to the Indonesians.

Mr. Masters at first replied, "Oh, sure," when asked if Mr. Martens told him about passing the list, the transcripts show, and he later added, "We knew where the names were going." But when asked several times if Ambassador Green or C.I.A. officials also knew or approved, he replied: "I'm not sure anyone could remember at this late date. Let's face it, an awful lot of things were going on out there. This was not No. 1."

Mr. Masters, now head of the Washington-based National Planning Association, later told Ms. Kadane that the Indonesian military was not a group of "village idiots" and that he believed they knew how to find Communist leaders without American help.

In a final conversation with Ms. Kadane, when he became aware of what would later appear in print, Mr. Masters said: "I certainly would not disagree with the fact that we had these lists, that we were using them to check off, O.K., what was happening to the party. But the thing that is giving me trouble, and that is absolutely not correct, is that we gave these lists to the Indonesians and that they went out and picked up and killed them."

"I don't believe it," he said. "And I was in a position to know."

The transcript of an interview with Mr. Lydman includes an assertion by Ms. Kadane that "top people" in the embassy coordinated the release of the list. Mr. Lydman replied, "Oh, yes, absolutely."

But in an interview last week in Washington, where he is retired, Mr. Lydman said his response was "absolutely not what I intended."

"I certainly wasn't focusing on the impact of what she was saying," Mr. Lydman said. He said many issues were coordinated at daily staff meetings at the embassy, but that he had no knowledge of any approval for the release of the lists.

C.I.A. Involvement: Ex-Officers Speak

When interviewed for her article, the deputy C.I.A. station chief in Jakarta at the time, Joseph Lazarsky, told Ms. Kadane that the Jakarta C.I.A. station "contributed quite a bit" to Mr. Martens's lists, contradicting Mr. Martens's assertion that the lists were assembled only from press clippings.

But the C.I.A. station chief in Jakarta at the time, B. Hugh Tovar, denied that his office gave any classified information on Indonesian Communist officials to Mr. Martens.

The article also said that William Colby, a former Director of Central Intelligence who headed the C.I.A.'s Far East division in 1965, "compared the embassy's campaign to identify the P.K.I. leadership to the C.I.A.'s controversial Phoenix Program in Vietnam." Phoenix was a C.I.A.-sponsored effort to identify Communist agents within the South Vietnamese civilian population, some of whom were later killed by South Vietnamese Army units.

Mr. Colby said in a telephone interview that his remarks were "misappropriated." He noted that he had repeatedly stated publicly that the C.I.A. had no covert involvement in the Indonesian coup or its aftermath.

One observer removed from the controversy is John Hughes, a former editor of the Christian Science Monitor who won a Pulitzer Prize for his reporting on the Indonesian coup and later wrote a book on the subject.

Reached in Maine, where he now edits The Camden Reporter and The Free Press in nearby Rockland, Mr. Hughes said the notion that the United States Embassy would have assisted the army in locating Communists seemed "pretty far out" to him.

"I don't think the Indonesian Army needed any help in going after Communists in Indonesia at that time," he said. "It sort of boggles the mind that the embassy would need to be giving out lists. There wasn't any problem about killing people. There was an abundance of names and targets. Everybody knew who was a P.K.I. cadre."

As Peru votes, insurgent's mystique casts shadow

Sam Dillon

Herald Staff Writer

LIMA, Peru—Many times since Abimael Guzman discovered his "Shining Path" to communism, recruited his insurgent army and plunged Peru into its bloodiest civil war in four centuries, police have declared him surrounded, wounded, about to die, or dead. But he appears to live on.

Guzman, the 55-year-old former philosophy professor who has guided the Shining Path for two decades, has extended his influence across 11 of Peru's 24 states. He has not been recognized in public for more than 10 years, yet the elusive ideologue is today one of Latin America's most powerful, if enigmatic, leaders.

Followers call him The Guide, The Fourth Sword of Marxism—after Marx, Lenin and Mao—and, in the vast Andean highlands where Shining Path is strong, even *Presidente Gonzalo*.

Today, in balloting that pits novelist Mario Vargas Llosa against Alberto Fujimori, an agricultural engineer, Peruvian voters are to choose the country's next official president. Guzman is not a candidate, but he's made his presence felt in the campaign, sending his followers to threaten voters, bomb election offices and murder candidates. The campaign's central issue has been how to confront the Shining Path, while bringing order to the chaotic economy Guzman has helped erode.

Peru's two most recent presidents, Fernando Belaunde and Alan Garcia, both vowed to defeat Guzman. Instead, their aspirations to reform and development foundered in the rising tide of Guzman's insurgency.

Washington until recently kept its distance. But after the Shining Path forged ties with the narcotics lords who finance Peru's coca leaf production, the Bush administration decided to dramatically increase U.S. military aid to Peru. Now Washington has joined the fight against Abimael Guzman. Yet to U.S. policy makers, as well as to most Peruvians, he remains a mercurial figure.

Born in 1934 in southern Arequipa province, Guzman was reared by his mother. At Arequipa's San Agustin University during the 1950s, he was known as a reserved student with a passion for classical music and literature. In 1961, Guzman presented his thesis for a doctorate in philosophy, *On Kant's Theory of Space,* to Miguel Angel Rodriguez, his professor, himself a distinguished Marxist.

"Extraordinarily brilliant," Rodriguez said of Guzman in 1982.

In 1962, Guzman took a teaching job at the University of Huamanga, in Ayacucho, high in the Peruvian Andes. He married one of his students, Augusta La Torre. They pledged not to rear children in order to devote themselves to revolution, according to Rodriguez.

"He's inspired by the belief that he can solve the problems of the country. He's given his life to that," Rodriguez said.

Peace Corps volunteers were working in the area, but Guzman organized protests—"Peace Corps, War Corps," his students chanted—forcing the Americans to withdraw, said Gustavo Gorriti, a Peruvian journalist who has studied Guzman's life.

Studied suffering Indians

Guzman, studying the exploitation suffered by Peru's Indians and drawing parallels with the Chinese peasants who fought for Mao Zedong three decades earlier, recruited his students into a Maoist party and sent them to agitate in Indian villages. In 1976, he took his movement underground, and in May 1980 launched his insurgency.

The Shining Path began to bomb government offices, ambush policemen, execute mayors and blow up power pylons. Peru's military reacted with a ruthless counterinsurgency campaign that has involved the massacre of entire Indian villages and, in 1986, the slaughter of more than 270 Shining Path inmates in two Lima prisons.

Ten years into Guzman's insurgency, Peru is in a shambles and the conflict is accelerating. More than 18,000 have died, and so far this year, political killings are up 80 percent, according to diplomats here.

Guzman has become a myth seemingly invincible despite constant rumors of his demise. The first came in 1982, when police, finding his personal documents after a battle, trumpeted Guzman's death. Three years later, police reported him "surrounded" near Cuzco and predicted his quick arrest. Later he was reported hiding in Bolivia. And Sweden. And Ecuador. In 1987 and 1988, police said they had Guzman cornered in, successively, Lima, southern Arequipa, northern Cajamarca and central Huanta. In April 1989, police displayed a corpse they believed to be Guzman. Fingerprints proved it wasn't.

Mystery increases influence

The uncertainty about his whereabouts has increased Guzman's influence, according to Sen. Enrique Bernales, who heads a Senate commission on Peruvian violence.

"Guzman has cultivated mystery as a process of deification," Bernales said. Is Guzman ailing? A kidnapped doctor taken to Guzman in 1982 diagnosed a strange neck malady: Hodgkin's disease, police said. In succeeding years, police decided he was suffering from psoriasis and psychotic depression.

Then, concluding he had kidney disease, they staked out every dialysis center in Peru. Guzman never arrived.

Guzman once had curly hair, spectacles, bushy eyebrows and a Roman nose. But today, police concede they have no idea what he looks like. The last known photo was taken in 1983, and police suspect he has had plastic surgery. Of the thousands of Shining Path members arrested, only a handful have ever seen Guzman.

Last week, police seized an elegant Lima safehouse jammed with Shining Path documents, many signed by Comrade Gonzalo himself. Police found a woman's wig they believe Guzman has used as a disguise. They also found hundreds of philosophical tomes, many meticulously annotated in Guzman's hand.

'Revolutionary Howard Hughes'

"It's the house of a man living in reclusion, studying," Interior Ministry spokesman Fernando Yovera said in an interview. "He's a kind of revolutionary Howard Hughes."

Some authorities suggested Guzman might be buried in the garden. Yovera, however, concluded that Guzman lives on. But in a world turning from communism, are his followers turning from Guzman?

An aging professor slips into a quiet Lima bar to talk to a foreign reporter. He knew Guzman in university days, and is still a follower.

Yes, the safehouse capture was an important blow. Yes, he's irritated by the carelessness that allowed this setback. Yes, the roll-up has forced an emergency reorganization. No, he's not worried. Nor is he concerned about Washington's deepening involvement in the war.

"That will change nothing," the professor says. "We don't fear the gringos."

A news flash on television interrupts. Terrorists have exploded a car bomb a block from Lima's presidential palace. Orange flames curl skyward from a torn chassis. Police shout. Pedestrians scream. The professor watches, transfixed.

"They didn't use enough dynamite. The newspaper stand next to the car wasn't even touched," he mutters. No, he says, there's been no ideological split. Comrade Gonzalo is still in charge.

State Terrorism

The application by the state apparatus of terrorist mechanisms is perhaps the most devastating of all forms of violence. In this sense, the twentieth century is the most terrorized in history. For the first time in history, it became technologically feasible for a government, if it chose to do so, to acquire all the instruments needed to wreak total havoc on its own population. Nor is a government bent on terrorism required to restrict its activities to its own indigenous citizenry. State terrorism can be transported beyond the borders of its jurisdiction to targets thousands of miles away.

There is a tragic irony to state terrorism. The purpose of the state is, after all, to safeguard and enhance the lives of the citizens who, in effect, created the state in the first place. Thus, state terrorism is the opposite of and is in blatant contradiction to the mainstream of Western political thought. Not that terrorist governments care about such niceties. In fact, a government employing state terrorism may be doing so not so much in ignorance of Western traditions but because of its hostility to such traditions.

"The State as Terrorist" provides a capsule summary of the variants (they range from bad to worse) and gradations of state terror. It is not at all uncommon for governments to resort to terror to remain in power, but they then proceed to follow state terror to its horrifying and even logical conclusion—genocide. Examples in the twentieth century abound and show no inclination of disappearing.

The next several articles reveal the almost democratic aspects of state terrorism. It is unnecessary to be a Nazi Germany or a Stalinist Russia to organize a terrorist enterprise—that is, unless a government bent on a program of state terror is intent on ruining the lives of tens of millions of people instead of several hundreds of thousands. Terror can be institutionalized by governments on the left or the right, on any continent, by any race, and even within some societies that practice democratic politics.

"Who Killed Jonathan Moyle?" is an especially intriguing article since it is a summary of the mysterious circumstances of a journalist's untimely death. The incident argues very strongly for the position that some terrorist governments do have a long reach and will not hesitate to murder those it considers dangerous.

Looking Ahead: Challenge Questions

What explains the tremendous lethality of state terrorism? How can governments get away with so much violence?

Why do some governments employ the services of death squads? What do the death squads accomplish that the government itself finds difficult?

What are the different circumstances for state terror in Africa and Latin America?

How do governments justify their usage of extremely harsh repressive measures, and how can they be termed terrorist?

Unit 4

The State as Terrorist

Martin Slann

Various social sciences have sought to identify and characterize the psychology, ideology, and goals of political movements using terrorist activities. Usually, those activities seek to undermine and discredit a society's governing process by making millions of individuals aware that, even as political innocents, they are vulnerable to violence. What is often unclear or overlooked is that the government itself may be utilizing violence, at least partially, to achieve its goals. As John McCamant has put it, "One searches in vain through the thousands of articles and books written by political scientists, political sociologists, economists, and anthropologists for references to the awful and bloody deeds of governments and for explanations of how and why these deeds are done."[1] This chapter attempts to illuminate the more brutal and sustained features of state terrorism.

Characteristics of State Terrorism

The most notorious historical examples of state terrorism—Stalin's purges in the 1930s and the Nazi regime's atrocities (1933–1945)—are especially frightening because they are so recent and because they were among the most lethal: coercion by the state was unchecked even by the usual norms of common sense and political prudence.[2] In these, as in numerous other instances, terror became so politically useful it seemed to develop a reckless permanency of its own.[3] State terrorism becomes institutionalized when this occurs.

Even though, predictably, terrorist organizations have often referred to the governments they oppose as "terrorist"—for example, the IRA in Northern Ireland and the Basque ETA in Spain consider their targets to be aggressors and occupiers of an exploited nation—for the purposes of this essay, however, an acceptable definition of state terror is "the more precise and deliberate act of inflicting harm on an individual or group in order to change the nature of their behavior and/or instill fear in other individuals or groups."[4]

This definition was first applied to South Africa, and for good reason. The psychological dimensions of the South African government's apartheid policies are obvious and have been most pronounced in the country's educational system, where the African school-age population is made aware in numerous ways years after year of its inferior social and political position. Certainly, the government prefers this form of "psychological terrorism" to more violent forms of pressure. State terrorism, then, does not always manifest as physical violence, although the threat is always present. This is an advantage that terrorists operating without government sanction conspicuously lack.

The state as terrorist is not a new concept or phenomenon. Anarchists (who often take on the appearance of terrorists themselves) have argued for centuries that the state, in any form, is an unmitigated and unnatural evil; and that physically and psychologically, it is an intimidating apparatus capable of any outrage.[5] The anarchists' message, however, is difficult to publicize, in part because the state most often controls the communications network. After all, "when state terrorism surfaces the government is usually quick in censoring the media. The net effect is an imbalance in the news coverage of terrorism. Informed only by the mass media, the average news consumer gets the impression of a unilateral upsurge in mainly left-wing insurgent terrorism,"[6] even though state terrorism is both more pronounced and more effective.

The state obviously has great potential to do harm. This is especially true if a government has at its disposal the tremendous resources offered by modern communication and transportation systems, which it usually does. The state ultimately controls or at least monitors extensively the exchange of information at all levels of society. Antistate terrorists have long appreciated this fact and have imitated the state's use of ruthless example to intimidate.[7] When a crowded marketplace is blown up or a plane hijacked, millions of people know about it within minutes. However, they are only temporarily horrified and intimidated; that is all any terrorist organization, even the most resourceful and well funded, can hope to accomplish. The apparatus of the state, however, can perpetuate continuing, relentless intimidation because of its maximum and often monopolized resources.

Certain forms of state terrorism actually enjoy a genuinely popular base. Iranian enthusiasm over the seizure of U.S. diplomatic personnel in 1979 is a case in point. When the hostages were seized, the students who took over the U.S. Embassy compound had only the most tenuous connection with the government. When the revolutionary regime realized the popular support for the act, it quickly condoned and eventually completely dominated the proceedings. The original act became an activity of state terrorism with widespread domestic support.[8]

A terrorist government can also seek to increase its influence abroad or sustain its effectiveness at home by exporting its version of revolutionary justice. In October 1986, for example, the Syrian Embassy in London became a virtual base for a terrorist effort to blow up an El Al flight. And less than two years earlier, the British had ordered the Libyan Embassy closed when a member of the embassy's staff (with full diplomatic immunity) shot and killed a British police officer. This transforming of a diplomatic headquarters into a terrorist enclave, which has become known as the "terrorist embassy,"[9] is almost without precedent in international relations. Embassies of rival states include spies on their staffs and even secret police detachments; however, even the tactics of Germany's embassies under the Nazis were more subtle and less violent than those of the terrorist state today. The Western political democracies, in particular, are now seeing in effect an outpost of the terrorist state established within their own capital cities. Using such means to extend its influence and presence, the terrorist state perpetuates its power and programs.

State terrorism is typically perceived by its perpetrators to be justified. "Government violence and even unjust violent policies are exempt from a definition of terrorism as long as we accord a legitimate monopoly of violence to the state and its duly authorized functionaries."[10] In other words, governments can get away with more violence than can any other institution in society, because of unrivaled resources, and because there is usually either some popular support for even the most brutal political regime or legitimization of the government from outside by the recognition of international law.

Gradations of State Terrorism

There are, of course, gradations of state terrorism, ranging from bad to worse. These are summarized below:

1. Intimidation—government attempts to anticipate and discourage dissent and opposition. Current noteworthy examples include Chile and South Africa, where intimidation occurs usually through control of the media and the widespread presence of police.
2. Coerced conversion—government seeks a complete overhaul of a national life-style, usually following a revolution. Nicaragua and Iran are obvious examples.
3. Selective genocide or autogenocide—government seeks to eliminate physically an entire class, ethnic or religious group, or other minority for ideological reasons. Two of the most pronounced examples are the Stalinist purge of the Ukrainian kulaks and the Nazi-perpetrated annihilation of European Jewry.

Obviously, there can be and often is some overlap among these categories. There is, for example, the charge that the Sandinistas of Nicaragua are pursuing a determined policy of near genocide against the Miskito Indians even as they attempt to indoctrinate the remainder of the population in Marxist ideology. And certainly the Nazi regime engaged in all three gradations of state terror.

Intimidation is almost universally used by terrorist governments. Conversion, on the other hand, appeals to those regimes that seek a profound change in a population's social and political environment. When conversion is coerced, of course, its effects can be brutal and even lethal. At least, though, conversion of a political or religious doctrine allows physical survival, which cannot be said of genocide. Here conversion is not considered a viable alternative. This most extreme form of state terrorism offers victims no hope at all of survival. When physical elimination of an entire community is the avowed purpose of a regime, the terror state can pursue the policy methodically and without interruption and usually without opposition. Moreover, a compelling ideology or charismatic leadership can be so persuasive that genocide assumes for its perpetrators a noble and even historically inevitable act.

A most lethal derivation of selective genocide is autogenocide, where the government is intent on destroying a large portion of its own citizenry. A recent example is Cambodia between 1975 and 1979, when the Pol Pot regime brutalized and starved between one and two million of the country's seven million inhabitants.[11] Had the regime endured, it is unlikely that any element of the population would have been able to oppose it.

Variants of State Terrorism

Once in power, a regime can indulge in a variety of terrorist enterprises. Besides settling old scores within the state, a regime can, as we have seen, export terror to foreign enemies and can also visit revenge on dissidents who have gone into exile. Examples of state sponsorship of terrorism are suggested in Table 1.

Obviously, state terrorism can become undifferentiated from the sporadic activities of terrorists' groups not aligned with the state. This is certainly the case in the second and third categories given in Table 1. In the first category, however, state involvement is immediate and direct. And all three types illustrate the fact that state terrorism is capable of assuming any sort of ideological posture, whether of the extreme right or left or of religious fundamentalism.[12]

TABLE 1
State Terrorism

Type	Description	Example
State-directed	Reign of terror	French Revolution, 1792–1794; Iran, early 1980s
State-tolerated	Private death squad	El Salvador and Guatemala, 1970s
State-exported	Selective assassination	Trotsky's murder in Mexico, 1940; Qaddafi exiles abroad

Primitivism and Zealotry

In some instances the terrorist state's goal is in essence to return to a purer, more primitive situation from the past. Many terrorist regimes have expressed such a desire. They regard the present as decadent and corrupt, and their attempts to return to an idealized past, while awkward and occasionally suicidal, are sincere. Some terrorist states have been criticized by their own advocates for not being firm enough in this regard. Julius Evola, for example, considered Mussolini's Italy to be a step in the right direction, but not fully committed to restoring the pristine values of the pre-Christian Roman state.[13]

In the 1980s, religious zealotry has become the most familiar characteristic of terrorist movements. This new terrorism is marked also by increasingly overt state sponsorship. The combination is both effective and frightening. Peter Merkl has written that "religious fanaticism and ethnic prejudice apparently can make the more selective *brigatisi* [Italian terrorists] and Baader-Meinhof terrorists look relatively humane."[14] Given the spectacle of a fully equipped state apparatus supporting theologically inspired terrorist acts, this is not an understatement.

This fundamentalism has become the primary motivation of contemporary terrorist states and has profoundly influenced their foreign policies as well. There are frequent references to the United States, Israel, and the West in general as "satanic." The more pronounced features of these "purist" regimes may be summarized as:

1. Compelling ideological or theological message
2. Total intolerance of dissent
3. Antipathy toward normal interplay of democratic polities
4. Extremist harassment of political, ethnic, or religious minorities
5. State inseparable from, and the self-designated enforcer of, the "truth"
6. Perennial conflict with external foes
7. Frequent denigration of and lack of concern with standard of living

As irrational as these may seem from a western viewpoint, it is important to keep in mind that even the most extreme form of fanaticism has, for the terrorist state, its own rationale. Terrorists do not see themselves as irrational and neither do terrorist states. Sartre implied a disconcerting parallel when he questioned whether, as repulsive as Palestinian terrorism may be, the Israeli state's destructive power is any less so when visited on Palestinian refugee camps?[15] Governments that sponsor or indulge in acts of terrorism have consistently claimed that, at best, they are simply vanguards in the fight for freedom and human progress and, at worst, they are engaging in the historically respected option of retaliation.

Moreover, the terrorist state seeks to preserve itself and assume legitimacy by joining the world political community and participating in its exchanges. It does not directly declare war against its perceived enemies, because it is not equipped to do so. Instead, like Libya, Syria, or Iran, the terrorist state opts for a policy of constant harassment against its foes.

The rational agenda of a terrorist regime should not be misunderstood or underestimated. Such an agenda may be hostile to democratic concerns and values, but it is supposed to be. The Iranian government or Iranian-inspired fanatics in Lebanon kidnapping or killing journalists, diplomats, or scholars is considered to be a legitimate method of bringing attention to a particular issue or securing compliance with a demand. Fundamentalist-based terrorist governments, after all, invoke a "higher" law than the international code that most countries accept as binding. It should be remembered that "terrorist-supporting nations will not surrender seriously held ambitions to expand their power and influence simply because the law is against them. Legal argument alone will not protect lawabiding nations and peoples against Quaddafi or Iran's Khomeini."[16]

Conclusion

In essence, state terrorism challenges, as well as departs from, the Western tradition of political philosophy. Possibly the terrorist state is simply a new formulation of the old conflict between despotism and democracy; between the point of view that the state precedes and is superior to the individual and the classical concept of individual sovereignty.

There is also the complementary concern that the most notorious terrorist states are also those most inspired by an absolutist, usually religious-based ideology. Fanaticism, however, in any form has never been compatible with political democracy and has consistently been in relentless opposition to it. Thus, state terrorism, regardless of the ideological direction of the regime, is basically antithetical to a Western political tradition that disavows extremism and insists on constitutional government. As authoritarian regimes headed by political or religious zealots become more plentiful than democratic polities,[17] it is incumbent upon democratic societies to fully understand the myriad dimensions of all forms of state terror.

NOTES

1. John F. McCamant, "Governance Without Blood: Social Science's Antiseptic View of Rule; or, The Neglect of Political Repression," in

Michael Stohl and George A. Lopez, eds., *The State as Terrorist: The Dynamics of Governmental Violence and Repression* (Westport, Connecticut: Greenwood Press, 1984), p. 11.

2. Stalin's purges, for example, decimated hundreds of thousands of loyal and talented communists; the Holocaust that consumed both Jews and non-Jews used up substantial amounts of German personnel and materiel needed for Germany's war effort.

3. It also developed a bureaucracy of its own, as suggested by the thousands of Nazi SS clerks who kept meticulous records on daily genocide.

4. Robert A. Denmark and Howard P. Lehman, "South Africa: The Costs of Containing Repression," in Stohl and Lopez, *The State as Terrorist,* p. 184.

5. However, before states developed, terrorism was practiced extensively in primitive societies by members of one clan against victims captured in conflict with another clan.

6. Alex Peter Schmid and Janny de Graaf, *Violence as Communication: Insurgent Terrorism and the Western News Media* (Beverly Hills, California: Sage Publications, 1982). p. 85.

7. For an example of this point, see Schmid and de Graaf, *Violence as Communication.*

8. An excellent account of this unusual sort of terrorism is found in Warren Christopher, et al., *American Hostages in Iran: The Conduct of a Crisis* (New Haven and London: Yale University Press, 1985).

9. See the commentary by Yoram-Eytan Ettinger, "Is There a Way to Find the Root Cause of International Terrorism?" *The Houston Post,* 19 September 1986, p. 3E.

10. Peter H. Merkl, "Approaches to the Study of Political Violence," in Peter H. Merkl, ed., *Political Violence and Terror: Motifs and Motivations* (Berkeley, Los Angeles, London: University of California Press, 1986), p. 20.

11. No one will ever be sure of the numbers. Some good guesses are made by Elizabeth Becker, *When the War Was Over: The Voices of Cambodia's Revolution and Its People* (New York: Simon and Schuster, 1986).

12. Religious fundamentalism itself is capable of springing from a variety of religious persuasions. Most, if not all, religions have the unpleasant and often contradictory ability to inspire both fanaticism and violence. See, for example, David C. Rapoport, "Fear and Trembling: Terrorism in Three Religious Traditions," *The American Political Science Review,* vol. 78, no. 3 (September 1983), pp. 658–676, and Bernard Schechterman, "Religious Fanaticism as a Factor in Political Violence" (Coral Gables, Florida: The International Freedom Foundation, 1984).

13. See Richard H. Drake, "Julius Evola and the Ideological Origins of the Radical Right in Contemporary Italy," in Merkl, *Political Violence and Terror: Motifs and Motivations,* pp. 61–89. Evola even traced the decline of the West from pagan times, where free inquiry helped to undermine traditional values and belief systems.

14. Peter H. Merkl, "Conclusion: Collective Purposes and Individual Motives," in Merkl, *Political Violence and Terror,* p. 361.

15. For a discussion of how confusing the sources of terrorism are, see Haim Gordon, *Dance, Dialogue, and Despair: Existentialist Philosophy and Education for Peace in Israel* (University, Alabama: University of Alabama Press, 1986).

16. Abraham D. Soafer, "Terrorism and the Law," *Foreign Affairs,* vol. 64, no. 5 (Summer 1986), p. 922.

17. See, for example, Juan J. Linz, *The Breakdown of Democratic Regimes: Crisis, Breakdown, and Equilibrium* (Baltimore, Maryland: The Johns Hopkins Press, 1986).

Iraq's Human-Rights Toll

Violations should spur an international effort to protect rights

M. Cherif Bassiouni

■ *M. Cherif Bassiouni is a professor of law and president of the DePaul University International Human Rights Law Institute in Chicago.*

THE United Nations Security Council's recent denunciation of Iraqi human-rights violations is neither effective nor enough. What is needed from the UN and from the world community are not political denunciations, but permanent, impartial, and effective means to protect human rights, without distinction as to perpetrators or victims.

A permanent international commission of inquiry should immediately be formed to investigate all human-rights violations – particularly cases of Iraqi policies and practices that violate the most elementary norms of human decency. These include: murder, torture, beating, physically and psychologically degrading treatment, pillage, robbery, theft, arbitrary arrest, detention, and expulsion.

These practices are carried out by Iraqi military and police personnel and even by civilians. They are directed mostly against other Arabs (primarily those whose countries are aligned with the US). Non-Arabs, though held as hostages in Iraq and Kuwait, are, from available accounts, treated fairly well.

Regrettably, the media have not sufficiently highlighted Iraq's abuse of its Arab brethren, seldom reporting the horrible, daily atrocities in Kuwait and Iraq. There has, of course, been extraordinary coverage of Western hostages who have not been treated with anything remotely resembling the savagery and harshness of Iraqi treatment of Arabs. For example:

■ Estimates put the murder toll of Kuwaiti civilians close to 1,000. Their bodies – not returned to their families – are reportedly buried in unmarked graves.

■ Torture and physical abuse of Kuwaitis are reported as particularly brutal. Reported incidents include babies taken out of incubators and left to die so that the equipment can be sent to Baghdad; rape of women and men (particularly Asian workers); random and wholesale beating and degrading treatment of Kuwaiti men during interrogation.

■ Widespread pillage not only of public property, but also of private Kuwaiti homes, stores, businesses, and industrial property.

■ More than 1,000 Egyptians who lived in Iraq have been murdered, and the killing continues. Since Aug. 3, an average of three caskets per day reach Cairo. Baghdad's accompanying death certificates usually state the cause of death as accidental. Most bodies, however, reveal gunshots, multiple fractures, and other marks indicating physical mistreatment.

■ More than 1 million Arabs and non-Arabs are estimated to have left or been forced to leave Kuwait and Iraq, their money, property, and personal possessions taken from them. Among them are an estimated 700,000 Jordanians, Palestinians, and Egyptians.

ALL these acts are clear violations of international law. They are specifically prohibited by the Fourth Geneva Convention of Aug. 12, 1949, which the Iraqi military is familiar with since the conventions are taught in their military academy and were invoked during the eight-year war with Iran. In addition, the 1979 Convention on the Taking of Hostages, the 1984 Convention Against Torture, the 1966 International Covenant for the Protection of Civil and Political Rights and the United Nations Charter all prohibit Iraq's actions.

Moreover, the protections established in these international instruments also are contained in the Sharia (Islamic Law). The Koran and the Sunna (deeds and sayings of the Prophet), which are the two principal sources of Islamic law, unequivocally prohibit such conduct.

Iraqi soldiers, officers in charge, and commanding officers, including Saddam Hussein, cannot claim ignorance that international and Islamic law prohibit this type of conduct. Those who commit these violations, order them, fail to prevent them, or fail to punish the perpetrators are criminally responsible.

Allegations and estimates are not, however, sufficient to bring charges for human-rights violations. Ascertainable facts are needed. The UN should set up an impartial international commission of inquiry to interview victims and witnesses, correlate data, and prepare dossiers on individual cases.

But the work of such a commission should begin quickly, before witnesses become unavailable or their recollection fades.

Recently, the Security Council resolved to establish an ad hoc commission to investigate Israel's killing of some 20 Palestinians at Jerusalem's Temple Mount. Appropriate as that is, no one who views human rights as universal can fail to note that the same measure was not resolved for Iraqi violations – or, for that matter, for other more serious ones. Lest one forgets, 1.5 million people have been killed by the Khmer Rouge in Cambodia, with muted condemnation by powers quick to condemn Israel and now Iraq. We must not have different scales to weigh human-rights violations, scales dependent upon who the violator or the victim may be.

The tragic incidents in the Middle East can be an opportunity to enhance human-rights protections by serving as an impetus to the establishment of an impartial, permanent fact-finding commission. The time has come to do something more than express selective verbal condemnations.

IRAN'S DISMAL RECORD

John Hughes

During the long and bloody Iran-Iraq war, the United States proclaimed a policy of neutrality between the two countries, but in fact "tilted" toward Iraq. The reasoning was that Iran, under the Ayatollah Khomeini, was barbarous and out of control. Iraq seemed the lesser of two evils.

Since the Iraqi invasion of Kuwait, we have come to know better. But in its campaign to rally the enemies of Iraq, the United States should beware any tendency this time around to "tilt" toward Iran.

Even though the Ayatollah has departed the scene, any suggestion that the mullahs who now wield power in Iran are more amenable to compromise and moderation is just not so.

Iran's record on human rights is as dismal as ever and even a UN investigation which at first attempted to whitewash Iran now is finding serious fault. Consider some of these excesses reported to the UN:

A woman prison inmate in Iran says she saw a woman and two teenagers thrown into a furnace by two prison guards she names.

A young bank employee, charged with robbery, is sentenced to 166 lashes, and then decapitated by the "just sword of Imam Ali."

A young vegetable vendor, charged with robbery, gets 50 lashes, amputation of a hand, and then is hanged.

Others charged with robbery have four fingers of their right hands amputated in front of a large crowd.

Security officers burn political slogans on a man's back with cigarette butts.

A man in prison is tied to a chair while dogs are incited to attack him.

There are allegations of sexual abuse of both male and female prisoners.

Arbitrary executions, trials without lawyers for the defense, and trials in secret without public monitoring all seem to be frequent. By the Iranian government's own accounting to the UN, there have been 113 executions in the past several months. The UN investigation frowns at these figures and says they are much higher than is reasonable in the civilized world. But in fact, outside critics of Iran say there are many more executions than the government reports.

The Iranian regime controls the press through restrictions on printing paper, and is said to monitor mail, letters, and telephone conversations. Many disabled veterans have reportedly been hired and placed in communications offices throughout the country to monitor telephone conversations between citizens.

Freedom of movement is restricted. The government is reported to maintain a computerized list of some 35,000 Iranians who are forbidden to travel abroad. Travel agencies issuing tickets for foreign travel must report details to the security authorities.

Members of the Bahai religious community are still subject to discrimination.

The repressive influence of the mullahs is not limited to Iran itself. As reported in this column last May, the Iranian regime reached out to Switzerland to assassinate Kazem Rajavi, an Iranian exile who had testified against the regime at the UN on a number of occasions. He was the brother of Massoud Rajavi, leader of the People's Mojahedin of Iran, which opposes the regime. Swiss police have since confirmed the involvement of "an official Iranian agency" in the killing.

A second, and tougher, report on Iranian human rights abuses has just been issued by the UN's special representative, Reynaldo Galindo Pohl. Professor Pohl, a citizen of El Salvador, issued a much-criticized report earlier this year that seemed to whitewash Iran. In his latest findings he confirmed that accused do appear in court without defense lawyers, and are even sentenced to death without defense counsel. Trials are supposed to be in public, but trials take place in prisons to which the public has no access.

Prisoners are sometimes never informed of the charges against them.

The enormous quantity of allegations from all sources, says the latest UN report, "provide a credible factual basis for the belief that human rights violations occur frequently [in Iran] and that government action has not been sufficient to end them."

While such a record continues it is difficult to see Iran as a potential ally of the United States.

DESTASIFYING GERMANY
The undergrowth of evil

United Germany has an ugly legacy from its eastern half: the Stasi, the old communist regime's snoopers, blackmailers, spies and allies of terrorism. They will be hard to root out—even if everyone really wants to see it done.

BERLIN

Of all the problems facing newly united Germany, the legacy of the Stasi—the former East German Ministry for State Security (*Staatssicherheit*)—looks the most pernicious. The worst strains of economic and political merger will be over after a few painful years. But the poison of the Stasi, for nearly four decades a master of spying abroad and snooping at home, could linger on much longer.

How so? The Stasi has been wound up and its boss, Mr Erich Mielke, is in jail. Police and intelligence services in the United Germany are subject to democratic control. True, but that does not mean a line can simply be drawn under the past. To see why, consider the moloch that the workaholic Mr Mielke, a man said to have trusted no one, not even himself, developed and ran for more than 30 years, from 1957 to 1989.

The Stasi had 85,000 employees, more than 30,000 of them at its sprawling headquarters in an East Berlin suburb. It also had around 50,000 part-time informers. It owned well over 2,000 properties, worked from nearly 6,000 others, amassed an arsenal of weapons second only to the army's, and even had a regiment named after Felix Dzerzhinsky, founder of the Russian Cheka, as its own "praetorian guard". Its budget for 1989 would have dazzled most intelligence agencies: 3.6 billion Ostmarks. Even in real money—and remember that at home the Stasi's costs were in Ostmarks—that was a lot: say $1 billion.

Small wonder the Stasi has been called a state within a state. But that implies it was an independent agent. It was not. It saw itself as "the shield and sword" of the ruling Socialist Unity—ie, communist—party. In fact, the two depended equally on each other. Without the Stasi, the party could not have stayed on top for so long; without the party, the Stasi was rudderless.

Mr Mielke, minister for state security with the rank of general, had a seat on the all-powerful Politburo from 1971, and reported personally to Mr Erich Honecker, the state and party leader, every Tuesday. Now aged 82, he seems to have been a loyal servant, though he kept files on Mr Honecker just in case, and eventually joined other Politburo bosses in replacing his chief with a younger man, Mr Egon Krenz. "But I love you all, really," he shouted in bewilderment to barracking deputies in the Volkskammer, the East German parliament, a year ago, the week after the Berlin Wall was breached. In his odd way, perhaps he did.

Only a relatively small part of the Mielke empire, department HV-A (Hauptverwaltung Aufklärung—the "enlightenment" department), with around 4,000 staff, was devoted to spying abroad, especially in West Germany. But that part was hugely successful, thanks mainly to Mr Markus "Mischa" Wolf, the Russian-trained spymaster who headed it from the 1950s until his surprise retirement in 1987.

Mr Wolf's most notorious agent was Günter Guillaume, the "spy in the chancellery" whose unmasking led to the resignation of Mr Will Brandt as West German chancellor in 1974. Recent revelations show that HV-A had other agents who may have been at least as damaging as Guillaume. One of them ran eastern-block double agents for West German counter-intelligence. He has turned out to have been a double agent himself. Another, now dead, had been the deputy chief of West Germany military intelligence. Yet another sent a weekly top-secret report from the West German spy services to the chancellor, Mr Helmut Kohl—and simultaneously to East Berlin, where it may have been read sooner than in Bonn. Inclined to ironic wit, Mr Wolf seems to have been thought too clever by half by the dogged Mr Mielke, who of course bugged his telephone, and that of his successor from 1987, Mr Werner Grossman.

Training terrorists

The Stasi was also deeply involved in international terrorism. It helped train Palestinian groups; it swapped tips about western intelligence services, including the Israeli Mossad, with Arab extremists; it tolerated, even if—which is unlikely—it did not actively assist in, the preparation in East Germany of terror attacks against targets in the West.

Why? For one thing, Arab states helped Mr Honecker bring East Germany out of international isolation in the early 1970s; so the Stasi and countries like Libya, Syria and Iraq were happy to help each other in the "anti-imperialist struggle". Secondly, East Germany insured itself against terrorists by giving them (at least) free passage. Among those to drift in and out of the country recognised but unhindered was "Carlos", the most notorious of the lot. Members of the West German terrorist Red Army

Faction, originally the Baader-Meinhof gang, got new identities and jobs in East Germany, thanks to the Stasi's ultra-secret "anti-terrorist" department 22. This department was so secret that Mr Honecker, now aged 78 and in a Soviet military hospital, swears he had no idea what it was up to. Intelligence sources in both east and west Germany say he must have known about it from Mr Mielke, and have given it his approval.

The snoopocracy

For all this activity abroad, it was the home front that really kept the Stasi busy. More than 20,000 of its full-time staff were actively involved in running its swarms of informers, who were graded with a punctiliousness close to farce. On the snoopers' scale an informer could be an IM (unofficial collaborator), FIM (unofficial collaborator running other unofficial collaborators), GMS (a kind of low-level IM), IMB, IME, IMK and so on. They shovelled their information through to the ZAIG, the Stasi's 1,000-strong central processing group, probably the busiest outfit in communist Germany, which in turn pushed mounds of briefing up to the Politburo.

In line with Mr Mielke's principle that "everyone is a potential security risk", Stasi eyes and ears had to be everywhere: in factories, offices, the armed forces and, of course, the churches and the dissident groups that emerged, mainly, in the 1980s. Stasi agents mingled with the crowds when East German sports teams played against visiting westerners, to see who was not cheering the home side. Stasi electronic bugs were stuck under restaurant tables, in public lavatories, even into the seats of the opera house in Dresden. More than 2,000 Stasi staff poked into mail, especially that bound for the West; another 1,500 monitored telephone calls. So many reports flooded in (laboriously accompanied by chits for even the tiniest expenses "on the job") that latterly the Stasi began to strangle in its own paper. It has left behind around 170 kilometres (more than 100 miles) of files, including reports on some 6m people, 2m of them West Germans. The file on one anti-regime writer, Mr Erich Loest, runs to several thousand pages.

How was the Stasi able to sign on so many helpers? Some argue that it was because of a "typical German overrespect for authority". Others note, more relevantly, that after 12 years of Nazi dictatorship, followed at once by Soviet occupation and a new German puppet dictatorship, most East Germans had no will to resist.

In the main, however, the answer is grimly straightforward. The Stasi recruited partly by claiming it was a patriotic duty to aid the state against spies and saboteurs from the West; partly by giving money and other perks; and often by blackmail. The latter was frequently banal, like threatening to tell on an extra-marital peccadillo or some drunken outburst against the regime. But there were plenty of more vicious cases too. For instance, a child caught shoplifting was told the crime would be hushed up if he reported on his parents. A pensioner was denied access to the western medicine he needed, unless he snooped on foreign journalists. The Stasi knew people's weak points; if it did not, it found them out, sometimes clearing whole blocks of flats on a spurious excuse, so that it could hunt undisturbed for incriminating evidence in a single one. Hence victims and collaborators were often one and the same. That is one of the trickiest problems for Germans trying to come to terms with the Stasi past.

Effort wasted

Despite all this effort, the country's doddering rulers, especially Mr Honecker, failed to draw realistic policy conclusions from the information they got. That was not because all the reports were slanted. Documents recovered since the Stasi fell show that the processors of the ZAIG regularly held up to their masters an accurate picture of East German life: few goods and rotten service; poor wages and foul working conditions; rising anger over rude bureaucrats, lying media and lack of scope to travel abroad.

The only notable result was that Mr Mielke decided to create an extra level of super-secret snoopers by boosting the role of his OIBES, "officers on special mission". Members of this elite band were channelled into senior jobs in public life, the economy and armed forces, from which they reported back, independently of other Stasi agents, on any and every danger they spotted. In the past few months close on 2,000 OIBES have been uncovered. But thousands more "in the field" are still unidentified. Many may remain so. For although the Stasi has been on the run since the Berlin wall came down, it has done much to cover its tracks.

Taking cover

To do this, it first infiltrated the "citizens" groups that occupied Stasi offices in East Berlin and elsewhere after the bloodless revolution last winter. Members of these groups, many of them left-wingers who at the time still hoped for a sovereign, socialist East Germany, now agree they were hoodwinked into destroying some Stasi records by "helpers" arguing that otherwise the CIA and West German intelligence would get hold of the stuff. Meanwhile, the staff of the HV-A, its offices not yet occupied, had turned their skills from spying abroad to shredding documents day and night.

That department's last boss, Mr Werner Grossmann, says happily that nothing was left that could endanger his agents. He also insists that no agents were passed on to the Soviet KGB. Western intelligence officials doubt this. The KGB had helped to set up the Stasi, and always worked closely with it, even in the Gorbachev era, when political ties between the two governments became strained. It is believed that the KGB has not only taken on some of the Stasi's top people but has lists of Stasi agents and informants in the West—several thousand of them in western Germany alone. If so, these people could be intimidated into working for the KGB, Gorbachev or no.

Second, the Stasi also infiltrated the state committee set up to dissolve it. That was hardly surprising, since the committee was established, under popular pressure, by the communist-led administration of Mr Hans Modrow which governed (or tried to) until the general election last March.

Third, and more curiously, the anti-Stasi campaign made little headway even after a freely elected government came to power in East Berlin and the committee was put under the authority of the new East German interior minister, Mr Peter-Michael Diestel, a Christian Democrat.

Mr Diestel seemed in no hurry to pursue the Stasi. Initially he proposed to appoint the spymaster Mr Wolf (who is still at large) as one of his advisers, dropping the idea only after a widespread outcry; and he ignored a list presented to him of OIBES said to be working in his own ministry. West Berlin justice officials also accuse him of foot-dragging in turning over Stasi files dealing with the La Belle affair, a Libyan terrorist attack on a West Berlin discotheque of that name in 1986, in which two people were killed and nearly 200 wounded. In the end the files turned up, but evidently tampered with. Mr Diestel came under fire in the Volkskammer, but survived a no-confidence vote, thanks not least to strong backing from Mr Lotha de Maizière, then East German prime minister and now a minister in the all-German cabinet under Mr Helmut Kohl.

The Volkskammer last June set up its own special committee to oversee the dissolution of the Stasi. This was far more active than Mr Diestel had been. But it ceased to exist when the two Germanies united in October, having barely had time to scratch the surface of its task.

Why worry?

Some people ask why all this matters. Despite the Stasi, the Wall came down and Germany is united. Isn't it time to stop the chase and burn the files (still enough of them, the wags say, to heat the east through a hard winter)? Surely there is more than enough to do building the future without raking over the past?

That view is more often heard in western than eastern Germany. It is arguable; indeed it is very much what the Americans thought of denazification once the cold war got under way. But, like that lamentable acquiescence in crime, it is mistaken.

Its critics make three main points. First, victims of Stasi crimes—those jailed on trumped-up charges, mentally and physically tortured, blackmailed—must have a chance to get justice. That does not mean a witch-hunt for all ex-Stasi staff down to janitors, drivers and cooks. But it does mean identifying the main string-pullers (itself no easy task), collecting the evidence and bringing charges. That process has hardly begun.

Second, top Stasi people need to be kept out of influential jobs in the civil service, judiciary, business, universities and armed forces of united Germany. That may prove hard. When the Stasi was formally wound up, thousands of its staff slipped into work in East German ministries, the customs and post office. Many others, including OIBES, have jobs in firms that have changed their legal form, from "people's businesses" to limited-liability companies, but which otherwise continue as before. Old boy networks are being fostered between ex-Stasi folk and the Party of Democratic Socialism (sic), the successor to the Socialist Unity party. These people do not lack influence or cash. Despite its recent pledge, under public pressure, to give up most of its wealth, the PDS is still flush with money.

Third, many Germans, just because they remember how denazification was allowed to falter in the late 1940s, feel uneasy about trying to sweep the Stasi past under the carpet. They doubt that it could be done anyway, pointing, as an example, to the last, shocking sessions of the Volkskammer just before German unity. Amid shouting, tears and a sit-in, the East German parliamentarians battled—after months of stalling—over whether the names of those among them allegedly connected with the Stasi should be made public. Some members confessed to a connection, others hedged, huge suspicion remained. Could there be similar scenes one day in the all-German Bundestag, which has 144 members (out of 656) from the east? There have been calls to screen these members for a Stasi connection after this weekend's general election. Why only these people?, critics ask. Parliamentary politics is not the only area of life that ought to be kept clean—and, even if it were, the Stasi had West German helpers too.

The dragon-slayer, maybe

These awkward issues are now in the hands of Mr Joachim Gauck, a Protestant pastor from Rostock, in eastern Germany, whom the all-German government has appointed to look into the Stasi files. Under the terms of the unity treaty, the files will not automatically be open to scrutiny by those claiming to be Stasi victims. But they are to be used both in the hunt for Stasi criminals and to help screen people seeking civil-service and political jobs.

Mr Gauck faces a difficult task. The government may have given him the job, but will it really give him firm political support in doing it, given that not everybody feels it is one that must be done? Even if he gets the help he needs, can he be sure that, among his staff of nearly 1,000, no Stasi sympathisers have crept in? Hardly. In any event, his work will be tricky. Apart from their sheer mass—still huge, despite Stasi filleting within the past year—the files are suspect as evidence. For instance, Stasi recruiters keen to shine sometimes described as collaborators people who were not.

Even to those wary—another legacy of the Stasi—of unreservedly trusting anyone from the east, Mr Gauck looks ideal for the job. He is 50. His father was deported by the Russians to Siberia, and the East German regime refused his children higher education, because he would not kow-tow. As a member of the Volkskammer for the "Alliance 90" opposition group, he led efforts in the few months available this year to chase the Stasi up. Already dubbed "St Gauck and the dragon"—it's a better pun if you remember Germans say Georg, not George—he will need a lot of solid backing if he is really to slay this many-headed monster. The next few months will show whether that is what in fact he gets.

El Salvador rights record challenged

Top military men linked to abuses

Martin McReynolds

Herald Washington Bureau

WASHINGTON—A congressional study released Monday [May 21] raises serious new questions about the Salvadoran armed forces' ability to control human rights abuses in their decade-long war against leftist guerrillas.

Fourteen of El Salvador's 15 highest-ranking officers have commanded troops responsible for killing civilians, torturing prisoners, causing disappearances and falsifying information to hide abuses, according to the report, released by Sen. Mark Hatfield, R-Ore., and Reps. Howard Berman and George Miller, both California Democrats.

"When we got involved in El Salvador, we gambled that we could reform the Salvadoran military," Berman said. "This report makes it tragically clear that this gamble failed."

A Salvadoran Embassy spokesman said Ambassador Miguel Angel Salaverria had received a copy of the 34-page report Monday afternoon and would be unable to comment on it until today.

The release of the report, the second critical congressional report on El Salvador in recent weeks, came on the eve of today's scheduled debate in the House over a proposed 50 percent cut in U.S. military aid to El Salvador to protest rights abuses, including the November slayings of six Jesuit priests and their two housekeepers.

A congressional report issued last month concluded that the investigation into the slayings was being stonewalled by the military, prompting several senators and congressmen to push for the aid cut amendment.

Supporters expect the amendment, to a bill authorizing $720 million in emergency aid to Panama and Nicaragua, to be approved.

Berman said the report calls into question the United States' 10-year effort to bolster democracy in El Salvador by spending a total of $1 billion to help the Salvadoran military defeat leftist guerrillas.

The report, prepared by the staff of the bipartisan Arms Control and Foreign Policy Caucus headed by Berman, matched Salvadoran government records of the officers' assignments with data from human rights organizations. It was said to be the first full review ever undertaken of the careers of the top Salvadoran military commanders.

"A key finding of the report is that 11 of these 14 commanders received U.S. training," Berman said. "This raises doubts not only about the Salvadoran military's ability to absorb human rights principles but consequently the relevance of the training itself.

"After 10 years, it is time to recognize that we have been unable to instill respect for basic democratic values or the rule of law in the Salvadoran military," Berman said.

Other major conclusions of the report:

■ Human rights abuses have been documented for troops under the command of 14 of the 15 top officers, including army Chief of Staff Col. Rene Emilio Ponce, the minister of defense and two vice ministers.

■ In more than 50 reported cases of abuse, not even junior officers have been brought to trial, "even though nearly every case would seem to point to officers either ordering the abuse, concealing or failing to investigate it."

■ Killings of civilians, often of people in custody, were documented under 12 of the officers; prisoners were reported tortured or abused under 12 officers; wounded victims were denied medical treatment for long periods under four of them; and disappearances were documented under three of them. Ten of the 15 commanders appear to have falsified reports or commanded troops to do so.

■ Of the 15 top officers, 12 are members of the *tandona,* or big class, that graduated from the Salvadoran military academy in 1966 and is resisting pressures to reform.

■ The commanders make key decisions by consensus rather than through a formal command structure. A group of eight to 10 top officers in the *tandona* known as the *compadres* mediates disputes among them. (*Compadres* are men who act as godfathers for each others' children.)

■ Widespread corruption appears to be a significant barrier to efforts to hold top officers accountable under the law. Many officers have detailed knowledge of each other's questionable business practices, making it nearly impossible to get any of them to testify about their fellow officers' rights abuses.

The report did not accuse any of the 15 Salvadoran officers of ordering human rights abuses or participating in the cover-ups.

The U.S. Military Group assigned to El Salvador said in March that human rights issues play a central role in the U.S. military effort in El Salvador.

"Human rights training is an integral part of many training courses" conducted by U.S. forces for the Salvadoran military, the military group said in response to questions from a Salvador task force headed by Rep. Joe Moakley, D-Mass.

Caleb Rossiter of the staff of the Arms Control and Foreign Policy Caucus said Monday, however, that there is rarely a specific human rights course in the American training programs for Salvadoran troops that he has reviewed.

"The U.S. military training package by design handles human rights implicitly—by exposure to U.S. values and U.S. trainers," Rossiter said. "They hope the Salvadorans will pick it up without preaching, because preaching can be counterproductive. They argue very strongly that it's been done by exposure, but I think that's a lot to ask of it."

RIGHTS ABUSES IN EL SALVADOR

Fourteen of 15 El Salvador military leaders have had human rights abuses committed by troops under their command, according to a report issued by three U.S. congressmen.

LEGEND
- (blank box) Received U.S. training
- (shaded box) No U.S. training

Officer	Noncombatants killed in custody	Other killings of noncombatants	Torture or abuse	Disappearances	Facts falsified	Medical care denied
Col. Rene Emilio Ponce	X		X	X	X	
Col. Gilberto Rubio		X	X		X	X
Gen. Rafael Humberto Larios	X		X		X	
Col. Juan Orlando Zepeda	X					
Col. Inocente Orlando Montano	X	X			X	X
Col. Juan Carlos Carrillo	X		X		X	X
Col. Dionisio Ismael Machuca	X		X	X		
Col. Ciro Lopez Roque	X	X	X		X	
Gen. Rafael Antonio Villamariona	X	X	X		X	
Col. Francisco Elena Fuentes	X		X	X	X	X
Col. Jose Humberto Gomez	X		X		X	
Col. Mauricio Ernesto Vargas	X	X	X			
Col. Roberto Pineda Guerra						
Col. Jose Emilio Chavez Caceres	X	X	X		X	
Col. Hector Heriberto Hernandez			X			

SOURCE: U.S. Congress Arms Control and Foreign Policy Caucus

WES ALBERS / Miami Herald Staff

Political Violence on the Rise Again in Guatemala, Tarnishing Civilian Rule

Lindsey Gruson

Special to The New York Times

GUATEMALA—Five months before elections, this country is being swept by growing waves of political violence and human rights abuses.

Prominent businessmen, politicians, diplomats and human rights campaigners have been killed or have just disappeared. More frequently, however, the victims are less well known—students, teachers, unionists, religious workers and members of peasant groups.

"We have a culture of violence, and that's hard to overcome," said an opposition member of the Guatemalan National Assembly. "We all expected a civilian Government would change it. But nothing happened. The mentality still plagues us because the criminals, the assassins and the kidnappers are still among us, still are members of the army and the police."

Abuses Said to Climb Sharply

Although comprehensive statistics have not been compiled, human rights monitors say the number of killings, kidnappings and disappearances have climbed sharply in the last two years.

In the first four days of June alone, 15 killings were reported by Central America Report, an authoritative Guatemala-based news weekly. Seven other bodies were found in places near Guatemala City frequently used to dump slain people.

In the most publicized recent case, Luis Miguel Solís Pajarito, a member of the National Council of Displaced, a refugee advocacy group, was kidnapped on May 3 while visiting the capital. At least two other members of his family had previously disappeared.

The kidnapping of Mr. Solís came two days after the slaying of José María Ixcayat, a leader of the Council of Ethnic Communities Runuje Junam, an organization working on behalf of Indians. He received several death threats in April and was killed by heavily armed men who had surrounded his house.

Among the victims in June was Julio César Valdez, the director of the Vocational and Technical School, who was killed while driving to meet students who were to repair his pickup truck.

Power Reported Ceded to Army

The abuses have not reached the level they did during much of the 16 years of military rule preceding the inauguration of President Vinicio Cerezo in 1986. But the rising toll has raised questions about Guatemala's claim to be a developing democracy. Many Western diplomats say that two right-wing coup attempts led Mr. Cerezo to cede most power to the armed forces and that the President is now little more than a facade for continued military rule.

"Human rights abuses have essentially been viewed as a public relations problem under President Cerezo," America's Watch, the New York-based monitor, asserted this year. "The military remains a law unto itself and human rights violations have risen sharply. Instead of bringing the perpetrators to justice, the Cerezo administration has consistently tolerated and, worse still, apologized for unspeakable abuses committed by the men the President supposedly commands."

In particular, Americas Watch criticized the Government for obstructing investigations into the massacre in November 1988 of 22 peasants near the hamlet of El Aguacate in Chimaltenango province. Leftist guerrillas were initially blamed for the killings. But several independent inquiries have tentatively concluded that the army was responsible.

Salvadorans Are Blamed

Some human rights advocates assert that the President's seeming indifference to abuses amounts to complicity. They say there is enough evidence to implicate Guatemalan intelligence officers in the kidnapping and murder in January of Héctor Oquelí Colindrés, a leader of El Salvador's centrist National Revolutionary Movement, and Gilda Flores, a local political leader. But Mr. Cerezo, Western diplomats said, has declined several requests to take action.

Mr. Cerezo's spokesmen said the President was too busy to be interviewed. But a report made public by his office blamed Salvadorans for the two killings. While even close advisers acknowledge that he does not control the military, they say he has made progress in building a free society.

"He's changed the culture of violence to one of negotiations," said José Luis Chea, an academic and a former deputy minister and ambassador. "The situation is changing a little bit at a time. The great achievement of Cerezo in history is that the right will vanish by institutional means."

A Landslide Victory

A Government human rights office has been set up. Dissent, while still dangerous, is no longer tantamount to suicide. Neither is organizing. More unions were registered in the first two years of the Cerezo administration than in the previous 16 years of military rule. Labor demonstrations and strikes are now almost common. That would have been inconceivable under previous governments, when this city was a free-fire zone for political extremists.

Human rights groups estimate that in the 16 years of military rule more than 100,000 people were slain and that at least 40,000 disappeared. Under intense international pressure, the military five years ago agreed to allow free elections.

Mr. Cerezo campaigned on a platform that promised to bring the military under civilian control and to provide an accounting of the repression. His landslide election in 1985 was widely seen as the end of a national nightmare.

"During his campaign, Vinicio promised an accounting for the disappearances and murders," said Edmond Mulet, a senior Congressman from the National Centrist Union, an opposition party. "But those pages in the book of Guatemalan history are still blank. There's nothing there. Absolutely nothing."

So far, the rate of human rights violations remains lower than in the early 1980's, when 200 or more people a month were slain. Attacks on monitors prevent the compilation of accurate statistics. But the Center for the Investigation, Study and Promotion of Human Rights said there were 270 killings in the first three months of the year. In contrast, there were about 100 in the first three months of President Cerezo's five-year term.

Spokesmen for the group emphasized that their statistics only demonstrate the trend, since the numbers are compiled from newspaper articles. Another rights group recently reported that in the first four years of civilian government, there were 5,300 killings and disappearances, most of them in the last two years.

'The Tip of the Iceberg'

Many diplomats and human rights monitors said they expect the situation to worsen as the far right and elements of the military seek to create uncertainty before the elections scheduled for November. "So far, we've only seen the tip of the iceberg," a Western diplomat said.

Many critics trace the roots of the renewed violence to an amnesty decreed by the departing military Government four days before Mr. Cerezo's inauguration. Human rights monitors say the amnesty permitted the death squads to survive by going underground and they criticize the President for failing to demand its repeal. But other officials say Mr. Cerezo would probably have been deposed if he had supported the decree's repeal.

Monitoring groups began to report a surge in human rights abuses shortly after a right-wing coup attempt in May, 1988. The army high command quickly suppressed the uprising, the first of two. In return, Mr. Cerezo was forced, among other things, to give the military a free hand in security policies, former Cabinet members said.

Attacks on human rights campaigners have once again become almost common. Monitors said three were killed in the six weeks between mid-March and the beginning of May.

Human rights demonstrators were attacked on March 2 in Chupol, in the northwestern province of Quiché, by about 100 members of a paramilitary civil patrol and plainclothed soldiers, the monitors said. They said at least 20 demonstrators were wounded when the attackers, shouting "Guerrilla assassins, go back to the mountains," hit them with sticks and threw stones.

The Defense Minister at the time, Héctor Alejandro Gramajo, dismissed the incident as a problem between "civilian neighbors." But Juan Morales, a 25-year-old member of the civil patrol, said in an interview that the patrol had been ordered to take part in the attack by soldiers.

COLOMBIA RIGHT-WING VIOLENCE

Death Squads Seek Negotiations

Stan Yarbro

Staff writer of The Christian Science Monitor

PUERTO BOYACA, COLOMBIA

THEIR leaders say they are self-defense groups formed to fight Colombia's leftist guerrillas. But human rights activists and some government officials say they are really death squads financed by drug traffickers.

Government officials accuse some members of the groups of perpetrating some of the worst massacres and political violence in Colombia's recent history.

Now, the extreme rightist groups based in the Central Magdalena River region have offered to lay down their weapons. Woven into their peace rhetoric, however, are calls for increased military presence in the zone and suggestions that the government should grant amnesty to citizens accused of committing atrocities.

"We want the government to know that we are neither assassins nor drug traffickers," says Puerto Boyaca Mayor Gustavo Londono. "We are proud residents of the anti-subversive capital of Colombia."

Mr. Londono and other representatives claim to be speaking, not about death squads, but about self-defense organizations, which have completed their mission of ridding the zone of leftist guerrillas and their sympathizers.

And the administration of President Virgilio Barco is apparently listening to their proposals. Interior Minister Horacio Berpa told El Tiempo newspaper last week that "accepting the offer of self-defense groups not linked to common crime is an important step toward national harmony."

SHIRLEY HORN - STAFF

Some human rights observers, however, see a Trojan horse in the making. They express fears that the government's eagerness to see the groups disarm may lead it to disregard atrocities committed by fanatical members.

"If the government accepts the disarmament proposal, it could generate a tendency to drop official charges against paramilitary squad members accused of mass killings," says Gustavo Gallon, a Bogotá lawyer and human rights investigator.

Minister Berpa said in the El Tiempo interview that the government has no intention of forgiving massacres such as the murder of 20 peasants in 1988 in the Uraba region of northern Colombia.

After carrying out an investigation into the massacre, the country's secret police accused Luis Rubio, then mayor of Puerto Boyaca, and two of the town's citizens, Gonzalo Pérez and his son Henry, of being its masterminds.

The suspects were all officials in Acdegam, a self-described association of cattle ranchers that officials say directs the region's paramilitary groups. A judge issued arrest warrants for the men, as well as for several military officials and two Medellín cartel leaders implicated in the massacre.

But the town's mayor, Londono, says the suspects are honest citizens who fought valiantly against the Revolutionary Armed Forces of Colombia (FARC), the rebel group that dominated the region until 1983, when the self-defense forces were formed.

Londono, also a member of Acdegam, says the so-called self-defense groups want peace more than anyone. "After they lay down their arms, the government will no longer be able to blame them for every massacre committed in the country," he says.

Ivan Duque, a Liberal Party Deputy Senator from Puerto Boyaca and the former head of Acdegam, says leftists in the Congress and the courts conspired to bring false charges against "defenders of our nation."

Mr. Duque says some 5,000 men in the Central Magdalena have offered to disarm to show their commitment to peace.

Cartel Influence Underlies Death Squads

PUERTO BOYACA, COLOMBIA

SOME of Colombia's death squads grew out of armed peasant self-defense organizations that were legally permitted by the government and openly supported by the military until last year.

Many of the peasant groups were formed in the late 1960s and early 1970s in response to kidnappings of wealthy farmers and other abuses by rebel leftist guerrillas of the Revolutionary Armed Forces of Colombia (FARC).

The peasant organizations controlled by local bosses soon shed their defensive garb. "At some point many of these groups became offensive rather than defensive and began attacking guerrillas and massacring peasants suspected of aiding them," says Emilio Aljure, the government's human rights adviser.

Most analysts agree that in the case of the Central Magdelena region, drug traffickers were principally responsible for transforming self-defense groups into right-wing death squads.

In the mid-1980s, members of the Medellín cartel began buying up the region's rich land.

The FARC still controlled much of the zone. They extorted payments from farmers there and often either kidnapped or killed those who would not cooperate.

But the drug traffickers refused to play by the rebels' rules.

Instead they decided to provide private counterinsurgency groups with sophisticated weaponry to confront the rebel problem.

The Central Magdelena squads have spread out over Colombia in what human rights activists say is a formula by traffickers and extreme rightists to take control of large sections of the country.

– S. Y.

"These self-defense groups have been charged with massacres that they never committed," he says. "The groups must respond to the accusations by demobilizing themselves to prove to the country that they don't have anything to do with death squads, massacres, and drug trafficking. They are simply armed peasants."

Duque pounds his fist on the table as he describes what he calls negotiations between the groups and the government. He says he has carried messages from one of the accused men, Henry Pérez, to Interior Minister Berpa. The police have accused Pérez of providing security for Medellín cartel cocaine processing labs.

Colombia's interior minister did not return this reporter's phone calls. But Barco peace adviser Rafael Pardo emphatically denies the government has been talking to the right-wing groups.

"There are not, nor will there be negotiations with them," Mr. Pardo says.

Alejandro Valencia, a political scientist at Bogotá's Los Andes University suggests that "the disarmament proposal is likely a trick to legitimize the paramilitary groups in the region and consolidate their power. "The groups have nothing to lose and everything to gain by offering to lay down weapons."

Others see the proposal, not as artifice, but as a response to government pressure on the rightist groups. The Barco administration has increased military operations in Central Magdalena as part of its anti-drug crackdown.

The secret police, known as the DAS, have exposed paramilitary schools operating near Puerto Boyaca and financed by the Medellín cartel. Warrants have been issued for British and Israeli mercenaries who entered the zone allegedly to train men at the schools.

Analysts say the civilian forces in Magdalena Medio may be reacting to what they perceive as an even darker future. Colombia's president-elect, Cesar Gaviria, has said the country's paramilitary groups are one of the main causes of violence. He has promised to move to dismantle them after taking office on Aug. 7.

"The paramilitary groups are afraid that Gaviria will move against them and are trying to seize the initiative to prevent it," says Luis Orujuela, a political scientist at Los Andes University.

Leaders in Puerto Boyaca, national officials, and independent observers agree that disarming the groups will not end the region's problems. The government must increase its presence to resolve the problems, they say.

Acdegam and the forces it directs gained power by providing an alternative to the control exercised by the FARC. Acdegam runs 35 community schools and provides a number of other community services, including medical care and legal advice, to Puerto Boyaca citizens.

"We took the place of the state here," says Deputy Senator Duque. "Now in exchange for disarming the self-defense groups, we want the state to provide community services."

Emilio Aljure, the government's human rights counselor, adds: "The government must find ways to increase its nonmilitary presence in the Central Magdalena. It must replace illegal organisms with legal ones."

Chinese Repression Threatens Tibet's Buddhist Tradition

James L. Tyson

Staff writer of The Christian Science Monitor

China's increasing persecution of religion in Tibet threatens to smother Tibetan Buddhism, says a report to be released today by the human rights organization International Campaign for Tibet.

In addition to abusing the rights of monks and lay Buddhists, Beijing has systematically eliminated the few autonomous monasteries carved out in the last decade. Tibetan Buddhism could wither in its native land as China hampers the training of novice monks and bars religious practice outside monasteries, says the Washington-based organization.

"Prompt measures must be taken in Tibet today to ensure the continued existence and vitality of Tibetan Buddhism and to halt the egregious human rights abuses being committed against monks, nuns, and lay Buddhists," the report says.

State persecution has escalated since demonstrations began in Tibet against Chinese rule three years ago. Despite official pronouncements of religious freedom, the heavy-handed treatment of Buddhists has intensified in tandem with the nationwide crackdown on dissent beginning in June 1989, the report says.

The 96-page study is based on documents, official reports from China, and interviews with Tibetan monks and nuns who recently took refuge in India. It is one of the most detailed investigations into Communist persecution in the Himalayas.

Beijing yesterday condemned the report prior to its release.

"What the Tibetan monks in India claim totally disregards the facts; they are persons with ulterior motives," says Ren Yinong, deputy director of culture and information at the State Nationality Affairs Commission.

The report reveals that China's excesses extend beyond reports of torture and other human rights abuses into virtually every kind of attempt by Tibetan Buddhists to revitalize their faith.

Police have jailed 91 monks and 487 have been expelled from monasteries since protests began in 1987.

The state governs finances, planning, and construction at monasteries and restricts the number of monks at each monastery. It also set a minimum age of 18 for monks and requires young Tibetans to gain permission of Communist officials before becoming novices, the report says.

In times of severe persecution like today, the state dispatches "work teams" of state cadres to the monasteries to enforce the most repressive measures. The teams collaborate with police interrogators and specialists in torture to identify dissident monks, according to the report. Work teams have been instrumental in the jailing of 91 monks and expulsion of 487 monks from lamaseries in the Lhasa area since a spate of protests began against China's rule in September 1987, the report says.

On the contrary, "Tibet now has a peaceful and auspicious atmosphere; it is Shangri-La in reality as well as in name," says Mr. Ren, of the State Nationality Affairs Commission.

The unrest in Tibet underscores how Beijing overlooked the paramount place of Buddhism in Tibetan identity when it condoned a limited revival of the faith early last decade, says Ronald Schwartz, a professor at Memorial University of Newfoundland.

Beijing believed that "by allowing Tibetans a carefully controlled form of religious expression, they would become happy and content with the Chinese government," Dr. Schwartz says.

"But the policy had the opposite effect: As the Tibetans pushed up against the limits of the policy, they realized how cynical the policy really was," says Schwartz, a sociologist who has studied persecution in Tibetan monasteries.

"For the Tibetans, religion is a cultural enterprise, a collective enterprise, and a national enterprise and China just simply can't tolerate that," he says. Beijing's dilemma is whether to grip monasteries tighter and worsen discontent, or ease controls and risk new calls for religious freedom, Schwartz says.

SRI LANKA PEACE TALKS COLLAPSE

Government Declares War on Tamils

John Colmey

Special to The Christian Science Monitor

COLOMBO, SRI LANKA

AFTER 13 months of negotiations and repeated attempts to secure a cease-fire, the government of Sri Lanka this week declared an "all-out war" on minority Tamil guerrillas fighting for a separate state within this small Indian Ocean island.

"I will go all out for the LTTE," Ranjan Wijeratne, state minister for defense, told Parliament Monday, referring to the Liberation Tigers of Tamil Elam. "There will be no mercy. I advise LTTE to come to talks before it's too late."

But while Sri Lanka descends into what may be the most-costly war in the country's history, many people are asking how it happened, how the negotiations failed.

Until this week, President Ranasinghe Premadasa's government had sought to bring the 17-year-old guerrilla army into the political mainstream through negotiations. But Shaul Hameed, the government's chief negotiator, said that talks since May 1989 with the rebels came to a standstill last week after their failure to observe two cease-fires.

The talks were going well, according to both sides, until they were shattered by a Tiger attack on a police station in the eastern city of Batticaloa over a civil dispute. A Muslim supporter for the LTTE reportedly had told the Tigers that he was assaulted by a Sinhalese policeman Sunday at a police station in the east.

After that, fighting quickly escalated as the Tigers captured more than 25 police stations and attacked Sri Lankan Army camps throughout the disputed north-east, where most of Sri Lanka's Tamil population lives.

The conflict has already claimed more than 500 lives, including more than 200 policemen, most of whom were executed by guerrillas. At least 600 policemen are also missing. And more than 70,000 people have fled the fighting in past weeks.

The rebels said their chief conditions for restoring the cease-fire are the withdrawal of all government soldiers and police from the north and east and the immediate creation of a Tiger-controlled police force.

The Tigers took virtual control of the Tamil-dominated north and east when India withdrew its peacekeeping forces in March, following an unsuccessful 32-month mission to disarm the rebels.

According to a Tamil professor and longtime observer of the LTTE, tensions gave way to war because the talks dragged on too long. "The basic problem is that the LTTE became restless," he says. "After 13 months of negotiations, they really hadn't achieved very much. The government should have moved faster."

But, he says, "it was due less to Machiavellian design than to folly at failing to grasp the opportunities for peace."

"Now it's too late," he says.

The government refutes this claim. "People must realize that this is a problem that has been here for almost half a century, and acute for the last 17 years of our history," says Mr. Hameed, the minister of justice.

But he admits, "my optimism has taken a beating."

Colombo opened peace talks with the Tigers 13 months ago in a bid to persuade them to abandon their armed struggle.

The Tigers said they would consider an alternative solution to independence that would give the northeast province, where most Tamils live, a measure of autonomy. Tamils, who make up 18 percent of Sri Lanka's 18 million people, say they are discriminated against by the majority Sinhalese, who control the top ranks of the government.

Now that the negotiations have failed, some Sri Lankans say the only chance left for peace lies in the hands of the international community. "There has to be some form of external presence," says Neelan Tiruchelvam, a Harvard-trained Tamil lawyer, "either a United Nations or European Commonwealth peacekeeping force. The hostility is so deep between the armies, they could never hold the peace while negotiations go on."

Mr. Tiruchelvam says the International Red Cross could also play a role to uphold the Geneva Convention, which ensures that there is an absence of torture, and that the wounded and prisoners receive proper treatment. "Without that," he says, "the society will descend into the worst form of barbarism."

The Red Cross already has a staff of 30 to 40 in Sri Lanka. Last week, they visited a refugee camp with more than 20,000 Tamils outside Trincomalee, where Sinhalese and police burned most of the Tamil shops and houses. According to one representative, there is a severe shortage of food and water. Two days ago, the government issued a call to international groups and nongovernment organizations to provide assistance to the displaced people.

Another group working in Sri Lanka is the Medecins Sans Frontières (MSF), a French-sponsored organization that sends volunteer doctors and nurses into militarized zones. According to Christine Neveu, the group's administrator, while the government asked other organizations for assistance, the Army made MSF withdraw from Batticaloa, the site of some of the worst fighting last week. She says MSF was asked to leave because the Tiger-built bunkers in front of the hospital put it in the direct line of artillery fire.

"They gave us about 15 minutes notice," she says.

According to Olivier Rouleau, MSF's medical coordinator, the group's withdrawal points out the need to keep hospitals neutral. Warring factions in Sri Lanka tend to use hospitals as strategic locations, he says.

For now, the war rages on.

"You have interest in a society when there is some hope," says the Tamil professor, "but you lose interest when you see only further deterioration."

Sri Lanka's South Rebuilds After Conflict

COLOMBO, SRI LANKA

As the north and east plunge into a Tamil-Sinhalese war, Sri Lanka's south emerges from a different guerrilla war fought among the majority Sinhalese. This saw the nation's youth carry out a massive uprising against the government under the Marxist banner of the People's Liberation Front or JVP.

"Things got so bad," says Ranjan Wijeratne, plantations minister and state minister of defense. "People thought the government would fall any moment."

Under Mr. Wijeratne's direction, the Sri Lankan security forces responded with ferocity and crushed the People's Liberation Front. But the conflict cost more than 30,000 lives, mostly civilians.

Chief among the causes of the conflict, according to a government commission, were high rates of unemployment and inflation, coupled with a political patronage system that controlled nearly every job in the government sector.

The situation was aggravated by the high literacy rate – almost 90 percent of the 16 million population – and the estimated 400,000 students who enter the job market each year.

Acting on the commission's recommendations, President Ranasinghe Premadasa has moved to solve those problems. He now backs merit-based recruitment for government jobs and is establishing regional colleges to provide rural youth with employment closer to home.

The economy has bounced back. Growth in gross national product is expected to top 5 percent in 1990 from a low of 1 percent last year.

Foreign investors are renewing their interest in buying state-owned enterprises as Mr. Premadasa moves further to privatize industry. Tourists are flocking back to the island's pristine beaches.

All that, however, is threatened by the newest outbreak of violence in the northeast.

– J. C.

What Became of Burma's Dissident Students

The student rebels in central Burma have been ruthlessly subdued by the Army.

Mya Maung

Mya Maung is a professor of finance at Boston College.

It has been almost two years since the Burmese student staged a protest against Burma's military dictatorship in March 1988.

For the next six months, massacres and crackdowns of students and other dissidents ensued, a bloodletting over the Golden Land unparalleled in the entire history of Burma.

Where have all the students gone, and what is happening inside Burma, now called Myanmar by the present military regime of Saw Maung? The answer is that thousands of them fled from the long arm of the fearful military intelligence service.

The student refugees have been housed along the Thai-Burmese border at various insurgent camps of the Karen National Union. They have formed an organization called All Burma Students Democratic Front, joining the Democratic Alliance of Burma, a coalition of 30 or so opposition parties inside and outside Burma.

The military crackdown of student dissidents and refugees was made in cooperation with the Thai government. Seventeen reception camps were opened, and refugees were promised amnesty. Later, however, they were detained or arrested. According to the Bangkok Post, over 1,200 dissident students seeking refuge in Thailand face imminent deportation. The New York Times reported last June that students in the border refugee camps were suffering from malaria, malnutrition, and lack of support from the West.

Most of the student rebels in central Burma have also been ruthlessly subdued by the Army, which emptied jails and released thousands of common criminals to make room for the political prisoners. Their fate and conditions inside the jails were revealed by the US Embassy in July in terms of fascist torture and dehumanization.

Amnesty International has put out a 70-page report detailing the arrest, torture, and sentencing to death of political dissidents and violations of basic human rights by the present illegitimate military government since September 1988. It also recorded that the number of students and other political prisoners sentenced to death was 100, while more than 3,000 people have been detained and 1,000 arrested since July 1989.

Among those arrested are the two foremost opposition leaders, Daw Aung San Suu Kyi and U Tin Oo of the National League for Democracy. They were put under house arrest on July 20, and their sentence extends far beyond the announced date of a multiparty democratic election on May 27, 1990. On Dec. 22 U Tin Oo was sentenced to three years hard labor. And deposed premier U Nu was put under house arrest on Dec. 29, to make certain no opposition leaders of significance are left to contest in the forthcoming election.

Since the fake military coup of September 1988 by Gen. Saw Maung, the present military regime has suppressed freedom of expression, dissent, and assembly by passing many laws, among which are the Order 2/88, Notification No. 8/88, Martial law Nos. 1/89 and 2/89, along with the revocation of the Press Registration Law of 1962.

These arbitrary laws empower the military tribunals to detain, arrest, torture, and sentence opponents without fair public hearings or trials. They make a mockery of the promised free and fair election in May 1990. The regime has also been striking deals with foreign investors from the free world to sell off Burma's teak, fishery, gems, oil, and other commodities under the charade of "an open economy" or "the Burmese Way to Capitalism." The sadness of all these successful foreign economic deals lies in the fortification of the military might of the oppressor and the prolongation of the dictatorship over the people of Burma.

George Orwell's description of colonial British Burma seems to fit the present state of conditions in Myanmar with respect to freedom and security. As he wrote in his "Burmese Days":

"It is a stifling, stifling world in which to live. It is a world in which every word and every thought is censored. . . . Free Speech is unthinkable. All other kinds of freedom are permitted. You are free to be a drunkard, a coward, a backbiter, a fornicator; but you are not free to think for yourself."

It is highly ludicrous that Gen. Saw Maung recently accused "foreign imperialists" of causing dissension and disunity of Myanmar; in view of his regime's ruthless and atrocious repression of political dissent and freedom of speech. This was evident in putting under house arrest the charismatic opposition leader, Daw Aung San Suu Kyi, for exercising free speech and opinion.

The repression of freedom by the present military regime is reminiscent of Orwell's colonial and imperial Burma. The political saga of Burma/Myanmar since September 1988 is nothing really new in the annals of military dictatorship around the world, as a student protest and demand for liberty are crushed by an armed oppressor.

The answer to the question of where have all the Burmese students gone was, therefore, given a long time ago in the chronicles of totalitarian regimes. They are out of the classrooms of colleges and universities, which have been closed for nearly two years, and a majority are in jails or stranded in refugee camps along the borders.

Who Killed Jonathan Moyle?

The unexplained death of a British investigative journalist forms part of the dark epic of Iraq's vast arms acquisition program

Louis Rapoport

JONATHAN MOYLE, a British journalist about to expose an Iraqi arms operation, was slain in March in Santiago, Chile. The killing of Moyle, less well known than Dr. Gerald Bull, may seem of only tangential importance in the epic horror story of Iraq's arms acquisition program. But the story of his death is instructive.

Last spring, when dictator Saddam Hussein made his now-infamous threat to exterminate "half of Israel," he concluded his long speech with a few appreciative words about Bull. The remarks got lost in the media onslaught, overshadowed by the chilling dose of chemical arms-rattling. But they were significant, nevertheless: "And what about the fate of Dr. Gerald Bull, a great scientist and a great friend of Iraq's?" Hussein asked. "The Israelis killed him, and no one speaks about it."

Quite the contrary—there was a lot of talk about Bull's fate; and, as parts of his doomsday weapon were being seized in various European cities, a general consensus emerged: Israel's secret service was invariably named as the chief suspect in the killing. Iran was usually second. America and England came further down.

One notable exception to this trend was a report by journalist Angelo Pergolini, in the Italian weekly *Panorama,* which quoted Italian secret service sources as saying that Bull was a double agent for Israel—and that he was murdered by the Iraqis.

But only sniggers greet such Italian reports, though the Italian secret service has a solid reputation among Westernintelligence experts. Most intelligence agencies have committed and continue to commit murder; there aren't many clean hands in the intelligence world. But in recent years, the security agencies of countries like Libya and Iraq have been leading the pack, perhaps even ahead of the Soviets.

The question of who killed Bull will probably never be answered authoritatively; and Jonathan Moyle's case may not be any different.

There are many other aspects to the story of Iraq's vast arms acquisition program, including nuclear triggering devices and other sophisticated weaponry ranging from advanced missiles to high-tech helicopters to the deadly Nazi-invented Tabun gas. The political and financial power underlining the whole affair could fill volumes, as could the intelligence story: It was the CIA which ordered the "sting operation" by U.S. Customs last year in the nuclear capacitors affair. And there must have been half a dozen intelligence agencies on Bull's trail. Apparently, there is an intelligence angle to Moyle's death, as well.

FOUR MONTHS before Saddam Hussein swallowed Kuwait and set off the first post–Cold War world crisis, an enterprising young journalist specializing in the helicopter world was hot on the trail of Iraq's illegal importing of a large number of combat helicopters through the auspices of a sinister South American arms dealer.

Jonathan Moyle, 28, editor of a British helicopter magazine and himself a copter pilot, was found dead in his hotel room in Santiago last March 31, nine days after Gerald Bull was slain. The death was at first ruled a suicide, but the circumstances were so suspicious—it was so clumsily done—that the reluctant Chilean authorities were eventually forced to reopen the case. They now regard it as a murder inquiry. Their reluctance may have stemmed from the fact that the country's former dictator, General Pinochet, has been linked to major Iraqi arms deals.

Anthony Moyle, Jonathan's father, told this reporter in a telephone interview from England that his son was killed "by drug-arms cartel people. Even the Iraqis.

"Jonathan was investigating an illegal shipment of military helicopters to Iraq by the Cardoen company. Carlos Cardoen is a big South American arms dealer who was trying to ship the [converted Bell-206] copters to Iraq as civilian helicopters.

"Jonathan had found out that they were equipped with Helos guided missile systems and he had drawings of them in his private notebooks.

"Cardoen, whose main base of operations is in Chile, is a personal friend of both Pinochet and Iraq's Saddam Hussein. My son interviewed him on the Wednesday [March 28] before his death [the following Saturday] at a diplomatic reception, but Cardoen now denies it. Five witnesses saw my son talking to Cardoen's PR man, Raoul Montesino, that week, and the Cardoen people also deny that this conversation ever took place."

Although the father knew of no direct tie between his son's death and that of Bull, there may be a link between Cardoen and Bull, both big arms dealers whose main client was Iraq.

According to Anthony Moyle, Jonathan was intensively engaged in gathering material on the Iraq-Cardoen story and on another article during the three days leading up to his death. On Wednesday night, following the reception, he had dinner with the South American editor of *Jane's Defence Weekly.* On Thursday and Friday, he went to Antarctica with the Chilean Air Force, returning to Santiago on Friday evening. The next day he was supposed to go to Bolivia. At 5.45 a.m. on Saturday morning, the former RAF pilot

Reprinted from *Jerusalem Post,* September 15, 1990, p. 13.

and helicopter expert spoke with his parents.

"He was in great form, telling us about his impending trip in a few hours to Bolivia. He was getting married in a fortnight. Anyone who knew him knows how impossible the idea of suicide was. He had his whole life before him. The world was his oyster."

His death came about 15 minutes after the phone call. His body was found stuffed in a small closet of the Hotel Carrera, hanging from his own shirt. The bar was barely three feet off the ground, and police experts believe it was simply impossible for anyone but a lightweight midget to hang himself in the tiny closet.

The maid who found Jonathan Moyle's corpse and the telephone operator who put through his last calls disappeared, and it soon became clear that the journalist had been murdered, just as surely as another British journalist, Farzad Bazoft, had been executed for "spying" by Saddam Hussein two weeks earlier, on March 15.

BUT THEN came a strange twist to the story: British intelligence apparently began spreading a story that Moyle had accidentally strangled himself while masturbating.

Chilean investigators expressed dismay. The new Chilean magistrate who has taken over the investigation, Lucia Vaganay, said that the rumor was generated "from a long way away, not from Chile. We are not taking it into account, and it seems designed to distract us from the direction our investigation is taking."

Jonathan Moyle himself reportedly had past links with the Special Branch of British intelligence, according to British sources.

Although no one can fathom the depths of British intelligence, this may provide at least a slim link: British intelligence covered up the Bull Gun story for two years, according to Conservative Member of Parliament Sir Hal Miller, and there are definite indications that the British, possibly for security reasons, are concealing crucial information about the Moyle case.

Sir Hal himself also reportedly has had intelligence links, though in a telephone interview with this reporter he said only that "I've been in the Ministry of Defense." His role in the Babylon gun affair is not as clear as he would have it—and some say he is trying to cover his own tracks as a consultant to Walter Somers, one of the two main British firms involved in manufacturing parts of Dr. Bull's gun.

He insists that two years before the gun affair broke into the news, he reported to the authorities the concerns of a Walter Somers director that the specifications of the so-called oil pipes had been changed to military ones. The "authorities" were the Ministry of Defense, the Department of Trade and Industry, and "a third party" (this is the way Sir Hal consistently referred to British intelligence).

Was he now making a threat against the third agency? "I can imagine," Sir Hal answered, "that third agencies would not appear in court."

As to the story that Israeli intelligence had tipped off Whitehall about the Iraqi gun, Sir Hal said: "I took credit for being some months ahead of [them] for once."

As in the supergun affair, there are similar indications that the British had long known about Saddam Hussein's acquisition of sophisticated helicopter gunships, and were trying to stop it, and that the reasons for obscuring the circumstances of Moyle's murder have to do with legitimate security concerns.

The British remain implacably opposed to Saddam's regime, and he is virulently anti-British, believing that British intelligence is the cat's paw of the CIA. There obviously was coordination between Western intelligence agencies in helping to expose Saddam and Bull's giant gun dream, the nuclear triggers, the renewed build-up of Saddam's atom bomb program, the supply of chemical-warfare parts by West German, East German, and Brazilian companies, and other arms affairs. For example, a little more than a year ago, the British and American intelligence agencies worked closely together to stop the Condor missile project involving Mubarak's Egypt, Iraq and Argentina.

Fifty combat helicopters may seem small potatoes in such a vast field, but it gives an indication of the scope of Saddam's acquisition of war machines, and of the long, secret battle to thwart him. There are probably other Jonathan Moyles we will never hear about, victims of "the game" whose names appear once in the newspapers, then sink into oblivion. Who, for example, recalls Jalil Saleh Neamy, a Swede of Iraqi origin executed by Saddam last month as "an Israeli spy"?

Whether Moyle was simply a crusading journalist or an agent actively acquiring intelligence doesn't really matter. He was murdered in the line of duty, exposing one small part of a vast and very sinister story.

Terrorism in America

Although the focus on terrorism is usually on overseas developments, there is increasing evidence of an intensification within the United States. Robert Reinhold's article, "Threats, Real or Not, Stir Fears Across the U.S.," underscores the jitters that have swept the country since the outbreak of war in the Persian Gulf. "Skinheads Target the Schools" provides strong data on the "skinheads" having emerged in their own right as a distinct movement despite connections with other politicized hate groups. "New Extremists Exceed 'Jim Crowism' " warns that the recent right-wing extremist movement in the United States is more sophisticated and, in some instances, more religiously inclined than that which was spearheaded by the old Ku Klux Klan. Some of its leaders have donned business suits and run for political office. Many are truly revolutionary in that they hope to carve out a state for whites only in the heartland of the North American continent. Evidence of this sophistication is found in "Stopping Terrorism . . ." where organizational infrastructures often pose problems for law enforcement agencies.

External-internal linkage concerns for the United States are addressed in "Borders Open to Terrorist Threat" as the "open borders" are treated as the central issue. Several social problems—including alien migration and narcotics—are brought into focus as a part of America's vulnerability to terrorism. The importance of effective police work is also cited as a preventive approach. "Officials Say They Have Leads in Killing of Judge in Alabama" speculates on the drug problem having dire implications for the safety and survival of judges and the judicial system.

The latest concern in domestic terrorism combines two contentious issues—ecology and animal rights. "Environmentalists Hurt, Then Held, in Blast" brings to the fore the ecoterrorism question, a growing prospect in America, that often crosses over to animal and wildlife issues as well.

Looking Ahead: Challenge Questions

What similarities exist between American terrorist groups and overseas terrorist groups? What aspects are unique to the American groups?

What are the prospects and the means to counter terrorism in America? Is terrorism a manageable phenomenon in the United States?

Unit 5

Stopping Terrorism - The Problems Posed by the Organizational Infrastructure of Terrorist Organizations

ABSTRACT

Law enforcement agencies have had little success in combating terrorism. This paper explores the premise that the reason law enforcement agencies are ineffectual in dealing with terrorists is because of the unique organizational structure of terrorist organizations. Terrorist organizations do not employ a bureaucratic style of organization. Rather they use a circular, or closed, organizational structure which is unfamiliar to law enforcement agencies. Specific aspects of this circular organizational structure which hinder law enforcement efforts are discussed.

Wayman C. Mullins

The author received his Ph.D. in Psychology from the University of Arkansas. He is presently an Associate Professor at Southwest Texas State University. He has published several articles in leading psychology and criminal justice journals and has presented numerous papers at national, professional conferences. In addition, he published a book on terrorism in the United States in 1988. Requests for reprints should be sent to the author at the Department of Criminal Justice, Southwest Texas State University, San Marcos, Texas 78666.

A major emphasis is given by all law enforcement agencies to intelligence gathering activities. In fact, it might be argued that over 90% of a law enforcement agency's crime fighting efforts are devoted to intelligence gathering. For organized criminal activities, the amount of effort given to intelligence gathering may approach 100%. By organized criminal activities, it is meant that two or more persons who, with continuity of purpose engage in (1) supplying illegal goods and services, and/or (2) engage in predatory crime (State of California; in Task Force on Organized Crime, 1976; 214). Burglary rings, loansharking operations, fencing operations, gangs, drug cartels, subversive groups, racketeering organizations, and terrorist organizations are all examples of organized crime operations.

For the majority of organized crime operations, intelligence gathering efforts have been quite successful. The use of tax records, business records, electronic surveillance, inter-agency file-sharing, informants, and undercover operations have all been used by law enforcement agencies to arrest, indict, and convict persons engaged in organized crime activities (see for example, Stewart, 1980). One form of organized crime activity has, however, proved to be virtually unaffected by repeated intelligence gathering efforts - terrorism.

To many people, terrorism and terrorist organizations are nonexistent in the United States. This is true not only of citizens, but is also true of law enforcement personnel. Recently, the author gave a presentation on the terrorist problem in the United States to a group of over 100 law enforcement personnel. Members of the audience included patrol officers, investigators, supervisors, and chiefs. The vast majority were amazed at the breadth and scope of the terrorist problem in the United States, and at the number of separate terrorist organizations operating in this country. Table 1 gives a listing of several of the larger terrorist organizations active in the United States. In total, there are over 150 terrorist organizations operating in the United States. Many of these organizations are small, having only three to five members, while others claim membership in the thousands (such as the Ku Klux Klan and Aryan Nations). As shown in Table 1, the United States has both right and left-wing terrorist organizations. Right-wing organizations tend to espouse a philosophy of racial and/or religious superiority, while left-wing organizations argue for the overthrow of the government and a replacement government couched in Marxist-Leninist doctrine. Most of the terrorist organizations in the United States are comprised of United States citizens. Very few foreign terrorist personnel or terrorist organizations operate in the United States.

Table 1. A partial listing of United States terrorist organizations

Left-wing Organizations	Right-wing Organizations
Armed Forces of National Liberation	American First Committee
Communist Party USA	Arizona Patriots
Ejercito Popular Boricua Army	Aryan Brotherhood
Irish Republican Army[1]	Aryan Nations
May 19 Communist Organization	Christian Defense League
New Afrikan Freedom Fighters League	Christian Patriots Defense
OVRP	Ku Klux Klan[2]
Red Guerrilla Resistance	Mountain Church of Jesus Christ
Republic of New Afrika	Neo-Nazis
	American Nazi Party
	National Socialist League
	National socialist White People's Party
	National State's Rights Party
	Security Services Action Group
Revolutionary Youth Movement	The Order
United Freedom Front	White American Resistance
	Yahweh Church

Notes:
[1]Most members of the IRA in the United States are American citizens.
[2]The Ku Klux Klan consists of several different Klan organizations.

From *Journal of Contemporary Criminal Justice*, Vol. 4, No. 4, December 1988, pp. 214-228. Reprinted by permission, *Journal of Contemporary Criminal Justice*, Department of Criminal Justice, California State University, Long Beach.

Intelligence gathering activities against these terrorist organizations have for the most part been unsuccessful. Between 1980-1986, 190 terrorist incidents occurred within the United States, accounting for 18 deaths and 82 injuries (Mullins, 1988). There have been isolated law enforcement successes. For example, the FBI claimed to have prevented over 25 terrorist incidents in 1986 (and there is no reason to doubt this claim). The FBI, however, like other law enforcement agencies, prevent the individual members of the terrorist organization from conducting a tactical operation. They do not put the terrorist organization out of business (a crucial distinction). Mostly, law enforcement efforts to halt terrorism have been accidental. For example, in 1972, in Chicago, Illinois, members of The Order of the Rising Sun were arrested en route to poison the Chicago water supply with typhoid bacillus (Clark, 1980). The arrest of these terrorists was accidental and came as the result of a routine traffic stop, not intelligence activities. When intelligence activities result in the arrest of terrorists, it is usually because the terrorists have engaged in some other criminal activity. As an example, in 1984, Robert Mathews, leader of the Order, was killed in a shootout with the FBI on Whidbey Island, Washington. The FBI was investigating Mathews because of his suspected participation in a Brinks Armored truck robbery. In the largest case in history, 14 leaders and members of various white supremist organizations were indicted in Fort Smith, Arkansas, in 1987 on charges of sedition (Haddigan, 1987). In 1988, in a trial that lasted less than four months, all 14 persons were acquitted. The government's intelligence gathering activities were for naught.

If law enforcement intelligence gathering activities are successful with other types of organized crime syndicates, why do they fail when it comes to the terrorist organization? First, some types of intelligence gathering activities as delineated by Stewert (198)0 do not apply to the terrorist organization. For example, terrorist organizations do not pay taxes (many avoid this by claiming to be a religious organization), do not operate illegitimate or illegal businesses, and maintain a low criminal profile. Law enforcement agencies cannot rely on informants, as the members of a terrorist organization tend to be fanatical to the cause of the organization (whether religious or political). The primary avenue open to law enforcement intelligence gathering activities is the undercover operative. The structure of the terrorist organizations makes undercover infiltration virtually impossible. Regardless of the type of intelligence gathering mechanism, the organizational structure of terrorist organizations successfully prevents compromise and successfully thwarts law enforcement intelligence gathering activities.

The Closed Organization

Most organized crime operations are similar in organizational structure to classic bureaucracies. Abadinsky (1987) for example, discussed the bureaucratic structure and format of Italian-American crime families. Salerno and Tompkins (1969), in discussing organizational flow-charts of organized crime syndicates, have stated; "The major difference between the diagram of an organized crime family and the chart of a major corporation is that the head of the enterprise-the boss-does not have a box over him labeled 'stockbroker'. Many of the other boxes are paralleled in the underworld". Part of the reason law enforcement agencies have been able to gather intelligence and infiltrate these organized crime units is that the law enforcement official is familiar with working in and under the constraints of a bureaucracy. The law enforcement official is familiar with the organizational workings of a bureaucracy and can deal with the organization dynamics of the organized crime syndicate. In addition, organized crime bureaucracies, like the bureaucracies in private and public business are very loose-knit organizations, with formal chains-of-command, excessive personnel, diverse missions, and people far removed from the core of the organization. It is very often the persons at the extremes of the organization that provide information to law enforcement personnel, and is at the extremes of the organization that law enforcement has been able to covertly enter the organization as undercover operatives.

The terrorist organization is totally dissimilar to the bureaucratic organization. The terrorist organization has been compared to a solar system (Zawodny, 1983), with the leader as the sun and the members as the planets surrounding him (the use of "him" to refer to the leader is illustrative of the fact that almost all terrorist leaders in the United States are male). Unlike the open-ended bureaucratic organization, the circular terrorist organization is a closed system which makes it almost impossible for law enforcement to conduct intelligence gathering activities. In addition to being a close organizational system, the circular structure of the organization provides certain other benefits for the organization (while providing additional detriments to law enforcement intelligence gathering efforts).

One, it is easy for the terrorist organization to remain anonymous to outsiders. The terrorist organization is its own support network. Other bureaucratic organized crime syndicates rely on outsiders, whether in loansharking, fencing, prostitution, drugs, etc. Terrorist organizations in the United States seldom engage in these types of organized crime activities, and thus, they do not have to deal with nonmember citizens. As such, law enforcement personnel find it difficult to make contacts with the terrorists for the purpose of intelligence gathering.

Two, the leaders of the terrorist organization are active participants in the organization's activities. In other organized crime syndicates the leaders seldom take an active part in activities. There are literally hundreds of instances where the underlings in organized crime syndicates have been caught engaging in illegal activities and sentenced by a court. Very seldom are the top "bosses" caught, much less sentenced since the bureaucratic organizational structure of the syndicate provides buffer layers of other people for the "bosses" protection. On the few occasions when terrorists are arrested, the leaders are typically arrested along with the members. This is the only potential benefit of the circular organization to law enforcement personnel. Should the law enforcement agency intercede in the terrorist's activities, the terrorist leader is sure to be involved. Even though it is difficult to gather intelligence on the terrorist organization, when law enforcement agencies do successfully catch terrorists, the leader is often caught along with the workers. In 1985, the FBI raided and arrested members of the right-wing terrorist organization, the Cross, the Sword, and the Arm of the Lord. Arrested and sentenced with the members was the leader of the CSA, Jim Ellison (Mullins, 1988).

Related to the above, the circular organization allows for the power of the leader to be directly reinforced to the members of the organization. As mentioned previously, very seldom does a terrorist turn informant. Part of the reason for this is obviously due to the fanaticism of the terrorist. The terrorist who is an idealist is trying to tear down the old world and rebuild an ideal, perfect world (Steinhoff, 1976). To the idealist, law enforcement personnel exemplify the old, established order and are a mortal enemy (Coleman, 1976). The true idealist is the minority member of the terrorist organization. Many terrorists do not start their careers in terrorism as fanatical idealists. Most are followers. That is, they are individuals looking for a purpose to life, and the terrorist organization has given them that purpose. Followers have a distorted sense of reality, perceive themselves to be inferior, helpless, and an outsider, are insecure, hostile, and believe the world is conspiring against them (see for example, Freedman, 1974; Kaplan, 1981; Freedman, 1983; Wilkinson, 1983; Crenshaw, 1985; & Strentz, 1987). Once they join the terrorist organization, the daily and direct contact with the leader soon turns the followers into fanatics. Most terrorists perceive their leader as a messiah, or god-like figure. The leader tries to foster this perception (Wilson, 1973). The clearest and most well-known example of this is the Manson family. The members of the Manson family truly believed that Charles Manson was operating on a higher level of existence than other mortals. Some members in fact, perceived Manson not as human, but as a supernatural figure. This messiacism does not occur in other organized crime syndicates. Very often the lower level workers in these syndicates have never met the leader, much less come in daily contact. Unlike syndicates, in the circular organizational system, it is almost impossible to convince a member to turn against a leader.

Three, and of critical importance in any explanation of why terrorist organization remain impervious to intelligence gathering efforts, is that the terrorist leader is the member of the organization who recruits new members. No person can join the organization (or even be admitted for consideration) without the leader's direct intervention. Some terrorist organizations even use a polygraph exam on potential members. Robert Mathews of the Order gave all potential members a voice-stress analyzer test to insure that the potential member was not an undercover law enforcement operative and to determine that candidate's sincerity of beliefs. Some embers were periodically reanalyzed to ensure that they had not become informants. To date, no other organized crime syndicates have resorted to measures such as these to screen potential members and it is unlikely that they will do so. The organized crime syndicate is not concerned with the political or religious beliefs of its members, but are only concerned with the member's knowledge of criminal conduct.

Four, the leader of the terrorist organization has direct control over the members, and can administer punishment rapidly and directly. In some respects, this is also true for other organized crime syndicates. These syndicates exercise close control over their members and use extreme punishment against those who deviate from the norm. But, members of the terrorist organization have the perception of this punishment that persons in other organized crime syndicates do not have, because of the leader being involved directly. In the terrorist organization, the leader administers punishment, usually within sight of the other members so as to reinforce the lesson. Again, this serves to produce a high degree of paranoia and fear in the membership, so that even if inclined to do so, the members will not turn against the organization.

Five, the terrorist organization does not need support networks. All members share in all tasks and the group as a whole does whatever work needs to be done, whether the work is legitimate or criminal. Other organized crime syndicates must rely on outside persons and businesses for certain tasks and operations. For example, many activities of the "mafia" (i.e., drugs, prostitution, loan sharking, etc.) require nonmembers as consumers. Without the nonmember consumers, the "mafia", drug cartels, fences, etc. cannot do business. This is not the case with the terrorist organization. If the organization needs weapons, the members (as a group) perform the necessary activities to obtain the weapons. In the United States, activities of this nature often involve a criminal activity such as burglarizing a weapons armory. To raise money for terrorist operations, the Order conducted a series of bank and armored car robberies (Mullins, 1988). It was, by the way, these criminal activities which led to the arrest, indictment, and conviction of several Order members, and not their terrorist activities.

Six, the terrorist organization can operate against targets of opportunity. This is not to imply that terrorist organization do not plan their operations, but rather that terrorist organizations can rapidly and easily change operational plans to fit the situation. Because all members (including the leaders) take part in operations, the terrorist organization can change operational plans as the situation dictates. Security consultants advise their clients to make themselves secure targets primarily because terrorists will choose a different, easier target to conduct an operation against. In Italy, Aldo Moro was not the initial target of the terrorist kidnapping (Scotti, 1986). The terrorists kidnapped Aldo Moro because the primary target of the terrorists made himself too secure. If law enforcement does manage to obtain intelligence concerning a terrorist tactical operation, the ability of the terrorist organization to change targets on the "spur-of-the-moment" can make the intelligence worthless. Other organized crime syndicates do not have this tactical flexibility, and once they make an operational plan they must then stick with that plan to fruition.

Seven, the terrorist organization is extremely efficient as an organization. There are no paper trails for law enforcement to follow, and no bureaucratic administrative details by which to build an intelligence case. Many organized crime syndicates, including "Mafia" families and drug cartels have been put out of business by law enforcement personnel because of bureaucratic paperwork. The most obvious examples of this have been the numerous syndicates members convicted on income tax evasion charges. In other instances, law enforcement can build a case against the syndicate by building a paper trail (i.e., bank deposit slips, cash withdrawals, etc.). This is not the case with the terrorist organization. No terrorist organization in the United States has been shut down because of a bureaucratic intelligence trail.

Eight, the terrorist organization has a very efficient communications network which does not involve paperwork or telecommunications. Communications in the terrorist organization flow vertically, not horizontally. Orders from the leader, or suggestions made to the leader are done verbally and directly. Other organized crime syndicates rely on typical bureaucratic chain-of-command communications. Very often this involves the use of standard type business communications (phone calls, letters, memos, etc.). When these types of communications are used, law enforcement can again build a paper trail or use electronic surveillance/eavesdropping equipment to build an intelligence case against the syndicate. Law enforcement cannot do this with the terrorist organization.

Nine, terrorist organizations only seek support from other terrorist organizations (Anable, 1978). Right-wing terrorist organizations in the United States have developed elaborate techniques for sharing information, manpower, equipment, and finances. All of this interaction is done within a close society, and even more important, each organization involved has a common purpose. Other organized crime syndicates do rely on each other for support, but by the same token, they also rely on outsiders for support. In many cases, these syndicates will turn informant on another syndicate to enhance their own activities and position. Once an outsider is used, that outsider becomes the weak link in the chain and can be used by law enforcement personnel to compromise the syndicate.

Ten, the terrorist organization is able to relieve internal stress quickly and efficiently. If stress begins to build up among the members of the organization, the leader can take immediate steps (such as conduct a quick operation) to relieve that stress (Zawodny, 1978). As a side benefit, these successful operations serve to increase group cohesiveness (Hacker, 1983). In bureaucratic organized crime syndicates, the leaders cannot do that. In many instances, the leaders are not even aware that there is a problem. Many members of these syndicates have become informants because of dissatisfaction with the organization due to a build-up of this internal stress.

Organizational Structure

In addition to having a unique circular structure, the structural make-up of the terrorist organization is highly specialized. Although individual members of the organization may be required to have many skills and be able to perform highly diverse functions, the organizational units will be highly specialized. The members assigned to an organizational unit can then be expected to concentrate on a specialty function. Members of a bureaucratic organized crime syndicate may be assigned to one unit but may be required to perform, on an ongoing basis, many other functions. A person involved in loansharking, for example, may be required to collect the "numbers", deliver drugs, arrange customers for prostitutes, etc. The terrorist, in contrast, once assigned to a specialized unit, can concentrate on the specific tasks expected of that unit. The terrorist organization employs two types of units; operational units and nonoperational units. Operational units are those organizational units entrusted with tactical responsibilities, while nonoperational units are responsible for performing nontactical functions, but functions necessary to keep the organization operating. It is important to mention at this point that only the larger terrorist organizations have as detailed an organizational structure as will be described.

Operational Units - The cell is the major organizational component of the terrorist organization (Sterling, 1982). The cell is the unit of the terrorist organization which engages in acts of terrorism. Cells are generally limited to between three and ten persons. The small size of the cell works to prevent infiltration by law enforcement personnel (Michel, 1972). Small terrorist organizations may only have one or two cells for the entire organization, and these cells may be multi-purpose. By multi-purpose it is meant that the cell will perform whatever type of operation the organization engages in. As the organization grows, cells become more and more specialized, until cells become operationally specialized. Dalager (1984) and Wolf (1978) have identified these specialized cells. The terrorist organization may have specialized cells which engage only in activities of assassination, communication, escape and evasion, intelligence, passive resistance, propaganda, sabotage, supply and finance, surveillance and security, and terrorist operations (bombing, hijacking, etc.). An assassination cell, for example, would do nothing but conduct tactical operations of assassination. This cell would not even plan their target acquisition or escape and evasion. This would be the task for the intelligence and escape and evasion cells.

Once the terrorist organization begins to specialize and fragment into different cells, each cell becomes autonomous. One cell does not know of the existence of any other cell. Thus, if law enforcement personnel are able to compromise one cell, other organizational units will be compromised.

This is not the case with bureaucratic organized crime syndicates. Very often, the lowest members know of and are aware of the entire bureaucratic structure and the names of the personnel who occupy each position of the hierarchy. Thus, if one member of the syndicate informs to law enforcement personnel, that member can easily identify a large group of syndicate members. Or, if law enforcement undercover personnel infiltrate the syndicates, the undercover operative will rapidly learn who's who in the bureaucracy.

Non-operational Units - As terrorist organizations grow in size, it is necessary for them to add non-operational personnel and form non-operational units. By non-operational, it is meant that the organization has personnel assigned to non-tactical or non-critical tasks. These personnel do, however, perform essential services for the organization. Non-operational personnel are not outsiders enlisted to perform these non-operational functions, but are trusted members of the organization. Additionally, these personnel, unlike in the bureaucratic organized crime syndicate, do not know who the other members of the organization are.

One non-operational unit may be the clandestine press unit. This unit is responsible for the preparation of and dissemination of the organization's propaganda releases, press releases (terrorist organizations often employ the press to take responsibility for a tactical operation, spread the organization's philosophy, and/or deny culpability for some operation), and disseminate general information about the organization. In some terrorist organizations, the clandestine press unit employs sophisticated satellite telecommunications to spread their philosophy. The Aryan Nations produces and airs a radio show to espouse their philosophy (Staff, 1987). Thomas Metzger, former Grand Dragon of the Ku Klux Klan, produces and hosts a television show for the White Armed Resistance. This television show, beamed over satellite call *Race and Reason*, is for the purpose of spreading the message of racial hatred and racial supremacy. The clandestine press may not even be aware of the organization's tactical operations until after the fact. Terrorist organizations are the only type of organized crime organization which employs a press unit. Other organized crime syndicates prefer to remain low key. Even with the terrorist organization's need to publicize their activities and become high profile, law enforcement agencies still find it almost impossible to build intelligence cases against terrorist organizations.

Terrorist organizations also make use of couriers. Couriers are highly trusted individuals who relay messages and information between cells. Couriers may only know two or three members of the terrorist organization. The use of drop points or cut-outs are commonly employed, so that the courier never comes into actual contact with any members of the terrorist organization. Drop points or cut-outs are locations where messages and communications are traded by members of the terrorist organization. Drop points help the organization to insure that members from the various cells never have to come in contact with one another. These drop points or cut-outs are constantly being changed and moved for the express purpose of thwarting law enforcement efforts to collect information and build a case (or capture a member of the organization) against the terrorist organization.

The terrorist organization may also make use of supporters. Supporters are individuals who voluntarily assist the terrorist organization and primarily provide monetary support to the organization. In many instances, supporters will not even be aware of the true nature and purpose of the terrorist organization, but will be given a false cover story. As an example of how supporters may be enlisted, the author recently received a letter asking for donations to support a congressional lobby concerned with pressuring Congress to demand a search for Vietnam MIA's. As it turned out, any money donated would have gone to a right-wing terrorist organization devoted to the subversion of blacks, Jews, and other minorities, and to overthrowing the United States government and replacing it with a white supremacist government.

The terrorist organization may also make use of umbrella businesses. The primary purpose of these businesses is to provide financial support for the terrorist organization. Many organized crime syndicates make use of umbrella businesses. The major difference lies in who operates these businesses. In the case of organized crime syndicates, many of the umbrella businesses are operated by nonmembers. For example, the "mafia" often makes loans to nonmember citizens to open legitimate businesses (Anderson, 1979). These businesses are then used by the "mafia" to turn a profit, launder money, provide a meeting place, provide a tax shelter, dispose of stolen merchandise, hire syndicate members who are on parole or probation, etc. The nonmember owner may tire of being under "mafia" control or of the illegal activities and turn informant. Even the supporting businesses the syndicate controls directly will be used in the same manner for illegal activities. Thus, law enforcement personnel can build an intelligence case using the operating records of these businesses. The terrorist organization, on the other hand, uses its members in the supporting business, and avoids direct involvement of the business in the operational aspects of the organization. Primarily, the umbrella business is used legitimately for the purpose of raising funds for the organization. Very seldom will the business be used for illegal purposes. The only exceptions are when the business is used as a drop point or cut-out (only in dire emergencies), to store equipment or supplies (never has one of these businesses been found to contain weapons or other essential material), or meeting places. For the terrorist organization, the umbrella business will most likely be a bookstore or an Army surplus-type store.

On rare occasions, the terrorist organization may employ mercenaries. Although this has not yet occurred in the United States (at least to anyone's knowledge), it is a possibility. Mercenaries are individuals who are not members of the organization, but are hired by the organization to conduct a specific tactical operation. Mercenaries are typically hired by the courier or some other representative of the organization's leader and do not know of the organization or the goals of the organization. Mercenaries are nothing more than "hired guns". Typically, mercenaries are hired only for larger tactical operations or when a specific area of expertise is needed. No other organized crime syndicate employ mercenaries (with the possible exception of Colombian drug cartels).

The Terrorist Organization Hierarchy

As the terrorist organization increases in size, the organization develops a limited hierarchical structure. Even the largest organizations, however, have a much more limited hierarchy than do other organized crime syndicates.

As the terrorist organization grows in size and develops specialized cells, the organization will make use of group leaders. Group leaders are trusted members of the organization who operate one or more cells. The number of cells a group leader is responsible for is limited, as the more cells a group leader commands, the more members that leader could compromise if captured by law enforcement personnel. The responsibility of the group leader is to not only command cells, but also to make detailed plans for tactical operations. The group leaders do not select the targets for operations, but only make the operational plans. Group leaders do not know of the overall objectives their tactical operation is supposed to accomplish. In contrast, supervisors in bureaucratic organized crime syndicates (analogous to group leaders) are aware of the overall objective of their operations within the syndicates' organizational framework and for the accomplishment of organizational goals. Thus, if compromised, these supervisors can reveal much more information about the syndicate organization than can the terrorist group leader.

The larger terrorist organizations also have organizers. Organizers are responsible for making tactical target selections and making recommendations to the leader. Organizers are comparable to the executive vice-president in the legitimate bureaucratic organization or underbosses and caporegime in organized crime syndicates (Cressey, 1967). Organizers are persons who have been long-standing members of the terrorist organization, are highly trusted, and are highly motivated to the terrorist's cause. When caught (on the rare occasions that this occurs) by law enforcement personnel, organizers will not provide information concerning the terrorist organization.

The central operations committee of the terrorist organization is comprised of the organizers and leaders. The central operations committee is similar to the board of directors in the normal bureaucratic organization. The central operations committee is responsible for establishing the short and long-term goals of the terrorist organization. At times, the central operations committees of similar terrorist organizations (i.e., same philosophies and goals) will meet together to plan joint strategy. This occurred in 1982, in Hayden Lake, Idaho, when the leaders and organizers from several different right-wing organizations met to draft a new "Constitution". Representatives from the

Ku Klux Klan, Aryan Nations, Mountain Church of Michigan, and Texas Emergency Reserves were present at that meeting (Sapp, 1986).

DISCUSSION

From strictly an organizational standpoint, the terrorist organization presents a formidable foe for law enforcement. The closed, or solar system, circular organization, the close personal contacts between the leader and members, the small size of organizational units (cells), and the autonomy and specialization of the units are all factors which work in harmony to make the terrorist organization virtually impenetrable to law enforcement efforts.

Law enforcement personnel are not only at a decided disadvantage with the terrorist organization, they are also often not sure of how to deal with the terrorist organization. The law enforcement official knows only the bureaucratic organization and how to function within the constraints of that organizational system. Like any person in any endeavor, when faced with the unknown and unfamiliar the law enforcement official does not know what to do. Law enforcement officials try to combat terrorism under the constraints of bureaucracy, and it does not work.

It is not being suggested that law enforcement suspend the rules of conduct and operate with no constraints, not that constitutional and legal requirements be discarded, not that force be met with force. To do any of the above would reduce the law enforcement official to the same level as the terrorist. What is being suggested is education and training concerning the organization structure of terrorism. American law enforcement personnel receive as much training as their foreign counterparts concerning the motivation of terrorists, terrorist philosophy and doctrine, terrorist operations and tactics, and terrorist training. Yet, American law enforcement is not nearly as effective as their foreign counterparts in dealing with terrorism. The Israeli Mossad, the English SAS, and the German GS-G9 (to name just three) anti-terrorist units have scored impressive victories against terrorist organizations. The success of these counter-terrorist units is due in large part to their understanding of the organizational dynamics of terrorist organizations. These counter-terrorist units are not only effective in collecting intelligence data on the individual terrorists, but are also effective in compromising the terrorist organization. To be effective, American law enforcement personnel must learn about and understand the ramifications concerning the uniqueness of the terrorist organizational structure. Only then will law enforcement make a significant impact on terrorism in this country.

REFERENCES

Abadinsky, H. (1987). *Organized crime* (2nd Ed.). Chicago: Nelson-Hall.

Anable, D. (1978). Loose net links diverse groups: No central plot. In Elliot, J. D., & Gibson, L. K. (Eds.). *Contemporary terrorism: Selected readings.* Gaithersburg, MD: IACP. Reprint from the *Christian Science Monitor*, 1977.

Anderson, A. G. (1979). *The business of organized crime: A Cosa Nostra family.* Stanford, CA: Hoover Institutional Press.

Clark, R. C. (1980). *Technological terrorism.* Old Greenwich, CT: Denin-Adair.

Coleman, J. C. (1976). *Abnormal psychology and modern life* (5th Ed.). Glenview, IL: Scott, Foresman.

Crenshaw, J. C. (1985). Ideological and psychological factors in international terrorism. *Defense Intelligence College Symposium Proceedings.* Washington, DC: Defense Intelligence Agency.

Cressey, D. R. (1967). The functions and structure of criminal syndicates. In *Task Force Report: Organized Crime*, 25-60. Task Force on Organized Crime. Washington, DC: US Government Printing Office.

Dalager, P. D. (1984). *Terrorist organizations and operations: A topical training guide.* College Station, TX: The Texas A & M University System.

Freedman, L. Z. (1974). Terrorism: Policy, pathology, politics—Problems of the polistaraxic. *The University of Chicago Magazine, Summer*, 7-10.

Freedman, L. Z. (1974). Terrorism: Problems of the polistaraxic. In Freedman, L. Z., & Alexander, Y. (Eds.). *Perspectives on terrorism.* Wilmington, DE: Scholarly Resources.

Hacker, F. J. (1983). Dialectic interrelationships of personal and political factors in terrorism. In Freedman, L. Z. & Alexander, Y. (Eds.). *Perspectives of terrorism.* Wilmington, DE: Scholarly Resources.

Haddigan, M. (1987). Profile of 15 persons names in indictments. *Arkansas Gazette, April 25*, 1 and 11A.

Kaplan, A. (1978). The psychodynamics of terrorism. *Terrorism: An International journal, 1*, 237-254.

Michel, H. (1972). *The shadow war: European resistance, 1939-1945.* New York: Harper & Row.

Mullins, W. C. (1988). *Terrorist organizations in the United States: An analysis of issues, organizations, tactics, and responses.* Springfield, IL: Charles C. Thomas, Pub.

Salerno, R., & Tompkins, J. S. (1969). *The crime confederation*, Garden City, NY: Doubleday.

Sapp, A. D. (1986). The Nehemiah Township Charter: Applied right-wing ideology. Paper presented at the Academy of Criminal Justice Sciences, Orlando, FL (April).

Scotti, A. J. (1986). *Executive safety and international terrorism.* Englewood Cliffs, NJ: Prentice-Hall, Inc.

Staff, (1987). Racist radio makes Utah debut. *San Antonio Light, Dec. 6*, 5A.

Steinhoff, P. G. (1976). Portrait of a terrorist: An interview with Kozo O. Kamoto. *Asian Survey, XVI*, 835.

Sterling, D. (1982). *The terror network.* New York: Berkley.

Stewert, R. C. (1980). *Identification and investigation of organized criminal activity.* Houston, TX: National College of District Attorneys.

Strentz, T. (1987). *Terrorism.* Law enforcement satellite training network. Kansas: Kansas City Police Department.

Task Force on Organized Crime (1976). *Organized crime.* Washington, DC: US Government Printing Office.

Wilkinson, P. (1983). *The new fascists.* (Rev. Ed.). London: Pan Books.

Wilson, J. Q. (1973). *Political organizations.* New York: Basic Books.

Wolf, J. B. (1978). Organizational and management practice of urban terrorist groups. *Terrorism: An International Journal, 1*, 169-186.

Zawodny, J. M. (1978). Internal organizational problems and the sources of tensions of terrorist movements as catalysts of violence. *Terrorism: An International Journal, 1*, 277-285.

Zawodny, J. K. (1983). Infrastructures of terrorist organizations. In Freedman, L. A., & Alexander, Y. (Eds.). *Perspectives on terrorism.* Wilmington, DE: Scholarly Resources.

Skinheads Target the Schools

Introduction

For the past two years the Anti-Defamation League has closely monitored the rise in the United States of neo-Nazi Skinheads. An import from Great Britain, the Skinhead movement first attracted our attention when a shaven-headed gang from Chicago calling itself "Romantic Violence" took part in a 1985 national conference of white supremacists in Michigan. Promoting a hoped-for American tour of a British white-power band (which never materialized), members of this group displayed all the by-now familiar characteristics: shaven heads, neo-Nazi tattoos, Doc Marten work boots and an outspokenly vulgar advocacy of racism and violence.

Although non-racist Skinheads (often called "baldies" or "two-tones") considerably outnumber racist ones in most areas of the country, a fact we have noted in all our earlier reports, a new nationwide ADL survey shows racist Skinheads active today in thirty-one states—compared with twenty-one last fall—numbering a total of about 3,000 members. The southeastern states have experienced the greatest amount of membership growth since the last ADL survey. The national figure of 3,000, as compared with 2,000 eight months ago, represents a 50% increase, and a still disturbingly high rate of growth. Even more troubling was the fact that the overall high level of violence continued apace. Since the time of our last report in October, 1988 there have been three additional murders attributed to Skinheads, two of them racially motivated. Assaults on members of minority groups as well as heavy vandalism of religious institutions (particularly synagogues) have continued.

Our recently-completed survey also indicates that two new trends are adding to the dangers posed by racist Skinheads: a growing pattern of recruitment and activity in high schools and the acquisition of deadlier weaponry.

Schools

Skinheads have been responsible for a variety of racially-motivated incidents in schools, often creating an atmosphere of tension and fear among students. Such was the case at Groves High School in Birmingham, a suburb of Detroit, which was the site of a racial brawl in late November, 1988. It began when three non-student Skinheads walked into the school and, joining with three students, roamed the halls, eventually confronting two other students, one black and the other white. A brawl broke out—finally brought to a halt by school coaches—and Groves remained tense for several days afterward with rumors of revenge. Police ringed the school during this period. Skinhead students were expelled and transferred to Seaholm High School, where officials were concerned because of the presence of another small Skinhead group.

But the problems at Groves were far from over. In mid-April, racist flyers were found taped to a tree, fence, telephone pole and to doors outside the school. Two weeks later, several black students found the word "nigger" scrawled across their lockers. Other lockers were defaced with swastikas. On May 14, the outside of the high school was spray-painted with swastikas and words "White Power" and "Skins". Police believe Skinheads to be responsible for these acts.

In Camarillo, located in Ventura County, California, Skinhead flyers have been found in schools where Skinheads have clashed with a non-Skinhead group called the "Suicidals". Ventura County Skinheads have tried to recruit elementary school students, reportedly beating those whom they had befriended but who refused to partake in their activities.

Douglas County High School in Castle Rock, Colorado has a group of approximately a dozen racist Skinheads who were responsible for a number of racial incidents during the past school year. In February, 1989, a black student was harassed by Skinheads shouting racial epithets at her. They followed her to a nearby store where they pushed and threatened her. In early May, the same student was harassed in the hall by the leader of the gang. Two weeks later, the Skinheads harassed the artist of an anti-racist poster with threats such as "any day now, any time now, we're going to get you." These Skinheads, reportedly heavy drug users, are considered a powerful presence on campus. An incident during homecoming weekend last fall in which a noose was hung on a black student's locker along with a sign "Wanted: Three Blacks, Reward", could not be pinned on members of the group, but it is believed that they were the perpetrators.

At Sprayberry High School, located in Cobb County, Georgia (suburban Atlanta), a large group of over two dozen Skinheads have reportedly hurled "Heil Hitler!" salutes during recitation of the Pledge of Allegiance. The group's members have Nazi insignias scrawled on their lockers and books, as well as their jackets. Members of a Harrisburg, Pennsylvania Skinhead group called "Blitzkrieg" are reportedly active in the Central Dauphin School District. Parents of both white and black children are said to be afraid to send their children to school.

Recruitment

Skinheads have tried, with varying levels of success, to recruit students directly on school campuses. They have distributed literature and even, in one case, sent a mass mailing to parents. This occurred in Waco, Texas, where parents of students at Waco High School received a letter from the Dallas-based Confederate Hammer Skins last fall. Addressed to "proud parents," the message warned of "the dangers posed by minority gangs and drug pushers", adding that "it is time that the common White Americans stand up and demand that their children attend schools not polluted with drugs, gangs, and anti-Christian immorality." The letter closed by offering those who write to the group additional information about the organization "and what we are doing to help the White schoolchildren of America."

Students in at least eight eastern Oregon school districts as well as youngsters in four communities in the western part of the state were selected to receive a special "Skinhead movement" newsletter by long-time neo-Nazi activist Ricky Cooper. Cooper also sent the publication, a special edition of his "NSV Report" (named after his group, the National Socialist Vanguard), to youngsters in two Idaho communities, Bonner's Ferry and Weiser. Cooper obtained the names from local newspapers by clipping honor roll lists and articles about student leaders and sports participants. He has indicated that the mailings will continue until "the climate is ripe" for young people to rally around the hate movements.

On June 2, 1989, students, teachers, and administrators arrived at Oak Ridge High School in Orlando, Florida to find two flags had been raised above the school, one proclaiming "White Power", the other bearing the insignia of the American Front, a San Francisco-based Skinhead group. Portable classrooms located on the school's premises were spray-painted with swastikas. The east coast organizer of the group, David Lynch, has been an active Skinhead recruiter in various parts of Florida, and has attempted with limited success, to make inroads in Orlando area high schools.

Lynch also attempted to recruit last year at two high schools located in Orange County, New York, where his mother once lived. According to authorities, he had little success there, despite his claims that he recruited 20 students for an Orange County chapter of the American Front. (Lynch, 18, was arrested in Edgewater, Florida in early May along with two other Skinheads for carrying concealed weapons, possession of drug paraphernalia, and other offenses.)

Recruitment efforts in high schools have also been made in the following communities: Phoenix, Arizona; Austin and Houston, Texas; and McKeesport, Pennsylvania. Scattered attempts at recruitment on college campuses have met with little success. Much of this effort has taken place at three universities in Ohio: Ohio State, the University of Ohio, and the University of Cincinnati, which are located in communities where Skinhead activity has stepped up in recent months.

Weaponry

The favored weapons of Skinheads continue to be simple and crude: knives, bats, chains and steel-toed Doc Marten boots. Nonetheless, possession of handguns, shotguns and semi-automatic weaponry is becoming more common among Skinheads, and there are disturbing signs that their weaponry is becoming increasingly deadly:

- In May, four Skinheads were stopped in Taveras, Florida, after two had pulled guns on an elderly couple. Police uncovered two AR-15's, two 9mm handguns, two shotguns, and live ammunition.
- When law enforcement authorities searched the home of a member of the Arizona White Battalion, a Skinhead group based in Phoenix, they found gunpowder, pipes and detonators.
- At an event for Skinheads in Napa County, California in March, participants came equipped with semi-automatic weapons, including AR-15, an AK-47, automatic pistols, and shotguns.

When three Portland Skinheads confronted Mulugeta Seraw, an Ethiopian immigrant in front of his apartment last November and clubbed him to death, their weapon was a simple baseball bat. One month later, when three Skinheads drove through a neighborhood in the Northeast section of Reno, Nevada looking for a black person to kill, one displayed a small round of ammunition and reportedly said, "This is a dead black man." He placed these bullets in a gun, and one of them hit a young black man named Tony Montgomery and killed him. Six other bullets riddled two nearby homes, missing a child by five feet.

The most recent murder attributed by authorities to Skinheads took place in Denver on March 18, when 33-year-old David Timoner was shot to death with a 9mm weapon and his car set afire. During a police chase the following day, one of the two Skinheads involved took a hostage and held him while brandishing a .22 caliber handgun, telling a police negotiator that he wanted "to go out in a blaze of glory".

Weapons Training

The acquisition of sophisticated weaponry by Skinheads is to some degree the result of the influence which organized hate groups continue to exercise. For example, Tom Metzger of the White Aryan Resistance (WAR) and his son, John, traveled to Phoenix in January to lead Skinheads in a march to commemorate the birthday of Robert Matthews, founder of The Order. Later, they accompanied members of the Arizona White Battalion into the nearby desert where they engaged in weapons training with semi-automatic weapons. Notices for the Metzger-sponsored "Aryan Woodstock" announced that there would be a "Grand Prize drawing of a fine new firearm". (The drawing never actually took place.)

In April, following Richard Butler's Skinhead fest held at the Aryan Nation's compound in Idaho, authorities found a .30 caliber carbine rifle and a 12-gauge shotgun in the trunk of a car driven by two Skinheads who spun their car out of the compound and swerved into a ditch. One, Wyatt J. Brooks, 19, was charged with driving with a suspended license. (Brooks, a private first class, is a member of the 44th Inner Defense Artillery Station in Fort Lewis, Washington. Army authorities are said to be weighing whether his participation at the conference violated military regulations.)

In Casper, Wyoming, 18-year-old Skinhead David Spethman was indicted in April by a federal grand jury for illegal possession of a sawed-off shotgun. Spethman served as campaign treasurer for the congressional candidacy of Daniel Johnson, author of the PACE Amendment, a blueprint for purging the U.S. of its minority population. At the time of Spethman's indictment, he was being held for another charge (unspecified because of his juvenile status in Wyoming). Because Spethman turned 18 this year he will be charged as an adult under federal law. According to U.S. Attorney Richard Stacey, the barrel and stock of the gun were cut off after it was purchased. He described the weapon as "a very short sawed-off shotgun" and added that it is "nothing more, nothing less than an antipersonnel weapon".

Long Island, New York organizer Kenneth Hill was arrested in late May for illegal weapons possession. He was carrying a 9mm handgun and an AR-15 assault weapon in the commercial van he was driving.

On April 1 of this year, the leader of the Indianapolis National White Resistance, Matthew Myer, was arrested and charged with recklessness with a dangerous weapon (an AK-47 assault rifle).

The Confederate Hammer Skins of Dallas have stockpiled approximately a dozen shotguns and handguns. " Anthony", a leader of the CHS-affiliated Memphis area Skinheads, boasts ownership of a Mossberg 12-gauge pump-action shotgun, which he says he carries in his car along with a combat knife. According to Anthony, his group does not seek confrontation, "but we are prepared".

Links Among Skinheads

Both the Chattanooga group, which calls itself the Chattanooga Area Confederate Hammer Skinheads and the Memphis group, MASH, are closely aligned with the Dallas-based Confederate Hammer Skins. That group has been at the core of Skinhead recruiting efforts in other states, including Arizona, Oklahoma, and Wisconsin, and maintains close ties to Tom and John Metzger. (During his trial on charges of attacking and vandalizing a Dallas synagogue and Jewish Community Center, CHS member Daniel Alvis Wood testified that he had discussed his problems with Tom Metzger on several occasions.)

One of the more active Skinhead groups of late has been the Old Glory Skins, based in Atlanta. One of its leaders, Terence Georges, has traveled to Orlando, Florida to set up a branch of his organization. Another member, Robert von Sura, has traveled to Birmingham to forge a link with the Birmingham Area Skinhead (BASH). Members of BASH were present at both the Democratic National Convention in Atlanta last July and at the annual Klan gathering at Stone Mountain on Labor Day Weekend, where they were joined by members of the Atlanta Skinhead group. Two Skinheads from the Fort Lauderdale area and another from Daytona Beach have also linked up with the Old Glory group, and a chapter was established this spring in Charlotte. The leaders of Old Glory have also developed a friendly relationship with the Metzgers.

Although the Confederate Hammer Skins and Old Glory Skins have succeeded in establishing a level or organization more sophisticated than most Skinhead groups, it is not uncommon for Skinheads to establish ties to others in different parts of the country. This usually takes the form of correspondence about points of common interest (particularly White Power music) and about movement activities. Skinheads also seek out their counterparts when they travel to other cities, often staying at communal residences.

War Youth

Much of the Skinhead organizing has centered around a number of charismatic figures (most in their twenties and therefore somewhat older than the rank and file) who have brought together Skinheads in different cities under a single umbrella. The most successful of these has been John Metzger (himself not a Skinhead), whose WAR Youth works in tandem with John's father Tom of the White Aryan Resistance to organize Skinheads throughout the country. But there are others, most notably Robert Heick, leader of the San Francisco-based American Front, and the aforementioned Michael Palasch. Heick has organized in Southern California, Florida and Maryland. Palasch, who heads the National White Resistance of Metairie, Louisiana, has formed chapters in Indianapolis, Cincinnati, Columbus and on New York's Long Island. NWR literature printed in Metairie has been distributed by Palasch's local affiliates with local addresses to contact for further information.

Metzger, Heick and Palasch have gained something of "celebrity" status through their numerous appearances on television talk shows, most notoriously on the installment of Geraldo Rivera's program where a brawl broke out, resulting in injury to the show's host. These programs have apparently been judged by their producers to be successful vis-a-vis audience ratings, because many have continued to invite Skinhead leaders to appear on them, resulting in a boon for Skinhead recruitment. John Metzger has claimed that he received about a thousand letters after appearing as a guest on both "Donahue" and "Oprah", some of his fans sending as much as a $500 contribution. He also says that thanks to national exposure, he possesses a list of "a thousand different people that would drop ten, twenty bucks if I told them to". (Both claims are probably exaggerated.)

Given their lack of discipline and anti-organizational impulses, it is unlikely that the Skinheads will unite as a single national entity. Nevertheless, the growth in the number of Skinhead networks reflects the movement's increasing ability to organize, a factor which should contribute to its long-term survival.

Non-Racist Skinheads

As indicated earlier in this report, non-racist Skinheads considerably outnumber the racist ones in most areas of the country. Careful observation of the Skinhead scene over the past several years, however, leads to the conclusion that the distinction between the racist and non-racist variety is often blurred. Some "baldies", for example, openly express hostility toward homosexuals and have been arrested for violently assaulting gays ("fag-bashing"). Furthermore, it is not unusual for Skinheads who claim they are not racists to avow a belief in "white pride", a notion which is intrinsically racist. It is not surprising therefore that a good many Skinheads started out as "baldies", but eventually joined a neo-Nazi gang.

At the same time, there is no doubt that many non-racist Skins do proudly and genuinely eschew bigotry. Indeed, it is not unusual for blacks and Hispanics to be members of non-racist groups. But this does not signify that the groups are non-violent. On the contrary, they often boast about how tough they are and how many scraps they've been involved in with neo-Nazi Skins. In fact, the entire Skinhead scene is a violent one. Eric Andrew Anderson, whose masters thesis at Washington State University focused on the Skinheads in Great Britain and San Francisco, has pointed out that violence and machismo are central ingredients of the Skinhead culture. The record of Skinhead activity throughout the country confirms the correctness of his view. Skinheads have beaten, stomped and stabbed other Skinheads, punk rockers, long-haired hippies, gays and, in the case of the racist Skins, members of racial and religious minorities. Often these battles have taken place in clubs, leading the owners to bar the Skinheads or the authorities to close down the clubs altogether.

Conclusions & Counteractive Measures

The movement of Skinheads from the streets into the schools coming as it does at a time when the nation's schools are already wrestling with a host of difficulties, is a serious development. The evidence shows its impact not only on the students directly involved—the Skinheads and those closest to them—but on the entire school community. Events such as assaults on minority students; the appearance of racist graffiti on lockers, walls and doors; the shouting of racial epithets and the distribution of racist flyers have the effect of poisoning the entire atmosphere in a school and making orderly study exceedingly difficult. Beyond that, the Skinheads' recruiting efforts have involved exploiting racial tensions which they themselves have helped to create, triggering a self-generating destructive cycle.

When such problems have arisen, school administrators have coped with them as best they could, using whatever techniques they have judged appropriate, with varying results. The one approach, however, that has proven singularly ineffectual has been the "head-in-the-sand" policy. Principals who have tended to ignore the problem, out of concern, perhaps, for their school's reputation, have found that rather than going away, the problem has festered. The wiser course is a candid recognition that the problem exists and a sober consideration of possible remedies.

The second trend disclosed by the new ADL survey is the acquisition by racist Skinheads of increasingly dangerous weapons. A growing number of neo-Nazi Skinheads are adding firearms, some of them semi-automatic, to their stockpile of weapons. Heretofore the typical Skinhead instrument of assault has been a baseball bat, a knife or a steel-toed Doc Marten boot. Even these primitive weapons in the hands of Skinheads have been shown to be capable of murdering innocent victims. With the acquisition of such weapons as AR-15's and sawed-off shotguns, plainly the danger grows.

Any firearms in the hands of political extremists need to be taken seriously. The history of the past several decades shows that revolutionaries of the far right and the far left have been responsible for numerous fatal shootings and bombings. But there is something especially troubling about the possession of weapons of death by volatile youngsters filled with racial and religious hatred. All the more reason why the dangers posed by neo-Nazi Skinheads warrants the urgent attention of parents, educators, community leaders and law enforcement officials.

The Anti-Defamation League has taken a number of steps to inform communities about the nature of the Skinhead threat. Our reports are widely distributed to law enforcement officials, educators, and the press. We continue to regard the growth of the Skinhead movement as both a national and local problem requiring an effective response at both levels.

In January a high-level ADL delegation met with U.S. Attorney General Dick Thornburgh and received assurances that the Department of Justice regards with concern the racially and religiously motivated violence committed by Skinheads against individuals and institutions. Last month, a federal grand jury was convened in Dallas, signalling a U.S. Justice Department investigation of Skinhead crime described by spokeswoman Deborah Wade as "a showcase effort". The grand jury inquiry and a related state-federal investigation of Skinhead crime are being conducted jointly by the F.B.I., the Dallas Police Department, the Civil Rights Division of the Justice Department and the Dallas County District Attorney's Office. ADL has provided information to investigators.

In addition to supplying information on an ongoing basis to law enforcement agencies investigating criminal acts committed by Skinheads, ADL officials have briefed police personnel at conferences in Arizona, California, Georgia, Ohio, and New Mexico as well as states' attorneys in Illinois and the Prosecuting Attorneys Research Council, a group of district attorneys from around the country. We continue to promote the adoption and use by prosecutors of ADL's Model Hate Crimes Statute, a form of which is now in effect in some 20 states. These statutes increase penalties for bias-related crimes. They have begun to be used in a number of jurisdictions to prosecute Skinheads. Finally, we have established reward funds for information leading to the arrest and conviction of Skinheads responsible for criminal activity, a tactic which has proven successful in a number of cases.

A measure that would help considerably in reducing the potential danger of Skinhead violence would be the adoption of legislation outlawing the sale of semi-automatic assault weapons. As this report has documented, these weapons are increasingly falling into the hands of racist Skinheads, a trend which could climax in tragedy.

New extremists exceed 'Jim Crowism' of KKK

Cheryl Sullivan

Staff writer of The Christian Science Monitor

San Francisco

White supremacy has been at the bottom of organized racism since the birth of the Ku Klux Klan in the Reconstruction era.

While it is still a common denominator, radical groups like The Order and the Arizona Patriots are now espousing themes that are different from—and to some more alarming than—the KKK's goals of yesteryear.

- Today's white-supremacist leaders have given up their nostalgia for the "Jim Crow" era of the past, replacing it with a "cockamamie" vision of the future, says Bill Stanton of Klanwatch. "Today they want to create a new order. They envision an all-white republic in North America in which minorities will be run out of the country or, if they won't leave, be exterminated."

The Aryan Nations, for example, dreams of establishing an all-white homeland, to be called the "Northwest Mountain Republic," in Washington, Oregon, Idaho, Montana, and Wyoming.

- Many right-wing racist organizations no longer seek to portray themselves as law-abiding, Constitution-protecting, patriotic fraternities. Instead, the federal government has become the avowed enemy of such groups, whose members believe United States leaders have betrayed and invalidated the Constitution.

Militant organizations like The Order have stockpiled weapons, provided military-type training for their members, and planned attacks against government institutions.

Hoods and robes are out, and the "Rambo" image is in, says one Klan watcher.

- Blacks have been and still are targets of violence and harassment, particularly by extremist groups in the South.

But, increasingly, Jews are also coming under attack, partly as a result of a growing neo-Nazi influence in the movement.

A common theme among hate groups today is that an "international Jewish conspiracy" is responsible for most of America's current troubles, including the trade deficit, the slump in the industrial Midwest, and the farm crisis. The economically depressed farm belt, in particular, has been fertile ground for anti-Semitic organizations to sow messages of hate in hopes of winning converts to their cause, says Dan Levitas of Prariefire Rural Action Inc., in Des Moines.

A poll that was conducted in Iowa and Nebraska by Louis Harris Associates showed that 27 percent of the respondents laid the responsibility for the farm crisis on the shoulders of international Jewish bankers.

Far-right groups in farm country have sought to win a mass following by infiltrating the farm-protest movement, he says.

Some people are attracted to these groups, observers say, by the fact that they identify themselves with fundamentalist Christianity.

Major white-supremacist groups in the US

EAST

Invisible Empire Knights of the KKK: New leader has moved headquarters to Connecticut, first Klan ever north of Mason-Dixon line. Membership down to a few hundred.

SOUTH

United Klans of America: largest Klan faction in US, possibly with 4,000 members. Led by Robert Shelton, longtime Klan activist. Active in Alabama, Georgia, Mississippi.

Knights of the KKK: started in Louisiana by David Duke, credited with Klan's resurgence in mid-'70s. Most militant Klan group in US, but leadership now divided. Headquartered in Tuscumbia, Ala.; also active in Chicago. Duke left, later founded National Association for the Advancement of White People in Metairie, La.

White Patriot Party (WPP): formerly the Confederate Knights of the KKK, based in North Carolina. Stephen S. Miller (second in command but not related to former leader Glenn Miller) and four others were indicted Jan. 7 on charges of conspiring to obtain weapons stolen from a US military installation. Glenn Miller ran a paramilitary training camp, intending to create a Southern homeland for white Christians by taking over several North Carolina counties. A court this year ordered him to sever all his WPP ties.

National Alliance: Neo-Nazi group led by William L. Pierce, who started a new white enclave in rural West Virginia. Pierce is author of "The Turner Diaries," novel about a race war that became blueprint for The Order's criminal campaign.

Covenant, Sword, and the Arm of the Lord (CSA): paramilitary survivalist group operating on the Arkansas-Missouri border. Eight leaders arrested on federal weapons charges in 1985, after US agents discovered illegal weapons, explosives, land mines, and an antitank rocket launcher. CSA disbanded after its leaders were jailed.

MIDWEST

Posse Comitatus: loosely linked chapters across the US, but attracts rural farmers. Claims Federal Reserve System and income tax are unconstitutional. Posse leaders have fused tax-protest doctrine with virulent anti-Semitism. Leader Gordon Kahl murdered two US marshals in North Dakota, was killed in a shootout in 1983. Posse-type groups today now identify themselves by other names.

National Agricultural Press Association (NAPA): Leader Rick Elliott crisscrossed the farm belt in 1983 with a loan-franchise scheme for desperate farmers, but this year was convicted of theft and conspiracy in home state of Colorado. Published anti-Semitic tabloid, which carried ads for neo-Nazi groups. NAPA torch falls to Colorado farmer Leon Silkman.

WEST

Aryan Nations: Leader Richard Butler of Hayden Lake, Idaho, is a major figure in Christian Identity movement, a pseudo-religious justification for white supremacy. The Nations recruits members from white prison gangs.

Urges migration of whites to Pacific Northwest to create a homeland. Runs a computer "bulletin board" to dispense white-supremacist propaganda. Hosts annual "World Congress," a gathering of neo-Nazis, KKK, Posse Comitatus, and other white supremacists. Associates are former Klan leaders Robert Miles of Michigan and Louis Beam of Texas.

The Order: Most violent of neo-Nazi groups; several members have ties to Aryan Nations. Responsible for murder of Jewish radio personality in Denver in 1984, and armored car heists totaling $4 million in Seattle, Wash., and Ukiah, Calif. Money intended to finance white-supremacist revolution; only $1 million accounted for. Leader killed in shootout with FBI; 23 others in prison. Three men arrested in connection with the setting off of three bombs in Coeur d'Alene last Sept. 29 in an abortive attempt to rob two local banks were part of a small group which tried to revive the outlaw band.

White Aryan Resistance: Led by Tom Metzger of Fallbrook, Calif., former leader of California KKK. Metzger was 1980 Democratic nominee for Congress in state's 43rd District in 1980; lost by wide margin, but got 43,000 votes. Currently produces "Race and Reason," a white-supremacist program shown on public-access channels of cable TV.

Terrorism

Threats, Real or Not, Stir Fears Across U.S.

ROBERT REINHOLD
Special to The New York Times

LOS ANGELES, Jan. 23 — It certainly looked suspicious, the taped shopping bag found outside the Louis Vuitton luggage boutique on Rodeo Drive in Beverly Hills the other morning.

Sheriff's deputies rushed in and closed off the street, and the bomb squad gingerly carted the bag off to an empty canyon, where it was exploded — with a puff of feathers. The suspected terrorist bomb turned out to be a pillow.

If Rodeo Drive, where high-price shops now cater largely to busloads of Japanese tourists, seemed an unlikely target for Iraqi terrorists, the episode underscored the jitters that have swept the country since the outbreak of war in the Persian Gulf.

And if all the scares have so far proved false alarms or hoaxes, many Americans are nonetheless wandering through a psychological twilight zone of enormous stress in which it is difficult to distinguish among reality, perception and fantasy.

"People are nervous — everyone is dealing with the issue of what is real and what is fantastic in a state of threat," said one expert, Dr. Mardi J. Horowitz, a psychiatrist who directs the Program on Conscious and Unconscious Mental Processes at the University of California at San Francisco.

'State of Hypervigilance'

"People are searching for information to make the distinction," he said. "It creates a state of hypervigilance." Dr. Horowitz confessed that he was uneasy about taking a planned flight to Washington this week.

He is not alone in an American public whose fears were only heightened this week by news pictures of grim-faced captured American pilots, the deadly Iraqi missile raid against Tel Aviv on Tuesday night and terrorist attacks today on two American organizations in Istanbul and at two banks partly owned by Saudi and French investors in Lebanon.

Psychologists and psychiatrists say the fears feed on, probably more than anything else, television images from the war zone as well as those of possible domestic targets.

Examples abound:

¶On an Amtrak Metroliner from Washington to New York the other morning, Melinda Lukasz, a video producer with the Bell Atlantic Corporation, was uneasy. "I thought twice about getting on this train," she said. Nearby, Phil Williams, a Washington lawyer, said he had felt in the train station at Washington "an eerie feeling of impending peril," as if "people felt they had to look over their shoulders."

¶Ara Soulahian, a Federal Express courier who works in the heavily Jewish Fairfax district of Los Angeles, mused on his fate: "I realize now how I probably will die — on the job. I'll be making a delivery, and it will blow up right in my face." He said that in the current climate some offices were not admitting him or anybody else who delivers packages for a living.

¶Steven L. Kaufman, a salesman in Cerritos, Calif., canceled his regular flight to Salt Lake City on Monday. "With the hostilities," he said, "the first thing I thought of was my 14-month-old daughter at home. It was more important for me to be here than risk flying." He added that he and his wife, Christine, had bought extra bottled water on the chance that terrorists might throw poison into the aqueducts that supply the Los Angeles area.

¶Bill Payne, a Hollywood screenwriter, has decided to drive from Los Angeles to Ohio on a family visit instead of taking a flight there. "I know I'm sounding silly," he said, "but I don't like flying anyway, and I know somebody's going to get blown up. So I'm trying to reduce my chances." He has also avoided seeing the new movie "Not Without My Daughter," starring Sally Field as an Iranian's American wife trying to flee Iran, because of bomb threats against theaters that show the movie. Ms. Field hired a bodyguard last week, as did many other celebrities.

Fears of Calamity

Probably not since the Cuban missile crisis of October 1962 have Americans felt a keener threat of calamity on American soil, a fear reinforced by televised images of Federal agents in gas masks practicing how they would combat terrorists at the Super Bowl in Tampa, Fla., this Sunday, of armed guards closing off public access to the Birmingham Water Works in Alabama and of new security rules at airports.

According to a New York Times/CBS News Poll of 2,135 adults taken Jan. 17 to 19, just after the war with Iraq began, 63 percent of American adults are "very concerned" about the possibility of a terrorist attack in the United States. A separate survey of 766 adults, taken about the same time by the Gallup Organization, found that only one in four Americans felt in personal danger, although the proportion was almost certainly higher in cities.

Clearly, it is easy to dismiss some of the fears as outpacing any objective reality. Flashes of lightning and thunder over Southern California, seeming to mimic the television images of antiaircraft fire over Baghdad, stirred a brief panic among some here Monday night.

But countless rational Americans see good reason to be worried and are taking precautions, especially Jews, many of whom see themselves as special targets.

"There is a legitimate reason to be fearful," said Rabbi Martin Hier, dean of the Simon Wiesenthal Center here. "We have to take a man like Saddam Hussein, who has a track record of using every weapon he has, including terrorism, at his word. It would be very naïve to dismiss it out of hand."

Dr. Barbara Cadow, a psychologist on the adjunct faculty at the University of Southern California, said she had at first thought that only the extremely neurotic would be fearful of a terrorist attack. But she soon found that even the "high-functioning professionals" among her patients were turning anxious.

She said live television scenes of Israelis' putting on gas masks, placing their small children in special protective devices and retreating to sealed rooms had a powerful effect, particularly on mothers. "It was very effective in heightening anxieties," she said. "It was hard not to be affected."

Indeed, Army surplus stores in numerous American cities reported a run on gas masks and chemical warfare suits this week, and gas masks sold out completely in Marysville, Calif.

Diagnosis: Overreaction

But others see in all this a vast overreaction to danger in farway places.

"Clearly there is a possibility of some type of terrorist activity, but certainly the reaction has been exaggerated," said Dr. Manuel Tanay, a clinical professor of psychiatry at Wayne State University in Detroit.

"My office is across from the General Motors Building, and they have almost transformed it," he said. "They have guards everywhere. Let's face it: these are overreactions. Overreactions usually indicate some type of emotional process is at work, and my interpretation is that it's a displacement of the war, where there is a real danger to our young men and women, onto the domestic situation."

Whether the current state of vigilance can be maintained is doubtful, said Shlomo Breznitz, a psychologist from the University of Haifa in Israel, who is a visiting professor at the New School in New York. Even in Israel, he said, attention to uncertain threats attentuates with time and with false alarms. Indeed, he said, false alarms are part of the terrorist arsenal, inducing people to let down their guard and making later attack easier.

NATIONAL SECURITY

Borders Open to Terrorist Threat

Experts say US is vulnerable, but has avoided incidents so far through good police work

John Dillin

Staff writer of The Christian Science Monitor

SAN YSIDRO, CALIF.

AMERICA'S borders are being breached every day by thousands of foreign nationals – a fact that chills experts on international terrorism.

When the latest bombings and bomb threats against the judiciary erupted five days ago, investigators first suspected it was the work of Colombian drug traffickers.

The initial explosion killed United States Appeals Court Judge Robert Vance of Alabama, whose court hears many drug cases. He was the highest ranking judge ever murdered in US history.

Later incidents, including the bomb death of Savannah, Ga., attorney Robert Robinson and delivery of a bomb package to the office of a Jacksonville, Fla., civil rights group—point to a possible racial motive for the attacks.

But federal authorities concede that the danger from international drug terrorists remains high. They say drug cartels and foreign governments can move terrorists, money, and weapons into the US with relative ease.

Furthermore, US officials point out that threats from narcotics criminals have reached an all-time high.

From a national security standpoint, the area here along the 1,953-mile boundary with Mexico is particularly worrisome to federal officials. Nobody really knows who – or what – comes across.

Most aliens who enter the US illegally here are Mexicans. But what troubles experts on worldwide terrorism is that thousands of aliens are slipping secretly into the US are from volatile nations in the Mideast, Asia, and South America. All are potential sources of terrorist infiltration, including hired killers working for drug cartels.

Some lawmen along the border now are so concerned about security that they refuse to permit their photos to be taken, or their names to be quoted because of possible retaliation.

"We never know what we're going to find out here at night," notes one border patrolman in California. On a recent night here, for example, agents captured six aliens from Guatemala, two from Uruguay, two from India, and one each from Honduras, Peru, and Argentina.

In Texas, agents report that in the past three years, they have captured aliens from 73 nations, including Iran, Iraq, and China.

Yonah Alexander, an expert on international terrorism, says border security is a "very critical" element in America's efforts to keep out political, criminal, and religious extremists.

Dr. Alexander is director of the Institute for Studies in International Terrorism at State University of New York, and research professor at the Elliott School of International Affairs, at George Washington University. He says there is no doubt that some terrorist organizations already have penetrated this country.

"You cannot set a hermetic fence to keep out all terrorists. Tragically, in the US the [terrorist] infrastructure is set in place, ready to be activated at any time."

He says foreign organizations run grave risks in spreading terrorism inside the US, however.

"My assessment is that they [will] strike in this country only as a last resort. [They don't want] to wake up the American giant."

Government officials, increasingly concerned about national security, deployed 50 US marines in late November to assist the Border Patrol along the Southwest frontier. Use of the Marines follows a one-month test, conducted last spring, in which the California National Guard set up observation posts on the border.

Six hundred guardsmen took up positions between San Diego and Arizona. They built camouflaged observation posts, including underground bunkers, in the deserts and mountains abutting Baja California. Their assignment: Watch, listen, report. They were not to arrest or stop anyone.

In 30 days, the troops reported 32 clandestine flights from Mexico. Many of the aircraft flew at night – lights out – sometimes skimming just 50 feet off the desert floor. Most of the aircraft, including a low-flying DC-3, were probably loaded with drugs.

Intelligence from the guard helped bring about 564 arrests by federal, state, and local law enforcement agencies, including 237 for narcotics violations and 113 for weapons violations during the one-month test.

The guardsmen also were instrumental in the seizure of 62

firearms, 970 pounds of cocaine, 93 pounds of heroin, and 3,053 pounds of marijuana.

US officials – Border Patrol, Customs, Drug Enforcement Administration – admit that with current manpower levels, the frontier can't be controlled. Many welcome help from the military.

The Marine unit already has seen action. Last week, the marines exchanged gunfire with drug smugglers who were crossing by horseback into Arizona from Mexico. No one was hit (the marines fired over the smugglers' heads), but the Border Patrol confiscated 537 pounds of marijuana and one horse.

Away from the borders, the threat of terrorism has forced government officials to boost security for top officials.

In September, Attorney General Dick Thornburgh began using a $100,000, armor-plated limousine for protection against terrorism.

The US Marshals Service, meanwhile, has assigned a permanent security detail to William Bennett, the president's drug policy coordinator.

Throughout the country, the Marshals Service has tightened security at federal courts where Colombian drug traffickers face charges. Under new security guidelines, judges are no longer supposed to list their home telephone numbers or give out their home addresses.

In Florida, security was boosted for Gov. Bob Martinez (R), an outspoken foe of the drug cartels. Narco-terrorism is "something we have to be concerned about now," he told the Monitor. "Now is when you are engaged in the destabilization of the narco-traffic in Colombia. Their reaction will have to be now.

"Obviously they [the drug cartels] have threatened and engaged in terrorism in their own country. They have threatened lives of American leaders if extradition occurs," the governor says. "If they are to retaliate, it will be [within the next] two years."

Alexander says the US so far has avoided "spectacular" incidents of terrorism, through good police work. "I think we've prevented dozens of incidents," he says. "You don't read about it in the paper every day, but there is no doubt that because of the very professional, quiet work by the [Federal] Bureau [of Investigation], as well as state and local police, they were successful in preventing activities."

The coming months could be critical, however. The drug cartels are under pressure. If they are going to strike back, the time may be now.

Officials Say They Have Leads In Killing of Judge in Alabama

But F.B.I. Discourages Speculation on a Link to Drug Trafficking

PETER APPLEBOME

Special to The New York Times

BIRMINGHAM, Ala., Dec. 17 — Federal officials here said today that they had unearthed and were pursuing a number of leads in the killing of a Federal appellate judge who died instantly Saturday in the explosion of a bomb in a package mailed to his suburban house.

The Federal Bureau of Investigation declined to provide specifics on the investigation other than to discourage speculation that the package bomb that killed the 58-year-old judge, Robert S. Vance, could be the work of Colombian drug traffickers.

But drug cases make up about 60 percent of the caseload of the United States Court of Appeals for the 11th Circuit, on which Judge Vance sat. And associates and other officials said they would not be surprised if drug violence was behind the judge's death.

Other Bombings Nearby

But officials suggested that the incident may have had nothing to do with his work as a judge. In the nearby Birmingham suburb of Hoover, officials say, about six pipe bombs have been left in mailboxes of residents over the past year.

Concern about drug violence led the United States Marshals Service to warn Federal judges and magistrates against opening any packages sent to them, an official of the service said today.

Judge Vance was killed in the kitchen of his spacious brick Colonial house, on a wooded hilltop in the affluent Birmingham suburb of Mountain Brook, shortly before 3 P.M. Saturday. He is the third Federal judge to be assassinated this century. His wife, Helen, who was injured in the blast, was reported in serious condition today with internal injuries, but she spoke with investigators about the incident.

Judge Vance, appointed to the bench by President Jimmy Carter in 1978, was the former Democratic state chairman, and led the Alabama delegation to the party's national convention in Chicago in 1968, the first Alabama delegation ever to include blacks.

The attack brought widespread expressions of sorrow and outrage in Birmingham and the nation. Attorney General Dick Thornburgh said in a statement: "My heart goes out to the family of Judge Vance, who has served with distinction on the 11th Circuit Court of Appeals. Violent acts such as that are at odds with the underlying belief of our nation in the rule of law."

Tom Moore, a special agent for the F.B.I. in Birmingham, said the first day of investigation had turned up numerous leads that were being pursued. He indicated that progress was being made but declined to say how much.

"We're doing so much, we have so many men working it — not just the F.B.I. but the whole law-enforcement community — that we're coming up with things," he said. "Then we're pursuing those, and that leads somewhere else."

Other bureau officials, calling the case "the F.B.I.'s most important investigation," said that the drug link was being investigated but that it was only one of several avenues being pursued.

"Many of his cases were drug cases, as is the situation for all Federal judges these days," Mr. Moore said. "So that's something we can't ignore. But it's no more significant in our investigation at this phase than any other aspect."

Dampening Speculation

Mr. Moore did take pains to dampen speculation that officials believed that the incident could be related to Colombian drug operations. "The slant that's been given to the Colombian drug lords is probably overstated," he said. "It's just one of many possibilities that we're pursuing, and I think there's been a rush to judgment in that regard."

But to people in and out of the judiciary, it was difficult not to see Judge Vance's involvement in drug cases as a major area of concern.

The 11th Circuit comprises Alabama, Georgia and Florida. Judge Vance has heard a number of drug cases in Florida, but court officials say no particularly significant case that came to mind.

John Fernandes, a spokesman for the Drug Enforcement Administration in Miami, said: "Everybody is looking for it to be drug-related because violence tends to be coming more from the drug world than anywhere.

"Most Federal judges hear a lot of drug cases. But this judge may have heard a variety of different types of appeals. These things are complicated. A judge makes a lot of enemies."

Mr. Fernandes added that Federal officials would now "go through a painstaking process to narrow down" Judge Vance's cases.

Other officials said they would begin by reviewing his most recent cases. F.B.I. bomb squad experts were sent here from Washington, and Allen P. Whitaker, the special agent in charge of the F.B.I. here, said his entire staff had been assigned to the case.

The Marshals Service office assigned to Judge Vance's court said he had not been the subject of any threats, and some experts said a trial judge might be a more likely target of a drug-related reprisal than an appellate judge.

But Judge James C. Hill, a senior judge on the court, said the number and violence of the drug cases that come before it make the drug connection an obvious possibility.

"With the violence we regularly see associated with drugs, you almost have to think of drug operations," he said. "It probably has produced more violence than anything that has happened in this country since the Civil War."

William M. Dempsey, a spokesman for the Marshals Service in Washington, said threats and threatening behavior directed at judges have risen dramatically in recent years.

Sorrow and outrage at a bombing in Alabama.

Mr. Dempsey said that judges had been warned in the past to be careful about opening packages. But he added that Judge Vance's death had prompted his office to repeat the message and to add that judges should be suspicious even of packages that seem to be coming from a family member or familiar address. Within 24 hours of Judge Vance's death, he said, marshals across the country were notified by wire to get in touch with each Federal judge or magistrate in their jurisdiction.

There are about 1,500 Federal judges and magistrates. The Marshals Service has 2,000 agents and 1,000 support personnel.

"You can't guard every one of them 24 hours a day," Mr. Dempsey said. "It's a matter of when there's a perceived threat, taking the necesaary action. There's not a day that goes by that we don't have a round-the-clock detail on some Federal judge." But he said protection was more difficult "when they're home and not in the courthouse."

Two Previous Murders

All three Federal judges murdered in this century were killed at home. Federal District Judge Richard Daranco, 56, was shot and killed at his home in May 1988 by a former New York City police officer who was angry at the judge for his dismissal of a sex discrimination suit filed by his daughter. The assailant, 67-year-old Charles Koster, then killed himself.

In 1979, Federal District Judge John H. Wood Jr., 63, was killed by a sniper outside his home in San Antonio. The authorities said the murder had been ordered by a drug trafficker who was to come to trial before Judge Wood.

Other Federal law-enforcement officials here said it was too early to draw any conclusions about a motive.

"The judge had ruled recently in a series of narcotics trafficking cases," said Jack Killorin, a spokesman in Washington for the Bureau of Alcohol, Tobacco and Firearms. "At this point it's only speculation about the motive." Mr. Killorin said he could not cite specific cases that officials were examining.

Judge Vance's caseload was varied. He sat on the three-judge panel last January that denied a stay of execution for the convicted murderer Theodore Bundy, who was then put to death. He recently sat on panels hearing a sex discrimination case against General Motors and the case of whether a 7-year-old AIDS victim could attend school in a glass booth.

Environmentalists Hurt, then Held, in Blast

Katherine Bishop

Special to The New York Times

Oakland, Calif., May 25—When a bomb went off here Thursday night in a car carrying two leaders of a radical environmental group, their supporters were quick to blame opponents of a protest aimed at stopping the logging of redwoods in northern California.

But today, even while environmentalists were calling for an investigation of the timber industry in connection with the bombing, Oakland police officers arrested the two leaders of the group, Earth First. One is under police guard in the hospital where she is being treated for serious injuries.

The two, 40-year-old Judi Bari and 33-year-old Darryl Cherney, were charged with possession and transportation of an explosive device.

'Meant to Be Used'

Lieut. Mike Sims of the Oakland Police Department's homicide unit said the authorities believed that the bomb had been placed in the car by its occupants and that it had detonated accidentally.

"We're making the assumption that if the bomb was built, it was meant to be used," he said.

The developments seemed certain to heighten tension that has been building in timber country since Earth First announced plans for a "Redwood Summer" of demonstrations aimed at stopping the harvesting of old-growth redwoods, and summoned hundreds of college students to Northern California.

Friends of the two people who were arrested and others in the environmental movement were quick to denounce the charges as ridiculous, asserting that timber industry interests or Government officials were responsible for the bombing. Many recalled that leaders of Earth First had reported receiving death threats as the date drew near for the beginning of the protest.

Other Groups Are Wary

The members of Earth First are among the most radical supporters of environmental causes. Indeed, other environmental groups have sought to distance themselves from Earth First, whose slogan is "No Compromise in Defense of Mother Earth." Last month, for example, the Sierra Club came out in opposition to "Redwood Summer," fearing that the protest might result in violence.

Earth First, a loosely organized group that puts its size at about 6,000 people, has carried out a number of actions in its campaign against the timber industry.

In California, the group has been known for its advocacy of a practice known as "tree spiking," in which 10-inch-long nails or other metal objects are driven into trees to prevent loggers from cutting them down. A millworker was seriously injured in California in 1987 when he was hit in the face by a shattered saw blade that had hit a spike in a tree.

In recent months, Ms. Bari has denounced the practice.

The arrests today are not the first charges of illegal activities against members of the group. Four people, including the group's founder, David Foreman, have been indicted in Arizona on charges of trying to fell a 137-foot-high electrical transmission tower that provides power to the Central Arizona Project, a mammoth irrigation system.

The F.B.I. said the attempt was a trial run for the destruction of power lines that provide electricity to the Palo Verdi nuclear power plant in Arizona, the Diablo Canyon nuclear plant in California and the Department of Energy's plutonium fabrication plant in Colorado.

No Other Explosives

The authorities here today declined to give details of their investigation, but they said they had not discovered any more explosives in their searches of Mr. Cherney's van or at a house in Berkeley that serves as the headquarters of Seeds of Peace, a support group for opponents of nuclear weapons. Ms. Bari and Mr. Cherney had attended an organizing meeting for "Redwood Summer" at the house on Wednesday night.

Friends said Ms. Bari and Mr. Cherney were traveling to the University of California at Santa Cruz to recruit students for the protest when the bomb exploded, about noon on Thursday.

Mr. Cherney, who suffered minor injuries, was being held today in the city jail. Ms. Bari was in Highland Hospital, where her condition was listed as serious, with injuries including a fractured pelvis.

Today Mr. Cherney used the one telephone call allowed him by the police to call radio station KMUD-FM, a community-owned station in Garberville, to give a brief interview.

"Somebody's trying to kill us," Mr. Cherney said. "We are demanding, demanding that the Oakland Police Department and the F.B.I. seek out this assassin and bring him to justice immediately."

Supporters Denounce Charges

Friends, family and activists in the environmental movement denounced the charges as ridiculous; some asserted that timber industry interests or Government officials were responsible for the bombing.

At a news conference here today, Susan B. Jordan, a lawyer representing Ms. Bari, said, "This is clearly an attempted murder by someone who did not want them to do nonviolent protest in the redwoods this summer."

Ms. Jordan continued: "This charge is insane. There's a person out there who attempted murder. Why aren't they looking for that person? It's real easy to solve the crime this way, by putting it on the victims. These are radical environmentalists. It's easy to pick on someone who's unpopular."

In a brief telephone interview from her home in Silver Spring, Md., Ruth Bari, Ms. Bari's mother, said: "I'm terribly upset. I don't believe what the police are doing. She has been really emphasizing nonviolence. I can't see any way she would be carrying bombs."

Elizabeth Ball, the coordinator of the Mendocino Environmental Center in Ukiah, about 150 miles north of San Francisco, said: "It's not even a remote possibility. These people are working for the life and survival of all species. Bombing is against everything they believe in. This is another case of blaming the victim."

Threats Were Reported

Ms. Ball said she and Ms. Bari had recently received threats by telephone and in unsigned notes. Three weeks ago, a note was found taped to the door of the center, which serves as the address for the "Redwood Summer" planning, that showed a picture of Ms. Bari's face through the cross hairs of a rifle scope.

Violence has also been directed against timber interests recently. The authorities refused to comment today on whether they believed that the car bombing on Thursday was related to a pipe bomb discovered May 8 at a lumber mill owned by the Louisiana-Pacific Company in Eureka.

Ms. Ball said the center had been flooded with calls today from people all over the country expressing concern for the two activists and promising to participate in "Redwood Summer," which is to begin June 20 with a demonstration in Eureka. The protest is patterned after the "Mississippi Summer" civil rights protests that drew thousands of college students to the South in 1964.

"This tragedy is only going to make 'Redwood Summer' bigger," she said. "It has brought a sense of urgency, solidarity and total commitment."

Terrorism and the Media

The articles in this section have three main emphases. First, they identify and delineate the critical connection between terrorism and the media that flows from the third factor in the terror triangle—the audience (the public). It is the audience that must be effectively intimidated. Second, the articles point up the particular nature of the problem facing democracies, which, with their free presses, offer the best opportunities as targets for terrorists. And third, they focus on the dilemmas and responsibilities of the various media in regard to this form of political violence.

What is immediately apparent in all the articles is the perception that terrorists have evolved about the use of the media, especially the Western media, for conveying their causes, demands, threats, and attempts at intimidation to a wide audience. The media are so critical to terrorists that they have developed special skills and personnel to handle their interactions with them. The terrorists have gained a sense of the value that the public attaches to high drama at the same time that the media have done so.

All five articles in this section identify the stakes in the terrorist-media interaction for those immediately involved. They also address subsequent ramifications (such as copycatism and media hostaging) of terrorist acts.

"Terrorism and the Media: Lessons From the British Experience" is an instructive essay in how different (but still democratic) societies deal with the relationship between the media and terrorism. The British experience might go against democratic values, in the view of many Americans, but it is one worth serious consideration.

Aside from noting the dilemmas for the media in democratic societies, these articles present some of the more sophisticated arguments from the media's perspective. One subtle argument asserts that refusal to cover a story could be construed as censorship, a self-defeating and antidemocratic proposition. By implication, the terrorist wins if the event is publicized; if the story is not told, on the other hand, democratic values are weakened.

The greatest strength of these articles is the inclusion of numerous examples of situations involving terrorism and the media that actually occurred over the years. These concrete cases help the reader to understand the nature and significance of the controversies that arise in the media coverage of terrorist acts.

Looking Ahead: Challenge Questions

How do we know the difference between a news story and terrorist propaganda?

What are the responsibilities of the media in a terrorist situation?

What have been the more common criticisms by governments and even by journalists of media handling of terrorist incidents?

How much of a priority are media considerations in the tactical operations of a terrorist group?

At what point (if any) can a democratic government draw the line on coverage of terrorist activities by the media?

Unit 6

Terrorism and the Media

L. Paul Bremer III

Following is an address by L. Paul Bremer III, Ambassador at Large for Counter-Terrorism, before the International Association of Airline Security Officers, Washington, D.C., June 25, 1987

It is a pleasure for me to be at this important conference and to speak to a group so dedicated to the prevention of terrorist attacks—a goal we share. Your efforts to enhance airline security are commendable. I see from the conference agenda that you are also wrestling with tough issues like international drug smuggling. I hope that your sincere efforts to oppose these threats to the airline industry will bear fruit.

In your business and in mine, terrorism presents a direct threat to our interests and our personnel. From 1980 through 1986 the airline industry was the target of over 300 terrorist attacks on airplanes, airport terminals, corporate and ticket offices, and tourist bureaus. During the same period, diplomats and diplomatic facilities throughout the world were targets in over 1,100 attacks. That means that during the decade to date, an airline or diplomatic establishment was attacked about every 38 hours. While many of these attacks amounted to little more than harassment, many caused catastrophic loss of life. These numbers make it clear just how pervasive terrorism has become.

The Threat to American Diplomats

For me terrorism has a personal side. There are memorial plaques in the State Department lobby listing the names of American diplomats who have died in the line of duty since 1776. When I joined the Foreign Service 21 years ago, there were 81 names on those plaques. All but seven of these diplomats died from earthquakes, plagues, and other nonpurposeful causes. But in the last 21 years, 73 additional names have been added to these plaques, names of Americans serving in U.S. diplomatic missions. In other words, for the first 190 years of our nation's existence, the Foreign Service lost a member to violent, purposeful death about once every 27 years. Since I joined, we have averaged one such loss about every 90 days.

But not just diplomats and not just airlines and not just Americans suffer. Terrorism occurs in most parts of the world, but it is the world's democracies that suffer most. For example, in 1986, 64% of all international terrorist attacks were directed against only three countries—the United States, Israel, and France.

The moral values upon which democracy is based—individual rights, equality under the law, freedom of thought, freedom of religion, and freedom of the press—all stand in the way of those who seek to impose their will or their ideology by force.

The challenge to democracies is to combat terrorism while preserving these deep democratic values. A particularly sensitive issue, and the one I would like to discuss today, is the interplay of the media and terrorism. While virtually all players on the international stage vie for attention and public support, terrorists are unique in the way they use violence against innocents to draw attention to a cause.

Media and Terrorism

Terrorist threats—to our people, to friendly countries, and to democracy itself—are all made more complex by the interplay among media, governments, and terrorists. The very nature of terrorism, its desire to gain the widest possible publicity for its act, makes this complexity inevitable.

Terrorists have always understood that the target was not the physical victim but the wider audience. Their goal is to terrorize citizens in an apparently random way, so that people might lose confidence in their governments. Nineteenth-century Russian terrorists spoke of "propaganda of the deed." Terrorists then could not imagine the power terrorist acts would have in the day of worldwide live television broadcasts.

I'm sure many of us in this room can remember the horror we all felt seeing the 1972 Olympic Games disintegrate into kidnaping, flames, and murder. No doubt the Black September faction of the Palestine Liberation Organization (PLO) chose to attack the Israelis at the Munich Olympics precisely because it guaranteed them a worldwide audience. How many times since then have we all been riveted to our television sets to watch some new act of barbarism unfold.

But we must not fall into the trap of confusing technology with people. The medium is not the message. The message is what reporters and editors decide should be aired, decide what should be printed. What you and I see, hear, and read about terrorism in mass media is the result of multiple decisions made by cameramen, reporters, producers, copywriters, editors, and managers throughout the news industry. When we explore the role of media in terrorism, we are in fact exploring the judgments of dozens of individuals.

Delicate Issues When Covering Terrorist Incidents

The most difficult issue involved is media

Reprinted from U.S. Department of State, *Current Policy #986,* June 25, 1987, pp. 1-3.

coverage of a terrorist incident in progress. Because news organizations, especially electronic media, can have a major impact on the outcome of a terrorist incident, journalists must exercise special care and judgment. Innocent lives can be lost by even the slightest miscalculation on the part of the media. That is why we hope responsible journalists will keep certain specific points in mind as they cover ongoing terrorist incidents.

Journalists covering an incident in progress might take a point from the Hippocratic oath: first, do no harm. We have to assume that terrorists have access to anything published or broadcast about them and the attack they are carrying out. The hand-held television is a fact of life; any airport duty-free shop has excellent, battery-powered shortwave receivers the size of a paperback book; two-way radios are cheap and readily available. It is now possible to put a cellular telephone, a two-way radio, a shortwave receiver, and a television in one ordinary briefcase.

The ability of terrorists to track outside responses to their actions in real or near-real time means that journalists are not just narrating the passing scene. They are players; like it or not, they are involved. This involvement imposes special responsibilities on journalists during a terrorist incident such as an airline hijacking. Just like those of us on the task force in the State Department's Operations Center, just like you ladies and gentlemen responsible for the safety of your passengers, journalists are making decisions which can mean life or death for specific, identifiable individuals.

During hijackings and other incidents of hostage taking, terrorists have—as during the Air France hijacking to Entebbe and the TWA 847 hijacking—segregated victims by race, religion, nationality, or occupation. Indeed, people have been murdered on the basis of these distinctions. Obviously news reports saying things like "22 of the 72 passengers are American citizens" is information which can be useful to terrorists and deadly for hostages.

Even revealing the exact number of hostages can be valuable to terrorists. Six of the American employees of the U.S. Embassy in Tehran spent several weeks hiding with our Canadian friends. Had the terrorists realized their absence they, too, could have been seized. Several news organizations learned of this situation, and—to their credit—did not report it.

The importance of not revealing the number or identity of hostages during hijacking situations was among the topics discussed at a coordinating meeting held in February involving the Department of State, the Federal Aviation Administration (FAA), and chief executive officers and security officers from this country's airlines. During this meeting and at a recent followup meeting, we discussed the proper procedures for channeling such information.

A wide range of people have suggested ways in which the media might address the problems inherent in covering hijackings and other hostage situations. Some have suggested that there be no live coverage of an incident in progress. Others have proposed formal guidelines, perhaps offered by the government, perhaps voluntarily set up by news organizations, perhaps by the two working in concert. After considerable reflection, I believe that U.S. law and custom, our country's profound commitment to freedom of the press, and the individual circumstances of each terrorist incident make it impractical to develop universally accepted guidelines on media's response to terrorism.

Questions for Media Coverage of an Incident

Still, given the media's involvement in terrorist incidents, it seems to me that journalists and their editors should be asking themselves some tough questions as they cover terrorist incidents. Let me suggest eight such questions.

- Have my competitive instincts run away with me? Journalism is a competitive business. Everyone wants to cover the story better, and where possible, sooner than the competition. Occasionally, competitive instinct has overridden common sense. One need only look at the tapes of the Damascus "press conference" with the TWA 847 hostages to see how the pressures for a better camera angle or an answer to a question turned professional journalists quite literally into a mob.
- What is the benefit in revealing the professional and personal history of a hostage before he or she is released? Hostages have been known to misrepresent their marital status, professional responsibilities, career histories and other material facts in their efforts to persuade their captors not to harm them. One former hostage is certain that the lies he told his captors saved his life. It is standard American journalistic practice to report information about victims, but in many other democratic countries that is not the case. In the unique circumstances of political terrorism, even facts verified by family members or coworkers could have deadly consequences.
- When reporting on the statements made by hostages and victims, a journalist might well ask himself or herself: have I given sufficient weight to the fact that all such statements are made under duress? If I decide to go ahead with the report, have I given my audience sufficient warning?
- Should I use statements, tapes and the like provided by the terrorists? How reflective of actual conditions are the materials provided by the terrorists? How much analysis should I offer? How much speculation? Former hostage David Jacobsen recounts the beatings he received when U.S. media reported that messages made at the direction of his captors were said to contain "hidden messages."
- How often should I use live coverage? Should I put a terrorist on TV live? Should I run an unedited statement on the air or in print? To what extent will I serve the terrorists' purposes by so doing? One of the things that distinguishes terrorism from other crimes is the use of real or threatened violence to amplify and advance a political position. Few news organizations run more than brief excerpts of statements by anyone but the President of the United States. Even then, reporting full texts of presidential remarks is limited to special occasions. Giving extensive coverage to terrorist statements may well encourage future acts of terrorism.
- Am I judging sources as critically as I would at other times? Devoting major chunks of space and time to a terrorist incident can create a situation in which it becomes difficult to generate enough solid material to "fill the hole." During terrorist incidents we have all seen reporting of what amounts to nothing more than rumor. Information based on sources responsible news organizations would not normally touch has been given broad circulation during incidents. I have seen stories which should have read something like: "According to the reports of a wire service known to be careless, a newspaper noted for its irresponsibility has reported that anonymous sources in a rumor-plagued city have said. . . ."
- Should I even try to report on possible military means to rescue the hostages? A particularly controversial practice by some news organizations is trying to discover and publish reports on the movements of military forces during a terrorist incident. Such reporting can only end up one of two ways: the report is correct and the news organization runs the risk of having served as an intelligence source for the terrorists; or the report is wrong, in which case it may unduly complicate the resolution of the incident. This subject deserves special attention. Reports on military activities designed to surprise an armed foe are just about as secret as things get.

• What about honest consideration for the family members of victims? One former hostage recounts how his teenage son received a telephone call at 2 a.m. The journalist calling had a question: "The latest reports indicate that your father will be executed in 2 hours. Any response?"

Progress in Media Coverage

It is encouraging to see that responsible journalists are paying increasing attention to the impact their actions have on terrorism. I know that some major news organizations have set up specific internal guidelines for handling terrorist incidents.

It was gratifying to note that major networks declined to broadcast a videotape made in March by one of the hostages in Lebanon. The substance of what was said was reported, but the tape itself—obviously a cynical attempt by the kidnapers to advance their demands—was not aired.

Just as we in government must defend our constitution without abandoning our traditional values, journalists must exercise their judgment in ways which do not jeopardize their traditional role as an independent watchdog. The media need no prompting to resist efforts at manipulation by government. One can hope they exercise the same care at resisting manipulation by terrorists.

How then are we to thwart terrorism? What can we as citizens, as company executives, as journalists, as government officials do to protect ourselves from the multiple threats of terrorism?

UNMASKING TERRORISM

MANIPULATION OF THE MEDIA

Rushworth M. Kidder

A free people needs a free press. But terrorism needs a propaganda platform. So the news media face a dilemma: Is it possible to keep citizens informed of daily events (including the often graphic tragedy of terrorism) without becoming, to some degree, propagandists for the perpetrators?

Belfast

He was out with guests at a restaurant late one evening when the phone call found him.

Rushing back to his office, James Hawthorne, head of the British Broadcasting Corporation (BBC) for Northern Ireland, was met by a slightly white-faced senior editor. The message: A correspondent had just gotten an interview with Evelyn Glenholmes. The question: Should the BBC broadcast it?

Some news executives would instantly have said "Yes!" Ms. Glenholmes was a hot property, a prime suspect in the attempted assassination of British Prime Minister Margaret Thatcher by the Irish Republican Army (IRA) at a Brighton hotel in 1984. Glenholmes had gone underground. Getting her on tape was something of a coup.

But under Britain's Prevention of Terrorism Act, the IRA is an illegal organization. Broadcasting Glenholmes's words might entangle the BBC in legal considerations. Here in Northern Ireland, only the finest of lines separates reporting on terrorism (which is legal) from providing a propaganda platform for terrorists (which is not).

Which was it here? When BBC correspondent Anne Cadwallader had been approached in Dublin by several IRA members, she didn't have time to call Belfast for advice. Her instincts told her to go with them in their car. She was hooded and taken to a house somewhere in Dublin, where she met a young woman who said her name was Evelyn Glenholmes.

Listening to the tape later, Mr. Hawthorne heard a woman's voice protesting her innocence. Was it really Glenholmes? The Dublin correspondent could not have been expected to recognize her. Even if authentic — and even if legal — would the broadcast stir up a hornet's nest of criticism?

In such a case, says Hawthorne, the news executive has

Reprinted by permission from *The Christian Science Monitor,* May 16, 1986, pp. 18-20.

to make "a very, very careful judgment as to where this inherently difficult decision is going to land [him] with public relations and the reputation of the BBC."

"I had a gut feeling that it was proper to do it — an instinct that this was *real* news. I made that decision between 1 a.m. and 3 a.m." Then Hawthorne did his legal duty: He phoned the relevant authorities at 3 a.m. — knowing he would get only a duty officer who would have to wait until morning to refer the information higher — and went home. The story went out with the first morning news.

Is it news or terrorist propaganda?

In the fast-paced world of breaking news, even such apparently simple stories can involve agonizing decisions. Yet when such stories do go out, what is their effect?

Do they contribute to the free marketplace of ideas, helping the citizenry to understand the central issues of their day? Or do they give terrorists a megaphone through which to spread their message of fear to their ultimate target — the public at large?

Do the news media, in Mrs. Thatcher's words, provide "the oxygen of publicity" on which terrorism thrives? Or do they in Hawthorne's words, "allow people of the most seditious views to speak them," so that in the end "they don't have to express them in the hard way?"

Does extensive media coverage lead to what Jerrold M. Post, a psychiatrist with Defense Systems Inc., in Washington, D.C., calls a "Robinhoodization" of the terrorists, inflating them to the proportion of folk heroes? Or does such coverage produce what Paul Wilkinson, a terrorism authority at the University of Aberdeen in Scotland, calls "the outrage effect" — public revulsion of terrorist acts and demands for tougher governmental measures?

Does journalism interfere with official efforts to resolve crises, either by giving away essential information or, as Die Zeit political editor Dieter Buhl notes, by putting "so much pressure on the government" that it acts without due care? Or does it provide needed information to officials, since in hostile situations reporters can sometimes go where government decisionmakers cannot?

Finally, are the media hooked on terrorism? "Terrorism is drama," says Noel Koch, who oversees the Pentagon's counterterrorism efforts. "It's got suspense, it's got grievance, it's got people at risk, it's got the families that are crying; you can't duplicate it in fiction."

So do the media, in an effort to captivate viewers, turn to terrorist incidents whenever possible? Or do they simply report what they find, and try hard, as Alan Protheroe, assistant director general of the BBC, says, to do it "responsibly, accurately, with total care, and with total fairness in the things that [we] do not advocate"?

On these and other points there are vehement disagreements, not only among students of terrorism but within the broader public. On three points, however, there is basic consensus:

- Television is the terrorist's medium of choice. It is far preferable to print or radio as the outlet with the most immediacy and the most terrifying impact.
- Television is no longer simply reporting *about* the story: It has become *part of* the story. Making that point, Lawrence K. Grossman, president of NBC, calls television "the stage on which terrorist incidents are played."
- In the never-ending debate about the role of the news media in a free democracy, television is at the center of an ongoing controversy — and terrorism is Exhibit A.

Terrorists' growing media skills

Paul Nahon, news director at France's second television channel, Antenne-2, has a front-seat view of the terrorists' news-management skills. One of his four-man camera crews is being held hostage in Lebanon. The terrorists have colleagues in France who monitor everything said about the situation and pass it back to the captors.

In deciding how to cover the story, he says, "we have to be very, very careful every day. [The terrorists] are managing all this like professionals — professional politics, professional dramatism."

One of the noticeable developments in recent years, in fact, lies in the increasingly skillful use of publicity by terrorist organizations. "The vice-president for media relations," says Dr. Post, referring only half in jest to the individual within nearly every terrorist group who orchestrates media coverage.

With the growth of inexpensive videotape equipment, these groups are increasingly able to provide news organizations with television-ready footage: messages from terrorist leaders, interviews with captives, and even (in the case of British journalist Alec Collett, who disappeared in Lebanon in March 1985) visual records of executions.

Yasser Arafat's Palestine Liberation Organization now owns a share in an Arab communications satellite, leading one observer to wonder whether the world will soon see a new network, "Television Arafat."

And, as last summer's hijacking of TWA Flight 847 in Beirut showed, terrorists are getting very good at organizing press conferences and handling requests for interviews: A tour of the plane was reportedly offered to the networks for $1,000, and a session with the hostages themselves could be had for $12,500.

While NBC's Mr. Grossman likes to recount figures from a Gallup poll showing that 89 percent of Americans applauded television's coverage of the TWA incident, other observers, especially overseas, where television coverage is more understated, are less approving. "What [the American] media did in Lebanon during the TWA hijacking was disastrous," says Hans Josef Horchem, former head of West German domestic security and a recognized expert on counterterrorism. "It not only hurt the interests of the security forces, it was a question of taste."

In retrospect, says Ari Rath, editor of the Jerusalem Post, the TWA incident "is probably a very good example of very sophisticated use by hijackers and terrorists of the media."

To report or not to report

Mr. Rath, who like all other Israeli editors operates under a carefully organized form of governmental censorship, feels the tug between journalist and citizen.

"When you work as an Israeli journalist, you also have the other part in you, and that is your security awareness." He cites an example of a terrorist bombing several years ago that made use of a new method: a bicycle frame filled with TNT. When his paper reported how the bomb was made, the censor chastised him, showing point by point how his article had hindered both immediate and long-term police work. "It was an eye-opener," says Rath, who remains persuaded that his paper did the wrong thing. "One could have given a very good and grim and realistic description of that particular bombing incident without giving away some details which really did harm the investigation."

THE ETHICS OF REPORTING TERRORISM

How do the Western news media see their role in reporting terrorism? Interviews with leading journalists and news executives in Europe, America, and Israel suggest agreement on one principle — the media should be as free as possible. Beyond that, there are widely divergent views.

Eberhard Pilz, commentator, Association of Public Broadcasting Stations (ARD Television), Bonn

"Is it the role of the press to fight terrorism, or is it the role of the press to report what's going on?"

"Censorship is to be ruled out, that's not even something we should seriously discuss. [But] I'm not feeling that I am betraying my profession if I say that we have to have self-restraint. There are no imposed regulations [in West Germany], but there is a certain degree of understanding among all the participants. We as journalists need to be aware of the role we are playing, and the risks for society if the journalist lets himself be used by the terrorists to magnify whatever their intentions are. But an event is an event — you can't mute the media. [Instead,] you have to educate the audience to behave differently . . . to get this competition a bit more civilized."

Nachman Shai, director, Galei Zahal (Army Radio), Tel Aviv

"[The news media] sometimes seem to create a situation which plays into their own hands. The press is not passive anymore."

"If there is a general understanding that we have to fight terrorism, why should we make it harder? In some cases, the media do not represent the public anymore. In some cases the media force the public to know more than it really wants. I don't trust the networks . . . and especially the American networks. They will not lose any picture which shows . . . tragedy, emotions, something which will help them to attract viewers. Afterwards they will be very sorry, and they will send condolences to the families, but when it takes place [another time] they will fight each other [again]. . . . If they have 100 producers, reporters, cameramen, [and other] crew all over, they need to find something to do. They need to show that their mission was not in vain, that they did something."

Alan Protheroe, assistant director general of the British Broadcasting Corporation, London

"You're living in a democracy . . . . I believe that the public is entitled to know what and why [terrorists] are doing what they're doing."

"[My] journalistic assessment goes like this: Does what I am reporting actually enhance and add to the sum of information available to the viewer so that he may make up his mind? I still have the highest regard for the three [American commercial] networks. I have to say that I'm a great fan of the American technology and a lot of the journalistic practices that you have. [But] I think a national broadcaster of that caliber, of that importance or relevance to the community, has got imposed upon him . . . certain standards and certain concepts and precepts that you don't run from. You draw a line and say, 'No, I am sorry, there are standards of taste and standards of decency and standards of journalistic behavior,' . . . you draw a line and nobody crosses it."

Ted Koppel, anchor, ABC Television's "Nightline"

"The American media stretch the outer boundaries of what may seem acceptable to our European allies."

"[American television is] particularly vulnerable to misuse. We are vulnerable to misuse by our own leaders. We are vulnerable to misuse by our international adversaries. And they obviously include terrorists. The fact that terrorism by definition tends to be dramatic, [and] the fact that by definition it tends to involve acts which are pictorial, makes us even more vulnerable. [But] don't make the mistake of jumping to the conclusion that the immediate impact of that day's visual message is the final impact. The American media . . . operate under what ultimately is our basic assumption in this country, a Jeffersonian notion, that if you allow the public access to all the information, no matter how dramatic or devastating it may be at any given point, ultimately they will reach the proper conclusions."

On one point, there is basic consensus: Television is the terrorists' medium of choice.

It is far preferable to print or radio as the outlet with the most immediacy and the most terrifying impact.

WAS IT NEWS OR A BULLY PULPIT?

The decision whether or not to broadcast or publish interviews with admitted terrorists brings journalists to the fine line between news and a forum for propaganda.

Should known terrorists be interviewed on television?

Wherever that question arises in the West, it provokes emotional discussion. Yes, say those who defend free and uncensored journalism. No, say those who complain that the news media are little more than collaborators in spreading terrorist propaganda.

When the question arose in Britain last August — over a BBC television interview with Irish Republican Army leader Martin McGuinness (which was pulled at the last minute by a skittish board of governors) — the furor rose to the prime minister's office before the program was eventually allowed to run.

This sort of flap has now crossed the Atlantic, in the form of two-minute interview on NBC News May 5. The subject: Abul Abbas, the alleged mastermind behind last October's seajacking of the Italian cruise liner Achille Lauro. According to Mr. Abbas, his 1,200-strong Palestine Liberation Front now plans to bring its campaign of terrorism to the United States, to "respond against America, in America itself." Abbas also noted that "[President] Reagan has now placed himself as enemy No. 1."

The interview caused an outcry. Ambassador Robert B. Oakley, head of the State Department's counterterrorism office, accused NBC of being an accomplice to terrorism by giving Abbas publicity. A State Department spokesman noted that NBC's action might "encourage the terrorist activities which we are all seeking to deter."

What galled many observers, however, was not what Abbas said but the circumstances under which he said it. Terrorists, whose central tactic is to inspire fear, typically bluster and threaten. But should they be allowed their bully pulpit during America's prime-time news? And was NBC right to have agreed, as a condition of getting the interview, not to disclose the name of the "Arabic-speaking country" where Abbas was interviewed?

New York Times foreign editor Warren Hoge noted that his paper refused to interview Abbas under similar conditions, since "the most important news was his whereabouts" and "not being able to say where he was, was just unacceptable."

NBC officials, however, defended their decision on classic freedom-of-the-press grounds: Abbas, they said, was a newsmaker, and the American people have a right to know about terrorism. Cable News Network's Ted Turner, quoted in Broadcasting magazine, sided with NBC. "Once you start not running interviews [with controversial personalities], where do you stop?"

"What is more important," muses Rath, "to have the one-time scoop or save lives?"

Should the media, then, not publicize full details of terrorist incidents? Ambassador Robert B. Oakley, director of the US State Department's Office of Counter-Terrorism and Emergency Planning, thinks not. "There's a long history of what you might call copycatism [and] competitiveness, [especially] among Middle East terrorist groups."

His point was substantiated when the Feb. 28 assassination of Swedish Prime Minister Olof Palme was followed less than 36 hours later by the assassination of Zafer Masri, the mayor of the West Bank city of Nablus, under almost identical circumstances.

Observers also call attention to the news media's reporting of counterterrorism measures taken by security forces. During the siege of the Iranian Embassy in London in 1980, recalls the BBC's Mr. Protheroe, journalists were puzzled when a Thames Gas Board van came through police cordons, parked very close to the building, and produced several men with jackhammers who drilled up the street.

At the time, journalists were told it was to shut off the gas in case of an explosion. Later, they learned that the jackhammers provided noise cover for the Special Air Service commandos, who were drilling peepholes through the embassy walls from the building next door.

"I think you've got to report that," says Protheroe, although he would not want it reported while the incident was under way. His reason: to keep the electorate as fully informed as possible.

Censorship vs. self-regulation

Throughout the debate on the media's role, one call stands out: the need for journalistic self-regulation and not censorship. First, censorship would clearly violate one of the treasured cornerstones of democracy: a free press. "One of the biggest victories terrorists could ever achieve," notes NBC's Grossman, "would be to force democracies to adopt the repressive press restrictions of dictatorships."

But there is a second and more subtle reason: Given the pace of today's technology, censorship simply would not work. The anticipated threat: satellite television, beamed from any part of the world and receivable by viewers anywhere. In Europe, where some of the state-run television networks have worked out (1) fairly high standards of taste and (2) agreements with national security forces to withhold or delay broadcasts in certain cases, there is broad concern about the effect of general access to the major US networks.

If European television had to face pressure from American television, says Peter Goebel of West Germany's second television channel, ZDF, "I'm almost sure [the European stations] won't be able to keep their principles."

Nachman Shai, director of Israeli Army Radio and a former television journalist, finds the situation doubly difficult in Israel, where foreign television crews are a constant presence. However much Israeli journalists might choose not to broadcast certain pictures, he says, "there is such competition it is almost impossible to stop pictures from getting out."

Is such competition good or bad? How free should the media be? Again, there is serious disagreement.

"The disadvantages of the public not being accurately informed, or being informed only by administration spokesman, are too severe in our society," says former Central Intelligence Agency chief Stansfield Turner. "While I decry the media releasing secrets as much as they do, I would never think of trying to organize a government censorship bureau."

But Rand Corporation scholar Paul B. Henze sees a need for greater controls on the media. "What has been gained by all of the minute media reporting on terrorism? Whose interests have been served? Who has learned something? I find it very hard to think very readily of what good has been done by just simply tantalizing people."

But, putting the problem in another perspective, he notes that the criticism may well be overblown. "If the media had had as much deleterious impact as many critics of the media think," he quips, "we'd all be finished."

Terrorism on TV — Who are the Real Hostages?

MICHAEL ELKIN
Special to the Tribune

Is television news being held hostage by terrorists? Are the networks, by their willingness to report hijackings and related incidents of terrorism, accomplices to the very crimes they cover? Is the evening news becoming more and more a forum for anti-Israeli sentiment as terrorists trade hostages' lives for the promise of two minutes of air time?

Television news and terrorism — an uneasy dance of two nervous partners.

"TV has a love affair with violence," said Daniel Schorr, former network correspondent for both CBS and Cable News Network. And terrorism, added Schorr, currently a correspondent for National Public Radio, is the medium's latest sweetheart, albeit one with a sordid past and an apparently more destructive future.

Should networks be held accountable for the news they broadcast? Is "terrorvision," as television news coverage of terrorism has been called, a public service or a public outrage?

Interviews with broadcasters, television news executives, government officials, specialists in terrorism and media critics reveal a complex and controversial picture of television policy regarding how to deal with hostages and hijackings. Depending on the individual interviewed, television news is either a victim of guilt by association or is guilty of sacrificing sound judgment in return for successful ratings.

"Television has unquestionably become a primary vehicle for terrorists in search of an audience," said Larry Grossman, president of NBC-TV News.

Addressing a gathering of radio and television news directors and journalists at a forum in Columbus, Ohio, Grossman concerned himself with the role television news is playing in a volatile global situation. "Television coverage gives terrorists status; it enables them, at least briefly, to transcend their underdog role," he said.

It also adds to the problem, Grossman believes. "The very existence of television undoubtedly bears some responsibility for the 'copycat' syndrome of terrorism today."

Nevertheless, Grossman endorses continuing coverage of terrorism. "If television ever failed to report major episodes, we would find ter-

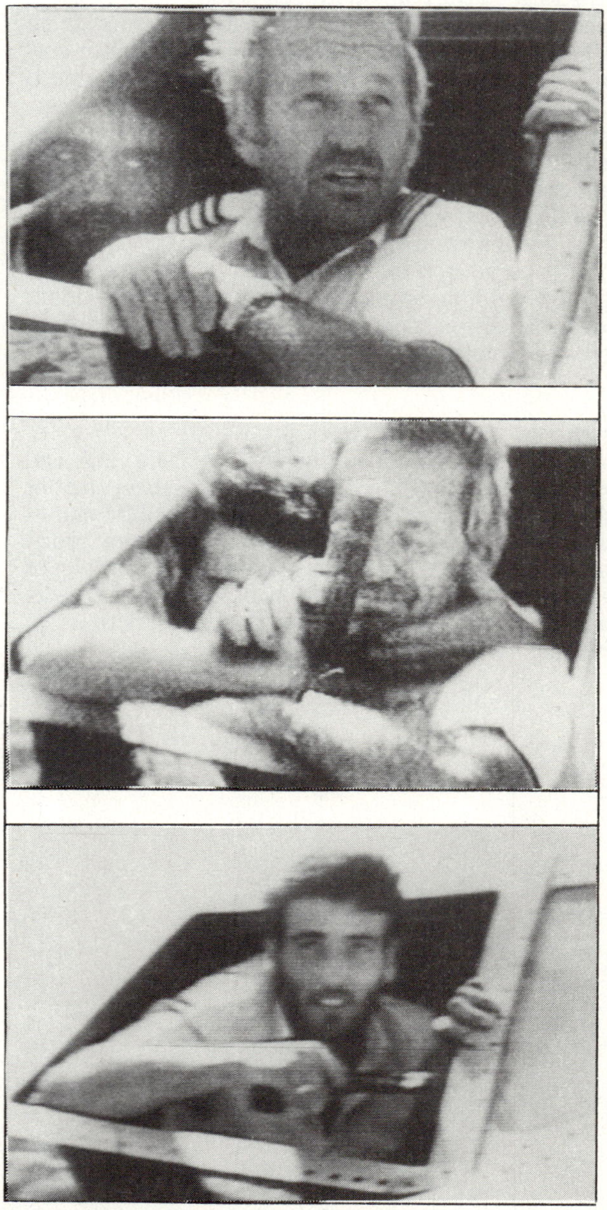

An armed terrorist holds a gun on Trans World Airlines pilot John Testrake at Beirut Airport, during the 1985 hijacking of the American airliner. From top to bottom, the gunman stands behind the pilot, waves his gun in front of the pilot and pulls him in, and tells the ABC news crew to leave. The photos were made off a television screen, courtesy of ABC News.
Photos by AP/Wide World

rorists escalating their actions to gain attention. Our guiding principle should be: It is always better to cover it than cover it up."

Whether better or not, it is undeniably good television. "It is hard to imagine a more seductive story for television" than terrorist activities, said William C. Adams, a professor in the public administration department of George Washington University and editor of *Television Coverage of the Middle East.*

Good Guys vs. Bad Guys

"It has every classic element — good guys vs. bad guys, a simple dramatic story with enormous human interest and with lives at stake. It's a continuing saga, with the element of 'stay tuned.' "

But this is no ordinary soap opera. While the terrorist victims of a "Dynasty" or "Dallas" can pick themselves up off the floor after being shot to death and go on to another series, real victims face real death.

"Terrorism on TV *is a simple dramatic story, with enormous human interest and with lives at stake. It's a continuing saga, with the element of 'stay tuned.'*"

George Will, a commentator on ABC-TV's *This Week With David Brinkley*, has addressed the problem in the past as part of a panel focusing on the issue. The competition among the three major networks virtually guarantees that there will be maximum coverage of anything spectacular and telegenic."

"Terrorists scare us into paying attention," added Roger Rosenblatt, essayist for *Time* magazine and contributor to PBS' *MacNeil/Lehrer News Hour*. "We're drawn in by our natural nose for noise."

But if there is no one there to hear the noise, would terrorism still exist? Joel Swerdlow, consultant to the Annenberg Washington Program in Communications Policy Studies of Northwestern University, is not so sure.

"To a large degree," said Swerdlow, "what defines terrorism is if it gets attention. Yet I've heard the argument that if terrorists don't get attention, they would just raise the ante."

L. Paul Bremer III, State Department ambassador at large for counter-terrorism, is firm in his belief that coverage ensures chaos. "Can there be anyone who believes that the Black September faction of the PLO chose to attack the Israelis at the Munich Olympics for any reason save the guarantee of a worldwide audience for their actions?"

"Terrorists make terrorism for the same reason people make potato chips," said Will. "It pays." Yet, the columnist added, terrorists know that viewers, like audiences who have seen one too many adventure films, are on the constant lookout for new thrills.

"The 'Indiana Jones phenomenon' will undoubtedly come to affect terrorism," he said. "That is, just when the sense of the public seems saturated, terrorists will find new ways to lacerate people's sensibilities."

And there will most likely be a camera crew awaiting them.

"Since outlaws cannot buy TV time, they have to earn it through terrorist acts," Charles Krauthammer, senior editor of the *New Republic*, has been quoted as saying. "Media terrorists now provide drama — murder and kidnapping, live — in return for advertising time."

Benjamin Bagdikian, media critic and dean of the journalism school at the University of California at Berkeley, thinks not all terrorists turn to television as their ultimate forum. "Not all terrorists want television coverage; they have other goals," he said. "For instance, there was the case of an Air India airline blown up in midair. There were no cameras there to show the event."

Media Collaboration

But that, according to many, may have been an anomaly. "Network news is being held hostage, metaphorically speaking," said Fred Friendly. Director of Columbia University seminars on "Media and Society," Friendly's broadcast career spans half a century, including his role as originator and executive producer of *CBS Reports* and producer of *See It Now* with Edward R. Murrow.

"There's a quote — it's not mine — that what the president wants is in the national interest; what the media wants is in the human interest. It's society that is being held hostage," said Friendly.

"The media are collaborators" on terrorism, argues Yoram Dinstein, a professor of international law at Tel Aviv University and currently a visiting professor at the New York University school of law. "The only sollution is censorship."

Israeli Ofra Bikel, a producer for PBS' *Frontline*, agreed that "the media are collaborators. Hostages don't have a choice in their situation; television networks do."

Offering a behind-the-scenes perspective, Ed Turner, executive vice president of CNN, contended that "coverage of terrorism is complicated by the knowledge that you are dealing with human lives. There's always the rationale to give a little air time to relieve pressure."

Dan Rather, anchor for the CBS Evening News, thinks the spotlight of attention is being misdirected. "The problem is the terrorists, not all the people who call attention to the terrorists and what they're doing," he said. "The press is being manipulated, we're being manipulated, all of us are being manipulated, but I'd rather be seeing these hostages alive and well at a press conference with television news cameras around than when cameras are not around."

Indeed, said Dick Wald, senior vice president of ABC-TV News, "the presence of cameras stopped terrorists from shooting more people" during the TWA hijacking in 1985.

There are those who contend that when networks do cover acts of terrorism, they do not do a very good job. "What they don't do very well," said Altheide, "is provide context; we get a real snapshot of history." Television journalists have "learned some minor and insignificant lessons."

There have been lessons to learn, agreed Ted Koppel, host of ABC-TV's *Nightline*, a program that evolved from a nightly report of the Iran hostage situation during the Jimmy Carter presidency. The hijacking of TWA Flight 847 in 1985 allowed for a lesson or two. "We learned to be more cautious," said Koppel. "We learned to exercise more care, to watch out more for manipulation."

Yet, Koppel has not been above reproach from those who question the value of having known terrorists interviewed on television. After the terrorist takeover of the *Achille Lauro* pleasure-cruise ship in 1985, *Nightline* featured Yasser Arafat as a guest. "There will always be people with whom we disagree," said Koppel at the time, defending the Arafat interview. "But I don't think we can maintain our consistency with the system we cherish so much if we single people out and do not cover them."

George Will contends that journalists really are not prepared to cover terrorism today. "The dominant kind of terrorism today, the kind we should be discussing, is what Secretary of State George Shultz has called state-sponsored terrorism.

"It is not a television psychodrama and thus is far beyond the capacity of journalists to deal with."

Yet deal with it they do. "The media," said Jeffrey Cohen of Fairness and Accuracy in Reporting, "covers terrorism like a sporting event,' with easy emphasis on "scoring wins."

"It trivializes." How can someone deal seriously with a medium, asks Cohen, whose motto is "If it bleeds, it leads."

Marvin Kalb, former chief diplomatic correspondent for NBC News and host of *Meet the Press*, finds that "there is some evidence that journalists are trying to be responsible. I know at NBC, there were guidelines on how to cover the next major event."

"We've all learned from every episode" of terrorism, said Tom Brokaw, anchor for NBC's evening news program. "Sure, there's a need to put incidents in context. But if the TV camera didn't exist, there would still be terrorism. These are deep-seated ideologies and passions that will be there without the cameras."

But the presence of cameras can make terrorism a more viable alternative to negotiation when it comes to winning demands.

"Television humanized the enemy," said Zbigniew Brzezinski, national security adviser from 1977 to 1981, addressing the problem for an article in the September 21, 1985, editor of *TV Guide*.

Former Secretary of State Henry Kissinger agreed in the same article. "I object to letting the terrorists stage performances for American television during which they state their demands," he said. "That may create an incentive to kidnap people in order to get on television."

While stating he is not calling for government censorship, Kissinger added, "I believe the networks might consider some self-limiting guidelines."

Encouraging Terrorism?

In a survey by *Glamour* magazine last year, 85 percent of those responding said that television news coverage encourages even more terrorism. More than 50 percent of those asked claimed that government should limit press coverage of terrorism, while 92 percent called for the press to monitor its way of handling such news.

"Terrorism has to be analyzed carefully," said Dr. John A. Sparks, president of the Public Policy Education Fund Inc., a non-profit research corporation in Grove City, Pa. Television, he said, should stress "over and over again that these are illegal, barbaric acts" terrorists are committing.

"What's missing from the stories being reported is the 'why'," said Jack G. Shaheen, professor of mass communications at Southern Illinois University at Edwardsville and author of *The TV Arab*. "We fail to go beyond the report itself. Commercial networks are a headline news service with an occasional in-depth report."

Television can serve as an arbiter of terrorist demands on a government. David Bar-Ilan, a founder of Artists and Writers for Peace in the Middle East, tackled this issue in *The Media's War Against Israel*.

The hijackers of the TWA flight had several demands, he notes, but television focused on but one: the release of 700 incarcerated Lebanese in Israel. "By sticking to this demand alone," said Bar-Ilan, the hijackers "had television networks throughout the West acting as their mouthpiece and at their disposal the round-the-clock service of the world's most influential opinion-makers."

Continued Bar-Ilan, "Like the media, they themselves quickly dropped all other demands and concentrated on Israel. Over and over again, television commentators, anchormen and reporters, alternating hints with accusations

What's missing from the stories is the 'why'. We fail to go beyond the report itself. Commercial networks are a headline news service, with an occasional in-depth report."

and assuming the roles of negotiators, arbiters and moralizers, portrayed Israel as an ungrateful ally, that had freed 1,150 convicted murderers in return for three Israeli soldiers, but would not free 700 innocent Lebanese to save the lives of American tourists."

The matter was not helped any, Bar-Ilan maintained, by the way questions were composed by other reporters. In an interview with Georgetown University fellow Geoffrey Kemp, Bryant Gumbel of the *Today* show asked, "Will Israel compromise on the TWA hostages or play fast and loose with American lives?"

Unelected Officials

In a way, television broadcasters serve as unelected public officials, helping to make public policy or, at the very least, shaping the opinions of millions.

"When TV reporters interview kidnappers, it inevitably complicates the job of the president," said Alexander Haig, former secretary of state. "Also, it risks making international outlaws seem like responsible personalities."

"There is no question that the press plays a major role in the evolution of public policy," said Marvin Kalb, director of the newly established Joan Shorenstein Barone Center on the Press, Politics and Public Policy at the John F. Kennedy School of Government at Harvard University." How does one handle that?"

Grossman has some thoughts on the topic. "In hostage situations, when millions get to see, and to some extent, get to know individual victims, the pressure to free the captives intensifies. The more the people know, the more authorities feel impelled to act — if only to overcome the appearance of impotence."

While this may influence public policy, government officials are not above using media coverage to promote their own goals. "The authorities themselves," added Grossman, "are not without major resources in using television's coverage of terrorist outrages to mobilize public opinion. Witness the Reagan administration's campaign against Muammar Ghadaffi."

Nevertheless, there are times when the networks play president themselves. NBC received some flak for broadcasting an exclusive interview with Abul Abbas, accused of plotting the *Achille Lauro* hijacking. The network refused to reveal Abbas' whereabouts at a time when the U.S. government was desperately seeking him.

Also under attack was David Hartman who, as co-host at the time of ABC-TV's *Good Morning, America,* asked Nabih Berri, involved in negotiations for the release of the TWA hostages, "Any final words to President Reagan this morning?"

Journalists should remember their priorities, said Fred Friendly. "I am a citizen first, a journalist second."

Exactly, noted Zbigniew Brzezinski at the time of the TWA hijacking. "A kidnapping or an act of terrorism is something akin to a wartime situation, and I would have thought that patriotism would have played some role in guiding their [networks] decision."

Patriotism has nothing to do with news coverage, argues Brokaw, who expressed "shock" over Friendly's statement of priorities. "Reporters have an obligation to be professional journalists," and national and jingoisitic concerns are secondary, he believes.

The Ratings Game

Is getting the best story the prime motivation for these reporters — or is there a less admirable reason?

"I think crass commercialism does dominate the medium," said Brzezinski. Altheide agrees. "Older rules are thrown aside in favor of technique and being first."

"Network executives are not naive," said Dr. Baruch Gitlis, director of the Harry Karren Institute for Propaganda Analysis in Tel Aviv. "They want to make money. They say they do it for the public service, but what service? The answer is money."

Ratings as the prime motivator for covering terrorism? "That's nonsense," says Turner of CNN. "We don't create the events. If you have a hostage-taking story, it would be truly irresponsible not to report it. If all we were after is ratings, networks would go after more tabloid stories."

Jody Powell, press secretary for President Carter from 1977 to 1981, begs to differ. He told one reporter, "The cause of excess by television in reporting hostage situations is not ideological basis; it's motivated by money.

"Excess tends to play into the hands of these yahoos and people who don't believe in the First Amendment and the free flow of information. The dumbest part of television's performance," he added, "was the tendency to jeopardize those fundamental things in the interest of some very short-termed striving for ratings."

Jack Shaheen agrees. "Network executives have to stop perceiving news as a means to make money," he said. "You've got to get back to the notion of news as a public service."

But can the public be served by what some call headline news coverage?

"Television has changed everything," said Ofra Bikel of *Frontline*. "There is no reality anymore; there is no truth."

According to NBC's Grossman and Dick Wald, senior vice president of ABC News, television coverage certainly has not helped the terrorists. "In view of the escalating public hostility toward terrorism, it does not appear that television has helped the terrorist's image any," said Grossman." In fact, the most vivid picture to emerge from the TWA crisis was that of the hooded terrorist with one hand clamped over the mouth of the TWA pilot and the other hand holding a gun, hardly an image calculated to win converts."

Wald agrees. "In the past decade," he said, "there has been no instance of terrorists gaining anything with the public but disapprobation. The public rejects terrorism. The public is not stupid."

Perception, of course, is relative. "We Chinese have an expression," said Bernard Yoh of the watchdog group Accuracy in Media. "The wise learn from other people's mistakes; the not-so-wise learn from their own mistakes; and those who do not learn from their own mistakes are doomed to eternal stupidity."

And where does that leave television journalism vis-a-vis its coverage of terrorism?

Doomed for eternity, answered Yoh.

The Silent Treatment for Terrorists

SUMMARY: Provoked by the dramatic increase in violence by Northern Ireland's terrorists, the British government is resorting to a crackdown that curbs their access to the media and denies accused terrorists the right to clam up under questioning with impunity. The broadcast ban is similar to one in effect in the Republic of Ireland since the 1970s.

Though Prime Minister Margaret Thatcher of Britain has enjoyed many successes throughout the 1980s, she has been afflicted with one persistent headache: how to deal with the Provisional Irish Republican Army and the situation in Northern Ireland. This is no accident. Already in the early Seventies, while incarcerated in the Maze prison outside of Belfast, Irish revolutionary Gerry Adams, writing under the code name Brownie, formulated the policies that would come to fruition under the Thatcher administration.

The primitive tactics of earlier generations were insufficient, he asserted. To update them, Adams, who later became leader of Sinn Fein, the political arm of the IRA, outlined a strategy that came to be known as "the Armalite and the ballot box" — guns and votes. Engaging in parliamentary politics while at the same time continuing bombings and other armed attacks was meant to give the IRA a more respectable image.

In its latest policy review, the British government has announced two new measures to counter the IRA strategy. One is a ban on television and radio broadcasts of interviews or direct statements by members of the outlawed IRA along with nine other organizations. These include Sinn Fein and the opposing Protestant Ulster Defense Association. Neither is proscribed, but the British government considers both of them apologists for those who resort to violence.

The other measure concerns the right of a suspect to remain silent. While in the past, the silence of a suspect could not be held against him, a judge will now be able to draw such inferences as he deems proper from the refusal of a suspect to speak. (This policy will also be extended to England and Wales to cover other serious crime.) The ban on the broadcasting of interviews immediately took effect; the law regarding the right of silence easily passed Nov. 9 in the House of Commons, where the Conservatives enjoy a 101-seat majority.

These steps were taken in response to increased IRA activity over the past year, most notably the Nov. 8, 1987, bombing in Enniskillen, Northern Ireland, which killed 11 persons at an outdoor service on Remembrance Day, the British equivalent of Veterans Day. The immediate cause of the policy review was the killing of eight soldiers during an IRA attack on a bus outside the town of Ballygawley in County Tyrone in August. Altogether, 88 persons have been killed in Northern Ireland so far this year, 51 of them civilians.

The broadcasting ban is designed, in the words of Thatcher, to deprive terrorists and their apologists of "the oxygen of publicity," which stimulates recruitment and confers an aura of respectability and legitimacy. Says Ian Stewart, minister of state for Northern Ireland, "We want to put an end to the practice of providing an easy platform for people who represent groups such as Sinn Fein and the UDA in Northern Ireland, who support political action by means of violence."

The rationale for limiting the lawful right to silence, according to Stewart, is that in recent years groups such as the IRA have developed a particular expertise in clamming up when taken into police custody. As a result, a growing number have had to be released.

In Northern Ireland, the jury system for trials of accused terrorists has been dispensed with since 1973 because of threats against jurors. Instead, accused terrorists are tried by a judge in so-called Diplock courts, named after a commission chaired by the late Lord Diplock, who held that "a frightened juror is a bad juror."

The measures also mark a new stage in the Thatcher government's long-running battle with the broadcast media. The government has repeatedly urged British broadcasters to be self-restrained in their reporting of terrorism. The prime minister is said to have become particularly angry when the British Broadcasting Corp. and Independent Television News initially refused to hand over to the Royal Ulster Constabulary film of a March incident in which two British army corporals were pulled out of a car by a furious mob attending a funeral and subsequently tortured and killed by the IRA.

Both measures immediately raised controversy. The British Broadcasting Corp. has stated that government interference in the news-gathering process may establish a dangerous precedent. Says one BBC journalist, "It suggests that broadcasters cannot be relied upon to behave responsibly when it comes to interviewing the IRA and IRA sympathizers. We are a little uncertain of where it may lead."

Broadcasters further stress the inconsistency of prohibiting Sinn Fein from having access to the broadcasting media, while at the same time allowing it to function openly as a political party.

In protest, BBC journalists called for a 24-hour news strike Nov. 10. Those in favor of the strike want the network to make clear in broadcasts from Northern Ireland that the reports are subject to restrictions, which the BBC already does in reports from South Africa.

On the political front, the opposition Labor Party has accused the government of overreacting and of eroding civil and human rights. Allowing judges to interpret a defendant's silence, so Labor Deputy Leader Roy Hattersley has opined, puts at risk the "verbally inadequate." According to Kevin MacNamara, chief Labor spokesman on Northern Ireland, the measures constitute an attack on one of the fundamental principles of British justice, the presumption of innocence. "To allow a cherished right in the British legal system to be altered is giving an additional victory to the Provisional IRA."

MacNamara also fears that it will harm the understanding of Britain's Northern Ireland policy abroad, particularly among Americans who hold their First and Fifth Amendment rights dear.

For their part, says one Sinn Fein member, the measures mark "one more attempt by the British to silence Sinn Fein." Adams has called them an attack on civil liberties and stated, "We are not going to take this lying down." Just prior to the announcement, Sinn Fein spokesman Danny Morrison said that if the measures are implemented, "the British public won't get our point of view. That is why the IRA carry out bombings. The British public listens to bombings."

As far as freedom of expression is concerned, says Stewart, the print media are not in any way prevented from carrying statements nor are British broadcast media prevented from using voice-overs or conveying the views of Sinn Fein or Ulster Defense Association spokesmen indirectly. Nor will the ban be applied at election time, as Sinn Fein is still permitted to operate as a party. (Totally proscribing Sinn Fein is considered impractical, since it would just regroup under another name.) Moreover, the ban does not apply to foreign news organizations.

What it does do, according to Stewart, is deprive terrorists and their apologists of a means for direct intimidation. Many British proponents of the measures also cite what they call the sheer offensiveness of the IRA's use of the media. In the case of the Enniskillen bombing, the IRA initially claimed that the bomb had been prematurely detonated by a British army electronic sweeping device. When this was proved to be a lie, the group backtracked and acknowledged it was a "mistake," for which Adams expressed his "regret."

Another often-cited example is the September bombing of the home of Sir Kenneth Bloomfield, Northern Ireland's top civil servant. Bloomfield and his family were lucky: Two of the four IRA bombs failed to explode. Within hours, Adams, who according to The (London) Sunday Times is considered by security specialists to be in the leadership of both Sinn Fein and the Irish Republican Army, went on BBC Radio Ulster, expressing a thinly veiled threat that civil servants advising British forces "run the risks" and that the IRA was giving them a chance to resign.

One commentator dryly noted in the British press, "After all, nobody calls it censorship when Mafia spokesmen are not allowed to explain, over the airwaves, why it is advisable to pay protection money."

As for the right to silence, Stewart points out, it still exists. The new proposal does not enable courts to convict people guilty simply on the grounds of their silence; there has to be corroborating evidence. But where a court in the past could not consider the silence of an accused as relevant to his trial, it now can draw whatever inferences it thinks are proper.

ASSOCIATED PRESS / WIDE WORLD PHOTOS

War memorial at Enniskillen, where Remembrance Day bomb last year killed 11

According to Bernhard Adamczewski of the Institute for the Study of Terrorism in London, the IRA carefully and methodically trains its men in methods designed to impede investigation into their acts of violence. Such techniques include lying down on the floor, standing on chairs or doing push-ups during questioning. In one case a man exposed himself to a woman detective. Such tactics require a special caution on the part of the police. Even attempts to make a suspect sit on a chair can be construed as a physical assault in court.

As a result, in an increasing number of cases, the courts have had to let people go, and judges in Northern Ireland complain that they have had to acquit people even when they have such evidence as fingerprints on explosives. The number of people charged with serious terrorist offenses has dropped from an average of about 1,200 a year a decade ago to about one-third of that figure today.

One recent case, according to Chief Inspector Herbert Norris of the Royal Ulster Constabulary, involved the arrest of five known terrorists found leaving a block of high-rise flats as the police arrived to carry out a search. While one group of officers apprehended the terrorists, another group radioed that three firearms found on the ground had been thrown from a flat. But because the men refused to speak when arrested and because none of them was a resident, the charges did not hold up.

A classic case from the early 1970s involved the hijacking of a bus, part of an IRA effort to disrupt life in west and north Belfast. The night before he was to give evidence, the driver was murdered, and the three people under suspicion, who kept silent throughout, had to be let go. Collapse of case.

Furthermore, Stewart points out that the legislation is in line with legislation already in force in the Republic of Ireland. Since the 1970s, a ban on direct broadcasting of terrorist statements has been in existence in the republic under Section 31 of the Broadcasting Act. The principle of drawing inference from silence has been established in Ireland since 1984, though Irish officials say that the British proposal is more far-reaching.

Nevertheless, it is in the Republic of Ireland that the new policy has found some of its strongest defenders. The Cork Examiner, a staunchly nationalist paper, recently editorialized: "On how many occasions have they [the paramilitaries] denied people in the North the most basic of human rights — the right to life itself, the right to work, the right to try to live ordinary decent lives, free from threat, intimidation, violence and murder? When they restore these rights, they will in turn have the right to complain."

— Henrik Bering-Jensen

Terrorism and the Media: Lessons from the British Experience

Abraham H. Miller

Abraham H. Miller is a Bradley Resident Scholar at The Heritage Foundation and Professor of Political Science at the University of Cincinnati.

In war, truth is the first casualty. In terrorism, truth never makes it to the casualty list. Its death silently precedes the first act of violence.

Warfare is about taking political power through force of arms. Terrorism is about seizing political power through force of propaganda. Terrorist violence is a facade behind which is concealed political and military impotency.

A terrorist leader is in a sense a dramatist. He produces violent spectacles designed to create the illusion of power through horror. What the terrorist lacks in real power, he compensates for in the production of attention-riveting visuals. Terrorism is theater played on the world stage to an audience of eager journalists—preferably those holding a camera.

The relationship between terrorists seeking publicity and journalists seeking news is at times called symbiotic, as the purveyors of violence-laced propaganda and the disseminators of news feed off one another.

It is this relationship—this production of violence for the camera—that presents the media with difficult ethical choices. Terrorists push the media into that grey area where distinctions blur between reporting the news and becoming part of the news, and frequently journalists have to ask themselves whether certain terrorist events would occur if not for the media's willingness to report them.

To ask that question, however, is not to suggest, as some regrettably have, that if the lens were to be capped, terrorism would somehow miraculously cease. Although terrorists do covet publicity, that is not their only motivation for violence. Terrorist violence is used for vengeance and as an instrument of negotiation.

Live Drama. Beyond that, capping the lens, even if legally permissible, is increasingly becoming bureaucratic whimsy. The same technology that makes contemporary terrorism live drama increasingly puts that drama beyond the effective reach of the censor—a fact that is underscored by recent events in Eastern Europe.

If there is any doubt as to terrorists' ability to function without the media, one only need be reminded that two of the most effective terrorist organizations on record, the Sicarii and the Zealots, functioned in the first century A.D. (And as even most American high school students know, that was before Dan Rather came to CBS.) These groups did rely on the propaganda of the deed, which they achieved by killing their victims in broad daylight on holy days amid large crowds, whose word-of-mouth accounts spread fear.

FRAMING THE ISSUE

Properly framed, the issue before us is not whether the media should cover terrorism, but how it should report it. The corollary question, of course, is who should decide how the media goes about its business.

If we are justifiably horrified at what havoc government can wreak with economic policy, contemplate momentarily what the bureaucracy could do if unleashed on the media. We might find that the media's rights under the First Amendment resemble nothing so much as First Amendment rights at some of our universities.

There would be the First Amendment hour, where freedom of speech would not be infringed if it did not run beyond prime time. Or there might be freedom of speech zones, the West coast on alternate Tuesdays and the East Coast on Mondays and Fridays.

And of course there would be decency rules, which would prohibit negative comments about both government-approved terrorist groups and state sponsors of terrorism. As the approval list would change frequently, it would be appropriate to check for updates with the State Department to see which terrorists were "in" and which were "out."

For those who believe the bureaucracy is incapable of such machinations, I suggest a short visit to the closest university that has adopted a so-called "decency standard."

Disregard of Ethics. Although I strongly believe that we conservatives do not desire to take the government out of the economy and put it into the newsroom, I also know that the risk of that tragic occurrence is the result of the media's own

From *The Heritage Lectures,* February 15, 1990, pp. 1-9. Reprinted by permission.

reckless disregard of basic journalistic ethics. Journalists of every stripe appear to learn ethics in the classroom and forget that they were meant to apply to something other than the final examination. As one thoughtful news expert put it, when we get discussions of ethics out of the classroom and into the boardroom, we will know then that ethics will have some influence on behavior.

The media is its own enemy. Nothing has been a greater threat to the media's continued access to its Constitutional rights than its coverage of terrorism and most notably its coverage of the hijacking of TWA Flight 847 to Beirut (June 1985). This event brought into focus, more than did any prior event, the media's general unwillingness to distinguish its rights from its responsibilities.

Whatever the media might have learned from its earlier coverage of the Iranian hostage crisis was quickly lost in the drama and competition of this new event. In their quest to beat the competition, the networks sent their superstars to Beirut, a device known as "bigfooting," where the resident and knowledgeable local correspondent is squashed into oblivion by the presence of a network's superstar.

TWA 847 became a media circus, and at one dramatic point Shiite gunmen had to discharge their weapons to preserve order at a press conference that had all the decorum of a school of ravenous barracudas encountering dinner in the open sea. But if that scene was the most dramatic and most memorable, it was so only because it came to symbolize the media's excesses. The media showed poor judgment at a number of points throughout the episode.

"Ratings Be Damned." As in the Iranian hostage situation—where in exchange for an interview with Marine Corporal William Gallegos, NBC permitted a fanatical spokeswoman called "Mary" to launch a five-minute tirade against America—all the networks gave airtime to people forcibly holding innocent Americans at gun point. The Iran hostage episode which became a soap opera for ratings so angered *TV Guide* (Dec. 22, 1979) that it published an editorial—which later appeared as an advertisement in the *Wall Street Journal*— noting, "We have seen enough unwashed Iranians chanting their slogans and waving their fists on cue to last a lifetime. . . . Let the ratings be damned."

TV Guide was alluding to an 18 percent rise in the size of the network news audience as a result of the coverage of the hostage crisis. Wild-eyed Shiites and captive Americans pushed up advertising revenue. Cloaked in the First Amendment, the networks showed us that captive Americans could be comfortably exploited for revenue.

If this exploitation of the hostages is infuriating, it seems to me that it is less so than the twisted rationale the media used to justify such interviews. Robert Siegenthaler, of ABC, [testifying before the House Subcommittee on Europe and the Middle East (July 1985)] claimed that his correspondent about to film an interview with a TWA hostage was able to say surreptitiously to the hostage that ABC would pack up and leave if the hostage did not want to be interviewed. Undoubtedly, this example will give new meaning to the concept of "informed consent."

Forget, if you can, that the networks are in a sense partners in this crime where Americans are being held in captivity because they are Americans and because they provide entree to the American media. Does anyone really believe that this hostage could have said to ABC, "Go home," and not suffered at the hands of his captors?

That a vice president of the network would use this episode to justify ABC's exploitation of the situation for "entertainment" purposes (it certainly is not news), indicates at best a certain sense of unreality and at worst a disdainful arrogance.

Congressman Thomas Luken in his outrage at Siegenthaler's response said, "This is so palpably offensive to me. He [the reporter] is still talking to people who are under complete control. He is still talking to people who had been given an indication by their captors as to what they should say. . . . You wouldn't even [have] had them on if the captors didn't deliver them to you. And you don't have the sophistication to recognize that the captors would have told them what to say? Privately or publicly?"

Cult of Objectivity. Charles Krauthammer writing in *Time* (July 15, 1985) refers to the media's arrogance as deriving from its cherished belief in the cult of objectivity. This doctrine is summed up for Krauthammer by veteran correspondent Sam Donaldson's remark, "It's our job to cover the story . . .we bring the information."

The act of observing and transmitting, however, even in the best of circumstances, alters the story. Every schoolboy learns that once he stains a slide to enhance its reflection under the microscope, he has intervened in what he observes. The media would have us believe that the camera does not alter the characteristics of events, even events staged by the propagandists of the deed.

Krauthammer finds the doctrine of objectivity to be little more than a self-serving rationale. I would argue, however, that the problem is not the doctrine of objectivity, for properly exercised it is as appropriate to the media as it is to science. The problem is that the media, unlike science, claims objectivity to conceal the intrusiveness of the process of observation.

One wonders if ABC would concede that David Hartman's solicitation of Nabih Berri—the good Shiite in this drama of good Shiite and bad Shiite—"Any final words to President Reagan this morning?" was something more than reporting the story?

It prompted enough reflection at ABC to put Hartman's, "Good Morning America," under the aegis of the news division the following day. Some said that this was done to make the program more sensitive to news guidelines. More cynical observers saw this as an attempt to wrap the program more tightly in the protection of the First Amendment.

Highjacking the Networks. TWA 847 presented us with other examples of the media becoming part of the story. The continual updates from Lebanon gave the appearance that the Shiites had not hijacked an airplane but had hijacked the networks. And all the lessons that were supposed to have been learned from the Iranian hostage situation were lost as TWA 847 was conducted like some instant replay of the Tehran soap opera. The media was not simply reporting the news; it was making the news. When Dan Rather asked one of the hostages what he would have President Reagan do, Rather demonstrated the ability of the media to be intrusive.

There was also the networks' subtle editorializing through the use of the doctrine of moral equivalence. Shiite gunmen held captive in Israel were portrayed as hostages, with tearful mothers and concerned families, no different from the mothers and families of the innocent Americans whose only crime was their citizenship. It would not be inappropriate to be reminded that one of the "equivalent" Shiites, subsequently released by Israel, was reported to have been involved in another act of terrorism, one which took place over Lockerbee, Scotland with the disintegration of Pan Am 103. So much for "objectivity" as applied to news analysis.

My concern here is not to excoriate the American news media for its reporting of TWA 847. As Jody Powell noted in testimony before the Congress (July 1985), the problem is not so much that the media will bring down the government or society, but that its excesses do damage to itself. And if the media wounds itself, we all suffer, for a free society is impossible without a free media.

It is one thing to depict media excesses. It is far and away another to prescribe an effective solution. Some have suggested that the media would act more responsibly if the media saw terrorism as threatening the social and political foundations of the society itself. How does the media report terrorism in a democratic society under siege? And would those experiences provide lessons for the American media's conduct of its business? To explore those issues I examined the behavior of the media in the United Kingdom.

THE BRITISH EXPERIENCE

Britain's experience with media coverage of terrorism casts these concerns against a backdrop where terrorist violence threatens the very integrity of the political system. For that reason, the British experience which tugs and pulls between concerns of freedom and order in a society that is directly under siege, might provide us with lessons about our own strengths and vulnerabilities. After all, media excesses might be tolerated when the reporting is from Beirut and the threat is to hostages and not to the very viability of the social and political system.

Cherishing Independence. To Americans, the British media appears to be only half free, for the British media can be subjected to prior restraint. But the similarities between the American and British media far overshadow their differences. Both function in liberal democracies that cherish as a primary value the media's independence from government intrusion—even if that value is sometimes practiced in the breach. For Britain, as for America, the major issue has been television coverage of terrorism. The intimacy, immediacy and reality of the electronic media elicits both a mental and visceral reaction that the print media cannot duplicate. And it is the impact of this that has greatly concerned British governments since "the troubles," as they are called, began in Northern Ireland in the late 1960s.

All British governments—and not just the Thatcher government—have attempted to influence the British Broadcasting Corporation (BBC) through either its Director General or the Chairman of its Board of Governors, generally, albeit not exclusively, to prevent the broadcast of televised interviews with terrorists involved in the conflict in Northern Ireland. There is, however, little concern about interviews with terrorists whose targets do not involve the integrity of the United Kingdom as a political structure. The Director General of the BBC never need fear that his phone will ring over a forthcoming program on SWAPO, the PLO, or even the dreaded Abu Nidal's Black June.

The BBC, an independent but government-funded corporation, is seen as more vulnerable to such influences than the IBA, the Independent Broadcast Authority which awards commercial franchises. But the IBA too is pressured to use its legal power to prevent networks from broadcasting programs, or, more commonly, to edit those it sees as being in conflict with the public interest. The government has pressured the IBA from time to time, but governmental concern is widely perceived as disproportionately directed against the BBC, which is seen as conveying a special legitimacy on those it interviews.

By American standards, the British government's intrusiveness into the media's conduct of its own affairs is appalling. From the government's perspective, however, the argument against interviewing terrorists is that a terrorist is an advocate of murder and such interviews are an incitement to commit murder in the future as well as a reward for having done so in the past.

For their part, the British media argues that such interviews enable the public to see the advocates of violence for what they really are and that the average viewer is revolted by terrorists' arrogant justifications of murder.

THE INLA INTERVIEW

These disparate perceptions clashed dramatically after a little-known Republican group calling itself the Irish National Liberation Army murdered Member of Parliament Airey Neave (March 30, 1979) as he drove toward the exit in Parliament's garage. In Dublin, the BBC televised an interview with an INLA spokesman. The INLA member not only admitted to the group's responsibility for the murder but reveled in it, calling Neave an advocate of torture. This charge was quickly challenged and disproved in the broadcast.

On the floor of Parliament the BBC was denounced. Prime Minister Thatcher said that she was appalled by the incident, and Lady Neave, the MP's widow, wrote to the *Daily Telegraph* (July 12, 1979) to express her distaste for the BBC's lack of sensitivity. Yet, 80 percent of the British public supported the broadcast, and despite Parliamentary pressure, Sir Michael Havers, the Attorney General, refused to prosecute the BBC.

On the floor of Parliament, Havers advised his colleagues that since the BBC interview had taken place in Dublin, the appropriate aspects of Britain's Prevention of Terrorism Act would be difficult to enforce. Some observers within Britain's law enforcement community suggested that a more compelling reason was that Britain as a society had to weigh the damage of prosecuting the BBC against the damage done by the broadcast. Even they acknowledged that Britain could live better with the consequences of the interview than the consequences of an attack on the media in the courts.

American vs. British Media. The idea of dragging the media before the courts for interviewing a terrorist is as appropriate a topic of discussion for the British as it is frightening to Americans. Nothing so separates the American media from the British as a common misperception of what "freedom of the press" means.

In January of 1972, for example, the *Times* (London) lavished praise on Ben Bradlee, editor of the *Washington Post,* and the *New York Times'* Abe Rosenthal for their vigorous defense of the press against, what the *Times* (London) called, the savage attacks against the media launched by Vice President Spiro Agnew. Mindful of a controversy surrounding the BBC's defense of journalistic freedom against the British government, as the government attempted to quash a televised program on Ulster, the *Times* concluded that freedom of the press might be good for the Americans but not for the BBC. The BBC, the *Times* reasoned, was a public corporation and thus had an obligation not to challenge the government.

But the BBC was challenging the government and persisted in doing so. Long before the INLA episode, in January of 1972, a BBC public affairs program, which openly debated the Ulster issue and in which the government refused to participate, drew strong condemnation on the floor of the Parliament and open threats to withdraw the BBC's charter when it came up for renewal. Lord Hill of Lutton, the Chair of the Corporation, took umbrage at this intrusion and lashed back at the government. In contrast to the BBC, the commercial authority refused permission to Granada Television to transmit a program for its "World in Action" series also depicting the conflict in Ulster.

But it is too facile to conclude from this juxtaposition that the BBC stood firm against censorship and that the commercial authority easily capitulated. Broadcast journalists continually complained of an atmosphere of self-censorship that permeated the industry, and the BBC was alleged to have imposed a series of restrictions that amounted to censorship. Journalists who broke ranks with the Corporation on this issue were said to have had their tapes blocked from transmission and their contracts dropped at renewal time.

NEW MEASURES IN RESPONSE TO TERRORISM

As the conflict in Northern Ireland crossed the Irish Sea and landed on the shores of Great Britain and IRA bombs took their toll on British soil, Parliament, in 1974, responded with legislation that its advocates called "draconian" and "unprecedented in peace time."

Initially this legislation, known as the Prevention of Terrorism Act, appeared not to be directed at the media. As terrorism escalated so did the legislation, and in 1976 two sections were added that originally were not directed at the media but ultimately came to have strong consequences for how journalists went about their business. The two new Sections were titled 10 and 11.

Section 10 prohibited anyone from giving aid that resulted in contributing to terrorism. Section 11 required everyone with knowledge of the whereabouts of actual or potential terrorists to bring that information to the police.

Threat to Civil Liberties. In 1978, in response to growing concerns about the Act's implications for civil liberties, Lord Shackleton was appointed to review the Act. Lord Shackleton's review showed no linkage between these sections and the media, but Section 11 was found to be threatening to civil liberties. Lord Shackleton recommended that it be dropped, but it was not.

When the BBC interviewed the INLA spokesman in Dublin, they exposed themselves to Section 11. In the aftermath of this broadcast, the attorney general entered into an exchange of private letters between the government and the corporation concerning the INLA broadcast. On the floor of Parliament, Conservative members wanted the letters disclosed, and in the process showed strong concern over the BBC's violation of the Prevention of Terrorism Act's Section 11. Here for the first time, and in contrast to the conclusion of Lord Shackleton, the attorney general interpreted Section 11 to apply to the media.

The BBC was unyielding. It argued that Section 11 if so interpreted would in effect prevent journalists from going about their business and subject them to terrorist retribution if they did comply with the government's order.

Clearly the issue was now framed in terms of civic obligation. Did a journalist have a civic obligation as a citizen first or as a journalist? And how could he function as a journalist if the two obligations were incompatible?

It is impossible in the context of this lecture to present each and every dispute between the British media and the government. If one were to look at the most important of those conflicts, one would be presented with an image of a society under siege attempting to cap the lens and a media attempting to go about its business weighing its journalistic responsibilities against its sense of civic obligation, with journalistic responsibilities in ascendance.

One might also see—as I have elsewhere—a society committed to basic journalistic freedom going through an elaborate ritual of lashing out at the messenger when it is incapable of lashing out against terrorism. Such perceptions are not inaccurate, but I no longer believe they totally describe the situation.

RETHINKING THE OBVIOUS

In thinking about the struggle between the British government and the media and how to analyze it, I am reminded of an episode that took place in a philosophy of science class of Abraham Kaplan's some twenty-five years ago. Kaplan began making a case for the intelligence and compassion of dolphins, by pointing out that almost as long as man has kept records there have been episodes of sailors being led to shore by schools of dolphins. Kaplan would cite evidence from different points of history and different points of geography. The accumulated account, which spanned both time and earthly space, seemed to make an impressive case.

Seeing how he had convinced his students, he then—as he often did on such occasions—would turn to them and present one crisp question. In this case, he asked, "Now what about the sailors who had been led out to sea?"

Too frequently we confront what might appear to us to be the zealotry of the media to commit excesses and to defend those excesses in terms of traditional values of freedom of inquiry. What we forget to consider is—the other side of the issue—the harm that comes from the zealotry of government censorship wrapped in the garb of the public interest.

For every widely-publicized episode where the media and the British government have come into conflict over a program on terrorism that the media aired over strong government objection, there are numerous, less publicized episodes where programs are not produced, not aired or severely edited because exchanges of letters, the threat of the Prevention of Terrorism Act, and Parliamentary criticism. All of this results in a creeping and insidious censorship.

THE MEDIA AND DEMOCRACY

A society under siege, in many ways, needs a critical and, yes, objective media more so than a society whose viability is not threatened. For siege itself produces societal reactions that are not in keeping with respect for individual liberty.

The policy of internment without trial in Northern Ireland; the sensory deprivation interrogations in Castlereagh and other prisons; and the British Government's attempt to obstruct the investigation of John Stalker into the RUC's (Royal Ulster Constabulary's) alleged shoot-to-kill policy are all grave threats to the integrity of a free society on both sides of the Irish Sea.

British society is best served by the continued vitality of its free media so that these issues—and the more recent ones concerning the killings at Gibraltar and the alleged collusion between the British Army and Protestant terrorists—see the light of public debate both within the halls of Westminster and across British airwaves.

In the face of such controversial issues that tear at the democratic fabric of Britain, she has been better served by their vigorous debate in the media than by those who would ultimately seek to censor these topics from public discussion. To the extent that the unions of broadcast journalists are correct in their accusations that an atmosphere of intimidation and censorship surround the production of television programs on Northern Ireland, terrorism has taken a strong toll on Britain.

In response to the BBC's initial refusal to air the controversial program, "The Edge of Union," Professor Paul Wilkinson, one of Britain's most respected authorities on terrorism, put the issue this way: "[A]ny suggestion that any external body is bringing pressure to bear and altering editorial judgement as a result of political considerations undermines not only the credibility of the media, but the credibility of democratic government. And there is plenty of evidence that the overall impact of good professional media reporting in democratic societies has been to harden the will of the decent majority against any submission to terrorist blackmail."

LESSONS YET TO BE LEARNED

The primary lesson for the American media is that as terrorism increasingly becomes a direct threat, there will be those in government who will desire some American version of the Prevention of Terrorism Act. It might start out innocuous, but like the Prevention of Terrorism Act, its interpretation will become more severe and its impact more insidious as the threat grows.

To restrict the media's freedom is to concede a victory to the terrorists. For ultimately, a society under siege will have all sorts of attacks on its basic liberties, and it will need a free—and yes responsible—media to make the public aware of the costs to balance freedom with order.

Terrorism and freedom do not exist well side by side. Few societies, even the most democratic, are going to avoid taking vigorous action and sometimes short-cutting civil liberties to defend themselves. Yet, such actions can be as threatening to democratic viability as the acts of terrorists.

Exploiting Hostages. I would prefer not to see an American television journalist conducting an interview with another American who is being held hostage, has a gun held to his head while he responds to questions, and is then forcibly yanked around the neck when the answer is not to his captor's liking. This is precisely what did happen to the captain of TWA 847. Such a scene is obscene. It exploits the hostage for perverse entertainment value. Equally insidious, it threatens the very freedom that enables the journalist to conduct the interview.

If journalists do not have more common sense and more ethical restraint than this, then the media's freedom—and ours as well—is in grave danger. American journalists might find themselves struggling as the British do to balance the responsibilities they have to their craft and to democratic traditions while evading the threat of an ever-intrusive government. What the journalist loses in this process fades in comparison to the price the rest of us will pay in the coin of individual liberty.

Freedom has to be tempered with responsibility. It is best tempered with the responsible exercise of journalistic ethics and not with the intrusiveness of government bureaucracy. Britain's bureaucratic intrusiveness into the media's conduct of its affairs has created the ridiculous situation where the Provisional IRA have less difficulty running for Parliament than getting on the BBC.

It is a situation that causes anguish in Britain. It is a situation that those in the American media who least desire it may through their own recklessness cause to occur. Let us hope that the American media can remember Mark Twain's advice on the issue—if I may interpret with some liberty—the blessing of freedom of the press was given to the American people with the corresponding blessing of the good sense to know when not to abuse it.

Tactics, Strategies, and Targeting

Terrorist tactics, strategies, and targeting provide a common basis for disparate terrorist groups. Different groups often exchange information and express sympathy with one another's goals. Many terrorist organizations have identical or very similar targets even if their motivations are quite different. Hence, it is easy for the Libyan government to help the IRA since it upsets the British, whom Gaddafi dislikes for being an ally of the United States and occasionally helping Israel.

Terrorism is not an inexpensive activity. Terrorist organizations usually require and even compete for assistance from supportive governments in the form of training and protection. Most of all, though, they are consistently in need of financial assistance.

Some terrorist groups are highly sophisticated organizations whose structures have been carefully formulated for efficiency and effectiveness. These unique organizational infrastructures often pose problems for law enforcement. Violence by design and methodology has become part and parcel of terrorist operations. Smaller terrorist groups can be especially dangerous if they do not rely on or answer to a state sponsor. These groups have the luxury of behaving irresponsibly, and they can thwart the more tangible goals of terrorist regimes and their proxies. "Linkages Between Sunni and Shi'i Radical Fundamentalist Organizations: A New Variable in Recent Middle Eastern Politics?" examines how the goals of terrorist organizations can coincide with one another.

"Why Hostage-Taking Is So Popular With Terrorists" examines the advantages that hostage-taking offers for terrorists. These include the low cost and the easy accessibility of kidnap victims. It is impossible for the United States or any other government to protect millions of soldiers, tourists, and business personnel stationed or traveling abroad at any given time.

"The IRA: Spreading a Wider Net" reminds us of the sorts of targets terrorists prefer. Favorites include government officials and soldiers leading the fight against terrorism.

"Narco-Terrorism 'Shooting Up' America" provides an understanding of the link between international drug trafficking and terrorism. Much of the vast quantities of money generated by the drug trade goes directly to terrorist groups, who use some of it to finance their own operations. Often this includes paying off government officials who allow terrorists to operate freely. To a very real extent, illicit drug consumers in the United States are the greatest financiers of terrorism.

Narco-terrorists are capable of brutality on a massive scale as "Peru's Shining Path Terrorists Open New Front in Drug War" reveals. In Peru, for example, the Shining Path is set on intimidating thousands of farmers to grow coca or face death. Crop substitution is not an option. "Colombian Journalists vs. Drug Terrorists" reveals the dangers faced by journalists who write (not very favorably) about narco-terrorists in Colombia.

Whether terrorists will at some point resort to using weapons of mass destruction is explored in "Will Terrorists Use Chemical Weapons?" Nuclear weapons are not yet a plausible choice at this stage, but chemical or biological weapons may very well be.

Terrorism is a complicated subject and, therefore, it is not unreasonable to suspect that even where it has been applied is not uniformly condemned. As "Terrorism and Public Opinion: A Five Country Comparison" indicates, public opinion and even support for terrorism can differ dramatically from society to society, especially when specifically targeted by the terrorists.

Looking Ahead: Challenge Questions

What are some of the important ways that terrorist organizations finance their operations?

How do the sometimes varying interests and goals of terrorist groups coincide? How do they on occasion compete against one another? What do terrorist groups representing the extreme left and right have in common?

What advantages are there in hostage-taking? What circumstances make it so easy?

What is the relationship between drug trafficking, drug users, and terrorism?

What are some weapons that may be used by terrorists in the future?

How is terrorism regarded in different societies and what accounts for the differences?

Unit 7

Linkages Between Sunni and Shi'i Radical Fundamentalist Organizations: A New Variable In Recent Middle Eastern Politics?

Bernard Schechterman and Bradford R. McGuinn

Linkages, Cooperation and Efforts to Promote Shi'i-Sunni Collaboration

To support and evaluate the efficacy of the concept of inter-sectarian cooperative activities, several sets of data, some more and some less developed than others are presented. The first deals with the most thoroughly documented example of Shi'i-Sunni organizational and behavioral linkage to date. From then on the available data base varies in comprehensiveness, not validity or reliability, because the area of subversive, terrorist and insurrectionary types of activities remain largely secretive.

On September 30, 1985, four Soviet officials were abducted in Beirut.[77] Although one of the Soviets was eventually killed,[78] the others were released within several weeks. In fact, given the routine chaos of Lebanon, the incident will perhaps only be remembered for the nationality of the victims.[79] Yet, there is strong evidence this event confirms the inter-sectarian hypothesis of this essay. The kidnapping operation was planned and executed through the cooperative efforts of Sunni and Shi'i fundamentalist groups, both sponsored by Iran.

For the antecedents of this incident one must look not to Shi'i controlled West Beirut,[80] but to Tripoli where Sunni radical fundamentalist prevailed.[81] Since the mid-seventies politics in this northern Lebanese city have been dominated by Syrian issue.[82] More specifically, the central political dynamics has been the tension between the Sunni Lebanese populace and the more recent arrivals, the Alawis, whose loyalties often extend toward their tribal kinsmen in secular (Ba'thi socialist) Syria.[83] In 1983 a major new force emerged in the Sunni community in the form of Shaykh Sa'id Sha'ban's Tawhid (Unity) Movement.[84] A charismatic radical fundamentalist, Sha'ban demanded that Lebanon be purged of all non-Islamic influences.[85] This was an indirect slap at Syria, whose Alawi leadership is held by many Sunnis to be heretical.[86] What distinguished Sha'ban from other anti-Syrian Sunni fundamentalists was his close relationship with and endorsement by Iran. [87] In fact, he is the "...only Lebanese or Syrian leader who is known to have been granted an audience with...Khomeini,"[88] repeated at length again the end of 1987, during an anti-Saudi conference on the holy places of Islam [88a]

During the weeks preceding the abductions in Beirut, Sha'ban's Sunni forces, allied with PLO elements (predominantly Sunni in background) loyal to Yasir Arafat, were engaged in a violent battle with Syrian-supported militias for control of Tripoli.[89] For Arafat it was to be his last stand on Lebanese soil, having been driven from the south earlier by the Israelis. It also reflected his disaffection with the Syrian support of dissidents in the PLO. Then, two weeks before the actual kidnappings, Syria initiated a full-scale assault on the city.[90] Even by Lebanese standards the ensuing destruction was extreme, no less the implications that even worse might occur. Various reports indicated five hundred people were killed from among the 200,000 remaining (500,000 having fled).[91] The level of violence was said to have been the highest since the Civil War of 1975/76.[92]

It was in this context that the four Soviets were abducted in Beirut. Two groups immediately claimed responsibility: the Islamic Jihad organization (Shi'i) and the hitherto unknown Islamic Liberation Organization (ILO).[93] The Islamic Jihad had been viewed all along as being linked to Iran.[94] The ILO was thought to be Sunni right from the beginning of its surfacing because its full name--the Khaled ibn al-Walid Forces---invoked a prominent Sunni figure in Islamic history.[95] It was assumed to be connected

 From *The Political Chronicle,* Vol. 1, No. 1, 1989, Journal of the Florida Political Association. Reprinted by permission.

with Sha'ban's Tawhid Movement because the nature of the demands, reiterated and supported by Islamic Jihad, were clearly the same.[96] In its initial communique the ILO states: "We have kidnapped four Soviet diplomats and demand a halt to the advance on Tripoli and retreat of the heretic forces..."[97] The ILO indicated its expectations were that the Soviet Union, a patron state, would pressure its client, Syria, to end the fighting in Tripoli.[98] Unquestionably, the Tawhid Movement had a clear motive for involvement in the abduction. Moreover, logic dictates, that a Sunni group could not have conducted this operation in Beirut without at least the approval of the preeminent Shi'i, no less their connivance.

To date the most detailed information concerning this group comes from the Kuwaiti daily newspaper **Al-Sayasah.**[98a] According to its political editor, the ILO emerged out of a deliberate Iranian effort to form a joint Sunni-Shi'i Islamic front in Lebanon. It's purpose was to counter the strength and influence of moderate elements such as the Amal and the Lebanese Mufti. Apparently Sunni groups such as Sha'ban's were well disposed to the idea, but some Shi'i leaders like Shaykh Muhammad Husayn Fadlallah, were either opposed or reticent. Interestingly, the Shaykh was not opposed on the basis of the other side being Sunni, but feared the impact such a union might have on their Syrian relationship. However, Khomeini was determined that the front be established, and Iranian representatives pushed forward with those agreeing to it, ignoring the rest. The end result was the ILO made up of 120 members---60 Sunnis and 60 Shi'a. The Iranian Revolutionary Guard Corps then undertook responsibility for the training missions and supply of arms in an area west of the Beirut-Tripopli highway (Shi'i territory). Three sub-groups, each of fifteen members, moved to Beirut. One of these, the Khalid ibn al-Walid group, actually abducted the four Soviets. The newspaper suggested that organizational confusion caused both the ILO and Islamic Jihad to initially claim responsibility. Once this condition was remedied, the ILO assumed sole authority over the operation.[99] It was agreed that the ILO:

> "...would be responsible for Muslim affairs in general and that the Islamic Jihad organization would devote attention to purely Shi'ite operations, provided that there is no contradiction between the operations of the two sides (emphasis added).[100]

This stipulation certainly appeared to conform to the "limited objective model" that could satisfy both sects individually and together. That is, tactical cooperation was possible because the base and strength of the Sunni and Shi'i movements were geographically separated. In other words., they could work in concert because neither represented a hegemonic or competitive threat to the other.

Lebanon provides several other examples of alliance patterns and operational unity between the two sectarian groups. As Hunter indicated:

> Since the Lebanese war, there have been reports that an increasing number of Palestinian refugees--most of whom are Sunnis--have become disenchanted with their secular leaders and are turning to the mosque as a source of hope. Nor is there any doubt that the war and its aftermath, especially the occupation of southern Lebanon, have radicalized the Lebanese Shi'as, thus providing countries like Iran with opportunities to recruit new sympathizers and agents for subversion.[101]

The Sidon area, both before and after Israeli withdrawal, offered a great opportunity to invoke and exploit Islamic fundamentalism, especially its most radical version. Anti-Israeli posturing and behavior produced general agreement among all factions of "the national and Islamic ranks," especially in undertaking military activities in the South. The long-term, with its stress on "liberating Jerusalem" and eliminating Israel also serves as a unifying factor for diverse elements. In the Sunni Muslim camp there was a clearly definable group also objecting to the Syrian regime. Islamic thought is conceived of as a means of bringing Sunni and Shi'is together. Sidon has become an arena reflecting links with the Islamic Unification Movement (Tawhid) in Tripoli and became intertwined with the newer Islamic movements in the Beirut area---Grouping of Muslim Scholars, Hizballah and others opposed to Israeli negotiations or peacemaking. Among the leading figures found in the Sunni camp espousing and cooperating with Shi'a elements have been Shaykh Mahir Hamud and Shaykh Salah Arqadan, both members of the Grouping of Muslim Scholars, again a group transcending the respective sects. Expressive of the Shi'a side of the political collaboration is Shaykh Muhammed Hamdi Shams al Din, deputy chairman of the Supreme Shi'ite Islamic Council, and the Grouping of Scholars of Jabal 'Amil, most prominent group for their belief in complete civil resistance in the South.[102]

Confusing the issue of Sunni-Shi'i linkages in Lebanon is the fact that collaboration takes on varying patterns of combinations. Secular Sunni leaders like Nazihg Bizri and Nassirist Mustapha Saad have "developed a tenuous working relationship with the Shi'ite Amal movement." In local politics, which often takes precedent over divisions at other times, the Sunni-Shi's cooperation was directed against the Lebanese Forces (Christian and/or central government).[103] A common Islamic background was also helpful.

Another combination that surfaced in 1985 was the link between the Palestine liberation organization (Arafat-led wing) and the Hizballah (Party of God) Shi'a zealots. The common and tactical enemy in this case was the Shi'a Amal, a more moderate and less receptive group to Iranian Islamic radical fundamentalism. The PLO's hoped for gains in the alliance pattern were two-fold: protection against repeated Amal attacks on Palestinian refugee camps and the ultimate permission to return to southern Lebanon to continue their war against Israel, a mutually shared objective. As the Arafat-led faction Fatah explained the situation:

> We were able to get on good terms with certain leading figures in Hezbollah...who opposed Arabs fighting each other.

The actual links remain "very limited, more on a personal than organizational level." The PLO provided both weapons and money to the Hezbollah, which were tendered to facilitate release of two Cypriot students kidnapped by the Shi'a group in Beirut. As much as Arafat and important segments of the PLO are often times characterized as "a traitor and infidel" by the religious fundamentalists, neither he nor they can overlook the essentialness of the Sunni religious background and factor among the Palestinian fedayeen and the refugees.[104] This was crucial to Arafat's last stand in Tripoli, where his alliance with Tawid, Iran's Sunni ally, paid off temporarily.

Even more expected and confirmed is the collaboration between Hezbollah, representing the Shi'a, and anti-Arafat PLO radicals in southern Lebanon. Although Hezbollah is in its ultimate ideology anti-Syrian and the PLO radicals are Marxists and pro-Syrian, the do share a common enmity with Israel and towards "American imperialism," if not the West overall. There are evidences they have cooperated in terrorist attacks in European countries where recently the Palestinians were incapacitated because of surveillance by those governments.[105] The emergence of an Islamic Jihad or Hezbollah affiliate labeled "Organization for Revolutionary Justice to Liberate Palestine"* seems to fit the PLO (Sunni)-Shi'a linking up for specific operations. Earlier events in the Middle East demonstrated the likelihood and viability of such alliances when the Khomeini revolution proceeded to turn the Israeli Embassy in Teheran over to the PLO. Although this was eventually reversed for political and ideological reasons by the Iranian government, it never precluded future contacts of convenience. Paradoxical behavior is common to the Middle East region and virtually all its inhabitants.

As early as 1979 Egypt's Islamic radicals, viewing themselves as an authentic indigenous force, derived both encouragement and sometimes material support from radical Islamic regimes outside Egypt. The refusal at that time to join oppositionist left radicals against the Sadat regime reflected an ego level belief in their chance for unilateral success in eventually winning power. The continuing successes on the higher education campuses, the penetration of governmental and military middle and lower ranks, led to their credible beliefs. Places like Minya and Assyut, both on the Nile, became hotbeds of militant demon strations against the government.[106] Sadat's cooption of the old Muslim Brotherhood as a tactic against the threats of the left, unleashed a severe negative reaction in radical fundamentalist quarters. They resented the conservatism of the Brotherhood and its connections with the regime. Former members and others gravitated to a series of new groups such as Jama[c] at al-Takfir wa-l-Hijira, Hizb al-Tahrir al-Islami, Jund Allah, Jama[c] at al-Jihad, Jama[c] at al-Muslimin li-l-Takfir, and Ansar Khumayni (The Followers of Khomeini). These groups represented a generational break with the radical fundamentalists of the 1950s and 1960s in several ways.[107] One, as the Arabic newspaper, **Al-Majallah**, characterized the 1970s on development:

> The other trend that actually exists in the arena, although not obviously apparent, is the extreme religious trend organized within the Islamic groups. The image of bearded young men is once again spreading among young people in the universities and villages. This image was evident during the last days of al-Sadat's rule. The reemergence of young men of this type can only indicate specific things--that the fundamentalist Islamic trend has strongly reappeared among youth.

The paper goes on to say that "These groups believe that Khomeyni's style is the most suitable and best among the styles that should be adopted in Islamic society." This included resort to violence.[108]

Secondly, coming increasingly from better educated backgrounds, some have used their educations in the Gulf region (as a form of Egyptian exports) to earn income for the home country; others have returned under the strong influence of Iranian fundamentalism. That is why so much of the pent up Islamic radical fundamentalism exploded upon the Egyptian scene in the spring of 1985.[108a]

The third factor that differentiates the new from the old Egyptian fundamentalism has been a climate conducive to religious activism by minority sects--Coptic Christians, Ismailis and Fatimids (Shi'a sects) etc. Both Shi'a offshoots are known to have adherents in the Minya and Assyut village areas, although most Ismailis are found in the Alexandria region of the Lower Nile. Undoubtedly, cross-fertilization of views has taken place.

Finally, the most daring break by indigenous radical fundamentalists from old patterns, was to attend an international get-together sponsored by Iran to honor the seventh anniversary of her Islamic Revolution. The 1986 gathering was made up of Islamic radical fundamentalists from all over the Arab and Islamic Worlds, including the *Jihad* (Holy War) *movements* in Egypt (see previous listing).[109]

South of Egypt is the Sudan, another country in which some evidence exists of the Sunni-Shi'i linkage in national politics. With an extended tradition of Islamic fundamentalism, dating to the Mahdist state of 1885, one would expect that the great grand son, Sadiq el Mahdi, head of the Umma party and leader of the traditional Ansar movement, would be in the forefront of current radical revivalism. Not so. The same holds true for the old version of the Muslims Brotherhood, an historical affiliate of the founding Egyptian organization, which has been reoriented to political compromise and is politically insignificant. The critical radical fundamentalists function nowadays under the name of The National Islamic Front (NIF), which was founded in 1985, and led by Hassan al Turabi. He views it as the "new" Muslim Brotherhood. It too, resembling the Egyptian setting, draws heavily from young fanantical students, and does well in urban areas among themiddle class (former rural-migrants?). The party is funded by wealthy local businessmen, Saudi interests opposed to left tendencies and the Iranian government. It has unusally close connections with the Iranian-inspired El Jihad el Islami movement, whose leader, Hassan Haj Ali, is actually a NIF member. This is the same Jihad movement associated with

*This group may be the same as the "Islamic Jihad for the Liberation of Palestine," which is made up of Palestinians working in the larger Islamic Jihad.[105a]

Egypt's version and in turn connected to the Iranian government. With the critical exception of the South where Christianity and Animism are prevalent, the central and northern Sudan are Sunni in makeup. Despite its violent methods and orientations, NIF participated openly in the 1986 elections, fielding 18 candidates in the key capital city of Khartoum. The El Jihad movement may be shadowy, but the NIF is quite public, even given its Khomeinist tendiencies.[110.]

During 1984 Jordanian officals revealed the existence of several clandestine pro-Iranian groups. Leaders of these organizations were said to have visisted Iran on several occasions.[110a] While the groups were unnamed by the government, one of the Islamic societies identified by Dekmejian fits this description. The Harakat al-Tawhid (Movement of Unicity) is thought to be a militant anti-Jordanian, anti-Iraqi, and a paro-Iranian Sunni group. Dekmejian even notes that it has ties in Israel, the West Bank, and the United States.[110b] But no evidence suggests any linkage to any specific local Shi'i movement, not surprising because of the dearth of members of that sect.

In the Arabian Peninsula the data is much sketchier on linkages and cooperation, but at least some evidences have already surfaced to support the existence of this phenomenon. In Saudi Arabia, following a continuing undertow of anger by Islamic fundamentalists against the westernization of the incumbent regime, there has been continuous plotting and actions directed at the government. John Bullock, writing in the **London Daily Telegraph**, noted "that hundreds of people are reported to have been arrested in Saudi Arabia in recent weeks on suspicion of trying to organize an Iranian-backed coup against King Fahd...The attempted coup was to have taken place last month. According to reports from Riad, most of those involved were middle class officials, school teachers and minor professional men. Those involved were *mainly Sunni Moslems*...The plotters were said to be fundamentalists incensed by the "worldliness" of the present Saudi regime."[111] By inference, if they were not all Sunni, the others were probably Shi'a, especially since they are found in profound numbers in the Eastern (al-Hasa) Province of Saudi Arabia. They have been involved in demonstrations many times heretofore, but have received their greatest notoriety during the annual Mecca pilgrmage, where Khomeini has encouraged them to be politically active amongst all Muslims.[112] Other rallying points for both Sunni and Shi'a radical fundamentalists have been the Iranian-sponsored Islamic Organization for the Liberation of the Arabian Peninsula[113] and the Mujahedin movement of Saudi Arabia, which also attended the seventh anniversary celebration of international terrorists in Tehran in 1986.[114]

In the overall Persian Gulf region, Iran has maintained contact with the Aldaveh movement of the Gulf States and the Amal Shi'a of Bahrain. They too attended the anniversary celebration. However, if Sunni Muslims are in no way involved inthe specific movements, they have been in touch with them via the intermediary of Iran, the instigator and sponsor in the different countries. At an international converence at least minimal linkage is evident by being at the same place at the same time. Even the Moro Communist front from the Philippines showed up at the international conclave. Since the Moro front is made up of predominantly Muslims and has regularly received aid and support form Libya and Saudi Arabia, both Sunni nations, Iran's participation indicates at least parallel, if not direct cooperation between Sunni and Shi'a support states.[115] As indicated in the Sudanese case, both Saudis and Iranians are likewise funding an Islamic radical fundamentalist party (NIF) and movement in that country (see preceding page).

In the case of Iraq, the evidence is highly circumstantial of any collaborative efforts by Sunni and Shi'a. The record is extensive on Iranian and Shi'a opposition to the regime of Saddam Hussein, and in turn his brutalization of any opposition, secular and sectarian, right or left. But **The Economist** reports that:

> Iraq is minus a town: Ad Dujayyl, 40 miles northeast of Baghdad, has been erased from the map. This town, with a mixed (emphasis mine) Sunni and Shi'a Moslem population of about 2,000, was the scene on July 11 (1982) of an assassination attempt on President Saddam Hussein. This was the second such attempt in Ad Dujayl. So Mr. Saddam Hussein decided to make an example of this center of disaffection. There were about 150 casualties in the two hours of fighting that followed the attempted assassination. After that 150 families simply disappeared. The remaining men were sent off to northern Iraq; the women and children were sent south. Bulldozers then demolished the town.[116]

Clearly, when no effort was made by the regime to sort out Shi'a, the traditional opponents, from the Sunni populace, then both were in common opposition to the government. And since fighting took place, both sects must have been contentious to have suffered the ultimate punishments of death, banishment and separation.

In a country like Senegal, where the ruling party is the *Parti Socialiste* (PS), past as well as current leaders have still had to rely on religious brotherhoods for basic political support. The struggle seems to be between the Mourides, previously influential via Leopold Senghor, and the Tidjianes, the current President Diouf's background. Because of the non-Islamic beliefs that have crept into the brotherhoods, Diouf has supported reformist tendencies. Still, this has failed to discourage formation and activities of Islamic radical fundamentalist groups, influenced by Iran. Two pro-Iranian publications, **Djamra and Wal Fadjri,** constantly attack the government with a radical Shi'ite ideology. The editor of one, Sidi Lamine Niasse, is the brother of the so-called Ayatollah of Kaolack, a center for great violent confrontations within the PS and a destabilizing factor in the general Casamance region. The radicalism is also propounded by the religious leader of the indigenous Lebanese community, Sheik Zein Mohsen and his acolytes at the *Centre Social Islamique*. Superficially one could conclude Iranian influence and connections exist only because of a Lebanese (and presumably Shi'a) community. However, most of the Senegalese are Sunni in background. Diouf's uncle, Badara Deme, and other influential leaders are marabouts, another term for Sunni identification. Elizabeth Diouf, the President's wife, is half Lebanese and half local tribe, thereby bridging the barrier between the Sunni and Shi'a elements in Senegal. Furthermore, an effective radical appeal, to be acceptable, has to be directed at the Sunni-backgrounded population, regardless of its origin.[117]

To the North, Iran has demonstrated its ability under Khomeini to forego its zealotry when dealing with Mummar Gaddafi and Libya, overwhelmingly Sunni in religious background and in its radical fundamentalism. Since both countries have felt very isolated at times in the broader Middle East/North African region, obvious differences have been overlooked to sustain their links and cooperation. In 1980 the Iranian government contemplated an initiative of an investigating team to Tripoli to resolve once and for all the disappearance of the missing Lebanese-Iranian leader, Imam Musa al-Sadr. The trip was canceled at the last minute due to the intervention of Ayatollah Montazeri and ex-Foreign Minister Yazdi, both friends of the Libyans. There argument put intergovernmental cooperation at the highest premium over Shi'a interests and radicalism. Thus a Sunni-based radical regime has been in fairly consistent alliance with a Shi'a-based radical regime.[118] Since 1983 the Iranians have found an additional role for this cooperative venture--helping facilitate their own terrorist goals through the Libyan regime as a means of avoiding direct complicity or condemnation.[119]

Moving further West in North Africa we come to Algeria. Of the three main strands of Islamic fundamentalists, one has certain connections, despite a Sunni background, with Iran and Lebanon, and a second one has more indirect or less certain linkage with the Iranians. In the first instance, we are concerned with *Le Djihad Islamique* (Islamic Jihad), led by Cheick Sadeck al Moundhiri. A violence-prone organization, it may well have succeeded in infiltrating the army and the *Gendarmerie Nationale* (National Guard). Like other North African Islamic Jihad's, it too is secretive, but integrates the two sects, at least by its external connections.

The second possibility is *Le Mouvement pour la Democratie en Algerie* (MDA), a modernist Islamic movement led by the perennial leader, Ahmed Ben Bella. With strong Berber support at home, both Libya and Iran have sought to use him against the incumbent regime which has recently shown a proclivity towards American contacts and anti-Gaddafi actions. The Ben Bella cooperation with Iran and Libya is a marriage of political convenience to the extent it exists, each using the other for separate and mutual goals of change in Algeria.[120]

The most rapidly mushrooming case is evolving in Tunisia in North Africa, some distance from Iran and with virtually no Shi'a population. It also is one of the most heavily documented cases in terms of available evidence. As early as February, 1985, the Iranians were surprised to find a group of Tunisians among the delegates to the Islamic Revolutionary Council in the World meeting in Libya. They indicated they represented the Islamic Tendency Movement (MTI), led by Rashed Ghanouchi, who had been heading the organization since at least 1981 when he was arrested by the government and imprisoned for three years. Though the Iranians were enthusiastic about using Libya as a vehicle for promoting Islamic revolution in countries like Tunisia and Morocco, they wanted a purely Islamic approach as opposed to Libya's united front approach including leftists.

> Al-Turayki (Iranian representative to the meeting) talked with one of the Tunisians, called Sadok Shimi, a representative of the Tunisian Islamic Tendency Movement, and he informed him that the Iranian deputy foreign minister, who visited Tunis at the end of last summer, was able, during his stay in Tunis, to contact one of the leader of the movement, notifying him of Teheran's decision to support the movement materially and morally.[121]

Because of surveillance and other problems they were unable to fulfill all their promises and needed Libyan geographic borders to facilitate movement into Tunisia proper. A lengthy report then followed on MTI operations from Libya, including Gaddafi's role and effort in behalf of the group.[122] In May, 1985, MTI denied any contact with a foreign government or ambitions to cause a revolution.[123]

In March, 1986, Kuwait's **KUNA** reported that Tunisian security authorities had uncovered a religious *political* organization whose leaders had received special religious teachings in the Iranian city of Qom the year before (1985). Since the same report noted that Tunisian security had also uncovered a small, *new* Iranian-oriented political party organization called. Hizballah al-Mukhtar (Chosen Party of God), the previous year's group was most likely the MTI.[124] Even the newer group was Iranian-connected since the Jihad movement, of which it was a part, also attended that now famous and oft-cited 1986 international terrorist conclave in Teheran.[125]

In response to the MTI attack on **Al-Dustur**, the newspaper that comprehensively reported the story of Teheran's relations in the first place, used its staff in Europe to run down the particulars of the relationship. On July 15, 1985, they produced a *detailed report* corroborating the accuracy of their first allegations. Details covered the mechanics on both sides of the cooperation and linkages, and went so far as to identify the further efforts and activities in neighboring Algeria and Morocco through religious organization branches also run from Iran.[126]

All of the Sunni-Shi'a linkages and cooperation would be either limited or unlikely were it not for the prime mover, fomenter and consolidator---Iran under the Ayatollah Khomeini. For most contemp[orary Sunni fundamentalist groups in the Middle East, Iran serves as an inspirational or aspirational model rather than as an ally.[127] But as already indicated in example after example, the line between model and ally has been crossed.. This, despite the cleavages wrought by the Gulf War. A theme of overriding commonality was echoed by Iran's President Khomeini when he declared:

> It is slanderous to describe the revolution in Iran as a sectarian revolution. Our revolution is the revolution of all Muslims, including Sunnis and Shi'is.[128]

Indeed, Khomeini has gone so far to

say: (t)he reasons which led Muslims at one time to become Sunnis and Shi'ites do not exist any longer..."[129] Kalim Saddiqui, head of the Moslem Institute in Britain, a pro-Khomeini intellectual, summarized the prevailing situation, clearly exploitable throughout the Islamic world, this way:

> Talk to the bus drivers and the rickshaw pullers in the Muslim world, Shia and Sunni alike, and you'll find that they approve of what Khomeini has done in Iran...They feel that Westernized elitist rulers have to go, in Saudi Arabia, the Gulf, Jordan, Iraq, Morocco, Indonesia, Sudan, Turkey, Somalia, and elsewhere.
>
> Iran now defines itself in Islamic terms...Its frontiers are not physical but Islamic...National boundary lines are artificial...I don't know where the new revolutions will be, or when, but they are coming, some within the next 10 years.[129a]

Obviously, these remarks underscore a preoccupation dually informed by idealism and *Realpolitik*. In a region overwhelmingly populated by the Sunnis[130] any hope for the spread of an Islamic revolution is tied to the interest and cooperation with Sunni radical fundamentalists. As such, the Khomeini regime has actively solicited their support as well as promoted their activism and influence. This is most evident in the institutionalized structure set up by the Iranian Islamic government, minimally a clearinghouse for other militant Islamic groups,[131] and maximally a proficient action-oriented vehicle forgetting its message across and facilitating terrorism as means to this end (see chart). Aside from an extensive overseas network arranged to deal with prominent Shi'a situations in places like Lebanon, Iraq and the Gulf States, other instrumentalities were as much or more concerned with impacting all Muslims or especially Sunni elements. The most remarkable role was exercised by Hojjat ol-Eslam Seyyed Hadi Khosrowshahi in his capacities as Ambassador to the Vatican (using his European Islamic Cultural Center) and as founder of the Islamic League Against Arab States. In each instance he performed the major tasks of dealing with and conveying the radical fundamentalist message to Sunni societies and groups whether in the Middle East, elsewhere throughout Asia, and among Muslim migrants in western Europe.[133]

But the overseas network and facilities represented one side of the extensive process committed to propagatying the Iranian view and the actual linkages anbd cooperative efforts. Over the course of the post-revolution period, evidence has mounted that Iran has become a critical meeting place and training center for subsequent political violence and activities by returnees to their homelands. Qom, Isfahan and Tehran have repetitively showed up on reports and analyses as waystations for terrorists and dissident causists from the Arab and non-Arab worlds. Dozens of Arab and Islamic nations have been represented at these gathering places. Put in perspective, given the distaste of Iranian fundamentalists for leftists, the obvious Shi'a segment expected and present, the solicitation of those with a Sunni background has been very obvious. The primary purpose of the various meetings and conferences was to agitate and inspire the Shi'a and Sunni participants to return home and work assertively in behalf of their common Islamic cause.[134] The end result has been the perception and labelling of Iran as on of the leading "terrorist states" in the world.[135]

Conclusion

Based on the available documented evidence and the conceptual/theoretical argumentation, the verdict on the linkages and cooperation assertion is highly supportable. While it cannot be claimed that radical Sunni and Shi'i groups will always cooperate in limited objective situations, neither should it be wholly dismissed. At the present time it can only be stated that this phenomenon has been occurring throught the Middle East and other regions of the world with some increasing frequency (at least until 1988).

Yet in the area of trend analysis, there are a number of factors which lend support to the belief that the collaborative activities of Islamic radical fundamentalists, rather than being an isolated incident, could represent a new factor in Middle Eastern politics. The following trends support this projection:

- The regional "crisis milieu" will continue to determine the style of politics in the Middle East.[136]
- Although Islamic fundamentalism may have lost some of its appeal among Middle Eastern intellectuals, it still remains the most potent radical force in the region.[137]
- The continuing decline inoil revenues and concomitant decrease in remittance funds to such dependent countries as Egypt, Jordan, the Sudan and the Yemens, coupled with existing economic development problems portends political instability easily exploitable by extremist elements.[138]
- The continued prospects of cooperation between radical Islamic and Palestinian terrorist organizations introduces the possibility of fundamentalist violence becoming an institutionalized variable in Middle Eastern politics.[139]
- The indications that Ayatollah Montazeri, a leading advocate of revolution for export, could succeed Khomeini in Iran, suggests that regime's subversive and across border politi cal activities will not abate.[140]
- The continued ability of Iran to use a surrogate state like Libya as a vehicle of entre and assertive influence in other Sunni-populated states has initiative and deflective advantages and is therefore likely to persist.[140a]
- A settlement of the Persion Gulf War in any fashion short of destruction of the Khomeini regime would further reduce intersectarian tensions and open up prospects of additional collaboration as well as Shi'a encroachment in Sunni societies.[141]
- While the outlook for peaceful political, economic and social development in the area has been negative for some time it is perhaps more appropriate nowadays to view the regional dynamics in terms of regression.[142] Finally, it should be emphasized that there is nothing inevitable in the further deterioration of stability in the Middle East (or Islamic World) or in the prospect of cooperation between Sunnis and Shi'i. Negative determinism is no

Iranian Overseas Network (1982 On)[132]

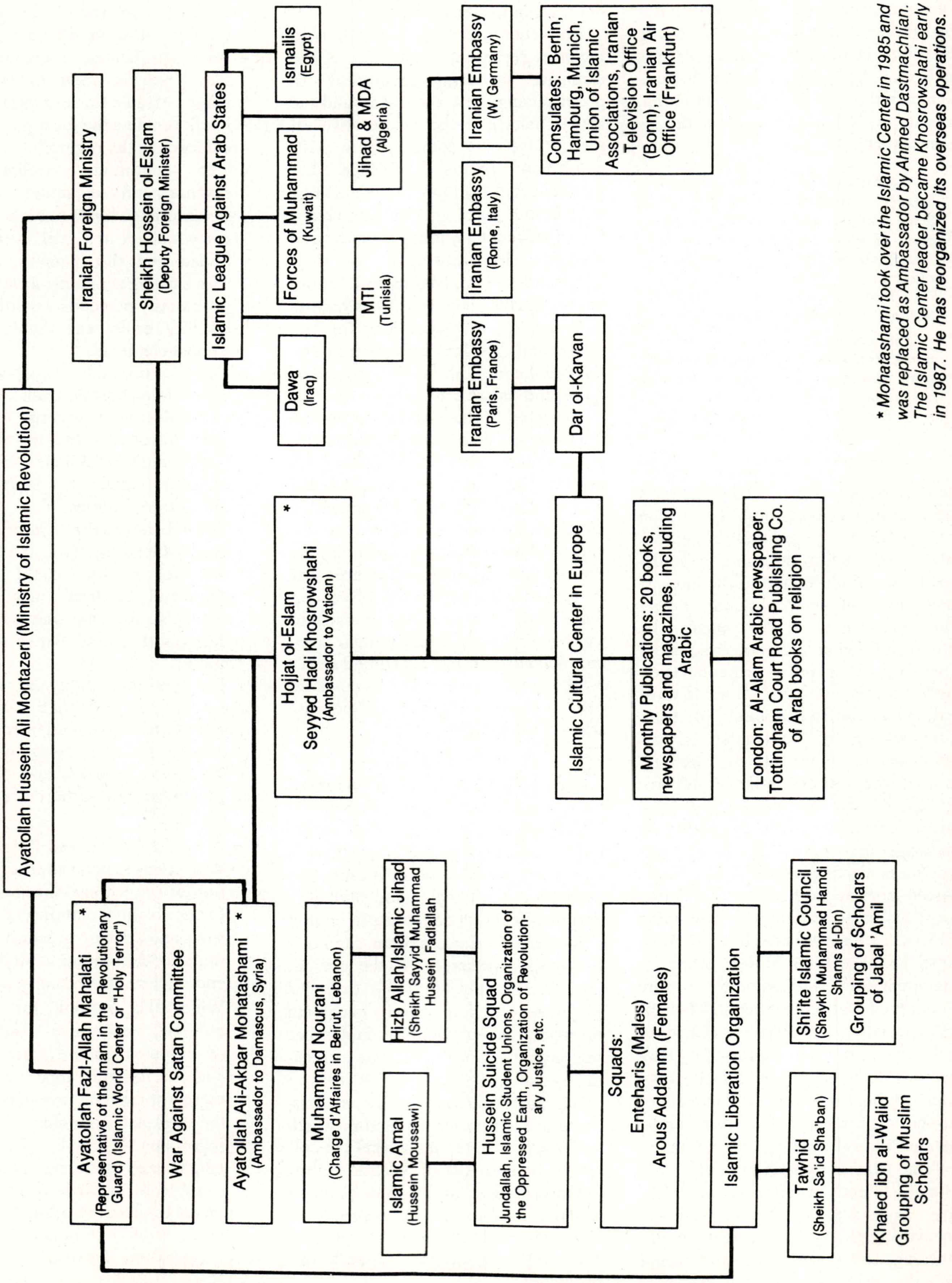

** Mohatashami took over the Islamic Center in 1985 and was replaced as Ambassador by Ahmed Dastmachlian. The Islamic Center leader became Khosrowshahi early in 1987. He has reorganized its overseas operations.*

less fatuous than its positive variant. Iran, a key sponsor of inter-sectarian collaboration, in a post-war decision might turn inward rather than sustain its outward aggressiveness. But clearly this would reflect "the end of the Khomeini Revolution" rather than its success and continuity. Unfortunately, the crisis which has the Arab/Islamic Worlds firmly in its grasp, of which cooperation between radical fundamentalist groups across sectarian lines constitutes only one part, reveals no immediate signs of weakening. An attuned observer of the regional dynamics would be well advised to pay deliberate attention to continued Sunni-Shi'i linkages as a critical variable in understanding and interpreting events.

77. See New York Times, October 1, 1985.

78. The body of Arkadi Katakov was found in West Beirut on October 2. See New York Times. Octover 3, 1985.

79. To be sure, this was not the first time Soviest have been attacked in the region. James Bill notes that "...over a dozen Soviet advisors were assassinated in 1980-1981 in Syria." See Bill, op. cit., p. 126.

80. Shi'i forces assumed control of this area on February 8, 1984. See Thomas L. Friedman, "The Lessons of Lebanon: A Personal Retrospective," Council on Foreign Relations, September 17, 1984.

81. Tripoli is Lebanon's second largest city and has the state's largest Sunni concentration (80%). See Yosef Olmert "Lebanon," in Colin Legum, Haim Shaked and Daniel Dishon, eds., Middle East Contemporary Survey (New York: Holmes and Meier, 1984, p. 670).

82. Ibid., p. 670.

83. Ibid., p. 670. According to The Economist, during the past two years, "...at least 5,000 Alawites have migrated from northern Syria into Tripoli, to add to the 50,000 Alawites already there. See The Economist, September 28, 1985.

84. In Islamic usage the term "tawahid" refers to the "oneness" of Allah. For information regarding the emergence of Sha'ban and Tawahid, see Olmert, op. cit., p. 671.

85. Ibid., p. 671.

86. Consistent with this anti-syrian orientation, Sha'ban is said to have lent support to members of the Syrian Muslim Brotherhood. See Olmert, op. cit., p. 671.

87. Ibid., p. 671, See New York Times, December 26, 1987, p.2.

88. See The Christian Science Monitor, October 2, 1985.

88. See The Christian Science Monitor, December 17, 1987.

89. The Beirut Voice of Lebanon indicated that 1,500 Palestinians from the Al- Jarmag Brigade, thought to be pro-Arafat, fought on the side of Sha'ban's Islamic Unifications Forces against the Syrian-backed militias. See The Foreign Broadcast Information Service (FBIS) "Lebanon" September 29, 1985. Also see New York Times, October 6, 1985.

90. See The Economist, September 28, 1985. p.39, and The Miami Herald, September 15, 1985.

91. Ibid.

92. The Economist, op. cit., p. 39.

93. Ihsan A. Hijazi, New York Times. October 2, 1985. Hijazi wrote; "(t)wo different organizations claimed responsibility today for the abduction of four Soviet diplomats here..." He identified one group as the Islamic Holy War and the other as the Islamic Liberation Organization-Khalid ben al- Walid Forces. See also A. R. Norton, "Estrangement and Fragmentation in Lebanon," Current History, February, 1986, p. 62.

94. Ibid. On the connection between Islamic Jihad and Iran, see The Christian Science Monitor, June 17,1985. Also a spokesman claiming to speak for Islamic Jihad claimed that it was "...coordinating its actions with the Islamic Liberation Forces of Kalid al Ibn al-Walid." See "Lebanon," FBIS, September 30, 1985.

95. New York Times, October 2, 1985.

96. Ibid. Also see, The Christian Science Monitor, October 2, 1985.

97. Ibid.

98. Ibid. Also see John Kifner, "Syria in Lebanon Declining Fortunes," New York Times, October 2, 1985.

98a. This account may be found in FBIS, October 22, 1985. According to William Rugh, Al-Syassah's political orientation may be described as "moderate, pro-government, less emotional than others, and pro-Egyptian." See William A. Rugh, The Arab Press (Syracuse: Syracuse University Press, 1979), p. 102.

99. FBIS, op. cit., p. A3. This correlates with a report published in New York Times, June 31, 1985. This analysis indicates that: "(t)here are about half a dozen Sunni Moslem leaders in West Beirut now allied with the Party of God, and in Sidon, south of Beirut, earlier this month an Islamic Front has formed under the direction of a shi'ite cleric with strong ties to Iran, Sheik Maher Hammond, that united Shite and Sunni clerics cooperating with the Party of God." The pro-Iranian bearing of Sha'ban was noted in the same report. Also New York Times, June 31, 1985 indicates that such a Sunni-Shi'i front had been established in June. A report in The Miami Herald, October 31, 1985 asserted that the kidnapers were believed to be linked to the Islamic Council of Ulemas "...a coalition of extremist Moslem Clergymen." In addition, the confusion regarding the responsibility for the abduction as reported in Al-Sayasah correlates with the pattern of statements published in FBIS. See FBIS, September, 1985.

100. FBIS, op. cit., p. A3.

101. Shireen T. Hunter, "Terrorism and Religion," Christian Science Monitor, November 7, 1984, p. 18.

102. FBIS, May 16, 1985, pp. 123-124; also see Note 99; R. Hrair Dekmejian, "Fundamentalist Islam, "Middle East Review, Summer, 1985, p. 32.

103. A. R. Norton, "Estrangement and Fragmentation in Lebanon, " Current History, February 1986, pp. 61-62.

104. "Lebanon: The Shi'i Factor," Middle East Intelligence Survey, p. 11; Juan Tamay, "Shiite Zealots Link with PLO to Battle Amal, a Hated Foe," Miami Herald, October 12, 1986, p. 26a.

105. Ibid.

105a. New York Times, Chart, February 11,1987.

106. Eric Davis, "Islam and Politics in Modern Egypt," SUNY-Binghamton Conference, March 13-14, 1981, pp. 12-15; "Egypt: Opposition to Sadat (II), "Middle East Intelligence Survey, Nov. 1-15, 1979, pp. 118-119.

107. Ibid., pp. 6, 27-30; Dekmejian, op. cit., pp. 28-33, especially p. 30.

108. FBIS, July 25, 1985, pp. 40-43.

108a. Davis, op. cit., pp. 24-25; Roger Owen, "Migrant Workers in the Gulf," Middle East Review, Spring, 1986, p. 25.

109. Brian Crozier, "The Problem of Crazy States," National Review, March 14, 1986, p. 24; "Egypt Arrests Key Islamic Cleric," New York Times, July 16, 1986; FBIS, July 13, 1987, c1-c2.

10. "Sudan. The Mahdi, Again?" Africa Confidential, March 12, 1986,pp. 2-3.

110a. See Wright, op. cit., p. 24.

110b. See Dekmejian, op. cit., p. 188.

111. "Potential Destabilizing Factors in the Saudi System," Contemporary Mideast Backgrounder, October 3, 1983, p. 5.

112. Ibid., "Tehran Urges Pilgrims to be Activists in Mecca," New York Times, July 19, 1986; "Internal Islamic Division as a Central Focus of Ferment in the Middle East," Weekly Media Abstract, July 17, 1986, p. 4. Also see Bernard Schechterman, "Politics of Instability in Saudi Arabia," Middle East Review, Fall/Winter, 1981-1982.

113. Crozier, op. cit., also see Chart and citations in #132.

114. Ibid.

115. Ibid.; also Crozier, op. cit., p. 24.

116. "The Iraq Internal Labyrinth, Contemporary Mideast Backgrounder, April 22, 1985, p. 5.

117. "Senegal: Handle With Care," Africa Confidential, February 27, 1985, pp, 4-6.

118. This anti-Iraqi coalition, known since 1978 as the "Front for Steadfastness and Resistance," was originally an anti-Sadat coalition. From the outset it was led by Syria. For a report on the joint Syrian-Libyan-Iranian terrorist connection, see The Wall Street Journal, June 19, 1985; FBIS September 6, 1985, p.35.

119. FBIS, June 17, 1985, p. 32, 33.

120. See Dekmejian, op. cit., p. 198; "Algeria: Playing with Splinters," Africa Confidential, November 27, 1985, pp. 3-4.

121. FBIS, June 17, 1985, pp. 32-33.

122. Ibid., p. 33.

123. Ibid., pp. 34-35.

124. FBIS, March 17,1986, Q8.

125. Crozier, op. cit., p. 24.

126. FBIS, September 6, 1985, pp. 33-35.

127. For examples of this inspirational/aspirational phenomenon in Algeria, Morocco, Tunisia, Egypt, the Sudan, Syria, the West Bank and within the PLO, see Pipes, op. cit., pp. 325-327; David K. Willis, "Fundamentalist Islam" Christian Science Monitor, 1985, p. 15; see also Robin Wright, "Sense of Persecution Fuels Shiite Resurgence," June 21, 1985, p. 11.

128. Quoted in Martin Kramer, "The Divided House of Islam," in Legum, Shaked and Dishon, op. cit., p. 240. Kramer notes that during January 1982, the Khomeini regime declared a week of Shi'i-Sunni unity to mark the Prophet's birthday. A small conference was held in Tehran attended by an undisclosed number of Sunnis. Given the dearth of information on this gathering, Kramer concludes that "...it was impossible to determine the extent of Sunni participation." Yet, it seems evident that unity was a major preoccupation for the regime.

129. Quoted in Wright, op. cit., p. 173.

129a. David K. Willis, " The Politics of Islam," Christian Science Monitor, July 25,1985, p. 15.

130. To be sure, Sunnis are in minority position in such states as Iraq, Lebanon, and Bahrain.

131. See Wright, op. cit., p. 27; also John Tagliabue "Terrorists Reportedly Trained in Iran," New York Times, December 30, 1985, p. 6.

132. Wright, op. cit., pp. 192, 108-9; Amir Taheri, "The Fruits of Terror," New Statesman, November 22, 1986, pp. 6-7; Amos Perlmutter, "Containment Strategy for the Islamic Holy War," Christian Science Monitor, 1983; Gary Thatcher, "New U.S. data show terrorism ebbed in 1986," Christian Science Monitor, February 3, 1987, pp. 3-4; "Chart," New York Times, February 11, 1987, FBIS, June 17, 1985, p. 32; FBIS, September 6, 1985, pp. 36-38; Lee Grady, "Islamic Jihad and the War on the West," The Miami Journal, August 1985, pp. 11-13; "Ivan's new terror plan," Foreign Report, The Economist, January 22, 1987, for reorganization of overseas network.

133. FBIS, September 6, 1985, pp. 36-38.

134. Wright, op. cit., pp. 27-31, 33-35. Kramer indicates that Montazeri was a major force in the Shi'i-Sunni unity effort. See Kramer, op. cit., p. 239. For a current discussion of Iranian involvement in PLO terrorist activities, see New York Times, December 30, 1985. She writes: "...some 380 men with various religious and revolutionary credentials met at the former Hilton conference hall." In her view, this seminar "symbolized a turning point" in the regime's commitment to export its revolution.

135. Tagliabue, op. cit., p. 6.

136. This style will likely be one of extremism. Regarding the future for Middle Eastern countries, Elie Kedourie writes: "(t)he long-term prospect in these societies is one of intellectual isolation, if not downright hostility, while the ideological style of politics which has made such inroads makes for activism and instability." See Kedourie, Islam and The Modern World, op. cit., p.66.

Regardless of its origin or causes, the crises which afflict this region preclude the possibility that moderation shall overcome extremism as the salient form of political expression--at least in the near future.

137. There is no indication that radical secular movements are regaining ascendancy over fundamentalism anywhere in the region. Even in Egypt, where a strong leftist movement once threatened the regime, Islamic militants constitute the principal opposition movement. See The Christian Science Monitor, June 14, 1985.

138. On the destabilizing ramifications of economic contraction in the Persian Gulf on such states as Egypt, Jordan, the Sudan and Yemen, as well as the potentialities for an upsurge in fundamentalism, see John Kifner and Judith Miller, "Wave of Arab Migration Ending with Oil Boom," The New York Times, October 5, 1985. Also see David K. Willis, "The Politics of Islam," Christian Science Monitor, July 25, 1985, p. 15.

139. See John Tagliabue, "Terrorists Reportedly Trained in Iran," New York Times, December 30, 1985, p. 6. Tagliabue indicates that it is widely believed that the terrorists responsible for recent attacks in the Rome and Vienna airports were trained in Isfahan, Iran. It is also suspected that the organizer of these operations, Abu Nidal, maintains training facilities in the Bekaa valley in Lebanon. This is also the area where the Iranian-sponsored Shi'i fundamentalist organization Hizballah is thought to be located. In fact, it has been noted that some interaction between the Palestinians and Hizballah has occurred. See Elaine Sciolino, "Wide Mideast Backing Reported for Abu Nidal," New York Times, January 19,1985. Also see p.

140. See The Economist, November 30, 1985.

141. See Dekmejian, op. cit., p. 168.

142. Analysis of the former colonial areas of Africa and Asia may increasingly involve this concept. While meliorists will always deny the possibility that regression may occur as readily as progress, the post-colonial experience of these areas gives cause to doubt the efficacy of their confident judgments. For example, in Africa, expectations of progressive democratic political systems have been eclipsed by the gruesome reality of tribal warfare, man-made famine, and corrupt despotism. By any account, the basic requirements of life are worse in the sub-Sahara region than they were at the time of independence.

The meliorists' vision does not appear to have faired any better in the Middle East. Obviously, to measure either regression or progress in this area by the standards of Western democracies would be pointless and unfair. Yet, as with Africa, the political, social, and economic achievements in these societies have been rather dubious. The inventory of such tribulations in this region, are by now well known. In fact, the power of radical Islam is often viewed as product of this condition. That the fundamentalist route may prove to be a dead end suggests not that a better route will be pursued, but that the situation there is indeed desperate.

Why Hostage-Taking Is So Popular With Terrorists

It's cheap, effective and the targets are plentiful

Brian Jenkins and Robin Wright

Brian Jenkins is chairman of the political science department at the Rand Corp. and director of research on political violence. Robin Wright, a senior associate at the Carnegie Endowment for International Peace, is a former Middle East correspondent based in Beirut.

Israel's invasion of Lebanon was just one month old on July 4, 1982, when a car carrying four Iranians—three diplomats and a journalist—headed toward East Beirut. At a checkpoint run by the Lebanese Forces, an Israeli-backed Christian militia, the Iranians' car was stopped even though it had diplomatic plates and, according to the Iranians, a police escort.

The four Iranians were taken hostage.

Tehran was outraged first by the kidnapping of high-level diplomats and then by the general disinterest in their fate, perhaps remembering the international furor and headlines devoted to the 52 Americans held in Iran between 1979 and 1981. But U.S. mediators and regional governments were all preoccupied with the war, and the four Iranians were practically forgotten. It turned out to be a costly oversight.

The incident, as recounted by both Iranian and U.S. officials, marked the genesis of the current foreign hostage phenomenon in Lebanon—a phenomenon that, as Lt. Col. Oliver North's recent testimony made all too clear, became a foreign policy obsession for the Reagan administration. More important, the abductions established the precedent and the initial motive for what has since become the most effective terrorism tactic in the Middle East in the 1980s. At least 130 foreigners from 18 nations have been held hostage in Lebanon since 1982.

Kidnapping has become a weapon of choice for terrorist groups for four reasons:

- Kidnapping is a relatively inexpensive tactic for small, poorly financed groups to make their presence known.
- Military and other forms of conventional power that major countries possess are virtually useless against kidnappers.
- Increased security awareness has made attacks on embassies and government officials as well as hijackings more difficult.
- The number of targets is almost limitless; they cannot all be defended or protected.

The 1982 incident that started the current wave of kidnappings is almost forgotten now. The four Iranians were never heard from again. Although few knew it at the time, the Christian militia had tripped on a major catch. The only name initially publicized was Mohsen Mousavi, chargé d' affaires at Iran's embassy in Moslem-dominated West Beirut. But also in the car was Ahmad Motevasselian. Tehran says he was merely an embassy political officer, but the State Department claims he was a commander of the Iranian Revolutionary Guards who had moved into Lebanon's eastern Bekaa Valley three weeks earlier.

Although the United States paid little attention to the incident in Beirut, Tehran's theocrats and their Lebanese allies never wrote off the Iranian hostages. In 1985 the United States received word through an independent channel that Iran would help with the half-dozen American hostages who had been seized since the 1982 incident if information was provided about the four Iranians. The United States again checked into the case; word came back that the Iranians were dead. Not much importance was attributed to the query, and the case again was forgotten.

With the benefit of hindsight, officials in Washington and diplomats who were serving in the Middle East at the time now recognize that the Iranian abductions established a new context and a new model for political violence against the various foreign forces in Lebanon that was later to be widely reenacted.

But in 1982 the United States did not calculate the long-term implications, despite the lessons both sides had learned during the prolonged hostage ordeal at the U.S. Embassy in Tehran. In the meantime, Iran and its Lebanese brethren have pursued and perfected an age-old practice.

Political kidnappings were not new to Lebanon. At least 2,000 local Moslems, Christians and Jews have disappeared over the past 12 years of civil strife, according to local relief agencies. Most are believed to have been immediately or eventually murdered, although all factions charge that their rivals still hold hostages.

But since the 1982 incident, the historic pattern of hostage-taking has changed dramatically in both proportions and political repercussions.

Governments are now locked in blind struggles with mysterious organizations they can barely identify. Direct communications are non-existent, normal ransom negotiations impossible. And the political consequences of the ensuing crises, unintended by any of the contestants, have gone far beyond the individual lives at stake.

After the 1982 abductions, the groups in Lebanon became more numerous and far murkier. Only in isolated cases have conventional militias been held responsible, such as the Lebanese Forces, which allegedly took the Iranians, or the predominantly Christian South Lebanese Army, which abducted

From *The Washington Post National Weekly Edition,* July 27, 1987, pp. 23-24.

21 Finnish United Nations troops for a week in 1985.

Based on information gleaned from freed hostages, most captors appear to be youths who come from poor areas and from communities that have the least political input. Their leaders are largely unknown. Some are not even groups in the conventional sense, but rather appear to be a constellation of ideologues and thugs often brought together on an ad hoc basis. A few cells appear to have been formed for a single operation or to have emerged almost accidentally from a family or a neighborhood gang.

A few are leftists, but the most active are the religious extremists, predominantly Shiite Moslems. Islamic politics, which is neither left nor right, adds a new variable to the hostage phenomenon as well as to the world's political spectrum. This new variable has befuddled both the constitutionally secular United States and the ideologically atheist Soviet Union.

Another key new component is state sponsorship. Outside powers have deeply confused the issue of responsibility—and inexorably complicated solutions—by skillfully exploiting hostage situations to achieve their own ends.

U.S. officials now believe that the intense American reaction to hostage situations planted ideas among the captors and their Iranian mentors about the latitude of their demands. In the process, the value of the hostages appreciated—and in terms of numbers held, the phenomenon grew out of proportion to any other terrorist tactic.

But the pattern of general violence indicated that the extremists also had a more ambitious goal—to purge the West from Lebanon and eventually the region. Two specific flashpoints in 1983—the U.S.-orchestrated troop-withdrawal agreement between Lebanon and Israel and U.S. warships shelling Moslem militias at the request of the Christian-dominated government—symbolized what was perceived by a growing number of extremists as Washington's anti-Islamic bias. The tension sparked a reaction.

"The Islamic Jihad organization claims it is responsible for the abductions in order to renew our acceptance of Reagan's challenge and to confirm our commitment," declared the first communiqué, "that we will not leave any American on Lebanese soil." This power play established the framework for a new variation on international warfare in which the weaker party consistently had the edge.

The role of Iran, which had an ax to grind because of its own "missing" envoys as well as a new ideology to propagate, was pivotal. Between the 1982 kidnappings and the new seizures in 1984, the Islamic republic had stoked the rising passions of religious zealotry in Lebanon. With help from local and imported mullahs, the Revolutionary Guards sent to Lebanon became missionaries more than fighters, drawing on the growing antagonism among Lebanon's Moslem majority toward the West and methodically building up a corps of cells among the faithful.

The tension was first played out in the 1983 bombings of the U.S. Embassy and the Marine and French barracks, during which more than 360 were killed. The Shiites, meanwhile, were rapidly becoming major players in Lebanon.

But by then the Marines were hidden in containers converted into underground bunkers and the temporary U.S. diplomatic quarters were barricaded. That left only civilian targets, such as Malcolm Kerr, president of the American University in Beirut, who was assassinated outside his campus office in January 1984. Although deeply mourned throughout the region, Kerr's death had little political impact.

And as the extremists quickly learned, the impact and protracted agony of a life hanging in the balance is far more effective than quickly forgotten murders carried out by an assassin or a suicide bomber. Deaths elicited anger; taking hostages provided leverage.

Holding foreigners also guaranteed status, power and attention, all important commodities to extremists from sects that had been ignored or discriminated against for decades. Like buying low-priced futures, holding hostages has been, in effect, an investment almost certain to grow in value over time—as recent events have proved.

In just over three years, Iran and Lebanese groups have elicited unprecedented political concessions directly related to hostage seizures, including millions of dollars' worth of arms from the United States and an agreement from France to negotiate the release of Iranian funds frozen by Paris since the 1979 revolution; more than $300 million has already been returned.

Even the release of the 766 Lebanese prisoners after the TWA 847 hijacking in 1985—the United States' second mass hostage trauma—was secondary to the captors' broader goals: world recognition that Israel was holding them in violation of international law and public questioning about the price of the U.S. commitment to Israel. And U.S. countermeasures, such as Washington's angry threats or the deployment of the Sixth Fleet off the Lebanese coast, served only to underscore American impotence in the face of this new movement. American warships did not impress the young fanatics. No terrorism tactic has ever been so effective.

Other groups with different agendas inevitably began to imitate. In later stages, U.S. officials believe that teams of "professional" kidnappers carried out the abductions on commission from extremist groups or on speculation, hoping later to sell their captives. "Trade" in hostages became lucrative business. Occasionally the two motives overlapped.

A new variable appears to be further changing the foreign-hostage phenomenon. The turning point was early 1986, when seizures resumed after a lull. Islamic Jihad had stopped abducting foreigners after June 1985, which coincided with the U.S.-Iran negotiations. With the exception of the four Soviets picked up by a Sunni group, not a single foreigner was kidnapped by any group in Lebanon for the next six months. And no more Americans were abducted for almost 15 months, until September 1986.

The change is the product of fragmentation, particularly among the various Shiite cells that still fall under the same umbrella. The breakup is similar to the evolution of the Palestine Liberation Organization over the past two decades. At its peak before the 1982 Israeli invasion, the PLO included eight disparate groups. The result in both cases has been even more labyrinthine politics—and new violence.

The recent proliferation of invisible and untraceable extremist groups has further complicated prevention of and reaction to hostage-takings. Until last fall, all but one of the U.S. hostages were believed to have been taken by Islamic Jihad. By January 1987, four different groups were involved, and at least three of them were predominantly Shiite.

But few who know the Middle East or the background to the hostage trend believe that Tehran any longer has total control over the hostages' fate. Release of Kuwait's 17 prisoners, release of Iranian, Lebanese and other prisoners in Europe, return of further Iranian assets held by the United States and France, or intervention by others, such as Syria, might end the current hostage crisis. But it will not end the phenomenon.

In light of the new framework established in Lebanon in 1982 and the way the trend has subsequently evolved, hostage-taking is likely to be the most vexing terrorism tactic for the foreseeable future. Hijackings are now more difficult because of increased security, and bombers may be discouraged by fortifications around diplomatic facilities. Compared with other options, abducting foreign hostages is physically and politically cost-efficient.

Last year, the West initiated unprecedented efforts to counter terrorism. The United States bombed Libya, while Washington and most of Europe imposed varied diplomatic and economic sanctions on Syria. Cooperation and intelligence exchanges increased among western allies.

But during the same time period, the United States and other nations with hostages in Lebanon made humiliating concessions. The captors could achieve gains far loftier than ransoms and prisoner releases; they were in a position to shape the foreign policy of major powers.

The greatest danger, however, is that the trend will begin affecting foreign interests in hot spots far beyond the Middle East. In light of the policy response by nations with hostage victims, seizing foreigners almost offers a model for other revolutionary or religious extremist groups. Two weeks ago three Americans and a Briton were taken hostage by Sudanese rebels.

Lebanon's unique chaos has certainly facilitated perpetrators of violence. But any area with a strong foreign presence or influence where central authority is breaking down is also vulnerable. Foreign hostage-taking has now become an "acceptable" norm in the international political arena, a way for outgunned and outmanned Third World countries or opposition movements to challenge powers of both East and West—and win.

The IRA

Spreading a wider net

Recent murders on the continent probably signal the entrenchment of a new strategy by the IRA, but its fundamental aim remains the same

THE latest arrests of IRA suspects on the continent have prompted the usual, understandable sense of jubilation in Britain. But if they mark the end of one IRA hit-squad, nobody should doubt that it will be replaced. It is gruesomely clear that the IRA has dug in for its "long war" on three fronts: mainland Britain and continental Europe as well as Northern Ireland.

The range and frequency of the attacks in the past few months strongly suggest that the IRA now has elaborate operational structures in place across several countries. If so, the security forces have to contend with a network that is only too likely to survive chance arrests and follow-up man-hunts.

At the same time, support for IRA prisoners on the continent has been formalised, on the model of the "welfare associations" which raise money for dependents in Northern Ireland, make travel arrangements for jail visits and lobby endlessly about prison conditions. Support organisations are useful to the IRA: they bind it more tightly into Northern Ireland's nationalist minority, most of whom have no truck with murder but do retain a sentimental ambivalence towards the IRA. IRA sympathisers claim that every prisoner draws up to 100 family members and friends into a reservoir of latent and not-so-latent IRA-supporters.

A triple-front strategy carries high risks for the IRA. Most directly, it poses the danger of heavy casualties. The security forces estimate that the IRA has no more than 200 active terrorists. Since 1988 it has lost 20 members (or alleged members) on the continent or in England—three shot dead in Gibraltar, 11 arrested on the continent and six in England. Police have identified others and must presumably have associates under surveillance. Less obviously, but nonetheless of great importance to the organisation, the strategy runs a higher risk of propaganda disasters: like the recent murder in Roermond of two Australian tourists, mistaken for off-duty British soldiers.

Against all this, three main motives probably account for the long-war strategy. The IRA's aim remains, as it has always been, simply to sicken Britain into withdrawing from Northern Ireland. Constant activity across as many countries as possible sustains the pressure on British public opinion. In this respect, protracted overseas trials and extradition rows are almost as welcome to the IRA as volunteers ready to mount bombing and shooting attacks.

Secondly, action against members of the security forces in Northern Ireland itself has become much harder in recent years. Advances in technology, plus bitter experience, have given the British army an unrivalled expertise in anti-terrorist warfare. Much easier to pick off a boy soldier on an English railway platform on his first weekend leave from army camp or a man driving home with his family in a German suburb, than to target a heavily armed and flak-jacketed infantryman backed up by electronic surveillance on the streets of Belfast.

Thirdly, the IRA has had to take stock of its failure in Northern Ireland. A campaign of violence restricted to the province has not had the demoralising impact on British opinion that the IRA had anticipated. Even so, the IRA has not reduced its murderous attacks on the Royal Ulster Constabulary and Ulster Defence Regiment. The army says the first half of 1990 has been one of the busiest periods it can recall, with use of Semtex on a wide scale and a new "lobbing bomb" technique used to some effect.

The sterility of the traditional strategy, sticking to Northern Ireland, was certainly apparent to the IRA's leaders by 1985-86. Unhappily for their victims, it was at this point—courtesy of Colonel Qaddafi's gift of explosives, guns and cash—that the organisation acquired the means to step up attacks overseas. Libyan munificence helped shape the international campaign, begun in earnest in 1988, which so many police forces are struggling to extinguish.

Winning few hearts, fewer minds

The sheer pace and range of the IRA's campaign have damaged the already waning fortunes of the IRA's political wing, Sinn Fein, by pointing up the contradiction of a legal political party that is linked to a killing machine. Sinn Fein once hoped to develop political clout to complement the IRA's military pressure: this was its "ballot-box and Armalite" strategy. But its 11% share of Northern Ireland's poll seems frozen. In the Irish Republic the last election brought the party just over 1% support. The Republic is repelled by what its people see as essentially "northern" violence.

In the bedrock communities of the North's nationalist minority—places like west Belfast, mid-Ulster, south Armagh and Londonderry—IRA killings are in general either justified or tolerated by more ordinary people than commentators outside the province usually like to acknowledge. But even there Sinn Fein admits that its vote is diminished by IRA "mistakes"—bound to multiply as the gunmen range wider.

Sinn Fein cannot influence the IRA, however. The political wing owes its existence to the military campaign's brutal articulation of the minority's grievance. At the height of Sinn Fein's electoral appeal, it was attracting one in three northern Catholics: this was in the aftermath of the 1981 IRA hunger-strikes, when ten prisoners starved themselves to death. The Sinn Fein president and MP, Mr Gerry Adams, may deplore particular IRA actions but he does not condemn a campaign of violence—even if, increasingly, he and others like him recognise how unlikely it is ever to achieve the aim of British withdrawal.

Narco-Terrorism "Shooting Up" America

David W. Balsiger

The unholy alliance between known terrorist groups and drug traffickers is a recent worldwide phenomenon that is growing. Well-equipped guerrilla and communist armies are providing the muscle needed to protect drug lords and their operations.

Colombian drug lord Carlos Lehder, recently arrested and waiting to be tried in the U.S. for drug trafficking, boasts that "coca has been transformed into a revolutionary weapon for the struggle against American imperialism." On national television he has also praised Adolf Hitler and threatened to raise a 500,000-man army to overthrow the Colombian government — something some believe he's capable of doing if he ever gets out of jail!

Narco-terrorism thrives on the American appetite for illegal drugs — estimated at $30 to $90 billion per year! Every drug user in America is helping to finance the narco-terrorism trade worldwide without realizing its implications.

While the drug lords control the narco trade, many governments are engaged in or directly linked to narco-terrorism. These include:

- **Cuba** — Fidel Castro charges $800,000 per boatload of drugs for safe passage through Cuban waters. Castro has bragged, "We are going to make the people up there [U.S.A.] white, white with cocaine."
- **Nicaragua** — Drug operations are directed by Tomas Borge, Nicaraguan Interior Minister and Humberto Ortega, the Defense Minister and brother of Marxist President Daniel Ortega. Drug loading operations have been photographed at Nicaraguan airports, and refining labs are operating in remote coastal areas of Nicaragua.
- **Syria** — Deeply involved in the drug trade, Syria is responsible for funneling most of the profits into anti-West revolutionary activities including international terrorism.
- **Iran** — The Hezbollah (Islamic Jihad) terrorist group uses narco money to terrorize the Middle East and hold American hostages.
- **Panama** — Gen. Manuel Noriega provided safe haven for drug cartel leaders and safe passage for marijuana and heroin headed for the U.S. Gen. Noriega has been recently indicted by the U.S. for involvement in drug trafficking, illicit arms trade, and gross human rights violations.
- **Bulgaria** — This Soviet surrogate channels drugs from the Middle East to Western Europe and North America. The Bulgarian secret police direct the drug-terror connection and have been implicated in the attempted assassination of Pope John Paul II.
- **Soviet Union** — Moscow has worked the drug-terror trade primarily through its three satellites — Bulgaria, Cuba, Nicaragua — although a Soviet cargo vessel had 200 kilograms of heroin seized in 1986.

Czechoslovakian defector Gen. Jan Sejna reported a Moscow meeting in 1962 with Nikita Khrushchev where the groundwork was put in place to use drugs to destabilize Western societies while generating hard currency.

Gen. Sejna, who now works for the U.S. Defense Department, said Khrushchev made the following comment for justifying drug trade involvement: "There were some who were concerned that this operation [drug trade] might be immoral. But we must state categorically that anything that speeds the destruction of capitalism is moral."

In addition to governments being involved in narco-terrorism, many well-known regional revolutionary terrorist groups are involved including the: IRA in Ireland, the PLO in the Middle East, M-19 and FARC in Colombia, Italy's Red Brigades, the right-wing Gray Wolves in Turkey, the Shan United Army, and the Burmese Communist Party in Burma. These radical or communist terrorist groups often use the drug money to buy weapons.

International Drug Lords

It's the excessive profit in the drug trade that keeps pushers, smugglers, growers, drug lords, dope cartels, and terrorist revolutionaries into this cash business. For example, cocaine ready to export from Colombia costs $8,000 to $9,000 wholesale per kilo (2.2 pounds) and sells for about $450,000 per kilo on the street in the U.S.

Colombia provides nearly 33 percent of the marijuana smoked by 20 million Americans and 75 percent of the cocaine consumed by America's five million addicted users.

No wonder drug lords and narco cartels have formed and operate like some of the world's largest business corporations. But the big difference between a corporate business enterprise and a drug cartel becomes apparent when examining a few of these cartels up close.

The Medellin drug cartel in Colombia which controls 80 percent of the cocaine coming into the U.S. had an annual income of $1.5 billion in 1984. During the past 10 years, the Medellin traffickers have ordered dozens of assassinations.

On November 5, 1985, the Medellin cartel financed M-19 guerrillas stormed the Palace of Justice in Bogota and killed 100 people including Colombia's 12 Supreme Court Justices.

One Medellin leader, Pablo Gaviria, employs 200 gunmen and runs two "schools for assassins" where killers are taught to shoot victims from the backs of motorbikes.

With the arrest of Lehder, cartel co-founder, Colombian drug lords have threatened to kill five Americans for every Colombian drug kingpin extradited to the U.S. for trial. American drug enforcement agents believe they have already dispatched a hit squad to attack anti-drug officials in the U.S.

Moving across the world to the Golden Triangle area of Burma, Laos, and Thailand, Burmese kingpin Khun Sa is the world's largest heroin trafficker.

For 25 years, Khun Sa and his private separatist army have fought the Burmese government while developing the opium-

Reprinted from *Family Protection Scoreboard,* Terrorism Special Edition, 1988. Authored by David Balsiger.

Crack Trafficking Groups

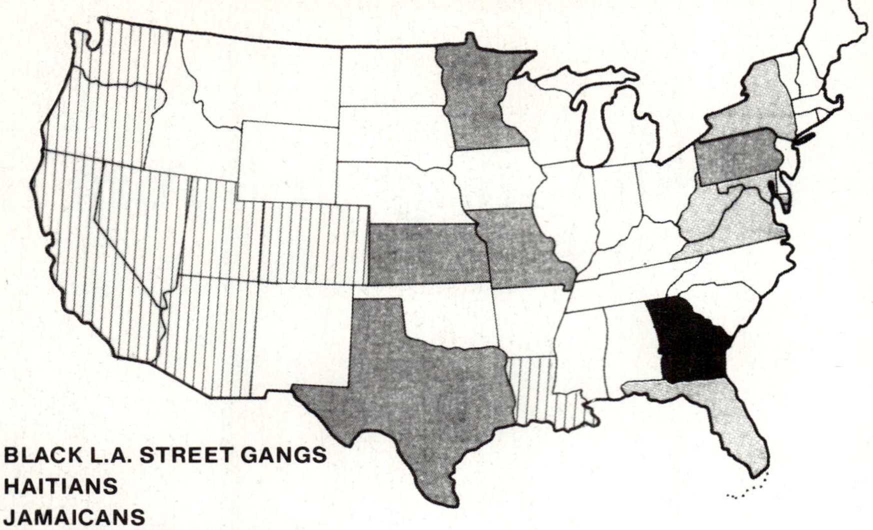

- BLACK L.A. STREET GANGS
- HAITIANS
- JAMAICANS
- HAITIANS AND JAMAICANS

SOURCE: DRUG ENFORCEMENT ADMINISTRATION

Sources of America's Narcotics

MARIJUANA (1987)

Colombia	33%
Mexico	28%
United States	25%
Jamaica	13%
Others	14%

COCAINE (1984)

Colombia	75%
Bolivia	10%
Peru	10%
Others	5%

HEROIN (1985)

Southwest Asia	47%
Mexico	39%
Southeast Asia	14%

SOURCE: DRUG ENFORCEMENT ADMINISTRATION

heroin business in the Golden Triangle.

While Khun Sa maintains a lavish lifestyle and sends his six children to European and U.S. schools, he is known for his harsh brutality.

Deserters from his well-equipped 15,000-man army are tracked down and shot, and informants are buried alive. He is said to have killed a barber who had given him a bad haircut.

Starting about 10 years ago, Khun Sa has tried to make deals with the U.S. government to stop sending dope to the U.S. in exchange for cash payments. The U.S. turned down the bizarre cash and crop-substitution program. Even more recently some have charged that unscrupulous CIA agents have operated a silent drug-money partnership with Khun Sa.

U.S. Customs Service Commissioner William Von Raab recently explained at a Senate committee hearing how one of the Cuban narco terrorism operations functioned with Cuba's full support:

"... A U.S. trafficking group was stealing shrimp boats in the United States, taking them to Cuba and there receiving fuel and a shipment of arms. The arms were then delivered by the boats to Nicaragua, after which they continued on to Colombia, picked up a load of marijuana, and returned to Cuba. In Cuba they were refueled and given a Cuban escort to a position south of Florida from which they would then proceed to their off-loading points in the United States, sort of a nifty 20th-century version of the old triangle trade, except this case involves Cuba and Nicaragua."

With corruption, global politics, and nature conspiring to hamper the drive to cut the narcotics flow into the U.S. and at the source drug officials are constantly fighting a losing battle.

America's War On Drugs

On the user level it's been hard to stop when drugs increasingly are related to crime. Three-quarters of all those arrested in Washington, DC for serious crimes tested positive for drug use in 1986, compared to 56 percent in 1984. Most believe if drug use is cut serious crimes will also decline.

To cut drug usage the U.S. federal policy has been three fold:

- Reduce the supply by attacking the production and the selling of the drugs.
- Reduce demand through education and public opinion.
- Provide drug users rehabilitation treatment on a voluntary basis.

At first glance, the strategy of interrupting supplies might seem to be successful. A doubling of Customs Service and Coast Guard outlays between 1981 and 1986 for drug interdiction activities, for instance, resulted in a 16-fold increase in seizures of cocaine, which rose from 1.7 tons in 1981 to 27.2 in 1986.

Beefed up domestic enforcement efforts have led to a large rise in the number of arrests and convictions for drug offenses. From 1982 to 1986, the number of Drug Enforcement Administration (DEA) drug convictions doubled, from about 6,000 to about 12,000, while the number of FBI convictions rose from just 42 to 2,791. Seizures of clandestine drug laboratories and marijuana eradication were up dramatically.

In total, the federal government will spend nearly $2.5 billion on drug law enforcement in fiscal 1988, up sharply from $806 million in fiscal 1981. Yet drugs continue to be widely available throughout the U.S.

Foreign eradication efforts have not prevented increases in foreign production. Said

DRUG USE CLUES

The following list prepared by *Good Housekeeping* magazine lists commonly used drugs and their resulting symptoms:

MARIJUANA: Diminished motivation, increased appetite, reddened eyes, impaired judgement, poor memory of recent events, decreased physical coordination.

COCAINE: Runny nose, tremors, nervousness and irritability, anxiety, decreased appetite.

HEROIN: Needle marks on arms, hands, knees, and abdomen, flushing, drowsiness, itching, decrease in physical activity.

HALLUCINOGENS (PCP,LSD): Dilated eye pupils, trembling of hands and feet, chills, cold and sweaty palms, decreased appetite, anxiety, disorientation.

THE WORLDWIDE SPREAD OF NARCO-TERRORISM

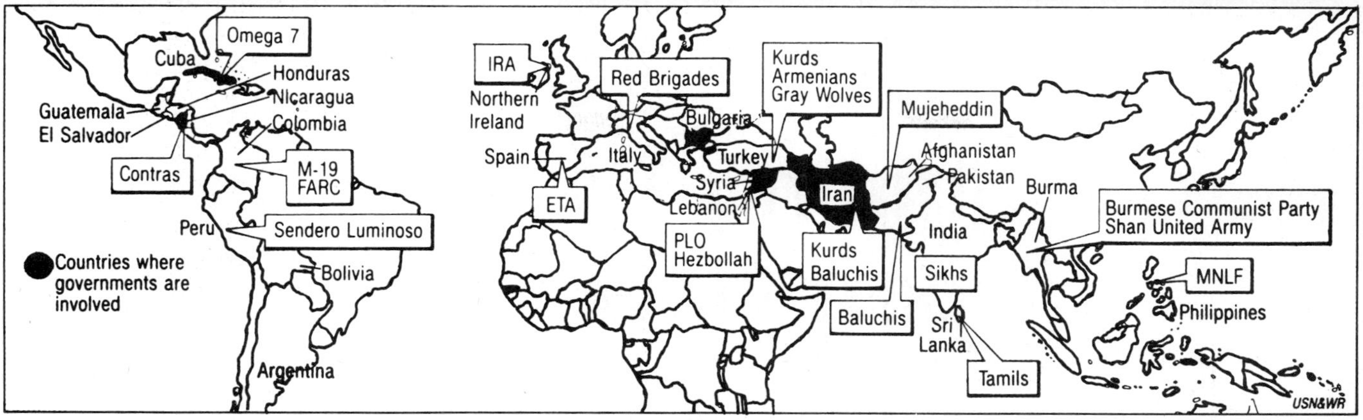

EDITOR'S NOTE -- Research conducted by *Scoreboard* editors with the U.S. State Department, the federal Drug Enforcement Administration and non-government sources found no evidence that the Contras or Omega 7 were involved in narco-terrorism. However, *Scoreboard* research does indicate that Cuba, Nicaragua and Panama should have been painted entirely in black, indicating heavy government involvement in narco-terrorism.

GANGS: Rise of Inner-City Warfare

by William G. Stearns

South-Central Los Angeles is ruled by gang terrorism.

The several dozen neighborhoods composing this urban war zone are plagued with daily drive-by shootings and black teenagers hawking cocaine crack from sidewalks as if they're running lemonade stands.

Violence rules the nights so severely that reporters covering gang activity have seen residents literally crawl across streets and lawns to reach the safety of their homes.

Police estimate that 40,000 teenagers and young adults belong to gangs in this section of Los Angeles alone. LA's two major gangs — the Bloods and the Crips — use Uzi submachine guns, AK-47 assault rifles, and AR-15 semiautomatics. And they're murderous:

- Last year 387 gang-related deaths were reported in Los Angeles County.
- Gangs were responsible for 299 drive-by shootings during the first five months of 1988. An enemy's house is targeted and, regardless of who is home, hundreds of rounds of semiautomatic fire are poured into the building from cruising cars.
- In just a seven-week period starting in mid-April, the Los Angeles Police Department made 12,500 gang-related arrests for crimes from assault to drug trafficking to murder.

Violence is a natural outgrowth of the LA gangs' power struggles over drug territory. Already the Crips and Bloods control the entire West Coast crack market, and their violence is expected to spread as splinter groups establish beachheads to deal in drugs and weapons in other major cities.

These splinter groups, according to Drug Enforcement Administration officers, are "highly organized and extremely violent." Crips groups are now entering Phoenix, Denver, Salt Lake City, Las Vegas, Portland, Seattle, and New Orleans. The Bloods have recently established networks in Sacramento and Tucson.

Noted expert on gang terrorism Phil Little of West Coast Detectives says the recent gang problems in Los Angeles "are not by chance, but are a direct effort to disrupt our inner cities. LA is just the first city to experience this well-armed and well-organized level of gang terror.

"The local police attempt to counter the gang violence is only a Band-Aid. When LA buys drugs," says Little, "it's arming gang terrorists to murder any of us on our own streets."

And LA is said to be just the beginning of what most major cities across America will be experiencing!

DRUG MONEY LAUNDERING COUNTRIES

Andorra	Luxembourg
Anguilla	Montserrat
Antigua	Netherlands Antilles
Bahamas	Panama
Bermuda	Switzerland
Cayman Islands	United Arab Emirates (Dubai)
Channel Islands	
Gibraltar	USA (Miami, New York City, Los Angeles, Houston)
Hong Kong	
Liechtenstein	

SOURCE: NATIONAL NARCOTICS INTELLIGENCE CONSUMERS COMMITTEE

the State Department 1987 report on the international drug trade: "Narcotics production was up all over the world." Nor have interdiction efforts reduced substantially the amount of drugs entering the U.S. A recent Rand Corporation study estimates that cocaine imports more than doubled between 1981 and 1985 while marijuana imports remained roughly constant.

In April 1986, President Reagan issued a "presidential directive" identifying the $110 billion-a-year drug trade as "a national security threat."

In disclosing the directive, Vice President George Bush said every American should "understand the very real link between drugs and terrorism. Too many families are already painfully aware of the connection between drugs and terror in our homes, in our streets, and in our schools. Now we must convey that when you buy drugs, you could also very well be subsidizing terrorist activities overseas. The message is just that simple and direct."

Peru's Shining Path Terrorists Open New Front in Drug War

Relentless atrocities intimidate farmers into shifting crops to coca

Sally Bowen

Special to The Christian Science Monitor

Satipo, Peru
Shining Path, Peru's Maoist guerrilla group, has found a new paradise in the central jungle province of Satipo.

Moving north from the Apurimac River, a coca-growing area it has long controlled, Shining Path, or Sendero Luminoso, is turning the Ene Valley into a new battleground for drug trafficking and its revolution against the Peruvian state.

The option the guerrillas have given local coffee and fruit farmers is brutally clear—cultivate coca and take up arms for us, or die.

Daily incursions and atrocities, albeit poorly publicized, emphasize the need for the new government of Alberto Fujimori to develop a coherent counter-subversive strategy, say security officials and church representatives in the region.

"The Ene Valley is a strategic zone," says Nemesjo Mejia, mayor of Satipo, a town of 30,000. "It is a breeding ground and hatchery for subversion."

Shining Path strategy in the eastern jungle appears to mimic its partly successful struggle to dominate the Upper Huallaga Valley, 300 miles farther north, where most of Peru's—and the world's—coca leaf crop is grown, say Peruvian antidrug police officials.

Since the guerrillas' big push into Satipo late last year, roughly 1,500 villagers are reported by locals to have been killed. Villagers tell of dozens of bodies floating in once-idyllic rivers.

SHIRLEY HORN – STAFF

President Fujimori's Sept. 26 rejection of a United States military aid package, worth $35.9 million, was received glumly by counterinsurgency officers. (A broader antidrug strategy was needed to support crop substitution and other forms of employment, Mr. Fujimori said. Officials also said clauses in the package would have breached Peruvian sovereignty.)

"Shining Path has to wipe out anything that opposes it," says a police intelligence officer. "It was a tremendous stupidity not to sign the military agreement" with the US.

Although the money had been specifically intended to equip six Army and Marine battalions for antidrug operations in the Upper Huallaga Valley, police here worry that government rejection of US military assistance will endanger their own hoped-for $20 million US aid package.

With a broken economy and desperately under-funded security forces, Peruvians in emergency zones must largely protect themselves. In Satipo Province, as in many other regions, this means forming community defense groups, or *rondas,* often at police or Army insistence.

But "how can we defend ourselves with only two old muskets and pitchforks against their machine guns and grenades," asks a villager, whose 30-family village was razed by the Shining Path.

Only the most atrocious Shining Path killings appear in Lima newspapers, much less the international press. The April 12 massacre at Naylam, an example of Shining Path revenge on a *ronda,* left behind 37 bodies, many mutilated. Smaller-scale murders are too commonplace to attract much attention. "Six killed in one village yesterday, two elsewhere the day before. But no one counts, no one cares," says a Franciscan priest working in the Satipo area.

For locals, who include native Indians as well as more recent immigrants from the poorest regions of the high Andean sierra, Shining Path violence is incomprehensible. Victor, a local manager of a small cocoa-processing plant, comes originally from Ayacucho, the town where Manuel Abimael Guzman launched the Shining Path movement in 1980.

"When the subversion started, I said fine. There was a lot of oppression and poverty. The state did nothing," Victor says. "But now I don't understand Shining Path's actions. They are all directed against the people."

By some estimates, 80 percent of those who farmed fertile lands stretching 100 miles southeast of Satipo have fled in the past 18 months. Some seek safety in small townships, while the Indians withdraw further into the jungle.

Along the banks of the Ene, Shining Path controls rudimentary cocaine-paste laboratories and at least 65 airstrips from which the basic material is flown out, destined for further refinement in Colombia or Brazil, says an antidrug police official.

In this lawless frontier, government presence is minimal. Mazamari, 15 miles from Satipo, is home to the "Sinchis," Peru's oldest elite antisubversive battalion. Notorious for tough antisubversive tactics and human rights abuses in the 1980s, the Sinchis now have terrorists in their own backyard. "It's ironic," says a senior Sinchi officer. "We're the main antisubversive base in Peru and now we are ourselves surrounded by terrorists."

The Sinchis, whose Quechua Indian name means "fierce warrior," are not paper tigers. Cadets on nightly training runs rhythmically chant "Blood, blood, I want blood," while two old Israeli command cars crawl around town. But they have no air transport and the Ene River, where Shining Path has its permanent bases, is a dangerous five-day march away.

During the first wave of guerrilla incursions in Satipo province, Ashaninka Indians also formed *rondas* and tried to resist with bows and poisoned arrows. Few such *rondas* remain. Instead, police intelligence officials report, Shining Path has forcibly recruited more than 250 Ashaninkas. Armed with automatic weapons, they move from one native community to another to persuade others to join them.

Faced with guerrilla-created power vacuums and continuing atrocities in emergency zones, Fujimori's government lacks the resources for an effective counterinsurgency or the economic development programs he believes are the only long-term solution.

The rejection of US military aid was correct, says Diego García Sayan, executive secretary of the Andean Commission of Jurists, a human rights organization. "But the ball is firmly back in Peru's court now," Mr. García says. "We have to come up with some concrete proposals for the development assistance we need."

Colombian Journalists Vs. Drug Terrorists

'It took tragedies to arouse interest in the U.S. press'

EL ESPECTADOR

This interview with José Salgar, acting editor in chief of the liberal "El Espectador" of Bogotá, was conducted by "World Press Review" associate editor C. Dominique van de Stadt:

How is 'El Espectador' coping after the bombing of its offices last fall in retaliation for the paper's crusade against drug traffickers?

Two hours after the near destruction of the newspaper offices in September by a truck filled with dynamite, all of the paper's personnel came to work. About three hours after that, amid the rubble, a 16-page edition was put together with magnificent photographs of the destruction. We had done our duty of publishing at our usual time and throughout the entire country. The paper has continued to operate with the pen as its only weapon. It has not missed printing a single issue.

No desertions have been registered among *El Espectador*'s 1,200 employees; there have been no resignations due to fear. Public opinion has supported us; the paper's circulation has risen. For some time, the paper has sold an average of 200,000 copies daily, and since the bombing it has increased by at least 20,000 copies daily. In subscriptions, especially, there has been a demonstration of solidarity. Advertisements have increased—that is one way for businesses to support *El Espectador*.

An extraordinary show of support has come from newspapers worldwide, which have formed a fund for aid to papers in difficulty. Through it, *El Espectador* hopes to obtain long-term credits to recover and to maintain our program to become a sort of laboratory of Latin American journalism for the 21st century. *El Espectador* has always trained its own journalists. But about a year ago, with our staff, we started courses to train journalists to report on problems common to all Latin American nations, to emphasize this area of Latin American journalism rather than nurture journalists who are experts only in issues affecting their respective countries. Every Wednesday, the paper publishes a supplement entitled *El Espectador del Mundo* prepared by these journalists under our supervision.

What is your own history with 'El Espectador'?

My story is a long one. I am 68. At 13, I had the opportunity to work at *El Espectador* as an editorial messenger and to study there. Thanks to the support I received from the editors at that time, I made headway in journalism studies without leaving the newspaper. I have had the opportunity to travel and take many courses abroad as well as at home. I have completed 55 years of continuous work at the paper, and I have lived through all of the most difficult periods that the paper has experienced. For a long time, I was editor in chief of an evening newspaper called *El Vespertino*, published by *El Espectador*.

When *El Espectador*'s previous editor, Guillermo Cano, was assassinated in 1986, it was agreed that his sons, Juan Guillermo, 35, and Fernando, 33, who have worked at the paper since their youth while continuing their studies, would be editors. But as I was the most senior person on staff, a shared editorship was ultimately decided upon, so I am actually a co-editor. Juan Guillermo and Fernando have often been absent, due to repeated threats against their lives. Since Cano's death, five of the newspaper's journalists and administrators have been killed by drug terrorists.

How do you manage to do your job, knowing the fate of your predecessor?

Maybe because we have had to suffer many hard blows, and those of us who are still alive have the obligation to follow that example and to continue at our battle stations with the same intensity. *El Espectador* was founded in Medellín 103 years ago precisely to struggle against injustice, to fight for freedom and for the good of Colombia. The editor at that time said that the paper was aimed at "not allowing good and bad actions to have the same name, not flattering those in power to gain their favor, and not applauding men or their acts unless our conscience so dictates." He said that we should be a sort of Don Quixote at the service of informing a great nation.

Aside from being Quixotes, idealists, always laboring to discover evil wherever it may be and attack it, we have created a great journalistic professionalism. Veteran journalists like us consider journalism a service to the country, to society, to the world—a service as obligatory as military service. We believe

Reprinted from *World Press Review*, January 1990, pp. 38-41. Taken from *El Espectador*.

that our job is like that of the missionaries who go to evangelize, to extend an idea throughout the world; that our office as journalists also contains something of the soldier who must sacrifice himself for his country, yield his life to defend the ideals for which he swore allegiance. So we carry out a journalism of conscience that is far superior to the material losses that we may incur. This is not the first war that *El Espectador* has suffered. Aside from battling drug trafficking, my newspaper has confronted corrupt powers, dictatorships, censorship, shutdowns, persecutions. As far as I know, it has always won its battles. This is not the battle it will lose.

Does this require sacrifices? Yes, and we have made ours. But that does not mean that we should slacken in our mission, even if the amount of blood we have to give is large.

Is 'El Espectador' making a difference with its coverage of the drug war?

We are using the professionalism of journalists to help not only our government, but also the governments of other countries, to confront drug trafficking and arrive at a just solution.

The Colombian press must overcome the conditions that have caused the virtual disappearance of investigative reporting. To deal with this, the press should produce reports compiled by teams of reporters. But there is too much pressure on journalists; this unanimity has not been achieved. The individual journalist lives in fear. If there were a united front, we could again publish investigative reports of value.

There is no lack of journalists. We are training journalists to form new, specialized teams of reporters. The students are 100-percent interested in confronting the Colombian problem.

Could what has happened to 'El Espectador' happen to other newspapers in Latin America?

Yes, possibly, if this war is not won in Colombia. If the newspapers do not wage this war, it is possible that it will continue to expand. If Colombia fell under the power of the drug traffickers, the wave would continue to spread through Latin America.

Why is it Colombia that has been most afflicted by the drug problem?

Colombia is ideally situated geographically to receive the coca leaf that is planted in the south—in Peru and Bolivia. The great cocaine processing plants were established in Colombia because it is in the middle of the Americas, with possibilities for immediate air and ship transportation with many connections. This is why Colombia has the greatest concentration of drug money in the world. Added to this are some political factors.

There is a zone in the Colombian interior called Magdalena Medio, where local self-defense groups, initially intended to combat communism, were formed with help from the paramilitary. The paramilitary do not belong to the official government forces but are friends of the military. Then these groups were joined by the drug traffickers. So what was going to be a political guerrilla group to fight communism became a force allied to the drug mafia for the destabilization of democracy.

What is the government doing to combat the drug barons and their allies?

One of Colombia's most serious problems is the infiltration of the drug world into all of its institutions—for example, the justice system and the armed forces. There has been a big cleanup in the police forces, which, in great part, had been dominated by the drug cartels. There have also been many changes in the army. There is more control now by the central government over its armed forces. The purge especially intensified after the assassination of leading presidential candidate Luis Carlos Galán in August.

Another problem is that the drug traffickers tell the judges, "Either you rule in our favor, or we will kill you. If you rule in our favor, we will pay you." So the judges are unprotected and often fearful. Colombia is searching for a means of effective protection of judges, like that achieved in Italy, for example. In Italy, during the "maxi trials" against the Mafia, a special building was constructed for the judges to live in.

Some say that Panama, under Gen. Manuel Noriega, is a country governed by drug money.

Yes, and it has been seen that this caused the repudiation of Panama by not only the U.S. but the entire world. It would be very serious if that example extended to other countries. I do not think that it will happen in Colombia.

Can you envision a Colombia without drug cartels?

It would be the return to what Colombia has always been: a poor, long-suffering country that based everything on work, the word of honor, the exercise of freedoms, but that did not have the vice that came from rapid, illicit enrichment. There was certainly political violence then; there were civil wars. Developing countries are always subjected to great pressures and great difficulties. But this is one of our most violent periods.

The drug story has recently overshadowed that of the guerrilla war. Are the M-19 leftist guerrillas and other groups still a threat to stability?

Yes. Currently the government is going ahead with a program to make peace with the M-19. Much progress has been made in negotiations, and it is hoped that soon there will be a demobilization and that the M-19 will surrender its arms to an international organization. In this case, the M-19 would become a political faction that would subject itself to the country's laws, peacefully.

But there are other subversive groups. There is the Army of National Liberation (ELN), which is very dangerous and highly organized. It wants to combat foreign capital in the oil industry and has been attacking oil pipelines. Another group is the nationalist Revolutionary Armed Forces of Colombia (FARC), which has been militant in its campaign for social justice but whose activities have deteriorated into common crimes. The government plans to try to achieve with FARC what was achieved with M-19.

Why doesn't the government hold talks with the drug terrorists?

There are many who believe that the crimes committed by the drug mafia are not political or economic crimes, but atrocious common crimes, committed by criminal bands that have no representation, no base from which to request any type of dialogue, that do not deserve to have talks but should be punished by the law. There should be no dialogue with these people.

We must not yield in trying to bring them to justice. We must not sit around a table with criminals who have trampled essential freedoms, such as the freedom of expression; who arrogate to themselves the right to censor the press with dynamite; who apply the death penalty in Colombian streets and request that the government negotiate with them. But I realize that, because drug trafficking is an international problem, some type of discussion will be held nevertheless.

Can the power of the drug mafia ever be broken?

Yes, I think so. I think that we can convince them that their crimes are driving away any possibility of an accord with the population. What has most damaged the Colombian environment is that these men have resorted to crime to combat those who do not agree with them. This has turned the national climate against them.

We must not admit the slightest probability of a coup d'état by the drug traffickers; we can stand fast by backing the drastic action of President Virgilio Barco. This is a great battle for the democracy of 30 million Colombians.

Is there a crop that could replace cocaine as Colombia's economic linchpin?

Coffee has been a victim of international ill treatment, of low international prices. If the price of coffee were higher, if the great consumer countries, such as the U.S., would pay better prices for it, surely many coca plantations would be replaced by coffee plantations.

Colombia has great export items. It is the No. 2 flower-producing country in the world, yet there are many trade barriers that hinder this flower trade. There are many regions that used to cultivate marijuana and coca and now produce fruit. The Federation of Coffee Growers has offered incentives to peasants to diversify crops. But if the price of coffee continues to fall at the current rate—it dropped almost 50 percent in 12 weeks after the worldwide coffee agreement was suspended last July—Colombian coffee farmers will have no other recourse but to stop producing coffee and dedicate themselves to coca, which is more profitable.

The best way for other countries to fight against the economic and social injustice in Colombia is to help us by buying our products at better prices. This will give the peasants better profits and will enable them to confront the illegal networks that are paying them to produce the drugs that are destroying the rest of humanity.

What is the status of the extradition debate now?

There is a minority, obviously headed by the drug traffickers, that opposes extradition. But national opinion in favor of the government's position on the need for extradition has grown. The support of all sectors of the country for energetic measures to detain the waves of crime is constantly rising. And one way to punish the criminals is to send those who commit crimes in another country to that country to be punished.

How is the drug war affecting the political scene?

My paper has been very severe in condemning the interference of drug money in political campaigns, and I have asked the public to vote for those candidates who expressly condemn drug trafficking and to oppose the financing of political campaigns with dirty money. Drug traffickers are trying to compromise many politicians by funding their campaigns.

How would you assess U.S. and other foreign coverage of Colombia and its drug war?

There are great injustices. When Colombia would not extradite drug traffickers to the U.S., that was reported and used against us. But when extradition was approved, it was not reported as great news. These are inconsistencies in the treatment of Colombia.

This attitude is more prevalent in the government than among journalists. But the journalists are also somewhat to blame in that they stress what is most sensational, the hottest news.

Washington's policies must change. We view with skepticism the anti-drug policies of the Bush administration. That administration supports repression in our countries but does not fight with equal intensity the drug consumption within the U.S.

The press should not let enthusiasm wane. Always, when there is a natural catastrophe, such as a flood or an earthquake, the world is moved at first, and then interest falls rapidly. It is imperative to keep alive the interest in defending all of the newspapers that are threatened by drug trafficking. The recently established Inter American Press Association fund, for example, provides loans to newspapers in difficulty.

More information about Colombia's true situation is needed in the international press. Its tradition of democracy is far older than the current violence. Medellín has a wonderful climate; it is a capital of medicine and of organ transplants. But this is never featured in the international press.

It took tragedies, threats against freedom of expression, and bombs to arouse U.S. press interest in Colombia. We journalists are very emotional. We only report the bad news. The last time that Colombia figured prominently in the international press was in 1985, when a volcano erupted, killing some 20,000 people. And even then it was not so much the collective deaths or the economic consequences that touched the world, but the plight of a young girl trapped by debris in a pit. Now there is an opportunity to better understand Colombia and its battle against an international crime network that is trying to take control of political and economic power in poor countries. This problem is not only Colombia's; it is the world's. And the world does not understand that it has to unite to combat it. The U.S. press should attach more value to issues other than vice and crime. Between blood and orchids, the U.S. always prefers blood.

Will Terrorists Use Chemical Weapons?

Yonah Alexander

Yonah Alexander, an authority on international terrorism, is a research professor at George Washington University's Elliott School of International Affairs and senior fellow of the U.S. Global Strategy Council.

News stories about Libya's Rabta Plant, which the United States believes produces chemical weapons, and the warning by President Saddam Hussein that Iraq will destroy half of Israel with chemical weapons if the Jewish state preemptively attacks his country, have refocused attention on the threat of unconventional warfare.

Development of chemical and biological weapons is easier than that of nuclear explosives. There are no insurmountable technical impediments in the use of chemical agents such as floroacetates, organophosphorous compounds and botulinum toxin.

They are relatively easy to obtain, their delivery systems are manageable and dispersal techniques are efficient. In fact, terrorists desiring to make nerve gases rather than obtain them directly from Libya, Iraq or even the commercial market, can still find the formulas at some libraries despite attempts by various governments, including that of Great Britain, to remove them from public access.

Once in possession of such information, a terrorist with some technical know-how could synthesize toxic chemical agents from raw materials or intermediates. In fact, many chemical toxins (e.g. Cobalt-60 and TEPP insecticides) are commercially available. They could be bought or stolen.

Also, covert and overt options for dispersing chemical agents are virtually limitless, including poisoning of water systems, contamination of food supplies, generation of gases in enclosed spaces with volatile agents, generation of aerosols in enclosed spaces with nonvolatile agents, and dispersal with explosives.

Early Attempts

There is no accurate statistical data on the number of chemical- and biological-related terrorist incidents because not all of them have been reported by governments and the news media. But there apparently are more than 100 known cases.

• In 1975, German authorities were threatened that mustard gas—stolen from an ammunition bunker—would be used in Stuttgart unless all political prisoners were granted immunity. Only some of the stolen canisters were found later.

• In 1978, an Israeli citrus fruit export to Europe was contaminated with liquid mercury. Israel had to cut back its orange exports by 40%. A similar incident on a smaller scale occurred in 1989.

As in the case of chemical violence, biological terrorism—the use of living organisms to cause disease or death in man, animals or plants—is technically possible. Warfare agents such as bruceliosis (undulant fever), coccidioidomycosis (San Joaquin Valley or desert fever) and psittacosis (parrot fever) are easy to acquire, cultivate and disseminate. The poison Ricin, for example, is developed from castor beans; about half a milligram is fatal.

Terrorists evidently have considered resorting to biological terrorism:

• In 1970, members of the Weather Underground planned to steal germs from the bacteriological warfare center at Fort Detrick, Maryland, for the purpose of contaminating a city water supply.

• In 1975, technical military manuals on germ warfare were found in a San Francisco hideout of the Symbionese Liberation Army.

To be sure, such forms of technological terrorism have been rare in comparison to the approximately 40,000 domestic and international incidents during the past 20 years. Terrorist operations typically have been limited in scope and not indiscriminate—owing to the perpetrators' desire to demonstrate their tactical capabilities rather than to commit a major violent act for its own sake.

Better-Trained Terrorists

However, technological developments offer new capabilities and targets.

Terrorists today are better organized, more professional and better-equipped than those in the 1970's. They are likely to take greater operational risks in the next decade. A few sophisticated terrorist groups could use higher leverage tactics to achieve mass disruption or political turmoil.

For example, Force 17, a terrorist body with special operational responsibility in Yasir Arafat's Fatah—the major constituent of the Palestine Liberation Organization (PLO)—had been trained in chemical weapons. Similarly, the Hezbollah (Islamic Jihad or the Party of God), operating with the support of Iran, might employ chemical terrorism against Western interests in the Middle East or against other adversaries such as Iraq or Saudi Arabia.

In addition to some of the Middle Eastern terrorist groups, some European extremists including Direct Action (French), the Irish Republican Army, and Red Army Faction (German) are likely candidates for unconventional terrorism.

Biological and chemical weapons have many advantages for terrorists. These include low cost, ease and speed of production, and the fact that they can be developed by individuals with limited education. Weapons production requires only a minimum of tools and space, and equipment can be improvised or purchased without arousing suspicion.

Other advantages include the reliability and availability of such weapons. Also, they are easier to disguise and transport than conventional arms.

Since chemical and biological weapons also are the "weak" states' answer to lack of nuclear arms, their proliferation, particularly in the third world, is disturbing. Libya and Iraq provide recent examples of this challenge.

In the longer term, nuclear terrorism—explosion of a nuclear bomb, use of fissionable material as radioactive poison or seizure and sabotage of nuclear facilities—also is plausible. And if only one terrorist group succeeds in achieving its goals through the use of weapons of mass destruction, then the temptation for other extremists to escalate will grow.

Reprinted from *JINSA Security Affairs,* June/July 1990, p. 10.

Terrorism and Public Opinion: A Five Country Comparison

Christopher Hewitt

This article examines public attitudes towards terrorism in five countries: Uruguay, Spain, Italy, Germany and Northern Ireland. It analyzes public concern over terrorism, images of the terrorists, support for the terrorists' goals, and public approval of anti-terrorist measures. There are significant differences between nationalist and revolutionary terrorism. Nationalist terrorists have a high degree of support from an ethnic constituency, while revolutionary terrorists attract a much smaller degree of support primarily from the educated young. It is concluded that public opinion towards terrorism is a product of complex historical situations, and that public attitudes are unaffected by the terrorist campaign itself.

The goal of insurgent terrorism is to alter the political situation by changing public opinion. The relationship between terrorism and public opinion is, therefore, an important issue that needs to be examined.

One purpose of terrorism is to draw attention to some cause or grievance. Schmid and de Graaf go so far as to claim that

> the genesis of contemporary insurgent terrorism ... (can be seen) primarily as the outgrowth of minority strategies to get into the news. The choice of this strategy to get grievances vented and redressed is ... probably due to the fact that the significance of parliaments as an intermediary between people and the executive has declined.[1]

Getting noticed is one thing – being understood is another.[2] Governments threatened by political insurgents usually dismiss them as common criminals, and, among the general public in England and the United States, terrorists are often seen as psychologically disturbed. For the terrorists, one of their initial problems is simply to be taken seriously, to be considered as having realistic political goals.

Even if the public regards terrorists as politically-motivated revolutionaries or nationalists, it still does not follow that they will support them or their goals. Those who advocate an urban guerrilla strategy believe, however, that terrorism itself can create a revolutionary situation. Two processes supposedly produce revolutionary consciousness. In the nineteenth century, many anarchists and social revolutionaries believed that the masses would be inspired by the 'propaganda of the deed' to rise up against oppression. The Narodnaya Volya's manifesto claimed that 'terrorist activity ... aims to undermine the prestige of the government, to demonstrate the possibility of struggle against the government [and] to arouse in this manner the revolutionary spirit of the people and their confidence in the success of their cause'. Kropotkin said that one terrorist act could 'make more propaganda than a thousand pamphlets. Above all, it awakens the spirit of revolt.' This view was echoed a century later by Latin American revolutionaries. Regis Debray wrote that 'the destruction of one troop transport truck is more effective propaganda for the local population than a thousand speeches'. According to the Tupamaros, 'revolutionary action in itself ... generates revolutionary consciousness, organization and conditions'.[3]

An alternative view of how to create a revolutionary situation is the 'provocation-repression' theory. By attacking the establishment and the security forces, the insurgents provoke the state into mass repression which alienates the general public, and increases support for the rebels.[4] The Basque insurgent group ETA believed that by attacks against the Spanish military and Guardia Civil, they would

> provoke Spanish authorities into an overreaction that would inflict heavy damage on the civilian Basque population. In attempting to stop ETA, Madrid would aggravate already strong but latent hostility against its policies among the Basques, and the previously inert civilian population would then commit itself to support ETA's armed struggle.[5]

In addition to mobilizing and radicalizing their own supporters, terrorists seek to destroy the morale of their enemies. To revolutionaries, the enemy is the ruling class and their agents, to nationalists, the enemy is the nation oppressing them. This produces markedly different campaigns, where revolutionaries selectively attack politicians and businessmen, while nationalists try to raise the costs to the foreign occupiers by killing large numbers of soldiers.[6]

Most counter-insurgency writers deny that terrorism produces support for the insurgents' goals, and argue that the strategy is actually counterproductive. According to Moss, 'in most cases, urban guerrillas are dangerous less for what they do than for what they inspire: the erosion of the consensus, a hardening of the political battle lines and a backlash that strikes back too hard and too indiscriminately', and he goes on to suggest that 'the usual response to terrorism is revulsion'.[7] Clutterbuck claims that, in both Germany and Italy, killing policemen with consequent 'TV pictures of their tearful working class families ... created widespread anger'.[8]

In the case of Uruguay, the consensus holds that public perceptions changed as the Tupamaro campaign became more deadly. Originally the Tupamaros carefully avoided unnecessary violence and attacked only the rich and elite. During Christmas they hijacked a food truck and distributed the groceries in the slums of Montevideo. They robbed the casino, but returned that share which would have gone to the employees. They broke into a financial institution and publicized its corrupt and illegal practices (which implicated a cabinet minister). When one of their kidnap victims had a heart attack, they kidnapped a specialist to treat him, and then released their prisoner when his condition worsened.

Such tactics created a favorable image for the Tupamaros, but the public supposedly turned against them once they began to murder people. 'They lost their original Robin Hood image as imaginative student pranksters who pilfered from the rich to give to the poor, by systematically murdering policemen as well as an American hostage, Dan Mitrione.'[9] This is a common view, usually supported by citing polls which show a dramatic decline in those thinking the Tupamaros were 'motivated by a concern for social justice' from 59 percent in 1971 to four per cent in 1972.[10]

There has, however, been no systematic cross-national analysis of the relation between public opinion and terrorism. This article attempts to remedy the omission by examining five societies, Uruguay, Germany, Italy, Spain/Basque provinces and United Kingdom/Northern Ireland, where significant terrorist campaigns have taken place. Since these cases do not constitute a representative sample, and were selected primarily

From *Terrorism and Political Violence*, Vol. 2, No. 2, Summer 1990, pp. 145-170. *Terrorism and Political Violence*, published by Frank Cass and Company, Ltd., England.

because of data availability, I shall discuss later the extent to which the findings can be generalized.

Insurgent terrorism has taken two forms. In Northern Ireland and the Basque provinces of Spain, nationalist terrorism by the Irish Republican Army (IRA) and Euzkadi ta Askatasuna (ETA) aims to drive out the British and Spanish, and to inspire the local population to support Irish unity or Basque independence. The Tupamaros in Uruguay, the Red Army Faction/Baader–Meinhof group in Germany, and the Red Brigades in Italy sought to bring about a revolution.

Terrorist groups see the public divided into two main categories: their constituency and their enemies. Their constituency consists of potential and actual supporters. For nationalist terrorists, their core constituency is defined by ethnicity: Catholics in Northern Ireland, ethnic Basques in Spain. Politically their support is organized in the militantly nationalist parties such as Provisional Sinn Fein (PSF) and Herri Batasuna (HB) or Euzkadiko Ezkerra (EE). Moderate nationalists such as the Social Democratic and Labour Party (SDLP) and the Partido Nacionalista Vasco (PNV) represent potential supporters, who hopefully can be won over to a militant position.

The revolutionary constituency is less clearly defined. Supposedly it is the proletariat, but *de facto* revolutionary terrorists draw their support from the educated young. Politically they lack an organized base, but are sympathetically, if critically, regarded by the extreme left. In a general sense their appeal is aimed at the left, whether communist, socialist or even social-democratic.

The available survey data are unfortunately, but not surprisingly, short of being ideal. On some topics we lack any information at all. If we wish to make comparisons between countries, the questions are rarely asked in the same form. Although we are interested in whether terrorism changes public attitudes, on several matters survey data exist for only one point in time.[11]

However, we do have sufficient information to consider four topics in some detail: the level of public concern, the image that the public has of the terrorists, the degree of support for the political goals of the terrorists, and public attitudes towards government anti-terrorist policies. Furthermore, although fragmentary, the data allow us to make comparisons between countries, as well as over time, and between groups within the same country. Thus we are able to suggest why people hold the opinions that they do and to link the description of public opinion to the theoretical literature on terrorism.

Terrorism as a Problem

The first question that needs to be asked about public opinion is to what extent terrorism is seen as a problem. One standard survey question asks what is the most important problem facing the country. In Table 1 the percentage selecting terrorism or a related topic is shown.

The answers are obviously affected by the list of topics suggested and by the wording of the topic. In so far as the question forces a single choice on respondents, it does not take account of those who see terrorism as a significant but not the most important problem. In Spain, if we include those who selected terrorism as the second most important problem, the number is much higher. Furthermore, for certain groups terrorism may be more important. In Northern Ireland, Protestants were more likely than Catholics to see terrorism as the most serious issue (41 per cent and 24 per cent).

The simplest explanation for the degree of public concern is that it is directly linked to the amount of terrorism: the more terrorism the more concern. This interpretation is supported by two pieces of evidence. First, cross-national differences in the proportion saying that terrorism is the most important problem do correspond to variations in the level of terrorism. If we consider terrorism-related deaths, for the period prior to when the polls were taken, the rank order is correct. Northern Ireland has the most deaths followed by Spain and then Italy with Uruguay and Germany having far fewer, and this corresponds to the concern expressed.

Second, within Spain, the changing level of concern is closely linked to the monthly death totals. Indeed, it is striking how quickly public attitudes change in respect to short-term fluctuations in the numbers killed (see Figure 1). Unfortunately, in none of the other countries are there a sufficient number of observations to examine changes over time.

Clearly, however, the amount of violence is not the only factor operating on public opinion. In the case of Spain, we can also examine regional differences to see whether there is more concern where terrorist violence is highest. Contrary to expectations, it is those areas with the highest levels of violence which are the *least* likely to see terrorism as a significant problem (see Table 2). This can be explained by considering the role of ethnicity in Barcelona and the Basque provinces, where most violence has taken place. Basques and Catalans have strong regional and ethnic identities, and sizeable minorities support separatist parties.[12] Terrorism is directed primarily not against fellow ethnics but against the Guardia Civil who are – as a deliberate policy – drawn from other regions of Spain.[13]

A similar explanation can be offered to explain the Northern Irish situation, where Catholics feel much less concern about terrorism than Protestants. By 1982 (when the survey was taken) the victims of terrorism were disproportionately Protestant.[14] On the other hand, the Catholic rate of unemployment was much higher than the Protestant rate. Not surprisingly Protestants rated terrorism the main problem facing Northern Ireland with unemployment the second ranked problem, while Catholics reversed the order.

TABLE 1
TERRORISM AS A PROBLEM

	Most Important Problem (%)		Deaths from Terrorism
(1) Northern Ireland 1982	Terrorism	34	2,340
(2) Spain 1979–82	Terrorism/public order	22	414
(3) Italy 1972–79	Public Order	16	227
(4) Great Britain 1971–2	Northern Ireland	13	678
(5) Uruguay 1968–69	Disorder/subversion	4	14
(6) Germany 1976	Public Order	8	12

Sources: *Attitudes to the Northern Ireland Assembly* (Survey conducted for BBC by Ulster Marketing Surveys, Oct. 1982).
Revista Espanola de Investigaciones Sociologicas (1972–82).
Gallup Political Index (London: Gallup Poll).
Indice Gallup de Opinion Publica (Montevideo: Gallup Uruguay).
Karl Cerny, *Germany at the Polls* (Washington: American Enterprise Institute, 1978), p.137.

FIGURE 1
TERRORISM AND THE LEVEL OF PUBLIC CONCERN IN SPAIN (1979–82)

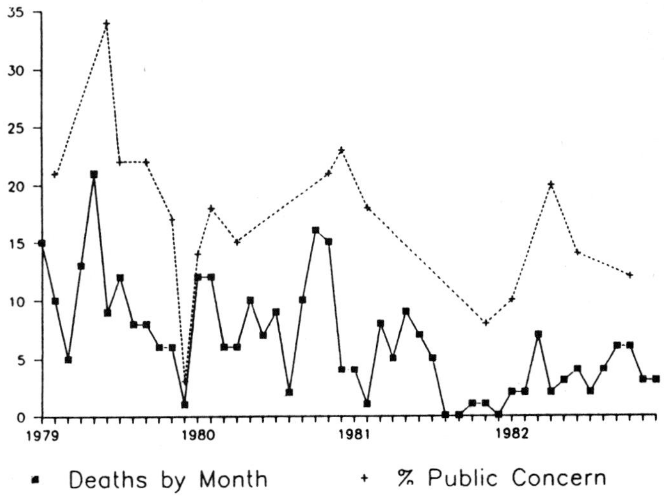

Source: *Revista Espanola de Investigaciones Sociologicas* (1979–82).

The importance of Northern Ireland to the British public can also be explained by considering who was being killed. During 1971–72 British concern reached a peak, with 13 per cent on average saying it was the most important problem for the country. The salience of the Northern Ireland issue was lower than would have been predicted given the number of deaths during the period (678). However, if we focus on the number of *British* soldiers killed (177), the concern expressed is at about the expected level. Since the early 1970s British interest in Northern Ireland has diminished considerably, paralleling the decline in the number of British soldiers killed.

TABLE 2

PUBLIC CONCERN IN SPAIN OVER TERRORISM BY PROVINCE AND DEATH RATE

	Terrorist killings/ m. population	Terrorism main problem (%)
Basque Provinces	191.9	10.5
Madrid	18.1	14.2
Barcelona	7.0	10.1
Galicia	1.8	16.5
Catalonia	0.8	15.7
Andalucia	0.8	18.4
Canaries	0.7	19.9
All other provinces	1.4	21.9

Source: *Revista Espanola de Investigaciones Sociologicas* (1979–82).

How the Public Views Terrorists

In most of the cases that we examine, survey data are available on public perceptions of the terrorists. In Uruguay, respondents were asked whether the Tupamaros were well-intentioned revolutionaries or common delinquents. In Italy, the public was asked to choose one or two phrases that best applied to the Red Brigade members. Three phrases were negative (instruments controlled from on high, dangerous assassins or crazy), but the others were ambivalent (pursuing a just end with the wrong means) or very positive (fighting for a better society). In Germany the question was whether the Baader–Meinhof gang acted out of political conviction or if they had become true criminals. In the Basque provinces, surveys have asked whether terrorists are patriots, idealists, madmen, criminals or individuals manipulated by outside forces. In Northern Ireland, respondents were asked whether they agreed or disagreed with statements about the IRA and the loyalist paramilitaries. (Were the IRA basically patriots and idealists? Were the actions of the loyalist paramilitaries a justified reaction to what has happened in Northern Ireland?) Given that the form of the question varies and furthermore that the answers change over time, somewhat procrustean procedures are necessary to compare the different cases. Table 3 shows the percentage of the public holding positive images of the different terrorist groups, and reveals that a significant proportion acknowledge the political nature of their actions.

TABLE 3

PERCENTAGE OF PUBLIC HOLDING POSITIVE IMAGE OF TERRORISTS

1.	Basque Provinces (ETA)	47.3
2.	N. Ireland (IRA)	38.6
3.	Uruguay (Tupamaros)	38.6
4.	N. Ireland (Loyalists)	37.6
5.	Italy (Red Brigades)	27.6
6.	Germany (Baader-Meinhof)	18.0

Sources: Juan Linz, *Conflicto en Euskadi* (Espasa Calpe: 1986).
E. Moxon-Browne, 'The Water and the Fish: Public Opinion and the Provisional IRA in Northern Ireland', *Terrorism*, Vol. 5 (1981), 41–72.
Indice Gallup de Opinion Publica (1967–72).
L'Espresso (10 Jan. 1982).
Allensbacher Jahrbuch (Institute für Demoskopie Allensbach, 1971).

Some groups are more likely to hold a favorable image of the terrorists. This is particularly true with regard to nationalist terrorists who are regarded very sympathetically by their fellow ethnics. In the Basque provinces, those who consider themselves as Basque are much more likely to see ETA as patriots and idealists than those who consider themselves to be Spanish. In Northern Ireland, Catholics and Protestants disagree significantly in how they view both the IRA and the Loyalist terrorists.

Revolutionary terrorists lack such a clearly defined constituency. Their Marxist rhetoric suggests that their support should be concentrated in the working class; yet, in fact, the Tupamaros and Baader–Meinhof are viewed most sympathetically by those of higher socio-economic status, although the differences are small. Demography rather than class is a differentiating factor with men somewhat more sympathetic than women, and the young noticeably more so than the old.

Political ideology is correlated with attitudes towards the terrorists.

TABLE 4

PERCENTAGE HOLDING POSITIVE IMAGE OF NATIONALIST TERRORISTS BY ETHNICITY

	By Fellow Ethnics	By Other Ethnics
Positive Image of ETA	65.9	15.5
Positive Image of IRA	46.3	34.7
Positive Image of Loyalists	43.9	25.0

Sources: Calculated from Clark, *The Basque Insurgents*, p.181; Moxon-Browne, 'The Water and the Fish ...', pp.41–72.

TABLE 5

PERCENTAGE HOLDING POSITIVE IMAGE OF REVOLUTIONARY TERRORISTS BY CLASS AND DEMOGRAPHIC CHARACTERISTICS

	Baader-Meinhof	Tupamaros
Men	20	36
Women	16	33
Young	25	47
Middle Aged	16	35
Elderly	13	27
Educated	18	37
Less Educated	17	31
Upper Class		37
Middle Class		35
Lower Class		32

Sources: *Allensbacher Jahrbuch* (1971), *Indice Gallup de Opinion Publica* (1967–72).

In the Basque provinces, supporters of the extremist Basque nationalist parties (HB and EE) hold very positive views of ETA, and in Northern Ireland, supporters of PSF hold very positive views of the IRA. Moderate nationalists like the Basque PNV and Catholic SDLP hold ambivalent but far more sympathetic attitudes than non-nationalists. A similar ideological polarization is seen in Uruguay, where supporters of the leftwing Frente Amplio were much more likely to view the Tupamaros as well-intentioned revolutionaries than were the center-left Blancos or center-right Colorados. In Germany, however, partisan differences were very slight between the conservative Christian Democrats and the Social Democrats. The Free Democrats, a middle class liberal group, were the most sympathetic.

Although plausible, the view that terrorists will damage their image by killing people is not supported by the evidence. Indeed, it is those groups that kill the most, like IRA and ETA, that have the most positive ratings, while the Red Brigades and the Baader–Meinhof gang, groups that have killed far fewer, have the most unfavorable images.

Only in the Uruguayan case are survey data available that allow us to examine how public attitudes actually changed over time as a result of terrorist violence. Three questions were asked repeatedly: whether a specific action was a legitimate revolutionary act or a crime; whether the Tupamaros were well-intentioned revolutionaries or common delinquents; and, whether there was any justification for the Tupamaros 'under the political conditions of our country'.

Some evidence does suggest that a soft-line campaign helps maintain a more favorable terrorist image. For example, the proportion of respondents who believed kidnappings to be legitimate revolutionary acts, increased *after* the victims were returned unharmed, as happened in the cases of Fly and Jackson.[14] When Fly was first kidnapped only 18 per cent of the individuals surveyed thought it a legitimate revolutionary act, but 32 per cent saw it as such after he was released. In the case of Jackson the figure rose from 30 per cent to 36 per cent. On the other hand, the killing of Mitrione brought about a dramatic decline in those thinking his abduction was justified. The week before his death, the public was evenly divided between those who thought it a legitimate revolutionary act (34 per cent) and those who considered it a crime (34 per cent). After his murder the division became 18 per cent and 44 per cent, respectively.

However, terrorist violence clearly has only a temporary effect. Figure 3, showing the proportion considering the Tupamaros 'well-intentioned revolutionaries' and their actions 'justified under the political conditions of the country', does not suggest any deterioration of their public image. The first killings of policemen were not until July 1969, but the public perception of them as well-intentioned revolutionaries averaged 38.7 per

FIGURE 2
PERCENTAGE HOLDING POSITIVE IMAGE OF TERRORISTS BY PARTY

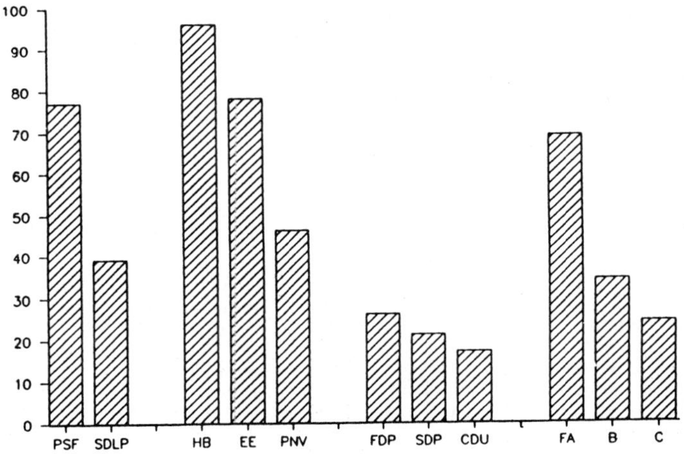

Sources: *From the Shadow of the Gun* (MORI, 1984).
W. Phillips Davison and Leon Gordenker, *Resolving Nationality Conflicts* (New York: Praeger, 1980), p.47.
Allensbacher Jahrbuch (1971).
Indice Gallup de Opinion Publica (1967–72).

cent before that date, compared to 38.9 per cent afterwards. Mitrione's murder had no discernible impact on public opinion either. Nor does the actual number of killings appear to be a negative factor. The percentage of respondents thinking the Tupamaros justified under the political conditions of the country increased substantially during the period when terrorist killings were at the their highest.

The often cited poll, showing a decline in public support for the Tupamaros, is doubly mistaken. Richard Clutterbuck erroneously cited statistics from an earlier article by Brian Crozier in the London *Times*.[16] Crozier, citing Gallup Uruguay, referred to the percentage who thought the Tupamaros 'well-intentioned' as dropping from 52 per cent to four per cent over the year. He compared this statistic to the proportion thinking that the armed forces were doing a good job, which had increased from 33 per cent to 59 per cent. Clutterbuck mixed up the two figures when he spoke of the decline being from 59 per cent to four per cent. However, Crozier also had gotten his figures wrong, since the actual July 1972 figure, approving the Tupamaros, is not four per cent but 36 per cent. The source of Crozier's four per cent is uncertain, but appears to be the July 1972 Gallup Uruguay poll. This poll also asked what *caused* the Tupamaros to appear, and reported that there was a decline from 11 per cent to four per cent in those who mentioned a 'lack of social justice'. Presumably this is the original source of the erroneous figure.

FIGURE 3
ATTITUDE TO TUPAMAROS

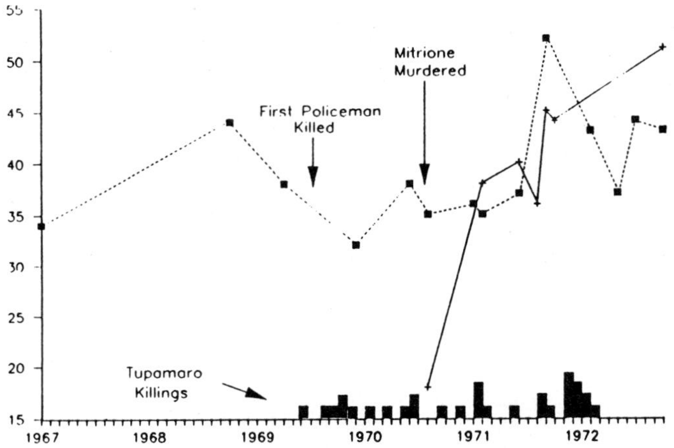

■ *Well-intentioned Revolutionaries*
+ *Justified*
Source: *Indice Gallup de Opinion Publica* (1967–72).

It seems, therefore, that a high level of violence does not in itself alienate the public. What appears crucial in creating a positive image of the terrorists as 'sincere patriots' and 'revolutionaries' is that they should behave like patriots and revolutionaries, and that such roles are understood within the society. Thus, the IRA operates within the context of a militant nationalist tradition deeply rooted in Irish history, and 'contemporary events so often evoke vivid and bitter memories'.[17] Basque nationalism and ETA's image are also the result of memories of past oppression by the Franco regime and popular resistance to it. In their campaigns the IRA and ETA usually behave like patriots fighting a national liberation struggle. Their targets are predominantly military, and they usually try to avoid killing innocent civilians.[18] Nationalist terrorists enjoy more legitimacy than do revolutionaries, particularly among their fellow ethnics, perhaps because revolutionary ideology is less easily understood by the general public. Even in Italy, a country with a well-established Marxist tradition, the Red Brigades had a much lower approval rating than the IRA or ETA.[19]

German political culture offered even less ideological support for revolutionary activity and Marxism has been largely supplanted by revisionist social democracy.[20] Pridham comments that 'it is difficult to measure the ideological dimensions of German terrorism' since the terrorist language 'has been both confused and confusing as a means of communicating ideas'.[21] Unlike Italy, the German system was working well, and hence demands for its revolutionary transformation were largely incomprehensible to the great majority of Germans.[22]

Attitudes Towards Revolution and Nationalism

Survey data are available for Uruguay, Italy, Germany and Spain on general ideological orientations and their changes over time. In Uruguay the population was asked whether they believed the solution to the country's problems lay in 'armed revolution' or 'law and order'. In Germany and Italy the options were 'radical change by revolutionary action', 'gradual improvement by reforms' and 'valiant defense against all subversive forces'. In Spain respondents were asked to locate themselves on a continuum from extreme left to extreme right. Figures 4 and 5 show the changes over time in the proportion supporting the various positions.

Does urban terrorism generate revolutionary consciousness? If it does, there should be an increase in the proportion of those defining themselves as revolutionaries or extreme leftists, but obviously this did not happen. In Uruguay and Italy, where major left-wing campaigns were mounted, the number favoring revolution declined steadily throughout the period of terrorist activity. In Germany and Spain, where leftist terrorism was conducted at a much lower level, the proportion of revolutionaries and extreme leftists remained virtually unchanged at a trivial level.

Does terrorism generate a backlash, with increased support for tough law and order measures? In Uruguay, Germany and Italy there is clear evidence of such a relationship. In Uruguay, the number of terrorist acts rose each year during 1968–72, and this is matched by a steady increase in the law and order category. The worst years for terrorism in Germany

FIGURE 4
POLITICAL ATTITUDES IN GERMANY AND ITALY

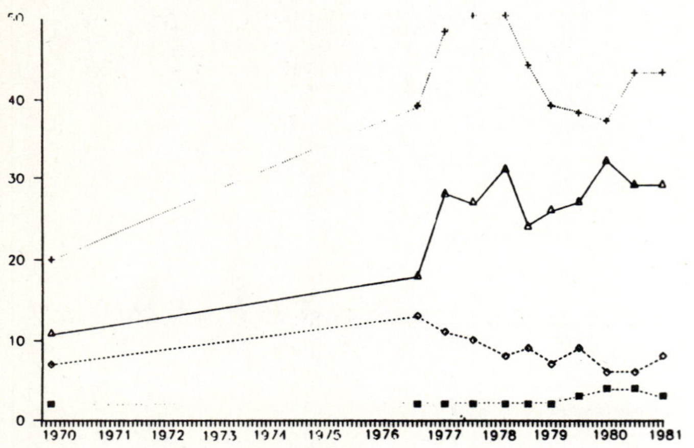

■ Germany Revolution
\+ Germany Defense
△ Italy Defense
◇ Italy Revolution

Source: *Index to International Public Opinion* (1981–82).

were 1977 and 1980 and in Italy 1978 and 1980, and during these years the percentage of the population favoring a 'valiant defense of society' reaches a maximum.

These shifts in Italy and Germany can be compared to those found in the EEC bloc as a whole to see whether the trend is due to a general change in political climate in the 1970s. In fact, the trend in the other EEC countries is different. From November 1976 to April 1981, the average of the other EEC countries (excluding Germany and Italy) shows a slight increase in

FIGURE 5
POLITICAL ATTITUDES IN URUGUAY

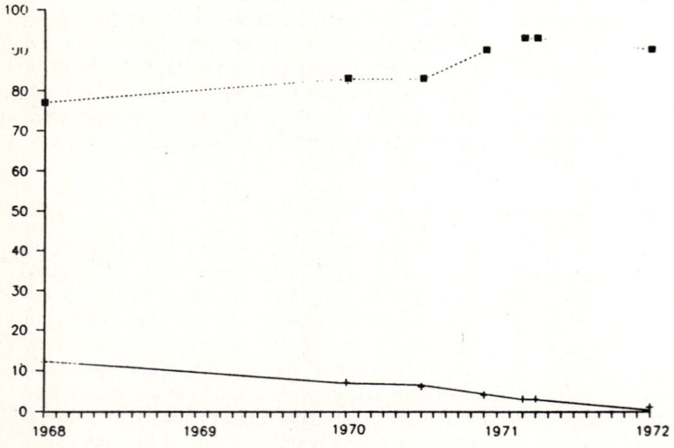

■ Law and Order
\+ Armed Revolution

Source: *Indice Gallup de Opinion Publica* (1968–72).

the proportion of revolutionaries (six per cent to seven per cent) and no change in the proportion favoring a valiant defense against subversion (27 per cent at both dates).[23]

Support for nationalism reveals a very different pattern from that for revolution, and seems unaffected by the level of violence. The people of Northern Ireland have been asked repeatedly for their views on 'the best solution to the Northern Irish problem' or their 'long-term constitutional preference', etc. Despite the fact that the options and the form of the question varies somewhat between the different polls, the answers can be compared over time. (Only a handful or respondents refuse to answer or have no opinion.) There is no sign that attitudes to Irish unity have changed within either the Catholic or Protestant community since the troubles began. Among Catholics, a united Ireland is usually favored by a plurality but not a majority, and there is no clear trend in the level of support. (The low point in nationalist sentiment coincides with the attempt at 'power sharing' during 1973–74). Of equal significance is the fact that Protestants show no sign of accepting the desirability of Irish unity, and continue overwhelmingly to support the British connection.

For the Basque provinces, Clark presents data from a large number of surveys on support for Basque independence. Unfortunately, as he notes, many respondents 'simply refuse to answer questions about ETA, terrorism, or politics in general'. There is no clear trend in the proportion that wanted full independence, although as the table points out the proportion seems to have declined after the granting of autonomy in 1979.[24]

FIGURE 6
SUPPORT FOR IRISH UNITY IN NORTHERN IRELAND BY RELIGION

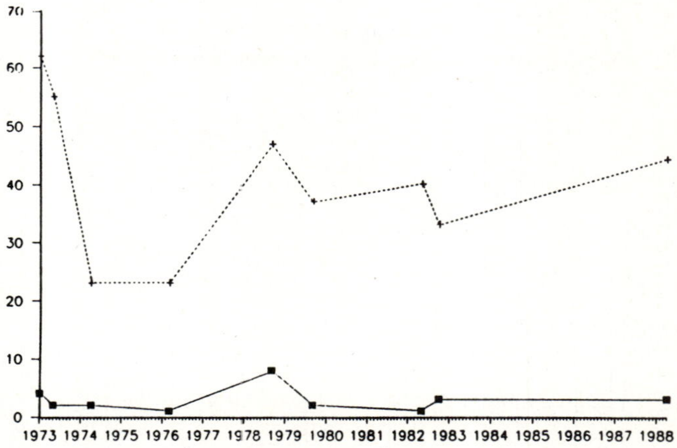

■ Protestant Support
\+ Catholic Support

Sources: 'What Ulster Thinks', *Belfast Telegraph* (19 Feb. 1973).
'Ulster 1973', *Carrick James Market Research.*
'Seven Out of Ten Back Power Sharing', *Belfast Telegraph* (19 April 1974).
ORC *Report* (5 June 1974).
Moxon-Browne, 'The Water and the Fish'.
'What the People of Ulster Think', *New Society* (6 Sept. 1979).
'Public Reaction in N. Ireland to Aspects of the Prior Proposals', *MRBI (Irish Times)* May 1982.
Fortnight (July–Aug. 1982).
Attitudes to the Northern Ireland Assembly.
From the Shadow of a Gun (MORI, 1984).

The social characteristics of revolutionaries and nationalists are shown in Tables 6 and 7, and it is clear that the pattern corresponds to that found in the previous section. Those who have a positive image of each terrorist group are similar to those who agree with the group's goals. Nationalism is strongly linked to ethnicity, and, whatever class differences exist, can be explained by the class composition of the different ethnic groups. Thus, Northern Irish Catholics are disproportionately working class, so Irish nationalists are more likely to be working class, but ethnic Basques are disproportionately middle class so Basque nationalists are more likely to be middle class. As would be expected, those favoring Herri Batasuna or Sinn Fein are usually nationalists. The lack of a definable class base for revolutionary ideology is again apparent, although revolutionaries are disproportionately young males.

TABLE 6

PERCENTAGE SUPPORTING NATIONALISM BY ETHNICITY AND PARTY

	Basques/ Catholics	Other Ethnics	HB/PSF
Basque Provinces	45	5	61
N. Ireland	33	3	69

Sources: Richard Gunther, Giacomo Sani and Goldie Shabad *Spain After Franco* (Berkeley, CA: University of California Press, 1986), pp.325–58.
Attitudes to the Northern Ireland Assembly.

TABLE 7

CHARACTERISTICS OF NATIONALISTS AND REVOLUTIONARIES

	Sex		Age			Class		
%Supporting Revolution in:	Men	Women	Young	Middle Aged	Older	High	Middle	Low
Uruguay	3.3	2.6	5.3	2.9	1.4	2.9	2.4	3.7
Italy			14.4	7.2		9.0		9.0
Germany			3.2	1.6		2.0		2.0
% Supporting Nationalism in:								
Basque Provinces						26.0	26.0	18.0
N. Ireland	18.0	10.0	17.0	12.0	13.0		13.0	15.0

Sources: *Indice Gallup de Opinion Publica* (1968–72).
Ronald Inglehart, *The Silent Revolution* (Princeton, NJ: Princeton University Press, 1977).
Commission of the European Communities, *The Young Europeans* (Brussels, 1982).
Clark, *Basque Insurgents*, p.183.
Attitudes to the Northern Ireland Assembly.

Public Opinion on Anti-Terrorist Policies

Faced with political violence, governments often respond with repression. People are arrested, shot by police or soldiers, stopped and questioned on the street, their houses searched, and their civil liberties and political rights restricted. Some survey data on attitudes towards anti-terrorist policies are available for all five countries, but the amount and quality vary significantly. The data for Northern Ireland, Germany and Uruguay are good, but those for Spain and Italy are fragmentary. Although precise comparisons between countries are difficult since questions are rarely asked in the same form, the data in Table 8 do suggest certain conclusions.

Usually, majorities or pluralities in all countries support getting tough with terrorists or rioters, and favor specific hard line policies. Cross-national comparisons reveal that public attitudes are more hard-line in Northern Ireland and Germany than in Uruguay, Italy or Spain. In Northern Ireland a large majority believe the Government 'should take a tougher line with the IRA', but in Uruguay those favoring a 'hard-line' approach are outnumbered three to one by those who favor a 'soft-line'. Taking a tough or hard-line approach can mean several things. Punishing terrorists is certainly popular in most countries. In Germany and Italy, there are majorities favoring more severe penalties for terrorist offenses, and in Northern Ireland, Italy and Germany for the restoration of the death penalty for terrorist murders. Uruguayans are obviously less enthusiastic about either policy. Terrorists who go on hunger strikes receive scant sympathy. More than three-quarters of those in Northern Ireland were against making any concessions to them, and in Germany, after Holger Meins starved to death, a similar proportion thought the authorities 'could not be held responsible'. Increasing the strength of the police is favored by a majority in both Northern Ireland and Germany, while a plurality is also willing to have them 'shoot to kill'. In Italy, a majority thought the police should intervene 'with force and decision' when political violence took place.

Restrictions on the legal rights of suspected terrorists are generally accepted. In Uruguay, most people approved the use of military courts, and in both Germany and Northern Ireland most thought that terrorists got a 'fair trial' despite special procedures. In Germany, measures such as supervision of defence lawyers, separating suspects and lawyers by glass panels, etc. were approved by overwhelming margins.

Attitudes towards preventive detention and internment show a reversal of the normal cross-national pattern. In Germany a proposal that terrorists who had served their sentence could be held in police custody 'when it

TABLE 8

SUPPORT FOR ANTI-TERRORIST POLICIES BY COUNTRY AND TYPE OF POLICY

	N. Ireland	Uruguay	Germany	Spain	Italy
PERCENTAGE SUPPORTING:					
Tougher/hardline policies in general	81	22	-	48	-
More severe penalities	-	43	85	-	87
Death penalty	53	21	61	43	54
Strengthening police	73	-	63	-	65
Shoot to kill policy	43	-	49	-	-
Trial procedures	53	48	60	-	-
Preventive detention/ internment	37	48	57	-	-
Hardline with hungerstrikers	77	-	78	-	-
Giving up civil liberties in interest of security	-	50	64	-	-
Censorship	-	38	77	-	-
ID checks	-	70	60	-	-
House searches	-	19	50	-	-
Positive rating of security forces	86	45	22	40	31

Sources: 'Public Attitudes to Internment', *Fortnight* (6 Sept. 1974).
Moxon-Browne, 'Water and the Fish'.
'What the People Think about Supergrasses', *Fortnight* (Nov. 1984).
'Opinion Poll', *BBC Spotlight* (May 1985).
Belfast Telegraph, 6 Feb. 1985.
John Finn, 'Public Support for Emergency Legislation in Northern Ireland: A Preliminary Analysis', *Terrorism*, Vol. 10 (1987).
Indice Gallup de Opinion Publica (1968–81).
Index to International Public Opinion (1979–81).
Allensbacher Jahrbuch (1968–81).
Revista Espanola de Investigaciones Sociologicas (April/June 1978).
'Imagen Publica de la Policia', *Revista Espanola de Investigaciones Sociologicas* (April/June 1982).
Cambio 16 (7 Jan. 1979).
L'Espresso (10 Jan. 1982).
Piergiorgio Corbetta, 'Perche piu indulgenza per i terroristi?' *Cattaneo*, Vol. 3 (June 1983).
Fabris, *Il comportamento politico degli italiani*, pp.225–6.

appears that they will commit other terrorist acts' was strongly supported and near majorities in Uruguay thought detention 'justified and well-handled'. However, those agreeing with internment in Northern Ireland, never constituted more than a substantial minority.

Throughout the period, the great majority of Germans declared themselves willing to give up 'some of their personal freedom in order to fight crime and terrorism', and in Uruguay a majority supported 'the suspension of individual guarantees' (that is, civil rights guaranteed by the constitution.) On specific issues, the Germans were willing to submit to identity checks and house searches by police, and to news blackouts for security reasons. On the other hand, Uruguayans, although conceding the necessity of identity checks, did not believe that censorship or house searches were justified.

There were noticeable differences between countries in how the public rated the conduct and competence of the security forces. By large majorities, both army and police were seen to be 'doing their job well' in Northern Ireland. In Uruguay throughout the period, almost half of those surveyed said their conduct was either good or very good. However, most Italians saw police measures to combat terrorism as both 'inefficient and insufficient', and only 31 per cent saw them as efficient or adequate. The German police were judged even less positively with only 22 per cent saying they 'took good care of security'. In Spain, public perceptions of the police were mixed. A majority thought they 'treated the public correctly' and 'protected and defended them'. However, almost half said they felt fear when coming into contact with the police, and only a minority thought the police had improved with democracy, had adapted to political change, or respected individual rights and liberties.

7. TACTICS, STRATEGIES, AND TARGETING

One might anticipate that support for tough policies would be greatest in those countries where terrorism poses the greatest threat, but this is not the case. German public opinion is as hardline as that of Northern Ireland, while Spaniards and Italians are no more hardline than Uruguayans. Historical factors may explain these cross national differences.[25]

An alternative view, that harsh security measures will alienate the public, is widely held. In the case of Uruguay, Moss claims that 'emergency measures alienated public opinion'.[26] Porzecanski says that the police 'became well known among the population for extensive and routine use of torture, as well as for heavy-handed citywide search operations'. These massive searches 'conducted clumsily at all hours of the night ... created great resentment among Montevideo's population'.[27] Labrousse describes how 'the population was incensed by the continual police controls'.[28] In the case of Northern Ireland, Moxon-Browne and Finn argue that harsh measures have 'alienated' public opinion and 'eroded' public confidence.[29] This view can be tested by examining differences in attitudes to security policies between groups, and also by examining changes over time.

Whether or not harsh security measures alienate the public seems to depend upon how selectively they are applied. In Northern Ireland, those arrested, interned, or shot by the security forces have been predominantly and disproportionately Catholic. Within Catholic areas, routine identity checks and house searches affect all the inhabitants, regardless of their politics or involvement in political violence. A similar situation obtains in Spain where the Basque provinces have experienced the full rigors of Spanish counter-insurgency policies. The result is widespread alienation among Catholics and Basques, and a polarization of attitudes towards security policy between Catholics and Protestants, Basques and non-Basques.

In Italy and Germany, security measures affect the general public only temporarily and during clearly defined crises, such as the Moro and Schleyer kidnappings. At other times 'since the terrorists proclaim themselves to be revolutionary leftists, radical left wing groups are naturally suspect and become targets of intensive investigation and sometimes harassment by the security forces'.[3] In Uruguay from mid-1970 onwards, mass searches and roadblocks affected the public at large, but most of those arrested and brutally interrogated were members of the radical left party, Frente Amplio. Table 9 compares attitudes towards security policy between those groups who were the targets of repression and the rest of the population. Without being overly cynical, one would conclude that those unaffected by government repression support it, while those who experience repression resent it. Indeed, there are indications that if the categories could be fine-tuned, the polarization would be even greater. Within the Basque provinces, for example, Basque nationalists are most likely to suffer detention and arrest, and are also the most hostile to hardline policies.[31]

Do public attitudes become more negative when repression continues over a long period, or when it is at a maximum? Sufficient data are available for Uruguay and Northern Ireland to explore this question. In Uruguay, four questions concerning security were asked repeatedly: should emergency measures reamin in effect, should individual guarantees be suspended, did the public favor a hard-line towards terrorism, and how was the conduct of the security forces rated?

Security force activity intensified in mid-1970 and extensive house searches were conducted in Fall 1970 and Spring 1971. There was a significant increase in the level of repression in April 1972, when a state of 'Internal War' was declared, and thousands were arrested. However, a comparison of attitudes towards security shows no sign that the public was alienated by the intensification of security activity.

In Northern Ireland, although several surveys have asked about security policies, they have not used the same questions. It is possible, nevertheless, to consider the differences between Catholics and Protestants in their support for security policies as a crude measure of Catholic alienation. Taking into account the number of civilians shot by the security forces, the number interned, and the number of houses searched, it appears that repression reached a peak during 1971–76, then declined erratically. However, the degree of Catholic alienation seems to be unrelated to the level of repression, and shows no obvious trend.[32]

Conclusion

The relationship between terrorism and public opinion is not a simple one. Terrorism seems as much a consequence of public opinion as it is a cause of changes in public opinion. Since there are important differences between nationalist and revolutionary terrorism, they will be discussed separately.

Nationalist terrorism emerges where there is a strong, historically-derived sense of nationalism linked to ethnicity. Nationalist ideology legitimates terrorist action and generates a positive image of the insurgents as long as the campaign follows proper tactics and does not lead to the killing of fellow ethnics. Support for militant nationalism does not decrease because of terrorist atrocities against the ethnic enemy.[33]

As a strategy for breaking the will of the occupying force, nationalist terrorism has had mixed results. The IRA's campaign has been greatly successful in affecting public opinion in Great Britain. Since 1974, the proportion favoring troop withdrawal has remained stable, with a clear majority favoring withdrawal and a plurality favoring a united Ireland.[34] The metropolitan Spaniards have been far more resistant and the most recent poll reveals that only 14 per cent favor giving in to terrorist demands or negotiating with the terrorists.[35]

Within the Basque provinces and within Northern Ireland, terrorism has reflected and exacerbated ethnic polarization. The different ethnic groups not only disagree about nationalism, but also about who is to blame for violence and what should be done about the situation.

Revolutionary terrorists usually start off with a much lower degree of popular sympathy than nationalists. Most people find their goals incomprehensible, and dismiss them as common criminals. Revolutionary terrorism does not increase revolutionary sentiments, either by 'propaganda of the deed' or by provoking repression. The revolutionaries are unable to broaden the basis of their support, which remains restricted to a small sector of the educated youth. Given their isolation, it is possible for the authorities to repress terrorist sympathizers, without alienating the public at large. The most obvious political consequence of revolutionary terrorism is a law and order backlash, which appears to benefit the conservative parties.

Attitudes towards political violence, whether revolutionary or nationalist, depend primarily upon structural-historical features, and are, therefore, little affected by either terrorist actions or by government policies. Those who advocate terrorism as a means of generating revolutionary consciousness are clearly following a false strategy, but those

TABLE 9
POLARIZATION OF ATTITUDES TOWARDS SECURITY POLICIES

% (Supporting Hardine Policies)

	Affected Group	Rest of Population
N. Ireland (Catholics)	27	73
Spain (Basque Provinces)	30	67
Italy (Proletarian Democrats)	11	66
Uruguay (Frente Amplio)	19	60

Sources: Same as Table 8. (Average of all polls which give breakdowns by relevant variables).

TABLE 10
CHANGING ATTITUDES TO SECURITY MEASURES IN URUGUAY (%)

Table 10: Changing Attitudes to Security Measures in Uruguay (%)

	Mild Repression (1968-Jun 1970)	Increasing Repression (Jul 1970-Mar 1972)	Intense Repression (Apr 1972-Oct 1972)
Favor Emergency measures	44	41	56
Favor Hardline		24	19
Approve Suspension of Guarantees		46	56
Conduct of security forces good	44	51	50

Source: *Indice Gallup de Opinion Publica* (1968–72).

who assume that terrorist sympathizers will be alienated by atrocities are equally deluded.

As noted, the data are fragmentary and it is hoped that additional material can be collected to fill in the lacunae, and to provide information on other terrorist groups in other countries. Whether this would lead us to modify our conclusions is uncertain. Israeli–Palestinian attitudes for example, seem very similar to those found in the nationalist conflicts in Spain and Northern Ireland.[36] On the other hand, our interpretation does not seem to be compatible with those cases where insurgencies were successful (for example, the Irish Rebellion of 1916–21, Algeria, Irgun in Palestine, Castro in Cuba), and where participants and observers argue that public attitudes did change dramatically as a result of terrorism and government repression.[37] Is the impact of terrorism on public opinion different between successful and unsuccessful campaigns? I trust that this attempt at a comparative analysis of public attitudes to terrorism will lead future studies to standardize their questions, so that cross-national comparisons can be made, and to replicate past questions, so as to allow an examination of changes over time.

NOTES

The author would like to thank the following organizations and individuals for providing me with survey data: Allensbach; Institut für Demoskopie, Zentral Archiv für Sozialforschung, Universitat zu Koln; Instituto di studi e richerche Carlo Cattaneo; *Belfast Telegraph*; *Irish Times*; BBC Northern Ireland; Professor Robert Clark, George Mason University; Professor Richard Rose, University of Strathclyde; Professor Juan Linz, Yale University; Professor Edward Moxon-Browne, Queens University of Belfast. The author is also grateful to the University of Maryland Baltimore County for purchasing the polls of Gallup Uruguay. The research for this article was partially funded by the United States Institute of Peace. The opinions, findings, and conclusions are those of the author and do not necessarily reflect the views of the United States Institute of Peace.

1. Alex Schmid and Janny de Graaf, *Violence as Communication* (Beverly Hills, CA: Sage, 1982), pp. 215–66.
2. David C. Rapoport, 'Fear and Trembling: Terrorism in Three Religious Traditions', *American Political Science Review*, 78, #3 (Sept. 1984), p. 665.
3. Schmid and de Graaf, pp. 13–14. Robert Moss, *Urban Guerrillas* (London: Temple Smith, 1972), p. 218. David C. Rapoport, 'The Politics of Atrocity', in Yonah Alexander and Seymour Finger (eds.), *Terrorism: Interdisciplinary Perspectives* (New York: John Jay Press, 1977), pp. 47–51.
4. The Brazilian revolutionary, Carlos Marighella, advocated this strategy in 'Mini Manual of the Urban Guerrilla', *Tri-Continental*, Vol. 6, (June 1969).
5. Robert Clark, *The Basque Insurgents: ETA 1951–80* (Madison, WI: University of Wisconsin Press, 1984), pp. 40–41.
6. For a discussion of the differences between nationalist and revolutionary terrorist campaigns, and the government policies used against them see Christopher Hewitt, *The Effectiveness of Anti-Terrorist Policies* (Lanham, MD: University Press of America, 1986).
7. Moss, pp. 247–8.
8. Richard Clutterbuck, *Kidnap and Ransom* (London: Faber, 1978), p. 38.
9. Moss, p. 223.
10. Richard Clutterbuck, *Protest and the Urban Guerrilla* (New York: Abelard Schuman, 1973), p. 230; Anthony Burton, *Urban Terrorism* (New York: Free Press, 1976), pp. 95–102; Stephen Goode, *Guerilla Warfare and Terrorism* (New York: Franklin Watts, 1977), p. 80; Bard O'Neill, *Insurgency in the Modern World* (Boulder, CO: Westview Press, 1980), p. 178.
11. In the tables following, when more than one survey is cited, a single statistic represents an average.
12. A statewide survey by J. Jimenez Blanco, *La Conciencia Regional En Espana* (Madrid: Editorial Cuadernos, 1977), on regional consciousness found that Barcelona and the Basque country expressed the most acute grievances over administrative centralization, were most likely to support independence, and were the most likely to vote for separatist parties.
13. On the basis of names, only 30 out of 403 victims of terrorism in the Basque provinces appear to have been ethnic Basques.
14. In the five years before the survey (1978–82), 61 Catholics and 199 Protestants, were victims of terrorism. Thus, Protestants, who make up 63 per cent of the population, suffered 77 per cent of the deaths.
15. Claude Fly, an American agricultural expert, was kidnapped in 1970 and Geoffrey Jackson, the British consul, in 1971.
16. See Clutterbuck, *Protest*, pp. 230, 239.
17. Moxon-Browne provides a good discussion of the historical factors which explain Catholic support for the IRA. 'The Water and the Fish: Public Opinion and the Provisional IRA in Northern Ireland', *Terrorism*, Vol. 5 (1981), 41–72.
18. Legitimate military or political targets constitute approximately 80 per cent of ETA's victims and 65 per cent of the IRA's victims. See Hewitt, *Effectiveness of Anti-Terrorist Policies*, p. 29.
19. The attitude of the Red Brigades to the PCI (Communist Party of Italy) was ambivalent. They saw the party leadership as having abandoned the goal of revolution, but hoped to win over the rank and file. Yet, among PCI supporters, 83 per cent were in 'total disagreement' with the actions of the extreme left (*L'Espresso*, 30 Oct. 1977).
20. Sympathy for the Baader–Meinhof gang was concentrated among students, but even in this group only 18 per cent agreed that 'terrorists are freedom fighters.' See Yonah Alexander and John Gleason (eds.), *Behavioral and Quantitative Perspectives on Terrorism* (New York: Pergamon, 1981), pp. 266–7.
21. Juliet Lodge, *Terrorism: A Challenge to the State* (New York: St. Martin's Press, 1981), pp. 24–5.
22. Questions on satisfaction with the way that 'democracy is working in my country' show consistently high levels of satisfaction in Germany and consistently low levels in Italy. In 1978, Germans had the highest satisfaction of all EEC countries and Italians the lowest. Survey Research Consultants International, *Index to International Public Opinion 1978–79* (Westport, CT: Greenwood Press, 1980), p. 287.
23. *Index to International Public Opinion 1981–2*, p. 582.
24. Clark, pp. 168–84.
25. The simplest explanation may be that Germans support law and order because they fear the emergence of a Weimar-type situation in which a weak government allowed extremist violence to flourish, while Spaniards fear a resurgence of Francoist repression.
26. Moss, p. 217.
27. Arturo Porzecanski, *Uruguay's Tupamaros* (New York: Praeger, 1973), pp. 55–6.
28. Alain Labrousse, *The Tupamaros* (Harmondsworth: Penguin, 1973), p. 130.
29. E. Moxon-Browne, 'Alienation: the Case of the Catholics in Northern Ireland', *Journal of Political Science*, Vol. 14, (Spring 1986), 74–89. John Finn, 'Public Support for Emergency Legislation in Northern Ireland: A Preliminary Analysis', *Terrorism*, Vol. 10, No. 2 (1987), pp. 113–124. 30. Andrew Mack, 'The Utility of Terrorism', *Australian and New Zealand Journal of Criminology*, Vol. 14, (Dec. 1981), 218.
31. See Richard Gunther, Giacomo Sani and Goldie Shabad, *Spain after Franco* (Berkeley, CA: University of California Press, 1986), p. 362. Their study found that nationally 88 per cent favored moderate-to-hard antiterrorist policies, but this position was held by only 43 per cent of the Basques and only 16 per cent of those supporting HB and EE. In Italy, the young and the educated are less likely to support the death penalty for terrorists. Piergiorgio Corbetta, 'Perche piu indulgenza per i terroristi', *Cattaneo*, Vol. 3, (June 1983), 21–35.
32. As measured in this fashion, Catholic alienation averaged 87 per cent in 1974, 83 per cent in 1982, and 73 per cent in the most recent 1985 survey.
33. A 1984 poll found 48 per cent of Catholics agreeing that the IRA are patriots and idealists (virtually the same as in Moxon-Browne's 1978 survey; see *From the Shadow of the Gun*, London: MORI, 1984). Even the bombing of a Remembrance Day memorial ceremony at Enniskillen produced only a five per cent decline in those saying they sympathized with the IRA. (*Fortnight*, April 1988). Within the Basque provinces, surveys carried out during the 1978–80 period show no trend, and those seeing ETA as 'patriots or idealists' constituted 48 per cent in 1978, 41 per cent in 1979, and 50 per cent in 1980. (Linz, *Conflicto en Euskadi*).
34. From 1974–1977 those favoring troop withdrawal averaged 57 per cent, and from 1978–81 those wanting to withdraw the troops immediately or within five years also averaged 57 per cent. Richard Rose, Ian McAlister and Peter Mair, *Is there a Concurring Majority about Northern Ireland?* (Glasgow: Centre for the Study of Public Policy, University of Strathclyde, 1978). For attitudes subsequent to 1977, see *Index to International Public Opinion*.
35. See Gunther, Sani and Shabad, p. 362. Earlier polls by Linz in 1978 and 1979 show a decline in those supporting negotiation or acceptance of terrorist demands from 24 per cent to 17 per cent. Leon Gordenker (ed.), *Resolving Nationality Conflicts: The Role of Public Opinion Research* (New York: Praeger, 1980), p. 48.
36. Palestinian support for anti-Israeli terrorism is certainly comparable to Catholic support for the IRA, or Basque support for ETA. A 1986 poll in the occupied territories found that 78 per cent believed violence to be justified. Meron Benvenisti, *West Bank Data Base Project: 1987 Report* (*Jerusalem Post*, 1987), pp. 45–6. See also Mohammed Shadid and Rick Seltzer, 'Political Attitudes of Palestinians in the West Bank and Gaza Strip', *Middle East Journal* (Winter 1988), 16–32.
37. Begin, for example, claims that Irgun attacks against the British produced an upsurge of support among the Jewish population. *The Revolt* (New York: Nash Publishing, 1977), pp. 193–6.

Countering Terrorism

The articles in this section focus on counterterrorist measures ranging from legalistic (and by inference, moralistic) responses to retaliation by means of force. Some approaches are at the unilateral end of the response continuum, and others at the multilateral (collaborative) end. Suggestions or discussions of combinations and mixed approaches abound in the articles as well.

"Counterterrorism in the 1990s," reflects the most recent thoughts and behavior of the U.S. government in countering terrorism as expressed by a leading official specializing in this area. Aside from identifying perceived geographic areas of concern, a list of successes and the need for additional responses, especially of the nonmilitary type, are summarized in this annual statement.

The next essay, "International Crime Requires International Punishment," discusses various aspects of an international law approach—bilateral and multilateral. International cooperation is stressed as an essential ingredient in countering terrorism. Unfortunately the United Nations has not been a fruitful arena where decisive counterterrorist actions have been taken. This circumstance, unsurprisingly, engenders a more visionary desire to set up an international court with jurisdiction over terrorist activities as criminal acts. One of the continuing controversial aspects of the legal approach is the use of extradition treaties to expedite access to and prosecution of terrorists in a second- or third-party country.

"When Reality Came Unglued: Antonio Savasta and the Italian Red Brigades" depicts the rise and fall of the Italian Red Brigades, a notorious chapter in that country's recent history. This essay is a fascinating case study of the making of a terrorist and his undoing.

The inherent difficulties of U.S. intelligence forces in the Middle East are highlighted in "Hezbollah Frustrates a Gulliver-Like U.S."

With Americans traveling abroad as a constant, the "advisories" of our government become critical in enhancing their safety. A data base is provided in "Advisories Help Keep U.S. Travelers Safe Abroad." Breakdowns or failures in this realm can lead to disasters such as Pan Am Flight 103. The on-again off-again attempts to conclude investigations of terrorist outrages are explained in "On the Trail of Terror." So much is known, yet so little responsibility is pinned on the culpable actors involved.

The next series of selections provide excellent summations of the continuing problems in countering terrorism. We are reminded, among other things, of the central importance of the "intelligence function" to effectively counter terrorism. "The Bush Administration's PLO Cover-Up" article especially raises the disturbing question of what consequences arise when the United States disregards intelligence information.

"Terror and Negotiation" explores the controversial issue of negotiating with terrorists in a hostage situation. Should it be an absolute moral prohibition or subject to qualification?

The concluding article, "Mission Improbable," categorically concludes that ten years after the Iranian hostage crisis the United States is still not prepared to fight terrorism. The author focuses on U.S. counterforce (military) capabilities and previous operations, and ends on a discouraged note.

Looking Ahead: Challenge Questions

What are the basic problems a government encounters in trying to direct its efforts against a terrorist group?

What are the hindrances in an international law approach to countering terrorism?

What are the political, legal, and ethical constraints on American use of military force against terrorists?

Unit 8

Counterterrorism in the 1990s

Morris D. Busby

Following is the address given by Morris D. Busby, Coordinator for Counter-Terrorism, to the International Seminar on Maritime and Port Security, Miami, Florida, January 3, 1990.

Today I would like to discuss U.S. counterterrorism policy and our priorities for the 1990s. Terrorism is still very much with us. In just over 1 year we have seen the bombing of Pan Am Flight 103 killing 270 people, 170 people were killed in the bombing of UTA [*Union des Transports Aeriens*] Flight 772 and 110 more in the recent bombing of a Colombian Avianca flight, Lt. Col. William Higgins was lost under grotesque circumstances in Lebanon, eight Americans are still held hostage in Lebanon, and five other Americans fell to assassins' bullets in the Philippines and Bolivia.

U.S. Counterterrorism Policy

We cannot expect to completely eradicate terrorism. It is now, and will remain, a persistent international problem. But we can, through our policies, reduce significantly the impact terrorism has on international life. We can make the terrorist's vicious work more difficult, and we can make it more costly for those states that continue to support terrorism. Our counterterrorism policy was initially developed during the 1970s. The basic principles remain as valid today as when first articulated.

First, we will not accede to terrorist demands. We will not pay ransom, release convicted terrorists, or pressure other countries to give in to terrorist demands; in other words, "no deals." Obviously, this aspect of our policy was damaged by the Iran-*contra* affair. That was a mistake, but for the past 3 years we have made crystal clear our steadfast commitment to the "no deals" principle. No country, no group, should believe there is gain in trying to blackmail the United States.

Let me add an important but little understood point—"no deals" doesn't mean "no talking." As we have consistently said, we will talk to anyone authoritative any time about the welfare and unconditional release of our hostages in Lebanon. But we will not reward the hostage takers and place others at risk by "buying" their freedom.

Second, we will continue to pressure states that support terrorist groups and use terrorism as a tool of their foreign policy. We want to convince such states that support for terrorists leads only to economic and political isolation, whereas turning away from these illegal and immoral practices will enable them to reenter the community of nations. Terrorist groups can't operate effectively without weapons, money, passports, training bases, and safehouses. And all too often, these essential items come from governments. We will not turn a blind eye to these activities. Where we have evidence, we will penalize these states with all means at our disposal and urge others to do the same. At the same time, as President Bush said in his inaugural speech—referring to Iran's influence over those who hold Americans hostage—"Assistance can be shown here and will be long remembered. Good will begets good will. Good faith can be a spiral that endlessly moves on."

There are signs that our policies are working. Some of the more notorious state supporters of terrorism have recently—publicly at least—attempted to distance themselves from terrorism.

Our 1986 airstrike on Libya's terrorist camps was a watershed event. European nations followed our lead by imposing political, economic, and security measures against the Qadhafi regime. They expelled more than 100 Libyan operatives and restricted the movements of others. Qadhafi learned that support for international terrorism is not cost-free and now professes to have changed his behavior, which after all is the objective of our policy. He has recently renounced terrorism and claims to no longer be supporting terrorism. We welcome this changed rheto-

Reprinted from U.S. Department of State, *Current Policy, #1243*, January 3, 1990, pp. 1-4.

ric and have called on him now to dismantle his terrorist apparatus, expel Abu Nidal and other terrorists to whom he has given sanctuary, close the training camps in Libya, and end funding for terrorist groups. This will be a true test of his intention.

Syria, another long-time supporter of terrorism, may also be rethinking its support for terrorism. In late 1986, British and West German courts established Syrian complicity in terrorist attacks in London and West Berlin. Together with Great Britain, the United States joined an international campaign employing diplomatic, political, and economic sanctions to convince Syria to reduce its links to terrorist groups.

These efforts have produced results. In 1985, Syria was implicated in 34 terrorist incidents, in 1986 only six. In 1987, we detected Syria's hand in only one incident and none during the past 2 years. Syria also expelled the violent Abu Nidal Organization in June 1987. Yet Syria continues to harbor terrorists. The PFLP–GC [Popular Front for the Liberation of Palestine-General Command] is headquartered in Damascus. The Japanese Red Army and other terrorist groups operate freely in Syrian-dominated Lebanon, openly provided with arms and supplies through Syria. There is no question that Syria, like Libya, bears responsibility for the activities of the groups it harbors. They should shut them down if they expect us to believe their antiterrorist rhetoric.

Looking at Iran, this country continues to support terrorism from the Middle East to Europe. And there is every indication that this is state policy. President Bush has clearly opened the door to better relations, but until Iran acts to abandon its policy of supporting terrorism and hostage taking, there will be no possibility of an improvement in the U.S.-Iranian relationship.

It would be an exaggeration to claim that U.S. Government policy has caused these terrorism-supporting nations to cease their support for international terrorist groups entirely. We believe they continue to provide such support. But we are modifying their behavior, and concerted, vigorous Western action does make them move more cautiously.

The third element of our policy is imposing the rule of law on terrorists. Terrorists are neither freedom fighters nor romantic warriors; they are criminals. We have on the books laws which give our law enforcement agencies powerful tools to combat terrorism. Popularly called the "long arm" statutes, these laws make terrorist acts committed overseas against Americans federal crimes. Without infringing on the sovereignty of others, it gives us the ability to act against terrorists in our own courts when we can.

This element of our program is maturing into a potent weapon for two basic reasons. There has been a sea change in international attitudes toward terrorists. Not long ago, many usually responsible countries granted terrorists dispensation for their crimes. Terrorists were considered victims of "oppression" and "imperialism"—victims or, worse, romantic adventurers whose behavior should be indulged.

Fortunately, no longer is this true. As terrorists widened their circle of targets in the late 1970s, they lost this international indulgence. In some instances, they even attacked their sympathizers and supporters. The shock of their brutal actions turned indulgence to revulsion. As popular disgust mounted, governments took strong action to counter the terrorists. Today, more and more terrorists are being brought to trial and convicted.

- One year ago a Maltese court sentenced the sole surviving terrorist in the November 1985 hijacking of an Egyptian airliner to 25 years imprisonment—the maximum sentence under Maltese law.
- In late 1988, a French court convicted *in absentia* the notorious Fatah [the military arm of the Palestine Liberation Organization] terrorist Colonel Hawari to 10 years in prison for complicity to transport arms, ammunition, and explosives and for criminal association. Hawari's sentence was the maximum allowed under the French law.
- Last February a court in Switzerland sentenced a Lebanese terrorist to life imprisonment for hijacking an Air Afrique flight the previous year.
- Last May a West German court sentenced Lebanese terrorist Muhammad Hamadei to life imprisonment for hijacking, hostage taking, and the murder of an innocent American seaman.
- Last March in Washington, D.C., a court sentenced Lebanese terrorist Fawaz Younis to 30 years for hijacking a Royal Jordanian Airlines flight in 1985 and for taking hostages, including American citizens.
- Just last month, terrorist trials took place in Paris and in Stockholm. In Paris an operative of the May 15 Middle Eastern terrorist group was sentenced to life imprisonment for murder and other charges for his involvement in a series of bombings in that city and in London during 1983–85.
- In Stockholm four members of the Palestine Popular Struggle Front were sentenced to terms up to life imprisonment for their bombing campaign in 1985–86 in Amsterdam, Copenhagen, and Stockholm.

So our policies are sound, and, step by step, we are having success. But terrorists still have the means to strike at us, outrage us, and force our attention on them. As we look to the 1990s, let me outline three areas of immediate concern.

Areas of Concern

In Latin America the use of terrorist tactics by narcotics traffickers and insurgent groups in this region is disturbing and on the rise throughout the Andes. In the past these groups have used terrorist tactics from time to time to suit their purposes. But now we see big-time narcotics dealers turning to terrorism to further their criminal enterprises. And we see classic insurgent or terrorist groups turning to drug trafficking to finance their activities.

In Colombia the drug cartels have unleashed an unprecedented wave of assassinations and bombings in a "war" against Colombia's democracy. Almost daily, drug cartel murder squads bomb newspaper offices, kill journalists, and assassinate judges. Last year Colombian narcotic traffickers and insurgent groups carried out more than 70 attacks aimed at American interests. In recent months we have seen a civilian aircraft bombed with all aboard killed and the destruction of the headquarters building of the security police leaving over 60 dead in that beleaguered country. President Barco and the Colombian Government have responded strongly. Colombia and its people have the full support of our government and all Americans. We are giving significant assistance to the Colombians and will continue to do so.

In Peru the terrorist activities of the *Sendero Luminoso* are a serious threat. *Sendero Luminoso* waged a brutal but unsuccessful effort to sabotage the municipal elections last November. Because of the *Sendero* terror, over 400 municipal officials have resigned during the last 2 years. Since 1980, when the *Sendero Luminoso* launched its terror campaign, more than 15,000 people have been killed.

In Ecuador the small but deadly Alfaro Vive group has been contained by the Ecuadorean Government. Although weakened, these urban terrorists are still capable of violent and coordinated action, especially when they receive help—as they have in the past—from the better organized Colombian terrorist groups.

Bolivia until recently had largely avoided the terrorist problems plaguing its neighbors. Now some groups are preparing and carrying out terrorist activities. There was a bombing attempt on Secretary [of State] Shultz's motorcade in August 1988, last May two American

Mormon missionaries were assassinated in La Paz, and the U.S. Embassy was recently bombed.

And in El Salvador, the insurgent Farabundo Marti National Liberation Front (FMLN) apparently miscalculated its own strength in launching its November offensive in San Salvador, losing many of its members. The FMLN has frequently resorted to terrorism against its own people. The FMLN has also targeted Americans. Four U.S. Marine Embassy guards and two American businessmen were among the dead in 1985 when FMLN gunmen machinegunned patrons at an outdoor cafe. The FMLN was also responsible for killing a U.S. Navy military adviser in 1983.

In another area of the world, the Philippines, we face another perilous challenge. The communist party's New People's Army (NPA) has frequently employed terrorism throughout its 20-year insurgency. In 1989, the NPA resumed targeting official Americans for assassination. Three Americans have been killed in the past year. In April, Vietnam War hero and former prisoner of war Col. James "Nick" Rowe was fatally ambushed while driving to work in Manila, and in September, during Vice President Quayle's official visit to the country, two Department of Defense civilian contractors were similarly killed near Clark Air Base. The NPA views the United States as its enemy and seeks to drive the U.S. military presence from the country. We fear its attacks on unarmed personnel will continue.

And, finally, radical Palestinian groups still represent an ongoing international danger. Combining a deep, visceral hostility toward the West with cold-blooded terrorism, these groups are responsible for some of the most vicious terrorist acts on record. We should expect these groups to remain active.

These issues—narcoterrorism in Latin America, terrorism in the Philippines, and Middle East terrorism—will certainly command our attention for the next few years. But there are other concerns. You have all read or heard apocalyptic stories of terrorists stealing or building their own nuclear weapons. This is the stuff of paperback thrillers. Most experts would agree that nuclear terrorism presents less of a potential danger than use of less dramatic, but no less potent means of mass destruction, such as chemical weapons or by exploiting more sophisticated technologies.

Terrorists have undoubtedly noted that the use of chemical weapons by the Soviets in Afghanistan and during the Iran-Iraq war seemed to provoke little public outrage. With increased security around their traditional targets—airports, embassies, government buildings—these favored terrorist targets are no longer easy marks. And, equally important, the international media have been relatively restrained lately in reporting on terrorist outrages, thus denying them the public stage they wish. Some terrorist groups might decide that these factors call for a new, more terrible approach, perhaps even the use of chemical weapons. A number of states that support terrorism have such weapons in their arsenals, and the technology is not difficult to acquire or develop.

We also anticipate that terrorists will make greater use of high technology in their attacks. To take one example, the Provisional IRA [Irish Republican Army], which has contact with Middle Eastern groups and Libya, has become expert in building bombs with long-delay timing devices, bombs which can be set to explode in days rather than hours. The IRA placed such a bomb in their 1985 attempt on [British] Prime Minister Thatcher at a seaside hotel during a party conference. And the recent assassination in Germany of Alfred Herrhausen used a particularly sophisticated device. Terrorists have been and will continue to make use of modern plastic explosives. These are much more powerful than traditional explosives like dynamite and TNT. And they are much more difficult to detect with current technology. Libya has already shipped several tons of a Czech plastic called Semtex to the Provisional IRA in recent years. And the IRA has used Semtex to devastating effect in Northern Ireland.

The December 1988 bombing of Pan Am 103 and last year's downing of UTA 772 may signal another change in terrorist tactics: A move away from the hijackings of the 1980s toward a more deadly strategy of simply killing large numbers of people by bombing commercial aircraft.

Response to Challenges

How should we respond to these challenges? Firmness and persistence must continue as the hallmarks of our country's counterterrorism effort. Only a sustained, relentless effort carried out over a period of years will suppress terrorism. We must maintain the patience and discipline to allow our current policy to work through the next decade. And we must be confident enough not to cut deals with hostage takers or other terrorists.

States supporting terrorism must be exposed to the sunlight. When necessary, international sanctions, including military force, should be imposed on these states to convince them that support for terrorism has a high cost and induce them to behave as responsible members of the world community. To further international cooperation against terrorist supporting states, we must expand our cooperation with Latin American, East Asian, and African countries. Terrorism is not limited to the Middle East or Europe.

During the past year, we have discussed terrorism with the Soviet Union as one of the transnational issues that we raise whenever the two sides meet. The Soviets have taken a more constructive approach recently and have condemned specific terrorist acts, but there is still much room for improvement. We will continue to press the Soviets to take concrete steps to make it more difficult for international terrorists to operate.

To further reinforce our law enforcement tactics, we and our friends must expand our sharing of information on terrorists as much as possible. To do so, we need closer cooperation, both on the policy and technical level. We already work very closely with our allies. As more countries join in the fight to eradicate terrorism, we must broaden our group until the terrorists and their supporters have no place to hide. On a less visible level, there will continue to be a place in the fight against terrorists for military and covert action. There are legitimate tools which we should use with discretion, but no one should doubt that we will employ these means to combat the terrorist threat.

We need to combat the terrorists' use of high technology. This means being willing to expend the time and money for research and development (R&D) activities. In the United States, counterterrorism R&D projects simply do not cross above the budgetary cut line for many of our government agencies. This must be remedied. To deal with this problem, we have created a national counterterrorism R&D program for which the State Department annually seeks funds. Unfortunately, the amount of funds appropriated by Congress for this purpose is never enough. We are working to increase funds for this vital program and make it a high priority.

We, too, can put new technologies to work. Progress in miniaturization has permitted the development of more accurate sensors better able to detect explosives and hazardous gases. Improved devices will make it easier to detect plastic explosives such as those used in recent airline bombings. Research into DNA technology is providing forensic scientists with significant biological tools. Refinements in computer software are enhancing our ability to gather and analyze information.

Terrorism, as we all know far too well, is an almost endless series of shifting tactics and differing targets. We have been largely successful in dealing with the threat posed by hijacking, for example, but now our efforts must address midair sabotage, which appears to be the current tactic of choice for terrorists.

The U.S. and other governments are working on a number of initiatives to help improve the security of air and sea travel. Our initiatives include:

- The development of sophisticated equipment to detect plastic explosives.
- Many of the nations represented at this conference are cooperating in a multination effort to develop an international agreement that will require the introduction of "taggants" into all plastic explosives which will make them easier to detect.
- The United States has supported the International Maritime Organization's (IMO) efforts to encourage worldwide implementation of its recommendations aimed at preventing unlawful acts against passengers and crews. These measures were a U.S. initiative developed in response to the 1985 *Achille Lauro* hijacking. The IMO, with U.S. Government support, is currently sponsoring regional seminars to encourage implementation of these measures.
- Effective training is also a crucial ingredient in improving security against terrorism. The United States offers training to many nations each year in antiterrorism skills, including aviation and maritime security.

No one can promise a world free of terrorism. But through hard-earned experience our country has developed a policy which is showing signs of success against the terrorists. They know we are serious. States which in the past routinely supported terrorists are now more cautious in their actions. Terrorists, once caught, are being put on trial and sentenced to lengthy jail terms. No longer are they being allowed to slip quietly away.

Our successes should encourage confidence that the tide is turning our way—that we are on the right path. We must understand, however, that suppressing terrorism will not be easy. We still have a long and difficult struggle before us. With heightened vigilance, clear thinking, and steady discipline, I am confident that we can prevail.

INTERNATIONAL CRIME
Requires International Punishment

To combat the twin crises of terrorism and international drug trafficking, the civilized world should establish an international criminal court.

Arlen Specter

Sen. Specter (R.-Pa.) is a member of the Judiciary Committee.

CRIMINAL justice, once thought to be a strictly local concern, now dominates the global agenda. There is dramatic movement toward the internationalization of law enforcement because of the development in the past 20 years of two transnational criminal offenses—terrorism and international drug trafficking.

These two modern problems call to mind the ancient crime of piracy. For centuries, ruthless pirates sailed through the waters along the Barbary Coast of North Africa, a menace to sailors and an impediment to the development of commerce. Finally, in the early 19th century, the U.S. and the European powers launched a concerted military effort to eradicate the scourge of piracy. Because the conduct of terrorists and drug traffickers, like the actions of these 19th-century pirates, shocks the conscience of the civilized international community, similar-minded nations of the world once again must utilize their collective authority to bring these bandits to justice.

As Director of National Drug Control Policy William Bennett has reminded us, there is no single solution to the problem of illicit narcotics use. Both the supply and demand sides of the equation must be addressed. Among the many steps that must be taken is improvement of our efforts to deter international drug trafficking by the meaningful threat of criminal sanctions.

Similarly, deterrence is the most important component of our efforts to combat terrorism, because the world is too large a place and the terrorists' opportunities too plentiful for law enforcement agents to stop any but a small fraction of attacks before they occur. Some fanatics will not be deterred by even the certain threat of harsh punishment, but others are more rational. If would-be terrorists became convinced that their prospects of finding a safe haven from prosecution were slim, there would be less terrorism in the world. Unfortunately, they receive precisely the opposite message today. Pariah nations such as Libya and Iran welcome them with open arms. More surprisingly, some American allies in Europe and the Middle East have displayed timidity when called upon to apprehend, detain, extradite, or prosecute terrorists.

The willingness of the U.S. to prosecute drug traffickers is well known. Not as many people are aware that we are willing to prosecute terrorist acts against American citizens, wherever they occur. In 1984, Congress made the taking of American hostages abroad a criminal act, and, in 1986, we passed legislation extending the reach of U.S. criminal jurisdiction to extra-territorial acts of violence against American nationals. The State Department has sought to maximize the effectiveness of these statutes by working to strengthen international extradition treaties.

Extradition—the legal process by which one nation surrenders a fugitive to another for criminal prosecution—is fraught with uncertainty. We have witnessed numerous incidents in recent years in which extradition has been rendered difficult or impossible because tremendous pressure to refuse it has been brought to bear upon nations that gain custody of suspected terrorists or drug traffickers. These include:

- The Fawaz Yunis case, in which the only legal mechanism for bringing a terrorist to justice was a dangerous, dramatic kidnapping on the high seas by American law enforcement agents.
- The Mohammed Hamadei case, in which international blackmailers seized German hostages in the Middle East in an attempt to derail the extradition of a terrorist from West Germany to the U.S. and an unsuccessful effort to prevent his trial in the German courts.
- The Abu Abbas case, in which Italy and Yugoslavia caved in to pressure and permitted a terrorist leader to escape prosecution for a vicious crime.
- The Mohammed Rashid case, in which a valid American extradition request, currently pending, has become a highly charged political issue in Greece.
- The Juan Ramon Mata Ballesteros case, in which the extradition of a suspected drug trafficker to the U.S. led to riots in the streets of Honduras.

In each instance, there has been heightened resistance to extradition requests from the U.S. because of anti-American sentiment in many parts of the world.

Some nations seek a middle ground by declining to extradite to the U.S. while agreeing to try the suspects themselves, but these countries often have become the targets of unbearable pressure as well. The fact remains that international extradition is an unreliable remedy in the toughest cases. We need an alternative mechanism—an international criminal court.

There is no question that such an institution would be a powerful weapon in the battle against drug trafficking and terrorism. I envision a court composed of jurists from many nations of the world with its own detention facility, its own prison, and a criminal code derived, through negotiation, from existing principles of international law and the various codes of the participating governments. It would serve as a neutral forum to which participating nations could extradite suspected terrorists and drug pushers. The court would try these criminals and, if they were convicted, provide a mechanism for international incarceration. To this end, I envision the establishment of a modern-day Devil's Island or, to choose a more up-to-date analogy, a new Spandau Prison.

I also propose that the President should initiate negotiations for the creation of a multilateral strike force capable of apprehending terrorists and major drug traffickers for extradition to the court. This international SWAT-team would be composed of highly skilled and specially trained combatants similar to those assigned to the U.S. Army's Delta Force. The inevitable criticism of U.S. military intervention would be blunted by the international composition of this group. The effort would not duplicate the mission of the UN Peacekeeping Forces. Rather, this international unit would be empowered to take the offensive against terrorists and drug traffickers, with one important restriction—the strike force only would be deployed at the invitation of the host country. Neither the strike force nor the international court should represent a threat to the sovereignty of nations.

There are many details to negotiate, but the premise of the court is sound. Recent history demonstrates that prosecuting and incarcerating these individuals is a burden upon the country to which the duty happens to fall. Sometimes, that responsibility is unbearable and a criminal goes free. The existence of an international court would enable the nations of the world to share this burden, making it tolerable and thereby enhancing the likelihood that terrorists and drug traffickers would be brought to justice.

American support for an international criminal court is growing. In 1986, Congress adopted an amendment to the Omnibus Diplomatic Security and Antiterrorism Act calling on the President to pursue negotiations to establish an international court to try terrorists. There also is a provision in the Omnibus Anti-Drug Abuse Act of 1988 seeking for the President to pursue negotiations to establish such a court with jurisdiction over drug trafficking and other violations of international criminal law. Similarly, the Congress has urged negotiations to create the multilateral strike force I have described and authorized the expenditure of funds should the strike force be established.

State Department officials have expressed guarded optimism about the concept of this international tribunal. I also have had discussions with a wide variety of foreign leaders on this subject, and the support it has garnered is very encouraging. Among the leaders who have endorsed, in whole or in part, the proposal to create such a court are Pres. Hosni Mubarak of Egypt, Pres. Hafez al-Assad of Syria, Defense Minister Yitzak Rabin of Israel, Prime Minister Hedi Baccouche of Tunisia, General Secretary Karoly Grosz of Hungary, Foreign Minister Guillermo Bedregal of Bolivia, and Prime Minister A.N.R. Robinson of Trinidad. One foreign leader who has taken a prominent role in the area of international law enforcement is Prime Minister Michael Manley of Jamaica, who repeatedly has urged the creation, under UN auspices, of a multilateral anti-drug strike force in the Western Hemisphere.

It is not surprising that the creation of an international criminal court has won widespread support because the strongest arguments in favor of the creation of such a body can be drawn from today's headlines. The need for an international forum in which to prosecute and maintain custody of terrorists is illustrated by the cases cited earlier.

Combating terrorism

Successes. On June 11, 1985, five heavily armed men, one of whom was Fawaz Yunis, seized a Royal Jordanian Airlines jet in Beirut, hijacking it for a 30-hour journey to Cyprus, Tunisia, and Sicily before returning to Lebanon. More than 50 passengers, including at least two American citizens, were aboard the plane throughout this ordeal.

During the hijacking, the terrorists severely beat Jordanian sky marshals on board and threatened to kill hostages one by one unless their demands were met. After two unsuccessful flights over Tunisia, they returned to Beirut, released the hostages, blew up the plane, and escaped.

Two years later, Yunis was brought to justice. An elaborate undercover operation executed by a team of U.S. law enforcement agents lured him onto a yacht moored in international waters off the coast of Cyprus. Yunis believed he was to take part in a drug deal, but instead found himself in American custody. He confessed to his crimes and was brought to the U.S. for trial. On March 14, 1989, Yunis was convicted in Federal district court in Washington, D.C., of hostage-taking, air piracy, and conspiracy, and sentenced to 30 years in prison.

I applaud the daring law enforcement operation that brought him into an American courtroom, but our long-term security interests require that the efforts to bring such outlaws to justice be institutionalized. Expeditions such as the one that netted Yunis are highly dangerous to the American personnel involved in them and are necessarily inflammatory. Anti-American sentiment throughout the world was fueled by the Yunis operation—a James Bond-like kidnapping on the high seas. U.S. citizens know that their government is well-intentioned, but foreigners are highly sensitive to what some perceive to be American imperialist tendencies. We should not need to act unilaterally, but be able to find a multilateral solution.

The TWA hijacking

The facts of the Hamadei case shock the conscience as well. On June 14, 1985, Trans World Airline Flight 847 departed Athens International Airport en route to Rome with 153 passengers and crew on board, most of them Americans. Approximately 10 minutes into the flight, two hijackers, later identified as Mohammed Hamadei and Hasan 'Izz-al-din, commandeered the aircraft and ran through the plane brandishing hand grenades and a pistol, while randomly striking the seated passengers with their weapons. The terrorists forced Chief Stewardess Uli Derickson to the flight deck area and gained access to the cockpit. The hijackers pistol-whipped the flight crew and ordered the pilot to fly to Algiers. The aircraft ultimately flew between Beirut and Algiers several times during the next two days while they retained control of the plane.

The hijackers had Derickson collect all passports and separated those of U.S. citizens and military personnel. The terrorists then ordered the military personnel into the first-class section one at a time for questioning, beginning with Navy diver Robert Stethem. The hijackers bound his arms together with an electrical cord, cutting off his circulation, and beat him until he was unconscious. Several other passengers also were beaten. Stethem regained consciousness, only to be shot in the head. The hijackers dumped his body onto the tarmac in Beirut before several more hijackers boarded the plane for its flight back to Algiers.

The terrorists eventually abandoned the plane after its final landing in Beirut. Thirty-nine passengers were removed from the aircraft and held hostage in various locations in Beirut before they finally were freed on June 30, 1985.

Hamadei, a Lebanese Shiite Muslim, was arrested in Frankfurt, West Germany. Immediately, the West German government came under tremendous pressure to reject the American request for prompt extradition of Hamadei. West German citizens were taken hostage in the Middle East, a shameless attempt to blackmail and intimidate a sovereign state. In the face of this unrelenting pressure, the German government refused extradition and decided to try Hamadei itself.

On May 17, 1989, he was convicted of murder and air piracy and received the maximum sentence available under German law—life imprisonment. I am pleased that the Hamadei case reached a satisfactory conclusion and commend the West German criminal justice system for its vigilance and courage. Nonetheless, the Hamadei case, like the Yunis one, vividly illustrates the need for an international criminal court. Why should West Germany have had to face a choice between the rule of law and the lives of its citizens? Perhaps the vicious conduct of a handful of extremists makes that choice inevitable, but why should any nation face it alone? The West Germans should have had the option of extraditing Hamadei to an international forum. An international court would be far less vulnerable than a single nation to kidnapping or other forms of terrorist intimidation.

Failure. The Yunis and Hamadei cases are, in large measure, success stories in the war on terrorism. In contrast, the case of Abu Abbas is an example of a dismal failure.

In October, 1985, four Palestinian gunmen hijacked the Italian cruise ship *Achille Lauro* in the Mediterranean Sea. The terrorists murdered Leon Klinghoffer, an elderly American confined to a wheelchair, and threw his body overboard. When the ship arrived at an Egyptian port, Italy and Egypt negotiated the return of the ship and the release of the remaining hostages, while the terrorists were promised safe passage out of the country.

Abu Abbas, head of the Tunis-based faction of the Palestine Liberation Front and trusted confidant of Yassir Arafat, was one of two PLO representatives who accompanied the hijackers in their escape aboard an Egyptian airliner. American F-14 fighters intercepted the Egyptian plane in international air space and forced it to land at Sigonella Air Force Base in Sicily, where American and Italian military forces immediately surrounded it. Because the crimes had been committed aboard an Italian vessel, the Italians insisted on asserting paramount jurisdiction and the U.S. troops withdrew. Prime Minister Bettino Craxi ordered the terrorists to stand trial, but, despite proper U.S. extradition requests, released Abbas, who promply fled to Yugoslavia.

The U.S. then requested that Yugoslavia extradite him. The Yugoslavs asserted that Abbas had diplomatic immunity through his position on the executive committee of the PLO, which Yugoslavia recognizes as the representative of the Palestinian people. Thus, the extradition request was rebuffed and Abbas was permitted to vanish back into the Arab underworld. He subsequently was tried, convicted, and sentenced in absentia by the Italian courts, but remains a free man today.

The Abbas case represents a dramatic setback for American anti-terrorist efforts. Not only did he slip through our fingers, but the incident created serious, although temporary, strains in our otherwise friendly relations with Egypt, Italy, and Yugoslavia. Egyptian Pres. Mubarak harshly criticized the U.S. action, although he was embarrassed by the incident. In Italy, the entire affair and the bitter recriminations that followed seriously undermined the Craxi goverment. In Yugoslavia, Pres. Lazar Mojsov reacted angrily to U.S. criticism that his country had acted improperly in releasing Abbas. Most of his criticism, however, was directed at Italy, which he castigated for having "put a rotten egg" into Yugoslavia's basket.

This entire diplomatic episode could have been avoided had there been an international forum to which Abbas could have been extradited. Egypt, Italy, and Yugoslavia all caved in to pressure by refusing to turn him over to the U.S., but any one of the three nations might have been willing to surrender him to an impartial international forum. Instead of countries dropping "rotten eggs" into each other's baskets, the international criminal court would become the appropriate receptacle for political "hot potatoes."

The aftermath of at least two other terrorist incidents remain unresolved as of this writing, First, the world awaits the apprehension of those responsible for the heinous destruction of Pan Am Flight 103 over Scotland in December, 1988. Second, there is the case of Muhammad Rashid, whose status is highly relevant to the discussion of an international court. Greece currently has custody of Rashid, who is wanted by U.S. prosecutors for allegedly placing a bomb on a Pan Am jet in 1982. The bomb exploded as the plane flew over Hawaii, killing a Japanese teenager and wounding 15 other passengers. In connection with that case, Rashid faces murder, assault, and sabotage charges in the U.S. Moreover, Rashid is a suspect in at least one other terrorist attack on an American airliner—the April 2, 1986, bombing of a TWA jet en route from Rome to Athens, in which four Americans were blown out of the plane at 15,000 feet.

On May 12, 1989, the Greek Supreme Court ruled that Rashid is eligible for extradition to the U.S., but the final decision rests with that nation's Justice Minister. The case has become a political issue in Greece, where there is much sympathy for the Palestinian cause. Once again, the country with the misfortune of having physical custody of a suspected terrorist becomes the target of terrorist pressure. On April 10, 1989, terrorists set off a bomb outside the Athens apartment of a Supreme Court judge. Other judges involved in the case have been threatened, causing the court to postpone consideration of the case on three occasions. Membership on the panel has changed three times, as five judges from the 52-member Supreme Court have withdrawn on the grounds of illness.

While we anxiously await the Justice Minister's decision on extradition, it is worthwhile to speculate about the potential benefit of an international criminal court in this situation. To be sure, there would be pressure on Greece to decline extradition even to an international forum, but the pressure would not be fueled by anti-U.S. sentiment. Extradition to the international criminal court might be seen as a reasonable alternative, palatable to both the U.S. government and the internal political forces.

Dealing with drug traffickers

The final example I will offer in support of the international court differs in that its protagonist is not a terrorist. Instead, the case involves international drug trafficking, the other major "docket" I propose for the new court.

In 1988, American and Honduran authorities jointly seized a major international cocaine trafficker, Juan Ramon Mata Ballesteros. With the consent and full cooperation of that nation's government, Mata was transported from Honduras to the U.S. for trial. A riot ensued and the American embassy in Honduras came under attack by angry mobs.

The Honduran people do not support drug pushers, but they do harbor understandable nationalist sentiments. These run particularly strong among the populations of Central and South America, where the U.S. often is seen as an overbearing and intrusive neighbor. If Honduras had had the option of surrendering the suspect to an international tribunal, the U.S. might not have been the focus of a mob's fury.

In a similar vein, the combination of an international court and an international strike force could be a powerful force for good in Colombia. If invited to intervene by its government, the strike force could assist the Colombian defense forces in the effort to locate drug cartel leaders in their embattled country. Once apprehended, these traffickers could be extradited either to the U.S. or to the international court, depending upon the prevailing political climate in Bogota. Americans might prefer extradition to a U.S. courtroom, but would settle gladly for the opportunity to participate in the prosecution of Medellin Cartel leaders Pablo Escobar and Jorge Luis Ochoa before an international criminal tribunal.

Many people deem the idea of an international court to be impractical. Surely, this "pie-in-the-sky" idea will never come to fruition, they say. Such a skeptical view ignores the solid historical foundation upon which the proposal is based. An international criminal court first was proposed in the aftermath of World War I, when some Allied leaders argued that Kaiser Wilhelm II of Germany and his key military officers should be prosecuted for war crimes. The trials never took place, in part because the Allies were unable to agree on the boundaries of international criminal law. The 1937 Convention Against Terrorism would have established the court, but only one nation (India) ratified the Convention before World War II broke out.

The most successful international criminal tribunal was created to prosecute war criminals following World War II. The War Crimes Commission, a cooperative effort of the U.S., Great Britain, France, and the Soviet Union, successfully conducted 13 trials in Nuremberg and one in Tokyo between 1945 and 1949. Another significant development following World War II was the establishment of the International Court of Justice. That court, which sits at the Peace Palace in The Hague, is empowered to resolve treaty disputes between nations, but has no criminal jurisdiction over individuals. In its early years, the UN sponsored several projects to initiate the creation of a court with criminal jurisdiction over individuals, but distrust between the superpowers thwarted these efforts.

Interestingly, developments in the Kremlin's view of the International Court of Justice may provide a golden opportunity for the creation of an international criminal court. For years, the U.S.S.R. all but ignored the Court. Then, in 1988, Soviet leader Mikhail Gorbachev proposed that the five permanent members of the UN Security Council—Britain, China, France, the Soviet Union, and the U.S.—agree to upgrade the World Court's status in resolving treaty disputes among them. The U.S., which had sent conflicting signals concerning the Court in recent years, responded with a proposal that the U.S. and the U.S.S.R. accept World Court jurisdiction in any dispute arising between them with respect to some 60 treaties or agreements signed by both nations. Negotiations are under way, and there is every reason to believe that the Court soon will be granted enhanced authority and recognition. In light of Gorbachev's interest, it might be useful to explore with the Soviets the structural advantages of establishing a criminal court as an adjunct to the International Court of Justice or, perhaps, granting the current court criminal jurisdiction over individuals.

I am confident that forward-thinking world leaders will recognize the potential benefits of an international criminal court. Once negotiations commence, it may become apparent that there are international crimes in addition to terrorism that should be incorporated in the court's mandate. For example, why not explore the creation of a court to try other international crimes such as torture and genocide? There are acute definitional controversies with respect to genocide, but they should not be insurmountable if the participating countries negotiate in good faith. Even if it should come to pass that only some nations can agree upon a suitable definition of genocide or, for that matter, of terrorism, it may be possible to structure a treaty that offers countries a *menu* of jurisdiction. Each signatory to the treaty would be able to choose the extent to which it will recognize the court's authority. Over time, as the court gains respect, signatories might choose to recognize a greater portion of its jurisdiction.

Some may fear that the establishment of a new international criminal court is another step down the slippery slope toward world government. Nothing could be further from the truth. The central purpose of the court is to enable each sovereign state to protect its citizens more effectively. Paradoxically, that nationalist goal can be furthered best by multilateral action. Participating in the search for multilateral solutions to global problems does not in any way imply a loss of sovereignty. Indeed, sovereignty is meaningless if a government can not protect the physical well-being of its citizens.

Therefore, I call for a multilateral solution to the twin crises of terrorism and international drug trafficking. The civilized world stands poised to condemn these evils once and for all, and the creation of an international criminal court would be an eloquent expression of that condemnation.

WHEN REALITY CAME UNGLUED: ANTONIO SAVASTA AND THE ITALIAN RED BRIGADES

Richard Oliver Collin D. Phil. (Ox.)

Coastal Carolina College
University of South Carolina

ABSTRACT

This article traces the life history of an unusual Italian terrorist, Antonio Savasta, a Roman Marxist-Leninist who rose in the 1970's to a senior position within the Italian Red Brigades. Savasta was captured during the celebrated 1981–82 abduction of an American General, James Lee Dozier, and his subsequent confession was primarily responsible for the virtual annihilation of continental Europe's most dangerous revolutionary movement.

Key Words: Terrorist, Red Brigades, Savasta, Italy

ORIGINS

While still in his teens, a young Roman named Antonio Savasta became persuaded that the Italian Government could and should be overthrown. In time, he became one of the pre-eminent leaders of the Red Brigades, carrying out knee-cappings, robberies, kidnappings, and political assassinations. Arrested during the celebrated abduction of an American general named James Dozier, Savasta unexpectedly turned state's evidence, virtually destroying his country's revolutionary movement.

While most revolutionaries can be neatly categorized as either intellectuals or gun-slingers, Antonio Savasta proved to be both thinker and shooter, combining extraordinary ruthlessness with a probing, restless mind (Scialoja, 1982). He does not fit easily into any stereotype of the "terrorist personality" and those who knew him before his capture have testified to his charm, charisma, and qualities of leadership. People meeting him in prison have described him as sensitive and thoughtful, albeit tormented by reflections on his past and the breakup of his one great romantic interest (De Luca, *Ragazzo*, 1982; Savasta, *Letter*, 1988). Despite his warm personality, students of his career continue to be stunned by the mayhem this otherwise engaging young man perpetrated in a few short years (Genova, 1987; Tumbarello, 1987).

While many European "New Left" radicals of the 1960's and 1970's emerged from comfortable bourgeois backgrounds, Antonio Savasta was one of the few authentic proletarians at the top of the revolutionary movement. Born December 30, 1955, he grew up in Centocelle, a vast, sprawling neighborhood of grey apartment buildings and shabby working class cottages near Rome's Via Prenestina. During Savasta's youth, Centocelle was a jungle of shacks and huts, temporary structures built in defiance of zoning regulations and often lacking even rudimentary sanitary facilities (Freid, 1973:46–94). As Savasta later commented:

> *Centocelle was a ghetto. There was chronic unemployment, violence and promiscuity, and a total lack of culture. We had the sense that the Italian government was absent and unreal, and that the Catholic Church was only for old ladies. Growing up there in the nineteen fifties, young people felt that it was impossible to alter anything or amount to anything. We felt that we had to try to change it. (Savasta, 1987)*

Savasta did not enjoy a good relationship with his father, who had joined Mussolini's Fascist police to avoid military service during World War Two (Andreoli, 1982). He continues to have, however, a warm and significant relationship with his mother, who had served with the *Resistenza* during World War Two, helping to smuggle prisoners-of-war to safety in the south (Savasta, 1987; Tumbarello, 1987). In the eyes of the then-legal Mussolini Government, members of the Resistance Movement were "terrorists," a fact which may have re-defined the word in Savasta's mind. In Italian revolutionary circles, a family connection to the Partisan War of 1943–1945 was important. Red Brigade activists saw themselves as legitimate heirs to the partisan tradition, and many senior *brigatisti* enjoyed

Reprinted with the permission of Richard Oliver Collin, Professor of Government at Coastal Carolina College, University of South Carolina, from *Violence, Aggression, and Terrorism*, Vol. 3, No. 4, 1989, pp. 269-294. His most recent publication is *Winter of Fire: The Abduction of General Dozier and the Downfall of the Red Brigades*.

some actual ancestral affiliation with the Resistance movement (Fani, 1985:30 ff.).

Savasta's parents met and married after the War, producing two sons, Paolo and Antonio. The family was poor and Savasta attended state-supported local elementary schools. By all accounts, "Toto" (as his friends nicknamed him) was bright and popular. In 1970, at the age of fourteen, Savasta enrolled at Centocelle's Lyceum of Benedetto da Norcia to prepare himself for university studies (Andreoli, 1982). To make ends meet, he did back-breaking work in the afternoons as a laborer at a nearby collective farm, earning extra money by playing his guitar and singing with a local rock group (Savasta, 1987; Genova, 1987; Tumbarello, 1987).

In post-war Italy, the axis of national political life ranged between the conservative Catholic *Democrazia Cristiana* (DC) and an increasingly bourgeois Italian Communist Party (PCI). In the marginal society of Centocelle, however, neither of these two great institutions had much impact. Savasta's friends were neither church-going Catholics likely to support the DC, nor the unionized factory workers who provided a power-base for the PCI. As a result, many young people drifted toward the margins of political life, gravitating into tiny Maoist or Trotskyite groups (Andreoli, 1972; Drake, 1982:123; Ferrarroti, 1970:41 ff.).

Their natural enemies came from Italy's neo-Fascist movement, the *Movimento sociale italiano* or MSI. Throughout Savasta's youth, ideologically opposed gangs conducted huge running fist-fights in corridors and cloak-rooms despite the efforts of police and school authorities to keep them apart. In fact, the sixteen year old Savasta was briefly detained by the police in 1972 after some neo-Fascist youngsters had been injured during one of these epic brawls (Andreoli, 1972). The obsessive conviction that there was imminent danger of a neo-Fascist *coup d'état* was later to become a cardinal element in Italian New Left thinking (Savasta, 1987; Galli, 1986:9–11; Peci, 1983:36).

Inspired by the revolutionary success of Mao's Chinese Red Army, the Viet Cong, and by what was expected to be the victory of the Tupamaros in Uruguay, a handful of university graduates in northern Italy decided to pass to open revolution as early as 1969 (Peci, 1983:38). Led by Renato Curcio, Margherita Cagol, and Alberto Franceschini, they called themselves the Red Brigades, but their early operations were most non-lethal and largely unsensational (Galli, 1986:5–7; Franceschini, 1988:30–62).

In Savasta's Rome, however, the dominant voice on the revolutionary left belonged to a university professor named Antonio Negri (*Senato*, IX, 1986:386; Drake, 1982:111–117). Denying that a quick, military-style revolution could be achieved, Negri called for the creation of "autonomous" organizations capable of hovering on the margins of legality, harnessing and channelling the revolutionary enthusiasms of Italy's young people while encouraging wide-spread resistance to authority. According to Negri, workers should sabotage industrial capitalism while students shut down the educational system; the resulting diffused criminality would create the environment for an authentic revolution (Negri, 1974; Drake, 1982 and 1984; *Senato*, I, 1983:14–15).

Young Italians responded with a network of semi-revolutionary, semi-legal organizations, all part of a nationwide movement first called *Potere Operaio* (Workers' Power) and, after 1973, known as Autonomy or *Autonomia* (Monicelli, 1978:43–135; Weinberg, 1987:55–61). In Savasta's Centocelle, young dissident Marxists found a vacant store to serve as the headquarters of a typical *Autonomia* neighborhood organization. Called the *Collettivo comunista di Centocelle* (or Centocelle Communist Collective), this political youth group was similar to hundreds of other "*collettivi*," the rich soil from which the Red Brigades would later grow (Savasta, 1987).

Antonio Savasta joined *Potere Operaio* in 1972 and when *Potere operaio* dissolved the following year, the *Collettivo* of Centocelle affiliated with the *Autonomia* movement (*Senato*, IX, 1986:266). In 1974, at a meeting of the *Collettivo*, Antonio Savasta met Emilia Libera, the young woman who was to be his partner in love and revolution for the next thirteen years. Together with their friends, Antonio and Emilia disrupted classes at the Lyceum, attacked neo-Fascist rallies, and mounted violent protests against the war in Vietnam (Andreoli, 1982).

As early as 1974, these neighborhood *Autonomia*-affiliated collectives began to form secret defense committees as protection against attacks by neo-Fascists and police. The clandestine committees changed their names periodically, but, by 1975, some were called the *Formazioni armate comuniste* (Formations of Armed Communists or *FAC*) while others were known as *CoCoRi* for *Comitati comunisti rivoluzionari* (Communist revolutionary committees). The acronyms notwithstanding, the Centocelle *FAC* was nothing more than a sub-committee of the more combative members of the Centocelle *Cellettivo;* the nineteen year old Antonio Savasta joined during his last semester at the Lyceum (*Senato*, IX, 1986:266).

These *FAC*'s were often called to defend housing occupations or "squats," a common reaction to the mid-seventies shortage of low-cost housing. This experience was emotionally significant for Savasta. As he later recalled:

> *We always felt that those of us who were going to make the revolution should not attempt to dictate the shape of society afterwards. But each of us had a private vision of what it would be like after the revolution and I thought we should try to imitate the kind of human relationships that emerged from those squat groups. There were a lot of meetings;*

everybody helped make every decision and every voice was heard. The women got a chance to talk about their special concerns and even the children were listened to. (Savasta, 1987)

In spring 1975, one of Savasta's close friends defied the police by leading a group of young couples into an empty apartment building in Rome's San Basilio district. A three-day battle ended when the police opened fire, killing Savasta's comrade (*Senato*, IX, 1986:263). This incident seems to have provided a kind of radicalizing moment in his life:

The police response demonstrated to us that what the Red Brigades had been saying for some time was absolutely true. Legal activities were getting us nowhere. At the emotional level, the death of my friend, who was only trying to establish his right to a house, weighed on me heavily. (*Senato*, IX, 1986:266)

A Rubicon had been crossed. Following the San Basilio incident, Savasta and his colleagues in the Centocelle *FAC* began making trips into the hills, practicing marksmanship with stolen weapons. In the summer of 1975, they took their first step toward outright illegality when they invaded a Roman jewelry store, waved their pistols at the clerk, and expropriated the contents of the cash register (*Senato*, IX, 1986:277).

THE IDEOLOGICAL BASIS FOR REVOLUTION

In June of 1976, the twenty-year old Antonio Savasta completed his studies at the Centocelle Lyceum (where he had become the unchallenged leader of the student body) and enrolled in a six-year literature course at the University of Rome (Andreoli, 1982; *Senato*, IX, 1986: 269). That first year, he read his way through the classics of revolutionary literature, bogging down in *Das Kapital* and disliking what he felt was the passivity of Antonio Gramsci, but thrilling to the energy of what became his bible, Lenin's *State and Revolution* (Savasta, 1987).

Most of Savasta's fellow-students could have been described loosely as "New Leftists," interested not only in collectivist solutions to social problems but also in human freedom, feminism, ecology, the third world, and sexual liberation. Few saw the Soviet Union as a model, especially after the 1968 invasion of Czechoslovakia; Savasta himself frequently referred to the Russians as "social imperialists" (*Senato*, IX, 1986:395; Savasta, *Letter*, 1987).

Throughout the seventies, Italian universities sheltered many students and faculty who came to believe that reforms could not be accomplished without a revolution against the Italian state (Acquaviva, 1979:61). The sociologist Sabino Acquaviva describes the violence created by Savasta's contemporaries as a reaction to the crises overtaking both of Italy's key social institutions. In the aftermath of Vatican II, the Roman Catholic Church was still metabolizing the reforms of John XXIII, while the Communist Party was shifting its ideological basis toward the center, abandoning both the Soviet Union and Leninist revolutionary aspirations (Acquaviva, 1979). Using the provocative term "Cathocommunism" to describe this phenomenon, historian Giorgio Bocca has suggested that the turmoil in both Church and Party left Savasta's generation intellectually homeless (Bocca, 1978: 7–16; Galli, 1986:13).

Certain foreign writers were also important in granting intellectual legitimacy to the revolutionary ideal, principally Jean-Paul Sartre and Herbert Marcuse, whose works were available in Italian translations by the early seventies. Sartre suggested that the common people were passive sheep who needed to be bullied into a revolution by a clear-sighted "pledged group" (Fenzi, 1987:249). The anti-Soviet Marcuse, in turn, provided a gleaming vision of a democratic collectivist future (Peci, 1983:53). Both Sartre and Marcuse are difficult in any language, and their ideas became primarily known to Savasta's generation through secondary sources. Nearly all future *brigatisti* had digested Franz Fanon's powerful *The Wretched of the Earth,* however. Savasta himself was seduced by Fanon's notion that violence could have an emotionally cathartic value, although the young Italian was later to discover that killing people gave him nightmares rather than catharsis (Savasta, 1987; Genova, 1985:94).

For Savasta and his contemporaries, however, the pivotal political experience was the failed American effort in Vietnam. For them, the war had been genocidal, a clear-cut evil that destroyed any residual moral legitimacy the US might have retained from the fight against Nazism in World War Two. And Savasta's generation regarded the Italian state as co-responsible for the Vietnam adventure, since the government had allowed the American military to use bases on Italian soil. Hence, when American legitimacy disappeared in the ashes of the Vietnamese conflict, the far more fragile legitimacy of the young Italian Republic collapsed with it.

While it is not difficult to see why Savasta and his friends wanted a violent social change, it is more complicated to explain how they managed to persuade themselves that a successful revolution in Italy was possible. Their conviction seems to have stemmed from two interrelated factors: an extremely mechanistic interpretation of Marx's celebrated views about the inevitable self-destruction of capitalism; and a narrow almost solipsistic vision of world events (Carlucci, 1982; Peci, 1983:44–48).

Clearly, the Italian economy was tormented during the middle and late 1970's. The annual rise in consumer prices between 1974 and 1982 averaged almost seventeen percent, while unemployment afflicted one person in ten and interest rates soared painfully (Hellman, 1987:373). As bad as it was, no one seriously anticipated the imminent collapse of the Italian financial system. For Savasta and his colleagues, however, Marx's magic moment was about to arrive, with the country trembling on the brink of spontaneous revolution. As multi-national capitalism crumbled, a vanguard party would be needed to play mid-wife to the birth of revolutionary communism (De Luca, *Ragazzo*, 1982).

How could intelligent, well-meaning young people have come to this astonishing conclusion? Savasta's colleagues seem to have missed what everyone else understood because of a kind of self-imposed solipsism in which they rejected information from the usual journalistic and academic sources, concentrating upon passionate newsletters published by student groups, political tracts written by revolutionaries like Negri and their own personalized interpretations of *Das Kapital* (Savasta, 1987; Genova, 1987).

Savasta and his colleagues even convinced themselves that the United States was collapsing as a world power. As he remembered the excitement of the period:

> *From all over the world, news was coming in that nations were rebelling against the omnipotent Americans and their puppet regimes. We were certain that the US could no longer impose its will on the world. Why not in Italy? Why shouldn't the chain of imperialism snap in Italy, its weakest link? Why not? (Savasta, Letter, 1987)*

In retrospect there were many good reasons why not, but with the Italian economy at its lowest ebb, with the Christian Democratic administration wracked by one horrific scandal after another, and with the US government adrift in a post-Watergate-post-Vietnam haze, there seemed to Savasta's generation no particularly compelling reason why the Italian government could not be overthrown with the application of determined violence. Savasta himself was later to refer to this period with a provocative phrase, *lo scollamento di realità* (reality coming unglued or un-stuck).

In September of 1976, Savasta and his companion, Emilia Libera, were approached by a Red Brigade recruiter who offered them the chance to play a role in the coming revolution. Unhesitatingly, they consented, and reality began to come unglued.

THE EARLY YEARS WITH THE ROME COLUMN

Insiders called it the *Organizzazione*, and Savasta became an insider thanks to the efforts of a quiet serious man named Bruno Seghetti (*Senato*, IX, 1986:268). Once a prominent member of the *FAC*, Seghetti argued that *Autonomia* had become a kind of debating society for intellectual rough-necks, admirable in its way but essentially going nowhere. Since the proletariat could not change this government they needed to get on with the task of overthrowing it (Savasta, 1987).

By 1976, most of the original Red Brigade leadership had disappeared, some into exile, many into prison and a few into the cemetery after shoot-outs with the police. The decimated *Organizzazione* was being rebuilt by the implacable Mario Moretti, a masterful conspirator destined to dominate the revolutionary left for the next six years. Working with a tall, hulking peasant from Reggio Emiliano named Prospero Gallinari, Moretti had come to Central Italy to put together a Rome Column (*Senato*, I, 1983: 13; Fanti, 1985:142–158).

Under Moretti, the *Organizzazione* was well-structured, flexible, and curiously democratic. At the national level, long-range policy was set by an elected parliamentary body of 25–30 members called the *Direzione strategica* (Strategic Directorate). To run the Red Brigades operationally on a day-to-day basis, Strategic Directorate in turn selected a small *Comitato esecutivo* (Executive Committee) of four or five experienced guerrillas who closely supervised all major operations (*Senato*, IX, 1986:372; Peci, 1983:59).

By the mid-seventies, several Red Brigade "columns" had been established, most of them based in a single city (e.g. Rome, Turin, Genoa, Milan, Naples) while the Veneto Column was regional in character, including brigades from Venice, Verona, Padua, and several smaller cities in the Veneto Region. Each column was led by a "directorate" of experienced brigadists and headed by an appointed column chief, or *capocolonna*. Each city-column was composed of a series of "*brigate*" (or brigades) of between five to ten members apiece (Genova, 1985:126–127; Peci, 1983:57).

Until the end of 1977, Mario Moretti committed his *Organizzazione* only to a low-risk program of kneecappings and political assassinations, targeting mostly middle-echelon people in an effort to undermine the morale of magistrates, police officers, and business executives accused of exploiting the working class (Drake, 1982:111). At the end of the year, however, Bruno Seghetti assigned Savasta the task of shadowing Italy's best-known political figure, Aldo Moro, who came to the University of Rome once a week to lecture on constitutional law. Savasta was able to find no moment of vulnerability in Moro's schedule. He played no further role in the Moro affair until the spring of 1978, when Seghetti gave him a stolen green Renault with orders to keep it safe, out of sight, full of gas and instantly available (*Senato*, I, 1983:84; *Senato*, IX, 1986:288).

On 16 March 1978, a Red Brigades team kidnapped Aldo Moro and slaughtered his five bodyguards, demonstrating the ruthlessness and the extraordinary technical competence reached by the brigades under Moretti's leadership. During the period of Moro's captivity, Savasta kept busy on the fringes of the operation. Among other things, he participated in a kneecapping, joining a team that fired an automatic pistol into the legs of a middle-ranking Christian Democratic politician named Girolamo Mechelli (*Senato,* IX, 1986:288). On the 7th of May 1978, Seghetti called for the stolen Renault.

Two days later, Aldo Moro was ordered to climb into the back of the Renault. He was then shot dead by Savasta's friend, Prospero Gallinari. The Renault was driven into downtown Rome and abandoned defiantly mid-way between the offices of the Communist Party and the Christian Democratic Party headquarters (Acciari 1984).

Individual members of the Red Brigades fell into two categories. Although Savasta and Emilia Libera began as unpaid "irregulars," they were expected to be totally committed to the *Organizzazione,* and—appropriately disguised—to participate in illegal operations, such as robberies and knee-cappings. At the same time, irregulars carried on a legal, apparently normal existence, continuing to use their real names and to maintain normal contacts with friends and family. A smaller and completely clandestine group within the Red Brigades was composed of salaried "regulars" who lived with false identity papers and under assumed names in a state of total illegality (Fenzi, 1987:58; Savasta, *Letter,* 1988).

Both categories however, were intended to enjoy equivalent standing within the organization, and the votes of regulars and "irregulars" were counted equally when elections for the Strategic Directorate were held. At the height of the movement in 1978–79, the total strength of the Red Brigades amounted to about three hundred regulars and fifteen hundred "irregulars," supported by an estimated twenty-five thousand sympathizers prepared to offer occasional logistical support (Bocca, 1978:270).

During the last months of 1976, Savasta seems to have won his spurs by spray-painting political slogans on the walls of the University, distributing pamphlets to potential recruits, and fire-bombing the automobiles of conservative professors (*Senato,* IX, 1986:288). Under his nom di guerre of Diego, he became the Red Brigades "ambassador" to Centocelle, entrusted with the task of organizing the veterans of the old Centocelle *FAC* into a small Red Brigade unit (Moran, 1986:95; *Senato,* IX, 1986:268).

In the spring of 1977, Antonio Negri's *Autonomia* sparked an explosion of political passion, later called the *Movimento del '77,* that brought thousands of young Italians into the streets for daily demonstrations and riots. In their sometimes heavy-handed efforts to restore order, the police occasionally opened fire, killing students and innocent by-standers. Capitalizing on the tension, Savasta and his colleagues infiltrated student demonstrations in order to raise the level of violence and, if possible, to provoke the police into using their guns. Dead policemen and dead students would radicalize society, the Red Brigades reasoned, creating a backlash effect and making the Italian state appear ruthless and violent (Carlucci, 1981; *Senato,* IX, 1986:269; Weinberg, 1987:67–68).

In March of 1977, a popular and prominent Communist politician named Luciano Lama came to the University of Rome to deliver a lecture. Anxious to show that the craven reformism of the Communist Party was a betrayal of the working class, Savasta and his friends launched a violent physical attack on Lama, forcing him to flee the University without making his speech (Carlucci, 1981; *Senato,* I, 1983:14; Drake, 1982:110).

While this was meant to demonstrate that the Communist Party was no longer the cutting edge of protest, it was a tactical set-back for Savasta because he was identified and secretly photographed by a police agent during the tumult. He was neither questioned nor arrested at the time, perhaps out of deference to his policeman father, but the police quietly opened a small file on him, a file destined to grow larger with the passing years (*Senato,* X, 1986:25).

Emilia Libera began her own university career in the autumn of 1977, registering as a part-time student in the Faculty of Science, where she worked on experiments in the chemistry lab and recruited members for a new university brigade (Moran, 1986:93–96).

THE RISE TO PROMINENCE

In September of 1978, Prospero Gallinari decided to restructure the Rome column. Savasta was moved up to work with the *Capo-colonna* himself and given a seat on the Rome Directorate, making him one of the top guerrilla leaders in the city (Moran, 1986:105; *Senato,* IX, 1986:299). This rapid rise in importance was partially due to his charismatic personality, noted by a senior Red Brigades intellectual:

> *Savasta was loved by everyone. This was partly because of his warm personality and partly because there was nothing he would not do for the Organization. Without exactly trying and certainly without striking any poses, Savasta exercised a certain natural authority. . . . He communicated a sense of unshakable and reassuring mental health. (Fenzi, 1987:183)*

His charisma notwithstanding, Savasta's rise was also related to his talents as a gunman; he has admitted to involvement in seventeen separate homicides during his career (Tumbarello, 1987). On 3 May 1979, Prospero Gallinari, Bruno Seghetti, Antonio Savasta, Emilia Libera, and a group of ten others launched a daring frontal assault on the central offices of the Christian Democratic Party in Rome's Piazza Nicosia. Terrifying the headquarters staff with automatic weapons fire, they confiscated a pile of secret documents, partially destroyed the building with an explosive charge, and fought their way to freedom past a police patrol, killing two officers in the process (Galli, 1986:234; De Luca, *Guida,* 1982; *Senato,* XII, 1986:109).

Savasta's next target was Lieutenant Colonel Antonio Varisco, a senior investigator for the Carabiniere National Police, who had been working energetically to smash the Rome Column. Varisco enjoyed the reputation of being an extreme right-winger in his political views, and had even been the subject of a popular novel (Cassola, 1973). Savasta picked up Varisco's trail on 13 July 1979, following the Carabiniere's BMW through the early morning traffic. With a colleague at the wheel of a stolen vehicle, he fired a smoke grenade through a window of the speeding car. When the stunned Carabiniere stamped on the brakes, Savasta shot him dead with two blasts from a shotgun (De Luca, *Guida*, 1982; Galli, 1986:241; Acciari, *Savasta*, 1982).

Four days after Savasta killed Colonel Varisco, the Sandinista Liberation Front overthrew Anastasio Somoza's government; encouraged, the Executive Committee considered the possibility of achieving a Nicaraguan-style victory in Sardinia, long regarded by the hard left as Italy's last colony. Choosing Savasta as the commander of Red Brigade resources in Sardinia, the Executive Committee brought Savasta and Emilia Libera into full-time status as salaried "regulars" (Savasta, 1987).

The task awaiting them in Sardinia was challenging. A nascent separatist movement already existed, but this group needed to be controlled and re-directed toward the long-range goals of the revolutionary left (Bellu, 1983). Perhaps more important to the Executive Committee was the fact that Renato Curcio and the other "Historic Leaders" of the Red Brigades were languishing in a Sardinian maximum security penitentiary. Gallinari had conceived an elaborate plan to bring them to freedom, but first Savasta had to create an operational base on the island (*Senato*, I, 1983:61).

Savasta and Libera had just gone to work in Cagliari, establishing contact with Sardinia's *Barbagia rossa*, when Prospero Gallinari was badly wounded in a gunfight with the police. Distraught, Savasta dashed back to the mainland to organize a ruthless rescue operation. Gallinari was recovering under police guard in a Rome hospital where the Red Brigades had a team of unsuspected irregulars in place, and Savasta plotted to have these covert *brigatisti* kill Gallinari's six guards by serving them poisoned coffee. From his hospital bed, however, Gallinari vetoed the plan, perhaps because he felt too ill to survive without medical attention (Fanti, 1985:155).

As a replacement for Gallinari, Savasta was promoted again at Christmas, being elected to the Strategic Directorate, the "parliament" of the Red Brigades (Moran, 1986:20). After the holidays, he and Emilia returned to Sardinia where disaster struck for the second time. On 15 February 1980, the couple were sitting in a waterfront bar in Cagliari, engaged in a quiet conversation with a group of Sardinian revolutionaries. Because his customers seemed to be whispering over their beer, the bartender decided on a whim that they had to be drug dealers and telephoned the police. Responding rather casually to the call, a patrol strolled in with drawn guns and ordered Emilia and Antonio to get into the back seat of one squad-car while the Sardinian revolutionaries were hustled into another (Zasso, 1983).

The moment the police took their eyes off him, Savasta drew his Browning automatic pistol and opened fire. In a moment's mayhem, dozens of shots were exchanged, and a bullet seared its way along the side of Emilia's skull. Throwing her over his shoulder, Savasta raced down a back alley and somehow managed to escape. Hungry, hurt, and desperate, they sheltered for several days of freezing winter weather in a deserted beach hut. When Emilia was once again able to walk, Savasta led her under cover of night to a friend's home; a month later, they fled back to the mainland, heavily disguised (Zasso, 1983; Savasta, 1987; Genova, 1987).

After the two Romans had abandoned the island, one of the arrested Sardinians identified Savasta and Libera from police mug-shots. Now in possession of their real names, the authorities interrogated both sets of stunned parents. Emilia's scalp wound healed quickly, but after the shoot-out she began to lose her passion for revolution. No one blamed Savasta, but the Sardinian interlude was a failure in every respect (Genova, 1985: 119–20; Bellu, 1983).

TRIUMPH AND DISASTER WITH THE VENETIAN COLUMN

Savasta returned to the mainland in the spring of 1980 to find that his beloved *Organizzazione* was crumbling into warring factions as *brigatisti* grappled with the prospect of defeat, or at least of continued non-victory. The Milan column had virtually seceded from the Red Brigades, believing that the *Brigate rosse* should postpone long-range political goals in favor of displaying their relevance to workers on the shop floor; in practice, this meant a reckless policy of assassinating low-level business executives who had offended Milanese workers (Fenzi, 1987:186–217).

A more serious problem, however, was posed by the so-called *movimentisti* (or "movementists"). Led by a former professor of criminology named Giovanni Senzani, the *movimentisti* viewed a short term military victory over the Italian state as unlikely and proposed instead the creation of a broadly-based underground movement with links to organized crime in the lawless slums of Rome and Naples (*Senato*, IX, 1986:373–376). As Savasta explained it:

> *The Movementists liked the idea of encouraging a widespread, uncontrolled resistance to the Italian government even if this resulted in petty criminality, industrial sabotage,*

or meaningless vandalism. Most of our historic leaders in prison sympathized with this point of view, even though it was undisciplined and essentially anarchistic. The overwhelming majority of those still in the field, however, remained faithful to the original objectives of the ***Organizzazione.*** *I remained firmly with the main body of the Red Brigades. The press called us the* ***militaristi,*** *but we were simply those who continued to believe in a vanguard organization that would launch attacks into the heart of the state. We also thought that our people needed to obey orders; you can't improvise a revolution and a guerrilla movement isn't a jazz band where everybody plays his own tune. Somebody has got to be in charge and it had always been the Executive Committee. (Savasta, 1987)*

Throughout the summer of 1980, Savasta attended a series of top-level *Direzione strategica* meetings during which he tried to heal the breach within the *Organizzazione.* While these meetings were ultimately unsuccessful, they did enhance Savasta's stature as one of the group's most trusted senior men, despite his youth (Fenzi, 1987:181–185).

While the revolutionaries feuded, the Italian police began a relentless counterattack. In the northeast, Carabiniere Major General Carlo Alberto Dalla Chiesa worked tirelessly to dismantle the Veneto Column, arresting several successive column chieftains and bringing Red Brigade activities in Venice to a halt (Fenzi, 1987:222). Threatened with the loss of an entire column, the Executive Committee dispatched Savasta to the northeast with orders to stabilize the situation. Throughout the autumn of 1980, Savasta worked furiously to staunch the hemorrhage of arrests; by December, he had largely succeeded, even managing to mount a few operations (Acciari, *Savasta,* 1982).

A grateful *Organizzazione* reacted by appointing Savasta to the leadership of the Veneto Column; a few weeks later, he was elected to a seat on the Executive Committee. Membership on this five-person *Esecutivo* represented the very top rung of the insurrectionary movement, and, at twenty-five, Savasta became one of the highest-ranking revolutionaries in Italy, attending regular meetings at a secret headquarters in Milan.

Their confidence partially restored, the Red Brigades surged into the winter of 1980–81 with a stunning campaign, designed to convince the outside world that the *Brigate rosse* were as strong as ever. In December 1980, they kidnapped the head of the Italian prison service, forcing the government into a series of humiliating concessions. Following hard on this success, a group of Professor Senzani's followers seized a well-connected Neopolitan politician, and "retailed" him back to the Christian Democratic Party for several million dollars (Galli, 1986:236–248).

In April of 1981, however, the *Esecutivo* lost its legendary leader, Mario Moretti, who stumbled into a police trap and disappeared into prison (Fenzi, 1987:26–28). With Moretti gone, the split between Giovanni Senzani's *Movimentisti* and Savasta's *Militaristi* became deep and permanent; there were now two rival Red Brigade organizations in the field (Savasta, *Letter,* 1988). The four remaining members of the Executive Committee, all *militaristi,* were determined to push on with Moretti's concept of a tightly-knit, highly disciplined, essentially Leninist organization, feeling that more successful, high-profile operations would reunify the movement (Savasta, 1987; Fenzi, 1987:236).

On 20 May 1981, Savasta directed the kidnapping of Giuseppe Taliercio, Chief Executive Officer of a giant petro-chemical firm named Montedison. The Red Brigades accused Montedison of polluting the Adriatic and exploiting its work-force, and in a previous operation, the Veneto Column had murdered one of Taliercio's predecessors. When the Montedison Company refused to negotiate for the life of the kidnapped chemist, the Executive Committee voted the death penalty (*Senato,* IX, 1986:380; Tumbarello, 1987). As Savasta remembered the episode:

There were differences of opinion over Taliercio. There were those who wanted to execute him and others who wanted to spare his life. Taliercio was not maltreated in any way, despite what the police later claimed. As a gesture of humanity, the prisoner was told that he would be released and invited to climb into a box so that he could be taken out of town. When he was in the box, I shot him with a silenced Beretta. (Savasta, 1987)

Inexplicably, Giuseppe Taliercio refused to die, and a horrified Savasta shot him a total of seventeen times before the engineer finally perished (De Luca, *Ragazzo,* 1982; Genova, 1985:94). The awfulness of the execution had a significant emotional impact upon Savasta, who began suffering from nightmares, as well as Emilia Libera, who was rapidly sinking into despair. Although her career as a revolutionary had been hampered by her reluctance to commit physical violence, Emilia Libera was regarded as one of the best brains in the Red Brigades, and her loss of faith was troubling (Savasta, *Letter,* 1988; Coppola, 1983). Savasta later commented:

Emilia had always been irritated at what the women called the ***maschilismo*** *of the Organization, the notion that revolution was a man's business and women could only have a subordinate role. But after Sardinia she began to have doubts, worrying that we were eventually going to lose. But our commitment to the Red Brigades was so central to our relationship that we were never able to discuss it openly. I knew she had begun to doubt that we would ever win, and I was beginning to worry as well, but I reacted by trying to convince her that everything was really all right, that one more successful campaign would set things right again. (Savasta, 1967)*

The campaign that would shake the Italian government, bring the *movimentisti* back to the fold, and renew Emilia's confidence was meant to be the Winter Campaign of 1981–82. As planned by an increasingly desperate Executive Committee, this campaign would involve the kidnapping of a senior anti-terrorist policeman, the president of the Fiat Corporation, and a ranking American general (*Senato*, X, 1986:387; Genova, 1965:134–5).

In retrospect, it ought to have been clear to everyone that the *Brigate rosse* would eventually turn their guns against NATO and the American military presence in Italy. Verbal attacks against American imperialism had long been a feature of Red Brigade propaganda statements, and the European "hard left" had always believed that US armed forces stationed abroad carried out an essentially imperialistic role. The newly-elected Ronald Reagan was seen as representing the most aggressive force in American political culture, and a broad spectrum of the Italian public resented the basing on Italian soil of a new generation of American nuclear weapons like the Cruise missile (Savasta, *Letter*, 1987).

Working from a safe-house in Verona, Savasta's team targeted James Lee Dozier, a tough, sometimes testy Brigadier General who had won the Silver Star in Vietnam. In Verona, the Florida-born West Pointer was serving in a humdrum administrative post; while Dozier liked Italy and spoke passable Italian, he was finding his NATO job to be more protocol than substance (Dozier, 1988). Understanding very little about the real operational structure of NATO and the complicated political relationships among members of the Atlantic Alliance, Savasta and his colleagues persuaded themselves that Dozier was actually the covert, behind-the-scenes commanding officer of all armed forces in Italy, both Italian and Allied, and the mastermind of American imperialism in Southern Europe. Reality had come unglued again.

From a technical point of view, the abduction was brilliant. Posing as plumbers intent upon repairing a leaky pipe, Savasta and his kidnap team knocked on Dozier's door in the early evening on 17 December 1981, while the General and his wife were preparing dinner. Despite vague advance warnings from Italian intelligence sources that a senior American might be the target of terrorist action, the General opened the door. After a struggle, both the General and his wife were immobilized. Dozier was spirited away to a safe-house in the nearby university town of Padua and six thousand Italian policemen, a bewildering variety of American, Italian, and NATO intelligence agencies, and the Mafia all took to the field to rescue him (Genova, 1985:124–6; Rabb, 1987).

During the forty-two days of the General's imprisonment, Dozier and Savasta dueled intellectually across the enormous ideological and cultural abyss that divided them, a process hampered by the fact that each considered the other to be an unmitigated scoundrel. Savasta worked hard to force from Dozier an admission that the American military was running Italy from behind the scenes and that the American crusade in Vietnam had been imperialistic and genocidal (Savasta, *Letter*, 1987). While Dozier was willing to engage in a dialogue on political and military issues, he stoutly refused to give them what they wanted, revealing no secrets and making no concessions that would be useful for propaganda purposes.

Savasta hoped to use Dozier to force the Italian Government into releasing imprisoned *brigatisti*, but he had badly misjudged the value of an American general as a hostage (*Senato*, IX, 1986:311). Several times since the death of Moro, the Italian government had indeed avoided trauma to the country's political or bureaucratic elite by surrendering to Red Brigade demands. But Dozier was not a part of the Italian elite, and it is the function of generals to die heroically. Prime Minister Giovanni Spadolini had come into office a few months earlier promising to get tough with the Red Brigades. Deciding that Dozier was ultimately expendable, Spadolini's cabinet pre-emptively refused to negotiate, committing unprecedented police resources to the rescue effort in the belief that they would win politically whether the General lived or died.

From the Red Brigade point of view, the abduction became an embarrassment when the rest of the 1981–82 campaign fizzled into failure. The *Esecutivo* began the familiar process of debating the execution of their hostage, with Savasta realizing grimly that there could be only one possible verdict (Savasta, *Letter*, 1988).

While the Italian *Polizia di Stato* justifiably claim the successful conclusion of the Dozier case as one of their greatest triumphs, the General's rescue from the Padua safe-house was partially fortuitous. In their desperate attempt to find some link to Savasta's organization, the State Police were questioning every known radical in the Veneto Region. During a midnight raid on the home of a leftist school-master, they found Ruggiero Volinia, a low-ranking irregular who had been Savasta's driver for the Dozier abduction, spending a romantic night with the teacher's sister. Had Volinia kept his mouth shut, he would have been released since the police had no reason to suspect him (Genova, 1985:203; Savasta, *Letter*, 1988).

Fortunately for General Dozier, Volinia was questioned by a capable anti-terrorist police commissioner named Salvatore Genova who tricked him into believing that the police knew his role in the Dozier abduction. Frightened of life imprisonment, Volinia led Commissioner Genova to Savasta's Padua safe-house in exchange for a suspended sentence and a financial reward. The *Polizia di Stato* quickly prepared a raid, employing a specialized Italian assault team (Genova, 1987).

The end for Savasta and his colleagues came mid-morning on 28 January 1982, when he looked out the kitchen window of the Padua safe-house:

> *I saw a man crossing the parking lot. . . . His features were covered with a ski-mask, and he was carrying a machine-*

gun. At first, I thought he was going to rob the supermarket. Then I realized that we were surrounded, that the police had somehow found us. I was not sure that we would be taken alive since we believed that the police sometimes preferred to kill us but I gave the order to Emilia [Libera] and the others to offer no resistance. (Savasta, 1987)

SAVASTA IN PRISON

A few minutes later, Commissioner Genova and his men broke into the safe-house and rescued General Dozier unhurt, taking Savasta, Libera, and three other prisoners. Given his physical toughness and his commitment to the revolution, no one anticipated that Savasta would confess, since most of his imprisoned colleagues were stoically and silently serving life sentences.

Why did he collaborate? Physical abuse of the prisoners clearly played an important part in the decision-making process and several policemen were later tried for their role in the interrogations (De Vito, 1982). All of Savasta's group later testified that maltreatment had begun immediately after their capture. For eighteen hours, they were struck, burned with cigarettes on the back of their hands, and subjected to mock executions, while Emilia Libera was stripped naked and threatened with rape. By early the next morning, both Savasta and Libera had begun to make partial confessions as a way of avoiding the immediacy of pain, although they tried for a while to protect their close friends (Genova, 1985:144–47; Coppola, 1983; Savasta, 1987; Bocca, 1985:280 ff.).

Savasta's decision, however, was influenced by his growing realization that the revolution was dead (Carlucci, 1982; Tumbarello, 1987). As he later commented:

I felt very fragile. And I began also to see that the revolution was not going to happen in the short term. Even before our arrest, I had been starting to think that it might be better for the Proletariat if the Red Brigades should cease activities. We were only strengthening the police and the government. The sooner we disappeared as an organization, the sooner the working class could proceed along some different path with its political evolution. We had failed. Capitalism was not yet collapsing, and it was time to clear the stage. (Savasta, 1987)

Once Savasta began confessing, he put his photographic memory at the service of the police, producing names, dates, addresses, phone numbers, a great stream of information. The newspapers began calling him "terrorism's accountant" because of the dry precision with which he revealed the secrets of the Red Brigades (Contu, 1984). Armed with this highly specific information, the Italian police rampaged through the rest of 1982 and into 1983, virtually dismantling the Red Brigades (Genova, 1985:37).

The two years following their arrest were emotionally difficult for both Savasta and Emilia Libera as they were carted around the country in chains, attending trial after trial, sometimes as defendants and sometimes as prosecution witnesses. Compounding their unhappiness, they were subjected to horrific abuse from their "unrepentant" former colleagues (De Luca, *Ragazzo,* 1982).

After her arrest, Emilia Libera began making revised plans for her own future, contacting her old professors at the University of Rome and arranging to begin an external studies course in medicine. After her prison sentence is completed, she will need just a few more years of study to qualify as a physician. In 1985, Libera notified Savasta that she regarded their relationship as ended; in 1988, prison authorities allowed her a short furlough to marry another prisoner (Savasta, *Letter,* 1988).

After his various trials, Antonio Savasta was sent to the Paliano Maximum Security Penitentiary to begin serving a seventeen year sentence (Mieli, 1983). Paliano Penitentiary is an enormous medieval castle thirty miles east of Rome in the foothills of the Ernici Mountains. The prison is reserved for prisoners who are "special" in some way, many of them repentant terrorists. While the accommodations are hardly luxurious, the environment is relatively pleasant.

Savasta today is a surprisingly cheerful man, in excellent health, who has been studying computer science for the past several years to prepare for the future (Savasta, *Letter,* 1988). Although he is still very radical in his views, he sees no further role for himself in either conventional or revolutionary politics (Tumbarello, 1987). While he still has very little patience with American leaders, he has come to admire Mikhail Gorbachev, and his previously intense anti-Soviet feelings have mellowed (Savasta, *Letter,* 1988). In letters to friends, he displays a new interest in environmental politics. Like many former *brigatisti,* he is concerned with history's verdict on the Red Brigades and continues to look for ways of justifying his years of struggle (Savasta, *Letter,* 1989).

How long will he remain in prison? A few weeks after his capture and confession, the Italian parliament passed legislation rewarding repentant terrorists with massively reduced prison sentences (Mellini, 1986: 11–17). Since Savasta is regarded by the police as the single most important factor in crushing the main body of the Red Brigades, many working policemen and judges would like to see him released (Genova, 1987).

Thanks to the "repentance" law, Savasta could be freed from prison in 1990, although there is some public resistance to the idea of releasing him at all, and the decision is essentially political (Contu, 1984; Andreoli, 1988; Acciari, *Proposta,* 1982). Since 1984, Red Brigade violence has declined to about one operation a year, and the last serious crime was the murder of Christian Democratic Senator Roberto Ruffili in early 1988 (Carlucci, 1988). Should operations of this kind stop altogether, there would be some public support for the release of Antonio Savasta as a reward for his role in bringing Red Brigade violence to an end.

Aside from the homicides for which he has admitted guilt, public opposition to Savasta's release stems largely from a public perception that his "repentance" is technical and limited (Contu, 1982). Certainly, his public statements have set him apart from other imprisoned *brigatisti,* many of whom have claimed genuine spiritual repentance, apologizing profusely for the madness of terrorism.

Savasta, on the other hand, has always maintained that the armed struggle of the seventies was an appropriate "gamble with history," but that the gamble was badly timed, since capitalism failed to collapse as expected. He has, in effect, apologized for an error in scheduling, and promised that some future generation of revolutionaries will get it right. As he noted when testifying to the Moro Commission:

> *The problem is how the armed struggle will finish, not whether or not the Red Brigades have failed. In fact, the Red Brigades were finished the moment that the movement split, when there was no longer a single point of view, and a single identity. . . . With all these contradictions, the Red Brigades failed. But the armed struggle will begin again. (Senato, X, 1986:381)*

ACKNOWLEDGEMENTS

I would like to thank colleagues at the University of South Carolina's Coastal Carolina College campus for their help with this article, especially Professors Roy Talbert, Fred Hicks, and James Henderson. My travel to Italy was partially funded by a University of South Carolina Venture Fund grant.

REFERENCES

Acciari, Sandro. Savasta rivela la geografia BR' di tutta Italia [Savasta reveals Italy's Red Brigade geography]. *Il Corriere della Sera,* February 18, 1982.

Acciari, Sandro. Proposta la modifica della legge sui pentiti per farne beneficiare anche Antonio Savasta. [Proposal to modify penitence legislation to benefit even Antonio Savasta]. *Il Corriere della Sera,* February 24, 1982.

Acciari, Sandro. Vi svelo io quei misteri [I will explain those mysteries]. *L'Espresso,* August 12, 1984.

Acciari, Sandro and Buffa, Pier Vittorio. Contro Chi? [Against whom?]. *L'Espresso,* April 7, 1985.

Acquaviva, Sabino. *Guerriglia e guerra rivoluzionario in Italia* [Guerrilla and Revolutionary Warfare in Italy]. Milan: Rizzoli, 1979.

Andreoli, Marcella. E sopratutto diciamo grazie a Curcio [And above all we thank Curcio]. *L'Europeo,* February 15, 1982.

Andreoli, Marcella. Io non perdono [I don't forgive]. *Panorama,* January 31, 1988.

Bellu, Giovanni Maria. Viva Cuba, abbasso Roma [Hurray for Cuba, down with Rome]. *L'Espresso.* September 4, 1983.

Bocca, Giorgio. *Il terrorismo italiano* [Italian Terrorism]. Milan: Rizzoli, 1978.

Bocca, Giorgio. *Il caso 7 aprile: Toni Negri e la grande inquisizione* [The 7 April Case: Toni Negri and the Grand Inquisition]. Milan: Feltrinelli, 1980.

Bocca, Giorgio. *Noi terroristi—12 anni di lotta armata ricostruiti e discussi con i protagonisiti* [We Terrorists—12 Years of Armed Struggle Reconstructed and Discussed with the Protagonists]. Milan: Garzanti, 1985.

Carlucci, Antonio. Volete sapere la verità? [Do you want to know the truth?] *Panorama,* July 5, 1982.

Carlucci, Antonio. Al Cuore di De Mita [At De Mita's heart], *Panorama,* May 1, 1988.

Cassola, Carlo. *Monte Mario.* [Mount Mario] Milan: Rizzoli, 1973.

Collin, Richard Oliver and Freedman, Gordon L. *Winter of Fire: The Abduction of General Dozier and the Downfall of the Red Brigades.* New York: Dutton, forthcoming in June 1990.

Contu, Ignazio. Ascoltando i falsi pentiti [Listening to the falsely repentant]. *Domenica del Corriere,* No. 20, Year 84, May 15, 1982, pp. 10–14.

Coppola, Franco. Anche Savasta e la Libera [Even Savasta and Libera]. *La Repubblica,* July 8, 1983.

Della Porta, Donatella. *Terrorismo in Italia* [Terrorism in Italy]. Bologna: Il Mulino, 1984.

De Luca, Maurizio. Guida al processo Moro [Guide to the Moro trial]. *L'Espresso,* April 18, 1982.

De Luca, Maurizio. Un ragazzo di buoni pentimenti [A youth of good repentances]. *L'Espresso,* April 25, 1982.

De Vito, Francesco. Torture [Tortures], *L'Espresso,* March 28, 1982.

Dozier, James Lee. Interview with author on November 21, 1986 in North Fort Meyers, Florida.

Drake, Richard. The Red Brigades and the Italian Political Tradition, In Y. Alexander and K. A. Myers, (eds.) *Terrorism in Europe.* London: Croom Helm, 1982, pp. 102–140.

Drake, Richard. The Red and the Black: Terrorism in contemporary Italy. *International Political Science Review,* 5:3 (1984), pp. 279–298.

Drake, Richard. *The Revolutionary Mystique and Terrorism in Contemporary Italy.* Bloomington: Indiana University Press, 1989.

Fanti, Liano. *S'avanza uno strano soldato: Genesi del brigatismo rosso reggiano* [A Strange Soldier Advances: The Origins of the Red Brigades in Reggio]. Milano: SugarCo Edizioni, 1985.

Fenzi, Enrico. *Armi e bagagli: un diario dalle Brigate rosse* [Arms and Baggage: A Red Brigades Diary]. Genoa: Costa e Nolan, 1987.

Ferrarotti, Franco. *Roma da capitale a periferia* [Rome from Caital to Periphery]. Bari: Laterza, 1970.

Franceschini, Alberto et al. *Mara, Renato e io.* [Mara, Renato and I]. Milan: Mondadori, 1988.

Fried, Robert C. *Planning the Eternal City: Roman Politics and Plannings Since World War II.* New Haven: Yale University Press, 1973.

Galleni, Mauro (ed.). *Rapporto sul terrorismo* [Report on Terrorism]. Milan: Rizzoli, 1981.

Galli, Giorgio. *Storia del partito armato 1968–1982* [History of the Armed Party 1968–1982]. Milan: Rizzoli, 1986.

Genova, Salvatore. *Missione antiterrorismo* [Anti-terrorist Mission]. Milan: Sugarco Edizioni, 1985.

Genova, Salvatore. Interview with author on June 23, 1987, Genoa, Italy. [Having arrested and interrogated Antonio Savasta, Commissioner Salvatore Genova of the Italian *Polizia di Stato* was an important source of information for this article].

Hellman, Stephen. "Italy," in Mark Kesselman and Joel Krieger's *European Politics in Transition.* Lexington, Mass: D. C. Heath, 1987, pp. 319–450.

Herman, Edward and Brodhead, Frank. *The Rise and Fall of the Bulgarian Connection.* New York: Sheridan Square, 1986.

Mellini, Mauro. *Il giudice e il pentito: dalla giustizia dell'energenza all'emergenza della giustizia* [The Judge and the Repentant Defendant: from the Justice of Emergency to an Emergency in Justice]. Milan: Sugarco Edizioni, 1986.

Mieli, Paolo. Delitto senza castigo [Crime without punishment] *L'Espresso,* December 11, 1983.

Monicelli, Mino. *La follia veneta: Come una regione bianca diviene culla del terrorismo* [Venetian Madness: How a Catholic Region Became a Hotbed of Terrorism]. Roma: Editori Riuniti, 1981.

Moran, Sue Ellen (ed). *Court Depositions of Three Red Brigadists: A Rand Note.* Santa Monica: Rand, 1986.

Negri, Antonio. *Crisi dello stato-piano: Comunismo e organizzazione rivoluzionaria* [Crisis of the Planned State: Communism and Revolutionary Organization]. Milano: Feltrinelli, 1974.

Negri, Antonio. *La fabbrica della strategia: 33 lezioni su Lenin* [The

Strategy Factory: 33 Lessons on Lenin]. Padova: C.L.E.U.P., 1976.

Negri, Antonio. *Proletari e stato: per una discussione su autonomia operaia e compromesso storico* [Proletarians and State: Towards a Discussion on the Autonomia of Workers and the Historical Compromise]. Milan: Feltrinelli, 1976.

Negri, Antonio. *La forma Stato* [The Form-State]. Milan: Feltrinelli, 1977.

Negri, Antonio. *Il dominio e il sabotaggio: sul metodo marxista della trasformazione sociale* [Dominion and Sabotage: On Marxist Methods and Social Transformation]. Milan: Feltrinelli, 1978.

Novelli, Diego and Tranfaglia, Nicola. *Vite sospese* [Suspended Lives]. Milan: Garzanti, 1989.

Peci, Patrizio. *Io l'infame* [I, The Infamous One]. Milan: Mondadori, 1983.

Rabb, Maxwell. Interview with author on July 6, 1987 at the American Embassy, Rome, Italy. Rabb was the American Ambassador in Italy between 1982 and 1989.

Reed, William. Interview with author on January 19, 1988. As the commanding officer of the Vicenza detachment of the US Army's 66th Military Intelligence Group, Reed was the ranking American intelligence officer in northern Italy during the Dozier abduction, and participated in the US Government's debriefing of General Dozier after his release.

Savasta, Antonio. Interview with author on July 25, 1987, Paliano Penitentiary, Paliano, Italy.

Savasta, Antonio. Letter of October 1987 to author.

Savasta, Antonio. Letter of February 1988 to author.

Savasta, Antonio. Letter of May 1989 to author.

Scialoja, Mario. Sei misteri pieni di mistero [Six mysteries full of mystery]. *L'Espresso*, May 16, 1982.

Senato della Repubblica—Camera dei Deputati, VIII Legislatura. [Senate of the Republic and Chamber of Deputies, Eighth Legislature]. *Commissione Parlamentare d'inchiesta sulla strage di via Fani sul sequestro e l'assassinio di Aldo Moro e sul terrorismo in Italia* [Parliamentary Committee Investigating the Massacre on Via Fani, the Abduction and Murder of Aldo Moro, and Italian Terrorism]. Rome: Tipografia del Senato. Thirteen volumes published between 1983–1988.

Seton-Watson, Christopher. Terrorism in Italy in Juliet Lodge (ed.), *The Threat of Terrorism.* London: Wheatsheaf, 1988, pp. 89–118.

Silj, Alessandro. *Mai piú senza fucile!: alle origini dei NAP e delle BR.* Bologna: Editore Vallecchi, 1977. Published in English as *Never Again Without a Rifle: The Origins of Italian Terrorism,* (trans. Salvator Attanasio) New York: Karz, 1979.

Tumbarello, Roberto. Una vedova mi ha salvato [A widow saved me]. *Oggi,* March 27, 1987.

Weinberg, Leonard and Eubank, William Lee. *The Rise and Fall of Italian Terrorism.* Boulder, Colorado: Westview, 1987.

Zasso, Gino. Per i pentiti Savasta e Libera pena ridotta di oltre 20 anni [For the repentant Savasta and Libera a sentence reduced below 20 years]. *Il Corriere della Sera,* February 20, 1983.

Hezbollah Frustrates a Gulliver-Like U.S.

Tiny Faction Plays Hostage Shell-Game, and Bush Can't Move

WALTER S. MOSSBERG
And BARBARA ROSEWICZ
Staff Reporters of THE WALL STREET JOURNAL

WASHINGTON – President Bush has some idea who is holding the American hostages in Beirut, but that doesn't mean he has the quality of intelligence he needs to act.

One of the likely captors is Imad Mugniyah, who is said to wear three guns at all times: one on each side and one on his back. Another is Hussein Musawi, a school teacher turned terrorist.

The president also knows which neighborhoods, and even which buildings, have been used to imprison the hostages at various times. Even now, Joseph Cicippio and the remaining American hostages are believed to be held in Chiyah, Borj El Brajne or another of the cinderblock slums of south Beirut.

But Mr. Bush has been unable to act because the U.S. has no way of pinpointing the hostages' locations at any moment. As a result, the U.S. has been paralyzed by perhaps 500 hard-core fanatics wedged into a few sectors of a country smaller than Connecticut.

"Nobody can look the President in the eye and say, 'I guarantee you if you move within the next X hours or days, they're there and there's a 90% chance of success,' " says Richard Murphy, who was President Reagan's assistant secretary of State for the Middle East. "It isn't that kind of situation."

No Outsiders Welcome

U.S. intelligence forces' embarrassing inability to penetrate the terrorists' world is due largely to the nature of Lebanon's Shiite Moslems, who comprise the most aggressive of that war-torn country's sects.

The religious warriors holding the hostages operate in a network of family alliances that nurture and protect them. They live in a rabbit warren of flat-roofed concrete buildings, where outsiders are quickly identified and confronted. No local government dares intrude. Their willingness to die for their cause is evident in the 1989 "Martyr of the Month" calendar, featuring pictures of fallen zealots.

They are members of the Shiite sect of Islam and of its militant Lebanese organization, the Party of God, or Hezbollah. Galvanized by generations of poverty and discrimination in their own country, they have taken their inspiration from Iran's late Ayatollah Khomeini, who was the world leader of the Shiites.

They hate the Israelis who invaded their southern Lebanese villages in 1982—and Israel's patron, the United States, which sent Marines into their domain until Shiite terrorists slaughtered 241 of them by driving a bomb into their barracks.

The importance of bloodlines is visible in the intensely personal aspects of the terror. Some of the Hezbollah captors—including those who have kidnapped Americans—are seeking to have their own relatives freed from captivity in Kuwaiti, Israeli and German jails.

Family Prisoners

Mr. Mugniyah, for instance, has a brother-in-law jailed in Kuwait after his conviction for bombing the U.S. and French embassies there in 1983. Mr. Mugniyah wants the U.S. to pressure Kuwait into releasing his brother-in-law. Mr. Mugniyah's wife works at his side wearing a dark Islamic veil.

Another Hezbollah clan holding hostages, the Hamadis, is pressuring West Germany for the release of one of its members, Mohamed Hamadi, who was convicted for his role in the 1985 hijacking of TWA Flight 847, in which an American sailor was murdered.

But even these details are sketchy, so poor is U.S. knowledge about Hezbollah. There is always a chance, of course, that the Central Intelligence Agency knows more than it is letting on. And it's possible that Israel's kidnapping of a local Hezbollah leader, Sheik Abdul Karim Obeid, could yield an intelligence bonanza sufficient to break the hostage case.

But U.S. officials, right up through Mr. Bush, insist they lack hard intelligence data on the hostages. From space, the U.S. can photograph a street intersection in south Beirut and it routinely intercepts telecommunications. But to no avail. "There is no substitute to people who are on the ground," says Sen. Sam Nunn, the Georgia Democrat who heads the Senate Armed Services Committee.

The situation on the ground is one of anarchy. Lebanon may be the least-governed patch of the planet. There is no civil government or police force worthy of the name that could help the U.S. The country is divided into sections controlled by Syria, allies of Israel, Christian warlords, Sunni Moslems, Druze, and at least two groups of Shiites, including Hezbollah.

'Law of Hezbollah'

"In the south of Beirut, there is no control at all. You have one law there, and it's the law of Hezbollah," says a leading

The Hezbollah, or Party of God, is a militant Lebanese organization whose members are of the Shiite sect of Islam. The Hezbollah is also made up of a number of blood-related clans that make infiltration all but impossible. The level of violence by this organization is extreme: the Marine barracks near Beirut, pictured above, were bombed in a suicide mission that resulted in 241 American Marines' deaths. (Photo credit UPI/Bettmann-Pierre Sabbagh)

French expert on terrorism who writes under the pen name of Xavier Raufer.

There is already much American blood on the hands of Hezbollah. It planned the bombing of the Marine barracks near Beirut in 1983, slaughtering 241 Marines who were on a peacekeeping mission. One of Hezbollah's leaders, Sheik Abbas Musawi—who himself is believed to be a relative of one of the hostage-takers—yesterday bragged about the Marine massacre, publicly taunting Mr. Bush about it.

The group has twice bombed U.S. embassy buildings in Beirut, killing a total of 72 people, including the CIA's top Middle East expert, Robert Ames, and several of his deputies. During two airline hijackings, in 1984 and 1985, Hezbollah members singled out American passengers and killed them. The murder toll also includes hostage William Buckley, who was the CIA station chief in Beirut; Malcolm Kerr, the president of the American University there, and now, presumably, Col. William Higgins, who headed a U.N. peacekeeping force.

To the extent they know much of anything, U.S. intelligence experts suspect that such Hezbollah groups as "Oppressed of the Earth," which claimed to kill Col. Higgins, and "Revolutionary Justice," which is threatening Mr. Cicippio, aren't really separate groups at all. Instead, those and other fearsome-sounding names, experts think, could be cover names for carrying out actions approved by Hezbollah's ruling council.

Even if the CIA could send a Lebanese-American agent into Hezbollah's south Beirut stronghold, experts say he wouldn't get far. "I wouldn't say it's difficult to infiltrate. I'd say it's impossible," says Mr.

Raufer, the French consultant. "You'd have to be not only an Arab, not only Lebanese, but able to show you came from some particular family in some particular village in southern Lebanon."

And if not? "You'd end up like William Buckley," Mr. Raufer says.

No Local Allies

The U.S. also lacks reliable local allies who might help. American intelligence was well-wired among Lebanon's Christians and Palestinians, but the Christians have no entree into Hezbollah areas and Palestinian leaders have been driven out of Lebanon by Israel.

Another problem is that Hezbollah is compartmentalized into small terrorist cells that move among multiple bases and that cooperate with each other. Former French hostages report that a French book taken from one of them later was given to a second who had supposedly been captured by an entirely different group. Some other former hostages report being moved—sometimes in car trunks, wrapped like mummies—from one building to another.

"These people aren't arrayed like conventional forces. They scatter like sand crabs," says Noel Koch, the Pentagon's former chief counter-terrorism official.

Hezbollah terrorists occupy, in addition to their south Beirut stronghold, several buildings in the town of Baalbek. The third home base for Hezbollah-affiliated families is in south Lebanon, where Shiite villages are clustered, and where Col. Higgins was seized.

These sites, including the Sheik Abdullah Barracks in Baalbek, have been photographed from the air by the Pentagon. Plans were drawn years ago for bombing them. But a French bombing raid in 1983 had little effect, and it's doubtful that the terrorists are staying there in large numbers during the current crisis.

Even if the U.S. could play on the Hezbollah's turf, it wouldn't be comfortable with the eye-for-an-eye rules. In 1985, for instance, after four Soviet diplomats in Lebanon were kidnapped and one killed, Moscow got the Druze to snatch some of the kidnappers' relatives. The Soviet hostages were freed after a body part from one of the relatives was mailed to the terrorists.

But the State Department the same year vetoed a CIA plan to kidnap Mr. Mugniyah while he was traveling in Paris. The State Department nixed the action to avoid offending France, according to an account in "Best Laid Plans," a book about the failed war on terrorism.

Advisories help keep U.S. travelers safe abroad

WILLIAM A. DAVIS
Boston Globe

Travelers going abroad these days need to ask many more questions than they used to.

Once it was considered enough to inquire: "Is it safe to drink the water?" Now, before visiting a country, sensible travelers want to know if there is a home-grown terrorist movement, an out-of-control epidemic, a soaring crime rate, a civil war, an imminent general strike or coup d'etat, flooding or earthquakes and a lot more.

The best place to get such vital questions answered is the U.S. Department of State's Citizens Emergency Center in Washington.

The State Department, which often has to aid Americans who get into trouble overseas, issues frequently updated "travel advisories," covering situations that might cause problems for unwary visitors. When you call the center's 24-hour number — (202) 647-5225 — you can hear advisories by pressing the indicated numbers on a Touch-Tone phone. Callers can also leave names and addresses to get printed copies of advisories.

Currently, there are 54 advisories in effect. Some are for troubled nations such as Libya, Cambodia and Iran, where the United States has no embassies and where Americans rarely travel. But advisories have also been issued for such frequently visited countries as India, Kenya, Peru and the Soviet Union.

"The State Department issues advisories to inform Americans about conditions of risk abroad which might affect them adversely," said spokeswoman Nyda Novodvorsky. "But just because we have an advisory doesn't mean we don't want people to travel; sometimes the problem is in a particular part of a country, and the rest is just fine."

In India, for example, Americans are advised to avoid travel to the state of Jammu and Kashmir, in Northern India, because of political unrest, and to use caution when traveling through the Punjab region — especially by bus or train — because of sporadic incidents of political violence.

The advisory for Kenya reports that visitors have been robbed and even killed in remote areas of the interior — including game parks — and along sections of the coast south of Mombasa. Visitors are advised to travel in groups rather than alone, question tour and safari lodge operators about security arrangements and keep valuables, including passports, in hotel safes. The advisory also notes that strains of malaria resistant to common anti-malarial medications exist in Kenya.

Most advisories refer to temporary conditions and are modified or rescinded as a situation gets better or worse. In recent months, for example, the area of Liberia that Americans were advised to avoid because of fighting between rebels and government troops has expanded steadily. U.S. citizens are now urged to defer travel to Liberia, and Americans already in the country are being advised to leave.

Some travel advisories cover a broad range of potentially troublesome situations. The three-page advisory on Peru, for example, points out that "both terrorism and crime are serious problems" and that revolutionaries may be planning to kidnap foreigners, "especially U.S. citizens." Because of robbery and assault, American tourists are advised to use caution when visiting Cuzco and Machu Picchu — popular travel destinations — and hikers to avoid the Inca Trail, except if traveling in large groups with guides.

Crime in the Soviet Union appears to be getting worse as the country's economic situation worsens.

"Crime is a very real threat in the Soviet Union," the travel advisory notes. "There has been a substantial increase in violent crime in the past year . . . the embassy in Moscow and consulate general in Leningrad have received increasing numbers of reports of muggings, robberies and pick-pocketing, burglaries, sexual assaults and beatings of American citizens visiting or resident in the Soviet Union."

The advisory points out that ethnic clashes have "occurred with growing intensity over the past year" but notes that violence hasn't been directed at American citizens or other foreigners. Some areas of the Soviet Union have been temporarily closed to foreign tourists, however, requiring changes in package-tour itineraries.

The State Department also wants American visitors to know that "organized tours in the USSR are strenuous: Daily schedules are heavy, distances long and flight delays and changed departure times common."

From *The Miami Herald,* July 22, 1990, p. 16K. Reprinted courtesy of *The Boston Globe.*

'Crime is a very real threat in the Soviet Union. There has been a substantial increase in violent crime in the past year.'

Travel Advisory
State Department

The advisory states that "medical care in the Soviet Union does not meet Western standards," and tourists in frail health are urged not to visit the Soviet Union. "Intourist, the Soviet travel organization, often will absolve itself of all responsibility for tourists who become so ill they cannot maintain the tour schedule."

The advisory for the Soviet Union also includes warnings about complying with Soviet customs regulation and the danger of selling hard currency on the black market, a common but illegal practice for which foreign tourists are sometimes detained.

Crime does not seem to be a major problem in China, but the advisory cautions travelers that, while most major scenic and historical sights are open to visitors without special travel permits, travel is still prohibited to certain areas and Lhasa remains under martial law, although it may be visited.

While some advisories are constantly being changed, others have remained unaltered for years. The advisory for Cuba, for example, explains that the American trade embargo — prohibiting tourism, among other things — has been in effect for a half-dozen years. The oldest standing advisory, for Malaysia, was issued in 1983 and outlines the country's tough antidrug laws: Conviction of drug trafficking or possession of relatively small quantities of marijuana or narcotics carries a mandatory death penalty.

The State Department also puts out "travel notices" concerning situations that may cause travelers inconvenience, such as hotel shortages during certain periods. Travel notices don't go on the emergency center hot line, but the information is disseminated to the press and travel industry and put into commonly used computer data systems.

Besides issuing travel advisories and notices, the Citizens Emergency Center assists Americans in distress abroad and helps relatives locate Americans missing overseas.

A number of government publications offer general travel advice, tips for older Americans and those residing abroad and tips for travelers to specific countries and regions such as the Caribbean, South Asia, sub-Saharan Africa and the Soviet Union. For information, write to Superintendent of Documents, U.S. Government Printing Office, Washington, D.C. 20402; or call (202) 783-3238.

Also helpful reading for international travelers are two recent books: *The Safe Travel Book — A Guide for the International Traveler* by Peter Savage (Lexington Books, $9.95); and *A Handbook for Citizens Living Abroad* (USA Today, $12.95).

On the trail of terror

Despite the infighting among intelligence agencies, the 'hicks' from Scotland are closing in on those who bombed Pan Am 103

In the year before a bomb sent Pan Am Flight 103 cartwheeling into the tiny village of Lockerbie, Scotland, the local police force had been pretty busy. They had captured a lot of stray dogs, 626 to be exact. And they had looked into plenty of cases of suspected sheep anthrax, 456, although none was ever confirmed. There was also the odd stolen car to be recovered and the occasional unpleasantness in one of the fine pubs along the High Street. Murder and terrorism were not things with which the Dumfries and Galloway Constabulary, as the local police force is known, had had a whole lot of truck, however. So it was not surprising after the Boeing jumbo jet crashed four days before Christmas last year, killing 270 people, that families of the victims, the general public and even other police investigators from Washington, London and Bonn began wondering aloud just why a tiny Scottish police force, the smallest in the United Kingdom, should take the lead in what had become the world's largest terrorism investigation ever. "Not to put too fine a point on it," says a senior Scottish official, "but I think a lot of people thought they were dealing with a bunch of hicks."

Nuts-and-bolts police work. It is beginning to look as if it's time to score one for the hicks. In the 10 months since the Lockerbie tragedy, while the world's most sophisticated intelligence agencies consulted their high-tech computers and half-billion-dollar spy satellites, the Scots, working side by side with their counterparts from the FBI, kept beavering away at plain old nuts-and-bolts police work. Though investigators still have many unanswered questions, they say they are closer than ever to identifying the suspects who collaborated in planting the bomb on the plane and are gathering the kind of evidence that could be used in a courtroom to convict them.

The biggest clue was uncovered the old-fashioned way—at the scene of the crime. Literally crawling on hands and knees in some areas, across a search area of roughly 845 square miles, the investigators recovered tons of aircraft debris and passengers' personal belongings. Among the latter were discovered a piece of a pair of pants, the torn remains of pajamas and a tweed sport coat and a scorched baby jumpsuit, nearly intact. The jumpsuit provided the best clue of the lot. On it was the label "Babygro." Scottish police and FBI agents traced the label and found the brand was sold only in Ireland and on the island of Malta. Malta was the key. A factory there, called Yorkie Clothing, Ltd., had manufactured the jumpsuit.

Forensic wizardry did the rest. Specialists at the British Defense Ministry's Royal Armaments Research and Development Establishment, probably the world's most sophisticated crime lab, linked the bits of pajamas, trousers and sport coat to Yorkie, as well. "We're very good on the forensics," says an FBI official close to the investigation. "But the Brits are very, *very* good." With the jumpsuit, the British experts determined, the other clothes had been stuffed into the copper-colored Samsonite suitcase they had already identified as containing the bomb. If they could determine who had bought the clothes, they would probably find the person who had planted the bomb on board Flight 103.

Scottish police and FBI agents descended on Malta several weeks ago to do just that. A shop owner provided the critical link. He recalled having sold the clothes to a man in his mid-40s. A police artist was brought to Malta to make a detailed sketch of the suspect. He is 5-foot-10, muscular and clean-shaven. The store owner said the man spoke with an Arabic accent and was probably from Libya. The investigators now believe that the man, who has not been located, checked the bag on an AirMalta flight to Frankfurt on the morning of December 21, the same day Flight 103 blew up over Lockerbie. Investigators believe the man was able to check the Samsonite with the bomb in it through Frankfurt and onto Flight 103, perhaps with the help of an airport employe in Valletta, Malta's capital.

Luggage transferred through airports from one carrier to another is known as "interline" baggage. Airline regulations prohibit any bag, interline or not, from being loaded onto a plane if its owner has not boarded. Somehow, the investigators believe, the man who bought the clothes arranged to check the Samsonite under the name of a passenger already on board the AirMalta flight. A spokesman for AirMalta says that the airline has checked and that the "rogue bag" theory is not true. The investigators nevertheless believe that AirMalta is the key and that, for the first time, they know how the bomb was placed on board in Frankfurt as a routine interline transfer.

The American and Scottish investigators have developed further evidence from other quarters about how the bombing was planned. Working with intelligence agencies in the U.S., Britain and Sweden, they have determined that a Palestinian now on trial in Stockholm on unrelated terrorism charges was in Malta in mid-October. They say they know now that Mohammed Abu Talb met a man there called Hafez Dalkamouni, a senior member of the Popular Front for the Liberation of Palestine –General Command. U.S. intelligence officials say the PFLP–GC, led by Ahmed Jibril, is the principal suspect in the Pan Am bombing, and they believe it was commissioned by officials in Teheran as revenge for the mistaken shooting down of an Iranian commercial airliner by a U.S. warship, the U.S.S. *Vincennes,* in the Persian Gulf in July, 1988.

The dark side. Dalkamouni was arrested by German police in a suburb of Düsseldorf in October, 1988, with 15 other men suspected of membership in the PFLP–GC. The police seized a bomb, bomb-making materials and other weapons (see box) in connection with a terrorist operation that U.S. and Scottish officials believe was linked directly to the bombing of Flight 103. But German authorities released everyone but Dalkamouni and one other man, citing insufficient evidence. Among those released was Marwan Kreeshat, who is thought to have manufactured the barometer-triggered bomb that blew up Flight 103. He is now missing and believed to be living in Jordan. The Lockerbie investigators believe that Dalkamouni and Talb

planned the Pan Am bombing. If they can find the man who bought the batch of clothes in Malta, they think they can prove it conclusively and make their case in court.

The persistence of the police effort, led by the Scots' senior investigator, John Orr, is the bright side of a much darker tale, however. Serious questions have been raised in investigative and intelligence circles about the performance of German authorities in the bombing inquiry. Though the West German federal police, the BKA, are co-investigators in the Pan Am bombing with the Scots and the FBI, officials close to the investigation say the Germans have been uncooperative and, at times, obstructive. Scottish authorities told the *London Sunday Times* and the British newspaper *The Independent* last week that German investigators knew of the AirMalta connection as long ago as last February. According to the reports, the BKA obtained a computerized baggage list from the Frankfurt airport showing the copper-colored Samsonite from Malta being checked through Frankfurt and placed aboard Flight 103.

The list was not turned over to the Scottish and U.S. investigators until August, the reports said, and then only after the British forensic specialists had linked the clothes from Malta to the suitcase with the bomb in it. German authorities issued a statement last week saying they are cooperating in the Pan Am inquiry, but investigators have been insisting for months now that that is not the case.

Underlying this friction is speculation that the Germans are being recalcitrant out of spite. A British intelligence official says that authorities in Bonn complained bitterly months before the Pan Am bombing about unauthorized British espionage activities in West Germany. The Germans believed that British operatives had targeted an Irish Republican Army terrorist cell in Germany without notifying the Bonn government. The British official said he knew of no unauthorized intelligence-gathering operation against the IRA in Germany, but he conceded that if the operation were being run by the Special Air Services, the elite military antiterror operatives who shot and killed three IRA members in Gibraltar last year, the Bonn government probably would not have been notified. In any case, the investigators in Lockerbie believe that that bad blood, as well as German embarrassment over the release of the terrorist suspects in October and the fact that the bomb was placed aboard the Pan Am plane in Frankfurt, is responsible for the lack of cooperation by the BKA.

The encouraging news, according to investigators, is that the BKA obstreperousness will not matter. If the Scots can make a case against the Lockerbie bombers, it will be thanks to good old-fashioned detective work.

by Brian Duffy

The Yugoslav bomb connection

Early in the afternoon of October 26, 1988, plainclothes German police broke down the door of a second-floor Frankfurt apartment frequented by an inept one-legged terrorist. The raid was part of a much larger police action, known as "Operation Autumn Leaves," that resulted in raids on 12 homes and offices across Germany and the detention of 16 suspected terrorists. Inside the Frankfurt flat at 28 Sandweg, the police officers found books, files and even a few rather nice pieces of furniture. But there were also automatic rifles, mortars, rifle grenades and an antitank gun, not to mention 14 blocks of dynamite, six strips of TNT and 5 kilograms of Semtex plastic explosive.

When the West German federal police, the BKA, began tracing the weapons, they found evidence that has become crucial to the Pan Am 103 investigation. Some of the weapons, intelligence officials say, had come from Army soldiers in Yugoslavia, a well-known terrorist crossroads. It was not until sometime after the Pan Am jet blew up over Scotland several weeks later that the German police began to press the Yugoslav connection. All 16 suspects besides Hafez Dalkamouni, the one-legged terrorist, and another man had been released by a German judge for lack of sufficient evidence. But the Germans wanted to reinterview one of the suspects, a man named Martin Kadourah. When the BKA learned Kadourah was in Yugoslavia, intelligence officials say, they asked authorities in Belgrade to arrest him and return him to Bonn; if they didn't, it was implied, the Germans would let the public know about the Yugoslav Army rifles. The intelligence officials say they believe the rifles were sold by Yugoslav soldiers to the suspected terrorists. Belgrade police arrested Kadourah and sent him to the Germans.

Then Bonn asked the Yugoslavs to raid a house in a small town called Krusevac, about 50 miles from the Bulgarian border. Under pressure, Belgrade again complied. In the house were found an unspecified quantity of Semtex and a recipe for turning it into a bomb. Months later, the BKA would seize another bomb in Germany, believed to be identical to the one that blew up Pan Am 103. That bomb came from the same batch of Semtex recovered in Krusevac. The Germans reportedly now have concluded that the terrorists operating in Yugoslavia are among the conspirators who brought down Pan Am 103.

This is hardly the first time that terrorists have found a haven in Yugoslavia. The Belgrade government publicly opposes terrorism. Yet Yugoslavia continues to figure prominently on the itineraries of some of the world's most notorious terrorists. Carlos, "the Jackal," who has been linked to terrorist attacks around the world, has visited there often. Mohammed Abbas, the mastermind of the *Achille Lauro* cruise-ship hijacking, fled there after he was detained briefly in Italy. The Abu Nidal terrorist organization has operated from there. It is never mentioned in the same breath as Iran, Iraq, Syria or Libya, but Yugoslavia, as the Pan Am-bombing inquiry shows, still looms large in the world of international terrorism.

MATT ZANG & DAVID S. MERRILL—USN&WR

FIGHTING INTERNATIONAL TERRORISM: WHAT DOES AND WHAT DOES NOT WORK

Yonah Alexander

Yonah Alexander is a research professor at the Elliott School of International Affairs, George Washington University; director, Institute for Studies in International Terrorism, State University of New York; and senior fellow, U.S. Global Strategy Council.

The powerful bomb that destroyed Pan Am Flight 103 over Scotland on December 21, 1988, killing a total of 270 people on the jumbo jet and on the ground at Lockerbie, has once again demonstrated the persistent challenge of contemporary terrorism to the United States and to its friends and allies abroad. During the Reagan presidency, two other mid-air bombings occurred on U.S. air carriers. On August 11, 1982, a boy was killed and 15 passengers were injured by a bomb on a Pan Am jet bound from Tokyo to Hawaii. And four Americans, including a nine-month-old baby, were sucked out a gaping hole of TWA Flight 840 en route from Rome to Athens after a bomb exploded under a seat. Other significant terrorist incidents involving U.S. citizens and targets during the Reagan administration include the following events:

1981

— Presence of Libyan hit squads in the United States

— Kidnapping of Brig. Gen. James Dozier by the Red Brigades in Italy

1982

— Assassination of Lt. Col. Charles Robert Ray, a military attaché at the U.S. Embassy in Paris, by Lebanese terrorists

1983

— Bombing of the U.S. Embassy in Beirut, killing 17 Americans

— Bombing of U.S. Marine headquarters at the Beirut airport by a Shi'ite suicide bomber, killing 241 Marines

> **U.S.** efforts in cooperating with other countries to develop practical measures to combat terrorism bore fruit.

— Bombing of the U.S. Embassy in Kuwait by Lebanese and Iraqi terrorists

1984

— Kidnapping of five Americans in Lebanon, including William Buckley, the CIA station chief in Beirut

— Murder of Malcolm Kerr, president of the American University of Beirut

— Bombing of the U.S. Embassy annex in East Beirut, killing two military officers

— Hijacking of a Kuwaiti airliner to Iran, killing two Americans

1985

— Hijacking of TWA Flight 847 by Shi'ite terrorists, lasting 17 days, with the torture and killing of a U.S. Navy diver

— Gunning down of six Americans in El Salvador

— Hijacking of the Italian cruise ship *Achille Lauro* by members of the Palestine Liberation Front and the murder of a crippled American tourist

— Simultaneous airport attacks on Rome and Vienna by Abu Nidal terrorists, killing 5 Americans

— Bombing at La Belle discotheque in West Berlin by Libyans, killing 2 and wounding 70 Americans

1986

— Hijacking of Pan Am Flight 73 in Karachi, killing two U.S. citizens

— Kidnapping of two Americans in Beirut

1987

— Attack on U.S. military bus in Greece by November 17 Revolutionary Organization, wounding 17 servicemen

— Attacks on U.S. military personnel in Spain and the Philippines

— Attacks on U.S. diplomatic missions in Europe and Latin America

— Kidnapping of four Americans and a U.S. resident in Lebanon

1988

— Assassination of a U.S. military attaché in Athens

— Kidnapping of U.S. Marine Lt. Col. William Higgins of the UN Observer Mission in Lebanon

— Attacks on U.S. military personnel in Greece and Italy and U.S. facilities in France, Spain, and West Germany

Anti-U.S. incidents multiplied during Ronald Reagan's presidency. The statistics are, indeed, staggering. A total of 1,385 inter-

From *The World & I*, March 1989, pp. 105-111. Reprinted with permission from *The World & I*, a publication of The Washington Times Corporation, copyright © 1989.

national terrorist attacks were launched against U.S. targets between 1981 and 1988 (January-October). Incidents in 1988 were some 31 percent over the 1987 level, making it the bloodiest year yet.

This reality clearly illustrates the grim fact that the Reagan administration was a prime target of both state-sponsored terrorism (such as Libya, Syria, Iran) and substate groups, including those that are Marxist-oriented (such as Germany's Red Army Faction), separatist (such as the Puerto Rican Armed Forces of National Liberation), Islamic fundamentalist (Hezbollah), Palestinian (such as Abu Nidal), and ideological mercenaries (such as the Japanese Red Army).

How successful was Reagan in combating international terrorism? What does the balance sheet look like? Which policies worked and which did not? And what are the lessons of these experiences for the Bush administration?

The record

An assessment of the Reagan counterterrorism experience, based on the availability of information from open sources, reveals both success and failure. The policies and actions that seemed to work include the following areas:

Greater U.S. Public Awareness of Terrorism. The administration's public affairs efforts (such as distributing documents and holding press conferences) resulted in more Americans becoming aware of the threat of international terrorism to the national security interests of the United States. For instance, public polls indicate that terrorism is now perceived as a major foreign policy challenge along with nuclear war and regional conflicts around the world. Indeed, the public's insistence on decisive U.S. responses to international terrorism, including military action, has intensified.

Shift in International Opinion from Tolerance of Terrorism to Revulsion. The tolerance toward terrorism that once prevailed in many Western and Third World countries has been reduced considerably as a consequence of U.S. public diplomacy efforts abroad (including briefings and publications). Earlier fascination with the "romantic" nature of the "root causes" of terrorism (as, for example, the struggle against "capitalism" and "imperialism") is being replaced by a growing public outrage at the globalization and brutalization of ideological and political violence.

Warning of Terrorist Threats. Keeping Americans alert to potential terrorist threats through special briefings and timely travel advisories has been instrumental in preventing a substantial number of incidents. Tourists and businesspeople have continuously been warned not to travel to high-risk areas such as Central America or to countries where airport security is lax. Government officials, diplomats, and the military have been advised accordingly, and various appropriate procedures have been instituted. As a by-product of these warnings, uncooperative states such as Greece were forced to upgrade their airport security measures, thereby assuring a more normal flow of tourism and commerce into their countries.

Improved Intelligence Crucial in Preventing Terrorism. The improvement of U.S. intelligence assets, both human and technological, proved to be the first line in counterterrorism operations. Timely collection, analysis, and dissemination of relevant information on the perpetrators, their ideologies, modus operandi, and other aspects helped to prevent incidents from occurring. In 1983, for example, a plot to firebomb a Seattle theater filled with hundreds of innocent people was prevented. In Ankara, a planned attack by members of the Islamic Jihad on NATO targets and the kidnapping of Americans was foiled in 1987. Many hundreds of other terrorist incidents were averted because of good U.S. intelligence and cooperation with friendly foreign governments.

Expanding Legislation and International Legal Structures. The statutory loopholes in U.S. law have gradually been bridged. A case in point is congressional action to pass the "long arm" statute that makes it a federal crime for a terrorist to threaten, detain, seize, injure, or kill an American citizen abroad. On the bilateral and multilateral levels, U.S. efforts to strengthen the rule of law were also effective. For instance, the "political offense" exception to the U.S.-U.K. Supplementary Extradition Treaty had been removed, and the United States initiated the convention on maritime safety through the International Maritime Organization.

Apprehension, Prosecution, and Punishment of Terrorists. Through improved intelligence and law enforcement work, the United States was successful in arresting terrorists in the United States. In 1987, three pro-Syrian Lebanese carrying explosives were apprehended when they attempted to cross into the United States from Canada. Last year, Yu Kikimura, a member of the Japanese Red Army, was arrested in New Jersey. Overseas, the FBI, in a sting operation in international waters off the coast of Cyprus, arrested Fawaz Younis, a Lebanese operative in the 1985 hijacking of a Jordanian airline during which Americans were taken hostage. These suspects are now awaiting trial in the United States.

The United States was also instrumental in encouraging other governments to arrest, bring to trial, and convict an increasing number of terrorists. In 1988 alone, five Abu Nidal terrorists were sentenced to death in Sudan, and another was sentenced to 25 years' imprisonment in Malta.

Unilateral U.S. Action. The United States has continuously formulated coherent policies that underscored the need to act unilaterally and multilaterally in the fight against terrorism. The major contribution to this effort had been the Task Force on Combating Terrorism, headed by then-Vice President George Bush. Its findings and 44 separate recommendations, which were published in a public report, provided the official framework for U.S. policies for the next decade. The report stated unequivocally U.S. "firm opposition to terrorism in all its forms and wherever it takes place" and detailed a wide range of responses to both domestic and international terrorism.

Some of the guidelines provided by this report as well as earlier pronouncements have been implemented. A case in point is the 1985 interception by U.S. Navy jets of an Egyptian aircraft carrying the hijackers of the *Achille Lauro*. Another dramatic illustration of the success of U.S. policy is the military action directed against Libya in 1986. As a consequence, the level of Libyan-sponsored terrorism declined considerably. In addition, European allies, which initially were reluctant to cooperate with the United States, undertook various political, economic, and security steps to penalize Tripoli, including the expulsion of Libyan diplomats.

Collective International Measures. U.S. efforts in cooperating with other countries to develop practical measures to combat terrorism bore fruit. Thousands of foreign officers received U.S. antiterrorism training assistance. An increasing number of countries have agreed to deny refuge and safe haven to known terrorists. U.S. allies resorted to effective diplomatic and economic sanctions against state-sponsored terrorism, such as Syria's involvement in abortive terrorist operations in England and Germany, which was established in 1986. As a result, Damascus reduced its complicity in state terrorism from 34 cases in 1985 to 1 in 1987.

Even the Soviet Union seemed to shift its disposition toward terrorism. Continuous U.S. dialogue with Moscow has been instrumental in persuading the Soviets to join in condemning terrorism unilaterally (such as the hijacking of Pan Am Flight 073 in Karachi) and to play a useful role in contributing to the drafting of international instruments (on aviation and maritime security).

The results of expanded international cooperation efforts initiated by the United States were most dramatically demonstrated when the Olympics in Los Angeles and Seoul were uneventful.

Continuous U.S. dialogue with Moscow has been instrumental in persuading the Soviets to join in condemning terrorism unilaterally.

The foregoing positive record of the Reagan administration must, however, be balanced against serious failures in policy and actions. Two major errors undermined U.S. counterterrorism efforts: the Iran-Contra affair and the misdirected use of military power.

The unambiguous policy that the United States will not accede to terrorist demands, will not pay ransom, and will not make deals with terrorists suffered a near-fatal blow with the exposure of the Iran-Contra affair. Reagan's apparent authorization of U.S. arms sales to Iran in January 1986 jeopardized the credibility of the United States at home and abroad. The perception that the president exchanged hostages for arms was reinforced by the congressional committees' final report, which placed the "ultimate responsibility" for the episode on Reagan. Although three American hostages were released as a result of this secret deal, two others were kidnapped subsequently. Currently nine Americans are still held captive.

This affair most dramatically demonstrated that making concessions does encourage more terrorism. The damage was self-inflicted, and its consequences will be felt in the years to come.

Moreover, Reagan's vow of "swift and effective retribution" against terrorists was perceived by both friend and foe as a pronouncement by a "paper tiger." In the first place, the administration's labeling of perpetrators as "terrorist states" was influenced by political rather than objective criteria. Thus, countries like the Soviet Union and Iraq, whose record of utilizing terrorism as an extension of their own foreign policy is clear, were excluded from the official list of terrorist states and thereby became immune to retaliation.

Second, the United States failed to inflict a proportionate penalty on terrorist groups or their sponsors, because the military power deployed was misdirected. For instance, the bombardment of Lebanon by the U.S. battleship *New Jersey* sent the wrong signal and backfired. Similarly, the use of U.S. military aircraft against Syrian antiaircraft missiles in 1983 had little effect on Damascus' capability to sponsor terrorism.

In sum, when Reagan left the Oval Office in January 1989, the United States remained a prime target to terrorism and in need of a more effective strategy to reduce the threat at home and abroad.

The Bush strategy

Based on the Reagan administration's hard-learned lessons on the viability and effectiveness of various counterterrorism approaches, it can be expected that President Bush will provide political vision and a firm and sustained will to reduce terrorism to a level at which it is no longer a perceived national security threat.

The president's agenda will inevitably include both short-term and long-range challenges. The major immediate tests that Bush faces are (1) regaining credibility lost by the Iran-Contra episode, (2) identifying the perpetrators of the bombing of Pan Am Flight 103 and undertaking appropriate responses, and (3) resolving satisfactorily the Libyan munitions plant problem.

In the long run, it would be prudent for the Bush administration to focus on a counterterrorism strategy that includes the following concepts:

Coherent, Persistent and Bipartisan Policy. High priority should be given to developing a disciplined policy that spells out the essential guidelines of U.S. determination to fight terrorism relentlessly, both unilaterally and in concert with other nations. Policy consolidation should include bipartisan support for U.S. efforts, restoration of public faith in the capability of the government to protect Americans at home and abroad, and a White House leadership that avoids a "Rose Garden hostage" profile.

An Effective Organizational Structure. The ability to fight terrorism effectively depends on a sound organizational command structure. Better coordination of civilian and military resources should be developed. It is essential to reduce interagency rivalries and devise realistic divisions of labor on the local, state, and federal levels.

Intelligence capabilities should be continuously upgraded, including increasing budgets and expanding the resources of indigenous foreign agents to allow greater disruption of the terrorists' infrastructures. Beefing up counterterrorism research and development projects is also essential. Refining computer software to improve information gathering and analytical capabilities is a case in point. Another important task is to develop more reliable sensors for explosives and hazardous gas detection.

A Strong Legal Foundation. Apprehension, prosecution, and punishment of terrorists require increased use of the rule of law on national, regional, and global levels. Review of existing legal measures should be undertaken. Reexamination of all legal frameworks, such as Executive Order 11905 of 1976, which bans assassination, and the 1988 Senate legislation requiring notice to Congress at least 48 hours before initiating covert action, seems prudent. Efforts to strike out the "political offense" exception to extradition treaties should be intensified. Exploration of new international conventions such as the protection of women and children should also be top priority.

Intelligence capabilities should be continuously upgraded, including increasing budgets and expanding the resources of indigenous foreign agents to allow greater disruption of the terrorists' infrastructures.

Vigorous International Diplomatic and Economic Pressures. Expansion of international diplomatic and economic pressures can be particularly effective in combating state-sponsored terrorism. Perpetrators should be exposed and appropriate sanctions imposed. Diplomatic options include suspending cultural exchanges, imposing travel restrictions, and severing relations. Economic alternatives vary from freezing an offending state's assets to trade embargoes and blockades.

State sponsors must be warned that the international community considers any manifestation of terrorism as unacceptable behavior that will not be tolerated. For instance, if Czechoslovakia had refused to cooperate in controlling the exportation of the plastic explosive Semtex, it should have been penalized accordingly. Similarly, pressure should be applied to countries such as Greece that release convicted terrorists and refuse to support extradition procedures.

Improving Covert and Overt Military Capabilities. A critical task for the United States is to upgrade covert military preemptive strike capabilities and overt military operations against terrorists. Allocation of required funding, recruitment and training of motivated personnel, and acquisition of adequate airlift and communication equipment are some of the needed responses. Improvement in both passive defense capabilities (such as contingency planning and crisis management) and active defense measures (such as rescue operations) are also required. Intensified covert support for foreign counterterrorist operations as well as the creation of overt regional counterterrorism forces should also be considered.

To be sure, these responses represent only several of the wide range of measures available to the Bush administration in dealing with terrorism. In facing the manifold challenges ahead, such as freeing the nine American hostages in Lebanon and reducing the threat of narcoterrorism, the president's steady leadership in the next four years will be critical to saving future lives and limiting the damage to U.S. security interests.

The Bush Administration's PLO Cover-Up

Steven Emerson

Mr. Emerson, who writes frequently on foreign and intelligence matters, is the coauthor of the book "The Fall of Pan Am 103: Inside the Lockerbie Investigation" (Putnam, 1990).

A month ago, terrorists opened fire on a bus of Israeli tourists near Cairo. Nine Israelis were machine-gunned to death. When the Palestine Liberation Organization issued a statement that appeared to justify the attack, the Egyptian government made its fury known to the PLO and the world media. And what was the official American reaction to the PLO statement? Nothing. Not a word.

Refusal to criticize the PLO has now become a cornerstone of Bush administration policy. The latest manifestation of this disposition to whitewash the Palestinian group is the report the State Department presented to Congress on Monday, as required by the PLO Commitments Compliance Act enacted last month.

In December 1988, Yasser Arafat told the world that he "renounced" terrorism and "recognized" the state of Israel. By uttering those magic words, Mr. Arafat immediately gained the recognition of the U.S. But Mr. Arafat has a long history of saying one thing and doing another. In fact, just one month before, Mr. Arafat had been denied a visa to the U.S. by the Reagan State Department because it found that, despite his claims that he had abandoned terror, he was directing terrorist acts through such front groups as Force 17 and the Hawari Organization.

Condemn Terror

At the first meeting between U.S. and PLO representatives in December 1988, the Americans told the PLO—according to a list of "talking points" recently published by the Israeli government—that the dialogue would be broken off if the PLO resumed terrorism: "No American administration can sustain the dialogue if terrorism continues by the PLO or any of its factions." In addition, the U.S. required the PLO to "publicly disassociate" itself from "terrorism by any Palestinian groups operating anywhere." Finally, the U.S. said that it expected the PLO to condemn any terrorist act carried out by "any element of the PLO" and to expel that element from the PLO.

The Bush administration maintains that the PLO has met those conditions. Monday's State Department report says, "the PLO has adhered to its commitment undertaken in 1988 to renounce terrorism."

But what about the numerous terrorist attacks on Israel since December 1988? The State Department report reluctantly acknowledges that nine "border attacks"—the new diplomatic euphemism for terrorist attacks—against Israel have been launched by "constituent groups of the PLO" over the past 14 months. Those incidents do not invalidate the report's conclusion, the report says, because "the intended target of the attack was unclear" except for three of the attacks in which the report concedes that "civilians appeared to be the target." But the three attacks directed at civilians were, the report insists, neither authorized nor approved by Mr. Arafat or the PLO Executive Committee.

All of this is dangerously misleading or positively untrue. The State Department report omits any mention of the multiple terrorist attacks carried out by groups that sit on the PLO Executive Committee, including raids by Mr. Arafat's Fatah group. Constituent groups of the PLO have openly taken credit for more than 18 attempted terrorist attacks on Israel from Lebanon, Egypt, Jordan and the Mediterranean over the past 14 months. In the West Bank and

Gaza, many Palestinians have been murdered at the explicit—and documented—direction of the PLO and Fatah.

As for the nine PLO that the State Department report does acknowledge, it is not true that there is no evidence about their targets. There is clear and compelling evidence that the intended target of each one of them was civilian.

To take just one example: On Jan. 26, three guerrillas armed with machine guns, grenades and explosives attempted to penetrate the northern Israeli border from Lebanon. Intercepted by Israeli soldiers, the squad was killed in a shootout. In the terrorists' possession, besides weapons, was a map revealing one—and only one—target: a kibbutz called Misgav Am. The group that claimed responsibility for the abortive Misgav Am attack—as well as five others that were equally unsuccessful—is the Democratic Front for the Liberation of Palestine, which sits on the PLO Executive Committee. One of the DFLP's senior officials, Yasser abd al-Rabbu, is the head of the PLO delegation to the U.S.-PLO dialogue in Tunis.

Confronted with this accumulation of evidence, State Department spokesman Adam Shub averred: "None of the cross-border attacks has succeeded, so we don't know what the targets would have been. Therefore we can't call them terrorist. We don't know what they were planning." The State Department dismisses the written evidence from the Misgav Am raid as "inconclusive." When offered transcripts of the confessions of captured terrorists by the Israeli government, the State Department said that the interrogations were not "reliable." When offered an opportunity to interview the captured guerrillas first-hand, the U.S. refused.

When the Bush administration finds itself unable to deny that an attack occurred, it blames some rogue Palestinian element, never the PLO itself. As Monday's report puts it, "We have no evidence in those cases or any others that the actions were authorized or approved by the PLO Executive Committee."

But this is to misunderstand how the PLO works. The PLO is an umbrella organization, and its central committees do not attempt to control the operations of its member groups. The issue is not, what does the PLO Executive Committee order or authorize; the issue is, are the groups that constitute the PLO complying with the commitment they collectively made to the U.S. in December 1988? As State Department spokesman Charles Redman said in March 1989, "If the PLO cannot or will not exercise such control, it raises questions concerning the commitment undertaken in the name of the PLO—indeed, questions about the PLO's ability to carry out its commitments."

Constituent groups of the PLO have openly taken credit for more than 18 attempted terrorist attacks on Israel over the past 14 months.

The Bush administration is particularly at pains to avoid criticism of Mr. Arafat's own Fatah wing of the PLO. On Dec. 5, five guerrillas infiltrated the Israeli Negev from the Egyptian Sinai. They carried no identification and the labels in their clothes had been cut out—all they had were Kalashnikov rifles, explosives and 51 grenades. Israeli soldiers intercepted them.

Faced with incontestable documentation that the five were affiliated with Fatah, John Kelly, assistant secretary of state for Near East and South Asian Affairs, argued before Congress three weeks ago that while "there may have been Fatah members involved," they were "operating without sanctions from their leadership." In private conversation, though, State Department officials have admitted Fatah sponsorship of the attack. It is highly unlikely that Mr. Arafat, a man who insists on approving the smallest actions of his Fatah organization, down to the purchase of its fax machines, could have been unaware of it. The attack is not mentioned in the State Department report.

The contortions the Bush administration goes through to protect the PLO can verge on the grotesque. Last August, a Palestinian fundamentalist from Gaza wrenched the steering wheel of an Israeli bus away from the driver. The bus plunged into a ravine: 15 Israelis and one American were killed. The terrorist act was captured on television, and within six hours of the incident, the Israeli government had provided a detailed accounting of the attack.

The usual unnamed State Department official termed the event "senseless" and "tragic"—but categorically refused to label it an act of terrorism.

Why the Delay?

Only after two days had elapsed—and after a bitter Israel protest that the Bush administration's failure to condemn the murder gave a "license to kill to every Palestinian individual or organization"—did the State Department see fit to label it a terrorist attack. Why the two day delay? A State Department spokesman said at the time that the U.S. had only belatedly acquired the necessary information. But in fact, according to a senior U.S. official, the real reason was that the Bush administration was afraid that the mass slaying had been a PLO operation. Only when PLO responsibility was ruled out did the administration feel free to call it a terrorist operation.

Last summer, the Israelis dispatched Yigal Carmon, the Israeli government's adviser on counter-terrorism, to Washington with proof—maps, documents, leaflets—that, despite the American "talking points," PLO groups had not ceased their terrorist raids. He also brought tapes of speeches in Arabic by Mr. Arafat in which he condoned terrorist attacks.

State Department officials at first refused to meet with Mr. Carmon, before finally agreeing to a perfunctory meeting. But the Bush administration apparently did not feel confident that others would find Mr. Carmon's documents qute so uninteresting—so he was instructed not to speak to Congress and the media.

On March 1, Secretary of State James Baker testified before Congress, ". . . we have not received or seen evidence of complicity or encouragement or acquiescence by [Mr. Arafat] of terrorist activity." If Mr. Baker has not seen the evidence, it is because he has ordered his underlings not to collect it.

INTELLIGENCE AND THE WAR AGAINST TERRORISM

DIMINISHING THE THREAT

Meir Amit

The author is a retired major general who served as director of IDF military intelligence and as head of the Mossad. He has also held senior positions in both government and industry. He is currently chairman of General Satellite Corporation, which is developing the Amos *communications satellite in conjuction with IAI.*

Aided by advances in technology, communications, transportation, and even diplomacy, a new plague has cursed the family of nations: terrorism. There are few activities today which require as much thorough and monotonous preparation as anti–terror campaigns. As the attacks themselves become increasingly sophisticated, the counter–measures must respond in kind, using first–class professionals who are well–trained to pinpoint their target.

Public relations is an important part of anti–terrorist activity. The enemy must be exposed, and the public must be convinced of the need for the steps to be taken against them.

Range of Measures

When determining what means to use against a particular terrorist threat, operational intelligence is of primary importance. Defensive measures, such as fencing off an area, can be combined with preventive measures, such as keeping weapons from being smuggled into a given area.

Preventive measures on the political level include detention, which aims to prevent potential trouble makers from being involved in expected operations. In addition, "agents of influence" are effective in shaping opinions, especially among youth who may be inclined to join terror organizations.

Retaliatory actions and punishment, of course, are always possible responses to a terrorist action. It should be emphasized that collective punishment is less effective than isolating those who are really responsible for a particular act. In addition, punishment doesn't really prevent terrorism. At best it can delay it, which is an important factor in a continuous struggle.

The retaliatory steps taken against Jordan in the late 1960s and early 1970, in response to terrorist actions emanating from that country, provide an interesting case in point. In September 1970, the Jordanian government decided to restore order. In one week, more Palestinian terrorists were killed in Jordan than had been killed by Israel during the preceding 20 years. There was no international reaction. The incident showed that sometimes pressure on others brings them to achieve your goals for you.

Another very important measure is education: preparing the public to behave correctly before, during, and after a terror attack. No matter how many agents the authorities place in areas sensitive to attack, there is no replacement for an alert public.

Cooperation, encompassing various possibilities from international cooperation to inter–service cooperation, is a component of the overall struggle against terrorism. Sometimes there are differences of opinion between the various services, a problem faced by Israel until the responsibilities between the different services combating terror were very clearly defined. It was not easy, and ideal results can never be achieved. Cooperation also means the flow of information, shared doctrine, and the coordination of retaliation and counter–terrorist activities.

Crucial Weapon

Intelligence is the most crucial weapon against terrorism. Only those anti–terror activities based on good intelligence can be effective.

With advance knowledge, we can be sure that 80–90 percent of terrorist incidents will be prevented. The majority of hostile actions within Israel do not take place at all because of early intelligence information. They are prevented before they begin. Reliable intelligence allows the authorities to concentrate on sensitive or suspected areas, which makes them more effective and saves a lot of resources.

While the intelligence community is active 24 hours a day, 365 days a year, its achievements cannot be publicized.

Reprinted by permission of the *IDF Journal* (Israel Defense Forces Journal), Fall 1989, pp. 8-10.

Only mishaps, fiascoes, and failures receive public attention. The large majority of intelligence actions are successful, but nobody knows about them.

Intelligence is also vital for effective retaliation. In 1973, three of the key Fatah terrorists in Beirut were killed. They had been personally involved in planning and executing terrorist acts. They had been the brains behind the operations. In planning retaliation against them, they were followed, and their habits and those of their families, whom we did not want to harm, were carefully studied. Intelligence played a decisive role not only in providing the information, but during the operation itself. Israeli agents went into Beirut and found their targets simultaneously in their homes in different high–rise buildings. Without very specific information these kinds of operations would be impossible to carry out.

Anti–Terrorist Planning

The first task is to set up a static network that collects data on a continuous basis, thereby establishing a database. This is not an easy job and it is not the most interesting work. On top of this static network you have to superimpose a dynamic network that supplies information in real time.

The next step is to establish priorities, which amount to warning lights or *Important Information Indicators.* To avoid a constant state of alert, priorities must be established for the collection agencies as well as for those who evaluate the information. There is an ocean of information and, although there are computers that use sophisticated processing methods, it is very difficult to cope with so much data. That is why it is necessary to set priorities and define important items.

Subsequently, information has to be processed, edited, and disseminated. Information that is not sent to the right people at the right time and in the right form is worthless. There is a dilemma here. Political leaders and decision makers want raw information. They want to feel the flavor, they don't want sterile processed information. This can be very dangerous.

When Moshe Dayan was Minister of Defense, he liked to *feel* information, to *sense* it. The danger was that he would draw conclusions from one set of facts, against all the rules. We worked hard to find the right way to present the information while also satisfying his need to be close to the raw input. This was not unique to Dayan, and whenever it occurs, it creates a real problem for intelligence officers.

The next step is to build a communications network that connects all the parties concerned. This is intended not only to establish links, but to keep them open and to see to it that the information will flow in real time. Even the best information, the best processing, and the best analysis will produce no results if they are not communicated to the decision–makers at the proper time.

International cooperation is also vital, including databases, exchanges of information, and open communication. There is a need to define a clear and unified terminology. Each country must decide its own order of priorities, which makes it difficult to combine efforts.

Decision–Making

There must be an efficient and quick decision–making process on both the national and international levels. Adequate resources must be allocated for intelligence, including money, people, organization, and even definition of areas of responsibility. There is no better investment than intelligence. It gives the best results, even better than any other investment in defensive or offensive activity.

Finally, the need for very close cooperation between intelligence and operations must be stressed. The operations staff must understand intelligence, while intelligence personnel must understand the operation.

As opposed to other modes of warfare, terrorism is irregular. It is a partisan war, and is highly compartmentalized. Terrorists operate in small mobile units. They are flexible and have almost no hierarchy. It is very difficult to mix in their crowd, as closed groups know one another. Any stranger who appears on the scene is immediately suspect, therefore, collecting information about terrorists in their own milieu is very difficult.

There are ethical problems as well. In conventional war, the rules of the game are different. But terror activity takes place in peacetime, when these rules are not applied. Martial law cannot be imposed, and the courts must be respected.

Finally, we face the problem of false alarms, since no chances can be taken when combating terror. Repeated diversions of false alarms add up to a major imposition which diminishes the reliability of intelligence.

Anti–terror activity is a continuous war. Although terrorism does not present a danger to our very existence, its cumulative effect has been a major drain on our resources, as well as on our national spirit. In the future, terrorists may turn to nuclear or chemical weapons, and the threat they pose will increase. We must be constantly vigilant. I do not think terrorism can be stopped altogether, but it can be diminished.

Terror and Negotiation

Martin Hughes

This article considers the claim that we should never negotiate with terrorists. The author argues that, although it may always be wrong to let terrorists dictate to us, negotiation may still be acceptable since to negotiate and to submit to dictation are different things. A ransom agreed in negotiation is a ransom which can be afforded and so should not be withheld. The claim that to ransom some victims is to endanger others is commonly exaggerated to the point of treating existing hostages as unconditionally expendable; a certain barbarism is reached at that point. Turning to the argument that negotiation concedes legitimacy to illegitimate political forces the author argues, firstly, that to deny that an opponent has any legitimacy is to risk brutalizing oneself and, secondly, that to seek legitimacy in opponents who have been evil hitherto is a useful means of securing peace. He concedes that the search for legitimacy in evil people may fail for years or even fail indefinitely and that during those years negotiations are useless; which makes ruthless repression on our part the only reply to terrorism which, during those years, is of any use. But this concession does not elevate 'Never negotiate with terrorists' into an absolute moral principle.

It is always wrong, according to the convictions of many people, to negotiate at all with terrorists because this always makes them stronger materially and – what is worse – confers legitimacy upon them. In opposition to this I argue that readiness to negotiate, though not readiness to accept any terms asked, is, in general, right. Refusal to negotiate means that we resolve to use force as our only means of dealing with certain enemies; to use force only, even against opponents of undeniably evil nature, is corrupting. This is a general moral point: I refer to particular cases but offer no manual for negotiators; I suggest only that the special features which each case is likely to have make it hard to find any maxim which is morally compelling every time. The maxim that a firm policy of refusing terrorist demands should be firmly followed,[1] a maxim which seems to rule negotiations out, except perhaps negotiations on such temporary matters as food supplies for the hostages, has a stark simplicity which I cannot accept and moral consequences which disturb me.

The consequence which most concerns me is falling into the trap noticed by Joseph Conrad in *The Secret Agent*. Conrad portrays a terrorist called 'the Professor'[2] whose aim is to put himself beyond arrest by carrying explosives which he will detonate when any attempt at arrest is made – he means to force the police to shoot him down illegally. He believes that by forcing the police into illegality, that is forcing society to rely on force alone, he can strike the heaviest blow against society, corrupting its soul rather than simply shedding some of its blood. Before arguing that he was right in this belief I offer some definitions and indicate the background in political philosophy from which I argue.

By 'terrorists' for present purposes I mean those who take and threaten hostages, using their hostages' lives as a bargaining counter. By 'anti-terrorists' I mean those who oppose terrorists, by 'counter-terrorists' those who try to oppose them by some equivalent threat, if necessary in disregard of legal restrictions. 'Hostages' may refer, in a narrow sense, to captives in a dungeon or a hijacked plane but also there are hostages in a wider sense: whole populations who must run their lives with an eye on on the shadowy presence of a private army, hostile to the legitimate government, in their midst. Plainly, hostages in the wider sense may be sympathizers with the terrorist cause or potential recruits to it; so, sometimes, may hostages in the narrow sense if the emotional circumstances are right. Terrorists may be able to create these circumstances – 'the Stockholm syndrome'[3] – by the manipulation of language.

Although not all brutality counts as terror it is possible under my definition for brutal methods used by governments to be counted as terror against the people and it is possible both for unofficial terrorists and for governments to terrorise their own supporters. Rulers in crisis, desperate to modernize their countries or to prepare for war, sometimes treat those supporters who are entrusted with any office or responsibility as hostages: if they do not fulfil the Plan they pay with their lives. But in current usage the term 'state terrorism' refers less to such domestic management by terror as to support by one state for terrorists operating against another state. In this paper I do not discuss international negotiation where one government is currently terrorist in either sense. Although I do mention negotiation with governments whose past is terrorist my main concern is with terror as part of internal or civil conflict.

I assume that terrorists are ruthless servants of a big idea and ruthless manipulators of language in the cause of their idea. Accordingly they belong to a category of people whose appearance in civil conflict is incisively described by Thucydides[4] and angrily discussed by Hobbes, who is much influenced by Thucydides and is the greatest philosopher of conflict, in Part IV of *Leviathan*,[5] where the perversion of ideas, particularly of Christian ideas, is the main topic. This topic has remarkable contemporary importance. The acrimony and fanaticism of the old religious wars has found rebirth in the terrorism of today: increasingly we find religion as a motive and terrorism as a means.

From *Terrorism and Political Violence*, Vol. 2, No. 1, Spring 1990, pp. 72-82. *Terrorism and Political Violence*, published by Frank Cass and Company, Ltd., England.

But Hobbes comes to the conclusion that it was a fault in the government of Charles I to repress people whose political ideas were perverted. So it was wrong, at least according to this phase of Hobbes' philosophy, to treat these dangerous people as if they had no legitimacy, wrong even though they had in truth no legitimacy: and this phase of Hobbes' philosophy is what I attempt to explore and apply in this article. Refusal to negotiate is the logical expression of the belief that the other side has no legitimacy and so should not be treated as if it had. From noticing why people refuse to negotiate we can see what negotiation truly is.

To understand the idea of negotiation we should first distinguish negotiation from dictation. If one side has no choice except the choice between its own destruction and the acceptance of dictated terms then the situation is a different one from those we consider here, where we presuppose that the choice between negotiation and hostilities (with some chance of success) is always open. Negotiation envisages compromise and therefore presupposes that the other party has, or can acquire, some predictable character: if that other party is completely unstable he cannot compromise or take any definite position. We can, of course, use negotiation to create the character we want. Facing a man who had seized a gun in desperate rage we might try to talk, offer him ways out and so calm him down: a minor but significant example of negotiation and of the search for common ground where people can converse without threats.

The aim of negotiation is to remove threats and so must be a search for legitimacy in the other party. This is exactly why some say 'Never negotiate with terrorists'. They say this because they demand absolute fidelity to our original principles: these were right and we should stick to them; the other side, who rejects our principles, is and always was hopelessly corrupt and should be treated accordingly. If we accept that there is any legitimacy in them we commit moral treason.

The tactical maxim of the upper hand, which says 'Never negotiate except from great strength and to great advantage' is rather different and concern trates on the material strength of the enemy, which, by this maxim, must never increase either directly or through any form of political gain which may recruit more supporters or increase morale. Thus even legitimate demands should be refused, once they have been pressed by terrorist means, unless you are already sure of victory over the terrorist forces. Postponing the central question of legitimacy, I consider first the practical arguements against letting the terrorists gain advantage in any way, even for a time.

II

Against the idea of negotiating with terrorists the 'more hostages' argument – that is the argument that negotiation to release actual hostages 'merely puts others at risk' – usually prevails. Furthermore it is argued that, if there is a ransom, the enemy will use the ransom to buy more arms which will bring more hostages within his reach; I call this the 'more guns, more hostages' argument. Still more important, if part of the ransom is release of captured terrorists, they will feel they can operate with impunity. We will have made them a present of renewed morale. I call this the'impunity argument'. All these arguments are variations on one theme, that the terrorist enemy must be denied all material and tactical advantages.

These arguments do not really have anything like the decisive force that people imagine. The 'more hostages' argument treats a contingent risk as if it were ineluctable. It is extraordinary that Western governments refuse or pretend to refuse to negotiate with terrorists who seize Western hostages on the streets of Beirut, a place where armed gangs, each based in a few crowded and impenetrable streets, have sometimes been the only power.[6] The refusal is justified because others must not be put at risk. But why not take the simple precaution of keeping our people out of Beirut and the tiny areas where the terrorists' writ runs? The fear of more hostages in the future loses its force completely if there other means sure to cut off the hostage supply; and it loses its force not completely, but significantly, if there are means simply likely to cut off that supply.

Here I might be challenged by people with better factual knowledge than I can claim of the situation in Beirut, who might scorn my remark that there is a 'simple precaution'. It may be that there will always be Westerners who cannot avoid venturing into the danger zone or that success in Beirut will tempt Lebanese terrorists to try their hand abroad, even in Western countries. But the conclusion is the same even if these objections are correct.

If the danger zone is not avoidable and there will always be people who are potential hostages but who must venture there, then the most important point is that there is no reason to think that refusal to negotiate over previous hostages protects them: the terrorists may take great satisfaction in creating impotent anger and gnawing fear in those whom they especially hate and they can achieve this by adding more victims to their collection, emphasizing once again the impossibility of rescue. Furthermore, even if there must be some venturers into the danger zone it is obvious that there cannot be many: only extreme commitment, necessity or folly will bring flies to the spider's web. So there is no serious fear that the number of hostages might become so high that the terrorists' bargaining position, should negotiations happen, will be unbearably strong.

Again, it may be that Lebanese terrorists will release present British hostages but then take more, not in Lebanon if none are available there, but in other countries, even in Britain itself. But then the battle would be on much better ground. The present hostages have languished for years: in Beirut no rescue is thinkable, elsewhere it would be. So, even if keeping our people out of Lebanon is not as complete a precaution as I believe it is, the future risks do not prohibit the negotiated release of the present hostages.

Another form of the argument I oppose suggests that, even if there are no more physical hostages, we can by negotiation make our sovereignty and government policy a hostage. Those who say this forget the distinction between negotiation and dictation. Of course, no government can accept dictation of policy by anyone else. But is it an inflexible principle that policy never changes in any respect to save the lives of our citizens? Surely there is neither fairness nor fidelity to the social contract in protecting some others from a hypothetical risk by means which submit the present hostages to real, unending misery. Moreover there is a certain barbarity in treating any individuals as utterly and unconditionally expendable, which is what this principle insists that we do to the present hostages.

Similarly, a few more guns and a bit more money are not too worrying if their effects can be neutralized by the enormous arsenals and treasuries of the anti-terrorists. The 'more guns, more hostages' argument treats an absolute increase in terrorists' power as if it were important; in reality it is the increase relative to the power of the anti-terrorists that matters and that relative increase, even when the absolute increase is substantial, may be completely trivial. My argument presupposes that the ransom will not be too great: which, I suggest, is a rational presupposition. No money ransom is likely to bring the overall armament of the terrorists to a point anywhere near that of the anti-terrorists: if it were it would not be paid. The central point is that ransoms by definition are set, if they are negotiated rather than dictated, by what the donor can afford. Ransom in kind, if it were (say) nuclear weapons able to turn the whole balance of power between terror and anti-terror, would not be granted.

If we turn to the impunity argument we should note that 'impunity' either refers to freedom from due and legal punishment under a social contract or to freedom from revenge by aggrieved people, including aggrieved governments.

Freedom from punishment outrages us in proportion to our commitment to protect the social contract which protects us all: to grant impunity is to strike a blow at the heart of the social contract. There is no question but that unrestricted impunity for terrorists would be a mortal blow but we cannot instantly conclude that lesser degrees of impunity have the same drastic effect. It is clear that not all demands, however extreme, made in negotiation can be met but not clear that negotiation should not start.

Terrorists have often seized hostages to secure the release of their own friends imprisoned for previous terrorism. The result of negotiation has sometimes been – as in the recent hijack involving Iran, Kuwait and Algeria in various roles, against which British opinion reacted very strongly – that the imprisoned terrorists stayed in prison but that the free terrorists stay free in exchange for the hostages' lives.[7] If – and it is a big if – an outcome on these terms is acceptable it follows that impunity is acceptable, at least impunity to a certain degree.

British government and public opinion had strong reservations about accepting even this degree of immunity for those who had perpetrated the Iran–Algeria hijack, which was hideously protracted and brutal. But this understandable movement of opinion may have been wrong. If we refuse to end any terrorist incident with immunity to the terrorists, and maintain this refusal even if we can see no other way to release the hostages, our refusal amounts to the absolute assertion that, as a matter of principle, the outcome in which hostages and terrorists all die is preferable to the outcome in which all live. But surely – to expand slightly on a point made above – the idea of social contract is to protect innocent lives and to create rulers, armed forces, courts of law and punishments, as means for this protection. The absolute, exception-free assertion demands that we sacrifice the end, protection of life, to the means, victorious use of armed force: which is illogical.

Punishments are a substitute under the social contract for the natural right of revenge, which is personal vindication of honour and reputation and which any social contract severely limits. But it is possible for governments or individuals to treat revenge as more important than punishment in extreme situations. They may think that contracts are meaningless unless the government can defend its honour. This is not necessarily a vainglorious idea: it appeals to the idea of honourable behaviour, meaning firm and consistent defence of what we believe in. That means, they suppose, no advantage to terrorists of any sort: all they deserve is retribution. This retribution or revenge must be claimed at all costs, since anything else dishonours and subverts government. Justice, on this view, becomes summary. The right to fair trial and treatment which ordinary criminals have is simply an advantage which terrorists will (as they so often have done) shamefully exploit. Terrorists have no rights.

But this at-all-costs retributionist view, adopted in the name of consistent and honourable moral effort, is disastrous to rulers, partly but not only because of the catastrophic loss of support that may occur if 'all costs' are willingly paid. The classic example is the excessive repression after the 1916 rising in Ireland.

But even apart from this kind of catastrophe, campaigns of all-out retribution and repression against terrorists are always, but for one exceptional class (which is the worst), fought inconsistently and by two kinds of force. First there are those genuinely under the control of the government and thus with rules of engagement that apply some limits to what they can do; secondly there are irregular forces who find these limits irksome. Irregular military forces are not necessarily mere scum or social outcasts transformed into mindless death squads. If the regular forces are weakened then good people may have to consider saving society by private means; if the regular forces are expensively strengthened and wear totalitarian trappings then there will be some who want to assert their independence of spirit by doing their job for them, quickly and cheaply. In the mind of Ulster Protestantism,[8] ever since it emerged as a political force, there have been appeals to both principles: the British government and its armed forces sometimes seem too weak, therefore in need of private citizens' help, and sometimes too overbearing, therefore in need of correction by true patriots. This is a necessary development. Governments can scarcely remain governments if they do not insist on controlling their supporters and in a violent scene this means serious tension: the government has wider policy questions to think of, its local supporters have an overwhelming concern with immediate problems and fears – with face-to-face enemies who may be waiting with a gun round the next corner. The immediate fear turns local loyalists into vigilantes, persons with a self-awarded licence to kill.

When the government calls for victory and retribution against the enemy at all costs it means victory for its own authority: when the vigilantes call for victory over the same enemy they mean that their right to self-defence (by attack if necessary) must be vindicated, even at a cost to the authority of the government which it would be self-defeating for the government to pay. Government restraint on vigilantes – which probably means painful restraint on the keenest members of the regular forces as well – is therefore a concession to the terrorists: they are to be treated as if they had rights after all. And that cancels the policy of retribution at all costs.

For example, de Gaulle was put into power by French Algerian forces that were, because they had decided to keep Algeria French at all costs, escaping constitutional control; once in power, he had, if he was truly to exercise government, to control them. It is plain that his decision to negotiate with the native Algerian terrorists led to a bloody conflict with French Algerian forces. The converse is just as true: his need to be genuinely in power forced him into conflict with his former supporters. Because he was fighting them he had to abandon their policy: so he, once the chosen representative of those who cried for victory at all costs, had to negotiate with the terrorists. This example illustrates how the policy of victory and retribution at all costs does not lead to a consistent effort but raises two forces, potentially in serious conflict, on what was once the same side.

There is, as mentioned, an exceptional and worst case typified by El Salvador: here the government is not genuinely in power[9] but formally in office while vigilantes – now official stormtroops and the only effective anti-terrorist force – act in their own way, the way of people trained only for violence. This is a recipe for barbarism. No one in this situation stands on a moral plane higher than that of the terrorists. We simply find a range of armed factions contending for victory at all costs. The only moral distinction between them now is in policy for the future. If we have to choose between them only on these grounds we might well hope for negotiation and compromise, so that after the fighting there will be some scope for policy rather than victory in a desert. Once again it is a mistake to think that refusal to compromise is the only sign of a consistent and honourable mind.

This completes my case as far as it concerns material and tactical advantages. The arguments I oppose overestimate the material advantages to be gained by the terrorists from negotiation and underestimate the costs paid by the government by refusing to negotiate, including the costs of vigilantism. I now turn to the question of legitimacy.

III

The slide from anti-terrorism to counter-terrorism and stormtroop behaviour is the slide by government to the same moral plane as the terrorists occupy. My argument above shows, I believe, that 'the Professor' was right: that to induce this slide is a most important objective for terrorists because it splits their opponents into vigilantes and legitimists. The opposite process is the one in which terrorists are raised above their original plane – that is, acquire legitimacy. Even though this may take generations to complete, or seriously to begin, it is the more desirable process. It demands entry into negotiations by representatives of non-terrorist traditions; the latter are bound to have suspicions which they need to keep within bounds if the process is ever to be completed. By far the most important example is that of the Soviet Union, a society that once attempted modernization through terror and whose rulers, heirs of the terror, now appreciate that further modernization requires the removal of the substantial remains of the system by which terror was inflicted. I accept that the example of the Soviet Union, now an established world power, raises rather different questions from those raised by my general topic, terrorist civil wars. But the differences do not make the example irrelevant. It should encourage us to believe that, even where there is not the slightest short-term prospect for negotiation, we should not rule it out on principle: the right time may come.

My central contention is that the best and most prudent thing we can do with terrorists or the heirs of terrorists is give them legitimacy, thus enabling them to abandon and leave behind the methods of terror: the means to this is negotiation, because negotiation is a search for legitimacy in the other side. If they will not accept the gift then, of course, the hostility must continue – and this may be the case for several generations. By parity of reasoning we on our part should refuse to offer the gift only if we ourselves want to ensure that the conflict or battle continues and so are ready to commit ourselves to the necessary campaigns of repression and to pay the price that these entail.

I support my contention as follows. I have already argued that repression 'at all costs' in the name of absolute fidelity to our original principles is detrimental in practical terms. I now suggest it brings with it a fundamental moral problem. Governments facing this problem may find their own legitimacy lost. The root of that problem is this, that to deny legitimacy to any group of human beings is to commend highly the job of controlling them and to condemn bitterly all their objections to our control. The more consistently we affirm these values and the more we embody them in the law the more we commit ourselves to a double standard and so become, after all, unfaithful to our original principles.

An example is to be found in certain events which form part of British dealings with Irish terror. In the 'Birmingham Six' judgement, recent at the time of writing, the Court rejected an appeal, mentioning among other points that those concerned were known IRA sympathizers, had 'signified approval'[10] of the IRA. There has been immense debate about the facts of this case; for the purposes of this argument I assume that the Court was right in every disputed matter of fact. Behind the apparent factual dispute there lies something quite different, in truth a dispute over the legitimacy of Irish nationalism.

Nothing could be more rational than the opinion that known sympathisers with a terrorist cause are more likely, in comparison with known opponents, to be terrorists themselves. This remains true however widely the word 'sympathy' is defined: Irish nationalism, which is support for the objectives of the IRA, is obviously more likely, compared with opposition to those objectives, to issue in active IRA membership. The sympathy makes the action more probable. Thus there is a valid inference: given his opinions he can reasonably be suspected of crime. From this there is a further inference: the opinions of Irish nationalists are illegitimate because of their criminal tendency. Because Irish nationalists reject this conclusion they reject the whole train of inferences and accuse the Court, in its assessment of facts, of gross unfairness and of travesty. These accusations are themselves unfair; all the same the Court's proceedings were one part of a picture which should give us grave concern.

At about the same time as the 'Birmingham Six' case a British soldier, convicted of murder in the course of service in the Northern Ireland terror zone, was pardoned and reinstated in the Army: he was, on an official view, merely involved in a 'tragic error'.[11] We may have no difficulty at all in sympathising with a young man under the intense pressure of war against lurking gunmen. But the official attitude (supported by public opinion) to this case was the logical counterpart to the attitude to terrorist sympathisers just described. From the fact that someone has dedicated himself against terrorism there is an inference to his essential justice and innocence, bestowed by the goodness and legitimacy of the cause.

These two cases taken together apply, if we consider the reasons given and the words used, a double standard to the idea of guilt, double because the essential question is 'Which side is he on?' We might imagine the opposite double standard applied to the two cases in the hardest Catholic areas of Belfast:

> A brutal army of occupation officially declares that this murder is an error rather than an evil: so we can conceive of patriotism only as violent opposition to those who so despise the Irish. Meanwhile British courts insult the Irish by using as evidence of guilt of violent crime simple belief in the nationalist cause, belief which is nothing but elementary patriotism.

From a British point of view we would readily see that the Thucydidean process, whereby the beautiful words of moral discourse become stupefying weapons of propaganda, was at work here. But I suggest that the examples show that the same process is also at work, though it may not be so advanced, in the British body politic.

The trains of thought underlying both the Court of Appeal judgment and the pardon for the soldier can readily be understood by anyone with British patriotic loyalties, the loyalties which I share. Indeed I believe public opinion supported both, with major protest only from those with Irish sympathies. But acceptance of both is very disturbing. Even if one of the two trains of thought is fully justified morally, it is impossible that both should be. We cannot approve of both unless our thought is dominated by the question 'Which side is he on?' But if that question is dominant we are no longer thinking in a moral spirit, since a moral spirit demands impartiality and impartiality is just what this question excludes. Not to think in a moral spirit is to lose integrity.

But this loss of integrity is hard to avoid if we insist that we are a legitimate political force and that others, with whom we are in conflict, are not legitimate. Then the question of which side someone is on, ours or theirs, must be of supreme importance when we judge his actions. To claim exclusive legitimacy is to lose moral integrity because it is to abandon impartial judgement, and to lose moral integrity is to put our claim to legitimate political authority at risk, perhaps to lay the foundations of tyranny or some other serious moral decline.

This problem connects with the problems of negotiation with terrorists because it arises from the claim to exclusive legitimacy, the claim which is most often advanced by those who rule out negotiation with terrorists completely and on principle. The moral danger inherent in making this claim is very serious, akin to the dangers of excessive zeal which Hobbes saw in the religious policy of Charles I: excessive even against people whose religious ideas were dangerously perverted.

Perhaps there are some people in whom we can never find good or even the shadow of some legitimate purpose. Still, I oppose the idea that we should, as a matter of principle, refuse to look for good in the other side during protracted years of conflict. The refusal to look is the rejection of the very idea of negotiation, the process by which we seek for legitimacy in opponents or seek to create it in them.

The practical alternative to negotiation is the apparatus of repression – blazing guns, bleak prisons, intrusive surveillance – always evil in themselves. I have never questioned that these means may have to be used, even intensively and over long stretches of time. I am aware that negotiation has been tried in Northern Ireland and has always failed abysmally. But the awareness of that failure should not make us nail our colours to the claim of exclusive legitimacy. This claim is corrupting. 'Never negotiate with terrorists' is a false moral principle.

NOTES

1. P. Wilkinson, *Terrorism and the Liberal State*, 2nd ed. (London: Macmillan 1986), p.301.
2. See E.K. Hay, *The Political Novels of Joseph Conrad* (Chicago, 1L: University of Chicago Press, 1963), pp.251–63.
3. M. Connor, *Terrorism: The Solutions* (London: Paladin Press, 1987), pp.127–9.
4. Thucydides, *Histories*, Book III, para.82.
5. T. Hobbes, *Leviathan*, especially Ch. 47.
6. J. Laffin, *The War of Desperation* (London: Osprey Publishing, 1985), p.204.
7. *The Times*, 21 April 1988.
8. S. Nelson, *Ulster's Uncertain Defenders* (Belfast: Appletree Press, 1984).
9. *The Economist*, 21 Nov. 1987.
10. *The Times*, 29 Jan. 1988.
11. *The Times*, 24 Feb. 1988.

MISSION IMPROBABLE

Why—10 years after Desert One—the U.S. still isn't ready to fight the war against terrorism

James Bennet

James Bennet is an editor of The Washington Monthly. *Research assistance provided by Bill Yelverton.*

The Cold War is over and you're ready for bed. So you pat the dog, kiss the wife, and set the alarm for a half hour later than usual. You pull the down comforter up to your chin and wriggle slightly, enjoying the rough feel of your new flannel PJs. Idly, you picture yourself casting, the line arcing through the air—20 yards, no, 50 yards—the lure striking the water . . . here he comes, big fellah, big ole bass . . . the phone rings. The wife sighs. It's Brent Scowcroft, sounding more tense than usual. You listen. Softly you mutter, "Darn Eye-rainians." You get out of bed and, robed, shuffle off for the Situation Room, trailed by the officer with the launch codes.

Actually, the Iranians evidently have nothing to do with this one. Meeting you at the door, Scowcroft explains that a group of terrorists have hijacked a Lloyd Aero Boliviano 727 bound for Miami from La Paz. On board are at least 40 Americans, including several businessmen and economists who were in Bolivia for a round of debt-reduction talks. The plane is now flying a crazy, zig-zag route up the spine of South America. You ask Scowcroft about the available military options, and he starts to look really nervous. Shouldn't we alert Delta Force? you ask. Can't they handle the job? Scowcroft quickly answers yessir to the first question. Then he clears his throat and gives you the only truthful answer available to the second one, which is that. . . .

There's no way of knowing, because Delta hasn't tried to rescue any hostages since the botched mission to Iran. But if the record of America's counterterrorist commandos through the eighties is any indication, the outlook's pretty grim. The United States has had a decade to apply the brutal lessons of Desert One to building counterterrorist forces that can supply the "swift and effective retribution" promised by Ronald Reagan—that can give the military the capacity for the quick-hit missions, ranging from rescue to retaliation, that it so clearly lacked. More than a billion dollars has gone to develop two commando units—Delta Force, which grew out of the Army, and SEAL Team Six, drawn from the Navy—and the support they require. The need for a better response to terrorism certainly hasn't disappeared: During the 1980s, terrorists killed 571 Americans around the world.

So with all that incentive, all that spending, and all that time, could we get the hostages out of Iran today? "No, no," says a former member of the Special Operations command, who, like most of his comrades, wouldn't allow his name to be printed since he continues to advise the command informally. The troops themselves, by all accounts, are excellent; the problems lie not with the men who pull the triggers but with the command that controls them and, ultimately, with the political leadership. Their Rambo rhetoric notwithstanding, first Ronald Reagan and now George Bush never pushed hard or long enough to bust through the roadblocks that cut off the Iran rescue mission at Desert One. Left to its own devices in the late eighties, the military side of the American counterterrorist effort became "a boondoggle," says a Defense Department source with several years' experience in special operations. "This whole force, the way it's configured, is a disaster." Even the more charitable assessments don't inspire much confidence. "If you put the right leadership in and give them five years, we'll have the forces we need," says Col. Charlie Beckwith, who led the troops on the ground in Iran. "And I think we've got the right leadership now." Five *more* years?

But you need those commandos in the air now. The plane, low on fuel, has requested permission to land in Caracas. Perez probably won't let American troops fight on his soil, but there's a chance he'd at least take some advice, if you could get a team there fast enough. You've gotten a clearer picture of the situation from information that's dribbled in as the pilot communicates with air-traffic controllers in Lima and Quito: There are at least four terrorists, all members of the Fuerzas Armadas Revolucionarias de Colombia (FARC). A communist guerrilla movement with close ties to Colombia's drug lords, the FARC has conducted a number of kidnappings and assassinations of Colombians and even some attacks on Americans over the past few years. Unfortunately, you don't know much more about the FARC than that. You do know that the terrorists are armed with handguns and grenades and apparently are carrying some sort of explosive, since they keep threatening to blow up the plane.

On an open line from Simon Bolivar International Airport, Kenneth Skoag, the chargé d'affaires, informs you that the Venezuelans have deployed their army to block all runways. The jet comes in anyway in an effort to force a landing—maybe hoping the barricades will be lifted at the last moment, as they were in Beirut during that nightmare TWA hijacking five years ago—but the pilot loses his game of chicken and pulls up at the last moment, banking to the northwest. Given his dwindling fuel supply, he must be planning to land at either Aruba or Curacao—neither of which has a standing military capable of dealing with the crisis. The U.S. might have to act, not just advise, after all.

Stealth vs. Sikhs

"Oddly enough," says Robert Kupperman of the Center for Strategic and International Studies, "we may yet yearn for a bipolar, Cold War world." Besides flooding the international arms market with sophisticated weapons, the retreat of the superpowers is creating a vacuum in which ethnic nationalist groups around the world—Tamils, Croatians, Igbos, Azerbaijanis, Sikhs—can press their demands. Many of their grievances are legitimate, but, as the Lithuanians are discovering, their desires for independence may not be fulfilled overnight. It's in that gap between a pressing, legitimate cause and its satisfaction that terrorism flourishes. As terrorist and insurgent groups like the PLO, the Shining Path in Peru, the New People's Army in the Philippines, and the Basque Fatherland and Liberty in northern Spain learned long ago, there's no better way to grab attention in the telecommunications age than with a sudden act of spectacular violence. Today, the means to do so are becoming more accessible and more deadly (see "Beyond Hijacking,").

In the United States, responsibility for dealing with international terrorism is parceled out, with some duplication, primarily among the CIA, the FBI, the Pentagon, the State Department, and the National Security Council. Of these, the Department of Defense seems least likely to play a continuous, useful role. Military force won't win the war on terrorism, just as hiring more cops alone will never put an end to urban crime. To sleep more peacefully, the world's leaders must recognize the just grievances at the core of many terrorist actions; the best commandos in the world—the British SAS and the Israeli paratroopers—haven't managed to subdue or placate Catholics in Northern Ireland or Palestinians on the West Bank.

But that doesn't mean the president should be deprived of an off-the-shelf military option, and that terrorists should be relieved of worrying about one, when Americans are threatened abroad. When a group of angry Sikhs threatens to blow up the U.S. embassy in New Delhi, you don't want to have to wait for the State Department to negotiate peace in the Punjab; you want to have a good intelligence network in place, solid logistical support, and a counterterrorist team that's armed and ready to go. The release of American hostages by terrorist groups in Lebanon may prove that the U.S. doesn't always need good counterterrorist forces; but the fact that the Americans were captive as long as three and a half years—and that others continue to be held hostage—suggests that those forces would be nice to have. Sure, the Czechoslovaks have stopped exporting Semtex; but they had already sent one million pounds of it to Libya, and, as Vaclav Havel pointed out, it takes only about six ounces to blow up an airplane. And while American customs agents may be able to stem the flow of nuclear triggers to Iraq, they can't shut down Iraq's nuclear weapons program or deter Saddam Hussein from using or selling the binary chemical weapons he calls "the fire."

As Sam Nunn commented in a 1986 Senate speech, since "Special Operations Forces"—including counterterrorist commandos—are more likely to conduct missions than conventional troops, "our entire armed forces—and hence our military capacity—will be judged on whether these forces succeed or fail." After four years, that message seems finally to have made it across the Potomac to the defense department, only to be transformed into a marketing ploy. The Pentagon is still pushing to build Stealth bombers, but now with the added claim that they'd make great counterterrorist weapons. "Right now, I don't think [Richard Cheney] has a clear idea of what the military needs of the future are, of how important terrorism and low-intensity conflict will be," says Gen. Edward "Shy" Meyer, former Army chief of staff. Indeed, the history of America's efforts to develop commando units should serve as a cautionary tale to anyone who expects the Pentagon to make good on its promises of trimming down to lean, flexible fighting forces.

It sure is sunny in Curacao, where CNN has once again beaten the U.S. military to the scene. Standing beside the plane, one of the terrorists issues the group's demands in excellent English: the release of several members of the FARC being held in Colombia; the withdrawal of all American advisers and drug interdiction officers in Colombia and Peru; the destruction of all military equipment supplied by the United States to Colombia; and the pardoning of Gen. Manuel Noriega. One of the terrorists' demands—a full tank of fuel—has evidently already been met. The young man swears to begin killing one passenger every four hours. To underscore the point, his comrades dump a bloody corpse onto the tarmac behind him. Moments later, you learn that the dead man was a banker from Columbus, Ohio. The ball's in your court, Mr. President.

You glance around the room. Colonel Needels, the gung-ho NSC aide, is yelling into a telephone. It seems that for some reason Delta still is not airborne. Scowcroft grabs your arm, and you look back at the television screen. The 727's wheels are just leaving the tarmac.

For most of the eighties, America's counterterrorist forces were on the defensive, waging a covert war for survival. Their battles weren't fought in the streets of Beirut or on the shores of Tripoli, but in the halls of the Pentagon. "The enemies are not overseas grabbing hostages or this and that," explains a retired Green Beret colonel who follows special operations. "The enemies are the other branches of the services." Counterterrorist forces (and special operations forces generally) are a threat to the conventional military—a budget threat.

To survive the struggle for a slice of the department's funding, any defense project needs friends in high places willing to fight for it. Since special operations don't revolve around large units wielding sophisticated, expensive hardware in conventional conflicts, they forfeit the support of crucial advocates: defense contractors and most congressmen, who want to keep the assembly lines humming, and generals and admirals, who expect to command sizable forces that fight in the fashion in which they themselves trained. Still, thanks to a few powerful believers in counterterrorist and other special operations forces on the Hill, Congress kept appropriating money for them during the 1980s. But, somehow, the

Beyond Hijacking

Igor Khripunov, first secretary at the Soviet embassy in Washington, D.C., tells an interesting story. It seems that, given the spirit of the times, an Eastern Bloc country decided to cancel an order it had placed for 12 Soviet-built tanks, to the great disappointment of the management of the factory that had produced them. "They were rather desperate as to how to dispose of these tanks," says Khripunov. So they turned to an international "mediator" who found them a buyer, an unnamed, third country. The factory secretly shipped the tanks to the Black Sea, where they would have been picked up by the buyer's freighter—had the KGB not caught on. According to Khripunov, deals like this are the result of the build-down of the superpowers' defenses, which is already glutting the international arms market and driving down prices for sophisticated weapons. "It's now a buyer's market," he says. Welcome to the multipolar world.

Tanks, of course, are not likely to become the terrorist weapon of choice. Terrorists prefer lethal weapons that are easy to conceal and transport and are unlikely to backfire on their users. The proliferation of a variety of weapons that satisfy these requirements is increasing the chances that some will fall into terrorists' hands. Terrorism, measured in terms of numbers of acts committed, declined in the second half of the 1980s, as it did in the second half of the 1970s. However, the overall changes are disturbing. "There's a trend toward killing people," observes Bruce Hoffman, a terrorism expert with the Rand Corporation. The number of terrorist incidents increased by a third in the 1980s over the 1970s; meanwhile, the number of incidents that left people dead climbed 75 percent, and the total number slain by terrorists doubled.

There are more terrorist organizations today than there were 10 years ago, and they are more technically sophisticated. They are also more likely to play for higher stakes. Contrary to their reputation, terrorists tend to be conservative in their methods, relying on familiar tactics. And most experts used to think they wouldn't resort to weapons of mass destruction, because they had no goal that could justify the carnage. But now, more nationalist groups around the world are trying to carve out their own states. "All of a sudden, you have a demand of a high enough order that it makes sense," says Hoffman. In addition to plastic explosives, terrorists might turn to any of the following to push such demands:

➤CHEMICAL WEAPONS: These include mustard gas, cyanide, phosgene, and nerve agents like Tabun, Sarin, and the extremely lethal VX, stockpiled by the U.S. Army, a drop of which on the skin can kill. Today, 15 to 30 nations—ranging in size from China to Burma and including, of course, Libya—have chemical weapons. The superpowers control the vast majority of the world's chemical stockpiles: the U.S.S.R. has about 50,000 tons, the U.S. about 30,000. (Because it is trying to bolster its arsenal, the U.S., after pushing for worldwide controls on exports of the building blocks for these weapons, is now in the ironic position of having either to import more chemical agents or to sue Amermoney kept disappearing into the conventional military. Nowhere was this struggle for survival more apparent than in the commandos' efforts to get dependable transportation.

Whoosh-whoosh, crash-crash

Although the cause of failure of the rescue attempt in Iran lay deeper, it manifested itself most obviously in the miserable airlift. Of eight helicopters on the mission, one apparently suffered a cracked blade; another lost its navigational system; a crucial hydraulic pump failed on a third. That left only five helicopters to press on from the refueling site, Desert One. Since the mission required at least six, the rescue force tried to abort. A helicopter collided with a C-130 transport, sending up an enormous fireball. The heat was so intense that no one could retrieve the bodies or intelligence material that, discovered later in the wreckage, probably led to the executions of some pro-American Iranians.

Never again, right? Well, during the *Achille Lauro* affair in October 1985, American counterterrorist forces were held up for 18 hours when their airplane broke down; on reaching Egypt, they had no helicopter with enough range to get them to the scene. One month later, Palestinian terrorists hijacked an Egyptair plane with American passengers aboard to Malta. Three Air Force planes that were supposed to carry American commandos to the scene couldn't fly. Rather than wait any longer for advice, Egyptian commandos blasted the doors off the plane and killed 60 passengers.

"The primary culprit in this sad story, unfortunately," said Sam Nunn on the Senate floor in 1986, "is the Air Force." He called the state of special operations airlift—then no better than at Desert One six years before—"a shameful indictment of Air Force priorities." Indeed, as *Military Logistics Forum* reported that year, the Air Force had ranked airlift for special operations 59th on its list of priorities for funding in fiscal year 1985. Items 53 and 54 paid for ferrying top Air Force officers and officials—and 60 was a modernization program for airplanes used to spray Agent Orange in Vietnam. The Air Force resisted the drudgery of its special ops "trash-hauling" responsibilities just as it has resisted the close-support role it's supposed to play for troops on the front line.

ican companies to produce them.) The performance of these weapons tends to be unpredictable (because they are dependent on weather conditions) and large quantities are needed to do widespread harm; last year, the Iraqis used several thousand tons, delivered by ballistic missiles, to kill about 3,000 Kurds.

➤BIOLOGICAL WEAPONS: In military cost/benefit terms, these provide the broadest coverage area per pound of payload of any weapons system, including nuclear bombs. From one bomb, the dispersion of anthrax (which can be extracted from an infected cow and then grown) could kill up to a million people. Islands contaminated with anthrax in tests by Britain during World War II are still uninhabitable. Biological weapons also include cholera, plague, and Q fever; saxitoxin, a toxin made from shellfish, is said to be 1,000 times more potent than even the Army's VX. At least 10 developing nations are trying to make biological weapons. One advantage they have over chemical weapons is that the agents that produce them can be used for legitimate purposes, so export controls can't stop their spread; and unlike nuclear weapons, biological ones emit no telltale radiation that make them traceable. They can be delivered, like chemical weapons, by bombs or missiles, or in discrete quantities placed in ventilation systems. One significant drawback from the terrorist perspective is that they are very dangerous to handle.

➤NUCLEAR WEAPONS: These can achieve even more effectively than biological weapons the basic objective of terrorists—sowing terror. To do that, terrorists need only convince their target government that they can explode a bomb—and there's a fair amount of convincing information already in circulation; simply sending the relevant official a scrawled version of the diagrams printed years ago in *The New York Review of Books* or *The Progressive* could go a long way.

Still, there's nothing like the real thing. The recent attempt by Iraq—the same nation that used chemical agents on its own people—to buy trigger components for nuclear weapons demonstrates that vigorous export controls can slow, but probably not stop, a nation's efforts to get the bomb. Some nations have tighter controls than others; between 1977 and 1980 a West German businessman shipped an entire nuclear plant, piece by piece, to Pakistan. In 1987, a U.S. Task Force on Nuclear Terrorism concluded that with three or four specialists, a terrorist group could build a crude nuclear bomb; the trick lies in getting the fuel (to kick off their nuclear weapons program, the Israelis stole plutonium from the United States). No one knows if a terrorist group could steal an atomic weapon, since the command and control systems of the five to eight nations that probably stockpile them are classified. But consider this fact: One of the largest stockpiles of the Soviets' 33,000 nuclear weapons is outside Baku, the capital of Azerbaijan. The weapons stashed there may number in the thousands. Rebels in the area have already attacked one military installation housing nuclear weapons.

—J.B.

With some exceptions, the Air Force needed to modify or build only a few more planes and helicopters, models of which were already in service, to meet the special operations requirements; nevertheless, because they were few in number, special operations aircraft were expensive, so they would cut into other procurement programs. And those aircraft generally were not the sophisticated planes—the Stealth bombers and Advanced Tactical Fighters—that attract generals. "You're talking about prop planes, basically," says a congressional aide. "The people who make the decisions are mostly Air Force fighter and bomber pilots." Noel Koch, former deputy assistant secretary of defense for special operations and counterterrorist operations, is particularly bitter about Air Force resistance to building the helicopters crucial to counterterrorist missions. "They want all this fancy aircraft they can imitate with their hands," he says. "You know, 'whoosh, whoosh.'"

The "whoosh whoosh" mentality has meant that, despite Sam Nunn's "indictment" and despite an Air Force lieutenant general's confession before Congress in 1988 that less airlift was then available than at Desert One, the commandos still lack the aircraft they need to carry out their missions. They have at their disposal the same 10 AC–130 gunships and 14 MC–130 Combat Talons that they had before the mission to Iran. The newest Combat Talon airframe dates back to the mid-sixties. The Air Force blamed problems with the Combat Talon's high-tech radar for delaying efforts to build new planes during the eighties. But it wasn't exactly pushing to get those bugs ironed out; it assigned eight different managers to oversee the program in one four-year period.

Thanks mostly to congressional pressure, the commandos' air support is showing signs of improvement. Most promising, nine new "Pave Low" helicopters, which can carry troops at night into enemy territory, recently rolled off the lines. If all goes according to plan, 12 new gunships will be delivered between January 1992 and May 1993. The first new Combat Talon is scheduled to arrive this October; by August 1993—10 years after the initial contract was signed—the Air Force should have 22 new planes. Of course, that October delivery date is contingent on the Combat Talon passing some further tests. After a decade, the remaining problem sounds depressingly familiar. "There are some functions of the radar that have not yet been tested," says Col. Paul Beggs, the program director.

Just before the main U.S. forces attacked during Operation Just Cause in Panama, Delta Force commandos stormed a prison (El Carcel Modelo) to release a CIA operative named Kurt Muse, who had been held there since April. They freed Muse and bundled him onto a helicopter waiting on the roof. The helicopter took off—and promptly crashed, injuring the man the commandos were trying to save. Why did the chopper go down? "Overloaded—too much weight," says a retired special operations officer familiar with the raid. "If they pay attention to anything after all these years," he adds, shaking his head, "it should be airlift."

Already, Delta deployed once to Puerto Rico in hopes of nabbing a narcotraficante—and blundered into an FBI-DEA operation to grab the same man, reportedly almost starting a firefight.

With rivals like that . . .

You decide to grab a couple of hours of sleep while the hijacked jet, after buzzing Howard Air Force Base in Panama, continues north over Costa Rica. As you lie down, you reflect on that hostage crisis last November, when 12 Green Berets were trapped in the Sheraton Hotel in San Salvador by FMLN guerrillas. On Air Force One *you announced to reporters that our commandos had "liberated with finality" the Americans, only to learn that the FMLN had simply melted away, letting the Green Berets (surrounded for protection by the darn press!) slip out of the hotel. You were embarrassed when you learned the truth, but the bottom line was that you were pretty lucky—no one was hurt. You didn't feel nearly as lousy as you do now.*

Some aide wakes you with the news that, according to the pilot's radio broadcasts, the terrorists have murdered two more passengers. Delta, he says, has holed up at MacDill in Florida, waiting for their moving target to come to roost. After crossing into Mexican airspace, the hijacked plane suddenly cuts to the east over the Caribbean. Cuba seems to be the probable destination, but the pilot never communicates with Havana; he must be headed for Haiti or the Dominican Republic. You issue instructions to the ambassadors in each country: Make sure that jet isn't allowed to take off again; and get permission for Delta to attack. Supposedly, the relevant area specialists from State are on their way to the White House to help out.

The commandos' constant struggle to get adequate airlift reveals the fundamental liability of American counterterrorist forces. More than any other type of military operation, counterterrorist missions demand that a wide variety of tools—men and equipment drawn from several services and agencies—function together seamlessly. That they've never been able to is a telling demonstration of the gaps separating the many institutions, from the DEA to the Navy, responsible for U.S. national security. In a massive operation there's more room to accommodate interservice rivalries: Just about everybody—from special operations to the Marines to two of the Air Force's Stealth fighters (both of which missed their targets)—got a crack at Noriega's troops; and during the air raid on Libya in 1986, the Air Force and the Navy divided the Gulf of Sidra in half, so that each got the chance to strut its stuff. In such large operations, each service may perform well (as most did in Panama) or poorly (as both did over Libya); in general, they are less likely to stumble over each other (although, as in Grenada, they still can).

It's much harder to cram representatives from all the services into a small force moving quickly to counter a terrorist threat. Although the poor airlift and failure to rehearse an abort were the most obvious flaws of the Iranian rescue mission, the operation failed primarily because the planners tried to throw together Marine pilots flying Navy helicopters to rendezvous with Air Force planes carrying Army troops. They couldn't fuse all the elements—even though they had six months to do it.

Compare that operation with the most famous counterterrorist mission of the past 20 years: the Israeli raid on Entebbe airfield in 1976. In eight days, the Israelis managed to gather intelligence to support the raid; to rehearse the operation with a small band of paratroopers—a unit not specifically trained for counterterrorism; and to fly the team (with a Mercedes to disguise the first wave of attackers as Ugandan dignitaries) seven hours through a storm to land 30 seconds behind schedule in hostile territory precisely where the planners intended. The terrorists were all dead within three minutes of touch-down. Of course, there was a large element of luck working for the Israelis. And the mission was not nearly as complicated as the one the U.S. attempted in Iran. Still, the comparison seemed to demonstrate that while the Israeli armed services could pull off a seat-of-the-pants, flexible response to terrorism, the American armed services, as then constituted, couldn't.

At least, that's what the handful of special operations advocates in the Pentagon concluded after the Iranian fiasco. The less the counterterrorist forces had to depend on the rest of the military, the reasoning seems to have been, the more likely they were to succeed. Acting on the recommendations of the Holloway Commission, which investigated the mission to Iran, the Pentagon moved to institutionalize the counterterrorist forces, stationing Delta at Fort Bragg under the newly created Joint Special Operations Command (JSOC, pronounced "jay-sock") and setting up SEAL Team Six, stationed in Norfolk.

But as Air Force resistance to supplying transport demonstrated, those moves proved insufficient to protect the commandos from Pentagon turf wars. So in 1986, Congress took unprecedented steps to insulate the forces further by making three principal changes: it created a "unified command" (one that cuts across all four services) to coordinate all special operations forces, which include, for example, the Rangers and the Green Berets; it established an assistant secretary of defense for special operations and low-intensity conflict to support the unified commander; and it set up a coordinating board at the NSC to be composed of representatives from all the agencies, from the FBI to JSOC, that can help fight terrorism. Congress also recommended, but did not require, that the president appoint a deputy assistant for "low-intensity conflict," who would advise him on counterterrorism and counterinsurgency.

The armed services and the White House didn't exactly trip over each other rushing to comply. Reagan never appointed a deputy assistant. DOD stuck the new command in Tampa, Florida (from where, without a powerful lobby in the capital, it wouldn't be able to bother anyone at the Pentagon) and waited for more than a year to appoint key staff members. Using the time-honored divide-and-conquer strategy, it understaffed the office of the assistant secretary and put half his people in a building far from the Pentagon. Even then, DOD wasn't willing to take any chances; the first appointee to the new office had recommended against its creation. In the first year of its existence, the special advisory group to the assistant secretary committed only one recommendation to writing: that DOD should not implement the new legislation.

But since the unified commander of special operations now controls his budget, the forces are no longer captive to the spending priorities of the other services. The command can commission its own procurement projects, and the troops and their pilots are able to train together regularly. The new, unified command structure apparently is overcoming the interservice rivalries that dogged the Iran rescue attempt. That's the good news. The bad news is that the old inter*agency* roadblocks are as formidable as ever.

Divide and lose

The mechanisms that are supposed to guarantee that other agencies, like the CIA and the State Department, are cooperating with Defense have never worked well. Of all the changes mandated by Congress, the assistant secretary of defense for special operations and low-intensity conflict "is the key," says Maj. Gen. Richard Scholtes, former commander of JSOC. The assistant secretary is supposed to fight for support for all special operations forces, including for the assistance of other agencies, and to keep his eye on hot spots worldwide. Unlike his predecessors, James Locher, the new assistant secretary, strongly believes in the office he holds (in fact, as a staff member of the Senate Armed Services Committee, he wrote the legislation that created it). But the Pentagon's longstanding resistance to the office has left him at a serious disadvantage. "There is a mini-groundswell among those of us in the low-intensity-conflict-aware group that Mr. Locher has just disappeared off the radar screen in Washington," says a longtime special operations officer, now retired. "He doesn't have a job, he doesn't have an office." "There's not much expertise in those offices," says a former counterterrorist officer, "and they're moving too slowly." For his part, Locher maintains that he just needs more personnel and more time. "We're essentially taking the slow and steady approach here. Small staff, big bureaucracy."

If the NSC coordinating board were effective, then Locher's job would be a lot easier. Drawing on deputy secretaries from assorted agencies, the board would have the authority to shove foot-dragging departments into line. Bush has appointed a deputy assistant, but, beyond counterterrorism, he has also saddled him with some other area responsibilities, including "Africa, the United Nations, refugees, public diplomacy, the international affairs budget." Under Bush, unlike under Reagan, the NSC board has met—but only once.

For some of the agencies fighting the long-range war on terrorism, most notably the FBI, the existing level of coordination seems fine. Legislation in 1984 and 1986 expanded the mandate of the FBI to investigate terrorist acts against Americans abroad and to bring those responsible to justice. With some 20 warrants against terrorists worldwide, the bureau has made real progress. "If you look at the arrest of Hamadi in Germany, the arrest of Rasheed in Greece, the arrest of Younis off the coast of Cyprus . . . we have had a coordinated response to terrorist actions and activities against American citizens," says Oliver "Buck" Revell, associate deputy director of the FBI, naming some successes of his agency in the past few years. In a counterterrorist operation, the FBI comes in after the fact on its own initiative and, through slow and steady detective work in a stable environment, tracks down the criminals. Although that work is vital, it won't do much good if some nut in Manila suddenly claims to have placed an anthrax-dispersion bomb on the grounds of our naval base at Subic Bay.

As the U.S. government has come to rely more and more on the FBI to grapple with terrorists, it seems to have given up on the idea of a military option. Somehow, in conversations with people like Revell who deal with terrorism policy daily, the idea of using force has become an afterthought, pushed between parentheses. A failure of careful planning and intelligence support—that is, of vigorous leadership to coordinate planning and support—is what put it there. "There is a tremendous gap at the highest level—at the National Security Council level—of an integrated, interdepartmental unit that sets not just policy but planning directed against the terrorist threat," says a defense department official with many years' experience in special operations.

Why did it have to be Haiti? And how the heck did CNN get there so fast? Pascal-Trouillot has not only refused to allow Delta to operate there, she's refused to let the small, advisory Emergency Support Team land. And now the darn plane is being refueled again. The camera abruptly swings around to focus on two trucks and three jeeps that are driving across the tarmac toward the jet. "Oh no," mutters someone behind you. For the first time, with a profound sinking feeling, you realize how carefully planned this operation is. Sure enough, in plain view, 40 or 50 hostages are marched down one of those mobile staircases into the waiting trucks. As the trucks drive off, turn left at the airport gates, disappear, all you can do is watch. Two bodies are stretched out on the concrete at the bottom of the steps. Standing beside them, the lead terrorist is signaling for another press conference. Scowcroft is on the phone with Webster, trying to find out how good our human intelligence in Haiti is.

The military's troubles with getting reliable intelligence predate the formation of elite counterterrorist units. In 1970, intelligence reports that a large number of American POWs were being held in the Son Tay camp, about 20 miles north of Hanoi, sparked a massive, five-month planning effort, spearheaded by the Army: dozens of briefings, planning sessions, and studies, involving several thousand support staff. Finally, in November, the raid was launched from bases in Thailand. The mission was executed flawlessly. The Americans killed 25 of the enemy and withdrew without losing a man. But they withdrew without gaining any, either. The camp was empty—the POWs had all been moved, and no one in intelligence had noticed.

1 Big Mac, hold the mission

Five years later, when Cambodians captured the *Mayaguez* (an American container ship) and her crew, the military commanders again couldn't get the information they needed. After four days, Gerald Ford sent in the Marines, though he had no idea where the Americans were being held. While 18 soldiers were dying in an assault on the island near the anchored *Mayaguez,* the crew, having been released from a makeshift prison on the mainland, were returning unharmed to the ship. In all, 41 American soldiers died as a result of the mission. Sadly enough, one can draw an almost unbroken line from Son Tay to the *Mayaguez* incident to the Marine barracks bombing in Lebanon to the telephone conversation George Bush recently had with a crank caller claiming to be the president of Iran.

Judging by the major operations of the eighties, the problem is not only that American intelligence-gathering is poor; it's also that the military can't manage to tap into what intelligence exists. While American troops were stationed in Lebanon, the Pentagon ignored warnings from its own agents that, though good information on terrorists existed, no one was making sure it reached the Marines.

Poor intelligence hobbled the Grenada operation, which followed on the heels of the Marine barracks bombing. As Reagan himself said after the invasion, the American troops had "little intelligence information about conditions on the island." The operation's troubles can perhaps be chalked up to the haste with which it was planned. At the last minute the CIA's one source refused to return to the island. And no one, evidently, thought to call any of the numerous rich Americans who keep summer homes down there—or to ask some of the students' parents to call up their kids and ask them where they were staying. As a result, the invading troops didn't even know that the American medical students were scattered across

Grenada. It took Delta—and the rest of the invasion force—two days to round them up.

The Panama invasion was planned over several months, so the architects had plenty of time to put the lessons learned on Grenada into play—if they had tried. Unfortunately, the Pentagon has a remarkable resistance to the conditioned response: No matter how many times it gets burned, it keeps making the same mistakes over and over again. Despite the debacle in Grenada, the CIA wasn't involved in planning Operation Just Cause, and the military forces had no way to tap CIA sources once they went in, contributing to their inability to find Noriega. Poor intelligence-gathering had other, more tragic effects as well. One SEAL team was assigned to disable planes at the Paitilla airfield. But as they approached the planes, the SEALs ran into unexpectedly heavy gunfire; four were killed and eight wounded. "Intelligence service to the SEALs was abysmal," says one man familiar with the operation. "They didn't know what the threat was." He pointed out that, given the enormous American presence in Panama, it wouldn't have been difficult to check out the airfield's defenses. "They could have asked a couple of the neighbors."

In contrast, the two major American counterterrorist successes of the 1980s, neither of which directly involved the Pentagon's counterterrorist forces, went off cleanly thanks to reliable intelligence-gathering. Although they had murdered an American, the hijackers of the *Achille Lauro* in 1985 were granted safe passage by Egypt, once they agreed to release their hostages. But, as Caspar Weinberger said at the time, "We had very good intelligence"—possibly thanks to Israel. In international airspace, American F–14s intercepted the airplane carrying the terrorists, forcing it to land at the U.S. Navy's Sigonella air base in Sicily. In 1987, in a more significant but less famous operation, three agencies and the Navy cooperated closely to bring Fawaz Younis, a Lebanese terrorist involved in at least two hijackings, to justice. The DEA found an informant who could get close to Younis; the CIA taped Younis bragging about his terrorist past; the FBI, which managed the operation, lured Younis from Cyprus into international waters and literally put the cuffs on him; and a Navy pilot carried him on a record flight through international airspace to the United States. Younis is now serving 30 years in maximum security.

That type of smooth coordination has eluded the special operations forces, largely because they haven't attempted it. "They don't know how to use the systems and the methods available to them," says a DOD source. "The military always wants to build units that are self-contained." JSOC now maintains a large computer database that stockpiles vital information on terrorists, airports, and American embassies around the world. But for intelligence gathering, Delta and SEAL Team Six are supposed to depend principally on the "Intelligence Support Activity," a secret unit within the Army that must seek CIA approval for its operations abroad. As Steven Emerson reported in his book *Secret Warriors,* the ISA has helped out other agencies and other governments—for example, it helped the Italian government locate U.S. General James Dozier, who was kidnapped by the Red Brigades in 1981.

The counterterrorist forces, however, tend not to use the ISA for long-range planning. "In Special Operations, the difficult missions are the ones that take a lot of time, a lot of planning," says a former member of ISA. But the ISA won't do that sort of brain work. "There's a lot more tendency to go with Direct Action—DA missions, the Rambo type missions. It's the McDonald's of Special Operations—instant gratification." It's partly that attitude, he says, which has turned rescuing hostages in Lebanon into a "mission impossible." Lebanon wasn't always that way, however. Directed through the NSC to come up with a rescue plan in the summer of 1986, ISA cultivated sources among the Christian militia, who supplied information that consistently checked out. By the fall, JSOC felt it had good enough intelligence and a sound enough plan to get at least three of the hostages out. But as the first agents were about to be deployed, the White House canceled the operation—apparently because a rescue attempt would have interfered with the arms-for-hostages negotiations being run out of the NSC (which were about to be exposed).

Look Ma—no hands!

Since 1986, no such long-range planning has been attempted. "The Pentagon routinely maintains and updates literally tons of plans and target folders against precise targets within the Soviet Union," Lt. Col. William Cowan, a retired ISA officer who still divides his time between Washington and Beirut, observed in a recent talk at the Johns Hopkins School for Advanced International Studies. But, incredibly, no such plans—for retaliation or rescue—are kept to respond to terrorists. For example, when photographs of the hostage William R. Higgins, hanging, were distributed by terrorists to the media last summer, according to Cowan "There were no prepared contingency plans to deal with the instance of a hostage being killed." As a result, the most potent military force in the world could do nothing.

The blame for this failure can't rest just with the counterterrorist command; JSOC is able to focus on "McDonald's" operations because no one up the chain is leaning on them to conduct more involved planning (and leaning on agencies like the CIA to help out). Based on that planning, a high-level NSC "interdepartmental unit," says one DOD source, could "set out the intelligence gaps and then continue to monitor and coordinate the closing of those gaps." Instead, the CIA is making "a separate, general effort, not focused on a mission, to penetrate the infrastructure of the terrorist groups." In other words, they're doing their own thing, just as the unified command in Tampa is. That missing "interdepartmental unit" is, of course, supposed to exist—the NSC board Congress created four years ago that can't seem to find the time to meet.

Rather than insisting on better cooperation from the existing mechanisms, the unified commander is now lobbying to have responsibility for approving some counterterrorist intelligence operations moved to the Department of Defense. (Under existing rules, the director of the CIA has to sign off on every intelligence gathering mission abroad.) Anyone with drive who's worked in the Washington bureaucracy understands the temptation to reinvent the wheel rather than rely on the old agencies that seem long ago to have rusted over (even the Department of Energy has its own agents, gathering intelligence on terrorist threats to U.S. nuclear facilities). But the Pentagon, in creating the ISA, has already reinvented the wheel. The argument of the unified commander is now that by detaching that wheel from the car, we'll reach our goal more quickly. Even Cowan, who reportedly infuriated Dick Cheney by going to Beirut last winter as a private citizen, but with the knowledge of the unified commander and without Cheney's or the CIA's approval, doesn't support eliminating the coordinating mechanism. "I take no exception to that process. . . . Special operations can't be off doing whatever they want to do." The trick, he says, is to make the mechanism work faster. To get the car to its destination, the thing we really need is a driver.

"Here guys!" calls out a commando, as he makes his way down the aisle of the liberated plane with a laden tray. "Budweisers!"

Of butts and Buds

In 1985 terrorists hijacked TWA Flight 847 on its way to Rome from Athens. It was a sophisticated operation: To forestall an attack, the terrorists kept the plane shuttling between Beirut and Algiers and split off some of the hostages to be held inside Beirut proper. They killed one American, a Navy diver named Robert Stetham. The next year, Hollywood came along and offered its own revision of the tragedy, in a movie called *The Delta Force*, starring Lee Marvin (as the hard-boiled colonel) and Chuck Norris (as the laconic, butt-kicking major). It's a movie that can't help but pump up the Ronald Reagan in all of us: Delta's planes all work, their plans are foolproof, their dune buggies never break down, their rockets, launched from motorcycles, all blast their targets. The right piece of equipment, from collapsible ladders to wire cutters, is always at hand. (The one poignant bit of cinema verité: Israel's Mossad supplies the intelligence.) The hostages are divided in three groups in Beirut, but Delta gets 'em all. "They're our guys—they're Americans—they're *Delta Force*!" exults a hostage, on the cusp of rescue. Chuck, wordless, kicks the lead terrorist's butt, then blows him up with a motorcycle-launched rocket. "Here guys!" calls out a commando as he makes his way down the aisle of the liberated plane with a laden tray: "Budweisers!"

Ronald Reagan himself, ironically, had the unpleasant task of facing reality during the actual hijacking. The U.S. quietly gave in, asking the Israelis to release a large number of Shiite prisoners. When the hostages were freed, the president announced on television that "the United States gives terrorists no reward and no guarantees. We make no concessions. We make no deals." Tastes great—but, somehow, compared to the movie version, it's a lot less filling.

Today, something approximating the Hollywood ending to a counterterrorist mission, such as the Haiti scenario, seems a long way off. (Meanwhile, Hollywood has had a taste of reality. During the filming of *Delta Force II* last year, a helicopter crashed, killing five.) The Panama raid provides few good clues to Delta's capabilities, since it wasn't an operation that required the instant response and hair-trigger expertise of America's precision commandos. The planners had months to prepare the operation. Kurt Muse regularly had American visitors who could describe his surroundings, and his captors weren't standing over him waiting to shoot or to detonate a bomb.

Fear of trying

Obviously, the persistent lack of good interagency support doesn't bode well for a more off-the-shelf operation. But even the apparent success the command has had in overcoming interservice divisions by collecting all the military components of the counterterrorist forces under one roof has had its costs. In Israel, the vast majority of the top military officers (and many of the political leaders) have served with special operations. This high-level awareness of the needs and potential of the commandos has meant that the units most likely to be used to fight terrorists have never had to be insulated from the rest of the services to survive. As a result, when a unit is needed it can be called up, combined with support (aircraft, intelligence), and sent into action. In the U.S., Congress set the commandos apart and pumped money into them to protect them from the Pentagon, while the executive branch left them alone. This odd mix of attention and inattention has meant that as the unified command has settled into its new, more independent role, some of the bad bureaucratic habits of the conventional military have begun to creep into the unconventional forces.

Now that, in the words of one former member of the special operations command, special operations has become a "growth industry," it has attracted a cluster of one-, two-, and three-star generals. Under the supervision of the Unified Command (which boasts three generals), JSOC alone has two generals, controlling a relatively tiny force. More generals mean more money and more attention from the Pentagon. But most of the high-ranking officers in special operations are trained in conventional tactics, and aren't used to trying to think like terrorists.

There's a more subtle influence working against unconventional missions as well. "JSOC has become another one of those good places to go to get promoted out of," says the former officer. The promotions are important, because they serve to attract capable, ambitious young officers to the command. The problem, however, is that these officers are being moved up without having conducted or planned difficult missions. In a democracy, a great burden of counterterrorist operations is that, though they may yield a political windfall, they are extremely risky—a lesson that Jimmy Carter's experience carved into every politician's mind. A promotion process with no regard for missions attempted—or, more important, even planned—transfers that risk-aversion to the military leadership, leaving a system that's all checks and no balance.

The one clear American retaliatory attack against a terrorist power in the past decade—the bombing raid on Libya in 1986—was a case study in risk-aversion. Commandos sent in on the ground could have, like terrorists themselves, placed bombs beside precise targets. Instead, as David Martin and John Walcott reported in their book *Best Laid Plans*, a Pentagon "no-loss policy" dictated the entire mission, from the size of the force to the timing of the assault. The result was a virtual no-hit air attack: Many of the planes never dropped their bombs, and of those that did most missed their targets. Almost five tons of explosives landed in residential neighborhoods. And in the end, two American airmen were lost, anyway.

The combination of a growing bureaucracy and the tremendous fear of screwing up has encouraged JSOC to become, in the words of one expert, "so monstrous that from a security standpoint and an effectiveness standpoint it can't rise above its own weight." The Pentagon has concluded that the best time to strike terrorists is within 24 hours of the start of a hostage-taking; in a preemptive mission, the commandos would probably have to move even faster than that. But it usually takes Delta at least that long just to cross the Atlantic, if not to get off the ground. The United States seems incapable of quickly dispatching the small, flexible teams that could approach terrorists quietly in a "nonpermissive environment" (on hostile territory, as at Entebbe).

For example, consider the case of the hijacking of TWA Flight 847. JSOC took 24 hours to assemble the right equipment and get its commandos airborne. The force landed at Sigonella to wait for a chance to strike. Eventually, JSOC sent in six planeloads of equipment and about 400 people, including 50 support staff, to Sigonella and then to a British base on Cyprus. The press—and consequently the terrorists—didn't have much trouble catching on. During the *Achille Lauro* affair, JSOC once again sent a massive force to Sigonella, including a dozen transport planes and 500 men. "When we go to some place like Sigonella," said a retired officer, "we leave footprints that are so huge that it wouldn't take a genius in some control tower to figure out something was up." You might think that, given the number of times they've had to descend on that base and leave such "footprints," JSOC would just pitch camp there. In fact, the idea of "forward-deploying" commandos, so that they would be closer to their probable targets, has been discussed for years. After the hijacking of TWA 847, George Bush wisely recommended placing commandos overseas in his much-vaunted counterterrorism report for the president. But the U.S. government has never pushed friendly governments for the permission to do so.

Just say no to counterterrorism

As the bipolar world breaks up, probably the worst news about America's ability to deal with terrorism abroad is that the unified command and JSOC may be giving up on fighting terrorists altogether. Instead, like practically every other agency in the government, they want to start fighting drugs. Last fall, the command gained greater freedom when the 14-year-old ban on assassinations was narrowed, so that commandos who kill a drug trafficker in the process of trying to take him alive would now not be breaking the law. Drug missions are attractive, says a former counterterrorist officer, because they're faster and easier, and require less complicated planning; there's also a higher probability of action. But if the forces begin to focus on this role they "will wind up leaving the counterterrorism mission behind." Capturing drug lords is a very different operation than taking out terrorists. In fact, it's a mission that the commandos are poorly equipped to handle, since it requires more diplomatic finesse than lethal, irresistible force. Many of the drug lords live in friendly countries, surrounded by innocent people. The commandos train by pumping an average of 20,000 rounds of ammunition into rubber dummies each month. Dispatching them to grab a drug lord is a lot like . . . sending bombers after Qadaffi. The odds are pretty high for causing a lot of what is euphemistically called "collateral damage": killing the wrong folks.

The drug war, involving as it does many more agencies, is more poorly coordinated even than the war on terrorism. Already, Delta deployed once to a staging area in Puerto Rico in hopes of nabbing a narcotraficante—and blundered into an FBI–DEA operation to grab the same man, reportedly almost starting a firefight. Says the retired officer of the growing emphasis on chasing drug lords, "In the long run, somewhere, we're going to do something very stupid." And in the meantime, as terrorists strike against Americans—in South and Central America, in the Philippines, in India, in a thousand potential hot spots around the world—we're likely to keep doing nothing at all.

Trends and Projections of Terrorism

In many respects, attempting to see into the future of terrorism is as difficult as defining terrorism or setting its boundaries. None of these articles, all written by specialists in the field, is encouraging about checkmating or eliminating terrorism in the world today or in the future. They all seem to share the perspective that terrorism is a phenomenon that has persisted throughout human history and will continue to do so.

"The Growing Threat of Terrorism" makes the point that terrorism has a future and it is very much a technological one. That means terrorism is a growing rather than a diminishing threat, especially as far as the United States is concerned. There is a definite likelihood of an explosion in the incidence of domestic terror in the United States in the next decade.

"The Contrasting Ethical Foundations of Terrorism in the 1980s" assumes that terrorism in the 1990s will continue, and may be worse than the terrorism of the previous generation. That is because terrorists, increasingly inspired by fundamentalist religious ideals and motivations, are becoming more aggressive as well as more numerous.

The general thread running through all of these articles is the point that the United States needs to develop insight and perspective in regard to the direction of terrorism. A key factor will be the speed and effectiveness of America's adjustment to and anticipation of developments.

Looking Ahead: Challenge Questions

What are the basic trends in present-day terrorism, and what trends are projected for the future?

What factors explain the specific dynamics of terrorism today?

What factors explain any recent and perhaps temporary downturns in terrorist activity?

How is orthodox religion influencing the conduct and ethical codes of terrorists?

Unit 9

TERRORIST THREAT TO COMMERCIAL AVIATION

Brian Michael Jenkins

The author is an expert on aviation security for the Rand Corporation in Los Angeles.

On July 22, 1968, an El Al Boeing 707 flying from Rome to Tel Aviv was hijacked by three members of the Popular Front for the Liberation of Palestine. The hijackers ordered the plane flown to Algiers, where they demanded the release of an unspecified number of Arabs imprisoned in Israel, in return for the release of the passengers and crew. The Algerian government removed the hijackers to a nearby army camp but kept the hostages and took over the negotiations. The non-Israeli passengers were released, and later the three female flight attendants and the women and children passengers were also let go. The 12 remaining Israeli crew members and passengers were held until September 1, when Algeria released all of them. On the following day, Israel announced the release of 16 Arab prisoners as a humanitarian gesture. Clearly, a deal had been struck.

The 1968 hijacking set a tactical precedent. There had been hijackings before, to be sure, but this was the first terrorist hijacking in which political demands were made. From the terrorists' point of view, it was a success. An El Al plane had been seized. That would never happen again. It had not been necessary to kill any of the hostages. In future episodes, hostages would die. The Israeli government had yielded. When faced with future hostage incidents, Israel would take a harder line. Other groups imitated the Palestinians, and by 1970, hijacking had become a well–established terrorist tactic.

The 1968 hijacking was also a strategic innovation. With it, terrorists defined commercial aviation as part of their battlefield. In this episode, the hijackers justified their action on the grounds that El Al had carried spare parts for the IDF during the Six Day War and therefore was a legitimate target. Later, terrorist hijackers ceased to offer any justifications. The world would spend the next 20 years trying to keep commercial aviation off the terrorists' battlefield. How well has it succeeded?

Why Choose Airliners?

Commercial airliners attract terrorists for both political and operational reasons. Airlines are symbols of nations, almost as much so as embassies and diplomats, and certainly as much so as big corporations with brand names. Statistically, these are the two favorite targets of terrorists. Airlines are not only symbols of nations, they are scepters of nationhood.

On the operational side, airplanes are convenient *containers* of hostages. They can be seized and controlled by a few people. They are *portable* and can be flown anywhere in the world. On international flights, the majority of the hostages will usually share the nationality of the carrier, thus providing a direct challenge to that government. The presence of hostages of other nationalities will involve other governments as well and will complicate things, often to the terrorists' advantage.

Hijackings account for half of all terrorist attacks on commercial aviation. Terrorist attacks on commercial aviation – hijackings, sabotage of aircraft, attacks at airports, and bombings of airline ticket offices – account for 13 percent of all international terrorist incidents. But, because of the heavy casualties resulting from airline bombings and the bloody terminations of some hijackings, they account for 34 percent of all fatalities.

Looked at another way, the 2,015 deaths resulting from terrorist attacks on commercial aviation over the past two decades account for nearly 10 percent of all commercial aviation deaths.

In response to the wave of hijackings and airline bombings that occurred in the late 1960s and early 1970s, airport security measures were increased. In 1973, passenger screening was introduced on all flights in the United States. El Al adopted even more rigorous search procedures. Analysts developed *profiles* of the types of passengers who were most likely to hijack planes: persons to be watched more carefully. For a while, some countries, including the United States, also deployed armed security guards on the planes themselves, a practice that a number of airlines continue. Pilots are divided on the use of these air marshals. Some consider their presence a significant deterrent to hijackers, while others worry more about the safety of the passengers and the aircraft if a gunfight should erupt while the plane is in flight.

International Cooperation

The physical security measures have been matched by efforts to put pressure

Reprinted by permission of the *IDF Journal* (Israel Defense Forces Journal), Fall 1989, pp. 11-12, 14, 16, 18.

on countries granting asylum to hijackers. During the 1968 El Al incident, the International Federation of Airline Pilots Associations as well as several airlines threatened to suspend flights to Algeria if the hostages were not released. A prerequisite to progress on the international front was a change in attitude. Until terrorists adopted the tactic for their own ends, hijackings were often seen in a positive light, as a means of escape from behind the Iron Curtain. The spate of hijackings to Cuba in the 1960s, however, caused people to review their thinking, and the later terrorist hijackings accelerated the shift. All hijackers had to be punished. If that meant people had to find another way to escape Communism, it was the price the West would pay to achieve international cooperation.

New conventions to guarantee the trial and punishment of terrorists who hijack or place bombs aboard airliners were negotiated and signed. They have been widely ratified and now represent one of the few areas where there is considerable international cooperation. A 1988 protocol extends the measures to cover airports as well as airliners. Governments also exerted direct pressure on organizations like the PLO to abandon hijackings and bombings of aircraft as a component of their armed struggle.

What were the results? Hijackings declined from 151 incidents, whether successful or not, between 1968–1970, to 56 incidents between 1971–1973, to 17 between 1974–1976. This represents an overall drop of nearly 90 percent. Most of the hijackings were still getaways in which the hijackers wanted only to change the destination of the airplane. Only 20 percent of the ostensibly politically–motivated hijackings were carried out by actual terrorist organizations. These declined too, from 27 in 1968–1970, to 25 in 1971–1973, to 13 in 1974–1976. This is an overall decline of nearly 50 percent. Terrorist hijackings remained at this level until the second half of the 1980s, when there was another drop.

Israeli Aviation Security Companies

The need to provide adequate security in Israel has resulted in the establishment of a number of Israeli security companies, including those specializing in aviation security. Three such companies are ICTS, ISDS, and MIPHA.

ICTS – Established in 1982, ICTS (International Consultants on Targeted Security Ltd.), is a world leader in providing security consulting services. The company's objective is to help corporations, organizations, government facilities, and individuals face and respond to terrorism, white collar crime, kidnapping, and other actions that may threaten them. The company was founded and is headed by a select group of former military commanding officers, veterans of government intelligence and security agencies, and business people.

ICTS is a specialist in aviation security. Due to the complex nature of airports and commercial airliners, they require special security measures and procedures that allow them to conduct daily operations without interfering with critical time schedules. In order to meet these demands, ICTS bases its security plans on a *screening* principle that focuses on the potential problem passenger, cargo shipment, etc. This method, when used in passenger security checks, is known as the *profile* method.

ICTS serves clients worldwide, and among their clients are three of the largest U.S. airlines with international routes.

ISDS – Established in 1982, ISDS (International Security and Defense Systems) offers consulting services in aviation security and provides training for security officers and personnel. ISDS's objective is to provide integrated security consultancy to public and private bodies through a security concept that stresses the prevention and deterrence of threatening acts. The company also supplies clients with a complete security package that includes equipment, manuals, training, and project establishment.

ISDS also offers a course entitled "Air Transport Protection for Security Officers." The course, held in Israel three times a year, covers a variety of areas of concern to aviation security officers including developing strategy in countering terrorist actions, gathering and protecting information and intelligence, and using air transport protection equipment.

ISDS has set up security systems in 17 countries throughout the world, and developed the security concept for the 1992 Summer Olympics to be held in Barcelona, Spain.

MIPHA – MIPHA International Ltd. specializes in a broad spectrum of security services including comprehensive consulting and training services as well as joint ventures covering every aspect of effective security. In aviation security, the company offers expertise in upgrading current airport security procedures, inspecting passengers and objects, conducting training programs for airport personnel, and providing aircraft security both on the ground and in the air.

Attack at Ben–Gurion

At the same time that terrorist hijackings were declining, terrorists were altering their tactics and shifting to easier commercial aviation targets. Terrorist attacks at airports began in 1972 with the bloody assault on passengers at Ben–Gurion Airport near Tel Aviv by Japanese terrorists, allies of the Palestinians. Twenty–five people were killed, and more than 70 were wounded, many of whom turned out to be Puerto Rican pilgrims on their way to visit the Holy Land. This episode shocked the world both by its ferocity and by its international character. How is it, people asked, that Japanese come to Israel in the name of Palestinians to kill Puerto Ricans? Terrorist assaults at airports increased during the following years. During the next decade (1973–1982), terrorists carried out 39 such attacks. Terrorist bombings of airline offices also increased beginning in 1974, and for 10 of the next 15 years, bombings at ticket offices outnumbered terrorist attacks on airliners. Overall, terrorist attacks of all types against commercial aviation increased, reaching a high point between 1980–1982. There has been another decline since 1983.

Despite the decline, hijackings remain a serious problem. They can be divided into two types: those in which terrorists hijack an airliner as a means of escape and perhaps to obtain a moment's publicity for their cause (41 percent of all terrorist hijackings), and those involving political demands and sometimes lengthy negotiations (59 percent). As security measures have required would–be hijackers to make a greater investment and take greater risks, terrorists want more in return. In recent years, hijackings have become more likely to involve demands beyond destination changes. Of the 13 terrorist hijackings in the last five years, 11 have involved demands beyond asylum or publicity.

Terrorist hijackings are also somewhat more likely to involve bloodshed than ordinary hijackings. Fatalities occurred in 23 percent of the terrorist hijackings, compared with 16 percent of the non–

terrorist hijackings. This is somewhat misleading, however. In ordinary hijackings, it is often the hijacker who is killed, while in terrorist hijackings, passengers are more likely to be counted among the casualties. It seems that terrorist hijackings are getting bloodier. Of the 13 hijackings carried out by terrorists during the past five years, seven incidents (53 percent) resulted in fatalities.

Crash of Pan Am 103

The crash of Pan Am flight 103 in Lockerbie, Scotland in December 1988 underlines the second major component of the terrorist threat to commercial aviation. Sabotage of aircraft is the biggest terrorist threat today. Since 1969, terrorists have placed or attempted to place bombs aboard commercial airliners on at least 46 occasions. Eleven of these have caused crashes, resulting in the deaths of 1,016 persons. However, not all the planes crash. In 1986, four passengers, including a mother and her infant daughter, were blown out the side of a TWA airliner over the Adriatic Sea. Despite the damage to the hull, the pilot was able to bring the plane down safely, but the incident still resulted in four fatalities.

In all, 1,128 persons have died during the past 20 years as a result of bombs going off aboard airliners in flight or in cargo containers on the ground. This represents 20 percent of all of the deaths in international terrorist incidents during the past two decades. There is a large number of fatalities in each incident: 329 were killed by a terrorist bomb on an Air India flight in 1986, and 115 were aboard the Korean Airlines flight brought down by a bomb in 1987. The fatalities attract intense media coverage and cause public alarm. Eleven of the 25 worst incidents of international terrorism, measured by the number of fatalities, resulted from terrorists planting bombs on commercial airliners. The other episodes were mainly car bombings. The threat of bombings, more than hijackings, now drives airline security.

The passenger screening procedures developed in the 1970s do not provide adequate protection against terrorist bombs. Standard X–ray machines and metal detectors will not necessarily alert operators to the presence of explosives. However, research into explosives–detection has accelerated during the last few years, and several technologies are being developed. One depends on the characteristic vapor emissions made by certain explosives. A machine using this technology can detect the most minute trace of explosives in luggage or on a person. Another device analyzes the unique *backscatter* patterns created when different materials are bombarded with neutrons.

Detection Technologies

The challenge has been to develop technologies that can accurately indicate the presence of explosives and that are still reliable and practical, given the tremendous volume of passengers and baggage that must be inspected at every major airport. The current vapor–detection machines require up to one–and–a–half minutes to detect the presence of explosives. At that speed, even with two machines, it would take several hours to check the passengers and baggage on a single Boeing 747 jumbo jet. Canadian officials look forward to an improved model that will require only three seconds per passenger, but even with a prototype in hand, deployment of bomb detection technology at airports around the world is still several years away. In the meantime, although improved X–ray machines can now alert operators to the possible presence of explosives in a suitcase, the most reliable procedure remains the tedious hand search of all luggage.

We may also want to think about additional ways to secure aircraft against bombs, for example, by hardening cargo holds to sustain or deflect explosions or by shielding vital controls to reduce the chances of an explosion resulting in loss of control and the crash of the airliner.

Bombings of airline ticket offices may be viewed as a substitute for attacks on airliners, a "poor man's" hijacking, a way to make a political point without running the risks. In contrast to airline sabotage, bombings of airline ticket offices are mainly symbolic forms of attack. Of 267 bombings, only eight incidents, or 3 percent, involved fatalities.

Bombings provide an indirect indicator of the threat to commercial airliners. They tell us which airlines terrorists would attack if security measures were less stringent. Terrorists, for example, have difficulty getting near El Al airliners, but they frequently attack El Al ticket offices. This is not to say that all terrorists planting bombs in front of airline ticket offices would hijack or blow up airliners if they could. One of the attractions in setting off a bomb at a ticket office is that casualties can be avoided. But these bombings do reflect grievances, anger, a willingness to resort to violence, and in some cases, a willingness to cause casualties. Thus, it could be argued that those airlines whose ticket offices are bombed most frequently are those whose aircraft are at greatest peril.

Who Gets Hit?

Who gets hit most often? Ten airlines account for 57 percent of all airline ticket office bombings. In descending order of frequency, these are Aeroflot, Pan American, Air France (and affiliated French carriers), El Al, THY (Turkish Airlines), Lufthansa, British Airways, Saudia, TWA, and Swissair.

How does this profile compare with attacks on airliners? Counting both terrorist hijackings and incidents of aircraft sabotage over the past 10 years (1979–1988), there have been 62 incidents, which point to some differences. First of all, the threat is diffuse. Thirty–two airliners from 30 countries have been attacked by terrorists. Air India heads the list, followed by Middle East Airways, Pan American, Air France (and other French carriers), Kuwaiti Airlines, El Al, Viansa (Venezuela), Avianca (and other Colombian carriers), Sahsa (Honduras), THY, and American Airlines, the last four with two attacks each.

Looking at both terrorist and ordinary hijackings, plus incidents of aircraft sabotage during the past five years, the 64 incidents give a somewhat different picture. Here, Middle East Airways heads the list, followed by Aeroflot, Iranair, Air India, and Air France. American carriers were targeted in nine of the 64 incidents, or 14 percent of the total.

Security consultants sometimes advise their clients to avoid certain carriers, certain routes, or certain airports to decrease their risk of becoming a victim of terrorism. To the extent that this advice is based on the historical record, I tend to be somewhat skeptical. As one can see from the preceding discussion, how secure an airline appears to be depends a great deal on how far back one wants to count and on how one counts. Does an unscheduled detour to Havana count the same as a terrorist hijacking to Beirut? Merely counting how many times an airline has been hijacked or bombed, without taking into account the number of its flights, may also give a misleading impression.

With these limitations in mind, and looking only at the period 1981–1988, one could safely tell frequent flyers to try to avoid, if they can, domestic flights in Iran, Poland, the Soviet Union, China, and Central America. Since 1981, eight flights out of Miami have been diverted to Havana. Flights from airports in Beirut, Athens, New York (another jumpoff point for hijackings to Cuba), and Frankfurt have each been targets of more than one terrorist attack. Attacks on U.S. carriers account for 19 percent of the total number of incidents, most of them being non-terrorist hijackings.

Who Hits Them?

Who are the adversaries? Individuals, groups, or persons not known to be affiliated with any terrorist group account for the largest share: 32 percent of all attacks on airliners since 1968. Arabs operating on behalf of various Palestinian groups and other Middle Eastern groups account for about 22 percent of the total. Various Latin American groups account for about 10 percent. The remaining attacks have been carried out by diverse European and Asian groups.

Focusing on terrorist hijackings and sabotage of aircraft yields a different picture. Various Palestinian organizations have claimed responsibility for 24 percent of all terrorist hijackings. Shi'ite extremists account for 12 percent. Other Middle Eastern groups account for another six percent. Together, they account for 42 percent of all terrorist hijackings. Palestinian, Shi'ite, and other Middle East organizations account for 45 percent of the sabotage incidents.

What are we likely to see in the future? Perhaps fewer, but deadlier and more sophisticated terrorist hijackings. The 1988 hijacking of Kuwaiti Airlines Flight 441 illustrates the problem. In that case, the hijackers were familiar with the cockpit and ground procedures and apparently even the tactical ploys used by negotiators, which they took steps to counter. The challenge, then, will be how to deal with hijackers who know accepted procedures and tactics.

Sabotage of aircraft is the most serious problem today. Even though it accounts for relatively few incidents, these incidents cause great numbers of casualties and widespread alarm. As their sophisticated devices show, terrorists are familiar with current security measures, and their bombs are becoming increasingly sophisticated. If the frequency of incidents like the crash of Pan Am 103 increases, passengers, particularly business flyers, may seek safe travel in corporate aircraft, or *membership* flights chartered by consortiums of companies that will vet and clear passengers beforehand.

Publicize the Problem?

Threats against airlines will remain a major problem. Should they be publicized? I think not. The fact is, airlines receive hundreds of threats. All are scrutinized. When they are specific, a flight may be delayed while the aircraft is searched. When they are general, security measures may be increased, depending on an assessment of credibility. We probably need to devote more attention to how to do this. But to publicly post threats would only inspire the pranksters, the fanatics, and the lunatics, thus multiplying the number of threats, increasing the noise level, and making it more difficult than it already is to assess credibility. Publicizing threats would tell passengers everything, but would provide them with no information. It's a bad idea.

Increased scrutiny of passengers and luggage will make it more difficult to smuggle weapons or explosives aboard aircraft through the *front door.* In some of the recent incidents, terrorists are suspected of having had confederates among the ground crew or of posing as members of flight crews or ground staff. We will have to pay more attention to locking the *back door,* that is, to controlling access to planes and cargo. This poses a major challenge. Major airports may have 25,000 to 50,000 workers. Aircraft cannot easily be sealed. Unlike boarding passengers, there are few obvious chokepoints.

With these trends in mind, we come to the most pressing question. Just how safe is air travel? More than 200 million passengers flew internationally in 1987. Two hundred fifty-nine of them died in the crash of Pan Am 103. The 2,015 fatalities since 1968 would give us a probability range of one chance in a million to several million of being killed by terrorists while flying on a commercial airliner or passing through an airport. One is in greater danger of being killed by a falling object. Several hundred million persons fly domestically each year in the U.S. alone. The odds against death at the hands of terrorists there would be even more remote. The best advice to frequent business flyers is still, drive carefully on the way to the airport.

This article was presented at the First International Seminar of Aviation Security.

The Growing Threat of Terrorism

Marvin J. Cetron

Marvin J. Cetron is founder and president of Forecasting International, Ltd., 1001 North Highland Street, Arlington, Virginia 22210. This article is excerpted from American Renaissance: Our Life at the Turn of the 21st Century, *co-authored by Cetron and Owen Davies, which was published by St. Martin's Press in August 1989 and will be available from the Futurist Bookstore.*

> International terrorism will continue to grow into the twenty-first century. Increasingly, home-grown terrorism will be a problem for the United States.

There can be no doubt that terrorism will continue into the next century. It is the primary way in which the weak and disenfranchised can ensure that their voices will be heard and that governments will feel the pressure to meet their demands, even when they are counter to the will of the majority. It is a war of psychology and perception. The terrorist's message to the targeted government is, "No matter how big and powerful you are, no matter how small we are, we can hurt you if you don't do what we want."

Bombing, assassination, and kidnapping will continue because they carry the terrorist message effectively. These crimes instill fear in the populace, because they never know when they will be hurt. As a result, citizens question the true power of their government.

Terrorist attacks are effective because the terrorist can use any damage done anywhere to get his or her point across. Since it is impossible to guard every person, every bus, or every place of business in a country all the time, the terrorist merely has to wait for a convenient moment to strike. No act of terrorism is ever "senseless," since a climate of fear and mistrust is precisely what the terrorist wants.

In 1986, the U.S. Joint Chiefs of Staff lumped all forms of Third World violence together under the term "low-intensity conflict." According to the joint chiefs, "Low-intensity conflict is a limited, politico-military struggle to achieve political, social, economic, or psychological objectives. It is often protracted and ranges from diplomatic, economic, and psychological pressures through terrorism and insurgency. Low-intensity conflict is generally confined to a geographical area and is often characterized by constraints on the weaponry, tactics, and level of violence." Former Secretary of Defense Caspar Weinberger says that "low-intensity conflict [is] the most immediate threat to free-world security for the rest of this century."

Since the 1960s, low-intensity conflict has undergone a worldwide revolution in its scope and organization. The United States and Great Britain organized special operations military and paramilitary forces to deal with insurrections in the Third World, while the Soviet Union began teaching the Palestine Liberation Organization how to fight effectively after Israel's victory in the Six-Day War in 1967.

Terrorist activity has always had its roots in specific political or religious conflicts within specific geographic areas. But when nations saw the chance to extend their spheres of influence without expending their own troops, they fostered this covert warfare, raising levels of training and even developing weapons specifically for terrorism and counterinsurgency. The quantum leap in the level of terrorist activity from 1960 to the present — both in numbers and sophistication — has left the superpowers struggling to catch up.

New Weapons

The traditional weapons of the terrorist were cheap, readily available, and would do the job. They ranged from the knife to the small automatic rifle to the plastic explosive. But now that they have the money and technical facilities of whole countries to back them, terrorists have a whole new range of weapons to use against a completely new set of targets:

- **Stinger hand-held rockets.** Small, light, and powerful, Stingers can be used — with almost no training — to knock out an airplane.

From *The Futurist*, July/August 1989, pp. 20-24. Excerpted from *American Renaissance: Our Life at the Turn of the 21st Century.* Copyright © St. Martin's Press, 1990. Reprinted by permission.

• **Computer viruses.** Viruses are programs that destroy data stored in a computer's memory. It is relatively easy for a programmer to write a program that will tell the computer to erase its memory or otherwise render its programs useless. What makes these viruses so hard to trace is that they often contain timing instructions, so that it might be months between the time a virus is introduced and the time it is triggered. The programmer simply embeds the codes into an otherwise harmless program, then tries to get the program into a victim's computer.

• **Electromagnetic pulse generators.** Put a pulse generator on the power line to an important computer, and the pulse will wipe out the data in the computer's memory.

• **Chemical and biological weapons.** Chemical weapons range from old-fashioned poison in the water and nerve gas to a new Liquid Metal Embrittlement agent (LME). Applied with a felt-tip type pen, LME is a clear, invisible substance that changes the chemical structure of a metal so that it is no longer resilient and flexible. The result: The metal can fracture under stress. Trucks, airplanes, or bridges would be vulnerable to catastrophic failure without advance warning.

The standard chemical weapons are frightening because they can be concocted from cheap and readily available materials. Common pesticide and fertilizer components can be used to make poison gas, while deadly chlorine gas can be obtained from the electrolysis of ocean water.

Some 20 countries are now developing chemical weapons, and at least 10 countries are working on biological weapons, according to CIA Director William Webster.

Chemical and biological weapons may become the "nuclear weapons" of small countries, since they are weapons of mass destruction that are easier to come by than nuclear weapons. Perhaps industrialized nations should consider banning from their schools and universities students from developing countries manufacturing biological or chemical weapons, since you can't produce these without a substantial technical education.

• **Nuclear weapons.** Technically, it is horrifyingly easy to produce an atomic bomb: Actual plans for building a bomb have been printed several times. The hardest part is obtaining the teaspoonful of weapons-grade plutonium that will produce an explosion the size of that produced by the Hiroshima bomb. Nuclear energy plants produce this substance as waste material. Though waste-storage sites and transports are closely guarded, there is at least 100 pounds of plutonium missing from various sites and shipments around the world. That's not very much over the course of the 40+ years since the development of nuclear power, but it means that it is possible that there are terrorists in possession of both the knowledge and the materials to build atomic bombs.

The Coming Rise in Domestic Terror

The biggest change in low-intensity conflict in the next decade will be an explosion in the incidence of domestic terror in the United States. Security measures currently in place around the world will help slow the spread of international terrorism, but the frustrated in the United States will begin to take their cue from terrorists abroad. Some of the groups that have already begun terrorist-type actions include:

• **Antiabortionists.** Planned Parenthood offices and women's health clinics that offer abortion have already been bombed. Attacks will get worse because religious groups believe that God's law puts them above civil law and other people's rights.

• **Drug dealers.** Terrorism by drug dealers will aim at breaking the resistance of city and state governments and law enforcement agencies. It will be sponsored by organized crime and "disorganized crime" — the kind of crazed violence observed in crack users that stuns those who haven't seen it. The methods may be inspired by the international terrorists, but the organized-crime armies have been trained and weaned in Colombian drug wars.

The U.S. government can muster tremendous resources to fight terrorism within its borders, and national leaders have always had to deal with threats from other countries. Few city mayors or state governments, however, are psychologically prepared or fiscally and strategically able to deal with sustained pressure from terrorism.

• **Counterterror from the right.** In Colombia, people who got tired of police inability to deal with ter-

Unlikely Terrorist Acts

Marvin Cetron says there are five terrorist attacks that are unlikely to occur in the near future in the United States, since such actions would be absolute acts of war, requiring high-power, violent retaliation:

1. There will be no attack on the U.S. Congress.
2. There will be no nuclear attack on any U.S. city.
3. Though there will be threats, no one will poison the water supply of a whole U.S. city.
4. There will be no well-coordinated, general attack on transport (e.g., blowing up railroad bridges), communications (destroying telephone centers), or the electrical power system (destroying many line transformers) to cripple a large part of the United States. Though small-scale individual attacks could occur at any time, a coordinated nationwide attack is beyond the means of most likely terrorist groups in the next decade.
5. No violent attacks or hostage taking will take place at TV or radio stations or newspaper offices, because terrorists know they need media publicity. The American media stick together against all outside attack.

rorism have formed death squads to "help out" the police. The same thing could happen in the United States.

New Targets

Many vital industries and resources are staggeringly vulnerable to attack. Even if there were the will to do so, it would be expensive and inconvenient to guard every office and factory. But some changes will have to be made to reduce their vulnerability to crippling terrorist attacks.

Computer attacks already account for some 60% of all terrorist attacks in the world. Twenty-four computer centers were bombed in West Germany in one year. Italy's Red Brigades and France's Action Directe have both targeted computer systems in Europe. It is only a matter of time before someone takes advantage of U.S. computer vulnerability.

France and Spain have already felt the terror when antinuclear groups broke into nuclear plants to protest their operation. These groups only shut down the power, but there is the threat of reactor meltdown and widespread radiation damage due to terrorist attacks on these facilities.

Only two pipelines supply virtually all the natural gas to the northeastern United States. Both are regulated by high-pressure pumps that are manufactured in foreign countries, with replacement times of more than a year. Both pipelines are essentially unprotected.

Two bridges, one over the Ohio River near Cincinnati, the other over the Potomac River near Washington, D.C., handle all the north–south railroad traffic in the eastern United States. Neither is guarded.

Fewer than 10 regional switching stations control virtually all the telephone communications in all the large cities of the United States. In May 1988, one of these stations caught fire in Hinsdale, Illinois, a suburb southwest of Chicago. It is an automated facility, with a single watchman on site and an overseer who monitors warning lights in a facility 100 miles away. By the time the technicians actually believed their warning lights and summoned help, the station was destroyed, plunging one-third of all western Chicago phones into silence. Because the station was between O'Hare Airport in Chicago and the regional air traffic control center in Aurora, Illinois, O'Hare was without much of its air traffic controls for hours.

Even with round-the-clock work crews, it took three months to repair the station. Phone service was not fully restored until August. With no phone transmission of any kind, many computer networks also went down. Only cellular phones using satellite transmission, such as car phones, were unaffected.

The telephone switching station fire points to a vexing problem for the increasingly high-tech industrial United States. There are fewer and fewer individuals who monitor the safety of the nation's highly automated industrial facilities. The human overseers who are there have enough experience with faulty equipment that they often distrust malfunction signals. The telephone overseer in Illinois disregarded his first "fire" signal because there was an electrical storm between his office and the switching station, and he knew that could cause a false display. Another problem is that these automated systems often have security systems that are tied to regular electric and phone transmission lines. If something happens to the electrical or telephone system, the security people are often "left in the dark."

Fighting the Plague

An effective war against terrorism must be fought on two fronts: the military and the political. Until very recently, the U.S. approach to fighting terrorism was completely defensive and reactive. According to Admiral Bobby Ray Inman, formerly chief of the CIA, "As late as 1980, there was no focused, ongoing intelligence-collection effort to try to pin down the scale of terrorist activity." In 1981, the Reagan administration set about correcting this situation. The president called on the State Department, the CIA, the FBI, and the military to pool their resources. They formulated strategies for dealing with terrorists and insurgents. From this brain trust came the notion of low-intensity conflict.

Police, military, intelligence, and security people are on alert now around the world. They look for concealed weapons, check for correct ID and passports, and watch borders for movements of known terrorists or suspicious characters. These measures should help prevent incidents like the bombing of the Marine barracks in Lebanon.

In combating terror, it is important to recognize that terrorists themselves differ widely in their motives and level of commitment. On a practical level, this means that some activists will be more open to dissuasion and more reachable than others. We can stop some violence — and we can tone down other acts — by our response to terrorist actions.

Fawaz Younis is a terrorist. He was the leader and spokesman for the group that hijacked and destroyed a Royal Jordanian airliner, and he took part in the hijack of TWA Flight 847, in which a U.S. Navy diver was killed. Younis was tracked by the FBI and CIA, then set up and lured into a trap. Arrested on international waters off Cyprus, Younis was brought by the Navy to stand trial for his crimes and was recently found guilty in a U.S. court. However, questions about the method of his arrest and the conditions under which he made a confession raised the serious possibility that Younis might be freed by a judge before he ever faced trial.

Alberto Franceschini represents a different type of activist — one much more like the type we are likely to find within the United States. One of the three founders of the Red Brigades, the terrorist organization that killed Italian Prime Minister Aldo Moro in 1978, Franceschini was betrayed and arrested. In prison, with time to analyze his experience, Franceschini decided to give up terrorism. "Armed struggle was useless," he says, "because Italy wanted not a revolution but simply to live well." Franceschini contrasts his Red Brigades with the Basque separatist movement, which has "a broad social base extending from the bourgeoisie to the proletariat . . . it is an independence movement, with deep cultural and historical roots, something the Red Brigades lack."

If we can better understand these different types of terrorism, we will be better able to deal with them. Younis is typical of international terrorism today. He is motivated by deep-seated nationalism and religion; for that reason, his political movement has widespread popular support. There was little question of his guilt, since he freely admitted his part in terrorist activities. Convicted in his trial, he will likely be seen by his supporters as a martyr to his cause. If he had been set free, he would have declared it a victory for his movement and vindication of their point of view, not a failure of the U.S. justice system.

"If ever we let known terrorists go free because of a technicality of the law, we only convince them further of the rightness of their cause."

The types of terrorists likely to surface in the United States in the next decade will be closer to the Franceschini type than to that of Younis. Like the Italians, most Americans want only to live well, so that violent activists must by their nature be tiny groups trying to impose their extreme views on the majority. In order to defeat terrorism, that majority must be unflinching in the face of extreme, unrelenting, painful attacks.

The justice system must never waiver in dealing as harshly as possible with those who resort to violence to enforce their will. Groups that advocate or condone violence must never be underestimated or overlooked. Granted, the most deeply committed of the terrorists will never be fazed by the threat of punishment. But group members may be persuaded to abandon violence. An activist faced with life in prison for terrorist acts may well decide that the risk is not worth the possible benefit gained.

The most dangerous of homegrown activists in the United States are, by this reasoning, the collection of groups with religious motivation, such as the antiabortionists. These groups, which have already been involved in a number of violent incidents around the United States, take God's word as their stepping-off point. It is but a small step for the most-fanatical antiabortionists to say that their stance is not merely prolife but pro-God; for them, violence, even murder, may no longer be a crime but a necessary if regrettable means to a necessary end. In this, they have much in common with Moslem fundamentalists, who swore to kill writer Salman Rushdie when his novel *The Satanic Verses* seemed to grant their religion less respect than they felt it was due.

If ever we let known terrorists go free because of a technicality of the law, we only convince them further of the rightness of their cause. If ever we negotiate with kidnappers, we only demonstrate our weakness and their correct selection of a target.

Former French Prime Minister Jacques Chirac made a statement about dealing with terrorists several years ago:

> When you negotiate with people who take hostages, you are obliged, in the negotiation, to give something. It may be just a little . . . but you have to give something. Once you have given something, the kidnapper gains from his action. So what is his normal . . . reaction? He does it again, thinking that it is a way of obtaining what he cannot obtain by other means.
>
> So you get caught in a process. . . . You can get two, three, or four hostages freed. But you give the kidnapper an inducement to seize another four, five, or six. So it is an extraordinarily dangerous and irresponsible process. That's why I don't negotiate.

Unfortunately, Chirac forgot his high principles when he was losing a presidential election and negotiated the release of three French citizens held captive in Lebanon in return for paying off a French loan in Iran.

Winning the War Against Terrorism

War with terrorists is a bit of a high-wire act. A country's response to a terrorist raid must be tough enough to encourage its allies and to convey the message that the country won't stop fighting after the first black eye. And the terrorists must be told that the nation will not be intimidated, no matter what the threats or crimes. On the other hand, the response must not be so harsh that the allies desert the cause or the terrorists and their backers are forced to escalate their response, starting a war.

U.S. law enforcement authorities will have their hands full coping with the new tide of domestic terrorism in the next century. Swamped by this flood of stateside terrorism, local governments and police forces will press the federal government to enact laws that allow extraordinary measures to be taken in certain situations. The new legislation will define terrorism and clarify the duties of federal and state authorities. Meanwhile, the decriminalization of drugs will take away the motivation for drug merchants to conduct a terrorist war against law enforcement authorities. After a number of attacks on industrial sites, the United States will finally get smart and post security forces around computer centers, reservoirs, electrical power stations, and phone switching stations.

Make no mistake about it: Terrorism is here to stay because it is still a useful tool for conveying an old message. It will take 10 to 15 years before the United States can get its act together to end the new terrorism. In the meantime, the best remedy against future terrorism is better preparation now: The United States must prepare psychologically, socially, and militarily. Security systems in the public and private sectors must be rethought — and hard questions about laws and theories of justice must be asked.

The Contrasting Ethical Foundations of Terrorism in the 1980s

Bruce Hoffman

Despite many other disagreements, experts on terrorism agree that during the 1980s there has been an increase not only in the total volume of terrorist incidents worldwide, but in the number of fatalities caused by terrorists as well. Indeed, terrorist operations claimed more than twice as many lives between 1980 and 1986 as in the previous seven years.[1]

A variety of reasons account for these increases. The most obvious explanation, perhaps, is the proliferation of terrorist groups and the attendant increases in the number of operations carried out and casualties caused. Ironically, another explanation might be the success of counterterrorist measures taken by the international community: heightened security measures have made earlier terrorist tactics, such as embassy takeovers and airline hijackings, more difficult to accomplish. Moreover, public attention is not as readily claimed as it once was. Terrorists have been forced to undertake more spectacular and, unfortunately, bloodier deeds in order to achieve the same effect. Another explanation might be that state-sponsorship has given some terrorists access to greater resources and thus the ability to mount increasingly destructive attacks.

But these explanations go only so far. Many of the terrorist organizations active throughout the 1970s are still active today. Groups such as the Red Army Faction, the Red Brigades, the IRA, ETA, and the PLO, to name but a few, have neither significantly altered their strategy and tactics nor embarked on bloodier or more destructive terrorist campaigns than a decade ago.

This article argues that the nature and character of the ethical foundations of terrorism have changed and that this change more accurately accounts for terrorism's growing lethality. In what appears to be an emerging trend, terrorism is increasingly perpetrated by groups with a dominant religious component in contrast to the largely politically oriented groups of the past two decades. Terrorism motivated by a religious imperative has shown itself to be considerably less discriminate than terrorism motivated by ostensibly political aims; consequently, it encompasses a far wider choice of targets and, indeed, of victims as well. Distinctions based on ideological polarity (for example, left versus right) or on nationalist or irredentist aims no longer usefully describe the way terrorists justify their violent campaigns. The causal link between the predominance of religion-based terrorism and terrorism's growing lethality is reinforced by the fact that although Shi'a Islamic groups committed only seven per cent of all international terrorist incidents since 1982, those incidents are responsible for 21 per cent of the total number of deaths.[2]

Certainly, any inquiry that attempts to match ethics with terrorist violence rests on tenuous moral ground. Terrorism is in itself widely regarded as fundamentally immoral, and the violence wrought against civilian targets, causing death and injury to innocent persons, vitiates any conception of an ethical terrorist code of conduct. But at the same time, it is impossible to ignore the proposition that the targets and tactics of various terrorist movements are in some – however idiosyncratic – way a reflection of ethical choices or considerations on the part of the terrorists.

This discussion admittedly involves a simplification that reduces a range of varied and complex phenomena to a few very general observations. However, in so doing, it attempts to delineate the contrasting ethical foundations of what, for purposes of polemical clarity, I broadly define as 'secular political' terrorism and 'religious political' terrorism. It further assumes that the justification and, more important, the legitimization of terrorist violence are fundamentally different in the two types of organizations.

The 'secular political' category embraces terrorist organizations such as nationalist or irredentist groups and left-wing and right-wing groups, whose aims are primarily political. Their campaigns are characterized in simplest terms by the quest for power, be it in a separate nation-state, a socialist state, or an authoritarian state. Another characteristic of this type of terrorist movement is the desire to attain socio-political changes *within* the existing world order and the use of terrorism as a means to that end.

'Religious political' terrorists also seek to realize wide-ranging changes in the existing world order based on a religious or theological imperative. Rather than regarding violence as a means to an end, these groups often view violence as an end in itself. The 'religious political' category includes Shi'a Islamic terrorist organizations, such as Islamic Jihad, Islamic Amal, *Hezbollah*, *Jundallah*, and *al-Dawa*, as well as American white supremacist groups, such as the Aryan Nations; The Order; The Covenant, the Sword and the Arm of the Lord; and, the Posse Comitatus. I am by no means arguing that Shi'a Islamic terrorists are at all like American white supremacist terrorists. Rather, I am indicating that there are similarities in their mindset, world view, and ethics which are useful not only for comparative purposes but also for underscoring the fact that 'religious political' terrorism is not restricted solely to Muslims in the Middle East.

In sum, whereas terrorism in the 1970s was characterized by groups with a 'secular political' ideology, today it is being carried forward by groups with a 'religious political' ideology – groups that, moreover, have a radically different perception of their constituencies and target audience and thus a very different ethic concerning the infliction of widespread destruction and bloodshed. The juxtaposition of these two types of terrorists makes for an interesting study of the contrasting ethical foundations of 'secular political' terrorism and 'religious political' terrorism since justification or legitimization of 'religious political' terrorism in the latter category is derived not from a secular political ideological framework, but from a religious political ideological one.

Secular Political Terrorism

For years, terrorism has been characterized by attacks on a limited number of individuals.[3] Even though terrorists have had the capability to inflict

From *Terrorism and Political Violence*, Vol. 1, No. 3, July 1989, pp. 361-377. *Terrorism and Political Violence*, published by Frank Cass and Company, Ltd., England.

large numbers of casualties with bombs in public areas, they have rarely done so or – perhaps more tellingly – even attempted to do so. Terrorists appear to act under self-imposed restraints. Mass, indiscriminate murder would alienate the very audience they wish to recruit or at least influence. Moreover, terrorists have generally been able to achieve publicity and other objectives through relatively more discrete acts of violence, without inflicting widespread casualties.[4]

This pattern has been observed consistently in the activities of the types of terrorist organizations that comprise the 'secular political' category. None of them commits acts randomly. For them, terrorism – like efficient warfare in general – seeks the maximum effect with the minimum of effort or sacrifice. This is not simply a product of sound tactics, but a reflection of ethical considerations. The ethical values embraced by this type of terrorist are directly related to the ethics of either their perceived constituents or their target audience. The terrorists appear to be cognizant of the likelihood that acts of mass destruction or bloodshed may result in public revulsion, alienating potential sympathizers, and triggering severe government measures.

The overriding tactical and ethical imperative for 'secular political' terrorists has been the deliberate tailoring of their violent acts to appeal to their perceived constituents. At the same time, they have use of violence to impress, intimidate, coerce, or otherwise embarrass their target audience – most often, the ruling government the terrorists are fighting against. In this respect, acts of terrorism are carried out in a way that situates them within the ethics of the terrorists' constituents or target audience.

This is especially true of left-wing terrorist organizations such as the Red Army Faction, Red Brigades, Direct Action, and Communist Combatant Cells. For example, Michael 'Bommi' Baumann, a member of the West German 2nd of June Movement, a less militant splinter group of the Red Army Faction, once explained that the 1978 hijacking of a Lufthansa jet by terrorists seeking the release of imprisoned RAF members was 'madness . . . you can't take your life and place it above that of children and Majorca holiday-makers and say: *My* life is more valuable! That is elitarian madness, bordering on Fascism'.[5]

For Baumann, the deliberate involvement of innocent civilians in that terrorist operation was not only counterproductive, but wrong. It was counterproductive in that it tarnished the left-wing terrorists' self-image of a 'revolutionary vanguard' – using violence both to draw attention to themselves and their cause and to 'educate' the public about what the terrorists perceive as the inequities of the democratic-capitalist state. It was also wrong in itself because innocent persons – no matter what the political justification – should not be the victims of terrorist acts directed against the state.

For this reason, left-wing terrorists' use of violence is narrowly proscribed. Their self-styled crusade for social justice is typically directed against governmental or commercial institutions or persons whom they believe represent capitalist exploitation and repression. Accordingly, the terrorists are careful not to undertake actions that might alienate potential supporters or their perceived constituency. Specific individuals – wealthy industrialists like Hanns Martin Schleyer, parliamentarians like Aldo Moro, or, more recently, businessmen or government officials connected with the arms industry – are targeted for assassination. When bombs are used the violence is often 'symbolic'. Although the damage and destruction that result are certainly not symbolic, the bombings are meant to dramatize or call attention to a political cause.[6]

The left-wing terrorists' role as a revolutionary vanguard, using symbolic acts of violence to 'educate' the masses, is apparent in the ongoing campaign against the United States military presence in Europe and NATO and the positioning of US nuclear missiles on European soil. The decision to base Pershing II and cruise missiles in Western Europe afforded the left-wing terrorists a new opportunity to broaden their base of support and appeal to a new constituency, that is, composed of persons opposed to the arms race. As a communiqué issued by Direct Action explained,

> Attacks on the multinational structures of NATO, on its bases and strategists, on its plans and propaganda, are bringing about a transformation of the awareness and practices of the proletariat, going beyond its national characteristics and bringing about an international organization advance.[7]

This approach is not so different from that of nationalist/irredentist terrorist groups like the PLO, IRA, and ETA. Although acts of terrorism committed by groups in this category have frequently been more destructive and have caused more casualties than those of their left-wing counterparts, many of the same aims and ethics are nevertheless present. The nationalist/irredentists also see themselves as a revolutionary vanguard – perhaps, not in classic Marxist-Leninist terms – but still as a spearhead, using violence to 'educate' their fellow nationals about the inequities imposed upon them by the ruling government, to underscore the powerlessness of the government and thereby embarrass and coerce it into acceding to the group's separatist/nationalist demands. In a broader sense, unlike left-wing terrorism, nationalist/irredentist terrorism is often designed to appeal to international opinion in support of the terrorists' separatist claims.

Even if nationalist/irredentist terrorists' violence is greater than that of left-wing terrorists, 'the "enemy" seems well identified, namely a member of the rival or dominant nationality'.[8] But, more important, to continue to receive the support of their constituency, generate sympathy among the international community, and forestall massive governmental countermeasures, the terrorists must also tightly control and direct their operations. The vast majority of victims of nationalist/irredentist terrorists, therefore, are low-ranking government officials, ordinary soldiers or policemen, other 'agents of the state', and members of rival communities or 'traitors' within their own community.

However, when these more 'typical' targets fail to sustain the momentum of a terrorist campaign or when other, unrelated events overshadow the terrorists and shunt their cause out of the public eye, the terrorists resort to more violent acts to dramatically refocus attention back upon themselves. But it would be a mistake to see these acts – which often involve the bombing of public gathering places or the hijacking of airliners – as random or senseless. For example, following the Palestinian terrorists' failure to mount a concerted guerrilla campaign against Israel on the occupied West Bank and Gaza Strip after the 1967 Six Day War, the Popular Front for the Liberation of Palestine began hijacking international airliners. The purpose of these operations was not to kill innocent persons, but to use them as pawns in the pursuit of publicity. One of the group's most famous hijackers, Leila Khaled said, 'Look, I had orders to seize the plane, not to blow it up . . . . I care about people. If I had wanted to blow up the plane no one could have prevented me.'[9]

Even when terrorist actions are not so deliberate or discriminate, and when their purpose is in fact to kill innocent civilians, the target is still regarded as 'justified' because it represents the terrorists' 'enemy'. Although incidents may be *quantitatively* different in the volume of death or destruction caused, they are still *qualitatively* identical in that a defined 'enemy' is being targeted. This distinction is often accepted by the terrorists' constituents, and at times it is accepted by the international community as well. The premier example of this was the killing of 11 Israeli athletes seized by Palestinian terrorists at the 1972 Munich Olympic Games. The terrorists declared, 'We are neither killers nor bandits. We are a persecuted people who have no land and no homeland.'[10] It is perhaps not coincidental that two years later, PLO Chairman Yasir Arafat was invited to address the United Nations General Assembly, and shortly afterwards the PLO was accorded observer status in that organization. In fact, the PLO now has diplomatic relations with 86 countries, while Israel has relations with only 78.

As a spokesman for the Popular Front for the Liberation of Palestine once explained,

> You must differentiate between the kind [of violence] used to exploit people and that used in self-defense: legitimate violence. The bullets that I shoot are not bullets used to exploit or subdue. They are just the opposite. They will remove exploitation inflicted upon me . . . . For violence to become fruitful, for it to get us to our aims, it should not be undertaken without a proper political base and intention. These should equip the movement with the right sources from which to draw its recruits.[11]

The ethical considerations in such a case may well be contrived, but nonetheless there is an appreciation that violence has its limits and, moreover, if it is used properly, it can result in significant dividends. In other words, the level of violence must be kept within the bounds of what the terrorists' constituents will accept. This is why 'secular political' terrorists, though capable of inflicting massive destruction and indiscriminate killing, generally avoid doing so.

But acts of terrorism, like battles in conventional wars, are difficult to limit and control once they are started, and they often result in tragedy to civilians who are inadvertently caught up in the violence. One example is the tragic bombing that occurred at Enniskillen, Northern Ireland, in November 1987, causing the deaths of 11 persons who were attending a memorial ceremony. The IRA was quick to describe the incident as an accident resulting from the 'catastrophic consequences' of an operation against British troops gone awry.[12] In this respect, an ethical distinction is still present, although self-serving justifications of 'catastrophic consequences' and 'accidents' are used to highlight that distinction.

Right-wing terrorism, on the other hand, has often been characterized as the most indiscriminate type of 'secular political' terrorism, primarily as a result of bombings in Italy, West Germany, and France during the summer and fall of 1980. These incidents took place at the Bologna train station (where 84 persons were killed and 180 wounded), the Munich Oktoberfest celebration (where 14 were killed and 215 were injured), and a Paris synagogue (where four persons were killed and 14 were wounded).[13] They seemed to herald a new and lethally indiscriminate campaign of terrorism. In the years since the bombings, however, these fears have not been confirmed by events. More significantly, many of the differences that were thought to exist between the aims and methods of right-wing and left-wing terrorists do not appear as vast today.

There has, in fact, been no sustained campaign of right-wing terrorism on any level comparable to that of European left-wing organizations or the various nationalist/irredentist groups throughout the world. Nor – with one exception – have right-wing terrorists carried out any further indiscriminate bombings. The lone incident occurred in December 1984, when a bomb exploded on the Naples–Milan express as it traveled through a tunnel between Florence and Bologna, killing 15 persons and wounding 100 others. Thus, although right-wing terrorism is at times indiscriminate, it is not always so. Except for the Oktoberfest bombing, neo-Fascist terrorism in Germany has been directed against specific targets – primarily refugee shelters and immigrant workers' hostels. In France, every attack has been directed against either Jewish-owned property or businesses or Arab and African student or workers' associations. Italy's record is spottier. But apart from the Bologna and express train bombings and an earlier incident that occurred at Milan's Piazza Fontana in 1969 (which killed 16 persons and wounded 88 others), right-wing extremists in that country have mostly attacked leftist targets, banks, political party offices, and policemen and police stations.

Accordingly, right-wing terrorism is based not on some pathological obsession to kill as many innocent people as possible, but on a deliberate policy of intimidating the general public into acceding to specific demands or pressure. The right-wing terrorists see themselves, if not as a revolutionary vanguard, then as a catalyst of events that will lead to the imposition of an authoritarian form of government. Thus, they tailor their violence to appeal to their perceived constituency – be it extreme nationalists, intransigent xenophobes, reactionary conservatives, or militant anti-communists – and, with the exception of a few indiscriminate bombings, they seek to keep it within the bounds of what the ruling government will tolerate without undertaking massive repressive actions against the terrorists themselves.

The basic aim of right-wing terrorists has long been the destruction of the liberal-democratic state to clear the way for a National Socialist ('Nazi') or fascist state. However, in recent years there has been an unexpected confluence of right-wing and left-wing terrorism goals and tactics in both Italy and Germany. In Italy, for example, the right-wing terrorist group calling itself 'Third Position', in reference to its hybrid ideology of 'Nazi-Maoism',[14] declares, 'Neither capitalism nor communism, neither reds nor reaction.'[15] And in Germany, a new right-wing ideology has emerged embodying a melange of 'people's socialist', 'anti-imperialist', 'national revolutionary', and 'ecological' dicta. As Henning Eichberg, a leading right-wing ideologue and lecturer in military history at the University of Stuttgart, explains, 'In order to unite the German nation anew, we must get away from the Vodka-Cola headquarters, from the cities, the colonies and the superpowers.'[16]

The objective of West German neo-Nazis has thus become, in the words of Manfred Roeder, leader of the 'German Action Group', one of that country's most active right-wing terrorist groups, 'the establishment of the first radical-democratic and anti-imperialist state on German soil'.[17] This can only be accomplished, he argues, by emulating left-wing revolutionary tactics[18] – and, presumably, by adhering to the ethical 'code of conduct' of selective, 'public relations-oriented' terrorism pursued by the leftists. The symmetry between the right and the left has also been voiced by neo-Nazis in other groups.[19] 'We have always said we are socialists', Michael Kuhnen, the leader of another right-wing terrorist group, stated. In addition, like its left-wing counterparts, his Action Front for National Socialists also opposes the deployment of United States nuclear missiles on German soil.[20]

The trend of both legal right-wing political parties and underground neo-Nazi organizations in this direction is also a reflection of their respective failures to attract large followings within the West German polity. The search for new constituencies and new sources of support is a familiar characteristic of terrorist organizations throughout the world. In this case, the pandering to causes which are ostensibly leftist represents a bid to broaden the rightists' appeal, impress a wider field of potential supporters, and acquire new popularity and strength. The emergence of popular, contentious issues such as the environment and the nuclear arms race is increasingly exploited by the neo-Nazi terrorists. As the West German Ministry of the Interior observed in its annual report on terrorism for 1985, these efforts 'often go hand in hand with militant anti-Americanism'.[21]

This shift in aims by right-wing terrorists has also manifested itself in attacks against the same targets favored today by the left: United States military facilities and personnel stationed in Germany. For the right-wing terrorists, there is yet another factor: envy of the attention, status, and occasional tactical victories won by left-wing terrorists in groups such as the RAF,[22] alongside of the realization that indiscriminate terrorist attacks will not result in the attainment of the right-wing groups' goals. Thus there is a confluence not only of ideals and tactics, but of ethics as well, if only to reap the benefits of support from new constituencies.

Religious Political Terrorism

Certainly, the relationship between terrorism and religion is not new. In fact, as David Rapoport points out in his seminal study of what he terms 'holy terror', until the nineteenth century, 'religion provided the only acceptable justifications for terror'.[23] This form of terrorism has occurred throughout history, although in recent decades it has largely been overshadowed by the more common 'secular political' terrorism. Admittedly, many contemporary 'secular political' terrorist groups have a strong religious element: the IRA, the Sikhs, the Armenians, and perhaps the PLO as well. However, the political aspect is the predominant characteristic of these groups, as evinced by their nationalist or irredentist aims.

At the same time, it would be a mistake to see the contemporary religion-motivated terrorist groups, such as the various Iranian-backed Shi'a organizations as apolitical entities. Although religion is their predominant motivation, their struggle inherently involves a quest for power – to be used to defend the faith, to defeat their 'enemies', and to establish a regional, if not global, hegemony. And the quest for power is, of course, at the heart of international politics.[24] In the Shi'a terrorist groups, Islam functions 'not just as a religion but a religious polity'.[25] Amir Taheri notes that the Shi'a terrorists who use 'violence and terror to promote their causes [and political objectives], would be insulted if described as political organizations seeking political change. They recruit their members in the name of Islam and are led by religious officials.'[26]

Most important for our purposes, there are a number of significant differences in the ethical foundations of 'religious political' terrorism and 'secular political' terrorism. For the 'religious political' terrorist violence is viewed as a sacramental act or a divine duty. Terrorism thus assumes a transcendental dimension,[27] and its perpetrators have none of the political, moral, or practical constraints that affect other terrorists. Whereas 'secular political' terrorists rarely attempt indiscriminate killing on a massive scale because such tactics are not consonant with their political aims,[28] the 'religious political' terrorists often seek the elimination of broadly defined categories of 'enemies'. Whereas 'secular political' terrorists generally consider indiscriminate violence immoral and counterproductive,[29] 'religious political' terrorists regard such violence as both morally justified and expedient for the attainment of their goals.

Another crucial difference is that 'religious political' terrorists do not have the kind of constituency or target audience the 'secular political' groups have. 'Religious political' terrorists are at once activists and constituents engaged in what they regard as a 'total war'. They seek to appeal to no other constituency but themselves. The absence of a constituency leads to a significant loosening of the ethics of violence. Religion is regarded as a legitimizing force, sanctioning wide-scale terrorism; moreover, it is open-ended in its range of targets. The restraints on terrorism that are imposed by the desire to appeal to a constituency are not relevant to the 'religious political' terrorist.

Moreover, where the aims of the 'secular political' terrorists can be described as utilitarian – seeking to bring about changes to achieve the greatest benefits for the greatest number – the aims of 'religious political' terrorists are more narrowly defined as the attainment of the greatest benefits for themselves. There is also a significant disparity between ends and means. Where the 'secular political' terrorist sees violence as a means to an end, violence is often an end in itself for the 'religious political' terrorist.[30]

Finally, the 'religious political' terrorists regard themselves not as components of a system, but as 'outsiders', seeking vast changes in the existing order. This sense of alienation enables the 'religious political' terrorist to contemplate far more destructive and deadly types of terrorist operations than 'secular political' terrorists. Taheri, for example, points out three key differences between Islamic terrorism and other forms of terrorism:

> First, it rejects all the contemporary ideologies in their various forms; it sees itself as the total outsider with no option but to take control or to fall, gun in hand . . . .
>
> The second characteristic that distinguishes the Islamic version from other forms of terrorism is that it is clearly conceived and conducted as a form of Holy War which can only end when total victory has been achieved . . . .
>
> The third specific characteristic of Islamic terrorism is that it forms the basis of a whole theory both of individual conduct and of state policy. To kill the enemies of Allah and to offer the infidels the choice between converting to Islam or being put to death is the duty of every individual believer, as well as the supreme – if not the sole – task of the Islamic state.[31]

Indeed, at the root of the present Iranian-backed Islamic terrorist campaign is the desire to extend the fundamentalist interpretation of Islamic law in Iran and, indeed, to export the revolution to other Muslim countries. 'We must strive', the Ayatollah Khomeini declared,

> to export our Revolution throughout the world, and must abandon all idea of not doing so, for not only does Islam refuse to recognize any difference between Muslim countries, it is the champion of all oppressed people . . . . We must make plain our stance toward the powers and superpowers and demonstrate to them despite the arduous problems that burden us. Our attitude to the world is dictated by our beliefs.[32]

These beliefs inherently embrace the notion that 'religion and politics are indivisible.'[33]

The revolution in Iran is held up as an example to Muslims throughout the world to reassert the fundamental teachings of the Koran and to resist the intrusion of Western – particularly United States – influence over the Middle East. This is also a reflection of the beliefs and history of Shi'a Islam as interpreted by Khomeini and subscribed to by his followers in Iran and other Middle Eastern countries. Three desiderata form the basis of this ideology:

> First, Shiites do not believe in the legitimate authority of secular governments. The 12th and last of the Shiite Imams, or successors to the Prophet Mohammed, is expected to reappear eventually to institute the rule of God's law on earth. Until then, all states are, on some level, inalienably illegitimate. Since Iran is the only state to have begun to implement 'true' Islam, however, it is thought to be the world's only legitimate state with a unique obligation of facilitating the worldwide implementation of Islamic law. Force and violence are not only acceptable but necessary means of doing so . . . .
>
> Second, the Shiites see themselves as a persecuted minority. They believe that through their special knowledge of the Koran . . . passed on to them by the Prophet Mohammed and the 12 Imams, they are the righteous few dominated by an innately wrongful majority . . . .
>
> Third, the Shiites view themselves as victims of injustice and oppression. Ayatollah Khomeini has interpreted this theme to make the Shiites the representatives, even vanguard, of the 'oppressed and innocent masses crushed under foot all over the world'.[34]

This sense of alienation and of the necessity for far-reaching changes in the world order is apparent in the works of a number of Shi'a theologians. 'The world as it is today is how others shaped it', wrote Ayatollah Baqer al-Sadr. 'We have two choices: either to accept it with submission, which means letting Islam die, or to destroy it, so that we can construct the world as Islam requires.' Mustafa Chamran has stated, 'We are not fighting within the rules of the world as it exists today. We reject all those rules.' Hussein Mussawi, the leader of Lebanon's *Islamic Amal,* puts it: 'We are not fighting so that the enemy recognizes us and offers us something. We are fighting to wipe out the enemy.'[35]

Many of these characteristics – the legitimization of violence based on religious precepts, the sense of alienation, preoccupation with the elimination of a broadly defined category of 'enemies', and the existence of a terrorist movement in which the activists are the constituents – are also apparent among militant white supremacists in the United States today. Although organized hate groups such as the Ku Klux Klan and various incarnations of Hitler's National Socialist (Nazi) party have existed in that country for decades, extremist white supremacist/paramilitary groups, oriented toward Christian fundamentalism, 'survivalism', outdoor skills, guerrilla training, and outright sedition – such as the Aryan Nations; the Order; the White Patriot Party; the Arizona Patriots; the Covenant, the Sword and the Arm of the Lord (CSA); and, the Posse Commitatus – are a newer phenomenon.[36] Indeed, whereas terrorism in the United States was once dominated by either ethnic/emigre or left-wing groups, in recent years, white supremacists have accounted for most of the United States' terrorist violence.

The magnitude of the threat posed by white supremacists in the United States is most clearly demonstrated by the wide-ranging geographical dimensions of the movement, the diversity of its adherents' causes, and their overlapping agendas. It is a movement with constituents, followers, and sympathizers stretching from Idaho, California, and Arizona in the west to North Carolina and Georgia in the east, from Texas to Canada and the Midwestern states in between. Moreover, their aims and motivations span a broad spectrum of anti-federalist and seditious beliefs, alongside racial and religious hatred cloaked in and justified by religious precepts. The white supremacists are bound together by their shared hostility to any form of government above the county level; their vilification of Jews and non-whites as 'the literal children of Satan'; their obsession with achieving the religious and racial purification of the United States; their belief in a conspiracy theory of powerful Jewish interests controlling the government, banks, and the media; and their advocacy of the overthrow of the United States government or 'Zionist Occupation Government' (ZOG), as they disparagingly refer to it.

The unifying thread in this patchwork ideology is the so-called Christian Identity movement.[37] The basic tenets of the Identity movement include the beliefs that Jesus Christ was not a Semite, but an Aryan; that the Lost Tribes of Israel are composed not of Jews, but of 'blue eyed Aryans'; that white Anglo-Saxons and not Jews are the true 'Chosen People'; and, that the United States is the 'Promised Land'. In this context, Jews are viewed as imposters and children of Satan who must be exterminated.

At the center of the white supremacist movement is the organization known as the Aryan Nations and its Church of Jesus Christ-Christian. The ideology espoused by the organization is a mixture of racist and seditious dicta. '*WE BELIEVE*', a brochure entitled *This is Aryan Nations* explains,

> there is a battle being fought this day between the children of darkness (today known as Jews) and the children of light (God), the Aryan race, the true Israel of the Bible . . . .
>
> *WE BELIEVE* in the preservation of our race individually and collectively as a people as demanded and directed by God. We believe a racial nation has a right and is under obligation to preserve itself and its members . . . . As His divine race, we have been commissioned to fulfill His divine purpose and plans . . . .
>
> *WE BELIEVE* that there is a day of reckoning. The usurper will be thrown out by the terrible might of Yahweh's people as they return to their roots and their special destiny.[38]

Indeed, the 'Aryan National State Platform' cites as Article VIII that 'A ruthless war must be waged against any whose activities are injurious to the common interest'.[39]

This 'cleansing' of the United States forms an immutable point of reference for the white supremacists' ideology. 'Aliens are pouring over as a flood into *each* of our ancestral lands', Aryan Nations founder and leader Richard Girnt Butler has written, 'threatening dispossession of the heritage, culture, and very life blood of our prosperity . . . . We know that as we return to our Father's natural Life Order, all power, prosperity, and liberty again comes to us as our possession, to establish justice forever on earth.'[40] Robert Matthews, the leader of an Aryan Nations splinter group called The Order, has declared that in order to stem this tide, all Jews, blacks, Hispanics, other so-called 'mud people', and white 'race traitors' must be exterminated in what has been described as 'a racial and religious Armageddon'.[41]

It is particularly alarming that the white supremacists' expressed *raison d'être* – racism, anti-Semitism and sedition – is justified and legitimized on theological grounds. It is at once a political and a grassroots religious movement. The leaders of the movement portray themselves as 'pastors' and 'reverends' and attempt to endow their organizations with a theological veneer that condones and justifies violence. In an article entitled, 'An All White Nation? – Why Not?', Roy B. Masker has explained how Aryan Nations members 'are in disobedience to our Father and God, Yahweh, for allowing the Nation He gave us to become the mongrelized cesspool in which we now find ourselves . . . . Indeed, it is incumbent upon us to BUILD A NEW, ALL-WHITE NATION! We are under command to do so! All scripture demands it!' Masker concludes with the admonition, 'Woe to those who stand in the way of the Aryan juggernaut!'[42]

The white supremacists do not appear to exhibit any of the political, moral, or practical considerations that constrain most other terrorist groups from causing mass-scale death and destruction. There are, in fact, striking parallels between these groups and religiously motivated Islamic Shi'a fanatics in the Middle East. Both groups transform abstract political ideologies and objectives into a religious imperative. Violence is not only sanctioned, it is viewed as a divine duty. Hence, the killing of persons described as 'infidels' by the Shi'a or as 'children of Satan' or 'race traitors' by the white supremacists becomes a sacramental act. Indeed, the elimination of Jews, blacks, 'mud people', and 'race traitors' is viewed by the white supremacists as both morally justified and essential for the attainment of the religious and racial 'purification' of the United States.

Although the white supremacists have thus far caused far less destruction and bloodshed than the Islamic Shi'a terrorists, evidence has come to light that at least some white supremacists have already laid plans to engage in indiscriminate, mass killing. According to a federal grand jury indictment recently handed down in Fort Smith, Arkansas, white supremacists from throughout the United States and Canada met at the Aryan Nations headquarters in Idaho in 1983 to plot the forcible overthrow of the federal government and the creation of a separate Aryan nation within the United States. The indictment states that they plan to 'finance their movement through robberies and counterfeiting. They agree to carry out assassinations of federal officials, politicians and Jews, *as well as bombings and polluting of municipal water supplies*' [my emphasis].[43] Any doubts of their seriousness of purpose were dispelled when police and federal agents who raided a white supremacist compound in rural Arkansas in April 1984, found a stockpile of some 30 gallons of cyanide to be used for this purpose.[44]

Such a scenario, in fact, is detailed in the novel, *The Turner Diaries*,[45] which has been cited as 'the Bible' of the white supremacists.[46] It describes a chain of events that begins with a white supremacist revolution in 1991 and culminates two years later in 'an all-out race war' and worldwide nuclear conflagration. In the book, a terrorist group called The Order embarks on a ruthless campaign of violence involving the assassination of public officials and prominent Jews, the shooting down of commercial airliners, the poisoning of water supplies, and bombings of public utilities. The book reaches its climax when the terrorists seize the US nuclear arsenal and obliterate several American cities before turning the weapons against targets in Israel and the Soviet Union.[47]

As incredible and lunatic as the events in *The Turner Diaries* may seem,[48] the strategy of the inchoate terrorist campaign waged in the United States between 1983 and 1984 by Robert Matthews and the real-life Order was in fact based on the battle plan detailed in the book. Furthermore, this apocalyptic vision forms part of the beliefs of many white supremacists today. Whereas most people harbour deep fears of a nuclear war, many white supremacists appear to welcome the prospect since a nuclear war would eliminate their avowed 'enemies' and permit the fulfillment of their objectives to create a world order peopled exclusively by the white race.

The self-described purpose of the Covenant, the Sword and the Arm of the Lord compound at Mountain Home, Arkansas (where the cyanide was discovered) is 'to build an Ark for God's people during the coming tribulations on the earth'.[49] Accordingly, the 100 or so men, women and children living in the compound have prepared themselves for the coming Armageddon by stockpiling weapons, food, and valuables, and undergoing training in survivalist techniques and guerrilla warfare. The group's journal describes the impending apocalypse as a limited nuclear war launched against the United States by 'Russia and possibly China and Japan'. As Terry Noble, a pastor and spokesman for the group explained, 'We are Christian survivalists who believe in preparing for the ultimate holocaust . . . . The coming war is a step toward God's government.'[50]

Conclusion

As this article has shown, the ethical values of 'secular political' terrorists are significantly different from those of 'religious political' terrorists. In this respect, distinctions among terrorist organizations based on ideological polarity or nationalist/irredentist aims no longer provide an adequate framework for explaining the contrasting ethical foundations of many contemporary terrorist movements. Terrorism today is increasingly being carried forward by 'religious political' groups, and this is, in fact, one of the main reasons for terrorism's increasing lethality.

The ethical considerations of 'secular political' terrorism are directly related to the constituency of the target audience to which the terrorists are appealing. Acts of 'secular political' terrorism are deliberately situated within the ethic of the constituency at large. All of the terrorist movements in this category seek targets that they consider lucrative. Terrorism is not random or senseless, but meant to appeal to and attract supporters, to focus attention on the terrorists themselves, and to attain tangible aims. Hence, publicity and attention are paramount aims, and the terrorists recognize that only if their violence is calculated or regulated will they be able to obtain the support or win the victories they desire. As an IRA terrorist once put it, 'You don't just bloody well kill people for the sake of killing them'.[51]

This is not the position taken by 'religious political' terrorists. Violence for them has a transcendent purpose and therefore becomes a sacramental act or divine duty. Religion is a legitimizing force, and terrorism becomes an end in itself. This is a direct reflection of the fact that 'religious political' terrorists do not seek to appeal to any constituency but themselves, and the changes they want to make are not for any utilitarian purpose, but are only to benefit themselves. The 'religious political' terrorist sees himself as an outsider from the society that he rejects, and this sense of alienation enables him to contemplate, and undertake, far more destructive and bloodier types of terrorist operations than his 'secular political' counterpart.

NOTES

Paper presented at the British International Studies Association's Annual Conference, University College of Wales, Aberystwyth, 16–18 December 1987. The author wishes to acknowledge the helpful suggestions made by Anders Stephanson, Benjamin Schwarz, Christina Schwarz, Konrad Kellen, Peter Lipton, and Janet DeLand, who read earlier drafts of this article.

1. A total of 3,225 persons were killed by terrorists between 1980 and 1986 as compared with the 1,573 killed between 1973 and 1979. Statistics compiled in The RAND Corporation Chronology of International Terrorism.
2. A total of 2,367 international terrorist incidents were recorded in The RAND Corporation Chronology of International Terrorism between 1982 and 1987. Shi'a terrorist groups committed only 160 of these incidents but were responsible for 592 deaths.
3. Brian M. Jenkins, 'Is Nuclear Terrorism Plausible?' in Paul Leventhal and Yonah Alexander (eds.), *Nuclear Terrorism: Defining the Threat* (New York: Pergamon-Brassey's, 1986), p.29.
4. See, for example, Brian M. Jenkins, *International Terrorism: The Other World War* (Santa Monica, CA: The RAND Corporation, R-3302-AF, Nov. 1985), p.23.
5. 'The Mind of a German Terrorist: Interview with Michael "Bommi" Baumann', *Encounter*, Vol.II, No.3, Sept. 1978, p.81.
6. For example, as a statement of the RAF's revolutionary 'philosophy' declared, 'Our original conception of the organization implied a connection between the urban guerrilla and the work at the base. We would like it if each and all of us could work at the neighborhoods and factories, in socialist groups that already exist, influence discussion, experience and learn. This has proved impossible . . . . Some say that the possibilities for agitation, propaganda and organization are far from being eradicated and that only when they are, should we pose the question of arms. We say: it will not really be possible to profit from any political actions as long as armed struggle does not appear clearly as the goal of the policisation [sic].' (See 'RAF Philosophy', in *The German Guerrilla: Terror, Reaction, and Resistance* (London: Cienfuegos Press, undated), p.98.)
7. Communiqué from Direct Action, claiming credit for the assassination of French General René Audran, 25 Jan. 1985.
8. Peter H. Merkl, 'Prologue', in Peter H. Merkl (ed.), *Political Violence and Terror* (Berkeley, CA: University of California Press, 1986), p.8.
9. Quoted in Gerald McKnight, *The Mind of the Terrorist* (London: Michael Joseph, 1974), p.26.
10. Christopher Dobson, *Black September* (London: Robert Hale, 1974), p.95.
11. Bassam Abu Sharif quoted in McKnight, *The Mind of the Terrorist*, p.26.
12. Quoted in *New York Times*, 15 Nov. 1987.
13. A French neo-Nazi group claimed responsibility for the synagogue bombing, but suspicion has also focused on Palestinian, Armenian, and domestic left-wing terrorist organizations.
14. See Bruce Hoffman, 'Right-Wing Terrorism in Europe', *Contemporary Affairs Briefing*, Vol.2, No.5, (Nov. 1982), pp.8–9.
15. Quoted in Thomas Sheehan, 'Italy: Terror on the Right', *New York Review of Books*, 22 Jan. 1981, p.25.

16. *Der Stern* (Hamburg), 4 March 1982.
17. Quoted in *Der Stern*, 29 Oct. 1981.
18. *Der Spiegel* (Hamburg), 11 Jan. 1981.
19. Additional expressions of 'revolutionary solidarity' with the left have been expressed by other neo-Nazis as well. See Bruce Hoffman, 'Right-Wing Terrorism in Europe Since 1980', *Orbis: A Journal of World Affairs*, Spring 1984, pp.23–4.
20. *The German Tribune*, 3 July 1983.
21. *Das Parlament* (Bonn) 28 June 1986.
22. *Stuttgarter Zeitung* (Stuttgart), 12 Dec. 1981.
23. David C. Rapoport, 'Fear and Trembling: Terrorism in Three Religious Traditions', *American Political Science Review*, Vol.78, No.3, Sept. 1984, p.659.
24. H. J. Morgenthau and Kenneth W Thompson, 'Principles and Problems of International Politics', in Brian Porter (ed.), *The Aberystwyth Papers: International Politics, 1919–1969*. It should be noted that of the three religious terror groups studied by Rapoport – the Thugs, the Assassins, and the Zealots – only the Zealots and the Assassins had a political aim. See Rapoport, 'Fear and Trembling: Terrorism in Three Religious Traditions', passim.
25. Robin Wright, 'Quiet Revolution: The Islamic Movement's New Phase', *Christian Science Monitor* (Washington, DC), 6 Nov. 1987.
26. Amir Taheri, *Holy Terror: The Inside Story of Islamic Terrorism* (London: Sphere Books, 1987), p.2.
27. See, for example, Rapoport, 'Fear and Trembling: Terrorism in Three Religious Traditions', p.674.
28. Brian M. Jenkins, *Will Terrorists Go Nuclear?* (Santa Monica, CA: The RAND Corporation, Nov. 1975, P-5541), pp.4–5.
29. Brian M. Jenkins, *The Likelihood of Nuclear Terrorism* (Santa Monica, CA: The RAND Corporation, July 1985, P-7119), pp.4–5.
30. See Rapoport, 'Fear and Trembling: Terrorism in Three Religious Traditions', p.659.
31. Taheri, *Holy Terror: The Inside Story of Islamic Terrorism*, pp.7–8.
32. Imam Khomeini, *Islam and Revolution* (Trans. by Hamid Algar) (London: KPI, 1981), pp.286–7.
33. Hussein Ali Montazeri, Khomeini's hand-picked successor, quoted in Colin Legum, 'Iran's Role in World Terrorism Depicted', *The Age* (Melbourne), 5 Jan. 1984.
34. Marvin Zonis and Daniel Brumberg, 'Behind Beirut Terrorism', *New York Times*, 8 Oct. 1984.
35. Quoted in Taheri, *Holy Terror*, pp.7–8.
36. For a detailed examination of many of these groups, see Bruce Hoffman, *Terrorism in the United States and the Potential Threat to Nuclear Facilities* (Santa Monica, CA: The RAND Corporation, R-3351-DOE, January 1986), pp.37–52; and Bruce Hoffman, 'Right-Wing Terrorism In The United States', *VAT Journal*, (Winter 1987).
37. The Identity movement is based on the Anglo–Israelism movement which emerged in Great Britain during the mid-nineteenth century. Anglo–Israelism embraced the notion that the ten lost tribes of ancient Israel were in fact composed of Anglo-Saxons and not Jews. In contrast to the present-day movement in the United States, this earlier movement was a pacifistic movement.
38. 'This is Aryan Nations', brochure distributed by the Aryan Nations (undated).
39. Aryan Nations, *Calling Our Nation*, No.53 (undated), p.2.
40. 'To Our New People', Open Letter from Richard G. Butler, Pastor, Aryan Nations (undated).
41. Quoted in *Washington Post*, 26 Dec. 1984.
42. Roy B. Masker, 'An All White Nation? – Why Not?', Aryan Nations, *Calling Our Nation*, No.53, p.23.
43. *Arkansas Gazette* (Little Rock), 27 April 1987.
44. Joseph M. Melnichak, 'A Chronicle of Hate: A Brief History of the Radical Right in America,' *TVI Report*, Vol.6, No.4 (undated), pp.41–2. This was also confirmed to me by an FBI agent present at the raid.
45. Andrew MacDonald, *The Turner Diaries* (Arlington, VA: The National Alliance/National Vanguard Books, 1985).
46. *New York Times*, 27 Dec. 1984.
47. MacDonald, *The Turner Diaries*, pp.38–9, 62, 174, and 190.
48. Turner's tale, although fictional, is in many ways like Adolf Hitler's *Mein Kampf,* which was not taken seriously at the time, only to be turned into terrible reality a mere ten years after its publication.
49. Quoted in Anti-Defamation League of B'nai B'rith, *Hate Groups in America: A Record of Bigotry and Violence* (New York: Anti-Defamation League of B'nai B'rith, 1982), p.52.
50. Quoted in ibid., pp.51 and 53.
51. Quoted in McKnight, *The Mind Of The Terrorist*, p.179.

Appendix

Worldwide Terrorism Since the World War II Period

Bernard Schechterman
University of Miami

	Terrorism by the State		Terrorism Directed Against the State	
State or Area	**Targets Within the State**	**Targets Outside the State**	**Outside Supporter of Terrorism (State Supported Terrorism)[a]**	**Domestic Revolutionary Terrorist Organization[a]**
Afghanistan	Muslim rebels, tribal groups			
Algeria			Ahl al-Dawah/Al-Qiyam (People of the Call, Muslim Brethren)—Egypt, Tunisia, Morocco; Jamaat al-Islamiyyah (Islamic Society)—Muslim Brethren, Egypt National Liberation Front (FLN)—Egypt	Ahl al-Dawah/Al-Qiyam (People of the Call, Muslim Brethren); Jamaat al-Islamiyyah (Muslim Brethren); National Liberation Front (FLN)
Argentina	Communists, the left		Ejercito Revolucionario del Pueblo (ERP)—Cuba, Trotskyites, USSR, Revolutionary Coordination Junta	Ejercito Revolucionario del Pueblo (ERP), Monteneros, Tacuara, Fuerzas Armados, Rebeldes (FAR), Movimento Argentino Nacional Organisacion (MANO), Argentine Anticommunist Alliance (AAA)
Bahrain			Jabhat al-Islamiyyah Lil-Tahrir al-Bahrain (Islamic Front for Liberation of Bahrain)—Iran, Iraq, Gulf States	Jabbat al-Islamiyyah Lil-Tahrir al-Bahrain (Shi'a)
Belgium			Fighting Communist Cells (CCC)—Direct Action	Fighting Communist Cells (CCC), Viaamse Militante Orden
Bolivia			Ejercito de Liberacion National (ELN)—Colombia, Peru ELN's, ERP	Ejercito de Liberacion National (ELN)
Brazil			M-19—Cuba, Nicaragua	Acao Liberidora Nacional (ALN), MR-8, Vanguardia Popular Revolucionaria (VPR), Vanguardia Armada Revolucionaria Palmares (VAR)
Bulgaria	Muslims	Italy		
Burma				Shan State Army
Cambodia	peasants (under Khmer Rouge)			
Canada				Front de Liberation du Quebec (FLQ)
Central African Republic	Tribal groups and individuals			
Chile	Communists, Socialists, the left		Movimento de Liberacion Nacional (MLN)—Tupamaros, Movimiento de la Izquierda Revolucionaria (MIR)—Peru, Venezuela MIR's, Manuel Rodrigues Patriotic Front)Libya	Movimento de Liberacion Nacional (MLN), Movimiento de la Izquierda Revolucionaria (MIR), Manuel Rodrigues Patriotic Front
Colombia			M-19—Cuba, Nicaragua; Ejercito de Liberacion Nacional (ELN)—Peru, Bolivia ELN's, Cuba; Fuerzas Armadas Revolucionarias de Colombia (FARC)—USSR	M-19, Ejercito de Liberacion Nacional (ELN), Ejercito Popular de Liberacion (EPL), Fuerzas Armadas Revolucionarias de Colombia (FARC), Quintin Lame (Indian)

State or Area	Terrorism by the State: Targets Within the State	Terrorism by the State: Targets Outside the State	Terrorism Directed Against the State: Outside Supporter of Terrorism (State Supported Terrorism)[a]	Terrorism Directed Against the State: Domestic Revolutionary Terrorist Organization[a]
Cuba	Batista elements and dissidents	Nicaragua, Dominican Republic, Colombia, Venezuela, Angola, Mozambique, Grenada		
Cyprus			Ethnki Organosis Kypriakou Agoniston (EOKA)—Greece	Ethniki Organosis, Kypriakou Agoniston (EOKA)
Czechoslovakia			Libya, Palestine Liberation Organization	
Dominican Republic			Macheteros—Cuba	Macheteros Partido Revolucionario Dominican (PRD)
East Germany		West Germany, Ethiopia		
Ecuador				Alfaro Vive, Carajo
Egypt (There are between 50–60 opposition groups, but only some use terrorism)		Israel (Gaza Strip), Lebanon	Hizb Allah (Party of God)—N. Yemen; Hizb al-Tahrir (Liberation Party)—Arab countries; Ikhwan al-Muslimim (Muslim Brethren)—Gulf States, Syria, Jordan, Maghrib, Europe, Saudi Arabia; Jamaat al-Harakiyyah (Society of Action)—Libya; Jamaat al-Islamiyyah (Islamic Society)—Saudi Arabia; Jamaat al Shariyyah (Society of Islamic Law)—Gulf States; Jamaat al-Tabligh (Society of Islamic Law)—Gulf States; Jamaat al-Tabligh (Society of Transmission)—Gulf States; Munazzamat al-Tahrir al-Islami (Islamic Liberation Organizational/Technical Military Academy Group)—Syria, Sudan, Jordan, West Bank; Takfir wal-Hijrah (Denouncement and Holy Flight or Society of Muslims)—Kuwait, Gulf States, Turkey, Jordan, Libya, Pakistan, Syria, Saudi Arabia	Hizb Allah (Sunni), Hizb al-Tahrir (Sunni), Ikhwan al-Muslimim (Muslim Brethren), Jamaat al-Ahram (Pyramid Society), Jamaat al-Fath (Society of Conquest), Jamaat al-Haq (Society of Truth), Jamaat al-Harakiyyah (Society of Action), Jamaat al-Islamiyyah (Islamic Society), Jamaat al-Shariyyah (Muslim Brethren), Jamaat al-Tabligh, Jamaat al-Khalifah (Caliph's Group), Jamaat al-Muslimin lil-Takfir (Society for Accusation of Disbelief), Jamaat al-Muslimin (Muslim Group), Jamaat al-Takfir (Society of Denouncement), Al-Jihad (Holy War), Junud Allah (Soldiers of the Compassionate), Mukaffaratiyyah (Denouncers of Infidels), Munazzamat al-Tahrir al-Islami (Islamic Organizational/Technical Military Academy Group), Munazzamat al-Jihad (Jihad Organization), Qif wa Tabayyin (Halt & Prove), Qutbiyyin (Followers of Qutb), Samawiyyah (The Heavenly), Shabab Muhammad (Youth of Muhammad), Takfir wal-Hirah (Denouncement and Holy Flight), Usbah al-Hashimiyyah (The Hashemite League)
Ethiopia	Urban Leninists, Menarchists, Tribal Groups, and Individual Dissidents	Sudan		Ethiopian People's Revolutionary Party (EPRP)
France			Direct Action—Fighting Communist Cells (Belgium), Corsican Front—Libya Breton Liberation Front/Breton Liberation Army (FLB-ARB)—Spanish ETA, Irish IRA	Direct Action, Corsican Front, Breton Liberation Front/Army
(West) German Republic			Baader-Meinhof or Red Army Faction (RAF)—PLO, Western European Marxist and Anarchist Groups; Revolutionare Zellen—Marxist and Anarchist Groups, Hoffman Military Sports Group—PLO	Baader-Meinhof or Red Army Faction, Bewegung 2. Juni, German Action Groups (Neo-Nazis), Revolutionare Zellen, Hoffman Military Sports Group
Great Britain			Provisional Irish Republican Army (PIRA)—Ireland and No. Ireland, Irish National Liberation Army (INLA)—Ireland and N. Ireland, Palestine Liberation Organization—Fatah, rejectionist factions, Iran-Iraqi officials, dissidents, Libyan dissidents	Provisional Irish Republican Army (PIRA), Irish National Liberation Army, Angry Brigade, Cadwyr Cymru (Keepers of Wales), Mudiad Amddiffyn Cymru (Movement for Defense of Wales)
Greece			International Solidarity/Christos Kassimis—Anarchists in West Europe	International Solidarity/Christos Kassimis, November 17 Movement

State or Area	Terrorism by the State: Targets Within the State	Terrorism by the State: Targets Outside the State	Terrorism Directed Against the State: Outside Supporter of Terrorism (State Supported Terrorism)[a]	Terrorism Directed Against the State: Domestic Revolutionary Terrorist Organization[a]
Guatemala	Indian Tribal Groups		Movimiento de Liberacion Nacional (MLN)—Tupamaros	Movimiento de Liberacion National (MLN), Fuerzas Armados Rebeldes (FAR), Mano Blanco (MANO), MR-13, Nueva Organisacion Anticommunista (NOA)
Gulf States			Ansar al-Dawah (Supporters of the Call)—Pakistan, India, Gulf States	Ansar al-Dawah (Supporters of the Call)
Haiti	Christian Sects and Individual Dissenters			
Holland			South Moluccans—Ambonese Indonesians	South Moluccans (Ambonese Indonesians)
India			Naxalites—Red China	Naxalites Sikhs
Indonesia	Timor Tribes			South Moluccans (Ambonese Indonesians)
Iran	Bahai, Jews, Mujahadeen, Shah supporters, Dissidents, Tudeh Communists, Kurds	Great Britain, Iraq, Saudi Arabia, Lebanon, Kuwait, Gulf States, France	Siakhal—Iraq, Libya, PLO; Kurdish Democratic Party (KDP)—USSR	Siakhal, Mujahadeen, Kurdish Democratic Party (KDP)
Iraq	Kurds, Shi'a, Communist Party, Tribal Groups, Islamic Groups	Iran, Syria, Lebanon, Kuwait, Bahrain, Saudi Arabia	Hizb al-Dawah al-Islamiyyah (Islamic Propagation Party)—Iran, Gulf States, Kuwait, Dubai, Lebanon, Bahrain; Rabitat al-Mara al-Muslimah (Muslim Women's Assn.)—Iran, Gulf States; Hizb al-Fatimi (The Fatima Party)—Iran, pro-Shah elements; Zaynab (Women's Assn.)—Iran; Hizb al-Thawri al-Islami (Islamic Revolutionary Party)—Iran; Ikhwan Muslimin (Muslim Brethren)—Egypt, Syria, Jordan, Saudi Arabia; Ijtihad al-Islami li-Talabat al-Iraqi (Islamic Iraqi Students Union)—Iran, Gulf States, USA, West Europe; Jamaat al-Ulama (Society of Ulama)—Iran; Majlis al-Thawra al-Islamiyyah (Islamic Revolutionary Council)—Iran; Mujahadeen (Fighters)—Iran; Munazzamat al-Amal al-Islami (Islamic Action Organization)—Iran; Rabitat al-Islamiyyah (Islamic Assn.)—Iran	Hizb al-Dawah al-Islamiyyah (Islami Propagation Party), Zaynab (Women's Assn.) Rabitat al-Mara al-Muslimah (Muslim Women's Assn.) Rabitat al-Islamiyyah (Islamic Assn.), Hizb al-Fatimi (the Fatima Party); Hizb al-Thawri al-Islami (Islamic Revolutionary Party), Ikhwan Muslimin (Muslim Brethren), Ittihad al-Islamic li-Talabat al-Iraqi (Islamic Iraqi Students Union), Jamaat al-Ulama (Society of Ulama), Majilis al-Thawra al-Islamiyyah (Islamic Revolutionary Council), Mujahadeen (Fighters), Munazzamat al-Amal al-Islami (Islamic Action Organization), Kurdish Liberation Movement (Barzani)
Ireland, North			Provisional Irish Republican Army (PIRA)—Ireland, PLO, Libya, USA; Irish National Liberation Army (INLA)—Marxist Groups, Ireland	Provisional Irish Republican Army (PIRA), Irish National Liberation Army (INLA), Ulster Freedom Fighters (UFF), Ulster Volunteer Fighters (UVF), Ulster Defense Association (UDA), Protestant Action Force
Israel		Lebanon	Palestine Struggle Front (PSF)—PLO; Popular Front for Liberation of Palestine (PFLP)—Syria, PLO, Iraq; Al Fatah-Jordan, Syria, Iraq, Egypt, Libya, Algeria, Saudi Arabia	Stern Gang (Lehi), Irgun Zvi Leumi (Jabotinski), Terrorists Against Terrorism (TNT)—West Bank, Ma'atz (Council of Young Delinquents), Palestine Struggle Front (PSF), Popular Front for Liberation of Palestine (PFLP), Al Fatah (Arafat), Usrah al-Jihad (Family of Jihad)
Italy			Red Brigades—Marxist/Anarchist Groups West Europe; League of Fighting Communists (LFC)—Marxist/Anarchist Groups West Europe	Red Brigades, Valpreda, Futurist Movement, League of Fighting Communists (LFC), Armed Proletarian Nuclei, NAR (Neo-Fascist), Ordine Nero (Neo-Fascist), MSI (Neo-Fascist)
Jordan	Al Fatah (PLO)	Israel, West Bank	Ansar Harakat Asna al-Quran (Supporters of the Sons of the Quran)—PLO; Harakat al-Tawhid (Movement of Unicity)—Anti-Arafat Palestinians, Iran; Hizb al-Tahrir al-Islami (Islamic Liberation Party)—Lebanon, Libya, Turkey, Palestinians; Al Fatah (Arafat)—Egypt, Syria, Iraq, Algeria, PLO, USSR, E. Europe	Ansar Harakat Asn al-Quran (Sons of The Quran), Harakat al-Tawhid (Movement of Unicity), Hizb al-Tahrir al-Islami (Islamic Liberation Party), Al Fatah (Arafat)
Korea (North)		South Korea		

State or Area	Terrorism by the State: Targets Within the State	Terrorism by the State: Targets Outside the State	Terrorism Directed Against the State: Outside Supporter of Terrorism (State Supported Terrorism)[a]	Terrorism Directed Against the State: Domestic Revolutionary Terrorist Organization[a]
Kuwait			Dar al-Tawhid (Unicity Publishers)—Iran, Iraq, Revolutionary Organization/Forces of the Prophet Muhammad—Lebanese Shi'a	Dar al-Tawhid (Unicity Publishers), Revolutionary Organization/Forces of the Prophet Muhammad
Laos			Pathet Laos—N. Vietnam	Pathet Laos
Lebanon		Israel	AMAL (Hope)/Afwaj al-Muqawamah al-Lubnaniyyah (Lebanese Resistance Detachments)—Syria, Iran; Al-Jamaah al-Islamiyyah (Islamic Society, Muslim Brethren)—Syria, Jordan, Egypt; Jihad al-Islami (Islamic Holy War)—Syria, Iran; Hizb Allah/Islamic Amal (Party of God)—Iran, Syria; Arab Knights (Tripoli)—Arafat PLO; Saiqa (Vanguard)—Syria; Popular Front for Liberation of Palestine (PFLP)—Syria, Iraq, USSR; Popular Democratic Front for Liberation of Palestine (PDFLP)—Syria, Iraq, E. Europe, USSR; Al Fatah—USSR, Syria, Algeria, Iraq, So. Yemen, Egypt; Palestine Liberation Front (PLF)—Syria; Fatah Uprising (Abu Musa)—Syria; Fatah Revolutionary Council (Abu Nidal)—Syria, Iraq; Arab Liberation Front (ALF)—Iraq; Palestinian Popular Struggle Front (PPSF)—Syria; Popular Command (Jabril)—Syria; Palestine Liberation Front Breakaway (Muhammad Abbes); Lebanese Armed Revolution Faction (LARF)—Syria, PLO, Algeria; Lebanese Communist Party—Syria, USSR; National Syrian Social Party—Syria	AMAL (Hope); Al-Jamaah al-Islamiyyah (Islamic Society, Muslim Brethren); Jihad al-Islami (Holy War); Hizb Allah/Islamic AMAL (Party of God); Saiqa (Vanguard); Al Fatah (Arafat PLO); Lebanese Armed Revolution Faction (LARF); Arab Democratic Party; Nasserite Organizations (Sidon and Beirut); Lebanese Communist Party; National Syrian Social Party (NSSP); Arab Socialist Union
Libya	Dissidents among students, businessmen, and military	Egypt, Nicaragua, Great Britain, Sudan, Lebanon, Malta, USA, Greece, West Germany, Tunisia, Algeria, Philippines, Jordan, West Bank, France, Israel, Morocco, El Salvador, Guatemala, Pakistan, Portugal, New Caledonia, Thailand, Chile, Colombia, Turkey		Holy War
Mexico				Frente Urbano Zapatista (Zapata), Southern Liberation Army (ELS), Fuerzas Revolucionarias Armadas del Pueblo (FRAP)
Morocco			Ikhwan al-Muslimin/Shabibah al-Islamiyyah (Muslim Brethren)—Egypt, French Brethren	Ikhwan al-Muslimin (Muslim Brethren), Shubban Islamiyyah (Islamic Youth)
New Caledonia			Kanak Socialist National Liberation Front—Libya	Kanak Socialist National Liberation Front
Nicaragua	Miskito Indians	El Salvador, Honduras	Frente Sandinista de Liberacion Nacional (FSLN)—Cuba, USSR, Libya, East Europe; Contra Groups—USA, Honduras, Costa Rica; Miskito Indians	Frente Sandinista de Liberacion Nacional (FSLN); Contra Groups; Miskito Indians
Oman			Omani Liberation Front (OLF)—USSR, So. Yemen	Omani Liberation Front (OLF)

State or Area	Terrorism by the State: Targets Within the State	Terrorism by the State: Targets Outside the State	Terrorism Directed Against the State: Outside Supporter of Terrorism (State Supported Terrorism)[a]	Terrorism Directed Against the State: Domestic Revolutionary Terrorist Organization[a]
Peru			Ejercito de Liberacion Nacional (ELN)—ELN in Bolivia, Colombia; Movimiento de la Izquierda Revolucionaria (MIR)—MIR in Chile, Venezuela	Ejerecito de Liberacion Nacional (ELN), Movimiento de la Izquierda Revolucionaria (MIR), Sendere Luminoso (Shining Path—Maoist), Tupac Amaru
Pakistan			Al-Zulfigar—Libya	Al-Zulfigar
Philippines			New People's Army—Libya, Saudi Arabia, Moro National Liberation Front—Libya	New People's Army, Moro National Liberation Front
Portugal			April 25 Movement (FP-25)—Libya	April 25 Movement (FP-25)
Puerto Rico			Macheteros—Cuba	Macheteros, Movimiento Independista Revolucionario Armado (MIRA), Commandos Armados de Liberacion (CAL), Fuerzas Armados de Liberacion Nacional (FALN)
El Salvador			Ejercito Revolucienario del Pueblo (ERP)—ERP Argentina, Farabundo Marti National Liberation Front (FMLN-5 groups)—Nicaragua, Cuba	Ejercito Revolucionario del Pueblo (ERP); Farabundo Marti National Liberation Front (FMLN)
Saudi Arabia			Hizb al-Tahrir al-Jazirah (Liberation Party of Jazirah)—Iran, Gulf States, Iraq, Bahrain; Al-Ikhwan (Muslim Brethren)—Egypt, Yemen, Pakistan, Gulf States; Jamaat al-Masjid (Mosque Society)—Gulf States, Oman; Munazzamat al-Thawrah al-Islamiyyah Shubuh fi al-Jazirah al-Aribiyyah (Islamic Revolutionary Organization in Arabian Peninsula)—Iran; Hejaz Liberation Front—Iraq	Hibz al-Tahrir al-Jazirah (Liberation Party of Jazirah), Al-Ikhwan (Muslim Brethren), Jamaat al-Masjid (Mosque Society), Munazzamat al-Thawrah al-Islamiyyah Shubuh fi al-Jazirah al-Arabiyyah (Islamic Revolutionary Organization in Arabian Peninsula), Hejaz Liberation Front
Senegal			Centre Social Islamique—Lebanon, Iran	Centre Social Islamique
South Africa	African National Congress, Black dissenters, Black unions	Southwest Africa (Namibia)	African National Congress (ANC)—OAU, Black African States, USSR; Umkhonto we Sizwe (MK)—Cuba, Angola, E. Germany	African National Congress, Afrikaner Weerstandbewegung (AWB-Neo-Fascist), Umhkonto we Sizwe (MK), Azarian People's Organization (AZAPO)
Southwest Africa (Namibia)			Southwest Africa People's Organizations (SWAPO)—Cuba, Angola	Southwest Africa People's Organization (SWAPO)
South Yemen (PDRY)		Oman, North Yemen, Lebanon		
Soviet Union (USSR)	Volga Germans, Tartars, Jews, Baltic Catholics, dissenters	Afghanistan, East European regimes, PLO (Arafat, rejectionist factions), some Communist parties in less developed countries		
Spain			Euzkadi ta Askatasanu (ETA V, VI)—Libya, PLO, French Basques; ETA VI-Liga Communista Revolucionari (LCR)—Anarchist/Marxist groups; Warriors of Christ the King—Italian, South American Fascist Groups; Call of Jesus Christ—Lebanese Maronites	Euzkadi ta Askatasanu (ETA V, VI); ETA VI—Liga Communista Revolucionari (LCR); Frente Revolucionario Anti-Fascista y Patriota (FRAP); GAL; Anti-Terrorism ETA; Anti-Communist Apostolic Alliance (AAA); Spanish Basque Battalion (Neo-Fascist); New Force (Neo-Fascist)
Sri Lanka			Tamil Groups—India Tamils	Tamil Groups
Sudan			Sudanese People's Liberation Army/Anya Nya II (SPLA)—Ethiopia, Libya	Sudanese People's Liberation Army/Anya Nya II (SPLA)
Sweden			Kurdish Workers Party (KKK)—Kurds in Iran and Iraq; Croation Ustasha—Yugoslavia Croats	

State or Area	Terrorism by the State: Targets Within the State	Terrorism by the State: Targets Outside the State	Terrorism Directed Against the State: Outside Supporter of Terrorism (State Supported Terrorism)[a]	Terrorism Directed Against the State: Domestic Revolutionary Terrorist Organization[a]
Syria	Muslim Brethren groups	Lebanon, Israel, Jordan, Egypt, Iraq	Ikhwan al-Muslimin (Muslim Brethren)—Egypt, Iraq, Jordan, Gulf States; Ikhwan al-Muslimin (Political Solution Group)—Egypt, Gulf States, Iraq; Kataib Muhammad (Muslim Brethren of the Interior)—Egypt; Salafiyyah (Puritans)—Egypt; Tahririal-Islami (Islamic Liberation Party)—Jordan; Talia al-Muqatila lil Mujahadeen (Combat Vanguard of Fighters)—Iraq, Egypt	Ansari (Supporters); Ikhwan al-Muslimin (Muslim Brethren), Ikhwan al-Muslimin (Political Solution Group), Al-Jihad (Holy War), Junud Allah (Soldiers of God), Kataib al-Haq (Phalanges of Truth), Khulasah (Puritans), Salafiyyah (Puritans), Tahrir al-Islami (Islamic Liberation Party), Talia al-Muqatila lil Mujahadeen (Combat Vanguard of Fighters)
Tanzania	Zanzibar Arabs, Tribal resettlement (Ujamaa villages)	South Africa		
Thailand			Muslim Groups—Libya	
Tunisia			Amal al-Islami/Khawanjia (Islamic Action/ Muslim Brethren)—Egypt; Hizb al-Islami (Islamic Party)—Egypt	Amal al-Islami/Khawanjia (Islamic Action), Progressive Socialist Gathering, Djihad Islamique, Ittijah al-Islami (Islamic Orientation), Jamiyyat Hifz al-Quran (Quran Preservation Societies), Hizb Allah al-Muktar, Parti de la Liberation Islamique (PLI) (Islamic Liberation Party), Movement of Popular Unity
Turkey	Kurds		Turkish People's Liberation Army (TPLA)—PLO, Syria, E. Germany, North Korea, USSR, Czechoslovakia; Armenian Secret Army (ASA)—USSR; ASALA (Armenian)—PLO, Libya, Syria, Greece	Nationalist Action Party, Turkish People's Liberation Army (TPLA), Armenian Secret Army (ASA), ASALA (Armenian), Kurdish Groups
Uganda	Tribes out of power			
United States			Aryan Nations—Neo-Nazis in Germany, Movimiento Independista Revolucionario Armado (MIRA)—Puerto Rico MIRA	Weathermen; Movimiento Independista Revolucionario Armado (MIRA); Symbionese Liberation Army (SLA); Aryan Nations; Covenant, Sword and Arm of the Lord (CSA); Posse Comitatus; The Order; White Aryan Resistance; White Patriot Party (WPP); National Alliance; Hanafi Muslims
Uruguay			Movimiento de Liberacion Nacional (Tupamaros)—Guatemala, Chile, Argentina Groups, USSR	Movimiento de Liberacion Nacional (Tupamaros)
Venezuela			Communist Party—Cuba, Movimiento de la Izquierda Revolucionaria (MIR)—Peru and Chile MIR's	Communist Party, Fuerzas Armados de Liberacion Nacional (FALN), Bandera Roja (Red Banner)
Vietnam (South and North)	South Vietnam officials (reeducation camps)	South Vietnam, Laos, Cambodia	Viet Cong—No. Vietnam	Viet Cong
Yemen (North)			Hizb Allah (Party of God)—Saudi Arabia, Gulf States	Hizb Allah (Party of God)
Yugoslavia			Croation Ustasha—USSR	Croation Ustasha
International			Muhammad Boudia Commando (Carlos)—Anarchist/Marxist Groups, PLO, Libya	

State or Area	Terrorism by the State: Targets Within the State	Terrorism by the State: Targets Outside the State	Terrorism Directed Against the State: Outside Supporter of Terrorism (State Supported Terrorism)[a]	Terrorism Directed Against the State: Domestic Revolutionary Terrorist Organization[a]
International[c]			Fatah (Arafat)—USSR, Arab League, Egypt, Libya, Syria, So. Yemen, Tunisia, Algeria, Lebanon, East Europe States, Jordan, Iraq, Iran, Sudan, Saudi Arabia, Kuwait, Gulf States; Arab Liberation Front (ALF)—Iraq; Palestine Liberation Front (PLF)—Iraq, Tunisia; Fatah Uprising (Abu Musa)—Syria; As Saiqa (Vanguard)—Syria; Palestine Front for Liberation of Palestine (PFLP) (Habash)—Syria, USSR; Palestine Front for Liberation of Palestine, General Command (Jibril)—Syria; Palestine Struggle Front (PSF)—Syria; Palestine Liberation Front (PLF)—Syria; Democratic Front for Liberation of Palestine (DFLP) (Hawatmeh)—Syria, USSR; Fatah Revolutionary Council (Abu Nidal)—Syria, Libya; Palestine Liberation Front Breakaway—Syria; PALM—Syria; May 15th Movement—Syria; Palestine Front for Liberation of Palestine, Security Command—Syria; Palestine Front for Liberation of Palestine, General Command Breakaway—Syria	

[a] It is not uncommon for a group to qualify under the heading of a domestic organization and also receive support from abroad. The domestic aspect indicates there is an indigenous basis for the origin and sustenance of the group apart from the overseas help.

[b] The Islamic Holy War and The Party of God operate by means of various subsidiary groups often brought into being for specific operations by members or by the leadership. Examples would be Organization of the Oppressed on Earth, Organization of Revolutionary Justice, etc. Many of the groups, particularly secular ones, are organized as part of the Lebanese National Democratic Front.

[c] The various Palestinian groups operate by means of various subsidiary groups often brought into being for specific operations by the leadership. Examples would be the Black September, Black June, Organization of Revolutionary Justice to Liberate Palestine, etc. The Palestinian groups most committed to "armed struggle" are also organized under the Palestine National Salvation Front. All are technically part of the larger organization popularly referred to and organized as the Palestine Liberation Organization.

Appendum

1990 Appendum: Survey of Worldwide Terrorism Since World War II (Political Form)

State or Area	Terrorism by the State: Targets Within the State	Terrorism by the State: Targets Outside the State	Terrorism Directed Against the State: Outside Supporter of Terrorism (State-Supported Terrorism)[a]	Terrorism Directed Against the State: Domestic Revolutionary Terrorist Organization[a]
Afghanistan		Pakistan		
Angola			UNITA-So. Africa, USA, Zaire Movimiento Popular Para a Liberacio de Angola (MPLA)—USSR, E. Europe, Cuba	UNITA, MPLA
Argentina			Motherland Movement-Nicaragua	Motherland Movement (MTP)
Botswana			Black Consciousness Movement (BCM)—PLO	Black Consciousness Movement (BCM)
Bolivia				Zarate Willca Fuerzas Armadas de Liberacion (ZWFAL), Commando Alejo Calatayno (CAC), Frente de Liberacion Nacional (FRELINA), Bolivian Labor Federation (COB), Commando Guerrilla Simon Bolivar (CGSP)
Canada			Direct Action—W. Europe Groups	Direct Action
Cape Verde (Portugal)				Portuguesa des Ilmas de Cape Verde

State or Area	Terrorism by the State: Targets Within the State	Terrorism by the State: Targets Outside the State	Terrorism Directed Against the State: Outside Supporter of Terrorism (State-Supported Terrorism)[a]	Terrorism Directed Against the State: Domestic Revolutionary Terrorist Organization[a]
Central African Republic			Ubangui Patriotic Front (MCLN)—Libya, Cuba, PLO, Angola	Ubangui Patriotic Front
Chad			National Liberation Front (FROLINAT)—Libya, PLO	National Liberation Front (FROLINAT), People's Revolutionary Movement (MPR)
Chile			Manuael Rodrigues Front (MPFR)—Cuba	Movimiento Juvenil Lautaro (MJL)
Colombia			American Battalion—Nicaragua	Extraditables (Narco-Group), American Battalion
Denmark				BZ (name not fully known)
Djibouti				Troops of Revolutionary Resistance (TRRF)
Dominican Republic				Maximiliano Gomez Revolutionary Brigade (MGRB)
Ecuador			American Battalion—Nicaragua	American Battalion
Egypt			Nasserites—Libya	Nasserites Egyptian Revolution
Ethiopia			Eritrean Liberation Front (ELF)—Saudi Arabia, Iraq, Other Arab States	Eritrean Liberation Front (ELF)
Fiji				Talkay Movement
France				Corsican Revolutionary Action
Greece			Popular Initiative Front—PLO	Social Resistance (SR), Popular Initiative Front, Revolutionary People's Struggle (ELA), Christos Tsoutsouris
Guadeloupe (France)			Caribbean Revolutionary Alliance—Cuba, Libya	Caribbean Revolutionary Alliance, Guadeloupe Liberation Army (GLA)
Guatemala				Guatemalan National Revolutionary Unity (URNG)
Guinea (Portugal)				Partido Africano da Independencia Guinea
Holland			Red Resistance Front—PLO Rode Hulp—W. Europe Anarchists/Syndicalists/Marxists	Revolutionary Anti-Fascist Action (RARA), Red Resistance Front, Rode Hulp
Honduras			Chinchonero People's Liberation Movement (CPLM)—Cuba, Contra Assassination Squads—Nicaragua, Lorenzo Zelaya—Cuba, Nicaragua	Chinchonero People's Liberation Movement, Lorenzo Zelaya Popular Revolutionary Force (LZPRF)
India			Dal Khalsa—PLO	Hizbul Mujahideen (Kashmir), Jammu and Kashmir Liberation Front, United Liberation Front Assam, National Socialist Council Nagaland, United Liberation Front Manipur, Dal Khalsa
Indonesia			Suma Ram (IRB)—Libya, FREITLIN (E. Timor)—PLO, Angola	Suma Ram, FREITLIN (E. Timor)
Iran		Spain, W. Germany, Turkey (Kurds, Islamic Fundamentalists)		
Israel		West Bank Gaza Strip	Japanese Red Army—PLO, Libya, Abu Nidal, Islamic Resistance Front—Muslim Brethren	Arab Freedom Front, Fatah Revolutionary Council (Abu Nidal), Sicarii, Rafik Salmi Bloc (Gaza Strip), Islamic Resistance Front, Keshet/Sicarii
Italy				Autonomia Operaia, Prima Linea, Third Position
Japan				Chukaku-Ha (MiddleCore)
Lebanon	Shi'i Factions (Amal vs. Hizballah), Maronites vs. Shi'i Factions	Spain, France, W. Germany, Great Britain	Islamic Liberation—Iran; Committee for Solidarity with Arab & Middle East Political Prisoners—PFLP-SC (LARF); Islamic Jihad for Liberation of Palestine—PLO	Progressive Socialist Party (Jumblatt), Islamic Liberation, Anti-Khomeinist Front, Vengeance Party, Tanyus Shahin Armed Unit (LARF)
Lesotho/ Swaziland				Pan African Congress of Azania (PAC), Basutoland Congress Party (Lesotho Liberation Army)
Libya		Chad, Kenya, Panama		Arab Nationalist Youth Organization (ANYO)

State or Area	Terrorism by the State: Targets Within the State	Terrorism by the State: Targets Outside the State	Terrorism Directed Against the State: Outside Supporter of Terrorism (State Supported Terrorism)[a]	Terrorism Directed Against the State: Domestic Revolutionary Terrorist Organization[a]
Malawi				Malawi Freedom Movement
Mexico				Movimiento de Accion Revolucionario (MAR), Commando International Simon Bolivar (CISB)
Rio de Oro (Morocco)			Saguiat el Hamra and Rio de Oro (SARIO)—Libya, Algeria	Polisario (People's Front-Western Sahara), Saguiat el Hamra and Rio de Oro (SARIO)
Mozambique			Frente Liberacion de Mozambique (FRELIMO)—USSR, East Europe	Frente Liberacion de Mozambique (FRELIMO), Mozambique National Resistance Movement (Renamo)
New Guinea				Papua Rebellion
Nicaragua		Colombia, Puerto Rico, Dominican Republic		Nicaragua Democratic Front
Panama				La Tendencia
Salvador			Central American Revolutionary Workers Party—Cuba, Nicaragua	PRTC, Clara Elizabeth Front, ARDE (Anti-Communists)
Somalia			Somali National Movement (SNM)—Ethiopia	Somali National Movement (SNM)
South Africa				White Wolves
Spain			October 1st Anti-Fascist Resistance Group (GRAPO)—Direct Action, Red Brigades	Iraultza (Basque Armed Revolutionary Workers Organization), Grupos Antiterroristas de Liberacion (GAL), Primero de Octubre Catalan Red Liberation Army (ERCA), Iparratarrek Terra Lliura (TL), GRAPO
Sri Lanka				Janatha Vimukhti Peramuna (JVP), Tamil Liberation Tigers
Surinam				National Liberation Union (NLU)
Thailand				Pattani (Shi'i) Rebellion, Patani United Liberation Front, Barbisan Revolusi Nasional
Tunisia			Islamic Trend Movement (MTI)—Iran, Libya	Islamic Trend Movement (MTI)
Turkey	Islamic Extremists		National Liberation Front of Kurdistan—Syria, Iran; Gray Wolves—Bulgaria Justice Commandos of the Armenian Genocide (JCAG)—Overseas Armenians Kurdish Workers Party (PKK)—Bulgaria	Armed Peoples Units, Jundallah (God's Warriors—Shi'i), Warriors of the 16th June, National Liberation Front of Kurdistan, Partiya Karkeren Kurdistan, JCAG, Der Sol, PKK, Apoist/Apocular (Kurds), Gray Wolves
Uganda			*National Resistance Council—Libya	Uganda People's Army, *National Resistance Council, National Liberation Front (UNLF)
United Arab States				National Democratic Front (NDF)
United States			Japanese Red Army—Abu Nidal, Libya	United Freedom Front; Ku Klux Klans, Black Liberation Army, Jewish Defense League
West German Republic			Partiya Karkeren Kurdistan-Turkish Kurds	
Zimbabwe				Zimbabwe African People's Union (ZAPU), Zimbabwe African National Union (ZANU)
International (Japanese Red Army)	Japan (Factional Killings)	USA, Israel	Anti-Imperialist International Brigade—PFLP-SC, Japanese Red Army—Abu Nidal, Libya	
International (Abu Nidal-Fatah Revolutionary Council)	Fatah (Yasir Arafat)	Israel, Americans, Egypt, Jordan	Japanese Red Army—Abu Nidal, Libya; Arab Revolutionary Cells; Revolutionary Organization of Socialist Moslems (ROSM)—Syria; Black September—Syria; Palestine National Salvation Front—Syria; Fatah Revolutionary Council—Syria, Libya, Iraq	

*State-run terrorist organization directed against internal tribes but organized and sponsored from abroad.

Index

Credits/ Acknowledgments

Cover design by Charles Vitelli

1. Concept of Terrorism
Facing overview—United Nations photo by Contact.

2. Causes and Scope of Terrorism
Facing overview—United Nations photo.

3. Terrorists: International, State-Sponsored, and State-Supported
Facing overview—United Nations photo by J. Isaac.

4. State Terrorism
Facing overview—Reuters/Bettmann Newsphotos.

5. Terrorism in America
Facing overview—UPI/Bettmann Newsphotos.

6. Terrorism and the Media
Facing overview—The Christian Science Monitor.

7. Tactics, Strategies, and Targeting
Facing overview—UPI/Bettmann Newsphotos.

8. Countering Terrorism
Facing overview—United Nations photo.

9. Trends and Projections of Terrorism
Facing overview—Reutters/Bettmann Newsphotos.

PHOTOCOPY THIS PAGE!!!*

ANNUAL EDITIONS ARTICLE REVIEW FORM

■ NAME: ______________________________ DATE: ______________________________

■ TITLE AND NUMBER OF ARTICLE: ______________________________

■ BRIEFLY STATE THE MAIN IDEA OF THIS ARTICLE: ______________________________

■ LIST THREE IMPORTANT FACTS THAT THE AUTHOR USES TO SUPPORT THE MAIN IDEA:

■ WHAT INFORMATION OR IDEAS DISCUSSED IN THIS ARTICLE ARE ALSO DISCUSSED IN YOUR TEXTBOOK OR OTHER READING YOU HAVE DONE? LIST THE TEXTBOOK CHAPTERS AND PAGE NUMBERS:

■ LIST ANY EXAMPLES OF BIAS OR FAULTY REASONING THAT YOU FOUND IN THE ARTICLE:

■ LIST ANY NEW TERMS/CONCEPTS THAT WERE DISCUSSED IN THE ARTICLE AND WRITE A SHORT DEFINITION:

*Your instructor may require you to use this Annual Editions Article Review Form in any number of ways: for articles that are assigned, for extra credit, as a tool to assist in developing assigned papers, or simply for your own reference. Even if it is not required, we encourage you to photocopy and use this page; you'll find that reflecting on the articles will greatly enhance the information from your text.

ANNUAL EDITIONS: VIOLENCE AND TERRORISM 91/92

Article Rating Form

Here is an opportunity for you to have direct input into the next revision of this volume. We would like you to rate each of the 67 articles listed below, using the following scale:

1. **Excellent: should definitely be retained**
2. **Above average: should probably be retained**
3. **Below average: should probably be deleted**
4. **Poor: should definitely be deleted**

Your ratings will play a vital part in the next revision. So please mail this prepaid form to us just as soon as you complete it. Thanks for your help!

Rating	Article	Rating	Article
	1. Defining Terrorism		36. New Extremists Exceed 'Jim Crowism' of KKK
	2. 'Terrorism'—A Term Notoriously Difficult to Pin Down		37. Threats, Real or Not, Stir Fears Across U.S.
	3. How to Tell a Terrorist		38. Borders Open to Terrorist Threat
	4. Terrorism: Myths and Reality		39. Officials Say They Have Leads in Killing of Judge in Alabama
	5. Unmasking Terrorism: The Fear of Fear Itself		40. Environmentalists Hurt, Then Held, in Blast
	6. "Holy Wars": The Ominous Side of Religion in Politics		41. Terrorism and the Media
	7. Unmasking Terrorism: The Terrorist Mentality		42. Unmasking Terrorism: Manipulation of the Media
	8. As Palestinian Revolt Continues, Violence Declines		43. Terrorism on TV—Who Are the Real Hostages?
	9. The Terrible Toll of Human Hatred		44. The Silent Treatment for Terrorists
	10. International Terrorism		45. Terrorism and the Media: Lessons From the British Experience
	11. Explaining Terrorism		46. Linkages Between Sunni and Shi'i Radical Fundamentalist Organizations: A New Variable in Recent Middle Eastern Politics?
	12. What Constitutes State Support of Terrorists?		47. Why Hostage-Taking Is So Popular With Terrorists
	13. Arming the IRA: The Libyan Connection		48. The IRA: Spreading a Wider Net
	14. Rafsanjani May Hold the Key That Releases the Hostages		49. Narco-Terrorism "Shooting Up" America
	15. Out From the Cellar		50. Peru's Shining Path Terrorists Open New Front in Drug War
	16. Interview With Abu Nidal		51. Colombian Journalists vs. Drug Terrorists
	17. A Terrorist Talks About Life, Warns of More Deaths		52. Will Terrorists Use Chemical Weapons?
	18. Neo-Nazis Stage Attacks		53. Terrorism and Public Opinion: A Five Country Comparison
	19. An Interview With Martin McGuinness of the Irish Republican Movement		54. Counterterrorism in the 1990s
	20. The Selling of Terrorism: Profit From a Lucrative Export		55. International Crime Requires International Punishment
	21. C.I.A. Tie Asserted in Indonesia Purge		56. When Reality Came Unglued: Antonio Savasta and the Italian Red Brigades
	22. As Peru Votes, Insurgent's Mystique Casts Shadow		57. Hezbollah Frustrates a Gulliver-Like U.S.
	23. The State as Terrorist		58. Advisories Help Keep U.S. Travelers Safe Abroad
	24. Iraq's Human-Rights Toll		59. On the Trail of Terror
	25. Iran's Dismal Record		60. Fighting International Terrorism: What Does and What Does Not Work
	26. Destasifying Germany: The Undergrowth of Evil		61. The Bush Administration's PLO Cover-Up
	27. El Salvador Rights Record Challenged		62. Diminishing the Threat Against Terrorism: Intelligence and the War Against Terrorism
	28. Political Violence on the Rise Again in Guatemala, Tarnishing Civilian Rule		63. Terror and Negotiation
	29. Death Squads Seek Negotiations		64. Mission Improbable
	30. Chinese Repression Threatens Tibet's Buddhist Tradition		65. Terrorist Threat to Commercial Aviation
	31. Government Declares War on Tamils		66. The Growing Threat of Terrorism
	32. What Became of Burma's Dissident Students?		67. The Contrasting Ethical Foundations of Terrorism in the 1980s
	33. Who Killed Jonathan Moyle?		
	34. Stopping Terrorism . . . The Problems Posed by the Organizational Infrastructure of Terrorist Organizations		
	35. Skinheads Target the Schools		

We Want Your Advice

Annual Editions revisions depend on two major opinion sources: one is our Advisory Board, listed in the front of this volume, which works with us in scanning the thousands of articles published in the public press each year; the other is you—the person actually using the book. Please help us and the users of the next edition by completing the prepaid article rating form on this page and returning it to us. Thank you.

ABOUT YOU

Name _______________________ Date __________

Are you a teacher? ☐ Or student? ☐

Your School Name _______________________

Department _______________________

Address _______________________

City _______________ State _______ Zip _______

School Telephone # _______________________

YOUR COMMENTS ARE IMPORTANT TO US!

Please fill in the following information:

For which course did you use this book? _______________________

Did you use a text with this Annual Edition? ☐ yes ☐ no

The title of the text? _______________________

What are your general reactions to the Annual Editions concept?

Have you read any particular articles recently that you think should be included in the next edition?

Are there any articles you feel should be replaced in the next edition? Why?

Are there other areas that you feel would utilize an Annual Edition?

May we contact you for editorial input?

May we quote you from above?

No Postage Necessary if Mailed in the United States

ANNUAL EDITIONS: VIOLENCE AND TERRORISM 91/92

BUSINESS REPLY MAIL

First Class Permit No. 84 Guilford, CT

Postage will be paid by addressee

The Dushkin Publishing Group, Inc.
Sluice Dock
Guilford, Connecticut 06437